PERSPECTIVES ON
AMERICAN
FOREIGN
POLICY

PERSPECTIVES ON AMERICAN FOREIGN POLICY

SELECTED READINGS

CHARLES W. KEGLEY, JR.
University of South Carolina

EUGENE R. WITTKOPF
University of Florida

ST. MARTIN'S PRESS
New York

For my father and the memory of my mother
CWK

For my mother and the memory of my father
ERW

Library of Congress Catalog Card Number: 82–60472
Copyright © 1983 by St. Martin's Press, Inc.
All Rights Reserved.
Manufactured in the United States of America.
765·
fedc
For information, write St. Martin's Press, Inc.
175 Fifth Avenue, New York, NY 10010

Book design: Robert Bull

ISBN: 0–312–60244–8

Contents

Part One
POST-WORLD WAR II
AMERICAN FOREIGN POLICY   **1**

1. **Stephen E. Ambrose**
   Globalism in American Foreign Policy   **10**

2. **John Lewis Gaddis**
   Containment: Its Past and Future   **16**

3. **Hans J. Morgenthau**
   Defining the National Interest—Again: Old Superstitions,
   New Realities   **32**

4. **George F. Kennan**
   Two Views of the Soviet Problem   **40**

5. **Spurgeon M. Keeny, Jr. and Wolfgang K. H. Panofsky**
   MAD Versus NUTS: Can Doctrine or Weaponry Remedy the
   Mutual Hostage Relationship of the Superpowers?   **47**

6. **Barry M. Blechman and Stephen S. Kaplan**
   U.S. Military Forces as a Political Instrument Since World War II   **62**

7. **Andrew K. Semmel**
   Evolving Patterns of U.S. Security Assistance, 1950–1980   **79**

Part Two
EXTERNAL SOURCES
OF AMERICAN FOREIGN POLICY   **97**

8. **Henry A. Kissinger**
   System Structures and American Foreign Policy   **103**

9. **Robert O. Keohane and Joseph S. Nye**
   Realism and Complex Interdependence   **119**

10. **U.S. Congress, Joint Economic Committee**
The International Economy: U.S. Role in a World Market   **133**

11. **John W. Sewell and John A. Mathieson**
The Third World: Exploring U.S. Interests   **148**

Part Three
SOCIETAL SOURCES
OF AMERICAN FOREIGN POLICY   **169**

12. **Carl Gershman**
The Rise and Fall of the New Foreign-Policy Establishment   **175**

13. **Ole R. Holsti and James N. Rosenau**
The Foreign Policy Beliefs of American Leaders, 1976–1980   **196**

14. **Lloyd Free and William Watts**
Internationalism Comes of Age . . . Again   **213**

15. **Bernard C. Cohen**
The Influence of Special-Interest Groups and Mass Media on
Security Policy in the United States   **222**

Part Four
GOVERNMENTAL SOURCES
OF AMERICAN FOREIGN POLICY   **243**

16. **Roger Hilsman**
Policy-Making is Politics   **250**

17. **I. M. Destler**
The Rise of the National Security Assistant 1961–1981   **260**

18. **Leslie H. Gelb**
Why Not the State Department?   **282**

19. **Harry Howe Ransom**
Strategic Intelligence and Intermestic Politics   **299**

20. **Thomas E. Cronin**
A Resurgent Congress and the Imperial Presidency   **320**

Part Five
POLICY-MAKER ROLES AS SOURCES
OF AMERICAN FOREIGN POLICY   **347**

21. **Stephen D. Cohen**
The Impact of Organization on U.S. International
Economic Policy   **352**

22. **Jerel A. Rosati**
Explaining SALT from a Bureaucratic Politics Perspective   **364**

23. **James C. Thomson, Jr.**
How Could Vietnam Happen? An Autopsy **379**

24. **Charles F. Hermann**
Bureaucratic Constraints on Innovation in American
Foreign Policy **390**

25. **Stephen D. Krasner**
Are Bureaucracies Important? A Re-examination of
Accounts of the Cuban Missile Crisis **410**

Part Six
INDIVIDUALS AS SOURCES
OF AMERICAN FOREIGN POLICY **425**

26. **Margaret G. Hermann**
Leaders, Leadership, and American Foreign Policy **429**

27. **John G. Stoessinger**
Crusaders and Pragmatists: Two Types of Foreign
Policy Makers **448**

28. **Alexander L. George**
Presidential Management Styles and Models **466**

29. **James David Barber**
President Reagan's Character: An Assessment **494**

Part Seven
THE FUTURE
OF AMERICAN FOREIGN POLICY **501**

30. The Global 2000 Report to the President **505**

31. **Henry Steele Commager**
Misconceptions Governing American Foreign Policy **510**

32. **Stanley Hoffmann**
Foreign Policy: What's to Be Done? **518**

Index **529**

Preface

This collection of thirty-two essays explores the central issues of post-World War II American foreign policy. Any anthology that seeks to examine both the substance of U.S. foreign policy and the process by which it is made should fulfill three basic requirements: (1) It should offer description and critical analysis, from a variety of perspectives, of change and continuity in America's relations with the rest of the world; (2) it should explain the multiple sources that have influenced the direction of American foreign policy; and (3) it should provide a framework for analyzing these sources.

This book, we believe, fulfills all these objectives, and it does so by presenting interesting selections, authored by authoritative observers, that offer diverse—even conflicting—points of view. Moreover, the essays are not only informative but also readable and up-to-date. In order to ensure that the most timely perspectives were included, nine essays were especially written or adapted for this volume. Such a broadly based collection, we feel, will enable the instructor to adapt this book for a variety of instructional purposes: as a supplement to any textbook in American foreign policy, or even, in a course based primarily on readings, as a core text itself.

Perspectives on American Foreign Policy is organized into seven parts, each of which begins with an introduction that provides a foundation for understanding the part's topic and that places the various articles of the part in the analytical framework that organizes the entire collection.

Part One begins with a discussion of the substantive aspects of America's foreign policy patterns after 1945. Particular attention is devoted to five themes that have been dominant in the formulation of U.S. foreign policy and that have remained constant throughout the postwar period. These themes are: globalism, anticommunism, containment, military strength, and interventionism. These five themes are also touched on in one way or another in most of the remaining essays in the book.

Parts Two through Six focus on the major sources of American foreign policy. Broadly defined, they are the international environment (the external source, Part Two), the domestic environment (the societal source, Part Three), the institutional features of the American government (the governmental source, Part Four), the roles that America's foreign policy makers occupy (the role source, Part Five), and the individual characteristics of these policy makers (the individual source, Part Six). Finally, the concluding part (Part Seven) examines the future of American foreign policy.

ACKNOWLEDGMENTS

We are particularly grateful to the following people who assisted us in the preparation of the manuscript: Stephen D. Hibbard, Lucia Wren Rawls, Joseph Sausnock, III, and Van Sturgeon. John A. Armitage of the University of Virginia, P. Terrence Hopmann of the University of Minnesota, and Lars Schoultz of the University of North Carolina at Chapel Hill provided thoughtful critiques of early versions of the manuscript. At St. Martin's Press we would like to thank Michael Weber, Editor; Richard Steins, Managing Editor; Marilyn Moller, Project Editor; and Christine Pearson, Production Supervisor.

PERSPECTIVES ON AMERICAN FOREIGN POLICY

Part One

POST-WORLD WAR II AMERICAN FOREIGN POLICY

Perhaps the most distinctive feature of American foreign policy since World War II has been its remarkable continuity. The principles and goals that have guided this policy through four decades have persisted in spite of a bewildering onslaught of complex and contradictory international and domestic events. As we examine American foreign policy, we will see its continuity captured in the following themes: *globalism, anticommunism, containment, military might,* and *interventionist means.*

The essays in Part I of this book illustrate the patterns of consistency in postwar American foreign policy touched on in these themes; the essays in the next five parts examine the forces that give rise to American foreign policy. To understand these forces, the essays focus on five sets of factors that may be considered the *sources* of America's foreign policy: (1) the international environment to which U.S. foreign policy must respond; (2) the domestic environment of the United States; (3) the institutional features of American government; (4) the roles occupied by American foreign policy decision makers; and (5) the individual characteristics of these policy makers. Finally, the essays in Part VII focus on the future of American foreign policy.

ANALYZING AMERICAN FOREIGN POLICY

Political commentators and analysts often have similar views about the dominant goals of postwar American foreign policy. But they differ widely in their explanations of the *causes* of that policy, especially because attention is focused on the day-to-day events highlighted in the news rather than on long-range perspectives. Disagreement exists because the sources of American foreign policy may be interpreted from many, often competing, perspectives. We think it is appropriate to acknowledge the existence of these contending perspectives and to direct attention to all of them rather than to only one. And we think that it is useful to organize discussion about alternate influences on American foreign policy making in terms of five basic categories, for it is in reference to one of these five sources that most analytic perspectives can be logically classified.

The five factors or determinants of American foreign policy (and the perspectives they invite) can be said to influence the course of America's response to external problems in the sense that they create the necessity for foreign policy decisions and, ultimately, for action abroad; and they affect the policy-making process that converts policy sources into policy outputs. In other words, they *stimulate* the nation's leaders to undertake action to cope with the external world; yet, at the same time, they also *constrain* the actual choices that leaders are able to make. Attention to only one of these sources would give us but one perspective on the determinants of American foreign policy. But understanding the breadth of postwar American foreign policy, and particularly its remarkable continuity, compels us to search for its multiple sources by investigating it from alternative perspectives. To reiterate, the five sources that influence American foreign policy in the dual sense described above are the *external* (world) environment, the *societal* environment of the nation, the *governmental* setting, the *roles* occupied by the nation's central decision makers, and the *individual* characteristics of those who make foreign policy.

Each of these factors can be thought of as a *source category* that encompasses a large number of variables that may interact with variables in other source categories. Such interaction shapes American foreign policy. For example, individual decision makers in government are both stimulated as well as constrained by their roles, roles that are defined largely by their policy-making positions within the foreign policy-making structure. Those governmental variables are in turn cast within the larger framework of American society, which operates within an even larger international environment that consists not only of a host of other nations but of nonstate actors as well. Thus, the five source categories provide the basis for formulating a *pre-theory* of American foreign policy.[1] That is, they help to order facts and concepts, to structure our observations about American foreign policy behavior in a theoretically meaningful way, and to suggest hypotheses that explain the performance of the United States in world affairs. The way the source categories facilitate an explanation of American foreign policy is illustrated in Figure 1.

The figure depicts the *inputs* to the foreign policy-making process as the external, societal, governmental, role, and individual source categories of the pre-theoretical framework. Those inputs may be considered policy "sources" because they give shape and direction to the kinds of behaviors the United States exhibits abroad. America's external behavior can be thought of as the *outputs* of the policy-making process. In most instances, foreign policy outputs are multifaceted; that is, they address concurrently a wide variety of issues and sometimes move simultaneously in divergent directions. At the same time, however, the broad concept of "foreign policy" also embraces certain *recurring* patterns of behavior, and these recurring patterns define the continuous efforts of the United States to cope with the environment beyond the water's edge. Note, however, that whether one

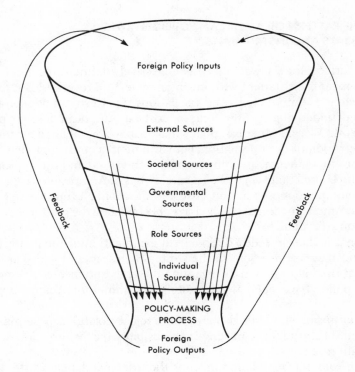

FIGURE 1 Sources of American Foreign Policy and Their Interrelationships

Source: Charles W. Kegley, Jr., and Eugene R. Wittkopf, *American Foreign Policy: Pattern and Process* (N.Y.: St. Martin's, 1982, 2nd ed.), p. 531.

is attempting to explain a single foreign policy event or a whole pattern of behaviors, no single source category fully determines output behavior; rather, the source categories are all interrelated and operate *in combination* to determine foreign policy decisions, and hence foreign policy outputs.

In the foreign policy-making process inputs are transformed into outputs. The process is complex because there are many participants and because policy making cannot be divorced from all of the interdependent sources which shape decision makers' responses to situations demanding action. But once decisions are reached by those in authority, action directed abroad commences—in the form of policy pronouncements and declarations, for example, or the granting of foreign aid, or even the sending of troops abroad. By monitoring the outcomes of this policy-making process, as we do in Part I, we can describe the patterns of postwar American foreign policy.

Our first task, then, is to examine the persistent patterns of American foreign policy as discerned from the goals the nation's officials seek to attain abroad, the values that give rise to those objectives, and the means or instruments through which they are pursued.

THE PATTERN OF AMERICAN FOREIGN POLICY: GOALS AND INSTRUMENTS

On the surface, the daily actions that collectively define American foreign policy appear to be fraught with inconsistencies and reversals. But despite these seeming contradictions and vacillations, a pattern can be seen in the goals and underlying assumptions of postwar American foreign policy. Since World War II, American policy makers have maintained a coherent, enduring vision of the international environment, a consistent view based on certain fundamental assumptions about the world and the appropriate role of the United States in it. To be sure, critics of American foreign policy have sometimes opposed its consensual foundation. Nevertheless, it is our view that American foreign policy since 1945 has been the product of a more or less consistent outlook.

What is that orthodox outlook? An examination of the major policy pronouncements and actions of the United States since World War II suggests that the following tenets regarding the ends and means of American foreign policy have been uppermost in the minds of American policy makers:

1. *Globalism:* The United States must reject isolationism permanently and substitute for it an active responsibility for the direction of international affairs.
2. *Anticommunism:* Communism is the principal danger in the world, and the United States must use its power to combat the spread of this presumed menace.
3. *Containment:* Because the Soviet Union is the spearhead of the com-

munist challenge, American foreign policy must be dedicated to the containment of Soviet expansionism and influence.

4. *Military might*: Military preparedness must be relied on to protect the nation's security and to influence the course of world events in a manner consistent with its interests.

5. *Interventionist means*: Intervention in the affairs of others may be necessary to protect the nation's security and to promote its interests.

The essays that follow elaborate each of these themes (from a variety of perspectives) and illustrate how they relate to the objectives and conduct of American foreign policy since 1945. A broad look at the messages they convey follows.

PERSPECTIVES ON THE POSTWAR PATTERN OF AMERICAN FOREIGN POLICY: AN OVERVIEW

Stephen E. Ambrose's "Globalism in American Foreign Policy," drawn from his book *Rise to Globalism*, outlines the basic features of the global responsibility the United States has assumed since World War II. The essay focuses particular attention on the intimate relationship between the nation's rejection of isolationism and its assumption of an active world role, on the one hand, and the perceived challenge of communism and a preference for military might and interventionist means as instruments for shaping world affairs, on the other. Ambrose reminds us that while the geographic reach of American interests and involvement, extending into every corner of the globe, may be taken for granted today, the extent of that globalism is largely a post-World War II phenomenon, and hence a feature which gives a distinctive character to postwar American foreign policy.

Anticommunism, and particularly opposition to the Soviet Union's expression of communism, have become so inextricably linked to the entire fabric of American public policy, domestic as well as international, that some have argued anticommunism has become *the* ideology of American foreign policy. The conviction that Marxist doctrine constitutes a threat to the United States has, in turn, defined the kinds of goals the United States has pursued abroad. The United States has appeared to define its mission not as much by what it stands *for* (other than the classic goals of self-preservation and national enrichment) as by what it stands *against*: communist ideology.

Anticommunism has been played out in the *containment* foreign policy posture. Viewed by many as an essentially defensive strategy for coping with the presumed expansive tendencies of the Soviet Union, containment first became the official foreign policy of the United States in 1947, when President Truman declared in the doctrine that bears his name: ". . . it must be the policy of the United States to support free peoples who are resisting attempted subjugation by armed minorities or by outside pressures." Truman's declaration was based on a view of international politics as a contest for world domination, with the Soviet Union an imperial power bent on world conquest. A distinctive view began to emerge, and it soon took on the characteristics of an American "grand crusade"—a Cold War with the Soviet Union. Containment thus became *the* foreign policy of the United States.

John Lewis Gaddis, a noted historian and student of the Cold War, traces the roots of containment and the Cold War in his article "Containment: Its Past and Future." Gaddis discusses not only the origins and evolutions of the Cold War, but also underscores the present relevance of issues and ideas associated with containment by reasoning that "containment . . . will very likely remain the goal of U.S. strategy toward the Soviet Union during the 1980s."

Whether containment *ought* to remain the focal point of American foreign policy is debatable. Hans J. Morgenthau, a strong critic of U.S. involvement in Vietnam and, until his death in 1980, a prolific and influential theorist of international relations, raises strong doubts about the wisdom of containment as it has been practiced. Basing his argument on the concept of the "national interest," a key idea in his writing over many decades, Morgenthau strongly criticizes the way that "indiscriminate opposition to communism" has led to "the indiscriminate support of governments and movements that profess and practice anti-communism." Morgenthau's wide-ranging article, "Defining the National Interest—Again: Old Superstitions, New Realities," written at the time of Jimmy Carter's inauguration as president (1977), also touches on the reasons underlying the persistence and continuity of postwar American foreign policy. The selection concludes with a discussion of U.S. relations with less developed nations in which Morgenthau argues that "the real issue that confronts American foreign policy is not whether a certain government professes and practices communism, but to what extent a government's foreign policy supports the foreign policies of the Soviet Union or of other governments hostile to the United States."

The intellectual father of containment is George F. Kennan. While head of the State Department's policy-planning staff in the late 1940s, Kennan published his now-famous article (signed "X") assessing "The Sources of Soviet Conduct" in the influential journal *Foreign Affairs*. In it, Kennan argued that Soviet leaders would forever feel insecure about their political ability to maintain power against forces both within Soviet society itself and in the outside world. Their insecurity would lead to an activist—and perhaps, toward the United States, hostile—foreign policy. Yet, Kennan reasoned, it was in the power of the United States to increase the strains under which the Soviet leadership would have to operate, perhaps thus leading to a gradual mellowing or even eventual end of Soviet power. Hence, Kennan made what was to become an often-repeated and accepted statement: ". . . [T]he main element of any United States policy toward the Soviet Union must be that of a long-term, patient but firm and vigilant containment of Russian expansive tendencies."

In time, Kennan became disturbed about how his conclusions were interpreted, and in particular with the identification of his ideas with the way containment was ultimately carried out as a foreign policy strategy. As he argued in his *Memoirs*, "I . . . naturally went to great lengths to disclaim the view, imputed to me by implication . . . that containment was a matter of stationing military forces around the Soviet borders and preventing any outbreak of Soviet military aggressiveness." In the essay reprinted here, "Two Views of the Soviet Problem," Kennan articulates what he sees as the differences between his ideas and those of his critics. The differences, he argues, lie essentially in discrepant views of the Soviet Union, the nature of its regime, and the motivations underlying its external behavior. He draws the important conclusion that different views of the Soviet Union lead to different policies for dealing with it. (This viewpoint is outlined in several other articles in this book, and the contrasts between differing views outlined by Kennan remain as pertinent today as they were throughout earlier periods of the postwar era.)

Kennan concludes with a critical view of the place that nuclear weapons have come to occupy in Soviet-American relations. Since World War II the United States has relied heavily on these weapons as an instrument of foreign policy to ensure its own physical security and survival and to accomplish its foreign policy objectives. The term *deterrence* describes the role that nuclear weapons have occupied in strategic thinking at least since the Kennedy administration in the early 1960s. *Deterrence* implies that potential adversaries will be dissuaded from hostile action against the United States by knowledge of the fact that the United States is able and willing to use nuclear weapons against them. Practically speaking, this means the United States has sought to deter the Soviet Union from attacking the United States (or its allies) by communicating to the Soviets that it possesses the capability and the will to destroy the Soviet Union with an effective retaliatory second strike. The Soviets, of course, have done the same thing. Hence, the superpowers find themselves in a mutual hostage relationship—neither can attack the other without the assurance of mutual destruction.

In recent years, many have argued that the principle of mutual assured destruction, identified by the acronym MAD, no longer guarantees the security and safety of the United States or its allies. Opponents of the principles underlying a MAD world, sometimes described as nuclear utilization theorists (NUTs), believe that a limited nuclear exchange with the Soviet Union may be possible—indeed necessary—and that a limited nuclear war may be winnable.

The issues joining those who embrace this view and those who believe that any nuclear exchange between the superpowers would necessarily and inevitably escalate to the point where both would suffer irreparable damage and destruction are complex and often exceedingly technical. Questions about the relative military capabilities of the United States and the Soviet Union are therefore focal points of discussion. Intimately related to these issues are questions about the adversaries' intentions. Often ignored, however, are the physical, emotional, and psychological consequences for American and Soviet citizens implied in the strategists' gobbledygook about "throw weight," "equivalent megatonnage," "circular error probability," and "overkill."

Spurgeon M. Keeny, Jr., and Wolfgang K. H. Panofsky bring us back to reality in their article, "MAD versus NUTS." Using language easily understood by the lay person, they discuss capabilities, intentions—and consequences. Their conclusion is that NUTS—an approach to nuclear war described as Nuclear Utilization Target Selection—remains suicidal and, one would hope, inconceivable, in a MAD world.

The United States has, of course, maintained throughout the postwar period formidable conventional military capabilities as well as an awesome nuclear arsenal. Often conventional military capabilities have been used directly to pursue particular foreign policy objectives. The postwar interventions in Korea, Lebanon, the Dominican Republic, and Vietnam are the primary examples. But in far more numerous cases, the United States has used its military might, not for the purpose of imposing a military solution on a political problem, but rather for the purpose of shaping political outcomes through the manipulation of military instruments of influence. Barry M. Blechman and Stephen S. Kaplan have identified 215 instances between 1946 and 1975 in which the United States used its military might for political purposes "without engaging in a continuing contest of violence." In their selection, "U.S. Military Forces as a Political Instrument since World War II," they seek to assess the effectiveness of past political-military operations. In the process, they illustrate vividly the multiple roles that military means have played in the postwar world as the United States pursued its self-defined global responsibilities.

The economically less developed countries of Asia, Africa, and Latin America, conventionally referred to as the Third World, have often been the targets of superpower intervention, as Blechman and Kaplan's article makes clear. The Third World has also witnessed some of the most violent conflicts of the postwar era. Foreign aid, both economic and military, propaganda efforts, and covert intelligence operations have been among the principal means the superpowers used to influence Third World political events. The efforts reflect the perception of the United States and the Soviet Union, particularly during the height of the Cold War in the late 1940s, 1950s, and early 1960s, of the need to secure Third World "allies" who would cooperate in the effort against "the enemy." As with other facets of U.S. foreign policy, the way aid, propaganda, and covert activities have been used has depended on the assumptions American decision makers have made about the objectives sought and on perceptions of Soviet intentions and capabilities.

During the past decade, the sale of military equipment to other countries became a preferred mechanism of U.S. policy makers for pursuing American interests. Andrew K. Semmel discusses the factors underlying this development in his article, "Evolving Patterns of U.S. Security Assistance, 1950-1980." Semmel examines the development of U.S. security assistance, the objectives of the program, and some of the major patterns and trends of the program the past three decades. Beginning with a definition of security assistance, Semmel focuses on the foreign and domestic rationales underlying this extensively used instrument of foreign policy. He then devotes attention to the shifting focus of security policy, as manifested in the type of assistance made available to other nations, the geographic distribution of security assistance, and the policy guidelines that have governed it. Examination of each of these areas reveals important conclusions about the linkage between security assistance as an instrument of policy and American foreign policy goals and objectives generally. The data on trends in military aid and sales also indicate the increasing use that has been made of these instruments in recent years, even as criticism of them has become more vocal at home and abroad.

The selections in Part I describe the salient features that characterize the foreign policy goals of the United States in the period since World War II and some of the instruments that have been used to realize them. Other elements of the objectives and means of American foreign policy could, of course, be added to the picture painted here. Nonetheless, the issues discussed in these essays relate to the ongoing, central questions of American foreign policy. The reader is thus asked to consider critically the timely controversies these essays illustrate, in order to understand the ingredients which give shape to the pattern of contemporary American foreign policy.

NOTE

1. James N. Rosenau, "Pre-theories and Theories of Foreign Policy," in R. Barry Farrell, ed., *Approaches to Comparative and International Politics* (Evanston, Ill.: Northwestern University Press, 1966), pp. 27–92. Rosenau's five categories of the sources of nations' foreign policy give the present volume its organization framework. For a book-length application of the pre-theory to the study of American foreign policy, see Charles W. Kegley, Jr., and Eugene R. Wittkopf, *American Foreign Policy: Pattern and Process*, 2nd ed. (New York: St. Martin's, 1982).

1

GLOBALISM IN AMERICAN FOREIGN POLICY

STEPHEN E. AMBROSE

In 1939, on the eve of World War II, the United States had an Army of 185,000 men with an annual budget of less than $500 million. America had no military alliances and no American troops were stationed in any foreign country. The dominant political mood was isolationism. America's physical security, the *sine qua non* of foreign policy, seemed assured, not because of American alliances or military strength, but because of the distance between America and any potential enemy.

Thirty years later the United States had a standing Army of well over one million men, with an Air Force and a Navy almost as large. The budget of the Department of Defense was over $100 billion. The United States had military alliances with forty-eight nations, 1.5 million soldiers, airmen, and sailors stationed in 119 countries, and an offensive capability sufficient to destroy the world many times over. It was deeply involved in a bloody conflict in Indochina, had used military force to intervene in Lebanon and the Dominican Republic, supported an invasion of Cuba, distributed enormous quantities of arms to friendly governments around the world, and fought a costly war in Korea. A clear majority of Americans supported a policy of intervention to prevent Communist expansion, an attitude that allowed American leaders to assume the role of world policemen. But despite all the money spent on armaments, and no matter how far outward America extended her power, the technological revolution had overcome distance, and with the loss of her protective insulation, America's national security was constantly in jeopardy.

The debacle in Vietnam, combined with the weakening of the office of the Presidency brought about by Richard Nixon's disgrace, started the pendulum swinging back again, away from intervention and toward a new isolationism. By the mid-seventies people were not so keen anymore about standing up to every Communist everywhere. They recognized that there were limits to American power. Although the military did not shrink in size, its rate of growth slowed and temptations to enter local conflicts in Africa and the Middle East were spurned. Relations with Russia and China had dominated the foreign policy of the forties, fifties, and sixties, but in the seventies the focus shifted to the Middle East and Africa.

Shifts in attitudes preceded the changes in policy. Before World War II most Americans believed in a natural harmony of interests between nations, assumed that there was a common commitment to peace, and argued that no nation or people could profit from a war. These beliefs implied that peace was the normal condition between states and that war, if it came, was an aberration resulting from the irrational acts of evil or psychotic men. It was odd that a nation that had come into existence through a victorious war, gained large portions of its territory through war, established its industrial revolution and national unity through a bloody civil war, and won a colonial empire through war, could believe that war profited no one. It was equally odd that a nation that had had one major war per generation of its existence, plus almost continuous warfare on its frontier, could assume that peace was the natural condition of states. Yet most Americans did so believe.

The American analysis of the basis of international relations made it difficult, perhaps impossible, for the United States to react effectively to the world crisis of the late thirties. America, England, and France wished to maintain the status quo without having to fight for it—thus they wished for peace. Germany, Italy, and Japan wished to change the status quo without having to fight in order to do so—thus they too wished for peace. But there was a basic difference in the wishing, and the American assumption that there was a world interest in peace was utopian. By making peace the object of their foreign policy, and by assuming that it represented rationality and the general good, American leaders found it difficult to influence events on the eve of World War II.

During and after that conflict Americans changed their attitudes. They did not come to relish war, but they did learn to accept it. They also became aware of their own vulnerability, which supported the belief, so popular after Pearl Harbor, that "if we don't fight them there, we'll have to fight them in San Francisco." Threats had to be met early and overseas. Certainly not all Americans accepted this analysis, but enough did to give the Cold War Presidents widespread support for adventures overseas, at almost any cost.

Technological change, especially in military weapons, gave added impetus to the new imperialism. For the first time in its history the United States could be threatened from abroad. High-speed ships, long-range bombers, jet aircraft, atomic weapons, and eventually intercontinental missiles all combined to endanger the physical security of the United States.

Simultaneously, America became vulnerable to foreign economic threats. Before World War II the United States was about as self-sufficient as any great nation is ever likely to be, especially in such basic items as energy resources, steel production, and agriculture. But an increasingly complex economy, coupled with the tremendous economic boom of the postwar years maintained by cheap energy, made America increasingly dependent on foreign sources. Before World War II the United States was the biggest seller of oil in the world; forty years later the United States was by far the biggest buyer of oil in the world.

And so, the irony. America had far more military power in the seventies than she had had in the late thirties, but she was less secure. America was far richer in the seventies than she had been during the Depression, but also more vulnerable to economic blackmail.

It was an unexpected outcome. At the conclusion of World War II America was at the top of the mountain. In all the world only the United States had a healthy economy, an intact physical plant capable of mass production of goods, and excess capital. American troops occupied Japan, the only important industrial power in the Pacific, while American influence was dominant in France, Britain, and western Germany, the industrial heart of Europe. The Pacific and the Mediterranean had become American lakes. Above all, the United States had a monopoly on the atomic bomb.

Yet despite the nation's preeminent position in the world, America's leaders in the summer of 1945 feared the future for three reasons. The first was political: The possibility of the emergence of another Hitler, a role Stalin seemed already to have assumed. The second was technological: The atomic secret could not be kept forever, and the German development of rocket weapons indicated that in the next war American cities would be targets. The third fear was economic: With the coming of peace there would be a return to depression. One way to avoid depression was through increased foreign trade, but if the rest of the world nationalized its basic industries and/or closed its markets, America would be unable to compete abroad.

To meet this threat the Americans hoped to shape the postwar world so that free enterprise, with an open door for trading, would become the rule rather than the exception. President Harry S Truman and other officials took it for granted that free, private enterprise was essential to a free, open, democratic society, and they were willing to save democracy at home by imposing it abroad. The program had some failures, along with some spectacular successes, primarily in Western Europe and Japan. Meanwhile the continuation of a war economy within the United States, an almost wholly unexpected development, helped ward off a return to depression. Indeed, the economy boomed in the postwar years, in part thanks to the arms race.

The arms race came about because the United States and the U.S.S.R. were deeply suspicious of each other, and with good reason. Economic rivalry and ideological differences helped fuel the race, but the most important factor was the pace of scientific and technological change in the postwar period. Nuclear weapons and the missiles to deliver them became the pivot around which much of the Cold War revolved. The fear that its opponents would move ahead on this or that weapons system drove each nation to make an all-out effort in the arms race. In the United States the resulting growth of the armed services and their suppliers—the military-industrial complex—gave generals, admirals, and industrialists new sources of power, leading to a situation in which Americans tended to find military solutions to political problems. The President was frequently tempted to accept advice to use military power, precisely because it was so easily available. No people or nation, it seemed, could stand against the American military. Not until the late sixties did large numbers of Americans learn the costly lesson that the power to destroy is not the power to control.

The United States of the Cold War period, like ancient Rome, was concerned with all political problems in the world. The loss of even one country to Communism, therefore, while not in itself a threat to American physical security, carried implications that officials in Washington found highly disturbing. They became greatly concerned with the appearance as well as the reality of events, and there was much talk of dominoes. Who ruled the Dominican Republic, for example, was of concern to one or two American corporations only, and clearly nothing that happened on that tiny island posed the slightest threat to American military or economic security. But the State Department, the White House, and the C.I.A. were certain that if the Communists won in the Dominican Republic, they would soon win elsewhere. In the early sixties, few important officials argued that South Vietnam was essential to the defense of the United States, but the attitude that "we have to prove that wars of national liberation don't work" (a curious attitude for the children of the American Revolution to hold) did carry the day, aided in no small measure by the argument that if Vietnam went Communist, all Southeast Asia would soon follow. The Pacific islands would come next, and eventually the fight would be on America's West Coast.

The attitude that what happened anywhere in the world was important to the United States differed radically from the American outlook of 1939. One reason for the change was the astonishing growth of America's overseas military bases. The American armed forces flowed into many vacuums at the end of the war, and once American troops were stationed on foreign soil, that soil was included in the list of America's "vital interests."

But America's rise to globalism was by no means mindless, just as it was not exclusively a reaction to the Communist challenge or a response to economic needs. A frequently heard expression during World War II was that "America has come of age." Americans had a sense of power, of bigness, of destiny. They had saved the world from Hitler; now they would save the world from Stalin. In the process, American influence and control would expand. During World War II, Henry Luce of *Life* magazine spoke for most political leaders as well as American businessmen, soldiers, and the public generally when he said that the twentieth century would be the American century. Politicians looked for areas in which American influence could dominate. Businessmen looked for profitable markets and new sources of cheap raw materials; the military looked for overseas bases. All found what they wanted as America inaugurated a program of expansion that had no inherent limits.

Americans who wanted to bring the blessings of democracy, capitalism, and stability to everyone meant just what they said—the whole world, in their view, should be a reflection of the United States. Americans launched a crusade for freedom that would be complete only when freedom reigned everywhere. Conservatives like Senator Robert Taft doubted that such a goal was obtainable, and old New Dealers like Henry Wallace argued that it could only be achieved at the cost of domestic reform. But most politicians and nearly all businessmen and soldiers signed on as crusaders.

While America's businessmen, soldiers, and politicians moved into South America, Europe, and Southeast Asia, her leaders rarely paused to wonder if there were limits to American power. The disorderly expansion and the astronomical growth of areas defined as constituting a vital American interest seemed to Washington, Wall Street, and the Pentagon to be entirely normal and natural. Almost no important public figure argued that the nation was overextended, just as no one could suggest any attitude toward Communism other than unrelieved hostility.

But ultimately, military reality, combined with the obvious truth that American empire builders were never as ruthless as they might have been without the restraints of their own moral heritage and culture, did put limits on American expansion. At no time after 1950 was the United States capable of destroying Russia or her allies without taking on totally unacceptable risks herself; at no time was the United States able to establish an imperial dominion free from her own moral constraints. The crusade against Communism, therefore, took the form of containment rather than attack. As a policy, containment, with its implication of an acceptance of a permanently divided world, led to widely felt frustration. These frustrations were deepened by self-imposed constraints on the use of force in Korea, Vietnam, and elsewhere. But scarcely anyone seriously considered an alternative to containment until that policy broke down so totally in Vietnam and Cambodia.

The failure of containment in Indochina led to another basic shift in attitude toward America's role in the world. It was not a return to isolationism, 1939 style—the pendulum did not swing that far. It was a general realization that, given the twin restraints of fear of provoking a Russian nuclear strike and America's reluctance to use her full military power, there was relatively little the United States could accomplish by force of arms.

After Vietnam there was also a shift in the focus of American foreign policy, especially after 1973, when the Arab oil boycott made Americans suddenly aware that the Middle East was more important than Europe to them. Nixon's 1972 trip to China, the emergence of black Africa, and the discovery of abundant raw materials in both Africa and South America, helped turn American eyes from the northern to the southern half of the globe. This shift emphasized the fundamentally changed nature of the American economy, from self-sufficiency to increasing dependency on others for basic supplies. As America entered the 1980s she was richer and more powerful—and more vulnerable—than at any time in her history.

2

CONTAINMENT
Its Past And Future

JOHN LEWIS GADDIS

N ations, like individuals, tend to be prisoners of their pasts. Rarely has this been more true than in the thirty-seven years of Soviet-American competition we know as the Cold War. That phenomenon, one of the longest-running in modern times, has appeared, more than once, to be on the verge of passing from the scene, but it never really has. Something always seems to happen to revive it—Korea, Hungary, the U-2, Vietnam, Czechoslovakia, Angola, the Carter human rights campaign, Afghanistan—just as pundits are about to consign the Cold War to those scavengers of dead issues and defunct controversies, the historians.

Why this extraordinary durability? How is it that a rivalry that arose three and a half decades ago over issues few leaders on either side today would be capable of recalling, much less discussing intelligently—how is it that such a competition can still preoccupy us today, in a world that could hardly be more different from that of 1945? And how is it that this rivalry, which, in any other age, would long ago have produced war, has not in fact done so, even though by anyone's standards there has been ample provocation? What are the prospects that this standoff between competition and caution will continue? What policies should the United States adopt in the 1980s to insure that it does?

I

The Cold War began as a direct outgrowth of the way World War II ended, with victorious powers on opposite sides of the globe separated, both in Europe and Northeast Asia, by power vacuums. If anything ever is inevitable in history, it was probably inevitable that the uneasy coalition Hitler had given rise to would break up, once the force that had brought it together had

John Lewis Gaddis, "Containment: Its Past and Future," pp. 1–21 in *Neither Cold War nor Détente? Soviet American Relations in the 1980s*, Richard Melanson, ed. (Charlottesville: University Press of Virginia, 1982). University Press of Virginia. Copyright © 1982 by the Rector & Visitors of the University of Virginia.

ceased to exist. The controversies that ensued over Eastern Europe, Germany and Berlin, the Balkans, Turkey, Iran, Japan, and Korea were all part of the process of postwar adjustment among the superpowers. They grew out of the probes and counter-probes by which great states demarcate respective spheres of influence, organize blocs, establish tacit "rules of the game," and in general settle down to the perpetual condition of wary coexistence that develops when neither side can dominate the other.

The ideological competition between communism and capitalism had been present, of course, since the days of the Bolshevik Revolution, but it was not a primary cause of the Cold War. Both Russians and Americans tended to view ideology more as a justification for action than as a guide to action; both, as they showed during World War II, were capable of subordinating ideological differences to pursue common interests where those existed. Once they disappeared, though, ideology did become the chief means by which each side differentiated friend from foe. The Soviet Union moved, somewhat belatedly, to consolidate its sphere of influence in Eastern Europe by imposing communist regimes there; the United States, also somewhat belatedly, came to see in the ideological orientation of states and movements reliable evidence of where they stood in the global competition for power. Admittedly, the pattern was not always perfect. The Soviet Union did not insist on imposing communist governments everywhere within its sphere of influence—Finland was the notable exception. Nor did the United States, as the case of Yugoslavia showed, consign to the outer darkness all communist states. In general, though, and with increasing frequency as the years went on, ideology did become the mechanism by which alignments were drawn in the Cold War, even to the point that the United States refused, for many years, to cooperate with the People's Republic of China in a task in which both had a strong interest—containing the Russians.

Once it was underway, the Cold War took on yet a third dimension— that of an arms race. Here, appearances were more important than reality. We now know that throughout the first two and a half decades of the Cold War, the Soviet Union was inferior to the United States in all major categories of weapons except manpower. But until the deployment of satellite reconnaissance capabilities in the early 1960s, Washington had no reliable means of verifying that fact, nor were the Russians cooperative in providing one. As a consequence, the arms race appeared to be closer than it actually was: Until 1961 the United States perceived itself as operating from a position of strategic inferiority, or something very near to it; after 1961, when Washington convinced itself that it was in fact ahead of the Russians, it was actually in the process of losing that advantage, thanks to the Kremlin's decision to switch, in the wake of the Cuban missile crisis, from an emphasis on rhetorical weapons to real ones.

A fourth dimension the Cold War took on was that of a competition for influence in the so-called Third, or Nonaligned, World. This, again, was an aspect of the struggle that did not surface immediately: Stalin's interest in supporting national liberation movements beyond his control was notoriously tepid. With Khrushchev, though, the arena of competition did shift to Asia, Africa, and Latin America, greatly aided by the grievances inhabitants of those regions had, rightly or not, against the industrialized West.

There is yet a fifth dimension of the Cold War that is more difficult to characterize than the others, but no less important: This is the Cold War as the product of internal influences within the two major countries involved. George F. Kennan had argued as early as 1946 that the Soviet leadership required the existence of a hostile outside world in order to justify its own repressive rule; there was nothing the West could do to allay Moscow's paranoia, he seemed to be saying, because the regime needed external threats to provide internal legitimacy.[1] Similarly, revisionist critics of American foreign policy have more recently made the argument that the requirements of capitalism force the United States into an imperial posture: It is we, not the Russians, they maintain, who find it necessary regularly to disrupt the international order.[2] Whether one accepts the argument or not, it is not too difficult to suggest groups or interests within the United States who might benefit from a continuation of the Cold War: defense contractors eager for arms sales, ethnic groups who for one reason or another nurse grudges against the Russians, career bureaucrats and military personnel whose budgets and promotion opportunities are tied to high levels of defense spending, and, perhaps most important, politicians attempting to win favor with the voters by the time-honored tactic of running against Moscow. Presumably parallel, though of course not precisely equivalent, impulses operate within the Soviet Union as well.

There have been, then, not one but several Cold Wars, and it is this multidimensional character that helps to explain the conflict's remarkable durability. It has had the capacity to shift from one arena of competition to another so that as settlements are reached in one area, rivalries break out elsewhere. It is as if a virus had the capacity to evolve into new and more resistant strains as each new antigen is developed against them. Although the last three dimensions of the Cold War—the arms race, the struggle for influence in the Third World, and external hostility as the product of internal interests—are the most virulent today, there is no reason to think that this process of shifting has ended, or is likely to anytime soon. It may be some time, then, before we can safely regard the Cold War, in its entirety, as history.

II

Before examining current aspects of the Cold War, though, some attempt should be made to address the tangled question of responsibility for it. Students of international affairs generally shy away from issues of responsibility: It is more important, they argue, to find out what happened; to get into arguments over "why" is to slide into the slippery realm of metaphysics.[3] That attitude may be appropriate enough for purely scholarly purposes, but when it comes to the policy implications of scholarly analysis, it will not do. To avoid judgments on responsibility for past events is to atrophy standards necessary for guidance in the future: We need careful thought about this question of responsibility if we are to avoid either the smug complacency of imagined moral superiority or the self-destructive effects of blaming everything that happens in this less-than-perfect world on ourselves.

In a sense, both superpowers have perceived themselves as acting primarily for defensive reasons during most of the Cold War. Whether justifiably or not, both the Soviet Union and the United States have explained their projection of influence over much of the rest of the world as necessary to protect themselves against the other. We will not get very far, then, by attempting to evaluate responsibility on the basis of where defensive motivations existed and where they did not. It is the nature of great powers that they often do offensive things for defensive reasons.

The more productive approach is to ask which great power was more capable of meeting its security requirements within the context of the existing international order and which required fundamental changes in that order to be secure. Here we come to the heart of the difference between American and Soviet behavior in the Cold War; it is from this perspective that we can best shed light on the issue of responsibility.

Americans have had the reputation, over the years, of wanting to change the international order. One thinks of Woodrow Wilson's Fourteen Points, Cordell Hull's schemes for reforming the world trade system, the Atlantic Charter, the original campaign for the United Nations. But not one of those initiatives was ever considered vital to the security of the United States: They were put forward, mostly sincerely, mostly with good intentions, but without that implacable determination—that unwillingness to compromise—that occurs when one's vital interests are at stake. Ours never really were in this somewhat utopian and certainly irregularly pursued effort to remake the world; as far as fundamental security interests were concerned, we were as content with the existing international system as the most cynical—and, in this country, most criticized—of our Old World allies.

Not so the Soviet Union. It is true that Stalin often spoke in traditional balance-of-power terms: All would be well, he implied, if the Soviet Union could only be granted its legitimate security interests. The problem was that he never made it clear how far those interests extended. The West was reluctantly prepared to grant Stalin the boundary concessions and subservient governments he wanted in Eastern Europe, nor did it balk at meeting his initial territorial demands in the Far East, despite the Soviet Union's minimal role in the war against Japan.[4] But Stalin wanted more; the northern provinces of Iran, for example, or control of the Turkish Straits, or a unified but subservient Germany, or the right to occupy Hokkaido. He also quite clearly refused to abide by promises he had made to hold free elections in the areas he occupied—notably Poland and North Korea—and he used (though somewhat cautiously) communist parties elsewhere to promote the objectives of the Soviet Union. It was not that Stalin had global ambitions or any fixed timetable for achieving them. It was just that he could not resist exploiting opportunities, and he had the patience to wait for them to arise.

There was, as a consequence, a fundamental difference in the way Soviet and American expansion proceeded in the postwar years. Soviet expansion reflected discontent with the world as it was, together with a determination to change it in such a way as to accommodate Moscow. American expansion took place, not so much out of dissatisfaction with the world as it was, as with the world as it would be if the Russians had their way. Soviet expansion took place for the most part against the wishes of the people involved; American expansion took place almost entirely at the fervent invitation of those worried about the Russians.[5]

This is not to say that both nations, once they acquired empires, did not behave in an imperial manner. Both fell into the habit of looking at the world in terms of a zero-sum game, in which gains for one invariably meant losses for the other. Both tended to lose sight, as a consequence, of the distinction between vital and peripheral interests. Both responded, at various times, by overcommitting themselves, although Americans, who tended to do their own fighting, allowed this to happen more often than did the Russians, who relied more heavily on proxies.

These similarities in behavior, however, should not be allowed to obscure the very real differences in motivation that give rise to them. The fact is that the United States throughout the history of the Cold War has, on the whole, been reconciled to living with the world as it is, while the Soviet Union, more for historical and institutional than ideological reasons, has seen its security as dependent on changing it. In this sense (though not in the classic Marxist-Leninist sense), the United States has been the status quo power, the Soviet Union the revolutionary power, and that fact ought not to be lost sight of in assessing responsibility for the Cold War.

III

If we can establish, then, that the dominant pattern in the Cold War has been one of Soviet action and American reaction (for this is what is suggested by the conclusion that the Soviet Union finds it more difficult to live with the existing world order than does the United States), then the question arises: How has the United States handled this problem over the years? How, and with what results, has it responded to Moscow's successive efforts to restructure the international system to its advantage?

The answer, of course, is containment, but it is immediately necessary to differentiate between the various approaches to that strategy that have been tried over the years. All postwar administrations have seen American security as tied up with the maintenance of a global balance of power. All have seen the Soviet Union as the major threat to that balance, though they have differed over the extent to which Moscow was capable of drawing other communist nations into that enterprise. All have sought to harness American resources, along with those of allies, in a joint effort to restrict the further growth of Soviet influence in the world, in order that the diversity upon which our system depends can be maintained.[6]

Nevertheless, there have been two distinct styles of containment in the postwar era—styles which can best be categorized as symmetrical and asymmetrical response. Symmetrical response simply means reacting to threats to the balance of power at the same location, time, and level of violence of the original provocation. It implies the idea of calibration: One tailors response to offense, doing no more but also no less than is necessary to counter the threat in question, without running the risk of escalation or suffering the humiliation of surrender. Asymmetrical response involves shifting the location or nature of one's reaction onto terrain better suited to the application of one's strengths against adversary weaknesses. One may, though, in the process run the risk of escalation or, by not countering the original provocation where it occurred, humiliation.

Both approaches have been tried at various times during the postwar period. George Kennan's original containment strategy was an example of asymmetrical response in that it sought to counter the fear brought about by the Soviet military presence in Europe and Northeast Asia after World War II, not by building up countervailing military force, but by relying on United States economic aid to rehabilitate war-shattered economies in Western Europe and Japan, thereby creating in those countries the self-confidence that would allow them to resist the Russians on their own. Containment would have been achieved, Kennan argued, if the four vital centers of industrial-military power not then in Soviet hands—the United States, the United Kingdom, the Rhine Valley, and Japan—could be prevented from becoming so.[7]

By 1950, though, out of a sense of the vulnerability the United States felt as a result of not matching perceived Soviet military capabilities (and especially after the unexpectedly early first test of a Soviet atomic bomb), Washington shifted, with NSC–68, to symmetrical response: We had to be prepared, the argument ran, to counter whatever aggression the Russians threw at us, but without resorting to nuclear weapons, where we no longer possessed a monopoly, and without capitulating, an action which, if it occurred anywhere, could lead to an erosion of credibility everywhere.[8] The way in which we fought the Korean War was an excellent example of symmetrical response: We countered an enemy provocation at the location, time, and in the manner of its original occurrence, without surrendering, but also without setting off a wider war.

The effort proved costly, though, and the American people grew impatient with it; those frustrations contributed to the victory at the polls in 1952 of General Eisenhower and the Republicans. Their objective was to maintain American interests throughout the world against what was seen as a centrally directed monolith controlled from Moscow, but to do it at less cost than the symmetrical response strategy of NSC–68 had entailed. Accordingly, they went back to the concept of asymmetrical response, but this time with reliance on the threat to use nuclear weapons as the primary deterrent: The idea was to create uncertainty in the minds of potential adversaries as to what the United States might do if aggression took place, thereby making the risks appear to outweigh the benefits.[9] We would respond to aggression, as Dulles liked to say, with ominous vagueness, "at times and in places of our own choosing."

Unfortunately, though, the Eisenhower-Dulles strategy of asymmetrical response had two major liabilities: It seemed to run the risk of nuclear war over minor matters (Quemoy and Matsu were conspicuous examples), and it seemed incapable of preventing communist victories under the guise of national liberation movements in the Third World. It was in part by capitalizing on these deficiencies that John F. Kennedy and the Democrats gained the White House in 1961; there was nothing very original about their strategy, though, as they took the country quickly back to the symmetrical response approach of NSC–68. Like the authors of that earlier document, Kennedy and his advisers regarded American interests in the world as indivisible, but they also saw means as expandable; therefore, they argued, the United State could afford to act to counter aggression wherever it occurred without either the dangers of nuclear war or the embarrassments of humiliation.

The chief result of this return to symmetry, of course, was the war in Vietnam, the most egregious American example in the postwar period of offensive actions taken for what were perceived to be defensive reasons; a war that, like Korea, was consistent with prevailing national strategy but also, by demonstrating the costs of the strategy, in the end discredited it. The debacle in Vietnam paved the way for the Nixon victory in 1968 and for a return, once again, to asymmetrical response.

The Nixon-Kissinger strategy reflected this emphasis in several respects. It called, through the Nixon Doctrine, for a cutting back of American commitments in the world: Allies, it implied, would bear a greater share of the burden of their defense, with the United States helping out, where needed, by furnishing technology but not manpower.[10] It called for countering Soviet challenges to the balance of power through a combination of pressures and inducements designed to get Moscow to accept certain "rules of the game"—to persuade the Russians that it was in their own best interests to accept the world as it was rather than to try to change it. This process was intended to work through the application of linkage—in itself an asymmetrical concept, implying the withholding of concessions in some areas until others were granted elsewhere. The goal was a multipolar world operating on balance-of-power principles—an idea not too different from what Kennan had sought some twenty-five years before.[11]

This emphasis on asymmetry continued through the end of the Ford administration, but not without coming under sharp attack from symmetrically minded critics who charged that détente had produced an erosion in American strategic and conventional capabilities relative to those of the Soviet Union.[12] Despite ample provocation from the Russians, the Carter administration never accepted that argument, less out of respect for the strategic legacy of Henry Kissinger, one gathers, than from the fact that no one has yet demonstrated how the nation can afford a return to symmetrical response in an era of energy dependency and double-digit inflation.

What is striking, in retrospect, about this oscillation between symmetry and asymmetry, is how little most of it has had to do with what the Russians were up to at any given point. Without exception, shifts in strategies of containment since 1947 have concided, not with new Kremlin initiatives, but with shifts in perceptions of means in Washington. Perceptions of means have played a larger role than perceptions of threats in shaping our policy toward the Soviet Union: The implications, it would seem, are not encouraging for those who seek a consistent and coherent foreign policy carefully insulated from domestic considerations.

IV

There have been several attempts at détente in postwar Soviet-American relations: the "thaw" following Stalin's death in 1953; Eisenhower's attempts, in 1959 and 1960, to establish a dialogue with Khrushchev; Kennedy's comparable efforts, partly successful after the Cuban missile crisis; Johnson's continuation of that approach, frustrated by the change of leadership in Moscow and American escalation in Vietnam. Not until 1969, though, did the same interest in a relaxation of tensions exist in roughly the same proportions on both sides: The decade that followed saw a sustained attempt on the part of both Moscow and Washington to move beyond Cold War rigidities that must now, in the light of Afghanistan and Poland, be regarded as having failed.

The reason, it would seem, is that both sides were to a greater extent prisoners of Cold War thinking than they realized at the time: Americans and Russians embraced détente with differing expectations of what it would produce—expectations colored, to a considerable degree, by legacies of the past.

Nixon and Kissinger, for example, thought of détente as an updated form of containment.[13] Their idea was to achieve nothing less than a modification of Soviet behavior by rewarding actions that showed a disposition to accept the world as it was and by discouraging, through the application of pressures and constraints, those that did not. It was a bit like trying to train a rat or a pigeon in a psychology laboratory to perform certain tricks in response to a carefully crafted and precisely measured series of rewards and punishments.[14]

The Russians, on the other hand, saw détente as a means of rendering safer the process of changing the international order. It was, they clearly said, a means of controlling competition in dangerous areas like nuclear weapons, while continuing it in others: The idea, in short, was compartmentalization.[15] True, the Soviet Union could benefit from certain concessions from the West, especially in the form of trading privileges. But it would not pay all that much to get them; in fact, Kremlin leaders probably believed they would not have to pay anything at all, given the abiding venality of Western capitalists eager to find buyers, even if communist buyers, for their products.

For a time, it seemed possible to paper over the differences. The Russians at Moscow in 1972 signed a statement of "Basic Principles" that appeared to rule out efforts to exploit Third World crises at the expense of the United States.[16] Summit meetings proceeded on more or less an annual basis during the early 1970s, with protestations of friendship covering up the fact that fewer and fewer meaningful agreements were being made. By the middle of the decade, though, cracks in the facade were becoming too noticeable to ignore.

One was Moscow's alleged failure to prevent the 1973 Egyptian attack on Israel and the 1975 North Vietnamese offensive against South Vietnam, acts of omission that seemed inconsistent with the injunctions against profiting from the discomfiture of others so solemnly invoked at the first Moscow summit. Another sign of strain came over the issue of human rights, with first Congress and then the Carter administration making changes in the Soviet treatment of Jews and dissidents a prerequisite for progress on economic and other issues. A third problem arose from the projection of Soviet power and influence into Africa, chiefly through the use of Cuban proxies, in what seemed to be a clear attempt to exploit remaining anticolonial sentiment there to the disadvantage of the West. Still another nail in the coffin of détente was the Soviet Union's continuing buildup in its strategic missile capabilities, a trend which, if it did not directly contravene the SALT I agreement, did at least seem ill-matched to the spirit of mutual restraint most Americans believed had been implied in those agreements. Afghanistan, of course, was the final blow.

It is not difficult, in retrospect, to pick out deficiencies in the American approach to détente during this period. The Nixon administration probably pushed linkage too vigorously, demanding that the Russians act to restrain countries over which they had limited leverage in the first place. It is not at all clear that the Russians could have stopped the Egyptians in 1973 or the North Vietnamese in 1975, even if they had wanted to. Then, too, linkage implied tight control—knowing just when to apply rewards and punishments, without going overboard on either. But the Nixon administration lost control of the linkage process almost at once, with the introduction in the fall of 1972 of the Jackson-Vanik amendment; in the years that followed Kissinger oscillated between yielding to and resisting congressional pressures to link détente to the Soviet performance on human rights, exerted without any clear notion on the part of the legislators of what precisely should be demanded or what should be granted in return. The Carter administration further compounded the confusion by first elevating the question of human rights to the level of universal principle but then abandoning the idea of linkage that seemed to offer the best hope of securing Soviet cooperation in that area in the first place.[17]

Similarly, on the issue of strategic arms, the administrations of Nixon, Ford, and Carter all tried, from an unfavorable position that saw American military power shrinking relative to that of the U.S.S.R., to negotiate arms-control treaties that would limit further Soviet gains without imposing dangerous restrictions on the United States. To a remarkable degree, they succeeded: Critics have yet to demonstrate convincingly how the SALT I agreements or their unratified SALT II counterparts left the United States inferior to the Russians in the overall calculus of strength that goes to make up deterrence.[18] But the agreements did require tolerating asymmetries, and that idea was difficult to sell to an uneasy public (and Congress) that saw quantitative indices of strategic power declining but failed to see the justification for freezing that disproportion permanently.

The United States also erred in not taking Brezhnev and his colleagues at their word when they said that détente would not preclude efforts to aid "liberation" movements in the Third World. As a result, Angola, Somalia, Ethiopia, and Yemen all became symbols of Soviet bad faith, when in fact the Russians were only honoring their own public promises, thereby meeting a standard to which Americans had often sought to hold them in the past. The most ridiculous manifestations of aggrieved American innocence came in the summer of 1979, when the Carter administration, hoping at once to defuse critics and avoid leaks, made public through Senator Frank Church the "unacceptable" presence of a Soviet combat brigade in Cuba— only to have to find it "acceptable" after all when it developed that the unit had been there for years and that Washington had no practical means of getting it out. Calling public attention to one's own impotence is, even in the best of circumstances, an unlikely way to enhance one's credibility.

Before carrying these criticisms too far, though, it is worth noting that things have not always worked out well for the Soviet Union, either. The effect of the 1973 Middle East war, despite the ensuing oil embargo, was to boost the reputation of Americans, not Russians, in the Arab world. The 1975 Helsinki agreement, proposed initially by Moscow as a means of legitimizing its control over Eastern Europe, is now remembered more for the attention it shed on human rights violations there and in the Soviet Union than for the purposes for which the Kremlin wanted it. Soviet incursions into Africa may have won Moscow temporary control in certain countries, but they are hardly all reliable allies today. Moreover, and as a consequence, Africans are coming to see Russians rather than Americans as inheritors of the imperialist tradition there: As one observer has put it, "U.S. policy in fact lost a country [Angola] and gained a continent."[19] Moscow's clumsy handling of its relations with Japan produced similar results: For the sake of a few barren islands in the Sea of Okhotsk the Russians have managed to drive the major powers in the Far East, Japan and China, into an "antihegemonal" alignment directed, however discreetly, against them. Finally, the Soviet military buildup has now set off corresponding trends in the West, just as the Russians may have reached the stage, for economic reasons, of needing to taper off.[20]

Afghanistan is, of course, a wholly new order of provocation. For the first time since World War II, the Soviet Union has used its own troops, not proxies, in an area that has not been generally regarded as lying within its immediate sphere of influence. It is startling to realize that the Red Army has suffered more combat casualties in the past year than in the previous thirty-five. Precedents thereby established are unsettling: We can no longer rely, as we have in recent years, on the cautious nonadventurism of the Kremlin gerontocracy: the old men did bestir themselves to act, this time, in an adventurous and unpredictable way.

Taking the longer view, though, Afghanistan is likely to be regarded as a strategic error of the first order on Moscow's part, akin, in the misjudgment it reflects, to the decision to blockade Berlin in 1948, or to authorize the North Korean invasion of South Korea in 1950, or to place missiles in Cuba in 1962. It is difficult to see how whatever gains the Russians have won there outweigh their losses: (1) within the Islamic world, which, before Afghanistan, had every reason, thanks to the Palestinian impasse and events in Iran, to be hostile to the United States; (2) in Western Europe, where NATO's sense of common danger has counterbalanced the potentially divisive effects of disproportionate energy deficiencies; (3) in American domestic politics, where the result has been to boost the fortunes of candidates the Russians would no doubt have preferred to have had defeated; (4) in the nonaligned world, where the painfully acquired leadership of a Soviet satellite, Cuba, has been abruptly discredited; and (5) in Eastern Europe and the Soviet Union itself, where the leadership has encountered as a consequence not only nuisances in the form of the American grain embargo and restrictions on technology transfers but also unaccustomed problems of public relations with regard to the Olympic boycott and, more significantly, the task of explaining what its troops are doing in Afghanistan.

One should not be too hasty, then, in deciding who gained the most from détente. All that can be said at the moment is that both sides went into it with differing expectations, that both, in varying degrees, have had their expectations disappointed, and that we are now entering a new and unpredictable stage in that long and complex phenomenon we call the Cold War.

V

Containment, therefore, will very likely remain the goal of our strategy toward the Soviet Union during the 1980s. . . . We may therefore consider what American interests are likely to be in the decade to come and what is most likely to threaten them.

Flights of contradictory rhetoric notwithstanding, United States officials have been surprisingly consistent in defining this nation's vital interests: John F. Kennedy was only saying more explicitly what his predecessors and successors have believed when he proclaimed, two months before his death, that "the interest of the United States of America is best served by preserving and protecting a world of diversity in which no one power or combination of powers can threaten the security of the United States."[21] It has been in the *balancing* of power, rather than in its unilateral or imperial exercise, that our security has most often been seen to rest: That there have been occasional departures from this pattern only demonstrates the untidiness of certain generalizations in history, not their overall invalidity.

What is it, then, that is most likely to threaten the existing distribution of power in the world in the 1980s? Despite Afghanistan, it is not the Russians, at least not in any immediate sense: Knowing the virtues of patience, they are unlikely to undertake overt and widescale challenges to the balance of power. It is certainly not communism, not in an age when the most strident calls for Western unity and strength regularly emanate from the proletarian mandarins in Peking. It is, rather, a small and poorly understood group of states, primitive, by most standards, in their economic development, medieval in their subordination of state and even multistate interests to the dictates of religion, unsophisticated in their knowledge of the outside world and for the most part heedless of the effects of their actions upon it, and yet in a position, thanks to accidents of geology and the insatiable appetite for fossil fuels of the industrialized West, to bring it literally grinding to a halt at any moment, whether on the whim of militant students, greedy sheikhs, or fanatical ayatollahs.

The Russians, it is important to note, did not create this situation—we did that ourselves. But they are in an excellent position to exploit it, whether by gaining control of the oil-producing regions, or by interdicting lines of supply, or by simply intimidating the shaky regimes of that area to such an extent that they dole out their principal commodity, not according to the laws of economics or the needs of the West, but by a rationing plan devised in Moscow.

Coupled with this is the less immediate but no less worrisome danger posed by the Soviet Union's attainment of parity, and in certain areas, superiority, in the arms race. This achievement stems from no recent decision on the part of Kremlin leaders—the military buildup has been steady since Brezhnev and Kosygin took office in 1964, greatly aided, it should be added, by the American involvement in Vietnam, which diverted resources away from measures needed to keep up with the Russians[22] and then, by debauching the currency, made it difficult if not impossible to afford to catch up. A condition of actual, as opposed to imagined, Western military inferiority is a new element in the history of the Cold War, the effects of which can be foreseen only to the point of surmising that they will not be reassuring.

What we face, then, is the task of defending our vital interests—the diversity that comes from having an international order in which no one power is dominant—from a position, not of military superiority or economic self-sufficiency, but of approaching military inferiority and already present resource dependency. It is not the most favorable position upon which to make a stand; within this general context, if not with reference to the immediate crisis in Afghanistan that gave rise to it, President Carter had some justification for making the statement that we now confront "the greatest threat to peace since the Second World War."[23]

VI

There are no quick solutions to this double problem of energy deficiency and declining military strength. Both can be dealt with, given time, but it will take years before substantial progress will be seen. What we need now are short-term measures to tide us over this crisis period, without at the same time disrupting the long-term initiatives necessary to eliminate it altogether.

Because we will be operating from a position of stringency, if not outright weakness, during this period, one thing is clear at the outset: Symmetrical response will not do. The United States and its allies cannot in the future afford to meet challenges to the balance of power on terrain and in circumstances selected by their adversaries. What this means is that we are going to have to persuade the Russians to play by our rules, rather than their own.

Moscow for years has seen détente as "compartmentalized competition"—one agrees not to compete in dangerous areas, but to do so in others. But this approach gives special advantage to the power that, by its own admission, is not content with the world as it is. It allows the Russians the luxury, in setting out to change the world, of picking how and where they will do it, with the knowledge that the United States, if it follows the rules of compartmentalized competition, will not be able to shift the theater of action onto more favorable terrain. It obliges us to contest the Russians on their terms, not our own, to respond to Soviet challenges where they occur, while carrying on business as usual elsewhere.

The Russian view of détente also poses problems for the West because of its fragmented structure of political authority. Compartmentalized competition requires not only an abundance of means but also tight coordination and control; where that is lacking, as it is to a considerable extent in the United States, the NATO countries, and Japan, the way is left open for divide-and-conquer tactics. The Russians can make advantageous offers to allies, or to special interest groups within the United States— farmers, businessmen, ethnic groups, even athletes—with the expectation that self-interest can usually be counted upon to overshadow the national interest, as officially defined in Washington.

Soviet "rules of the game," not surprisingly, thus offer greater benefits to the Russians than to us. The alternative, of course, is linkage—the idea, developed by Henry Kissinger, that all elements in the Soviet-American relationship are interconnected and that concessions in one area must be compensated for by roughly equivalent concessions in others.

There are, to be sure, problems with linkage, not the least of which is that the Russians have never really accepted it. It implies leverage where none may in fact exist. It can easily be overloaded, as Congress has already demonstrated. It runs the risk of escalation—of dragging in areas, issues, or weapons previously unrelated to the question at hand for the purpose of gaining points of pressure. Given the disadvantages of compartmentalized competition, though, linkage, with all its faults, seems the preferable alternative.

How do we do it, though? What do we link? One of the lessons of the Kissinger years is that linkage ought not to be a tit-for-tat arrangement: Progress on SALT, for example, in return for restraint in Africa. The problem with such bargaining has been that it creates artificial confrontations over questions of common interest (like SALT); it assumes Moscow's willingness to attach the same value we do to the various stakes in the game; it relies on the administration's ability to insulate the linkage process from outside pressures. What we need, instead, are linkages that do not require precise calculation but will nonetheless allow the West to apply its own strengths against Soviet weaknesses, to retain the initiative while minimizing costs.

One way to do this might be to incorporate into the idea of linkage a concept not unfamiliar to the Russians—that of the "correlation of forces," the overall direction of movement in world affairs which, Kremlin ideologists believe, is progressing inexorably toward the triumph of socialism as a matter of historical imperative. It is to our advantage to do this because world trends are not in fact proceeding in that direction—if by *socialism* one means, as the Russians do, a world congenial to their own domestic institutions. The world may be moving in a confused variety of directions at once—toward triumphs of nationalism, religion, ethnicity, irrationality, even anarchy—but there is no evidence of spontaneous movement toward the kind of world Kremlin leaders would choose, if they could.

A major, if curiously unremarked, phenomenon of the 1960s and 1970s has been the declining appeal of Soviet institutions as models elsewhere.[24] Whatever gains the Russians may have made in Angola, Vietnam, Ethiopia, Yemen, or Afghanistan, they can hardly compensate for their loss of influence in China, Indonesia, Egypt, Iraq, and among the communist parties of Western Europe. The Soviet Union is bucking the trend toward diversity that characterizes the contemporary world, and that is the West's great advantage. Survival, whether one is dealing with wind, water, or world politics, is largely a matter of accommodating one's self to irresistible forces, not fighting them. And the West (using the term loosely to include Japan) is in a far better position to do that than the Soviet Union.

The objective of containment, in this context, then, should be to bring home to Soviet leaders something Americans and many of their allies found out long ago: that the "correlation of forces" in the world favors the hegemonal aspirations of no one, and that the superpower that can bring itself to accommodate diversity now will be the one most likely to maintain its status and position over the long haul. It is in this sense—relating irreversible trends to immediate situations—that a revised strategy of linkage can be made to work. . . .

[The author concludes with a discussion of the ways containment may be continued successfully through a revised linkage strategy—*eds.*]

NOTES

1. See Kennan's telegrams from Moscow of February 22 and March 20, 1946, in U.S., Department of State, *Foreign Relations of the United States: 1946, Diplomatic Papers, vol. 6, Eastern Europe; The Soviet Union* (Washington, D.C., 1969), pp. 696–709, 721–23.

2. Robert W. Tucker, *The Radical Left and American Foreign Policy* (Baltimore, 1971), pp. 28–39, provides a succinct summary of the revisionist argument.

3. See, for example, Daniel Yergin, *Shattered Peace: The Origins of the Cold War and the National Security State* (Boston, 1977), p. 7; also, from a methodological perspective, David Hackett Fischer, *Historians' Fallacies: Toward a Logic of Historical Thought* (New York, 1970), pp. 14–15, 182–83; and Robert Stover, "Responsibility for the Cold War—A Case Study in Historical Responsibility," *History and Theory* 11 (1972): 145–78.

4. Further details can be found in John Lewis Gaddis, *The United States and the Origins of the Cold War: 1941–1947* (New York, 1972), pp. 77–79, 133–73.

5. For a recent confirmation of this thesis, see Bruce R. Kuniholm, *The Origins of the Cold War in the Near East: Great Power Conflict and Diplomacy in Iran, Turkey, and Greece* (Princeton, 1980), pp. 345, 381–82.

6. Seyom Brown, *The Faces of Power: Constancy and Change in United States Foreign Policy from Truman to Johnson* (New York, 1968), pp. 7–14.

7. George F. Kennan, *Memoirs: 1925–1965* (Boston, 1967), p. 359. See also John Lewis Gaddis, "Containment: A Reassessment," *Foreign Affairs* 55 (July 1977): 873–87.

8. NSC–68, "United States Objectives and Programs for National Security," April 14, 1950, *Foreign Relations of the United States: 1950*, 1: 237–92. For a recent reassessment, see Samuel F. Wells, Jr., "Sounding the Tocsin: NSC 68 and the Soviet Threat," *International Security* 4 (Fall 1979): 116–58, and subsequent commentaries on that article by Paul Nitze and the present author in 4 (Spring 1980): 164–76.

9. The best analysis is Glenn H. Snyder, "The 'New Look' of 1953," in Warner R. Schilling, Paul Y. Hammond, and Glenn H. Snyder, *Strategy, Politics, and Defense Budgets* (New York, 1962), pp. 379–524.

10. The clearest formulation of the Nixon Doctrine is in Nixon's first annual foreign policy report, February 18, 1970, *Public Papers of the Presidents: Richard M. Nixon: 1970* (Washington, D.C., 1971), pp. 905–6.

11. See especially, in this connection, Nixon's speech at Kansas City, July 6, 1971, *Nixon Public Papers: 1971* (Washington, D.C., 1972), p. 806; and the interview with him in *Time*, January 3, 1972, p. 15.

12. Alan Tonelson, "Nitze's World," *Foreign Policy*, no. 35 (Summer 1979), pp. 74–90.

13. Coral Bell, *The Diplomacy of Détente: The Kissinger Era* (New York, 1977), pp. 1–3.
14. The analogy is Stanley Hoffmann's, in *Primacy or World Order: American Foreign Policy since the Cold War* (New York, 1978), p. 46.
15. A succinct statement of the Soviet view of détente can be found in Leonid Brezhnev, *On the Policy of the Soviet Union and the International Situation* (Garden City, N.Y., 1973), pp. 230–31.
16. U.S., Department of State, *Bulletin* 66 (June 26, 1972), 898–99.
17. See, on this point, Strobe Talbott, *Endgame: The Inside Story of SALT II* (New York, 1979), pp. 48–49, 146–47.
18. Hoffmann, *Primacy or World Order*, p. 54. See also the record of Soviet concessions on SALT II detailed in Talbott, *Endgame*, especially pp. 134–35, 181–83.
19. Peter Jay, "Regionalism or Geopolitics," *Foreign Affairs* 58 ("America and the World: 1979"): 500.
20. Andrew Marshall, "Sources of Soviet Power: The Military Potential in the 1980's," in *Prospects of Soviet Power in the 1980's*, Part II, *Adelphi Papers*, no. 152 (London, 1979), p. 11.
21. Kennedy speech at Salt Lake City, September 26, 1963, *Public Papers of the Presidents: John F. Kennedy: 1963* (Washington, D.C., 1964), p. 736.
22. See, on this point, Harland B. Moulton, *From Superiority to Parity: The United States and the Strategic Arms Race, 1961–1971* (Westport, Conn., 1973), pp. 283–87; and, for the complaint of one who had to live with the consequences of these decisions, Henry A. Kissinger, *White House Years* (New York, 1979), p. 196.
23. Remarks at White House briefing for members of Congress, January 8, 1980, *Weekly Compilation of Presidential Documents* 16 (January 14, 1980): 40.
24. Helmut Sonnenfeldt, "Russia, America, and Détente," *Foreign Affairs* 56 (January 1979): 285–86.

3

DEFINING THE NATIONAL INTEREST—AGAIN
Old Superstitions, New Realities

HANS J. MORGENTHAU

Every four years, we welcome a new administration with great expectations for a new American foreign policy. We know of course that in the past a new administration has confirmed rather than altered the foreign policy of its predecessor and that in consequence American foreign policy since the end of World War II appears to the retrospective observer as a monument to consistency, in error and in truth, rather than as a progression toward truth, drawing lessons from the errors of the past. We know also that continuity in the ranking personnel of the foreign policy establishment is likely to spell continuity in policy since the new men responsible for foreign policy are likely to bring the same defects of intellectual judgment and moral character to bear upon the new problems of foreign policy as they did upon the old.

When John Foster Dulles took over in 1953, he promised friend and foe alike a new foreign policy, only to offer us Dean Acheson's in new rhetorical garb. When in 1961 Dean Rusk succeeded Dulles and Christian Herter, he supported the foreign policies his predecessors pursued or would have pursued, such as military intervention in Vietnam, if President Eisenhower's caution had not stood in their way. Lyndon Johnson as President embarked upon the very same foreign policies which candidate Johnson had opposed and which were in logical succession to those of his immediate predecessor. Similarly, Richard Nixon gained the presidency in 1969 on the promise of changing American policy in Indochina from war to peace but pursued as President a policy which, at least in its immediate manifestations, continued and escalated the policy of his predecessor. This consistency of American foreign policy over the long stretches of history is due to two factors: one resulting from a general quality of foreign policy, the other peculiar to the United States.

A rational foreign policy seeking the security of the nation in relation to other nations and the protection and promotion of its interests abroad is

Reprinted by permission of *The New Republic*, © 1977, The New Republic, Inc.

bipartisan by its very nature. The national interest which provided the reasoning for a rational foreign policy is not defined by the whim of a man or the partisanship of party but imposes itself as an objective datum upon all men applying their rational faculties to the conduct of foreign policy. Thus the national interest in the preservation and, if need be, the restoration of the continental balance of power has survived four centuries of radical changes in the composition and outlook of the British ruling class, as the national interest of Russia in the control of the Western accesses to its empire has survived the most radical domestic changes. Similarly, the American national interest in the tenets of the Monroe Doctrine and in the European and Asian balance of power has guided the foreign policy of the United States during the two centuries of the nation's existence.

More particularly, in view of those permanent interests, American foreign policy since 1945 has inevitably pursued the containment of the Soviet Union and of China, and has to that end supported the nations of Western Europe, Japan and South Korea as well as anti-Communist governments and movements throughout the world. These ends and means have remained unchanged for a quarter of a century. What has changed is the rhetoric through which American foreign policy has been rationalized and justified. What have also changed are the tactics of implementing the basic tenets of American foreign policy in certain regions, such as Southeast Asia. What have not changed are the basic tenets themselves.

That consistency of American foreign policy, reflecting the permanence of the interests which American foreign policy is supposed to serve, is accentuated by the identity of high officials responsible for the conduct of American foreign policy. Many observers have noted the paradox that the new foreign policies on which the new [Carter] administration is said to be embarking are to be executed by a group of men who are identified with the disastrous policies of the past, especially those in Vietnam. Common sense dictates that a group of physicians who have given the wrong diagnosis, suggested the wrong therapy, and covered their mistakes with the wrong prognosis will not be employed again to take care of the patient's medical problems. Why does a President-elect in preparation for the presidency pursue a course of action which he would find irrational if he pursued it in his private affairs?

The answer lies in a characteristic of American politics which is rarely mentioned although it explains much which at first glance defies rational explanation. We are referring to the enormous staying power of the conservative element in American society. The concentrations of private power which have actually governed America since the Civil War have withstood all attempts to control, let alone dissolve them. They have survived all such attempts from Populism to the Great Society. They have adjusted legal forms and procedures to political pressures and have coopted their one-time opponents, such as the labor unions. Democratic and Republican administrations have followed each other, and so have activist and passive, reformist and conservative Presidents, but the concentrations of private power have preserved their hold upon the levers of political decision. So it is but consistent for an incoming administration to staff the command posts of foreign and military policy with the same personnel that served its immediate predecessors. By the same token, the odds are against men who 10 years ago failed the moral and intellectual tests of statesmanship now advocating wise new foreign policies against a reluctant White House and a hostile public opinion.

While it is therefore futile to expect the new team responsible for foreign and military policies wisely and audaciously to break new ground, or to speculate what they will or will not do, it is in order to define and analyze certain fundamental issues which have been neglected or mistreated in the past. While it is vain to expect drastic changes in foreign policy because a new administration has taken over, it may not be *a priori* hopeless to change slowly and at first imperceptibly the ways we think about foreign policy. Changes in foreign policy must follow changes in the modes of thinking we bring to bear upon the fundamental issues of foreign policy. Four such issues call for our attention: first, our political and military modes of thought and action must be brought into harmony with the political and military realities of the age. Second, we must exchange the demonological interpretation of political reality, a reality peopled by evil persons, for understanding the depersonalized objective issues. Third, we must stop substituting pleasant but illusory verbalizations for a threatening reality. Last, we must cease, especially in our relations with the Third World, to act on the belief that a seemingly obstreperous reality will yield to good intentions and the expenditure of large amounts of money.

It is no exaggeration to say that the very structure of international relations, as reflected in political institutions, diplomatic procedures and legal arrangements, is utterly at variance with, and in large measure irrelevant to, the reality of international politics. While the former assumes the "sovereign equality" of all nations, the latter is dominated by an extreme inequality of nations, two of which are called superpowers because they hold in their hands the unprecedented power of total destruction, and many of which are called "ministates" because their power is minuscule even compared with that of the traditional nation-states. It is this contrast and incompatibility between the reality of international politics and the concepts, institutions and procedures designed to make intelligible and control the former which has caused, at least below the great-power level, the unmanageability of international relations bordering on anarchy. International terrorism and the different reactions of governments to it, the involvement of foreign governments in the Lebanese civil war, the military operations of the United States in Southeast Asia, the military interventions of the Soviet Union in Eastern Europe, cannot be explained or justified by reference to traditional concepts, institutions and procedures. Nor can the claimed moral responsibility of the industrialized nations for the economic welfare of the Third World. The same holds true for the obligation of the oil-producing nations to supply the industrial nations with their main source of energy at tolerable cost.

All these situations have one common characteristic: the fact of interdependence requires a political order which takes that fact into account, while in reality the legal and institutional superstructure, harking back to the 19th century, assumes the existence of a multiplicity of self-sufficient, impenetrable sovereign nation-states. These residues of an obsolescent legal and institutional order not only stand in the way of a rational transformation of international relations in the light of the inequality of power and the interdependence of interests, but they also render precarious, if not impossible, major rational policies within the defective framework of such a system.

The prime specific example is nuclear energy. Military strategy has been dominated throughout history by certain concepts, such as competitive armaments, attack and defense, victory and defeat, which derive of necessity from the nature of things military. While these concepts retain their validity for conventional war, they have lost their meaning for nuclear strategy. In contrast to the conventional arms race, the nuclear competition can reach an optimum—the ability to inflict unacceptable damage in a second strike. Once defense against strategic nuclear attack is impossible, avoidance of nuclear war through deterrence is the only rational response to the nuclear threat; [then] the destructiveness of nuclear war obliterates the distinction between victory and defeat.

It testifies to the persistence of conventional concepts that, in spite of their obvious obsolescence, they have not lost their hold upon the thinking and policies of governments. The nuclear arms race, long since having overtaken the optimum, has become a wasteful futility, aping the competition for conventional arms. Neither superpower has given up the search, however disguised, for a nuclear weapon that would promise to give a new meaning to the traditional distinction between victory and defeat. More particularly, the United States has continuously searched for a variant of, or substitute for, strategic nuclear war, in the form of counterforce strategy and tactical nuclear war, which would avoid indiscriminate total destruction and thereby restore the traditional distinction between victory and defeat. The lingering-on of these ideas, hallowed by their legitimate use during all of recorded history before 1945, which have become misconceptions when applied to nuclear strategy, has not only led us astray in the competition for ever more and better nuclear weapons, but has also caused us to underrate the strategic importance of conventional weapons.

American military policy, by overemphasizing, to the detriment of conventional weapons, nuclear preparedness in the surreptitious expectation of a winnable and not unacceptably destructive nuclear war, has reversed the true order of things: it wastes scarce human and material resources upon already excessive nuclear weapon systems, and accepts as permanent an inferiority in conventional weapons, which not only makes conventional war more likely and its outcome doubtful, but also increases the likelihood of escalation from conventional to nuclear war, provided the stakes are high enough for the prospective loser not to accept defeat in a conventional war.

As William Graham Sumner put it: "The amount of superstition is not much changed, but it now attaches to politics, not to religion." Superstition in politics tends to reduce variegated phenomena, difficult to understand and apparently impossible to master, to a simple, personalized factor. War-mongers of Wall Street, the Jewish conspiracy of the Elders of Zion, and the wirepullers of world communism are held responsible for the world's major evils. While the "spectre of communism" has influenced, to the point of obsession, the thinking of friend and foe alike, it was the coincidence, since 1917, of adherence to the Communist doctrine with the power of a state in the form of Russian Bolshevism that has created a continuing problem for American foreign policy.

What is the ultimate purpose of Soviet foreign policy? Is it the security and expansion of the Russian state, or is it the transformation of the world in the image of Soviet communism? The answer to these questions is not of mere academic interest, but determines the kind of foreign policy the United States ought to pursue *vis-à-vis* the Soviet Union and other Commu-nist nations and movements. American policy, in its rhetoric and from time to time in its practice, has been satisfied with a blanket opposition to com-munism, a stance that requires no more than the identification of a govern-ment or a political movement as Communist to make it an enemy of the United States. The Communist identification is the only mental operation required, and opposition is the only legitimate practical conclusion.

The corollary of this indiscriminate opposition to communism is the indiscriminate support of governments and movements that profess and practice anti-communism. American policies in Asia and Latin America have derived from this simplistic position. The Vietnam war and our inabil-ity to come to terms with mainland China find here their rationale. So do the theory and practice of counter-insurgency, including large-scale assassina-tions under the Phoenix program in Vietnam and the assassinations of indi-vidual statesmen.

Our relations with Communist governments and movements must be determined in view of all the factors that bear upon interests and power and of which communism, itself of different weight in different countries according to interests and power, constitutes but one among many. Once we pursue consistently this differentiated approach to communism, we will also be relieved of the compulsion, which is a mirror image of the blanket opposition to Communist governments and movements on ideological grounds, to support indiscriminately all governments which invoke ideologi-cal anti-communism as their reason of state.

The demonological approach to foreign policy strengthens another pathological tendency, which is the refusal to acknowledge in thought, and cope effectively with, a threatening reality. The demonological approach has shifted our attention and concern toward the adherents of communism—individuals at home and abroad, political movements, foreign governments—and away from the real threat: the power of states, Communist or not. An example of the same intellectual error is the contemporary emphasis upon détente as an alternative American policy toward the Soviet Union, presumably less hostile and more conducive to mutually advantageous cooperation than the policies that preceded it.

To recommend or reject a particular foreign policy carries the implication that the policy-maker has a choice between the policy recommended or rejected and some other kinds of policy. If no such choice exists, the recommendation or rejection may have its uses for purposes of propaganda, domestic and international, but it offers no genuine alternative. To do justice to détente as a recommended or rejected American policy one would have to raise the question of an alternative foreign policy, better or worse than détente. The answer to that question is bound to be that no such rational alternative exists.

The two nuclear superpowers, capable of destroying each other utterly in a matter of hours, have no rational choice but to pursue a policy of détente, that is, of decreasing and, if possible, eliminating tensions. It is exactly this kind of foreign policy the two superpowers have pursued since the end of the World War II. They were settled peacefully because both sides approached the outstanding issues in the spirit of détente, that is, of decreasing and eliminating tensions which otherwise might have led to a self-destructive nuclear war. Thus Secretary of State Kissinger is right when he has repeatedly defined détente as the policy to avoid nuclear war. The concept of détente is not susceptible to rational debate. Rather it serves the ideological function of justifying in moral terms whatever policy happens to be pursued. The concept of détente has a positive moral connotation. It is impossible to oppose détente in favor of bigger and better tensions.

Mr. Carter deems it "likely in the near future that issues of war and peace will be more a function of economic and social problems than of the military security problems which have dominated international relations in the world since World War II." This statement is but a particular expression of the widely held view that the most important issue facing the foreign policy of the United States and the one most likely to cause war is not the East-West confrontation with the Soviet Union, but the North-South relationship between the few industrialized, rich nations, and the great mass of the underdeveloped and mainly agricultural poor ones.

This view assumes that the highly developed and rich nations of the world are responsible, both in terms of cause and effect and in moral terms, for the plight of the Third World. The developed, rich nations, so the argument runs, owe their development and wealth primarily to the colonial exploitation of the nations of the Third World; hence, they are morally obligated to compensate the nations of the Third World for what the latter have been unjustly deprived. That moral obligation emanating from the specific evils of colonialism is reinforced by the general moral principle of equality which frowns upon the extreme inequality among nations and imposes upon the advantaged the moral obligation to share their advantages with the disadvantaged.

Regardless of the merits of this moral argument, the United States has a politico-military interest in the Third World which is a special manifestation of its general interest in the maintenance of a world-wide balance of power under present world conditions. In the practice of American foreign policy, that interest has taken on the aspects of opposition to the expansion of communism in the Third World. That opposition assumes that while individual Communist governments may have no direct influence upon the world balance of power, they have a psychological impact presaging further inevitable Communist gains. These psychological expectations become self-fulfilling prophecies; each gain, however insignificant in itself, psychologically prepares for further gains, and so forth. To that psychological preparation for gradual Communist expansion corresponds that expansion itself, which is assumed to go forward insignificant step by insignificant step until the sum total of such steps will amount to a significant change of the world balance of power in favor of communism.

Two flaws qualify, if not invalidate, this argument. On the one hand, it assumes within communism a uniform aggressive hostility to American interests and, on the other, it assumes within the Third World a uniform receptivity to aggressive anti-American communism. That is to say, it assumes the monolithic dominance of this particular variety of communism among its promotors and recipients in the Third World. At the same time, it assumes the ability of the United States to stop the spread of this kind of communism throughout the Third World. These assumptions are obviously open to serious doubt; if one were to take them without qualification at face value, one would come very close to the demonological approach which we have discussed above.

The polycentric character of communism, that is, the determination of its philosophy and policies by considerations of differing national interests rather than of dogmatic consistency, is by now well established. The real issue that confronts American foreign policy is not whether a certain government professes and practices communism, but to what extent a government's foreign policy supports the foreign policies of the Soviet Union or of other governments hostile to the United States. If one applies this criterion, one realizes that Communist philosophy and policies are by no means coterminous with Soviet influence. Anti-Communist military dictatorships support Soviet foreign policies, and governments who proclaim their "socialism" and practice what they at least think are Socialist domestic policies pursue foreign policies which are at least not necessarily hostile to the interests of the United States. The receptivity of the nations of the Third

World to competing foreign ideologies has been very much exaggerated by the three main contestants—the United States, the Soviet Union and China. The main motivating force in the Third World is not Western ideologies, of which Marxism is one, but indigenous nationalism, and most nations of the Third World prefer to be miserable in their own way to being happy in the American, Soviet or Chinese way.

It follows from the great diversity of interests pursued by the nations of the Third World and the great disparity of power they are able to bring to bear upon those interests that the North-South confrontation, as an alternative to the East-West confrontation, refers to nothing real. In the East-West confrontation, the United States and the Soviet Union confront each other as the two superpowers, supported by their respective allies and capable of destroying each other. What the United States and the other industrial nations confront in the North-South confrontation is not another power bloc of at least approximately equal strength, which could be dealt with on the level of power, but near-anarchy uncontrollable from within or without. When the United States enters the Third World, it confronts primarily not a particular country or group of countries of the Third World, but the Soviet Union, and the countries of the Third World participate in the confrontation only as the associates of one or the other superpower and as the object of their ambitions. What distinguishes the North-South from the East-West confrontation is not the identity of the principals but the geographic space in which they meet and the object over which they confront each other.

It is, then, a fundamental error to think about the nations of the Third World in terms of economic development, supported by the United States and international organizations and frustrated by the indigenous handicaps of culture and politics. It is pleasant to imagine that the United States can escape world politics by exchanging the East-West confrontation for a North-South one. For better or worse, there is no escape from the most dangerous confrontation the United States has ever experienced. It is the mission of the new administration to face that confrontation with wisdom and fortitude rather than spending itself in futile attempts to evade it.

4

TWO VIEWS OF THE SOVIET PROBLEM

GEORGE F. KENNAN

Looking back over the whole course of the differences between my own view of East-West relations and the views of my various critics and opponents in recent years, I have to conclude that the differences have been, essentially, not ones of interpretation of phenomena whose reality we all agree on but, rather, differences over the nature and significance of the observable phenomena themselves—in other words, differences not about the meaning of what we see but, rather, about what it is that we see in the first place.

Let me illustrate this first with the example of our differing views of the nature of the Soviet regime.

My opponents, if I do not misinterpret their position, see the Soviet leaders as a group of men animated primarily by a desire to achieve further expansion of their effective power, and this at the expense of the independence and the liberties of other people—at the expense of the stability, and perhaps the peace, of international life. They see these men as pursuing a reckless and gigantic buildup of their own armed forces—a buildup of such dimensions that it cannot be explained by defensive considerations alone and must therefore, it is reasoned, reflect aggressive ones. They see them as eager to bring other countries, in the Third World and elsewhere, under their domination, in order to use those countries as pawns against the United States and other nations of the Western alliance; and they see the situations existing today in such places as Angola and Ethiopia and Afghanistan as examples of the dangerous success of their endeavors. My opponents reject the suggestion that Soviet policy might be motivated in any important degree by defensive considerations. In their view, the Soviet leaders do not feel politically encircled or in any other way significantly threatened. And though it is recognized that Moscow faces serious internal problems, it is not thought that these problems impose any very serious limitations on the freedom of the regime to pursue aggressive external intentions. What emerges from this vision is, of course, an image of the Soviet regime not greatly different from the image of the Nazi regime as it existed shortly before the outbreak of the Second World War. This being the case, it is not surprising that the conclusion should be drawn that the main task for Western statesmanship at this time must be to avoid what are now generally regarded as the great mistakes of the Western powers in the late nineteen-thirties; that is, to avoid what is called appeasement, to give a low priority to the possibilities for negotiation and accommodation, and to concentrate on the building up of a military posture so imposing and forbidding, and a Western unity so unshakable, that the Soviet leaders will perceive the futility and the danger of their aggressive plans, and will accept the necessity of learning to live side by side with other nations on a basis compatible with the security of those other nations and with the general requirements of world stability and peace. I do not question the good faith of American governmental personalities when they say that once this new relationship of military and political power has been established they will be prepared to sit down with their Soviet counterparts and discuss with them the prerequisites for a safer world; but I fear that they see the success of any such discussions as something to which the Soviet leaders could be brought only reluctantly, with gnashing of teeth, and this seems to me to be a poor augury for the lasting quality of any results that might be achieved.

Now, all this, as I say, is what I believe my opponents see when they turn their eyes in the direction of the Kremlin. What I see is something quite different. I see a group of troubled men—elderly men, for the most part—whose choices and possibilities are severely constrained. I see these men as prisoners of many circumstances: prisoners of their own past and their country's past; prisoners of the antiquated ideology to which their extreme sense of orthodoxy binds them; prisoners of the rigid system of power that has given them their authority; but prisoners, too, of certain ingrained peculiarities of the Russian statesmanship of earlier ages—the congenital sense of insecurity, the lack of inner self-confidence, the distrust of the foreigner and the foreigner's world, the passion for secrecy, the neurotic fear of penetration by other powers into areas close to their borders, and a persistent tendency, resulting from all these other factors, to overdo the creation of military strength. I see here men deeply preoccupied, as were their Czarist Russian predecessors, with questions of prestige—preoccupied more, in many instances, with the appearances than with the realities. I do not see them as men anxious to expand their power by the direct use of their armed forces, although they could easily be frightened into taking actions that would seem to have this aim. I see them as indeed concerned—and rather naturally concerned—to increase their influence among Third World countries. This neither surprises me nor alarms me. Most great powers have similar desires. And the methods adopted by the Soviet Union are not very different from those adopted by some of the others. Besides, what has distinguished these Soviet efforts, historically viewed, seems to be not their success but precisely their lack of it. I see no recent Soviet achievements in this direction which would remotely outweigh the great failures of the postwar period: in Yugoslavia, in China, and in Egypt.

But, beyond that, a wish to expand one's *influence* is not the same thing as a wish to expand the formal limits of one's power and responsibility. This I do not think the Soviet leaders at all wish to do. Specifically, I have seen no evidence that they are at all disposed to invade Western Europe and thereby to take any further parts of it formally under their authority. They are having trouble enough with the responsibilities they have already undertaken in Eastern Europe. They have no reason to wish to increase these burdens. I can conceive that there might be certain European regions, outside the limits of their present hegemony, where they would be happy, for defensive purposes, to have some sort of military control, if such control could be acquired safely and easily, without severe disruption of international stability; but it is a far cry from this to the assumption that they would be disposed to invade any of these areas out of the blue, in peacetime, at the cost of unleashing another world war.

It is my belief that these men do indeed consider the Soviet Union to have been increasingly isolated and in danger of encirclement by hostile powers in recent years. I do not see how they could otherwise interpret the American military relationship with Iran in the time of the Shah or the more recent American military relationships with Pakistan and China. And these, I believe, are not the only considerations that would limit the freedom of the Soviet leaders to indulge themselves in dreams of external expansion, even if they were inclined toward such dreams. They are obviously very conscious of the dangers of a disintegration of their dominant position in Eastern Europe, and particularly in Poland; and this not because they have any conscious desire to mistreat or oppress the peoples involved but because they see any further deterioration of the situation there as a threat to their political and strategic interests in Germany—interests that are unquestionably highly defensive in origin.

I believe, too, that internal developments in the Soviet Union present a heavy claim on the attention and the priorities of the Soviet leaders. They are deeply committed to the completion of their existing programs for the economic and social development of the Soviet peoples, and I am sure that they are very seriously concerned over the numerous problems that have recently been impeding that completion: the perennial agricultural failures; the many signs of public apathy, demoralization, drunkenness, and labor absenteeism; the imbalance in population growth between the Russian center and the non-Russian periphery; the increasing shortage of skilled labor; and the widespread economic corruption and indiscipline. They may differ among themselves as to how these problems should be approached, but I doubt whether there are any of them who think that the problems could be solved by the unleashing of another world war. I emphatically reject the primitive thesis, drawn largely from misleading and outdated nineteeth-century examples, that the Kremlin might be inclined to resort to war as a means of resolving its internal difficulties. Nothing in Russian history or psychology supports such a thesis.

In saying these things, I do not mean to deny that there exist, interwoven with the rest of the pattern of Soviet diplomacy, certain disquieting tendencies, which oblige Western policymakers to exercise a sharp vigilance even as they pursue their efforts toward peace. I believe that these tendencies reflect not so much any thirst for direct aggression as an oversuspiciousness, a fear of being tricked or outsmarted, an exaggerated sense of prestige, and an interpretation of Russia's defensive needs so extreme—so extravagant and so far-reaching—that it becomes in itself a threat, or an apparent threat, to the security of other nations. While these weaknesses probably affect all Soviet statesmen to one extent or another, the evidence suggests to me that they are concentrated particularly in specific elements of the Soviet power structure—notably, in the military and naval commands, in the vast police establishment, and in certain sections of the Party apparatus. So far, these tendencies do not seem to me to have dominated Soviet policy, except in the case of the decision to intervene in Afghanistan—a decision that was taken in somewhat abnormal circumstances and is now, I believe, largely recognized, even in Moscow, as a mistake. But there will soon have to be extensive changes in the occupancy of the senior political positions in Moscow, and Western policymakers should consider that a Western policy that offers no encouragement to the more moderate elements in the Soviet hierarchy must inevitably strengthen the hand, and the political position, of those who are not moderate at all.

So much, then, for our differences of view with respect to the Soviet regime. It is not unnatural that anyone who sees the phenomenon of Soviet power so differently from certain others should also differ from those others in his view of the best response to it. It is clear that my opponents see the Soviet regime primarily as a great, immediate, and growing military danger, and that this conditions their idea of the best response. I have no argument with them about the existence of a great danger. I do differ from them with regard to the *causes* of this danger. I see these causes not in the supposed "aggressiveness" of either side but in the weapons race itself. I see it in the compulsions that this, like any other weapons race between sovereign powers, engenders within all the participants. I see it in the terrible militarization of outlook to which this sort of competition conduces: a species of obsession which causes those who have succumbed to it to direct their vision and their efforts exclusively to the hopeless contingencies of military conflict, to ignore the more hopeful ones of communication and accommodation, and in this way to enhance the very dangers against which they fancy themselves to be working.

Leaving aside for the moment the problems of nuclear weaponry, I shall say a word about the military balance in conventional weapons. An impression has been created that there has recently been a new and enormous buildup of Soviet conventional strength on the European Continent, changing the balance of forces in this respect strongly to the disadvantage of the West. This view has found expression in the statements of a number of distinguished Western personalities. I cannot flatly deny the correctness of this thesis. I am only a private citizen. I do not have access to all the information at the disposition of the governments. But, with all respect for the sincerity and good faith of those who advance this view, I am disinclined to accept it just on the basis of their say-so. I am so disinclined because I think I have made a reasonable effort, in these last few years, to follow such information as appears in the press and the other media about the military balance and I find this body of information confused, contradictory, statistically questionable, and often misleading. Most of it seems to derive from data leaked to the media by one or another of the Western military-intelligence services, and one cannot avoid the impression that it reflects a tendency to paint an exaggerated and frightening picture of Soviet capacities and intentions—a so-called worst-case image. This is done, no doubt, partly out of an excessive professional prudence but partly, too, I am afraid, with an eye to the reactions of various Western parliamentary bodies, which require to be frightened (or so it is believed) before they will make reasonable appropriations for defense. I can only say that if the NATO governments really wish us, the public, to believe in the reality of a recent dramatic increase in the Soviet conventional threat to Western Europe they will have to place before us a more consistent and plausible statistical basis for that view than anything they have given us to date. In terms neither of the number of divisions nor of total manpower nor of any of the other major indicators does the information now available to the ordinary newspaper reader prove that the balance of conventional military strength in Central Europe is significantly less favorable to the Western side than it was ten or twenty years ago.

To say this is not to claim that the present balance is satisfactory. That is not my contention. Of course there is a preponderance of strength on the Soviet side. Such a preponderance has existed since the Second World War. Of course it is not desirable. I myself favor a strengthening of NATO's conventional capacities, particularly if the strengthening be taken to mean an improvement of morale, of discipline, of training and alertness, and not just a heaping up of fancy and expensive new equipment that we do not have the manpower to operate or the money to maintain. But if this strengthening is to be effected I think it should be presented and defended to the public as a normal policy of prudence—a reasonable long-term precaution in a troubled time—and not as something responding to any specific threat from any specific quarter. The Western governments, in particular, should not try to gain support for such a program by painting on the wall an exaggerated and unnecessarily alarming image of Soviet intentions and capacities. This procedure represents, in my view, an abuse of public confidence, and one that, in the end, is invariably revenged.

So much for the conventional weapons. Now—with a sigh and a sinking of the heart—for the nuclear ones. Here, I am sorry to say, I have differences with every single one of the premises on which our government and some of the other NATO governments seem to act in designing their policies in this field. First of all, my opponents seem to see the nuclear explosive as just a weapon like any other weapon, only more destructive; and they think that because it is more destructive it is a better and more powerful weapon. I deny that the nuclear explosive is a proper weapon. It conforms, in my view, to none of the criteria traditionally applied to conventional weapons. It can serve no useful purpose. It cannot be used without bringing disaster upon everyone concerned. I regard it as the reflection of a vast misunderstanding of the true purposes of warfare and the true usefulness of weaponry.

My opponents see the Soviet Union as having sought and achieved some sort of statistical superiority over the NATO powers in this kind of weaponry. I myself have not seen the evidence that it has achieved that sort of superiority; nor do I see any reason to assume that that is what it would like to do. The evidence seems to me to suggest that it is striving for what it would view as equivalence, in the statistical sense—not for superiority. My opponents believe that differences of superiority or inferiority, in the statistical sense, have meaning: that if you have more of these weapons than your adversary has, you are in a stronger position to stand up against intimidation or against an actual attack. I challenge that view. I submit that if you are talking, as all of us are talking today, about what are in reality grotesque quantities of overkill—arsenals so excessive that they would suffice to destroy the adversary's homeland many times over—statistical disparities between the arsenals on the two sides are quite meaningless. But precisely that—the absurd excessiveness of the existing nuclear arsenals—is the situation we have before us.

My opponents maintain that the reason we must have the nuclear weapons is that in a conflict we would not be able to match the Soviet Union with the conventional ones. I would say: If this is true, let us correct the situation at once. Neither in respect to manpower nor in respect to industrial potential are we lacking in the means to put up conventional forces fully as strong as those deployed against us in Europe.

My opponents say: We must have these weapons for purposes of deterrence. The use of this term carries two implications: first, that it is the Russians who have taken the lead in the development of these weapons, and that we are only reacting to what they have done; and, secondly, that the Russians are such monsters that unless they are deterred they would assuredly launch upon us a nuclear attack, with all the horrors and sufferings that that would bring. I question both these implications; and I question in particular the wisdom of suggesting the latter implication thousands of times a year to the general public, thus schooling the public mind to believe that our Soviet adversary has lost every semblance of humanity and is concerned only with wreaking unlimited destruction for destruction's sake. I am not sure, furthermore, that the stationing of these weapons on one's territory is not more of a provocation of their use by others than a means of dissuading others from using them. I have never been an advocate of unilateral disarmament, and I see no necessity for anything of that sort today. But I must say that if we Americans had no nuclear weapons whatsoever on our soil instead of the tens of thousands of nuclear warheads we are now said to have deployed, I would feel the future of my children and grandchildren to be far safer than I do at this moment; for if there is any incentive for the Russians to use such weapons against us, it surely comes in overwhelming degree— probably, in fact, entirely— from our own enormous deployment of them.

Finally, there are many people who consider it useless, or even undesirable, to try to get rid of these weapons entirely, and believe that a satisfactory solution can somehow be found by halfway measures of one sort or another—agreements that would limit their numbers or their destructiveness or the areas of their deployment. Such speculations come particularly easily to a government such as our own, which has long regarded nuclear weapons as essential to its defensive posture and has not been willing to contemplate a future without them. I have no confidence in any of these schemes. I see the danger not in the number or quality of the weapons or in the intentions of those who hold them but in the very existence of weapons of this nature, regardless of whose hands they are in. I believe that until we consent to recognize that the nuclear weapons we hold in our own hands are as much a danger to us as those that repose in the hands of our supposed adversaries there will be no escape from the confusions and dilemmas to which such weapons have now brought us, and must bring us increasingly as time goes on. For this reason, I see no solution to the problem other than the complete elimination of these and all other weapons of mass destruction from national arsenals; and the sooner we move toward that solution, and the greater courage we show in doing so, the safer we will be.

5

MAD VERSUS NUTS
Can Doctrine or Weaponry Remedy the Mutual Hostage Relationship of the Superpowers?

SPURGEON M. KEENY, JR.
WOLFGANG K. H. PANOFSKY

Since World War II there has been a continuing debate on military doctrine concerning the actual utility of nuclear weapons in war. This debate, irrespective of the merits of the divergent points of view, tends to create the perception that the outcome and scale of a nuclear conflict could be controlled by the doctrine or the types of nuclear weapons employed. Is this the case?

We believe not. In reality, the unprecedented risks of nuclear conflict are largely independent of doctrine or its application. The principal danger of doctrines that are directed at limiting nuclear conflicts is that they might be believed and form the basis for action without appreciation of the physical facts and uncertainties of nuclear conflict. The failure of policymakers to understand the truly revolutionary nature of nuclear weapons as instruments of war and the staggering size of the nuclear stockpiles of the United States and the Soviet Union could have catastrophic consequences for the entire world.

Military planners and strategic thinkers for 35 years have sought ways to apply the tremendous power of nuclear weapons against target systems that might contribute to the winning of a future war. In fact, as long as the United States held a virtual nuclear monopoly, the targeting of atomic weapons was looked upon essentially as a more effective extension of the strategic bombing concepts of World War II. With the advent in the mid-1950s of a substantial Soviet nuclear capability, including multimegaton thermonuclear weapons, it was soon apparent that the populations and societies of both the United States and the Soviet Union were mutual hostages. A portion of the nuclear stockpile of either side could inflict on the other as many

Reprinted by permission of *Foreign Affairs*, Winter 1981/82. Copyright © 1981 by the Council on Foreign Relations, Inc.

as 100 million fatalities and destroy it as a functioning society. Thus, although the rhetoric of declaratory strategic doctrine has changed over the years, mutual deterrence has in fact remained the central fact of the strategic relationship of the two superpowers and of the NATO and Warsaw Pact alliances.

Most observers would agree that a major conflict between the two hostile blocs on a worldwide scale during this period may well have been prevented by the specter of catastrophic nuclear war. At the same time, few would argue that this state of mutual deterrence is a very reassuring foundation on which to build world peace. In the 1960s the perception of the basic strategic relationship of mutual deterrence came to be characterized as "Mutual Assured Destruction," which critics were quick to note had the acronym of MAD. The notion of MAD has been frequently attacked not only as militarily unacceptable but also as immoral since it holds the entire civilian populations of both countries as hostages.[1]

As an alternative to MAD, critics and strategic innovators have over the years sought to develop various war-fighting targeting doctrines that would somehow retain the use of nuclear weapons on the battlefield or even in controlled strategic war scenarios, while sparing the general civilian population from the devastating consequences of nuclear war. Other critics have found an alternative in a defense-oriented military posture designed to defend the civilian population against the consequences of nuclear war.

These concepts are clearly interrelated since such a defense-oriented strategy would also make a nuclear war-fighting doctrine more credible. But both alternatives depend on the solution of staggering technical problems. A defense-oriented military posture requires a nearly impenetrable air and missile defense over a large portion of the population. And any attempt to have a controlled war-fighting capability during a nuclear exchange places tremendous requirements not only on decisions made under incredible pressure by men in senior positions of responsibility but on the technical performance of command, control, communications and intelligence functions—called in professional circles "C^3I" and which for the sake of simplicity we shall hereafter describe as "control mechanisms." It is not sufficient as the basis for defense policy to assert that science will "somehow" find solutions to critical technical problems on which the policy is dependent, when technical solutions are nowhere in sight.

In considering these doctrinal issues, it should be recognized that there tends to be a very major gap between declaratory policy and actual implementation expressed as targeting doctrine. Whatever the declaratory policy might be, those responsible for the strategic forces must generate real target lists and develop procedures under which various combinations of targets could be attacked. In consequence, the perceived need to attack every listed target, even after absorbing the worst imaginable first strike from the adversary, creates procurement "requirements," even though the military or economic importance of many of the targets is small.

In fact, it is not at all clear in the real world of war planning whether declaratory doctrine has generated requirements or whether the availability of weapons for targeting has created doctrine. With an estimated 30,000 warheads at the disposal of the United States, including more than 10,000 avowed to be strategic in character, it is necessary to target redundantly all urban areas and economic targets and to cover a wide range of military targets in order to frame uses for the stockpile. And, once one tries to deal with elusive mobile and secondary military targets, one can always make a case for requirements for more weapons and for more specialized weapon designs.

These doctrinal considerations, combined with the superabundance of nuclear weapons, have led to a conceptual approach to nuclear war which can be described as Nuclear Utilization Target Selection. For convenience, and not in any spirit of trading epithets, we have chosen the acronym of NUTS to characterize the various doctrines that seek to utilize nuclear weapons against specific targets in a complex of nuclear war-fighting situations intended to be limited, as well as the management over an extended period of a general nuclear war between the superpowers.[2]

While some elements of NUTS may be involved in extending the credibility of our nuclear deterrent, this consideration in no way changes the fact that mutual assured destruction, or MAD, is inherent in the existence of large numbers of nuclear weapons in the real world. In promulgating the doctrine of "countervailing strategy" in the summer of 1980, President Carter's Secretary of Defense, Harold Brown, called for a buildup of nuclear war-fighting capability in order to provide greater deterrence by demonstrating the ability of the United States to respond in a credible fashion without having to escalate immediately to all-out nuclear war. He was very careful, however, to note that he thought that it was "very likely" that the use of nuclear weapons by the superpowers at any level would escalate into general nuclear war.[3] This situation is not peculiar to present force structures or technologies; and, regardless of future technical developments, it will persist as long as substantial nuclear weapon stockpiles remain.

Despite its possible contribution to the deterrence of nuclear war, the NUTS approach to military doctrine and planning can very easily become a serious danger in itself. The availability of increasing numbers of nuclear weapons in a variety of designs and delivery packages at all levels of the military establishment inevitably encourages the illusion that somehow nuclear weapons can be applied in selected circumstances without unleashing a catastrophic series of consequences. As we shall see in more detail below, the recent uninformed debate on the virtue of the so-called neutron bomb as a selective device to deal with tank attacks is a depressing case in point. NUTS creates its own endless pressure for expanded nuclear stockpiles with increasing danger of accidents, accidental use, diversions to terrorists, etc. But more fundamentally, it tends to obscure the fact that the nuclear world is in fact MAD.

The NUTS approach to nuclear war-fighting will not eliminate the essential MAD character of nuclear war for two basic reasons, which are rooted in the nature of nuclear weapons and the practical limits of technology. First, the destructive power of nuclear weapons, individually and most certainly in the large numbers discussed for even specialized application, is so great that the collateral effects on persons and property would be enormous and, in scenarios which are seriously discussed, would be hard to distinguish from the onset of general nuclear war. But more fundamentally, it does not seem possible, even in the most specialized utilization of nuclear weapons, to envisage any situation where escalation to general nuclear war would probably not occur given the dynamics of the situation and the limits of the control mechanisms that could be made available to manage a limited nuclear war. In the case of a protracted general nuclear war, the control problem becomes completely unmanageable. Finally, there does not appear to be any prospect for the foreseeable future that technology will provide a secure shield behind which the citizens of the two superpowers can safely observe the course of a limited nuclear war on other people's territory.

II

So much has been said and written about the terrible consequences of nuclear war that any brief characterization of the problem seems strangely banal. Yet it is not clear how deeply the horror of such an event has penetrated the public consciousness or even the thinking of knowledgeable policymakers who in theory have access to the relevant information. The lack of public response to authoritative estimates that general nuclear war could result in 100 million fatalities in the United States suggests a general denial psychosis when the public is confronted with the prospect of such an unimaginable catastrophe. It is interesting, however, that there has been a considerable reaction to the campaign by medical doctors in several countries (including the United States and the Soviet Union), which calls attention to the hopeless plight of the tens of millions of casualties who would die over an extended period due to the total inability of surviving medical personnel and facilities to cope with the situation. One can stoically ignore the inevitability of death, but the haunting image of being among the injured survivors who would eventually die unattended is a prospect that few can easily accept fatalistically.

It is worth repeating the oft-stated, but little comprehended, fact that a *single* modern strategic nuclear weapon could have a million times the yield of the high explosive strategic bombs of World War II, or one hundred to a thousand times the yield of the atomic bombs that destroyed Hiroshima and Nagasaki, killing 250,000 people. The blast from a single one-megaton weapon detonated over the White House in Washington, D.C. would destroy multistory concrete buildings out to a distance of about three miles (ten pounds per square inch overpressure with winds of 300 miles per hour)—a circle of almost complete destruction reaching the National Cathedral to the northwest, the Kennedy Stadium to the east, and across the National Airport to the south. Most people in this area would be killed immediately. The thermal radiation from the same weapon would cause spontaneous ignition of clothing and household combustibles to a distance of about five miles (25 calories per centimeter squared)—a circle of raging fires reaching out to the District line. Out to a distance of almost nine miles there would be severe damage to ordinary frame buildings and second-degree burns to exposed individuals. Beyond these immediate effects the innumerable separate fires that had been ignited would either merge into an outward-moving conflagration or more likely create a giant fire storm of the type Hamburg and Tokyo experienced on a much smaller scale in World War II. While the inrushing winds would tend to limit the spread of the fire storm, the area within five to six miles of the explosion would be totally burned out, killing most of the people who might have escaped initial injury in shelters.

The point has been forcefully made recently by members of the medical community that the vast numbers of injured who escape death at the margin of this holocaust could expect little medical help. But beyond this, if the fireball of the explosion touched ground, the resulting radioactive debris would produce fallout with lethal effects far beyond the site of the explosion. Assuming the prevailing westerly wind conditions, a typical fallout pattern would indicate that there would be levels of fallout greater than 1,000 rems (450 rems produce 50 percent fatalities) over an area of some 500 square miles, and more than 100 rems (the level above which there will be significant health effects) over some 4,000 square miles reaching all the way to the Atlantic Ocean. In the case of a single explosion the impact of the fallout would be secondary to the immediate weapons effects, but when there are many explosions the fallout becomes a major component of the threat, since the fallout effects from each weapon are additive and the overlapping fallout patterns would soon cover large portions of the country with lethal levels of radiation.

Such levels of human and physical destruction are difficult for anyone, layman or specialist, to comprehend even for a single city, but when extended to an attack on an entire country they become a dehumanized maze of statistics. Comparison with past natural disasters is of little value. Such events as dam breaks and earthquakes result in an island of destruction surrounded by sources of help and reconstruction. Nuclear war involving many weapons would deny the possibility of relief by others.

When General David Jones, Chairman of the Joint Chiefs of Staff, was asked at a hearing of the Senate Foreign Relations Committee on November 3, 1981, what would be the consequences in the northern hemisphere of an all-out nuclear exchange, he had the following stark response:

> We have examined that over many, many years. There are many assumptions that you have as to where the weapons are targeted.

Clearly, the casualties in the northern hemisphere could be, under the worst conditions, into the hundreds of millions of fatalities. It is not to the extent that there would be no life in the northern hemisphere, but if all weapons were targeted in such a way as to give maximum damage to urban and industrial areas, you are talking about the greatest catastrophe in history by many orders of magnitude.

A devastating attack on the urban societies of the United States and Soviet Union would in fact require only a very small fraction of the more than 50,000 nuclear weapons currently in the arsenals of the two superpowers. The United States is commonly credited with having some 30,000 nuclear warheads of which well over 10,000 are carried by strategic systems capable of hitting the Soviet Union. It is estimated that the Soviet Union will soon have some 10,000 warheads in its strategic forces capable of hitting the United States. An exchange of a few thousand of these weapons could kill most of the urban population and destroy most of the industry of both sides.

But such figures are in themselves misleading because they are already high on a curve of diminishing returns, and much smaller attacks could have very severe consequences. A *single* Poseidon submarine captain could fire some 160 independently targetable nuclear warheads (each with a yield several times larger than those of the weapons that destroyed Hiroshima and Nagasaki) against as many Soviet cities. If optimally targeted against the Soviet population, this alone could inflict some 30 million fatalities. One clear fact of the present strategic relationship is that the urban societies of both the United States and the Soviet Union are completely vulnerable to even a small fraction of the other side's accumulated stockpile of nuclear weapons.

III

The theme that nuclear weapons can be successfully employed in war-fighting roles somehow shielded from the MAD world appears to be recurring with increasing frequency and seriousness.[4] Support for Nuclear Utilization Target Selection—NUTS—comes from diverse sources: those who believe that nuclear weapons should be used selectively in anticipated hostilities; those who believe that such capabilities deter a wider range of aggressive Soviet acts; those who assert that we must duplicate an alleged Soviet interest in war-fighting; and those who are simply trying to carry out their military responsibilities in a more "rational" or cost-effective manner. The net effect of this increasing, publicized interest in NUTS is to obscure the almost inevitable link between any use of nuclear weapons and the grim "mutual hostage" realities of the MAD world. The two forces generating this link are the collateral damage associated with the use of nuclear weapons against selected targets and the pressures for escalation of the level of nuclear force once it is used in conflict. Collateral effects and pressures for escalation are themselves closely linked.

To appreciate the significance of the collateral effects of nuclear weapons and the pressure for escalation, one must look at actual war-fighting scenarios that have been seriously proposed. The two scenarios that are most often considered are Soviet attempts to carry out a disarming, or partially disarming, attack against U.S. strategic forces in order to force the surrender of the United States without war, and the selective use of nuclear weapons by the United States in Western Europe to prevent the collapse of NATO forces in the face of an overwhelming Soviet conventional attack. One can expect to hear more about the selective use of nuclear weapons by the United States in the Middle East in the face of an overwhelming Soviet conventional attack on that area.

The much-discussed "window of vulnerability" is based on the fear that the Soviets might launch a "surgical" attack against vulnerable Minuteman ICBM silos—the land-based component of the U.S. strategic triad—to partially disarm the U.S. retaliatory forces, confident that the United States would not retaliate. The scenario then calls for the United States to capitulate to Soviet-dictated peace terms.

Simple arithmetic based on intelligence assessments of the accuracy and yields of the warheads on Soviet missiles and the estimated hardness of Minuteman silos does indeed show that a Soviet attack leaving only a relatively small number of surviving Minuteman ICBMs is mathematically possible in the near future. There is much valid controversy about whether such an attack is in fact operationally feasible with the confidence that a rational decision-maker would require. But what is significant here is the question whether the vulnerability of Minuteman, real or perceptual, could in fact be exploited by the Soviets without risking general nuclear war. Would a U.S. President react any differently in response to an attack against the Minuteman force than to an attack of comparable weight against other targets?

Despite the relatively isolated location of the Minuteman ICBM fields, there would be tremendous collateral damage from such an attack, which under the mathematical scenario would involve at least 2,000 weapons with megaton yields. It has been estimated by the Congressional Office of Technology Assessment that such an attack would result in from two to 20 million American fatalities, primarily from fallout, since at least half the weapons would probably be ground burst to maximize the effect of the attack on the silos. The range of estimated fatalities reflects the inherent uncertainties in fallout calculations due to different assumptions on such factors as meteorological conditions, weapon yield and design, height of burst and amount of protection available and used. Estimates of fatalities below eight to ten million require quite optimistic assumptions.

It seems incredible that any Soviet leader would count on any President suing for peace in circumstances where some ten million American citizens were doomed to a slow and cruel death but the United States still retained 75 percent of the strategic forces and its entire economic base. Instead, Soviet leadership would perceive a President, confronted with an incoming missile attack of at least 2,000 warheads and possibly many more to follow in minutes, and with the action options of retaliating on warning with his vulnerable land-based forces or riding out the attack and retaliating at a level and manner of his own choosing with substantial surviving air and sea-based strategic forces.

It is hard to imagine that this scenario would give the Soviets much confidence in their ability to control escalation of the conflict. If the Soviets did not choose to attack U.S. command, control, communications and intelligence (C^3I) capabilities, the United States would clearly be in a position to retaliate massively or to launch a more selective initial response. If vulnerable control assets were concurrently attacked, selective responses might be jeopardized, but the possibility of an automatic massive response would be increased since the nature of the attack would be unclear. But even if these control assets were initially untouched, the Soviets could not be so overly confident of their own control mechanisms or so overly impressed with those of the United States as to imagine that either system could long control such massive levels of violence, with increasing collateral damage, without the situation very rapidly degenerating into general nuclear war.

The question of nuclear war-fighting in Europe has a long and esoteric history. Tactical nuclear weapons have been considered an additional deterrent to a massive Soviet conventional attack by threatening escalation to general nuclear war involving strategic forces—the so-called coupling effect. At the same time, tactical nuclear forces have been looked on as a necessary counterbalance to Soviet conventional forces in a limited war-fighting situation. To this end, the United States is said to have some 6,000 to 7,000 tactical nuclear weapons in Europe.[5] The existence of this stockpile has been public knowledge so long that it is largely taken for granted and the power of the weapons, which range in yield from around a kiloton to around a megaton, is not appreciated. It is interesting to note that we have in Europe one nuclear weapon (with an average yield probably comparable to the weapon that destroyed Hiroshima) for every 50 American soldiers stationed there including support troops. Tactical nuclear weapons are, of course, no longer a U.S. monopoly. The Soviets are building up comparable forces and have had for some time long-range theater nuclear missiles, earlier the SS-4 and SS-5, and now the SS-20, for which the United States does not have a strict counterpart. In this regard, it must be remembered that it is always feasible for the United States or the Soviet Union to employ some of their long-range strategic missiles against targets in Europe.

There is now a great debate, particularly in Europe, about the proposed deployment on European soil of U.S.-controlled long-range Pershing II and ground-based cruise missiles capable of reaching the territory of the Soviet Union, in response to the growing deployment of Soviet SS-20 mobile medium-range ballistic missiles. This discussion tends to consider the SS-20s and the proposed new forces as a separate issue from the short- and medium-range nuclear weapons already deployed in Europe. There is indeed a technical difference: the proposed Pershing II missile is of sufficient range to reach Soviet territory in only a few minutes, and the SS-20 is a much more accurate and flexible weapons system than earlier Soviet intermediate-range nuclear systems. Yet, the overriding issue which tends to be submerged in the current debate is the fact that *any* use of nuclear weapons in theater warfare in Europe would almost certainly lead to massive civilian casualties even in the unlikely event the conflict did not escalate to involve the homelands of the two superpowers.

Calculations of collateral casualties accompanying nuclear warfare in Europe tend to be simplistic in the extreme. First, the likely proximity of highly populated areas to the combat zone must be taken into account. One simply cannot assume that invading enemy columns will position themselves so that they offer the most favorable isolated target to nuclear attack. Populated areas could not remain isolated from the battle. Cities would have to be defended or they would become a safe stepping-stone for the enemy's advance. In either case, it is difficult to imagine cities and populated areas remaining sanctuaries in the midst of a tactical nuclear war raging around them. Then one must remember that during past wars in Europe as much as one-half of the population was on the road in the form of masses of refugees. Above all, in the confusion of battle, there is no control system that could assure that weapons would not inadvertently strike populated areas. Beyond immediate effects, nuclear fallout would not recognize restrictions based on population density.

The common feature of the above examples is that specialized use of nuclear weapons will as a practical matter be difficult to distinguish from unselective use in the chaos of tactical warfare. A case in point is the much-publicized neutron bomb, which has been promoted as a specialized anti-tank weapon since neutrons can penetrate tank armor and kill the crew. It is frequently overlooked that the neutron bomb is in fact a nuclear weapon with significant yield. While it does emit some ten times as many neutrons as a comparable "ordinary" small nuclear weapon, it also kills by blast, heat, and prompt radiation. For instance, one of the proposed neutron warheads for the Lance missile has a one-kiloton yield, which would produce the same levels of blast damage experienced at Hiroshima at a little less than one-half the distance from the point of detonation.

An attack on tanks near a populated area or a targeting error in the heat of battle would clearly have a far-reaching effect on civilians and structures in the vicinity. Moreover, the lethal effects of the neutrons are not sharply defined. There would be attenuation by intervening structures or earth prominences, and there is a wide gap (from 500 to 10,000 rems) between a dose which would eventually be fatal and that which would immediately prevent a soldier from continuing combat. Under actual war conditions no local commander, much less a national decision-maker, could readily tell whether a neutron weapon or some other kind of nuclear weapon had been employed by the enemy. Thus, the threat of escalation from local to all-out conflict, the problems of collateral damage of nuclear weapons, and the disastrous consequences of errors in targeting are not changed by the nature of the nuclear weapons.

In short, whatever the utility of the neutron bomb or any other "tactical" nuclear weapon in *deterring* Soviet conventional or nuclear attack, any actual use of such weapons is extremely unlikely to remain limited. We come back to the fundamental point that the only meaningful "firebreak" in modern warfare, be it strategic or tactical, is between nuclear and conventional weapons, not between self-proclaimed categories of nuclear weapons.

IV

The thesis that we live in an inherently MAD world rests ultimately on the technical conclusion that effective protection of the population against large-scale nuclear attack is not possible. This pessimistic technical assessment, which follows inexorably from the devastating power of nuclear weapons, is dramatically illustrated by the fundamental difference between air defense against conventional and nuclear attack. Against bombers carrying conventional bombs, an air defense system destroying only 10 percent of the incoming bombers per sortie would, as a practical matter, defeat sustained air raids such as the ones during World War II. After ten attacks against such a defense, the bomber force would be reduced to less than one-third of its initial size, a very high price to pay given the limited damage from conventional weapons even when over 90 percent of the bombers penetrate. In contrast, against a bomber attack with nuclear bombs, an air defense capable of destroying even 90 percent of the incoming bombers on each sortie would be totally inadequate since the damage produced by the penetrating 10 percent of the bombers would be devastating against urban targets.

When one extends this air defense analogy to ballistic missile defenses intended to protect population and industry against large numbers of nuclear missiles, it becomes clear that such a defense would have to be almost leakproof since the penetration of even a single warhead would cause great destruction to a soft target. In fact, such a ballistic missile defense would have to be not only almost leakproof but also nationwide in coverage since the attacker could always choose the centers of population or industry he wished to target. The attacker has the further advantage that he can not only choose his targets but also decide what fraction of his total resources to expend against any particular target. Thus, an effective defense would have to be extremely heavy across the entire defended territory, not at just a few priority targets. The technical problem of providing an almost leakproof missile defense is further compounded by the many technical measures the attacking force can employ to interfere with the defense by blinding or confusing its radars or other sensors and overwhelming the system's traffic-handling capacity with decoys.

When these general arguments are reduced to specific analysis, the conclusion is inescapable that effective protection of the population or industry of either of the superpowers against missile attack by the other is unattainable with present ABM (anti-ballistic missile) defense technology, since even the most elaborate systems could be penetrated by the other side at far less cost. This conclusion is not altered by prospective improvements in the components of present systems or by the introduction of new concepts such as lasers or particle beams into system design.

These conclusions, which address the inability of ballistic missile defense to eliminate the MAD character of the strategic relationship, do not necessarily apply to defense of very hard point targets, such as missile silos or shelters for mobile missiles. The defense of these hardened military targets does offer a more attractive technical opportunity since only the immediate vicinity of the hardened site needs to be defended and the survival of only a fraction of the defended silos is necessary to serve as a deterrent. Thus, the technical requirements for the system are much less stringent than for population or industrial defense and a much higher leakage rate can be tolerated. When these general remarks are translated into specific analysis which takes into account the many options available to the offense, hard site defense still does not look particularly attractive. Moreover, such a defense, even if partially successful, would not prevent the serious collateral fallout effects from the attack on the population discussed above. Nevertheless, the fact that these systems are technically feasible, and are advocated by some as effective, tends to confuse the public on the broader issue of the feasibility of urban defense against ballistic missiles.

The United States has a substantial research and development effort on ballistic missile defenses of land-based ICBMs as a possible approach to increase survivability of this leg of the strategic triad. The only program under serious consideration that could be deployed in this decade is the so-called LOAD (Low Altitude Defense) system. This system, which would utilize very small hardened radars and small missiles with small nuclear warheads, is designed to intercept at very close range those attacking missiles that might detonate close enough to the defended ICBM to destroy it. This last ditch defense is possible with nuclear weapons since the defended target is extremely hard and can tolerate nuclear detonations if they are not too close. While such a system for the defense of hard sites is technically feasible, there has been serious question as to whether it would be cost-effective in defending the MX in fixed Titan or Minuteman silos since the system could be overwhelmed relatively easily. In the case of the defense of a mobile MX in a multiple shelter system, the economics of the exchange ratios are substantially improved if the location of the mobile MX and mobile defense system are in fact unknown to the attacker; however, there are serious questions whether the presence of radiating radar systems might not actually compromise the location of the MX during an attack.

Looking further into the future, the U.S. research program is considering a much more sophisticated "layered" system for hard site defense. The outer layer would involve an extremely complex system using infrared sensors that would be launched on warning of a Soviet attack to identify and track incoming warheads. Based on this information, many interceptors, each carrying multiple, infrared-homing rockets with non-nuclear warheads, would be launched against the cloud of incoming warheads and attack them well outside the atmosphere. The warheads that leaked through this outer exoatmospheric layer would then be engaged by a close-in layer along the lines of the LOAD last ditch system described above.

It has been suggested that the outer layer exoatmospheric system might evolve into an effective area defense for population and industry. Actually, there are many rather fundamental technical questions that will take some time to answer about the ability of such a system to work at all against a determined adversary in the time frame needed to deploy it. For example, such a system would probably be defeated by properly designed decoys or blinded by nuclear explosions and, above all, may well be far too complex for even prospective control capabilities to operate. Whatever the value of these types of systems for hard site defense to support the MAD role of the deterrent, it is clear that the system holds no promise for population or industry defense and simply illustrates the technical difficulty of dealing with that problem.

While the government struggles with the much less demanding problem whether it is possible to design a plausible, cost-effective defense of hardened ICBM silos, the public is bombarded with recurring reports that some new technological "breakthrough" will suddenly generate an "impenetrable umbrella" which would obviate the MAD strategic relationship. Such irresponsible reports usually rehash claims for "directed energy" weapons which are based on the propagation of extremely energetic beams of either light (lasers) or atomic particles propagated at the speed of light to the target. Some of the proposals are technically infeasible, but in all cases one must remember that for urban defense only a system with country-wide coverage and extraordinarily effective performance would have an impact on the MAD condition. To constitute a ballistic missile defense system, directed energy devices would have to be integrated with detection and tracking devices for the incoming warheads, an extremely effective and fast data-handling system, the necessary power supplies for the extraordinarily high demand of energy to feed the directed energy weapons, and would have to be very precisely oriented to score a direct hit to destroy the target—as opposed to nuclear warheads that would only have to get in the general vicinity to destroy the target.

There are fundamental considerations that severely limit the application of directed energy weapons to ballistic missile defense. Particle beams do not penetrate the atmosphere. Thus, if such a system were ground-based, it would have to bore a hole through the atmosphere and then the beam would have to be focused through that hole in a subsequent pulse. All analyses have indicated that it is physically impossible to accomplish this feat stably. Among other things, laser systems suffer from the fact that they can only operate in good weather since clouds interfere with the beam.

These problems involving the atmosphere could be avoided by basing the system in space. Moreover, a space-based system has the desirable feature of potentially being able to attack missiles during the vulnerable launch phase before the reentry vehicles are dispersed. However, space-based systems involve putting a very complex system with a large power requirement into orbit. Analysis indicates that a comprehensive defensive system of this type would require over a hundred satellites, which in turn would need literally thousands of space shuttle sorties to assemble. It has been estimated that such a system would cost several hundred billion dollars. Even if the control mechanisms were available to operate such a system, there are serious questions as to the vulnerability of the satellites to physical attack and to various measures that would interfere with the system's operation. In short, no responsible analysis has indicated that for at least the next two decades such "death ray weapons" have any bearing on the ABM problem, or that there is any prospect that they would subsequently change the MAD character of our world.

Defense against aircraft further illustrates the inherently MAD nature of today's world. Although the Soviets have made enormous investments in air defense, the airborne component of the U.S. strategic triad has not had its damage potential substantially reduced. Most analyses indicate that a large fraction of the "aging" B-52 fleet would penetrate present Soviet defenses, with the aid of electronic countermeasures and defense suppression by missiles. It is true that the ability of B-52s to penetrate will gradually be impaired as the Soviets deploy "look down" radar planes similar to the much-publicized AWACS (Airborne Warning and Control System). However, these systems will not be effective against the air-launched cruise missiles whose deployment on B-52s will begin shortly; their ability to penetrate will not be endangered until a totally new generation of Soviet air defenses enters the picture. At that time, one can foresee major improvements in the ability of both bombers and cruise missiles to penetrate through a number of techniques, in particular the so-called "stealth" technology which will reduce by a large factor the visibility of both airplanes and cruise missiles to radar.

In short, there is little question that in the defense-offense race between air defenses and the airborne leg of the triad, the offense will retain its enormous damage potential. For its part, the United States does not now have a significant air defense, and the limited buildup proposed in President Reagan's program would have little effect on the ability of the Soviets to deliver nuclear weapons by aircraft against this country. Consequently, the "mutual hostage" relationship between the two countries will continue, even if only the airborne component of the triad is considered.

It is sometimes asserted that civil defense could provide an escape from the consequences of the MAD world and make even a general nuclear war between the superpowers winnable. This assertion is coupled with a continuing controversy as to the actual effectiveness of civil defense and the scope of the present Soviet civil defense program. Much of this debate reflects the complete failure of some civil defense advocates to comprehend the actual consequences of nuclear war. There is no question that civil defense could save lives and that the Soviet effort in this field is substantially greater than that of the United States. Yet all analyses have made it abundantly clear that to have a significant impact in a general nuclear war, civil defense would have to involve a much greater effort than now practiced on either side and that no amount of effort would protect a large portion of the population or the ability of either nation to continue as a functioning society. . . .

V

In sum, we are fated to live in a MAD world. This is inherent in the tremendous power of nuclear weapons, the size of nuclear stockpiles, the collateral damage associated with the use of nuclear weapons against military targets, the technical limitations on strategic area defense, and the uncertainties involved in efforts to control the escalation of nuclear war. There is no reason to believe that this situation will change for the foreseeable future since the problem is far too profound and the pace of technical military development far too slow to overcome the fundamental technical considerations that underlie the mutual hostage relationship of the superpowers.

What is clear above all is that the profusion of proposed NUTS approaches has not offered an escape from the MAD world, but rather constitutes a major danger in encouraging the illusion that limited or controlled nuclear war can be waged free from the grim realities of a MAD world. The principal hope at this time will not be found in seeking NUTS doctrines that ignore the MAD realities but rather in recognizing the nuclear world for what it is and seeking to make it more stable and less dangerous.

NOTES

1. See, for example, Fred Charles Iklé, "Can Nuclear Deterrence Last Out the Century?", *Foreign Affairs*, January 1973, pp. 267–85.
2. The acronym NUT for Nuclear Utilization Theory was used by Howard Margolis and Jack Ruina, "SALT II: Notes on Shadow and Substance," *Technology Review*, October 1979, pp. 31–41. We prefer Nuclear Utilization Target Selection, which relates the line of thinking more closely to the operational problem of target selection. Readers not familiar with colloquial American usage may need to be told that "nuts" is an adjective meaning "crazy or demented." For everyday purposes it is a synonym for "mad."

3. See Harold Brown, Speech at the Naval War College, August 20, 1980, the most authoritative public statement on the significance of Presidential Directive 59, which had been approved by President Carter shortly before.

4. For a particularly clear statement of this view, see Colin S. Gray and Keith Payne, "Victory Is Possible," *Foreign Policy*, Summer 1980, pp. 14–27. For opposing arguments, see Michael E. Howard, "On Fighting a Nuclear War," *International Security*, Spring 1981, pp. 3–17, and a further exchange between Messrs. Gray and Howard in *International Security*, Summer 1981, pp. 185–87.

5. For a discussion of the usefulness of theater nuclear forces in NATO as of that date, see Alain C. Enthoven, "U.S. Forces in Europe: How Many? Doing What?", *Foreign Affairs*, April 1975, pp. 523–31.

6

U.S. MILITARY FORCES AS A POLITICAL INSTRUMENT SINCE WORLD WAR II

BARRY M. BLECHMAN
STEPHEN S. KAPLAN

On November 11, 1944, the Turkish ambassador to the United States, Mehmet Munir Ertegün, died in Washington; not a very important event at a time when Allied forces were sweeping across France and Eastern Europe toward Germany, and Berlin and Tokyo were approaching *Götterdämmerung*. Sixteen months later, however, the ambassador's remains were the focus of world attention as the curtain went up on a classic act in the use of armed forces as a political instrument. On March 6, 1946, the U.S. Department of State announced that the late Ambassador Ertegün's remains would be sent home to Turkey aboard the U.S.S. *Missouri*, visibly the most powerful warship in the U.S. Navy and the ship on board which General Douglas MacArthur had recently accepted Japan's surrender.

Between the ambassador's death and this announcement, not only had World War II ended, the cold war—as yet untitled—had begun. In addition to conflicts between the United States and the Soviet Union over Poland, Germany, Iran, and other areas, the Soviet Union had demanded from the Turkish government the concession of two of its provinces in the east and, in the west, a base in the area of the Dardanelles.

On March 22, the *Missouri* began a slow journey from New York harbor to Turkey. At Gibraltar the British governor had a wreath placed on board. Accompanied by the destroyer *Power*, the great battleship was met on April 3 in the eastern Mediterranean by the light cruiser *Providence*. Finally, on the morning of April 5, the *Missouri* and her escorts anchored in the harbor at Istanbul.[1]

The research for this article was supported by the Advanced Research Projects Agency of the Department of Defense and was reviewed by the Office of Naval Research under Contract N00014-75-C-0140. The views expressed are the authors' alone and should not be interpreted as representing the official policies, either expressed or implied, of the Advanced Research Projects Agency, the Department of the Navy, or the U.S. government; nor should they be ascribed to the officers, trustees, or other staff members of the Brookings Institution.

Reprinted with permission from the *Political Science Quarterly* 94 (Summer 1979): 193–209.

The meaning of this event was missed by no one; Washington had not so subtly reminded the Soviet Union and others that the United States was a great military power and that it could project this power abroad, even to shores far distant. Whether the visit of the *Missouri*, or subsequent U.S. actions, deterred the Soviet Union from implementing any further planned or potential hostile acts toward Turkey will probably never be known. What is clear is that no forceful Soviet actions followed the visit. Moreover, as a symbol of American support for Turkey vis-à-vis the Soviet Union, the visit of the *Missouri* was well received and deeply appreciated by the government of Turkey, the Turkish press, and presumably by the Turkish citizenry at large. The American ambassador stated that to the Turks the visit indicated that "the United States has now decided that its own interests in this area require it to oppose any effort by the USSR to destroy Turk[ey's] independence and integrity."[2]

In this incident, as in hundreds of others since 1945, U.S. military forces were used without significant violence to underscore verbal and diplomatic expressions of American foreign policy. Recently we concluded a study concerned with some of these uses of the armed forces: those in which the various branches of the U.S. military were used in a discrete way for specific political objectives in a particular situation.[3] Historically, of course, the United States has not been the only nation to use its armed forces for political objectives; all the great powers have engaged in such activity, and in the last three decades the Soviet Union has been a frequent practitioner of the political use of the armed forces.

A principal objective of our study was to evaluate the effectiveness of the U.S. military as a political instrument, in the short term and over a longer period, by analyzing the consequences of such factors as: the size, type, and activity of military units involved in the incident; the nature of the situation at which they were directed; the character of U.S. objectives; the international and domestic context in which the incident occurred; and the extent and type of diplomatic activity that accompanied the use of the armed forces. We concluded, generally, that discrete demonstrative uses of the military were often effective political instruments in the short term, but that effectiveness declined when situations were reexamined after longer periods of time had elapsed. We also found that each of the variables mentioned above had important consequences for the effectiveness of these uses of the military.

METHODOLOGY

Armed forces serve foreign policy functions in many ways—by their existence and character alone, by their location abroad, by their routine exercises and visits, by their provision of military assistance and other forms of support. The United States has used military units often and in a wide variety of ways since World War II. Most of these uses have had a political dimension;

that is, they were liable to influence the perceptions and behavior of political leaders in foreign countries to some degree.

For the purposes of the study described in this article, we define a political use of the armed forces as a physical action taken by one or more components of the uniformed military services as part of a deliberate attempt by the national authorities to influence, or to be prepared to influence, specific behavior of individuals in another nation without engaging in a continuing contest of violence.

Using this definition, 215 incidents were identified in which the United States used its armed forces for political objectives between January 1, 1946, and December 31, 1975—an arbitrary cutoff date. We are confident that the list of incidents adequately represents all those instances in which U.S. armed forces were used in a way that would fit the terms of the definition.[4]

The use of military power as a tool of diplomacy can risk the security and well being of the United States and importantly effect U.S. and other international relationships both immediately and for a long time afterward. Although on some occasions the risks of intervention may be small, in many instances it is difficult to determine all possible dangers and the likelihood of their being realized. Military action in still other situations may clearly entail great risk—particularly if the USSR is an actor and is committed to a different result, or if another opponent is prepared to use violence as a last resort. The discrete political use of military power may also lead to unwanted dependency on the United States and the hostility, not only of antagonists, but of other nations in the affected region. U.S. relations with the USSR, China, and uninvolved U.S. allies may be made more difficult. In light of the Vietnam War experience, the effects of U.S. military activities abroad on the political culture of the United States and the fabric of American politics should also be considered. Before reaching a judgment that military intervention is necessary for the preservation of important U.S. interests and accepting the immediate and long-term risks that may be apparent, policymakers would be wise to consider also the utility of past political-military operations.

To evaluate this past effectiveness, two approaches, aggregate analysis and case study, which present macro- and micro-views of the same phenomena, were adopted. The value of the first is that it permits broad generalizations that might be applicable in the future when the armed forces are used for political objectives. Individual case studies can confirm or disprove these generalizations, allow the inference of propositions related to the peculiarities and complexities of specific situations, and provide a sense of the psychological climate and individual concerns that condition the choices of policymakers. In short, the two approaches are complementary; each has advantages and disadvantages, but together they afford greater understanding than either can provide separately.

For the aggregate analysis, a sample of thirty-three incidents, 15 percent of the total number of cases examined, was selected for systematic and rigorous analysis of outcomes. For each of the incidents in the sample, the available literature, documents, and newspaper accounts were investigated so as to determine:

- U.S. objectives vis-à-vis each participant, and whether those objectives were satisfied within six months and retained over three years following the use of U.S. armed forces;
- the size, type, and activity of U.S. armed forces involved in the incident;
- the character of the targets in relation to U.S. objectives;
- other activities (for example, diplomatic) undertaken in support of U.S. objectives along with the use of the armed forces;
- certain U.S. domestic conditions.

In the analysis, the degree of satisfaction of U.S. objectives was related to each of these other factors with the aim of highlighting the crucial variables determining whether a political use of the armed forces was likely to be successful or not. Five specialists made detailed assessments of the specific mechanisms through which military operations affected the perceptions and decisions of foreign policymakers in ten case studies.

What have been the results of discrete U.S. political-military operations? Are the prospects for success in such ventures good enough that policymakers should consider the armed forces an important option in these situations? Or should they view use of the military with great caution, since this type of activity often fails to meet its objectives and sometimes backfires? More to the point, under what circumstances are discrete uses of the armed forces for political objectives more likely to succeed, and when are they more likely to fail?

THE UTILITY OF MILITARY FORCE

The evidence supports the hypothesis that discrete uses of the armed forces are often an effective way of achieving short-term foreign policy objectives. The aggregate analyses show clearly that the outcomes of United States political-military activities were most often favorable from the perspective of U.S. decision makers—at least in the short term.

In a very large proportion of the incidents, however, this "success rate" eroded sharply over time. Thus, it would seem that, to the degree that they did influence events, discrete uses of military forces for political objectives served mainly to delay, rather than resolve, unwanted developments abroad. Though there is some value in "buying time"—that is, keeping a situation open and flexible enough to prevent an adverse fait accompli—it should be recognized that these military operations cannot substitute for more fundamental policies and actions that can form the basis either for sound and successful alliances or for stable adversary relations, such as diplomacy, close economic and cultural relations, an affinity of mutual interests and perceptions. What political-military operations perhaps can do is provide a respite, a means of postponing adverse developments long enough to formulate and implement new policies that may be sustained over the longer term. Or, if that is not possible, the political use of armed forces may serve to lessen the consequences of detrimental events. However, some of the case studies suggest that even these delaying and minimizing accomplishments do not always obtain.

In some cases the discrete use of force clearly has been ineffectual. For example, U.S. support for Pakistan during the 1971 war with India was a relatively empty gesture because the target actors recognized that under virtually no circumstances would the United States become militarily involved in the war. Consequently, the deployment of the *Enterprise* task force to the Indian Ocean had almost no effect on the decisions of either the immediate actors, India and Pakistan, or the actors indirectly involved, China and the Soviet Union.

In other cases, a discrete political application of the armed forces seems to have been associated with the creation of a situation that remained tolerable for a period of months or, in some cases, years. The intervention in Laos in 1962 was such an incident; the landing of U.S. Marines in Thailand coincided with the negotiation of a settlement that kept the peace in Laos for several years. U.S. actions to oust the Trujillo family from the Dominican Republic following Rafael Trujillo's assassination, and subsequent actions to support the new government, were of a similar character. These actions precipitated a more acceptable political situation in the Dominican Republic that persisted for several years, even though it ultimately foundered in 1965.

Was it worthwhile to use armed forces to obtain positive outcomes that could be sustained only temporarily, whether the duration was of several months or several years? We believe the answer is yes, insofar as an opportunity was gained for diplomacy.

When a positive outcome did not endure, it was usually attributable not to an absence of follow-up diplomatic effort, but to the fact that the internal situation within a state, or a specific interstate relationship, was strong and durable and thus not subject to penetration by either single or periodic U.S. military actions or by the use of other U.S. policy instruments. Realizing that this was the situation in Vietnam in 1964-65, American policymakers chose war as the solution, which contrasts with U.S. policy in the late 1940s in China when Communist forces there triumphed and forced the Kuomintang government of Chiang Kai-shek to flee to Taiwan; or in the early 1960s over Cuba when Fidel Castro identified his regime with communism and the Soviet Union; or in the late 1960s against North Korea after the *Pueblo* was seized and a U.S. Navy EC-121 aircraft was shot down.

Finally, in some cases with very special circumstances, discrete political uses of the armed forces contributed to the establishment of new international relationships, such that U.S. interests were protected for decades. For example, following the 1946 visit to Turkey by the battleship *Missouri* and further displays of U.S. military support for Ankara, Soviet pressures on Turkey declined; they have not been renewed in a serious way since. Displays of American military support for Italy prior to the 1948 elections seem to have contributed, along with such other instruments of policy as economic aid and covert support for democratic political parties, to the defeat of the Italian Communist party. The dominance of the Christian Democratic party, which resulted from that election, persisted for more than two decades. Political uses of the armed forces during the Berlin crises of 1958-59 and 1961 helped create stable conditions in Central Europe that continue to exist.

The Effects of the Military Demonstration

What is the mechanism at work here? How do the armed forces play their special role? The process begins when a given framework of relations among several countries, or a domestic political configuration abroad, is disrupted by something unexpected or at least unwelcome: a domestic upheaval, a new departure in a major power's foreign policy, or perhaps an unexpected armed clash between the military units of hostile states. Regardless of cause, this development often creates uncertainties and a distinct psychological unease among interested parties; at other times it leads directly to an unraveling of the fabric of relations that previously had been established and maintained by existing policies. Under such circumstances (and mindful of the fact that even when favorable outcomes do occur they are likely to persist only over the short term), a discrete demonstration of U.S. military capability can have a stabilizing and otherwise beneficial effect, perhaps persuading the target that the wise course of action is to alter the undesirable policy.

The effect of the military demonstration will depend to a large extent on whether the target finds the threat credible. A prime example was the arrival of U.S. military forces off the coast of the Dominican Republic in November 1961, an event that changed the perceptions of the Trujillo family and their lieutenants as to the United States' willingness to act. Coupled as it was with a clear ultimatum, the action seems to have exerted a powerful influence.

Such a military demonstration may be particularly effective when the target state is not fully committed to the course from which the United States hopes to dissuade it. We will never know for sure, but U.S. actions in support of Yugoslavia following President Tito's break with Stalin may have lessened Stalin's inclination to take more aggressive measures against Yugoslavia. Moscow may also have been somewhat deterred from taking action against Rumania following the intervention in Czechoslovakia in 1968. We will return to these distinctions. First, however, it is helpful to examine the mechanisms at work more closely.

In some of the cases studied, the insertion (even symbolically) of U.S. military forces may have provided leverage to U.S. decision makers where previously there had not been any. A U.S. military presence or operation may furnish an incentive to a foreign leader to consider the wishes of U.S. policymakers. After U.S. Marines landed in Thailand in 1962, and the threat of a U.S. intervention in Laos became credible, for example, the United States may have gained a decided edge at the negotiating table. In such a case the prime result is to lessen the potential U.S. loss. Foreign decision makers may act to avoid those extreme choices that they fear would precipitate a violent U.S. response. Unless the United States is willing to extend its new military presence into a permanent operation, however, any such demonstrative action is likely to be successful, to the degree it is successful at all, only for a limited time.

The intervention in Lebanon in 1958 provides a pointed example of this phenomenon. Although President Eisenhower authorized the landing of U.S. Marines and other forces in Lebanon in July 1958, the president—or at least Secretary of State Dulles—recognized that an American-imposed solution in Lebanon would be unacceptable to most of the Lebanese actors and therefore short-lived. Thus the United States adopted a twofold approach. On the one hand, a massive demonstration of American military power was staged, involving the landing of thousands of American troops. On the other hand, Deputy Under Secretary of State Robert Murphy was dispatched to Lebanon, where, recognizing the political realities of the situation, he negotiated a settlement that was probably more favorable to the actors who opposed U.S. policy than to the presumed American client, President Camille Chamoun. In other words, to the degree that it did influence the situation, the U.S. military demonstration seems to have bought sufficient time to reach new political arrangements that more realistically reflected the distribution of power among competing ethnic and political groups in Lebanon. Without the more realistic political solution negotiated by Murphy, the 1958 U.S. intervention in Lebanon would probably have been associated with a much less favorable outcome. At the same time, without the leverage provided by the U.S. military presence in Lebanon, with its implied threat of greater violence, Murphy might well have failed in his attempt to negotiate a political solution.

Military demonstrations also can ease domestic political pressures on the president from groups demanding more forceful action. In less serious incidents, these pressures—which can originate from ethnic groups, the Congress, friends and political associates of the decision makers, and executive branch uniformed and civilian officials, among others—are directed at lower-ranking foreign policy managers. Insofar as they can help to stabilize a situation, thereby postponing perceived adverse consequences of unexpected changes in international relations or the internal politics of foreign nations, discrete uses of the armed forces may diminish calls for more decisive action. The postponement provides the time needed to gather support within the bureaucracy and in the Congress and the public for the fundamental changes in policy required to accommodate developments. In the absence of the time bought by the military demonstration, these fundamental changes in policy may be more difficult to bring about, and the president might fear that his constituencies, both at home and abroad, will see him as bowing to foreign pressures.

This phenomenon was also demonstrated pointedly by the intervention in Lebanon in 1958. During the spring of 1958, President Eisenhower resisted several requests from President Chamoun for American military assistance. An unexpected event—the coup in Iraq in July—made it impossible to avoid the request any longer. Eisenhower feared that further inaction, after the seeming wholesale defeat of American clients in the Middle East, would have negative effects both on the perceptions of decision makers in foreign nations and on domestic opinion in this nation. American support for the realistic solution to the Lebanese problem negotiated by Murphy might have been difficult to muster without the symbolism of American strength suggested by the military intervention. In the absence of the intervention, President Eisenhower may have feared the effects of such an apparent concession on opinion both at home and abroad.

Similarly, following American intervention in the Dominican Republic in 1965, Ambassador Ellsworth Bunker negotiated an agreement in which it was all but explicit that the president elected the following year would be either Joaquin Balaguer or Juan Bosch. Balaguer was the last president during the Trujillo era, and a person the United States took pains to keep out of the Dominican Republic in later years; Bosch was strongly disliked by many American officials and suspected of tendencies that might allow an eventual takeover by the extreme left. The emplacement of U.S. forces in the Dominican Republic thus not only made an election there possible, it also made it possible for the United States to accept results of that election which it previously could not have tolerated.

None of this is meant to imply that the gains seemingly associated with discrete uses of the armed forces for political objectives have been fraudulent. The amelioration of pressures for extreme actions is an important benefit, as is the provision of time necessary to build a consensus for a new U.S. policy; so too is the provision of leverage to negotiators.

CORRELATES OF SUCCESS

Four groups of factors have been associated with the relative success or failure of political uses of the U.S. armed forces: the type of objective; involvement by the Soviet Union; the context of the incident; and the nature and activity of the U.S. military forces involved. (Unless noted otherwise, these conclusions refer mainly to short-term outcomes.)

U.S. Objectives

The nature of U.S. objectives may be an important determinant of whether a political use of force is successful. Favorable outcomes occurred most often when the objective of U.S. policymakers was to maintain the authority of a specific regime abroad. Such was the case, for example, when naval movements and other activities were undertaken in support of King Hussein during the 1970 civil war in Jordan. Indeed, the aggregate analyses suggest that maintenance of regime authority was the one type of objective associated with the persistence of a favorable outcome over the longer term. The armed forces were least often associated with favorable outcomes when the objectives concerned the provision of support by actors to third parties—for example, the many incidents in which U.S. military activities were undertaken in order to persuade the Soviet Union to cease supporting hostile political initiatives by its allies or clients.

Between these two extremes there were a reasonable number of favorable outcomes when discrete political uses of the armed forces were undertaken to offset the use of force by another actor. Over the longer term, however, frequencies of favorable outcomes were low when discrete political uses of the military were aimed at either the use of force by another actor or another actor's support of a third nation's use of force. Illustrative are the futile attempts during the late 1950s and early 1960s to convince the Pathet Lao and Viet Cong to terminate their insurgencies in Laos and South Vietnam.

Perhaps more significant, the mode in which the armed forces are used as a political instrument may also be an important determinant of success. It is evident from the aggregate analyses that discrete uses of the armed forces for political purposes were more often associated with favorable outcomes when the U.S. objective was to reinforce, rather than modify, the behavior of a target state. This stands to reason. Nikita Khrushchev, no doubt, found it much easier not to follow through on the various threats he made concerning Europe and the Middle East than he did to withdraw Soviet missiles from Cuba; just as deterring the outbreak of violence is usually an easier task than bringing violence to a satisfactory conclusion.

Human behavior is difficult to change. Individuals tend to be more aware of the risks of change than they are of the dangers of continuing their prevailing course. After all, established policies are known entities; even when the risks in continuing established policies are evident, the dangers of change will often appear more threatening. More to the point, no one—least of all the head of a nation—can afford to be told publicly what he should be doing. Thus, national leaders will resist demands for policy modifications most strenuously when such demands are made publicly, which is usually unavoidable when military power is used.

In short, whether a discrete application of military power was made in order to coerce a hostile target state to change its behavior or to encourage a friendly target state to change its behavior, the outcomes were similar; most often they were unfavorable from the U.S. perspective. On the other hand, when U.S. policymakers used the armed forces to coerce a hostile target state to continue to do something (for example, stay at peace), or to encourage a friendly state to remain on the same course, military demonstrations were relatively more often associated with favorable outcomes.

Consider, for example, the starkly different outcomes of the Berlin crisis of 1958–59 and 1961 and the several incidents in Southeast Asia in the late 1950s and early 1960s. In the former situation the United States sought essentially to assure allies and to deter certain threatened actions by the USSR and East Germany. Both types of objectives required only that the targets not change their behavior, and both were achieved. Not so favorable, especially over the longer term, were the outcomes of the Southeast Asian incidents, in which the United States sought to compel various Communist actors to stop using force and to induce the government of South Vietnam to behave differently (that is, more assertively). Here both types of objectives required a change of behavior on the part of target states, and only rarely were these outcomes achieved.

To some extent this conclusion may reflect Tolstoy's view that the only decisions that are carried out are those corresponding to what would have happened if the decisions had not been made. In many of the incidents, although U.S. decision makers may have thought—or feared—that a target state was prepared or intending to change its behavior, and thus used the armed forces to reinforce existing behavior, the target state actually may have had no such intention. A good example is the U.S. military activity that followed the Soviet occupation of Czechoslovakia, consisting primarily of increases in the readiness for war of U.S. forces in Europe. One objective of that action was to deter a Soviet invasion of Rumania. No invasion occurred; hence the military demonstration appears to have been effective. The question, however, is whether Soviet leaders ever seriously contemplated such an invasion. The same may be said about the Soviet Union not taking violent action against President Tito and Yugoslavia almost two decades earlier. This is not necessarily to discount the importance of the U.S. military activity. U.S. policymakers had other important objectives in mind as well. Still, the proportion of favorable "reinforcement" outcomes that are accounted for by the "unreality" of the feared target state behavior may be high. Unfortunately, that proportion is impossible to determine empirically.

Political uses of the armed forces were often associated with favorable outcomes when U.S. objectives were at least loosely consistent with prior U.S. policies. The purpose of discrete political uses of force must fit within a fundamental framework of expectations held by decision makers both in this country and abroad if the military activity is to be associated with a favorable outcome. With regard to the incidents in the sample, although prior diplomacy was closely associated with positive outcomes, diplomacy during the course of the incidents themselves was not.

When a treaty exists, or when policymakers have taken pains to make clear that the United States perceives itself to have a commitment, antagonists are less likely to probe, or to probe only within narrower limits than would have been the case otherwise, and to leave themselves a way open for retreat. In other words, antagonists may be less likely to try to present the United States with a fait accompli that could be reversed only through a major use of the armed forces. Prior diplomacy may have reinforced the antagonists' continued performance of desired behavior, and thus lessened the significance of a breakdown in relations or the severity of a crisis. Rather than have to cope with hostile actions, policymakers in these cases might have only had to respond to hostile rhetoric; alternatively, the degree of desired behavior modification of foreign decision makers might have been less.

Hence, although China initiated the 1958 Offshore Islands crisis by shelling Quemoy and Matsu, and Khrushchev threatened Berlin on several occasions, both Peking and Moscow carefully controlled their behavior during these incidents because they perceived a prior U.S. commitment (or at least feared the strength of announced U.S. commitments). In the absence of a prior U.S. commitment, as in Korea in 1950, we might surmise that not only would China and the USSR have gone further in their initial actions, but also that sudden U.S. diplomatic action, even if supported by a discrete political use of force, might have had a lesser effect. Skilled diplomacy during incidents—for example, by Robert Murphy in Lebanon, Averell Harriman in Laos, and Ellsworth Bunker in the Dominican Republic—has typically borne fruit only after ambiguous U.S. military commitments have been clarified by the movement of major military units. Thus, the United States should not count on skilled diplomacy as being effective in controlling crises in the absence of prior commitments and reinforcing uses of the armed forces; it should, however, aim to avoid such difficult tests in the first place by being quite clear as to what its commitments are.

Similarly, the aggregate analyses suggest that prior U.S. military engagement in conflicts in a region was often associated with favorable outcomes when subsequent demonstrative uses of military force took place. The fact that the United States previously had been willing to engage in violence in the region may have made the threats or assurances implied by the subsequent military activity more credible. Much less often associated with favorable outcomes were previous demonstrative uses of force in the region; the willingness to engage in violence seems to have been the key. Previous discrete political uses of force were associated with favorable outcomes more often, however, when the U.S. objective was to assure that a target state would continue to do something. Good examples are provided by U.S. naval demonstrations in the Mediterranean. U.S. military forces have not fought in that region since 1945, yet as concerns the assurance of Israel (and less frequently, Jordan), these displays of naval power were often associated with favorable outcomes. U.S. objectives in situations were far less often attained, however, when the political use of force was meant to modify the behavior of Israel's (or Jordan's) enemies.

In short, prior demonstrative uses of force or even prior military engagements did not seem to be sufficient to compensate for the previously noted difficulty of modifying a target state's behavior. Indeed, very little seemed to compensate for the difficulty of modifying behavior; more than any other factor this was the basic determinant of when a discrete political use of force would or would not be associated with the attainment of foreign policy objectives. It overshadowed the diplomacy that accompanied the military activity, the nature of the situation, and the timing, size, composition, and activity of the military units themselves.

Soviet Activity

A second group of factors that seemed to be associated with favorable outcomes in the aggregate analyses included the character of United States-Soviet relations and the specific role played by the Soviet Union in an incident.

One conclusion that runs counter to prevailing views concerns the possible effects of the United States-Soviet strategic nuclear balance on the relative fortunes of the superpowers. We did not find that the United States was less often successful as the Soviet Union closed the U.S. lead in strategic nuclear weapons that had been maintained for the first twenty or so years following World War II. Whether discrete political uses of U.S. armed forces were associated with positive outcomes seems to have been independent of relative United States-Soviet aggregate strategic capabilities. Of course, the United States may have engaged less often in these incidents since the late 1960s precisely because it understood that its chances of success were smaller; as the USSR closed the nuclear gap, the United States may have chosen to participate in incidents more selectively, choosing only those cases in which its chances of success were greatest.

Since this study was not designed to test the effects of the strategic balance, the findings in this regard are clearly tentative. Still, both the aggregate analyses and the case studies provide little support for the notion that decisions during crises are strongly influenced by aggregate strategic capabilities. Studies of Lebanon and Jordan, for example, indicate that, to the extent that evaluations of the military balance played any role, decision makers in the United States and Soviet Union, as well as those in the nations directly involved, were more concerned with the local balance of conventional power. More to the point, most local actors in these incidents seem to have had only a rudimentary and impressionistic sense of relative military capabilities in general.

Soviet political and/or military involvement in the incident itself, on the other hand, was clearly associated with the frequency of outcomes favorable to the United States, which were less often favorable when the Soviet

Union was involved, particularly when the Soviet Union threatened to employ, or actually employed, its own armed forces in the incident. The seemingly pernicious effect of Soviet involvement was tempered at times when broader United States-Soviet relations had been improving, and outcomes were more often favorable when overall United States-Soviet relations were characterized by greater cooperation. As in the previous finding, this conclusion is stronger when just those incidents in which the Soviet Union participated were considered, and stronger still when just those incidents were considered in which Soviet military forces were involved.

Nature of the Situation

Outcomes were favorable more frequently when discrete political uses of force were directed at intranational, as contrasted to international, situations. We are not confident about this finding, however, because two other factors that are also closely associated with favorable outcomes are highly correlated with intranational situations: lesser amounts of force tend to be used in intranational situations; and the U.S. objective in these situations is more often reinforcement, not modification, of behavior.

In the international situations, a positive outcome was most likely if the United States was involved from the very onset of a conflict. This finding complements the previous finding concerning the need for the U.S. objective and the specific use of force to be consistent with the prior framework of relations between the United States and the nations involved in the incident. In those situations in which the United States was involved initially, such as the Berlin crises of 1958-59 and 1961, U.S. statements of aims and objectives were more likely to be considered seriously. Similarly, U.S. threats or promises implied by the use of armed forces were more likely to be perceived as credible. In international situations where the United States intervened in affairs that did not concern it directly (or at least not initially), however, there seems to have been some question in the minds of the other actors whether U.S. threats or promises were credible. Consider the perceptions of Hanoi in the late 1950s and early 1960s and those of the Gandhi government in India during the crisis and then war with Pakistan in 1971, for example. The U.S. military demonstrations then were not taken too seriously at first. Why, North Vietnamese and Indian leaders might have asked, would the United States become involved militarily? Such questions were less likely to be raised in those situations in which U.S. interests were directly and obviously threatened.

Boding ill for the future, the proportion of incidents involving hostility between states appears to be increasing, while there is a decline in situations of an intrastate nature. Less and less is the United States being called upon by governments for support against internal dissidents; rather, the trend is toward being asked by one state for support against another. Insofar as such a shift is discernible, the risks of involvement to the United States, especially in a situation of violence, can only increase. The shift away from an intrastate focus means that the instruments brought to bear by regional actors will often be more powerful, both diplomatically and militarily. Allies usually act more overtly when they are supporting a state rather than a subnational group; hence, the facing-off of states is more likely to occasion the facing-off of alliances, whether formal or otherwise. Most important, the likelihood of superpower confrontation is increased.

States, unlike subnational groups, also have air forces, navies, and heavily armed ground forces. Thus the level of violence that can be threatened in a crisis or manifested in a conflict is much greater. For a threat by U.S. policymakers to be credible in these circumstances, large and technologically sophisticated forces must be available. Should these forces be committed in a conflict, they might have to be used in strength and be prepared to take significant casualties. The danger that U.S. action of this sort might stimulate a Soviet military response is obvious.

Size, Activity, and Type of U.S. Military Forces

The firmer the commitment implied by the military operation, the more often the outcome of the situation was favorable to the United States. Forces actually emplaced on foreign soil were more frequently associated with positive outcomes than were deployments of naval forces, which can be withdrawn almost as easily as they can be moved toward the disturbed area. The movement of land-based forces, on the other hand, involves both real economic costs and a certain psychological commitment that are difficult to reverse, at least in the short term. This is an interesting finding, not so much because of its novelty—after all, it only confirms the common perception—but because its implications run counter to common U.S. practice. The navy has been the preeminent military force in discrete political operations. Naval forces participated in more than 80 percent of the incidents; and reliance on the Navy was the case regardless of region, time period, type of situation, and whether or not the Soviet Union participated in the incident.

Naval forces can be used more subtly to support foreign policy initiatives—to underscore threats, warnings, promises, or commitments—than can land-based units, and they can do so without inalterably tying the president's hands. But it is precisely this last fact that probably diminishes the effectiveness of naval forces in a political role. Foreign decision makers also recognize that warships can be withdrawn as easily as they can enter a region of tension and, hence, that the commitment they imply is not so firm as that implied by land-based units.

Positive outcomes were particularly frequent when land-based combat aircraft were involved in an incident. This would suggest, particularly in view of the much greater mobility of modern land-based tactical air units, that the air force might be used more frequently in political-military operations than has been the case in the past.

Such a shift in U.S. practice would not be without its costs, because the use of land-based forces is perceived by foreign decision makers as greater evidence of commitment. If the U.S. objective is not so certain, if all that is desired is to take an action that signifies interest and concern but leaves room for maneuver—such as U.S. naval deployments during the Cyprus crises of 1964, 1967, and 1974—then the use of land-based forces would not be advisable. Moreover, in situations in which a military move is intended as a bluff or to screen a political defeat—as seems the case in the Indo-Pakistani War in 1971—the use of land-based air forces would not be advisable. In all these types of situations, naval forces would provide greater flexibility to decision makers and thus would be more appropriate even if their probability of succeeding may be less.

There are other ways to enhance the effectiveness of the armed forces. Outcomes were more often favorable when the units involved actually did something, instead of merely emphasizing their potential capability to intervene—for example, by reducing the time delay between a decision to intervene and the actual operation by moving toward the scene of the incident or by increasing their state of alert. The involvement of the military unit in a specific operation, such as mine-laying, or mine-clearing, or patrolling—and certainly when the actual exercise of firepower was involved—seems to have indicated a more serious intent on the United States' part. The movement of the force toward the region of concern by itself could be an ambiguous signal; it might not be clear to foreign decision makers what the United States had in mind, or the movement might pass unobserved. A more specific action, one that gave a clearer signal, thus was more often associated with favorable outcomes.

Positive outcomes were also more likely when the forces involved included strategic nuclear forces. Foreign decision makers seem to have perceived the use of strategic nuclear forces—whether or not it was accompanied by a specific threat to use nuclear weapons—as an important signal that the United States perceived the situation in a most serious way. Thus, the employment of nuclear-associated forces, such as Strategic Air Command aircraft or Sixth Fleet carriers when they were central to U.S. plans for nuclear war, served the same purpose as the involvement of military units in a specific activity or the use of ground forces as compared to naval forces: they bolstered U.S. credibility.

The risks of such a policy should be evident. There is no guarantee that any military demonstration will be successful. When nuclear weapons are involved, and the demonstration is not successful, the result could be disastrous; U.S. policymakers may be faced with the choice of admitting the emptiness of the nuclear threat, and thus undermining the credibility of fundamental U.S. commitments, or actually employing nuclear weapons.

Moreover, it may be that positive outcomes have more often occurred when nuclear forces were involved simply because these weapons have been used infrequently. The more U.S. decision makers turn to nuclear forces, even demonstratively, to ensure the credibility of signals in incidents such as we have described, the more quickly the special message now associated with nuclear weapons might erode. Eventually the movement of nuclear forces would not receive much more attention and would not convey any more credibility than movements of conventional forces.

A LAST WORD

The discrete use of the armed forces for political objectives should not be an option that decision makers turn to frequently or quickly to secure political objectives abroad; it should be used only in very special circumstances. We have found that over the longer term such uses of the armed forces were not often associated with positive outcomes. Decision makers thus should not expect them to serve as substitutes for broader and more fundamental policies tailored to the realities of politics abroad, and incorporating diplomacy and the many other potential instruments available to U.S. foreign policy.

Moreover, there are dangers in using the armed forces as a discrete political instrument. Symbolic low-level uses of force may be disregarded by antagonists or friends in a situation in which U.S. policymakers have not seriously contemplated the need for, or the consequences of, using larger forces in a more manifest way. Foreign decision makers may not perceive important U.S. interests to be involved; the initial U.S. military action may be seen as symbolic of U.S. interest but not of a commitment; foreign decision makers may calculate that they will be able to cope successfully with the forces that they expect the United States to bring to bear; or, when an actor feels its very existence is at stake, the calculus may not matter at all. In all these situations there is a risk that lesser military actions may lead to pressures for greater U.S. involvement.

Case studies bear this out: The Castro regime did not yield at the Bay of Pigs; Hanoi and the Viet Cong were not swayed in the early 1960s; and India dismembered Pakistan in 1971. In each case, either the United States suffered humiliation, or the fear of exposure embarrassed decision makers into escalation and war.

Still, in particular circumstances, discrete political uses of the armed forces often were associated—at least in the short term—with the securing of U.S. objectives or the stabilization of adverse situations while more fundamental policies could be formulated. Thus, at times, and although decision makers should view this option with some caution, the discrete use of the armed forces for political objectives seems to have been a useful step in shoring up situations enough to avoid dramatic setbacks, to mitigate domestic and international pressures for more forceful and perhaps counterproductive actions, and to gain time for sounder policies to be formulated and implemented.

To reach this conclusion about the apparent effectiveness of the armed forces as a political instrument is not to reach any judgment about the wisdom of using the armed forces for these purposes. That is a more difficult question, which can only be answered in the context of the specific choices—and the various costs and benefits associated with each choice—facing decision makers at that time.

NOTES

1. Log of the U.S.S. *Missouri*, Washington National Records Center, Suitland, Md.
2. U.S., Department of State, *Foreign Relations of the United States, 1946*, vol. 7, *The Near East and Africa* (Washington, D.C.: Government Printing Office, 1969), p. 822.
3. Barry M. Blechman and Stephen S. Kaplan, *Force Without War: U.S. Armed Forces as a Political Instrument* (Washington, D.C.: The Brookings Institution, 1978).
4. Analysts undertaking a similar study on a classified basis have indicated that there is a correlation of 0.89 between our incident list and a list of incidents which, under the terms of the definition employed in this study, their data would indicate took place. See Robert B. Mahoney, Jr., "A Comparison of the Brookings and CNA International Incidents Projects," Center for Naval Analyses, Professional Paper 174 (Washington, D.C.: February, 1977), processed.

7

EVOLVING PATTERNS OF U.S. SECURITY ASSISTANCE 1950–1980

ANDREW K. SEMMEL

The transfer of military arms, training, and services by the United States to foreign governments has been a controversial foreign policy issue for most of the postwar period. With the exception of the early Cold War years, security assistance policies have never been free of polemic or concern. Indeed, the history of U.S. international relations after World War II is filled with examples of U.S. security assistance: the Truman Doctrine, containment, European rearmament, and the Korean conflict in the late '40s and '50s; U.S. involvement in the protracted conflict in Southeast Asia in the late '60s and early '70s; the security guarantees to Israel and Egypt leading up to the Camp David Accords in the '70s; and the assurances to states coping with rising tensions in the Persian Gulf, the Indian Ocean, and the Caribbean in the early '80s. Critics and proponents of security assistance may differ on the relative contribution it has made to U.S. security and to the resolution of regional conflicts, but they would agree that, in practice, it has been a key agent in the conduct of U.S. foreign and defense policy over the past thirty years.

This essay examines the evolution of U.S. security assistance, the objectives of the program, and some of its major patterns and trends between 1950 and 1980. At the outset, it should be noted that security assistance—like foreign aid in general—is one of the most misunderstood aspects of U.S. foreign policy. It has been both maligned and praised, and because it continues to evoke strong partisanship on the part of critics and advocates alike, misinformation or selective information about security assistance has become a dominant factor contributing to widespread public

This essay was written specially for this book. Dr. Semmel is currently a Foreign Affairs Specialist in the Defense Security Assistance Agency of the United States Department of Defense. He taught previously at the University of Cincinnati and is currently writing a book on U.S. security assistance policy. The views expressed herein reflect those of the author and do not necessarily represent those of the U.S. Government or the Department of Defense.

misunderstanding. It is, indeed, difficult to even write about security assistance in a purely descriptive and dispassionate manner, since numerous and conflicting empirical examples can easily be mined from the historical records to support the charges and countercharges on the relative merits of the program.

WHAT IS SECURITY ASSISTANCE?

What is security assistance and why does it arouse such partisanship? In general, security assistance may be defined as the transfer of military equipment, training, services, and support from the United States to recipient countries. These transfers typically are made through direct cash purchases, sales financed by credits provided by the United States, grant transfers, and in some cases, barter arrangements. Security assistance is designed to improve the mutual security interests of both the United States and recipient countries. The distinction between security assistance and economic aid is less clear. Both serve interrelated goals—economic growth and political stability can not develop without adequate security, and national security would be meaningless without parallel political and economic improvements.[1] Both types of aid are included in the same foreign aid legislation, and statutory responsibility for both rests with the Department of State. No Department of Defense budget resources are ordinarily used or earmarked in support of security assistance, although the Defense Department has a major role in managing, planning, and implementing the security assistance portion of foreign aid.

The United States has several different security assistance programs; they include the following:

- *Foreign Military Sales (FMS).* The FMS involves straight cash sales to eligible governments of U.S. defense articles, services and training. It has been the major portion of security assistance in recent years. By 1980, there were more than 100 countries and three intergovernmental organizations authorized to participate in this program. Congress reviews proposed major sales and has extensive oversight authority, but cash transactions under this program have no impact on the budget of the U.S. government. Congress has never legislated a ceiling on the program, but has, from time to time, passed legislation to restrict FMS sales.
- *Foreign Military Sales Credit Program (FMSCR).* Unlike the FMS cash program, which requires no U.S. government funding, FMSCR is a government-funded program in the form of loans or credits under which governments can purchase defense articles, training, and services. FMS credits, which were begun in 1955, are normally loaned at repayable rates equal to what it costs the U.S. Treasury to borrow. FMSCR, however, consists of both *direct credits* and *guaranteed credits*; the former are extended by the Defense Department and may carry no obligation for repayment; the latter require repayment at the

going market interest rate. Normal repayment terms include one to three years grace on principal and an additional seven to eight years to repay the principal and interest, but these periods can be extended. It has been, in recent years, the largest government-financed program.

- *The Military Assistance Program (MAP)*. The MAP program is more than thirty years old and authorizes the transfer of defense articles to other governments on a grant basis. Although once the dominant security assistance program (reaching its peak in the early 1950s), it had been nearly phased out by 1980.
- *The International Military Education and Training Program (IMET)*. This is a grant program which enables the U.S. to provide training and education support to foreign military personnel. It is the smallest of the security assistance programs but is generally regarded as the most cost-effective. Before fiscal year (FY) 1976, such training was included in the MAP program. In the early '80s, more than seventy countries were receiving funds for training.
- *Economic Support Funds (ESF)*. Generally considered part of security assistance (though not military assistance), ESF provides both grants and loans to countries where the United States has a special security interest. These funds are often used to help balance-of-payments accounts or to ease chronic capital shortfalls. They may not be used to buy defense articles or services. In recent years, it has been the second largest government-funded program after the FMSCR program.

Several other programs fall under the rubric of security assistance. These include funds for multilateral *Peacekeeping Operations* (PKO), *Commercial Sales*, through export licenses, by private firms to foreign governments, and, from an historical standpoint, the so-called *Military Assistance Service Funded* account (MASF), which provided sizable grant military assistance to five Asian countries allied with the United States in the Vietnam War. Unlike the other programs described above, the MASF program was funded directly out of the military service budgets of the Department of Defense. Each of the programs listed, except FMS cash sales and commercial licenses, are, or have been, U.S.-government financed.

PURPOSES OF SECURITY ASSISTANCE

The purposes of security assistance are multifaceted—they are subject to periodic shifts and are intended to further both the foreign and domestic goals of the United States.

External Goals

Through the medium of the programs sketched above, security assistance is designed to assist other countries defend against threats to their national security and to improve the defense posture of the United States. It is commonly argued that security assistance, prudently planned and executed, will help accomplish the following foreign and defense policy goals:

- enhance the capability of U.S. forces to act in foreign conflicts.
- improve the defense and deterrent capabilities of friendly and allied states.
- promote the implementation of various U.S. regional strategies through the use of foreign military facilities, the use of facilities *en route* to conflicts, the right to overflight privileges, and to U.S. bases abroad.
- complement U.S. military capabilities through common weaponry, shared doctrine and training with other armed forces.
- establish U.S. influence in other countries and minimize the influence of the Soviet Union or its surrogates.
- help improve access to critical raw materials.

Each of these objectives has been important historically and when successfully implemented, has helped improve the geopolitical posture of the United States. Having strong friends and allies relieves the burden on the United States to provide ready deterrence and reduces the likelihood that U.S. armed force will be called upon to intercede on the behalf of its allies. Moreover, security assistance complements the U.S. defense effort overseas by enabling the United States to project power to distant areas by means of reliable bases, access to air and port facilities, and transit rights in troubled areas as well as en route. The medium of security assistance has been a key vehicle for obtaining these assets and has been the *quid* which most foreign governments expect in exchange for these benefits.

Security assistance has also been a valuable instrument for promoting the commonality between U.S. and allied and friendly forces. Greater commonality in weapon systems, communications equipment, military doctrine, and overall force structure would mean a more effective joint operation of U.S. and foreign forces. Such a commonality has been a constant aim of U.S. sales policy to NATO allies and NATO sales policy to the U.S. Similar, though less ambitious, goals have also been advanced in support of military transfers to non-NATO countries as well. By far, the overriding goal of foreign military assistance has been to contain, preempt, or lessen Soviet or Soviet-allied influence in other countries. From an historical standpoint, this has been the sine qua non of security assistance.

Domestic Goals

In addition to promoting foreign policy and defense goals, security assistance has been justified by the contribution it makes to the domestic economy and the defense industrial base. A viable export program, for example, may help:

- reduce the unit cost of U.S. military equipment for both foreign governments and U.S. armed services.[2]

• generate foreign exchange earnings and improve the U.S. balance of payments account.[3]
• reduce unemployment in critical labor sectors of the U.S. economy.[4]
• improve the defense industrial mobilization base.

There are, of course, countervailing views that arms production—whether for foreign sales or for U.S. inventories—is a misdirection of human and financial resources that is ultimately injurious to the U.S. economy and to U.S. interests (see Center for Defense Information, 1982). Such arguments may have some merit but, given the small size of the security assistance program, are more appropriately applied to defense spending in general.[5] Moreover, security assistance generates revenue through foreign cash sales and FMSCR receipts; the Congress has even set legal guidelines requiring full recovery of the costs of managing all FMS sales. Despite some comparatively small economic budgetary impact and some governmental outlays required, the adverse economic impact of the program is not very substantial.

HISTORICAL TRENDS

There are several discernible trends in the evolution of U.S. security assistance. These trends provide clues to the relative priority the United States has given to different regions of the world and to the kinds of commitments it has been willing to make to back up its concerns. This section focuses on three major trends which highlight past patterns of security assistance, provide valuable contextual information about the current program, and indicate possible future directions in U.S. security assistance. The three themes are: (1) the ebb and flow of different types of military assistance over time; (2) geographic shifts in the distributions of security assistance through time; and (3) significant policy changes in the way security assistance is managed.

Types of Security Assistance

As noted above, security assistance, until the mid-'60s, was dominated by the grant Military Assistance Program (MAP). The MAP program was designed to assist in the rearmament of Western Europe and NATO allies at a time when their economies and military capabilities were insufficient for meeting the perceived threat from the Soviet Union. The grant assistance provided under MAP consisted largely of older surplus war materiel drawn from U.S. service stocks being replaced by new advanced systems coming on line at the time. By the early '60s, however, most European nations had achieved sustained economic growth and acquired the economic and technological skills needed to develop their indigenous arms industries at capacities adequate to meet many of their needs. Moreover, surplus U.S. stocks had begun to lessen and European countries, by the '60s, were no longer content with dated technology and obsolete military hardware. At about the same time, pressure was growing in the United States to transform the grant

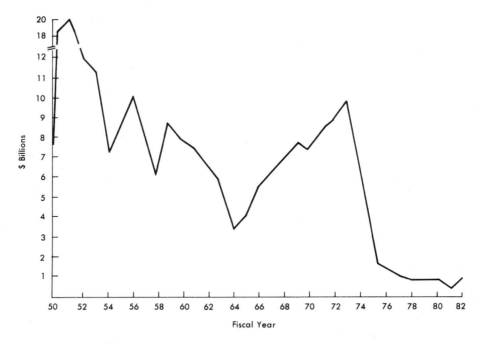

FIGURE 1 Grant Program (Constant FY 82 $: Billions)

military program to a more cost-effective system that would impose less drain on government outlays.

When measured in *constant* FY 1982 terms, the total grant element of U.S. security assistance actually peaked in the early '50s at more than $20 billion ($4.46 billion in current dollars). In FY 1981, total grants dropped below $1 billion or less than one-twentieth the FY 1952 level (in constant terms).[6] Through successive legislation, Congress mandated the winding down of the grant MAP program and pared down requests for increased grant assistance. The grant military training program (IMET), the forgiven or nonrepayable portion of the Foreign Military Sales credit program (FMSCR)[7] and the remnants of the MAP program are now the major elements of the once-dominant grant assistance. Figure 1 shows the steady erosion of the combined grant programs from FY 1950 to FY 1982. With the exception of the MASF-related upward spurt during the Vietnam period (FY 1966–1975), grant security assistance has experienced a continuous decline.

In FY 1955, the United States initiated the FMS credit, or guaranteed loan (FMSCR), program by which U.S. credits were made available to foreign governments for purchase of U.S. military articles, training, and services. The FMS credit program grew steadily through the '60s and began to accelerate in the '70s as the geographic focus of aid shifted from Europe to

TABLE 1
MILITARY ASSISTANCE: AGREEMENTS[1] AND GRANTS[2] ($ BILLIONS)

	FMS Agreements			MAP & MASF		
	1950–1970	1970–1980	1950–1980	1950–1970	1970–1980	1950–1980
East Asia Pacific	$1.44 (12.4%)	$10.24 (87.6%)	$11.68	$15.87 (55.2%)	$12.90 (44.8%)	$28.77
Near East South Asia	2.70 (3.1)	63.00 (95.9)	65.70	1.71 (78.8)	0.46 (21.2)	2.17
Europe/NATO	8.14 (17.3)	21.63 (72.7)	29.77	18.03 (96.2)	0.72 (3.8)	18.75
Africa	0.01 (1.4)	0.68 (98.6)	0.69	0.17 (81.8)	0.04 (18.2)	0.22
American Republics	0.41 (19.7)	0.97 (70.3)	1.38	0.63 (94)	0.04 (6.0)	0.67
International Organizations	0.24 (18.2)	1.08 (81.8)	1.32	1.60 (100)	0.0 (0.0)	1.60
General Costs	—	—	—	1.44 (79.1)	0.38 (20.9)	1.82
Totals:	$12.94 (11.7)	$97.60 (88.3)	$110.54	$39.45 (73.1)	$14.54 (26.9)	$54.00

[1] Agreements includes cash and credit sales.
[2] Grants include both the Military Assistance Program and the Military Assistance Service Funded Accounts but excludes training and forgiven credits.

Southeast Asia and then to the Middle East/Persian Gulf areas. At the same time, cash sales—both FMS and commercial—were rising to meet growing foreign demand made possible, in part, by the proliferation in the number of states, the sudden affluence of certain militarily weak countries, the mounting security requirements of many post-colonial regimes, and especially the chronic turmoil in the Middle East. The credit program did not surpass the combined grant element until FY 1974, but it has been the largest government-financed security assistance program since then. It was the simultaneous decline of the MAP program, the steady increase in the volume of international arms transfers, the transition from dated military technology to more sophisticated equipment transfers, and the shift in transfers from the industrialized world to the Third World that marked a new phase for U.S. security assistance and stimulated heightened concern among an attentive public in and out of the U.S. government.

The data in Table I show an unmistakable shift to foreign military sales agreements (cash and credit) from grant assistance (MAP and MASF) over the past three decades. The data are partitioned into dollar values for the 1950–1970 period, the past ten years, and the entire thirty year period. The bottom line tells the story. For the full thirty years, the United States signed

FMS agreements with foreign governments worth more than $110 billion and extended grant military assistance equalling $54 billion for a combined assistance of about $164 billion. (There has been an additional $10 billion in commercial exports; during the same period, FMS financing totalled almost $22 billion.) Most of this amount—roughly two-thirds—was consummated through FMS agreements and almost all of the contracts (about 88 percent) were signed during the '70s. Less than thirty percent of all grant assistance was extended in the '70s but nearly three-quarters of all military assistance was provided through grant aid in the 1950–1970 period.

Thus, the United States shifted the emphasis of military assistance to direct cash sales and credit loans during the very period when the international economy experienced stresses and strains growing out of escalating oil and food prices, low productivity, international economic stagflation, and mounting security problems. This may have been a rational adaptation to adverse economic realities by the United States, but it has imposed hardships on foreign customers. Because of this shift, the bulk of U.S. military aid agreements have been signed with a small number of capital surplus countries in the Middle East and selected industrialized countries in Western Europe and the Far East.

Geographic Trends

The original objective of U.S. military training in the immediate postwar period was to provide assistance to Western European and NATO countries to resist perceived Soviet aggression. The aid was aimed at rebuilding the defense capabilities of European armed forces at a time when both economic recovery and military rearmament were deemed impossible without U.S. assistance. Until as late as 1965, more than half of all U.S. military assistance went to NATO countries in Western Europe. It is not difficult to conclude that this program was enormously successful. Military aid to Europe—largely in the form of grant military assistance from 1950 through 1965 and cash sales after 1965—has helped keep Europe free of war for the longest period yet in the twentieth century. For most of the period, security assistance and arms sales served what one writer has termed the "mortar of the NATO alliance" (Lewis, 1980: 189).

Most of the weapons transferred to Europe by the United States consisted of surplus equipment dating from World War II, equipment the United States was replacing with more sophisticated weapon systems. Thus, military assistance served two related purposes: to deter Soviet aggression in Europe and to facilitate the modernization of U.S. forces by providing a plausible rationale for replacing obsolescent weapons in U.S. service inventories.

During the '50s, the United States also provided military assistance to South Korea, a policy decision which, in effect, broadened the geographic scope of containment and increased the military proportion of all foreign aid. One feature of these early years was the concentration of military aid in forward-based countries, that is, in countries located on the periphery of the Soviet Union—or China. In the case of European nations, U.S. assistance was required for a relatively short time—a decade or so for the more advanced countries—to help revitalize their national defense industries and to bridge the transition from grant-based assistance to mostly cash and/or credit sales. This pattern has been less true for most recipients in the Third World; for most, but not all countries (for example, Taiwan), there is no likely end to U.S. military assistance.

By the mid-'60s, the geographic focus of U.S. military assistance shifted dramatically to Southeast Asia, where the United States became embroiled in a protracted war supplying both U.S. forces and the armed forces of five allied Asian nations. This period heralded an important change in the rationale for military aid: away from countries on the periphery of the Soviet Union and so-called forward-based countries to disparate areas of the Third World. The nomenclature *security assistance* also changed: the parlance was expanded beyond aid to "allies" to include aid for "friends and allies." It also was expanded to include assistance for dealing with regional balances, internal instability, and counterinsurgency.

Virtually all the military assistance provided to South Vietnam, Korea, Cambodia, Laos, and the Philippines during the period 1966–1975 was grant assistance, and these funds came from the Defense Department's MASF account. Because of the infusion of grant assistance to East Asian countries, this region has been the principal recipient of grant assistance between 1950 and 1980.

During the '60s and the '70s, the major historic European colonial powers—all allies of the United States—continued their disengagement from the Middle East, the Persian Gulf, and Sub-Saharan Africa. The French withdrawal from Indochina in 1954, the British decision to terminate its military presence "east of Suez," the Belgian pullout from Central Africa in the early '60s, and the Portuguese retreat from Southern Africa in the mid-'70s all nurtured fears in the United States that the resulting power vacuums would be ripe for Soviet exploitation. Security assistance provided one of the most visible available means of responding (short of sending troops) to signal U.S. resolve to limit Soviet or Soviet-sponsored opportunities for seeking gains at Western expense.

Following the British withdrawal from the Persian Gulf region in 1971, U.S. assistance to key states in the Gulf area, particularly Iran and Saudi Arabia, grew sharply. The Arab-Israeli war in 1967, the so-called war of attrition which followed, and the Yom Kippur War in 1973 radically transformed the geographic focus of U.S. military assistance. The large credit transfers to Israel— and later to Egypt—and the high volume sales to Saudi Arabia and Iran, plus new programs with other states in the region, including Oman and Pakistan, swelled the arms flow to this part of the world. Geographically, this region now dominates the entire program. The pie charts in Figure 2 vividly show that the four programs have been skewed heavily toward the Middle

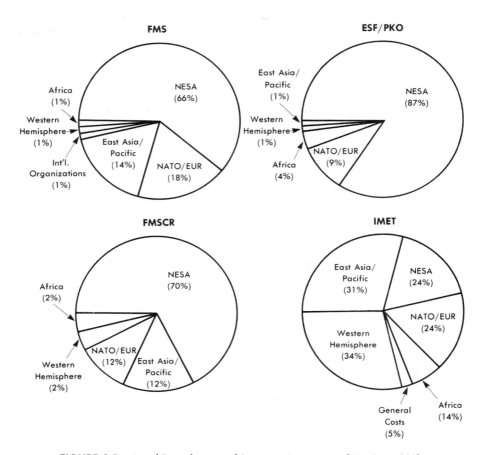

FIGURE 2 Regional Distribution of Security Assistance (FY 1976-1980)

East (designated as NESA on the charts); not shown is the fact that government-financed programs have been heavily dominated by assistance to Israel in this time period.

In all but the grant military training program (IMET), the Middle East received the overwhelming proportion of U.S. assistance funds—as much as 70 percent in FMS credits and nearly 90 percent of the Economic Support Funds in the five-year period shown.[8]

In the past decade, the government-financed portion of security assistance has been programed almost exclusively for developing countries. Apart from cash transactions, only Greece, Turkey, and Spain (and later, Portugal) in Europe received FMS credits. In the Far East, Korea and Taiwan have been major recipients of military aid since 1950 (excluding MASF countries), but the region received only a small fraction of the total assistance in recent years—although major cash sales go to industrialized countries in the region. The United States has never provided large quantities of military aid to Latin America or Sub-Saharan Africa, a pattern likely to change somewhat in the '80s. As a result, European suppliers and the Soviet Union have stepped in as the major providers of military equipment to these two regions.

During the '70s the U.S. security assistance program revolved around the nucleus of the Israeli program. In the '70s alone, the value of Israeli FMS credits in any single year exceeded the combined value of credits provided to all countries in Africa and Latin America for those same years. In FY 1974 and in each year from FY 1976 through FY 1980, Israeli credits surpassed the total credits programed for all Latin America during the entire thirty-year period; the same comparison is even more disproportionate for Africa. One should not necessarily conclude from these figures that the high levels of assistance provided Israel have deprived other recipients of U.S. aid. Given the general inclination of the U.S. Congress to cut military assistance while at the same time increasing aid to Israel, it is fair to state that the existence of the Israeli program in the '70s made funding possible for other countries including, to some degree, Arab nations.[9] In order to gain the passage of Israeli aid, supporters in both chambers have been compelled to vote for assistance to other countries to get a final bill.

Policy Changes

Security assistance is governed by two basic legislative statutes—the Foreign Assistance Act (FAA) of 1961 and the Arms Export Control Act (AECA) of 1976. In addition, Congress passes annual authorization and appropriation measures which, in effect, amend the existing laws and set funding ceilings for all government-financed programs during the fiscal year. If Congress desires, it may modify the existing law by mandating new reporting requirements, placing restrictions on aid to specified countries, and establish additional oversight controls or any other legal controls.

Over the years, various administrations have responded to international events, to public pressures, or to strongly held beliefs about the utility of arms exports by defining the standards under which such transactions are to take place. The chronology of these policy changes has been identified with the presidents who have announced them. The Truman Doctrine is associated with postwar aid programs to Greece and Turkey, the Eisenhower Doctrine with authority to rush assistance to Middle East countries threatened by communist aggression, and the Nixon Doctrine with the principle that the United States would provide arms and the military wherewithal (but *not* the armed forces) to help other countries meet legitimate national security threats.

During the Nixon and Ford administrations, there was no arms sales policy as such, and critics, including members of Congress, sought to limit the freewheeling way in which U.S. weapons were being provided to foreign governments. In 1975, Congress adopted the Nelson Amendment, which required that Congress approve any proposed sale of $25 million or more. This veto power was retained in the all-important International Security Assistance and Arms Export Control Act of 1976 (AECA). The act also extended the time for consideration of proposed sales (to 30 days), imposed controls on commercial sales of $25 million or more to non-NATO countries, restricted the arms-sales activities that could be performed by U.S. military advisory groups overseas, and elevated human rights as a criterion for judging a country's eligibility for security assistance.

The most important attempts to revamp the U.S. procedures and substance of security assistance and arms transfers to other countries in recent years have been the arms-transfer policies of the Carter and Reagan administrations. Both the Carter and the Reagan policies sought to capture the prevailing national mood at the time they were announced.

In May 1977, the Carter administration announced Presidential Directive 13, which most analysts now describe as a bold attempt to manage and restrain the international flow of arms. PD-13 actually grew out of strong national sentiment about the painful experience in Vietnam and out of persistent Congressional efforts to impose greater control over the export of arms. It must be remembered that successive Congresses during the Nixon and Ford administrations had legislated or voiced many of the very same restraint provisions embodied in PD-13.

PD-13 expressed the basic assumption that arms transfers to other governments created more potential dangers than any benefits to U.S. interests and should, therefore, be approved only under "exceptional" circumstances. This premise ran against the grain of the belief that arms aid was an essential tool of foreign policy; instead, it stated that the approval of arms requests would be viewed as an exception and not a rule of U.S. foreign policy. The policy set down the goal of transferring fewer weapons and established a number of controls on what to sell, to whom, and for what purpose. It also sought to enlist other supplier nations to restrain their military exports. The major controls in the Carter policy included the following:

- the United States would not be the first supplier to introduce advanced weapons into a region.
- there would be no commitment by the United States to sell advanced weapon systems until they were operationally deployed by U.S. forces.
- the United States would not approve the production of a unique or modified weapons system solely for export.
- coproduction arrangements with other nations would be prohibited.
- U.S. diplomatic and military personnel abroad would not promote arms sales.

PD-13 also set an annual goal of reducing the dollar value of arms sales and reiterated existing provisions of the law which gave prominence to the human-rights practices of foreign governments.

PD-13 also contained a presidential waiver which authorized the president to make exceptions to any of the restraint provisions. In sum, PD-13 was the most restrictive policy on arms transfers the United States had adopted, but because of the presidential waiver authority, it became, in practice, an extremely flexible document. The Carter policy of restraint on arms sales soon yielded to policy exceptions (especially on coproduction), mounting international tensions after the Soviet invasion of Afghanistan, and growing instability in the Persian Gulf region. Sales levels actually grew during the Carter presidency and, by 1979, the administration all but admitted that the annual dollar ceiling was no longer operative. The coup d' grace came when it was learned that Soviet military exports to the Third World in 1980 had surpassed those of the United States. Moreover, the initiative on multilateral arms restraint sputtered to a halt over conflicting views within the U.S. government, sensitivities to U.S. interests in the Middle East and the Far East, rising exports from European suppliers, and deteriorating relations with the Soviet Union in general (Blechman et al., 1982). By the time President Carter left office, his arms transfer policy had attracted at least as much criticism as it had received praise when first announced in 1977.[10]

Approximately six months after taking office, the Reagan administration unveiled its arms transfer policy, which attempted to maximize U.S. decision flexibility and was based on the unambiguous premise that arms transfers are an essential instrument of U.S. foreign policy. The Reagan policy distanced itself from PD-13, set no annual ceiling, softened (but did not eliminate) the human rights criterion, and treated arms sales as a morally neutral factor in the conduct of foreign policy. It also sought to replace universal criteria—for example, human rights—with more specific criteria that were related to the countries or regions under consideration. Thus any foreign request for arms were to be considered on a case-by-case basis. The policy stated that the United States retained a serious interest in restraining arms transfers but only after the cooperation of other major suppliers was assured. The key factors to be used in making decisions on foreign requests for U.S. arms would include the following:

- the military threat which the requesting nation faced.
- the priorities of U.S. armed services.
- the ability of requesting nations to absorb defense materiel without overburdening their military support system or their financial resources.
- the need to safeguard advanced, sensitive U.S. technologies.
- the impact of the arms transfer on the maintenance of regional stability.

The Reagan policy does not set forth any guidelines on coproduction but it does permit U.S. overseas personnel to assist defense industry representatives in conducting business with foreign governments, though they still may not promote U.S. arms sales. In sum, the Reagan policy, thus far, has been a more activist (that is, less passive) approach to the transfer of international arms. It elevates above all other considerations the perceived contribution which any sale makes to the national security interests of the United States.

FUTURE TRENDS

Many analysts have asserted that the Reagan arms transfer policy and the increase in security assistance funding evidenced in the FY 1981 and FY 1982 security assistance programs herald a surge in the value and volume of U.S. military assistance. Some preliminary indications in early 1982 point to total U.S. foreign military sales in the range of between $25 billion and $30 billion—a sum which would be the highest single year total ever (Pierre, 1981/82; Center for Defense Information, 1982). Forecasting the level of arms sales, however, is not a precise science and is subject to so many variables as to render most projections an approximation at best.[11]

U.S. arms sales in the future—FY 1983 through FY 1986—are projected at about $15 billion per annum. Based on burgeoning foreign demand for U.S. military assistance and the increased support by the Reagan administration for defense and defense-related spending, it would seem that the value of sales and the volume of transfers would accelerate rapidly.

There are, however, several factors which will likely dampen future U.S. sales. The proliferation in the number of supplier nations competing for the same market will, on occasion, squeeze out U.S. sales through the offer of better terms, faster deliveries, and viable alternatives. In addition, numerous countries have started their own indigenous arms industry which will enable them to reduce imports from abroad. A second key factor holding down future arms transfers will be the effects a weakened international economy will have on interest rates, slower economic growth, and rapidly rising international debt service ratios for many—but not all—governments. Many foreign regimes will respond with cautious procurement and think carefully about utilizing their scarce national resources for the latest state-of-the-art military systems (for example, modern fighter aircraft or battle tanks); instead, they may opt to spend their resources on operation and maintenance needs in order to stretch out the life-cycles of existing equipment already in their inventories.

Still another factor inhibiting sharp increases in future arms sales could be the high cost of U.S. military equipment and technology as well as the increasingly stiff repayment terms the United States requires for most recipients of FMS credits. Even if the dollar levels climb over the next several years, the high unit costs for modern technology and the high interest rates charged by the United States may hold down the numbers of items that will actually be sold. The amount and type of equipment and not its dollar value provide a more useful index of the actual military capabilities a country achieves. Additionally, foreign governments may press hard in the future for the participation of industry in arms production—for instance in codevelopment, coassembly, or licensed production—as a means to offset the cost of major purchases. If successful, such arrangements might drive up sales in the short run but down in the long term.

Finally, Congress may act to limit future increases in government-financed security assistance programs. If this happens, most Third World countries receiving U.S. assistance funds will find it difficult to procure major military equipment from the United States. They would be compelled to use their own resources for cash purchases, seek better terms from alternative suppliers, or even forego improvements in their force structures.

Paradoxically, the unfavorable international economic climate coupled with the high price of U.S. military technology and the stiff repayment terms of U.S. military loans may operate as a kind of arms control mechanism to slow down—but not reverse—the historic pattern of upward growth in arms exports.

CONCLUSION

There have been several major intersecting themes in postwar U.S. security assistance. Always a visible program with high stakes and significant dollar outlays, security assistance has continuously evoked criticism and praise among different segments of the U.S. population. Despite variations in approach, successive administrations from the early '50s to the present have employed security assistance as a vehicle for enhancing U.S. influence abroad and for complementing the overseas defense mission. The alleged domestic benefits of the program, such as lower unemployment and increased foreign exchange earnings, have been secondary because the United States—unlike most other major and minor supplier nations—has not had to rely upon foreign military exports to sustain a viable arms industry.

From its inception, the security assistance program was predicated on global security interests of the United States in a profoundly altered international environment after 1945. The United States had neither the political will nor the economic resources to police the entire international system but had to rely upon the self-survival instincts of allied and friendly governments to cooperate in developing a system of collective security through the bilateral transfer of military aid. The program demonstrates examples of unqualified success (Western Europe), qualified success (Israel), unqualified setback (Iran), and qualified failure (Peru); on balance, however, security assistance has been a positive investment for the United States. Whether the United States could have achieved the same benefits through other means will never be known, but one thing is clear: partisans on all sides of the debate will continue to infuse it with controversy for the indefinite future.

NOTES
1. In the case of one government-funded program, Economic Support Funds (ESF), the line between security and economic assistance is even more blurred. Economic Support Funds are provided to those countries in which the United

States has a particular security or political interest even though these funds cannot be used to purchase military equipment, training, or services. The ESF program is considered part of security assistance but *not* part of military assistance.

2. A Congressional Budget Office study, for example, found that an $8.2 billion sales program generates about $560 million in cost savings annually. The major portion of these savings are recoupments of research and development costs (R&D) from foreign purchases. The savings are primarily from high technology systems such as fighter aircraft and missiles (Congressional Budget Office, 1976b).

3. Another Congressional Budget Office study has equated $8.2 billion in foreign military sales to about $7.5 billion in export earnings based on the FY 1976 pattern of FMS new orders (Congressional Budget Office, 1976a).

4. Still another Congressional Budget Office study concluded that about 350,000 jobs in the U.S. are dependent on an $8.2 billion FMS program assuming a program mix of weapons, services and construction comparable to that of FY 1976 (Congressional Budget Office, 1976c).

5. The size of the security assistance program is such that in the '80s the ratio of security assistance to defense spending was less than two percent and the burden on the U.S. taxpayer to support the program was less than $15 per capita. Moreover, the largest single program—FMSCR—is "off-budget" and as such has no direct budgetary impact. As in the past, the budgetary impact remains small.

6. Total U.S. grant value at any one time may include the summed value of the MAP, the MASF, and the IMET programs as well as forgiven FMS credits and MAP excess articles.

7. Forgiven FMS credits in the past decade have almost exclusively been earmarked for the state of Israel. Normally at one-half billion dollars per year, these credits are nonrepayable, similar to grant aid and provided to Israel to meet its huge defense needs without causing a buildup of large foreign debt obligations. An additional reason has been to enable Israel to reach the level of security necessary to pursue the peace process with Egypt. Recently, forgiven credits have been provided to Egypt for similar reasons.

8. The term Middle East region as used here includes North Africa (Morocco and Tunisia), the traditional Middle East running from Egypt through the Levant to the Persian Gulf, and South Asia.

9. One study pointed to an interesting phenomenon in Congressional behavior toward security assistance for the period 1969–1976. The House consistently reduced the administration's requests but at the same time voted to increase the Israeli program. Indeed, success for the entire security assistance program has very much depended upon the willingness of Congress to fund the Israeli program: without aid to Israel, it is possible that many other country programs would not be funded. (See Feuerwerger, 1979.)

10. There has been considerable criticism and scepticism about the sincerity and practicality of the Carter policy. Among the more prominent expressions of insincerity are the following: (1) the policy exempted from annual ceiling totals commercial sales, sales to NATO allies, to ANZUS, and to Japan, and military construction under FMS; (2) presidential exceptions to the policy were frequent; (3) the production of an intermediate fighter aircraft (FX) solely for

export was authorized; and (4) the sales totals rose over the years.
11. The Defense Security Assistance Agency (DSAA) projected sales for FY 1982 to be about $25 billion but, by mid fiscal year, anticipated that total sales would be less than this figure.

REFERENCES

Blechman, Barry M., Janne E. Nolan, and Alan Platt. (1982) "Pushing Arms." *Foreign Affairs* (Spring): 138–154.

Center for Defense Information. (1982) *U.S. Weapons Exports Headed for Record Level.* Vol. XI: 3. Washington, D.C.

Committee on Foreign Affairs, U.S. House of Representatives. (1981) *U.S. Security Assistance and Arms Transfer Policies for the 1980's.* (March) Washington, D.C.: U.S. Government Printing Office.

Congressional Budget Office, U.S. Congress. (1976a) *Budgetary Cost Savings to the Department of Defense Resulting from Foreign Military Sales.* Staff Working Paper (May) Washington, D.C.: U.S. Government Printing Office.

———. (1976b) *Foreign Military Sales and U.S. Weapons Cost.* Staff Working Paper (May) Washington, D.C.: U.S. Government Printing Office.

———. (1976c) *The Effect of Foreign Military Sales on the U.S. Economy.* Staff Working Paper (July) Washington, D.C.: U.S. Government Printing Office.

Department of Defense, Defense Security Assistance Agency. (1980) *Foreign Military Sales and Military Assistance Facts.* Washington, D.C.

Farley, Philip J., Stephen S. Kaplan, and William H. Lewis. (1978) *Arms Across the Sea.* Washington, D.C.: The Brookings Institution.

Feuerwerger, Marvin C. (1979) *Congress and Israel: Foreign Aid Decision Making in the House of Representatives 1969–1976.* Westport, Conn.: Greenwood Press.

Gibert, Stephen. (1981) "Arsenal Diplomacy: Problems and Prospects," *International Security Review* 5, 3: 375–406.

Lewis, William H. (1980) "Political Influence: The Diminished Capacity," pp. 184–199 in Stephanie G. Neumann and Robert E. Harkavy (eds.) *Arms Transfers in the Modern World.* New York: Praeger.

Neumann, Stephanie G. and Robert E. Harkavy (eds.) (1980) *Arms Transfers in the Modern World.* New York: Praeger.

Pierre, Andrew. (1981/82) "Arms Sales: The New Diplomacy." *Foreign Affairs* 60:2: 266–286.

Semmel, Andrew K. (1982) "Security Assistance: U.S. and Soviet Patterns," pp. 267–290 in Charles W. Kegley and Pat J. McGowan (eds.) *Foreign Policy: USA/ USSR.* Beverly Hills, California: Sage Publishing Company.

U.S. Arms Control and Disarmament Agency. (1981) *World Military Expenditures and Arms Transfers 1970–1979.* Washington, D.C.: U.S. Government Printing Office.

Part Two
EXTERNAL SOURCES OF AMERICAN FOREIGN POLICY

The essays in Part I discussed aspects of the persistent elements of postwar American foreign policy captured in the themes of globalism, anticommunism, containment, military might, and interventionist means. Parts II through VI will turn to the forces underlying these persistent elements. Each part will introduce the variables that fall within the corresponding source category. We begin with the most comprehensive category, the one that subsumes the attributes that collectively define the nature of America's external environment.

EXTERNAL SOURCES OF AMERICAN FOREIGN POLICY

The external category refers to the condition of the global environment beyond the borders of the United States. It includes all variables related to the kind of international system in which the United States lives and to which it reacts. James N. Rosenau, who first proposed the pre-theoretical framework that is the organizational basis of this book, defines the external category as including the "aspects of a society's external environment or any actions occurring abroad that condition or otherwise influence the choices made by its officials.[1] He notes that "geographical 'realities' and ideological challenges from potential aggressors" are obvious examples of external variables which can shape the decisions of foreign policy officials. Another way of defining this category is to say that external variables refer broadly to the impact of the state of the world on the United States.[2] Thus the external source category draws attention to the kinds of behavior others direct toward the United States and to all developments abroad generally and explores how these influence the response of the United States. It also draws attention to the attributes of other societies, focusing on how the *kinds* of nations with which the United States deals shape U.S. foreign policy and behavior.

Because the external source category consists of so many variables (entailing *all* the characteristics common to the global arena), the questions derived from it are innumerable. How many sovereign nations are there in the international system? What types of governments do they have? Are these governments friendly toward the United States or hostile? How many formal alliances and other military coalitions exist in the system? Do they have sufficient military might and internal cohesion to deter attack from outsiders? Are existing international organizations able effectively to shape the behavior of nation-states or only mirror it? Does the international legal system effectively prohibit certain kinds of behavior while encouraging other kinds?

The answers to these questions and many others are assumed to influence significantly the kind of behavior the United States (or for that matter any nation) is likely to pursue. Thus the external environment is seen as one potentially powerful source of American foreign policy, and changes in the international environment may be hypothesized to stimulate changes in the nation's external conduct. At the same time, changes in American behavior may affect the external environment.

The analytic tradition that emphasizes a causal relationship between the international system and American foreign policy enjoys a wide following. "Political realists," in particular, argue that the nature of the international system, more than anything else, influences how its nation-members act. Beginning with a conception of human nature as inherently evil, political realists believe that international politics is nothing more than a Hobbsian struggle for power and influence. Accordingly, conceptions of "power" and "national interest" become focal points of concern, with realists arguing that nations ought to pursue these rather than abstract moral or legal principles. Hans J. Morgenthau's "Defining the National Interest—Again: Old Superstitions, New Realities," included in the preceding section of this book, illustrates this genre of thinking. Because all states are assumed to be motivated by the same drives, the principal way to understand international politics and foreign policy, according to this perspective, is to follow the interactions of states in the international arena—in other words, to focus on the external source category.

Political realism as a school of thought is not without its critics, as we will see in the essays that follow. However, the argument that the external environment is a principal cause of a nation's external behavior is a powerful one. Indeed, the anticommunist and containment themes discussed in Part I suggest that the United States has become so obsessed with one aspect of the external environment—namely, the capabilities, intentions, and behaviors of communism in general and the Soviet Union in particular—that to a substantial extent American foreign policy has become Soviet-centric.

There are examples to support the related proposition that changes in the external environment cause changes in American foreign policy. For instance, could the Reagan administration's enthusiasm for massive increases in military spending in a period of chronic domestic economic difficulties have received the support it did in the absence of substantial Soviet defense expenditures? Similarly, would American policy toward the Middle East and the continuing Arab-Israeli conflict have become more "balanced" in the absence of the oil embargo and subsequent oil price hikes initiated by the Middle Eastern oil exporting nations in 1973? Or could the Sino-American rapprochement of the 1970s have unfolded as it did without the continuing deterioration of relations between Moscow and Peking? Clearly, in these and many other examples, American foreign policy has responded to the behavior of other states, and developments abroad have precipitated changes in it.

As important as the external environment is, it would be wrong to think that it alone dictates foreign policy. External variables help define the limits of the possible; they preclude certain options and reduce the utility of others. In this way the international system imposes restrictions on American decision makers and limits their freedom to take policy initiatives. In other words, it promotes policy continuity by narrowing the range of workable choice. But the external environment can also operate as a stimulus to change by presenting the nation with opportunities—opportunities that are subject, of course, to the perception of decision makers—for the realization of foreign policy objectives. Note, however, that how (or even whether) an opportunity is perceived is as important as the actual events that precede the action finally taken. As one analyst put it,

> factors external to the actor can become determinants only as they affect the mind, the heart, and the will of the decision-makers. A human decision to act in a specific way . . . necessarily represents the last link in the chain of antecedents of any act of policy. A geographical set of conditions, for instance, can affect the behavior of a nation only as specific persons perceive and interpret these conditions.[3]

Hence, we can think of the external environment as a number of variables that define what is both possible and probable and that at any time may create opportunities for achieving foreign policy goals, or, alternatively, for accommodating new realities. Yet care must be exercised lest we assume that such opportunities will necessarily be seized or that such accommodations will automatically occur.

PERSPECTIVES ON EXTERNAL SOURCES OF AMERICAN FOREIGN POLICY: AN OVERVIEW

The concept of *bipolarity* describes a configuration of world power that effectively concentrates power and influence in the hands of two states which make up the "poles" in the system. It refers to the distribution of power between the United States and the Soviet Union between the late 1940s and the early 1960s, as well as the consequent clustering of many other nations into alliance systems managed and directed by the superpowers.

The bipolar distribution of power contributed to the periodic crises associated with Soviet-American behavior during the Cold War. With the nations of the international system grouped into two blocs—symbolized by the North Atlantic Treaty Organization (NATO), led by the United States, and the Warsaw Pact, led by the Soviet Union—the bipolar configuration bred insecurity among all.[4] The balance was constantly at stake. What one side gained was viewed as a loss by the other (what is known in the mathematical theory of games as a zero-sum outcome). Utmost importance was therefore attached by each side to recruiting new friends and allies, and fear that an old ally might desert the fold was ever present. Little room was left for compromise in the bipolar world. Every maneuver was seen as a new initiative toward world conquest; hence every perceived act of hostility was to be met with retaliation. Endemic to the struggle was the belief that conciliation was impossible, that the most that could be hoped for was a momentary pause in overt hostilities based on a mutual respect for the geopolitical status quo.

Since the 1960s the configuration of world power, and the foreign policy behaviors flowing from it, have defied easy description. *Tripolarity* is appropriate for describing a future in which the United States, the Soviet Union, and China all have extensive nuclear weapons capabilities. Today, however, the concept of *bipolycentrism* is more appropriate. It implies continued military superiority on the part of the United States and the Soviet Union and the continued reliance, at least ultimately, of each superpower's weaker alliance partners on their respective patrons for security. At the same time, the bipolycentric system allows considerable room to maneuver on the part of weaker members; hence the term *polycentrism*, connoting the possibility of many centers of power. While the superpowers remain dominant militarily, alliance members have greater fluidity in their diplomacy than is true in a strictly bipolar system.[5] And new foreign policy roles (other than simply "aligned" or "nonaligned") are created for actors in this less rigid system.

In his essay, "System Structures and American Foreign Policy," Henry A. Kissinger speculates about the causes and especially the consequences for American foreign policy of the shifting distribution of world power which has been occurring in the postwar era. The article was first published in 1968, but it retains extraordinarily contemporary relevance. Moreover, it defines key elements of the world view of one of the most important personalities in contemporary American foreign policy. Much of the logic underlying Kissinger's diplomacy during the Nixon and Ford presidencies is spelled out here. So, too, is his view of American political institutions, and especially his disdain for bureaucracy—a disdain which he maintained while at the same time manipulating bureaucracy for his own objectives.

As both scholar and policy maker, Kissinger embraced the assumptions of political realism which, as noted earlier, define the purpose of foreign policy as protecting the "national interest" in a global system characterized by the struggle for power and influence. The record of postwar American foreign policy supports the view that most American foreign policy makers have accepted these premises. Robert O. Keohane and Joseph S. Nye challenge the assumptions, world view, and policy prescriptions associated with political realism. They do not argue in their article, "Realism and Complex Interdependence," that "power"—especially military might—does not matter. They do argue that it does not matter in all places and times on all issues. Because these provocative ideas challenge others that have long been widely shared and deeply held among both students and practitioners of foreign policy, they have deservedly received wide circulation and commentary.

The challenge to political realism is especially apparent in matters of economic policy. The implied linkage between politics and economics is captured in the term *political economy,* the intellectual forerunner of political science which has gained renewed interest among scholars in recent years. "The International Economy: U.S. Role in a World Market," an analysis written for the U.S. Congress, spells out clearly and concisely the formidable challenge that current economic policy issues pose to the United States and the intimate connections of that challenge to questions traditionally regarded as "political." Implicitly, the analysis questions whether the distinction between "high politics" and "low politics" any longer makes sense. The term "high politics"—encompassed in the concept of political realism—refers to concerns of national security, which traditionally have been the foreign policy focus of postwar American leaders. "Low politics," on the other hand—implicit in the concept of interdependence—are matters of economic policy, which historically have been left to the devices of lower-level bureaucrats. In an interdependent world, however, the distinction drawn in practice as well as theory between high and low politics may be artificial or even dysfunctional. For interdependence implies not only a world sensitive to the United States but also an American economic and political system intertwined with developments abroad over which the United States often has little influence.

United States' interests in the Third World encompass national security as well as economic issues. They involve matters of high politics and low. This is the message of the essay, "The Third World: Exploring U.S. Interests," by John W. Sewell and John A. Mathieson.

Some policy makers and theorists have argued that Third World nations are largely irrelevant to the central concerns of American foreign policy. The technological superiority of the United States assures it the ability to innovate despite its dependence on foreign sources of supply, so this argument runs, while the technological requirements of modern warfare mean that Third World nations can not materially affect the national security of the United States. Sewell and Mathieson challenge both views, the latter on grounds that Third World nations are able to involve the United States and the Soviet Union in their conflicts, the former on grounds that the United States not only imports a great deal from Third World countries but also, *inter alia*, has come to depend heavily on them as markets for its own exports.

NOTES

1. "Pre-theories and Theories of Foreign Policy," in R. Barry Farrell, ed., *Approaches to Comparative and International Politics* (Evanston, Ill.: Northwestern University Press, 1966), p. 43.
2. In practice, most analysts using Rosenau's framework have found it useful to distinguish between "systemic" sources of foreign policy and "external" sources. The former are aggregate or general attributes of the international environment (e.g., the number of alliances or the frequency of war) which all states share. The latter are relationships between particular states (e.g., interactions between the United States and the Soviet Union). Based on this distinction, the elaboration of the external source category in Part II will emphasize primarily external rather than systemic explanations of American foreign policy.
3. Arnold Wolfers, *Discord and Collaboration* (Baltimore: Johns Hopkins University Press, 1962), p. 42.
4. See John Spanier, *Games Nations Play*, 2nd ed. (New York: Praeger, 1975).
5. Ibid., pp. 81–90.

8

SYSTEM STRUCTURES AND AMERICAN FOREIGN POLICY

HENRY A. KISSINGER

The twentieth century has known little repose. Since the turn of the century, international crises have been increasing in both frequency and severity. The contemporary unrest, although less apocalyptic than the two world wars which spawned it, is even more profoundly revolutionary in nature.

The essence of a revolution is that it appears to contemporaries as a series of more or less unrelated upheavals. The temptation is great to treat each issue as an immediate and isolated problem which once surmounted will permit the fundamental stability of the international order to reassert itself. But the crises which form the headlines of the day are symptoms of deep-seated structural problems. The international system which produced stability for a century collapsed under the impact of two world wars. The age of the superpowers, which temporarily replaced it, is nearing its end. The current international environment is in turmoil because its essential elements are all in flux simultaneously. . . .

I. THE STRUCTURAL PROBLEMS

For the first time, foreign policy has become global. In the past, the various continents conducted their foreign policy essentially in isolation. . . . Today, statesmen face the unprecedented problem of formulating policy for well over a hundred countries. Every nation, no matter how insignificant, participates in international affairs. Ideas are transmitted almost instantaneously. What used to be considered domestic events can now have world-wide consequences.

The revolutionary character of our age can be summed up in three general statements: (a) the number of participants in the international order has increased and their nature has altered; (b) their technical ability to affect each other has vastly grown; (c) the scope of their purposes has expanded.

From Henry A. Kissinger, "Central Issues of American Foreign Policy," pp. 51–97 in *American Foreign Policy* (New York: Norton, 1977). Copyright © 1968 by The Brookings Institution.

Whenever the participants in the international system change, a period of profound dislocation is inevitable. They can change because new states enter the political system, or because there is a change in values as to what constitutes legitimate rule, or, finally, because of the reduction in influence of some traditional units. In our period, all of these factors have combined. Since the end of the Second World War, several score of new states have come into being. . . . Our age has yet to find a structure which matches the responsibilities of the new nations to their aspirations.

As the number of participants has increased, technology has multiplied the resources available for the conduct of foreign policy. A scientific revolution has, for all practical purposes, removed technical limits from the exercise of power in foreign policy. It has magnified insecurities because it has made survival seem to depend on the accidents of a technological breakthrough.

This trend has been compounded by the nature of contemporary domestic structures. As long as the states' ability to mobilize resources was limited, the severity of their conflicts had definite bounds. . . . It is an ironic result of the democratization of politics [world-wide] that it has enabled states to marshal ever more resources for their competition.

Ideological conflict compounds these instabilities. In the great periods of cabinet diplomacy, diplomats spoke the same language, not only in the sense that French was the lingua franca, but more importantly because they tended to understand intangibles in the same manner. A similar outlook about aims and methods eases the tasks of diplomacy—it may even be a precondition for it. In the absence of such a consensus, diplomats can still meet, but they lose the ability to persuade. More time is spent on defining contending positions than in resolving them. What seems most reasonable to one side will appear most problematical to the other.

When there is ideological conflict, political loyalties no longer coincide with political boundaries. Conflicts among states merge with divisions within nations; the dividing line between domestic and foreign policy begins to disappear. At least some states feel threatened not only by the foreign policy of other countries but also, and perhaps especially, by domestic transformations. . . .

The tensions produced by ideological conflict are exacerbated by the reduction in influence of the states that were considered great powers before the First World War. The world has become militarily bipolar. Only two powers—the United States and the Union of Soviet Socialist Republics—possess the full panoply of military might. Over the next decade, no other country or group of countries will be capable of challenging their physical preeminence. Indeed, the gap in military strength between the two giant nuclear countries and the rest of the world is likely to increase rather than diminish over that period.

Military bipolarity is a source of rigidity in foreign policy. The guardians of the equilibrium of the nineteenth century were prepared to respond to change with counteradjustment; the policy-makers of the superpowers in the second half of the twentieth century have much less confidence in the ability of the equilibrium to right itself after disturbance. Whatever "balance" there is between the superpowers is regarded as both precarious and inflexible. A bipolar world loses the perspective for nuance; a gain for one side appears as an absolute loss for the other. Every issue seems to involve a question of survival. The smaller countries are torn between a desire for protection and a wish to escape big-power dominance. Each of the super-powers is beset by the desire to maintain its preeminence among its allies, to increase its influence among the uncommitted, and to enhance its security vis-à-vis its opponent. The fact that some of these objectives may well prove incompatible adds to the strain on the international system.

But the age of the superpowers is now drawing to an end. Military bipolarity has not only failed to prevent, it has actually encouraged political multipolarity. Weaker allies have good reason to believe that their defense is in the overwhelming interest of their senior partner. Hence, they see no need to purchase its support by acquiescence in its policies. The new nations feel protected by the rivalry of the superpowers, and their national-ism leads to ever bolder assertions of self-will. Traditional uses of power have become less feasible, and new forms of pressure have emerged as a result of transnational loyalties and weak domestic structures.

This political multipolarity does not necessarily guarantee stability. Rigidity is diminished, but so is manageability. Nationalism may succeed in curbing the preeminence of the superpowers; it remains to be seen whether it can supply an integrating concept more successfully in this century than in the last. Few countries have the interest and only the superpowers have the resources to become informed about global issues. As a result, diplo-macy is often geared to domestic politics and more concerned with striking a pose than contributing to international order. Equilibrium is difficult to achieve among states widely divergent in values, goals, expectations, and previous experience.

The greatest need of the contemporary international system is an agreed concept of order. In its absence, the awesome available power is unrestrained by any consensus as to legitimacy; ideology and nationalism, in their different ways, deepen international schisms. Many of the elements of stability which characterized the international system in the nineteenth century cannot be re-created in the modern age. The stable technology, the multiplicity of major powers, the limited domestic claims, and the frontiers which permitted adjustments are gone forever. A new concept of interna-tional order is essential; without it stability will prove elusive.

This problem is particularly serious for the United States. Whatever our intentions or policies, the fact that the United States disposes of the greatest single aggregate of material power in the world is inescapable. A new international order is inconceivable without a significant American contribution. But the nature of this contribution has altered. For the two decades after 1945, our international activities were based on the assumption that technology plus managerial skills gave us the ability to reshape the international system and to bring about domestic transformations in "emerging countries." This direct "operational" concept of international order has proved too simple. Political multipolarity makes it impossible to impose an American design. Our deepest challenge will be to evoke the creativity of a pluralistic world, to base order on political multipolarity even though overwhelming military strength will remain with the two superpowers.

II. THE LIMITS OF BIPOLARITY: THE NATURE OF POWER IN THE MODERN PERIOD

Throughout history, military power was considered the final recourse. Statesmen treated the acquisition of additional power as an obvious and paramount objective. As recently as twenty-five years ago, it would have been inconceivable that a country could possess *too much* strength for effective political use; every increment of power was—at least theoretically—politically effective. The minimum aim was to assure the impermeability of the territory. Until the Second World War, a state's strength could be measured by its ability to protect its population from attack.

The nuclear age has destroyed this traditional measure. Increasing strength no longer necessarily confers the ability to protect the population. No foreseeable force level . . . can prevent levels of damage eclipsing those of the two world wars. In these conditions, the major problem is to discipline power so that it bears a rational relationship to the objectives likely to be in dispute. The paradox of contemporary military strength is that a gargantuan increase in power has eroded its relationship to policy. The major nuclear powers are capable of devastating each other. But they have great difficulty translating this capability into policy except to prevent direct challenges to their own survival—and this condition is interpreted with increasing strictness. The capacity to destroy is difficult to translate into a plausible threat even against countries with no capacity for retaliation. The margin of superiority of the superpowers over the other states is widening; yet other nations have an unprecedented scope for autonomous action. . . . This does not mean that impotence increases influence, only that power does not automatically confer it.

This state of affairs has profound consequences for traditional notions of balance of power. In the past, stability has always presupposed the existence of an equilibrium of power which prevented one state from imposing its will on the others.

The traditional criteria for the balance of power were territorial. A state could gain overwhelming superiority only by conquest; hence, as long as territorial expansion was foreclosed, or severely limited, the equilibrium was likely to be preserved. In the contemporary period, this is no longer true. Some conquests add little to effective military strength; major increases in power are possible entirely through developments within the territory of a sovereign state. China gained more in real military power through the acquisition of nuclear weapons than if it had conquered all of Southeast Asia. If the Soviet Union had occupied Western Europe but had remained without nuclear weapons, it would be less powerful than it is now with its existing nuclear arsenal within its present borders. In other words, the really fundamental changes in the balance of power have all occurred *within* the territorial limits of sovereign states. Clearly, there is an urgent need to analyze just what is understood by power—as well as by balance of power—in the nuclear age.

This would be difficult enough were technology stable. It becomes enormously complicated when a scientific revolution produces an upheaval in weapons technology at five-year intervals. Slogans like "superiority," "parity," "assured destruction," compete unencumbered by clear definitions of their operational military significance, much less a consensus on their political implications. The gap between experts and decision-makers is widening.

In short, as power has grown more awesome, it has also turned abstract, intangible, elusive. Deterrence has become the dominant military policy. But deterrence depends above all on psychological criteria. It seeks to keep an opponent from a given course by posing unacceptable risks. . . . For political purposes, the meaningful measurement of military strength is the assessment of it by the other side. Psychological criteria vie in importance with strategic doctrine.

The abstract nature of modern power affects domestic disputes profoundly. Deterrence is tested negatively by things which do *not* happen. But it is never possible to demonstrate *why* something has not occurred. Is it because we are pursuing the best possible policy or only a marginally effective one? Bitter debate even among those who believe in the necessity of defense policy is inevitable and bound to be inconclusive. Moreover, the longer peace is maintained—or the more successful deterrence is—the more it furnishes arguments for those who are opposed to the very premises of defense policy. Perhaps there was no need for preparedness in the first place because the opponent never meant to attack. In the modern state, national security is likely to be a highly divisive domestic issue.

The enormity of modern power has destroyed its cumulative impact to a considerable extent. Throughout history the use of force set a precedent; it demonstrated a capacity to use power for national ends. In the twentieth century any use of force sets up inhibitions against resorting to it again. . . .

III. POLITICAL MULTIPOLARITY: THE CHANGED NATURE OF ALLIANCES

No area of policy illustrates more dramatically the tensions between political multipolarity and military bipolarity than the field of alliance policy. For a decade and a half after the Second World War, the United States identified security with alliances. A global network of relationships grew up based on the proposition that deterrence of aggression required the largest possible grouping of powers.

This system of alliances was always in difficulty outside the Atlantic area because it tried to apply principles drawn from the multipolar world of the eighteenth and nineteenth centuries when several major powers of roughly equal strength existed. Then, indeed, it was impossible for one country to achieve dominance if several others combined to prevent it. But this was not the case in the era of the superpowers of the forties and fifties. Outside Europe, our allies added to our strength only marginally; they were in no position to reinforce each other's capabilities.

Alliances, to be effective, must meet four conditions: (1) a common objective—usually defense against a common danger; (2) a degree of joint policy at least sufficient to define the *casus belli*; (3) some technical means of cooperation in case common action is decided upon; (4) a penalty for noncooperation—that is, the possibility of being refused assistance must exist—otherwise protection will be taken for granted and the mutuality of obligation will break down.

In the system of alliances developed by the United States after the Second World War, these conditions have never been met outside the North Atlantic Treaty Organization (NATO). . . . Lacking a conception of common interests, the members of these [other] alliances have never been able to develop common policies with respect to issues of war and peace. Had they been able to do so, such policies might well have been stillborn anyway, because the technical means of cooperation have been lacking. Most allies have neither the resources nor the will to render mutual support. . . .

The case is different with NATO. Here we are united with countries of similar traditions and domestic structures. At the start, there was a common conception of the threat. The technical means for cooperation existed. Mechanisms for developing common policies came into being—especially in the military field. Thus in its first decade and a half, NATO was a dynamic and creative institution.

Today, however, NATO is in disarray as well. Actions by the United States—above all, frequent unilateral changes of policy—are partially responsible. But the most important cause is the transformation of the international environment, specifically the decline in the preeminence of the superpowers and the emergence of political multipolarity. Where the alliances outside of Europe have never been vital because they failed to take into account the military bipolarity of the fifties, NATO is in difficulties because it has yet to adjust to the political multipolarity of the late sixties.

When NATO was founded in 1949, Europeans had a dual fear: the danger of an imminent Soviet attack and the prospect of eventual U.S. withdrawal. In the late 1960s, however, the fear of Soviet invasion . . . declined. . . . At the same time, two decades of American military presence in Europe coupled with American predominance in NATO planning have sharply reduced the fear that America might wash its hands of European concerns.

When NATO was formed, moreover, the principal threat to world peace seemed to lie in a Soviet attack on Europe. In recent years, the view has grown that equally grave risks are likely to arise in trouble spots outside Europe. To most Europeans, these do not appear as immediate threats to their independence or security. The irony here is striking. In the fifties, Europeans were asking for American assistance in Asia and the Middle East with the argument that they were defending the greater interests of freedom. The United States replied that these very interests required American aloofness. Today, the roles are precisely reversed. It is Europe that evades our entreaties to play a global role; that is to say, Europeans do not consider their interests at stake in America's extra-European involvement.

These are symptoms of deeper, structural problems, however. One problem, paradoxically, is the growth of European economic strength and political self-confidence. At the end of the Second World War, Europe was dependent on the United States for economic assistance, political stability, and military protection. As long as Europe needed the shelter of a superpower, American predominance was inevitable. . . .

Tutelage is a comfortable relationship for the senior partner, but it is demoralizing in the long run. It breeds illusions of omniscience on one side and attitudes of impotent irresponsibility on the other. In any event, the United States could not expect to perpetuate the accident of Europe's postwar exhaustion into a permanent pattern of international relations. Europe's economic recovery inevitably led to a return to more traditional political pressures.

These changes in Europe were bound to lead to a difficult transitional period. They could have resulted in a new partnership between the United States and an economically resurgent and politically united Europe. . . . But European unity is stymied, and domestic politics has almost everywhere dominated security policy. The result is a massive frustration which expresses itself in special testiness toward the United States.

These strains have been complicated by the growth of Soviet nuclear power. The changed nature of power in the modern period has affected NATO profoundly. As the risks of nuclear war have become enormous, the credibility of traditional pledges of support has inevitably been reduced. In the past, a country would carry out a commitment because, it could plausibly be argued, the consequences of not doing so were worse than those of coming to the ally's assistance. This is no longer self-evident. . . .

The consciousness of nuclear threat by the two superpowers has undermined allied relationships in yet another way. For understandable reasons, the superpowers have sought to make the nuclear environment more predictable—witness the nuclear test ban treaty and the nonproliferation treaty. But the blind spot in our policy has been the failure to understand that, in the absence of full consultation, our allies see in these talks the possible forerunner of a more comprehensive arrangement affecting their vital interests negotiated without them. Strategic arms talks thus emphasize the need of political understanding in acute form. The pattern of negotiating an agreement first and then giving our allies an opportunity—even a full one—to comment is intolerable in the long run. It puts the onus of failure on them, and it prevents them from doing more than quibble about a framework with which they may disagree. . . .

It is far from self-evident, however, that more extensive consultation within the existing framework can be more than a palliative. One problem concerns technical competence. In any large bureaucracy—and an international consultative process has many similarities to domestic administrative procedures—the weight given to advice bears some relation to the competence it reflects. If one partner possesses all the technical competence, the process of consultation is likely to remain barren. The minimum requirement for effective consultation is that each ally have enough knowledge to give meaningful advice.

But there are even more important limits to the process of consultation. The losing party in a domestic dispute has three choices: (a) it can accept the setback with the expectation of winning another battle later on—this is the usual bureaucratic attitude and it is based on the assurance of another hearing; (b) if advice is consistently ignored, it can resign and go into opposition; (c) as the opposition party, it can have the purpose either of inducing the existing government to change its course or of replacing it. If all these avenues are closed, violence or mounting frustration are the consequences.

Only the first option is open to sovereign states bound together by an alliance, since they obviously cannot resign or go into opposition without wrecking the alliance. They cannot affect the process by which their partners' decision-makers are chosen despite the fact that this may be crucial for their fate. Indeed, as long as the need to maintain the alliance overrides all other concerns, disagreement is likely to be stifled. Advice without responsibility and disagreement without an outlet can turn consultation into a frustrating exercise which compounds rather than alleviates discord. . . .

IV. BIPOLARITY AND MULTIPOLARITY: THE CONCEPTUAL PROBLEM

In the years ahead, the most profound challenge to American policy will be philosophical: to develop some concept of order in a world which is bipolar militarily but multipolar politically. But a philosophical deepening will not come easily to those brought up in the American tradition of foreign policy.

Our political society was one of the few which was *consciously* created at a point in time. At least until the emergence of the race problem, we were blessed by the absence of conflicts between classes and over ultimate ends. These factors produced the characteristic aspects of American foreign policy: a certain manipulativeness and pragmatism, a conviction that the normal pattern of international relations was harmonious, a reluctance to think in structural terms, a belief in final answers—all qualities which reflect a sense of self-sufficiency not far removed from a sense of omnipotence. Yet the contemporary dilemma is that there are no total solutions; we live in a world gripped by revolutions in technology, values, and institutions. We are immersed in an unending process, not in a quest for a final destination. The deepest problems of equilibrium are not physical but psychological or moral. The shape of the future will depend ultimately on convictions which far transcend the physical balance of power.

The New Nations and Political Legitimacy. This challenge is especially crucial with respect to the new nations. Future historians are likely to class the confusion and torment in the emerging countries with the great movements of religious awakening. Continents which had been dormant for centuries suddenly develop political consciousness. Regions which for scores of years had considered foreign rule as natural struggle for independence. Yet it is a curious nationalism which defines itself not as in Europe by common language or culture but often primarily by the common experience of foreign rule. Boundaries—especially in Africa—have tended to follow the administrative convenience of the colonial powers rather than linguistic or tribal lines. The new nations have faced problems both of identity and of political authority. They often lack social cohesiveness entirely, or they are split into competing groups, each with a highly developed sense of identity. . . .

It is in the new countries that questions of the purpose of political life and the meaning of political legitimacy—key issues also in the modern state—pose themselves in their most acute form. The new nations weigh little in the physical balance of power. But the forces unleashed in the emergence of so many new states may well affect the moral balance of the world—the convictions which form the structure for the world of tomorrow. This adds a new dimension to the problem of multipolarity.

Almost all of the new countries suffer from a revolutionary malaise: revolutions succeed through the coming together of all resentments. But the elimination of existing structures compounds the difficulty of establishing political consensus. A successful revolution leaves as its legacy a profound dislocation. In the new countries, contrary to all revolutionary expectations, the task of construction emerges as less glamorous and more complex than the struggle for freedom; the exaltation of the quest for independence cannot be perpetuated. Sooner or later, positive goals must replace resentment of the former colonial power as a motive force. In the absence of autonomous social forces, this unifying role tends to be performed by the state.

But the assumption of this role by the state does not produce stability. When social cohesiveness is slight, the struggle for control of authority is correspondingly more bitter. When government is the principal, sometimes the sole, expression of national identity, opposition comes to be considered treason. The profound social or religious schisms of many of the new nations turn the control of political authority quite literally into a matter of life and death. Where political obligation follows racial, religious, or tribal lines, self-restraint breaks down. Domestic conflicts assume the character of civil war. Such traditional authority as exists is personal or feudal. The problem is to make it "legitimate"—to develop a notion of political obligation which depends on legal norms rather than on coercive power or personal loyalty.

This process took centuries in Europe. It must be accomplished in decades in the new nations, where preconditions of success are less favorable than at comparable periods in Europe. The new countries are subject to outside pressures; there is a premium on foreign adventures to bring about domestic cohesiveness. Their lack of domestic structure compounds the already great international instabilities.

The American role in the new nations' efforts to build legitimate authority is in need of serious reexamination. The dominant American view about political structure has been that it will follow more or less automatically upon economic progress and that it will take the form of constitutional democracy.

Both assumptions are subject to serious questions. In every advanced country, political stability preceded rather than emerged from the process of industrialization. Where the rudiments of popular institutions did not exist at the beginning of the Industrial Revolution, they did not receive their impetus from it. To be sure, representative institutions were broadened and elaborated as the countries prospered, but their significant features antedated economic development and are not attributable to it. In fact, the system of government which brought about industrialization—whether popular or authoritarian—has tended to be confirmed rather than radically changed by this achievement.

Nor is democracy a natural evolution of nationalism. In the last century, democracy was accepted by a ruling class whose estimate of itself was founded outside the political process. It was buttressed by a middle class, holding a political philosophy in which the state was considered to be a referee of the ultimately important social forces rather than the principal focus of national consciousness. Professional revolutionaries were rarely involved; their bias is seldom democratic.

The pluralism of the West had many causes which cannot be duplicated elsewhere. . . . This is why Communism has never succeeded in the industrialized Western countries for which its theory was devised; its greatest successes have been in developing societies. This is no accident. Industrialization—in its early phases—multiplies dislocations. It smashes the traditional framework. It requires a system of values which makes the sacrifices involved in capital formation tolerable and which furnishes some integrating principles to contain psychological frustrations.

Communism is able to supply legitimacy for the sacrifices inseparably connected with capital formation in an age when the maxims of laissez faire are no longer acceptable. And Leninism has the attraction of providing a rationale for holding on to power. Many of the leaders of the new countries are revolutionaries who sustained themselves through the struggle for independence by visions of the transformations to be brought about after victory. They are not predisposed even to admit the possibility of giving up power in their hour of triumph. Since they usually began their struggle for independence while in a small minority and sustained it against heavy odds, they are not likely to be repelled by the notion that it is possible to "force men to be free."

The ironic feature of the current situation is that Marxism, professing a materialistic philosophy, is accepted only where it does not exist: in some new countries and among protest movements of the advanced democratic countries. Its appeal is its idealistic component and not its economic theory. It offers a doctrine of substantive change and an explanation of final purposes. Its philosophy has totally failed to inspire the younger generation in Communist countries, where its bureaucratic reality is obvious.

On the other hand, the United States, professing an idealistic philosophy, often fails to gain acceptance for democratic values because of its heavy reliance on economic factors. It has answers to technical dislocations but has not been able to contribute much to building a political and moral consensus. It offers a procedure for change but little content for it.

The problem of political legitimacy is the key to political stability in regions containing two-thirds of the world's population. A stable domestic system in the new countries will not automatically produce international order, but international order is impossible without it. An American agenda must include some conception of what we understand by political legitimacy. In an age of instantaneous communication, we cannot pretend that what happens to over two-thirds of humanity is of no concern or interest to the United States. This does not mean that our goal should be to transfer American institutions to the new nations—even less that we should impose them. Nor should we define the problem as how to prevent the spread of Communism. Our goal should be to build a moral consensus which can make a pluralistic world creative rather than destructive.

Irrelevance to one of the great revolutions of our time will mean that we will ultimately be engulfed by it—if not physically, then psychologically. . . .

A world which is bipolar militarily and multipolar politically thus confronts an additional problem. Side by side with the physical balance of power, there exists a psychological balance based on intangibles of value and belief. The presuppositions of the physical equilibrium have changed drastically; those of the psychological balance remain to be discovered.

The Problem of Soviet Intentions. Nothing has been more difficult for Americans to assimilate in the nuclear age than the fact that even enmity is complex. In the Soviet Union, we confront an opponent whose public pronouncements are insistently hostile. Yet the nuclear age imposes a degree of cooperation and an absolute limit to conflicts.

The military relationship with the Soviet Union is difficult enough; the political one confronts us with a profound conceptual problem. A society which regards peace as the normal condition tends to ascribe tension not to structural causes but to wicked or shortsighted individuals. Peace is thought to result either from the automatic operation of economic forces or from the emergence of a more benign leadership abroad.

The debate about Soviet trends between "hard-liners" and "soft-liners" illustrates this problem. Both sides tend to agree that the purpose of American policy is to encourage a more benign evolution of Soviet society—the original purpose of containment was, after all, to bring about the *domestic* transformation of the U.S.S.R. . . .

In fact, the difference between the "hawks" and "doves" has usually concerned timing: the hawks have maintained that a Soviet change of heart, while inevitable, was still in the future, whereas the doves have argued that it has already taken place. . . .

The difference affects—and sometimes poisons—the entire American debate about foreign policy. Left-wing critics of American foreign policy seem incapable of attacking U.S. actions without elevating our opponent . . . to a pedestal. If they discern some stupidity or self-interest on our side, they assume that the other side must be virtuous. They then criticize the United States for opposing the other side. The right follows the same logic in reverse: they presuppose *our* good intentions and conclude that the other side must be perverse in opposing us. Both the left and the right judge largely in terms of intentions. In the process, whatever the issue . . . more attention is paid to whether to get to the conference room than what to do once we arrive there. The dispute over Communist intentions has diverted attention from elaborating our own purposes. In some quarters, the test of dedication to peace has been whether one interprets Soviet intentions in the most favorable manner.

It should be obvious, however, that the Soviet domestic situation is complex and its relationship to foreign policy far from obvious. It is true that the risks of general nuclear war should be as unacceptable to Moscow as to Washington; but this truism does not automatically produce détente. It also seems to lessen the risks involved in local intervention. No doubt the current generation of Communist leaders lacks the ideological dynamism of their predecessors who made the revolution; at the same time, they have at their disposal a military machine of unprecedented strength, and they must deal with a bureaucracy of formidable vested interests. Unquestionably, Soviet consumers press their leaders to satisfy their demands; but it is equally true that an expanding modern economy is able to supply *both* guns and butter. Some Soviet leaders may have become more pragmatic; but in an elaborated Communist state, the results of pragmatism are complex. Once power is seized and industrialization is largely accomplished, the Communist Party faces a difficult situation. It is not needed to conduct the government, and it has no real function in running the economy (though it tries to do both). In order to justify its continued existence and command, it may develop a vested interest in vigilance against outside danger and thus in perpetuating a fairly high level of tension. . . .

If we focus our policy discussions on Soviet purposes, we confuse the debate in two ways: Soviet trends are too ambiguous to offer a reliable guide—it is possible that not even Soviet leaders fully understand the dynamics of their system; it deflects us from articulating the purposes we should pursue, whatever Soviet intentions. Peace will not, in any event, result from one grand settlement but from a long diplomatic process, and this process requires some clarity as to our destination. Confusing foreign policy with psychotherapy deprives us of criteria by which to judge the political foundations of international order.

The obsession with Soviet intentions causes the West to be smug during periods of détente and panicky during crises. A benign Soviet tone is equated with the achievement of peace; Soviet hostility is considered to be the signal for a new period of tension and usually evokes purely military countermeasures. The West is thus never ready for a Soviet change of course; it has been equally unprepared for détente and intransigence. . . .

V. AN INQUIRY INTO THE AMERICAN NATIONAL INTEREST

Wherever we turn, then, the central task of American foreign policy is to analyze anew the current international environment and to develop some concepts which will enable us to contribute to the emergence of a stable order.

First, we must recognize the existence of profound structural problems that are to a considerable extent independent of the intentions of the principal protagonists and that cannot be solved merely by good will. . . .

To understand the structural issue, it is necessary to undertake an inquiry, from which we have historically shied away, into the essence of our national interest and into the premises of our foreign policy. It is part of American folklore that, while other nations have interests, we have responsibilities; while other nations are concerned with equilibrium, we are concerned with the legal requirements of peace. We have a tendency to offer our altruism as a guarantee of our reliability: "We have no quarrel with the Communists," Secretary of State Rusk said on one occasion; "all our quarrels are on behalf of other people."

Such an attitude makes it difficult to develop a conception of our role in the world. It inhibits other nations from gearing their policy to ours in a confident way—a "disinterested" policy is likely to be considered "unreliable." A mature conception of our interest in the world would obviously have to take into account the widespread interest in stability and peaceful change. It would deal with two fundamental questions: What is it in our interest to prevent? What should we seek to accomplish?

The answer to the first question is complicated by an often-repeated proposition that we must resist aggression anywhere it occurs since peace is indivisible. A corollary is the argument that we do not oppose the fact of particular changes but the method by which they are brought about. We find it hard to articulate a truly vital interest which we would defend however "legal" the challenge. This leads to an undifferentiated concept of globalism and confusion about our purposes. The abstract concept of aggression causes us to multiply our commitments. But the denial that our interests are involved diminishes our staying power when we try to carry out these commitments.

Part of the reason for our difficulties is our reluctance to think in terms of power and equilibrium. In 1949, for example, a State Department memorandum justified NATO as follows: "[The treaty] obligates the parties to defend the purposes and principles of the United Nations, the freedom, common heritage and civilization of the parties and their free institutions based upon the principles of democracy, individual liberty and the role of law. It obligates them to act in defense of peace and security. It is directed against no one; it is directed solely against aggression. It seeks not to influence any shifting balance of power but to strengthen a balance of principle."

But principle, however lofty, must at some point be related to practice; historically, stability has always coincided with an equilibrium that made physical domination difficult. Interest is not necessarily amoral; moral consequences can spring from interested acts. . . .

The task of defining positive goals is more difficult but even more important. The first two decades after the end of the Second World War posed problems well suited to the American approach to international relations. Wherever we turned, massive dislocations required attention. Our pragmatic, *ad hoc* tendency was an advantage in a world clamoring for technical remedies. Our legal bent contributed to the development of many instruments of stability.

. . . The United States is no longer in a position to operate programs globally; it has to encourage them. It can no longer impose its preferred solution; it must seek to evoke it. . . . We are a superpower physically, but our designs can be meaningful only if they generate willing cooperation. We can continue to contribute to defense and positive programs, but we must seek to encourage and not stifle a sense of local responsibility. Our contribution should not be the sole or principal effort, but it should make the difference between success and failure.

This task requires a different kind of creativity and another form of patience than we have displayed in the past. Enthusiasm, belief in progress, and the invincible conviction that American remedies can work everywhere must give way to an understanding of historical trends, an ordering of our preferences, and above all an understanding of the difference our preferences can in fact make.

The dilemma is that there can be no stability without equilibrium but, equally, equilibrium is not a purpose with which we can respond to the travail of our world. A sense of mission is clearly a legacy of American history; to most Americans, America has always stood for something other than its own grandeur. But a clearer understanding of America's interests and of the requirements of equilibrium can give perspective to our idealism and lead to humane and moderate objectives, especially in relation to political and social change. Thus our conception of world order must have deeper purposes than stability but greater restraints on our behavior than would result if it were approached only in a fit of enthusiasm.

Whether such a leap of the imagination is possible in the modern bureaucratic state remains to be seen. New administrations come to power convinced of the need for goals and for comprehensive concepts. Sooner, rather than later, they find themselves subjected to the pressures of the immediate and the particular. Part of the reason is the pragmatic, issue-oriented bias of our decision-makers. But the fundamental reason may be the pervasiveness of modern bureaucracy. What started out as an aid to decision-making has developed a momentum of its own. Increasingly, the policy-maker is more conscious of the pressures and the morale of his staff than of the purpose this staff is supposed to serve. The policy-maker becomes a referee among quasi-autonomous bureaucratic bodies. Success consists of moving the administrative machinery to the point of decision, leaving relatively little energy for analyzing the decision's merit. The modern bureaucratic state widens the range of technical choices while limiting the capacity to make them.

An even more serious problem is posed by the change of ethic of precisely the most idealistic element of American youth. The idealism of the fifties during the Kennedy era expressed itself in self-confident, often zealous, institution building. Today, however, many in the younger generation consider the management of power irrelevant, perhaps even immoral. . . . Management is equated with manipulation. Structural designs are perceived as systems of "domination"—not of order. The generation which has come of age after the fifties has had Vietnam as its introduction to world politics. It has no memory of occasions when American-supported structural innovations were successful or of the motivations which prompted these enterprises.

Partly as a result of the generation gap, the American mood oscillates dangerously between being ashamed of power and expecting too much of it. The former attitude deprecates the use or possession of force; the latter is overly receptive to the possibilities of absolute action and overly indifferent to the likely consequences. The danger of a rejection of power is that it may result in a nihilistic perfectionism which disdains the gradual and seeks to destroy what does not conform to its notion of utopia. The danger of an overconcern with force is that policy-makers may respond to clamor by a series of spasmodic gestures and stylistic maneuvers and then recoil before their implications.

These essentially psychological problems cannot be overemphasized. It is the essence of a satisfied, advanced society that it puts a premium on operating within familiar procedures and concepts. It draws its motivation from the present, and it defines excellence by the ability to manipulate an established framework. But for the major part of humanity, the present becomes endurable only through a vision of the future. To most Americans—including most American leaders—the significant reality is what they see around them. But for most of the world—including many of the leaders of the new nations—the significant reality is what they wish to bring about. If we remain nothing but the managers of our physical patrimony, we will grow increasingly irrelevant. And since there can be no stability without us, the prospects of world order will decline. . . .

9

REALISM AND COMPLEX INTERDEPENDENCE

ROBERT O. KEOHANE
JOSEPH S. NYE

One's assumptions about world politics profoundly affect what one sees and how one constructs theories to explain events. We believe that the assumptions of political realists, whose theories dominated the postwar period, are often an inadequate basis for analyzing the politics of interdependence. The realist assumptions about world politics can be seen as defining an extreme set of conditions or *ideal type*. One could also imagine very different conditions. In this chapter, we shall construct another ideal type, the opposite of realism. We call it *complex interdependence*. After establishing the differences between realism and complex interdependence, we shall argue that complex interdependence sometimes comes closer to reality than does realism. When it does, traditional explanations of change in international regimes become questionable and the search for new explanatory models becomes more urgent.

For political realists, international politics, like all other politics, is a struggle for power but, unlike domestic politics, a struggle dominated by organized violence. In the words of the most influential postwar textbook, "All history shows that nations active in international politics are continuously preparing for, actively involved in, or recovering from organized violence in the form of war."[1] Three assumptions are integral to the realist vision. First, states as coherent units are the dominant actors in world politics. This is a double assumption: states are predominant; and they act as coherent units. Second, realists assume that force is a usable and effective instrument of policy. Other instruments may also be employed, but using or threatening force is the most effective means of wielding power. Third, partly because of their second assumption, realists assume a hierarchy of issues in world politics, headed by questions of military security: the "high politics" of military security dominates the "low politics" of economic and social affairs.

These realist assumptions define an ideal type of world politics. They allow us to imagine a world in which politics is continually characterized by active or potential conflict among states, with the use of force possible at any time. Each state attempts to defend its territory and interests from real or perceived threats. Political integration among states is slight and lasts only as long as it serves the national interests of the most powerful states. Transnational actors either do not exist or are politically unimportant. Only the adept exercise of force or the threat of force permits states to survive, and only while statesmen succeed in adjusting their interests, as in a well-functioning balance of power, is the system stable.

Each of the realist assumptions can be challenged. If we challenge them all simultaneously, we can imagine a world in which actors other than states participate directly in world politics, in which a clear hierarchy of issues does not exist, and in which force is an ineffective instrument of policy. Under these conditions—which we call the characteristics of complex interdependence—one would expect world politics to be very different than under realist conditions.

We will explore these differences in the next section of this chapter. We do not argue, however, that complex interdependence faithfully reflects world political reality. Quite the contrary: both it and the realist portrait are ideal types. Most situations will fall somewhere between these two extremes. Sometimes, realist assumptions will be accurate, or largely accurate, but frequently complex interdependence will provide a better portrayal of reality. Before one decides what explanatory model to apply to a situation or problem, one will need to understand the degree to which realist or complex interdependence assumptions correspond to the situation.

THE CHARACTERISTICS OF COMPLEX INTERDEPENDENCE

Complex interdependence has three main characteristics:

1. *Multiple channels* connect societies, including: informal ties between governmental elites as well as formal foreign office arrangements; informal ties among nongovernmental elites (face-to-face and through telecommunications); and transnational organizations (such as multinational banks or corporations). These channels can be summarized as interstate, transgovernmental, and transnational relations. *Interstate* relations are the normal channels assumed by realists. *Transgovernmental* applies when we relax the realist assumption that states act coherently as units; *transnational* applies when we relax the assumption that states are the only units.

2. The agenda of interstate relationships consists of multiple issues that are not arranged in a clear or consistent hierarchy. This *absence of hierarchy among issues* means, among other things, that military security does not consistently dominate the agenda. Many issues arise from what used to be considered domestic policy, and the distinction

between domestic and foreign issues becomes blurred. These issues are considered in several government departments (not just foreign offices), and at several levels. Inadequate policy coordination on these issues involves significant costs. Different issues generate different coalitions, both within governments and across them, and involve different degrees of conflict. Politics does not stop at the waters' edge.
3. Military force is not used by governments toward other governments within the region, or on the issues, when complex interdependence prevails. It may, however, be important in these governments' relations with governments outside that region, or on other issues. Military force could, for instance, be irrelevant to resolving disagreements on economic issues among members of an alliance, yet at the same time be very important for that alliance's political and military relations with a rival bloc. For the former relationships this condition of complex interdependence would be met; for the latter, it would not.

Traditional theories of international politics implicitly or explicitly deny the accuracy of these three assumptions. Traditionalists are therefore tempted also to deny the relevance of criticisms based on the complex interdependence ideal type. We believe, however, that our three conditions are fairly well approximated on some global issues of economic and ecological interdependence and that they come close to characterizing the entire relationship between some countries. . . .

Multiple Channels

A visit to any major airport is a dramatic way to confirm the existence of multiple channels of contact among advanced industrial countries; there is a voluminous literature to prove it.[2] Bureaucrats from different countries deal directly with one another at meetings and on the telephone as well as in writing. Similarly, nongovernmental elites frequently get together in the normal course of business, in organizations such as the Trilateral Commission, and in conferences sponsored by private foundations.

In addition, multinational firms and banks affect both domestic and interstate relations. The limits on private firms, or the closeness of ties between government and business, vary considerably from one society to another; but the participation of large and dynamic organizations, not controlled entirely by governments, has become a normal part of foreign as well as domestic relations.

These actors are important not only because of their activities in pursuit of their own interests, but also because they act as transmission belts, making government policies in various countries more sensitive to one another. As the scope of governments' domestic activities has broadened, and as corporations, banks, and (to a lesser extent) trade unions have made decisions that transcend national boundaries, the domestic policies of different countries impinge on one another more and more. Transnational communications reinforce these effects. Thus, foreign economic policies touch more domestic economic activity than in the past, blurring the lines between domestic and foreign policy and increasing the number of issues relevant to foreign policy. Parallel developments in issues of environmental regulation and control over technology reinforce this trend.

Absence of Hierarchy among Issues

Foreign affairs agendas—that is, sets of issues relevant to foreign policy with which governments are concerned—have become larger and more diverse. No longer can all issues be subordinated to military security. As Secretary of State Kissinger described the situation in 1975:

> progress in dealing with the traditional agenda is no longer enough. A new and unprecedented kind of issue has emerged. The problems of energy, resources, environment, population, the uses of space and the seas now rank with questions of military security, ideology and territorial rivalry which have traditionally made up the diplomatic agenda.[3]

Kissinger's list, which could be expanded, illustrates how governments' policies, even those previously considered merely domestic, impinge on one another. The extensive consultative arrangements developed by the OECD, as well as the GATT, IMF, and the European Community indicate how characteristic the overlap of domestic and foreign policy is among developed pluralist countries. The organization within nine major departments of the United States government (Agriculture, Commerce, Defense, Health and Human Services, Interior, Justice, Labor, State, and Treasury) and many other agencies reflects their extensive international commitments. The multiple, overlapping issues that result make a nightmare of governmental organization.[4]

When there are multiple issues on the agenda, many of which threaten the interests of domestic groups but do not clearly threaten the nation as a whole, the problems of formulating a coherent and consistent foreign policy increase. In 1975 energy was a foreign policy problem, but specific remedies, such as a tax on gasoline and automobiles, involved domestic legislation opposed by auto workers and companies alike. As one commentator observed, "virtually every time Congress has set a national policy that changed the way people live . . . the action came after a consensus had developed, bit by bit, over the years, that a problem existed and that there was one best way to solve it."[5] Opportunities for delay, for special protection, for inconsistency and incoherence abound when international politics requires aligning the domestic policies of pluralist democratic countries.

Minor Role of Military Force

Political scientists have traditionally emphasized the role of military force in international politics. . . . [F]orce dominates other means of power: *if* there are no constraints on one's choice of instruments (a hypothetical situation that has only been approximated in the two world wars), the state with superior military force will prevail. If the security dilemma for all states were extremely acute, military force, supported by economic and other resources, would clearly be the dominant source of power. Survival is the primary goal of all states, and in the worst situations, force is ultimately necessary to guarantee survival. Thus military force is always a central component of national power.

Yet particularly among industrialized, pluralist countries, the perceived margin of safety has widened: fears of attack in general have declined, and fears of attacks *by one another* are virtually nonexistent. France has abandoned the *tous azimuts* (defense in all directions) strategy that President de Gaulle advocated (it was not taken entirely seriously even at the time). Canada's last war plans for fighting the United States were abandoned half a century ago. Britain and Germany no longer feel threatened by each other. Intense relationships of mutual influence exist between these countries, but in most of them force is irrelevant or unimportant as an instrument of policy.

Moreover, force is often not an appropriate way of achieving other goals (such as economic and ecological warfare) that are becoming more important. It is not impossible to imagine dramatic conflict or revolutionary change in which the use or threat of military force over an economic issue or among advanced industrial countries might become plausible. Then realist assumptions would again be a reliable guide to events. But in most situations, the effects of military force are both costly and uncertain.[6]

Even when the direct use of force is barred among a group of countries, however, military power can still be used politically. Each superpower continues to use the threat of force to deter attacks by other superpowers on itself or its allies; its deterrence ability thus serves an indirect, protective role, which it can use in bargaining on other issues with its allies. This bargaining tool is particularly important for the United States, whose allies are concerned about potential Soviet threats and which has fewer other means of influence over its allies than does the Soviet Union over its Eastern European partners. The United States has, accordingly, taken advantage of the Europeans' (particularly the Germans') desire for protection and linked the issue of troop levels in Europe to trade and monetary negotiations. Thus, although the first-order effect of deterrent force is essentially negative—to deny effective offensive power to a superpower opponent—a state can use that force positively: to gain political influence.

Thus, even for countries whose relations approximate complex interdependence, two serious qualifications remain: (1) drastic social and political change could cause force again to become an important direct instrument of policy; and (2) even when elites' interests are complementary, a country that uses military force to protect another may have significant political influence over the other country.

In North-South relations, or relations among Third World countries, as well as in East-West relations, force is often important. Military power helps the Soviet Union to dominate Eastern Europe economically as well as politically. The threat of open or covert American military intervention has helped to limit revolutionary changes in the Caribbean, especially in Guatemala in 1954 and in the Dominican Republic in 1965. Secretary of State Kissinger, in January 1975, issued a veiled warning to members of the Organization of Petroleum Exporting Countries (OPEC) that the United States might use force against them "where there is some actual strangulation of the industrialized world."[7]

Even in these rather conflictual situations, however, the recourse to force seems less likely now than at most times during the century before 1945. The destructiveness of nuclear weapons makes any attack against a nuclear power dangerous. Nuclear weapons are mostly used as a deterrent. Threats of nuclear action against much weaker countries may occasionally be efficacious, but they are equally or more likely to solidify relations between one's adversaries. The limited usefulness of conventional force to control socially mobilized populations has been shown by the United States failure in Vietnam as well as by the rapid decline of colonialism in Africa. Furthermore, employing force on one issue against an independent state with which one has a variety of relationships is likely to rupture mutually profitable relations on other issues. In other words, the use of force often has costly effects on nonsecurity goals. And finally, in Western democracies, popular opposition to prolonged military conflicts is very high.[8]

It is clear that these constraints bear unequally on various countries, or on the same countries in different situations. Risks of nuclear escalation affect everyone, but domestic opinion is far less constraining for communist states, or for authoritarian regional powers, than for the United States, Europe, or Japan. Even authoritarian countries may be reluctant to use force to obtain economic objectives when such use might be ineffective and disrupt other relationships. Both the difficulty of controlling socially mobilized populations with foreign troops and the changing technology of weaponry may actually enhance the ability of certain countries, or nonstate groups, to use terrorism as a political weapon without effective fear of reprisal.

The fact that the changing role of force has uneven effects does not make the change less important, but it does make matters more complex. This complexity is compounded by differences in the usability of force among issue areas. When an issue arouses little interest or passion, force may be unthinkable. In such instances, complex interdependence may be a valuable concept for analyzing the political process. But if that issue becomes a matter of life and death—as some people thought oil might become—the use or threat of force could become decisive again. Realist assumptions would then be more relevant.

It is thus important to determine the applicability of realism or of complex interdependence to each situation. Without this determination, further analysis is likely to be confused. Our purpose in developing an alternative to the realist description of world politics is to encourage a differentiated approach that distinguishes among dimensions and areas of world politics—not (as some modernist observers do) to replace one oversimplification with another.

THE POLITICAL PROCESSES OF COMPLEX INTERDEPENDENCE

The three main characteristics of complex interdependence give rise to distinctive political processes, which translate power resources into power as control of outcomes. . . . [S]omething is usually lost or added in the translation. Under conditions of complex interdependence the translation will be different than under realist conditions, and our predictions about outcomes will need to be adjusted accordingly.

In the realist world, military security will be the dominant goal of states. It will even affect issues that are not directly involved with military power or territorial defense. Nonmilitary problems will not only be subordinated to military ones; they will be studied for their politico-military implications. Balance of payments issues, for instance, will be considered at least as much in the light of their implications for world power generally as for their purely financial ramifications. McGeorge Bundy conformed to realist expectations when he argued in 1964 that devaluation of the dollar should be seriously considered if necessary to fight the war in Vietnam.[9] To some extent, so did former Treasury Secretary Henry Fowler when he contended in 1971 that the United States needed a trade surplus of $4 billion to $6 billion in order to lead in Western defense.[10]

In a world of complex interdependence, however, one expects some officials, particularly at lower levels, to emphasize the *variety* of state goals that must be pursued. In the absence of a clear hierarchy of issues, goals will vary by issue, and may not be closely related. Each bureaucracy will pursue its own concerns; and although several agencies may reach compromises on issues that affect them all, they will find that a consistent pattern of policy is difficult to maintain. Moreover, transnational actors will introduce different goals into various groups of issues.

Linkage Strategies

Goals will therefore vary by issue area under complex interdependence, but so will the distribution of power and the typical political processes. Traditional analysis focuses on *the* international system, and leads us to anticipate similar political processes on a variety of issues. Militarily and economically strong states will dominate a variety of organizations and a variety of issues, by linking their own policies on some issues to other states' policies on other issues. By using their overall dominance to prevail on their weak issues, the strongest states will, in the traditional model, ensure a congruence between the overall structure of military and economic power and the pattern of outcomes on any one issue area. Thus world politics can be treated as a seamless web.

Under complex interdependence, such congruence is less likely to occur. As military force is devalued, militarily strong states will find it more difficult to use their overall dominance to control outcomes on issues in which they are weak. And since the distribution of power resources in trade, shipping, or oil, for example, may be quite different, patterns of outcomes and distinctive political processes are likely to vary from one set of issues to another. If force were readily applicable, and military security were the highest foreign policy goal, these variations in the issue structures of power would not matter very much. The linkages drawn from them to military issues would ensure consistent dominance by the overall strongest states. But when military force is largely immobilized, strong states will find the linkage is less effective. They may still attempt such links, but in the absence of a hierarchy of issues, their success will be problematic.

Dominant states may try to secure much the same result by using overall economic power to affect results on other issues. If only economic objectives are at stake, they may succeed: money, after all, is fungible. But economic objectives have political implications, and economic linkage by the strong is limited by domestic, transnational, and transgovernmental actors who resist having their interests traded off. Furthermore, the international actors may be different on different issues, and the international organizations in which negotiations take place are often quite separate. Thus it is difficult, for example, to imagine a militarily or economically strong state linking concessions on monetary policy to reciprocal concessions in oceans policy. On the other hand, poor weak states are not similarly inhibited from linking unrelated issues, partly because their domestic interests are less complex. Linkage of unrelated issues is often a means of extracting concessions or side payments from rich and powerful states. And unlike powerful states whose instrument for linkage (military force) is often too costly to use, the linkage instrument used by poor weak states—international organization—is available and inexpensive.

Thus as the utility of force declines, and as issues become more equal in importance, the distribution of power within each issue will become more important. If linkages become less effective on the whole, outcomes of political bargaining will increasingly vary by issue area.

The differentiation among issue areas in complex interdependence means that linkages among issues will become more problematic and will tend to reduce rather than reinforce international hierarchy. Linkage strategies, and defense against them, will pose critical strategic choices for states. Should issues be considered separately or as a package? If linkages are to be drawn, which issues should be linked, and on which of the linked issues should concessions be made? How far can one push a linkage before it becomes counterproductive? For instance, should one seek formal agreements or informal, but less politically sensitive, understandings? The fact that world politics under complex interdependence is not a seamless web leads us to expect that efforts to stitch seams together advantageously, as reflected in linkage strategies, will, very often, determine the shape of the fabric.

The negligible role of force leads us to expect states to rely more on other instruments in order to wield power. . . . [L]ess vulnerable states will try to use asymmetrical interdependence in particular groups of issues as a source of power; they will also try to use international organizations and transnational actors and flows. States will approach economic interdependence in terms of power as well as its effects on citizens' welfare, although welfare considerations will limit their attempts to maximize power. Most economic and ecological interdependence involves the possibility of joint gains, or joint losses. Mutual awareness of potential gains and losses and the danger of worsening each actor's position through overly rigorous struggles over the distribution of the gains can limit the use of asymmetrical interdependence.

Agenda Setting
Our second assumption of complex interdependence, the lack of clear hierarchy among multiple issues, leads us to expect that the politics of agenda formation and control will become more important. Traditional analyses lead statesmen to focus on politico-military issues and to pay little attention to the broader politics of agenda formation. Statesmen assume that the agenda will be set by shifts in the balance of power, actual or anticipated, and by perceived threats to the security of states. Other issues will only be very important when they seem to affect security and military power. In these cases, agendas will be influenced strongly by considerations of the overall balance of power.

Yet, today, some nonmilitary issues are emphasized in interstate relations at one time, whereas others of seemingly equal importance are neglected or quietly handled at a technical level. International monetary politics, problems of commodity terms of trade, oil, food, and multinational corporations have all been important during the last decade; but not all have been high on interstate agendas throughout that period.

Traditional analysts of international politics have paid little attention to agenda formation: to how issues come to receive sustained attention by high officials. The traditional orientation toward military and security affairs implies that the crucial problems of foreign policy are imposed on states by the actions or threats of other states. These are high politics as opposed to the low politics of economic affairs. Yet, as the complexity of actors and issues in world politics increases, the utility of force declines and the line between domestic policy and foreign policy becomes blurred: as the conditions of complex interdependence are more closely approximated, the politics of agenda formation becomes more subtle and differentiated.

Under complex interdependence we can expect the agenda to be affected by . . . international and domestic problems created by economic growth and increasing sensitivity interdependence. . . .Discontented domestic groups will politicize issues and force more issues once considered domestic onto the interstate agenda. Shifts in the distribution of power resources within sets of issues will also affect agendas. During the early

1970s the increased power of oil-producing governments over the transnational corporations and the consumer countries dramatically altered the policy agenda. Moreover, agendas for one group of issues may change as a result of linkages from other groups in which power resources are changing; for example, the broader agenda of North-South trade issues changed ofter the OPEC price rises and the oil embargo of 1973–74. Even if capabilities among states do not change, agendas may be affected by shifts in the importance of transnational actors. The publicity surrounding multinational corporations in the early 1970s, coupled with their rapid growth over the past twenty years, put the regulation of such corporations higher on both the United Nations agenda and national agendas.

Politicization—agitation and controversy over an issue that tend to raise it to the top of the agenda—can have many sources, as we have seen. Governments whose strength is increasing may politicize issues, by linking them to other issues. An international regime that is becoming ineffective or is not serving important issues may cause increasing politicization, as dissatisfied governments press for change. Politicization, however, can also come from below. Domestic groups may become upset enough to raise a dormant issue, or to interfere with interstate bargaining at high levels. In 1974 the American secretary of state's tacit linkage of a Soviet-American trade pact with progress in détente was upset by the success of domestic American groups working through Congress to link a trade agreement with Soviet policies on emigration.

The technical characteristics and institutional setting in which issues are raised will strongly affect politicization patterns. In the United States, congressional attention is an effective instrument of politicization. Generally, we expect transnational economic organizations and transgovernmental networks of bureaucrats to seek to avoid politicization. Domestically based groups (such as trade unions) and domestically oriented bureaucracies will tend to use politicization (particularly congressional attention) against their transnationally mobile competitors. At the international level, we expect states and actors to "shop among forums" and struggle to get issues raised in international organizations that will maximize their advantage by broadening or narrowing the agenda.

Transnational and Transgovernmental Relations

Our third condition of complex interdependence, multiple channels of contact among societies, further blurs the distinction between domestic and international politics. The availability of partners in political coalitions is not necessarily limited by national boundaries as traditional analysis assumes. The nearer a situation is to complex interdependence, the more we expect the outcomes of political bargaining to be affected by transnational relations. Multinational corporations may be significant both as independent actors and as instruments manipulated by governments. The attitudes and policy stands of domestic groups are likely to be affected by communications, organized or not, between them and their counterparts abroad.

Thus the existence of multiple channels of contact leads us to expect limits beyond those normally found in domestic politics, on the ability of statesmen to calculate the manipulation of interdependence or follow a consistent strategy of linkage. Statesmen must consider differential as well as aggregate effects of interdependence strategies and their likely implications for politicization and agenda control. Transactions among societies— economic and social transactions more than security ones—affect groups differently. Opportunities and costs from increased transnational ties may be greater for certain groups—for instance, American workers in the textile or shoe industries—than for others. Some organizations or groups may interact directly with actors in other societies or with other governments to increase their benefits from a network of interaction. Some actors may therefore be less vulnerable as well as less sensitive to changes elsewhere in the network than are others, and this will affect patterns of political action.

The multiple channels of contact found in complex interdependence are not limited to nongovernmental actors. Contacts between governmental bureaucracies charged with similar tasks may not only alter their perspectives but lead to transgovernmental coalitions on particular policy questions. To improve their chances of success, government agencies attempt to bring actors from other governments into their own decision-making processes as allies. Agencies of powerful states such as the United States have used such coalitions to penetrate weaker governments. . . . They have also been used to help agencies of other governments penetrate the United States bureaucracy.[11] . . .

The existence of transgovernmental policy networks leads to a different interpretation of one of the standard propositions about international politics—that states act in their own interest. Under complex interdependence, this conventional wisdom begs two important questions: which self and which interest? A government agency may pursue its own interests under the guise of the national interest; and recurrent interactions can change official perceptions of their interests. As a careful study of the politics of United States trade policy has documented, concentrating only on pressures of various interests for decisions leads to an overly mechanistic view of a continuous process and neglects the important role of communications in slowly changing perceptions of self-interest.[12]

The ambiguity of the national interest raises serious problems for the top political leaders of governments. As bureaucracies contact each other directly across national borders (without going through foreign offices), centralized control becomes more difficult. There is less assurance that the state will be united when dealing with foreign governments or that its components will interpret national interests similarly when negotiating with foreigners. The state may prove to be multifaceted, even schizophrenic. National interests will be defined differently on different issues, at different times, and by different governmental units. States that are better placed to maintain their coherence (because of a centralized political tradition such as France's) will be better able to manipulate uneven interdependence than fragmented states that at first glance seem to have more resources in an issue area.

Role of International Organizations

Finally, the existence of multiple channels leads one to predict a different and significant role for international organizations in world politics. Realists in the tradition of Hans J. Morgenthau have portrayed a world in which states, acting from self-interest, struggle for "power and peace." Security issues are dominant; war threatens. In such a world, one may assume that international institutions will have a minor role, limited by the rare congruence of such interests. International organizations are then clearly peripheral to world politics. But in a world of multiple issues imperfectly linked, in which coalitions are formed transnationally and transgovernmentally, the potential role of international institutions in political bargaining is greatly increased. In particular, they help set the international agenda, and act as catalysts for coalition-formation and as arenas for political initiatives and linkage by weak states.

Governments must organize themselves to cope with the flow of business generated by international organizations. By defining the salient issues, and deciding which issues can be grouped together, organizations may help to determine governmental priorities and the nature of interdepartmental committees and other arrangements within governments. The 1972 Stockholm Environment Conference strengthened the position of environmental agencies in various governments. The 1974 World Food Conference focused the attention of important parts of the United States government on prevention of food shortages. The September 1975 United Nations special session on proposals for a New International Economic Order generated an intragovernmental debate about policies toward the Third World in general. The International Monetary Fund and the General Agreement on Tariffs and Trade have focused governmental activity on money and trade instead of on private direct investment, which has no comparable international organization.

By bringing officials together, international organizations help to activate potential coalitions in world politics. It is quite obvious that international organizations have been very important in bringing together representatives of less developed countries, most of which do not maintain embassies in one another's capitals. Third World strategies of solidarity among poor countries have been developed in and for a series of international conferences mostly under the auspices of the United Nations.[13] International organizations also allow agencies of governments, which might not otherwise come into contact, to turn potential or tacit coalitions into explicit transgovernmental coalitions characterized by direct communications. In some cases, international secretariats deliberately promote this process by forming coalitions with groups of governments, or with units of governments, as well as with nongovernmental organizations having similar interests.[14]

International organizations are frequently congenial institutions for weak states. The one-state-one-vote norm of the United Nations system favors coalitions of the small and powerless. Secretariats are often responsive to Third World demands. Furthermore, the substantive norms of most international organizations, as they have developed over the years, stress social and economic equity as well as the equality of states. Past resolutions expressing Third World positions, sometimes agreed to with reservations by industrialized countries, are used to legitimize other demands. These agreements are rarely binding, but up to a point the norms of the institution make opposition look more harshly self-interested and less defensible.

International organizations also allow small and weak states to pursue linkage strategies. In the discussions on a New International Economic Order, Third World states insisted on linking oil price and availability to other questions on which they had traditionally been unable to achieve their

POLITICAL PROCESSES UNDER CONDITIONS OF REALISM AND COMPLEX INTERDEPENDENCE

	Realism	Complex interdependence
Goals of actors	Military security will be the dominant goal.	Goals of states will vary by issue area. Transgovernmental politics will make goals difficult to define. Transnational actors will pursue their own goals.
Instruments of state policy	Military force will be most effective, although economic and other instruments will also be used.	Power resources specific to issue areas will be most relevant. Manipulation of interdependence, international organizations, and transnational actors will be major instruments.
Agenda formation	Potential shifts in the balance of power and security threats will set the agenda in high politics and will strongly influence other agendas.	Agenda will be affected by changes in the distribution of power resources within issue areas; the status of international regimes; changes in the importance of transnational actors; linkages from other issues and politicization as a result of rising sensitivity interdependence.
Linkages of issues	Linkages will reduce differences in outcomes among issue areas and reinforce international hierarchy.	Linkages by strong states will be more difficult to make since force will be ineffective. Linkages by weak states through international organizations will erode rather than reinforce hierarchy.
Roles of international organizations	Roles are minor, limited by state power and the importance of military force.	Organizations will set agendas, induce coalition-formation, and act as arenas for political action by weak states. Ability to choose the organizational forum for an issue and to mobilize votes will be an important political resource.

objectives. . . . [S]mall and weak states have also followed a strategy of linkage in the series of Law of the Sea conferences sponsored by the United Nations.

Complex interdependence therefore yields different political patterns than does the realist conception of the world. [The preceding table] summarizes these differences. Thus, one would expect traditional theories to fail to explain international regime change in situations of complex interdependence. But, for a situation that approximates realist conditions, traditional theories should be appropriate. . . .

NOTES

1. Hans J. Morgenthau, *Politics Among Nations: The Struggle for Power and Peace*, 4th ed. (New York: Knopf, 1967), p. 36.
2. See Edward L. Morse, "Transnational Economic Processes," in Robert O. Keohane and Joseph S. Nye, Jr. (eds.), *Transnational Relations and World Politics* (Cambridge, Mass.: Harvard University Press, 1972).
3. Henry A. Kissinger, "A New National Partnership," *Department of State Bulletin*, February 17, 1975, p. 199.
4. See the report of the Commission on the Organization of the Government for the Conduct of Foreign Policy (Murphy Commission) (Washington, D.C.: U.S. Government Printing Office, 1975), and the studies prepared for that report. See also Raymond Hopkins, "The International Role of 'Domestic' Bureaucracy," *International Organization* 30, no. 3 (Summer 1976).
5. *New York Times*, May 22, 1975.
6. For a valuable discussion, see Klaus Knorr, *The Power of Nations: The Political Economy of International Relations* (New York: Basic Books, 1975).
7. *Business Week*, January 13, 1975.
8. Stanley Hoffmann, "The Acceptability of Military Force," and Laurence Martin, "The Utility of Military Force," in *Force in Modern Societies: Its Place in International Politics* (Adelphi Paper, International Institute for Strategic Studies, 1973). See also Knorr, *The Power of Nations*.
9. Henry Brandon, *The Retreat of American Power* (New York: Doubleday, 1974), P. 218.
10. *International Implications of the New Economic Policy*, U.S. Congress, House of Representatives, Committee on Foreign Affairs, Subcommittee on Foreign Economic Policy, Hearings, September 16, 1971.
11. For a more detailed discussion, see Robert O. Keohane and Joseph S. Nye, Jr., "Transgovernmental Relations and International Organizations," *World Politics* 27, no. 1 (October 1974): 39–62.
12. Raymond Bauer, Ithiel de Sola Pool, and Lewis Dexter, *American Business and Foreign Policy* (New York: Atherton, 1963) chap. 35, esp. pp. 472–75.
13. Branislav Gosovic and John Gerard Ruggie, "On the Creation of a New International Economic Order: Issue Linkage and the Seventh Special Session of the UN General Assembly," *International Organization* 30, no. 2 (Spring 1976): 309–46.
14. Robert W. Cox, "The Executive Head," *International Organization* 23, no. 2 (Spring 1969): 205–30.

10

THE INTERNATIONAL ECONOMY
U.S. Role in a World Market

A STAFF STUDY FOR THE JOINT ECONOMIC COMMITTEE, U.S. CONGRESS

The United States emerged from World War II as the world's preeminent military, political, and economic power. The American industrial base had been broadened and modernized by war while the industrial plant of America's allies and adversaries had been virtually destroyed. America was self-sufficient in most key raw materials, including petroleum, and had only limited economic ties to the rest of the world.

The end of the war, however, marked the beginning of a new era in U.S. international economic policy. Profound global economic and political changes gradually transformed the position of the United States from relative economic independence to much greater involvement with, and even dependence on, the economies of other countries. Of the many economic changes in the 1970's, one stands out above the others: the eight-fold jump in U.S. oil import prices from 1973 to 1979. After decades of cheap abundance, the soaring cost and restricted supply of oil threatened to limit world economic expansion.

Among other significant changes were the following:
- Worldwide development of chronic inflation plagued governments and citizens.
- A slowdown in world economic growth, following a long period of rapid rise, coincided with increased competition in world markets.
- The Bretton Woods system of fixed exchange rates tied to the dollar and gold expired, to be replaced by flexible rates with intermittent governmental intervention largely based on perceived national interests.
- Sharp fluctuations in the dollar exchange rate and the emergence of other strong currencies contributed, and will continue to contribute,

From U.S. Congress, Joint Economic Committee, Special Study on Economic Change, *The International Economy: U.S. Role in a World Market*, December, 1980.

to a gradual reduction in the role of the dollar as the world's primary monetary reserve unit.

- The United States swung from a position of trade surpluses during most of the postwar period to one of heavy deficits in the late 1970's, because of the cost of oil imports and other fundamental factors, including poor productivity performance.
- Multinational corporations and banks extended their industrial and financial operations in markets throughout the world.
- The colonial system came to an end, replaced by a multiplicity of new independent states concerned with raising living standards and improving their economic positions.
- Technical production skills spread to the developing countries, reducing the traditional comparative advantage of the older industrialized economies.
- Control over the major reserves of world mineral resources by the less developed countries sharpened the conflict with consuming countries over the supply and prices of basic commodities and raised the possibility of competition among the major powers for access to these resources.
- The countries of Eastern Europe, the Soviet Union, and the People's Republic of China gradually moved toward integration with the world economy.

While America's strategic position in the Western alliance remains largely unchanged, the emergence of a number of other economic and political powers . . . has diffused its economic and political influence. At the same time, the creation of myriad economic ties among the world's nations has made them sufficiently dependent on a regular flow of trade and capital so that their domestic economic policies increasingly are constrained by the flux of international markets and by decisions made in other capitals. Unfortunately, this growing economic interdependence has not brought with it greater political harmony, as evidenced by the differences between the industrialized "North" and the developing "South."

By the close of the 1950's, the dozens of new postwar nations began to exert their own political and economic influence in world affairs. Several developing countries have become major manufacturers and are likely to be competitors for world markets in the 1980's. A few oil-rich developing countries have generated immense financial surpluses and have become an important force in the international financial system.

The Position of the United States

As the world has changed, so has America's place in it. Where America was once self-sufficient in key natural resources, it now imports more than 20 percent of its total energy needs and is even more dependent on imports of other raw materials. Developing countries have become important sources of low-priced manufactured goods and also markets for a large and growing share of America's manufactured exports. The American-based multinational corporation has spread American capital, technology, and management techniques throughout the world. The flow of repatriated profits from foreign investments has helped limit the size of U.S. current account deficits, and thus has helped strengthen the dollar's exchange rate. Major capital centers are so closely linked and flows of capital so large that independent monetary policy has become difficult even for the United States.

In all cases, the U.S. response to the impact of external events on the domestic economy has been constrained by the fact that the United States is an "open economy" fully integrated into a world trade and monetary system characterized by flexible but managed exchange rates and considerable capital mobility—the ease which investments may be made both here (by foreigners) and abroad (by Americans).

The total of American transactions with the rest of the world—the balance of payments—can be measured in various ways. Probably the most meaningful is the current account, which includes all transactions except international loans and other inflows and outflows of capital. Within the current account, the most important single item is the balance of export and import trade in goods, but a trade deficit can be offset by surpluses in other accounts, including various service transactions and the remittance of profits from foreign investment made in previous years.

In the 20 years 1960–79, with surpluses in some years and deficits in others, the United States had a modest net current account surplus of about $30 billion, though in the . . . period of 1975–79 there [was] a deficit of about $6.5 billion. While in many periods inflows and outflows of capital can swamp the current account results, over the long run the current account measures the productive competitiveness of the economy and tends to determine the dollar's exchange rate. Had the U.S. current account been stronger in the past 20 years, the dollar's exchange rate would not have depreciated against the other leading currencies, as it did during the decade of the 1970's. Although this depreciation was probably unavoidable and helped to bring the trade and other accounts back toward balance, it also was a factor in the serious inflation problem in the United States by adding to the cost of imports and domestically produced goods competitive with imports or subject to export demand.

Therefore, concern over the balance of payments and, particularly, U.S. international competitiveness is understandable. The [United States] must produce more if it is to earn more and consume more. A key area of concern is lagging productivity, or output per hour worked.

U.S. productivity, after a long moderate advance, not only has slowed but, most recently, even fallen. At the same time, other nations have gained in productivity per person employed. For example, in the last three decades, Japan has multiplied its productivity four times as rapidly as the United

States. Japanese output per person employed rose from about 15 percent of the U.S. level in 1950 to 63 percent in 1978. West Germany, France, and Italy each more than doubled the rate of productivity advance of the United States. The Netherlands and Belgium advanced about three-fifths faster. Even the United Kingdom, the poorest performer among West Europeans, gained on the United States.

While the relative increase in the economic power of other nations and America's growing dependence on the rest of the world have challenged the traditional concept of American leadership, the United States still enjoys a preeminent position in the world economy. Its per capita income, by most reasonable measures, still averages higher than that of any other advanced country, though the gap has been closing in the last 20 or 30 years. With about one-twentieth of the world's people, the United States has perhaps one-fifth of the world's income.

Compared to other western industrial powers, the United States is rich in resources. The dollar remains the world's leading reserve currency and world trade still focuses on the immense American market. Although trade is a smaller fraction of the U.S. economy than in other countries, the U.S. economy is so large that U.S. exports and imports of all commodities and services will be in the range of $325 billion each way. The "direct" investments of Americans abroad, which involve controlling responsibilities for the production of goods and services, now carry a "book" value, which understates the true value, in excess of $200 billion. In 1980, American income from these direct investments [was projected to] exceed $40 billion. The primary importance of American money and finance in the world economy is suggested by the fact that some two-thirds of all international economic transactions are in U.S. dollars.

Though several other large countries, particularly in Western Europe, approach the United States in current level of per capita income, at least in one respect the situation of the United States is unique. Most of these other countries have stable or declining population and labor forces, and hence can anticipate stable or declining employment needs. The United States, on the other hand, must anticipate an increase in the demand for employment of up to 1.5 percent a year in the 1980's, and perhaps a further increase of about one percent a year in the 1990's.

The natural labor force growth is augmented by the immigration factor. During the 1970's the number of legal immigrants to the United States, including refugees with immigrant status, averaged about 450,000 a year. While there is no exact information on the number of illegal immigrants in the country, estimates range from 3 million to 12 million. The United States must show substantial economic growth in the future—faster than in other industrial nations—merely to keep its growing native and immigrant labor force employed. Thus, while per capita income in the United States may or may not rise relative to the other advanced economies, the absolute size of the U.S. economy is likely to be even larger, compared with the others, than it is today. Despite some loss of relative economic power, the United States will remain a giant by any measure.

[In] the decade of the 1980's . . . the United States confronts a mix of economic problems characterized by inflation, unemployment, slowing growth and productivity. These problems of the domestic economy now are inextricably linked with issues of world-wide economic cooperation as well as competition. The issues include trade with industrialized nations and with middle-income developing countries; oil and energy; aid to the poorest countries and peoples; and capital flows including overseas investment, the international monetary system and international banking. . . .

TRADE ISSUES AND POLICY

Foreign trade policy—typically described in shorthand as "free trade" vs. "protectionism"—has been an issue throughout U.S. history. In the period since World War II, the debate has not ceased, but the clear direction of policy has been toward fewer and lower trade barriers. This is true despite the fact that during the 1970's, the United States experienced a growing deficit in its foreign trade, an oil crisis, several recessions, and a relatively high level of unemployment.

There were, to be sure, several actions of a "protectionist" nature affecting specific products, including such devices as Orderly Marketing Agreements, Voluntary Export Restraints and countervailing duties. But it is fair to say that neither in the Congress nor in the Executive Branch is there now a strong school in favor of a general policy of high tariffs or other devices to protect American industry and agriculture against imports. . . .

International Competitiveness

. . . [T]here have been some profound changes in recent years that have a bearing on U.S. trade policy. Four stand out.

First, the United States has suffered a decline in overall competitiveness in international markets as the other industrial economies grew strongly. For example, throughout the decade of the 1970's, West Germany surpassed the United States as the leading exporter of manufactured goods, a position the United States had held for many years. Germany's lead, a narrow $1.4 billion in 1970, rose to $33.9 billion in 1979, a percentage differential of only 0.5 percent in 1970, but 22 percent in 1979. The value of Japan's manufactured exports, 62 percent of the U.S. level in 1970, rose to 85 percent in 1979. In each case, these gains were not due to significantly lower wage rates, but rather to more rapidly rising productivity coupled with industry and government export promotion efforts.

A corollary is that it is no longer true that the United States must import more in order to provide the world with the dollars needed to buy American exports. The rest of the world has ample dollars. If there is a policy priority now, it is export expansion rather than import expansion. . . .

Second, there is the appearance on the world scene of highly competitive exports of manufactured goods from nations that long have been regarded as "underdeveloped," and are now rapidly industrializing. The star performers in this respect are a handful of Asian countries (South Korea, Taiwan, Hong Kong, Singapore) but a number of others (Brazil, Mexico, India) are becoming important.

In these cases, of course, relatively low wage rates make a significant difference. The result of these two types of competition is that U.S. industry has sustained losses in some industries, such as cutlery and flatware, ceramics and dinnerware, motorcycles and bicycles, footwear, hats, radios, TV, textiles, and apparel. More important in the long run, competition has been growing for domestic and international markets in some of the largest and most basic U.S. industries—steel, some types of machinery, and automobiles.

However, in some manufactured products—especially capital-intensive and high technology goods from heavy power equipment to computers, and certainly in agricultural products—the United States still stands first. In 1979, the United States had a surplus of $17.9 billion in agricultural exports, a $32 billion surplus in capital goods, with a $30.2 billion deficit in consumer goods. Overall, the U.S. share of the world's exports of manufactures has declined in line with the decline in the U.S. share of world GNP, as the economies of other countries have grown faster than America's.

Despite a slower growth in U.S. exports of manufactures than has been the typical experience of other industrial countries, these exports have grown nonetheless, reinforcing the continued strong performance of agricultural exports which rose from less than $10 billion to $35 billion in the last decade. The large deficit in the overall trade balance in the later years of the decade was accounted for by the dramatic increase in the *price* of imported oil; after rising steadily, the *volume* of oil imports had begun to decline as the decade ended. While the oil imports generated some offsetting exports to the OPEC countries, the fact remains that if the cost of oil imports had been the same at the end of the decade as it was at the beginning, the U.S. trade accounts could well have been in surplus, though the balance will always fluctuate from year to year in response to cyclical influences here and abroad. . . .

Third, the move of the world economy toward far more flexible currency exchange rates has greatly changed the meaning of familiar trade-influencing devices such as tariffs. The day to day price of internationally traded goods to the importer—and hence their competitiveness against home-produced products—now is typically a function more of fluctuations of exchange rates than of small changes in the rate of duty. . . .

The move to flexible exchange rates, with its accompanying depreciation of the dollar—primarily in the first half of the 1970's—tended to correct that part of the U.S. problem of competitiveness that arose from an over-valued dollar. But it did not completely halt the downward drift of the U.S. share in total world exports of manufactures.

Fourth, world trade—aided by the anti-protectionist climate that generally prevailed both at home and abroad—has grown spectacularly, rising substantially faster than world output. In the United States the share of both exports and imports in GNP has almost doubled in the past 10 years: In the case of movable goods (leaving out services), each now represents about one-fifth of U.S. total output. A similar pattern holds for other countries. France, for example, had a highly protected economy for centuries and now, thanks in part to the European Common Market, has become a more open economy, though a number of trade barriers remain, particularly in agriculture and some high technology industries.

While this growth of world trade undoubtedly has been of great benefit to the general welfare and prosperity, it also poses a new kind of problem. As exports make up a higher and higher share of each nation's production, more and more jobs depend on them. And thus the temptation grows to promote exports through various government devices, including outright subsidies; in the cases of individual firms, the need to obtain and retain markets abroad creates a strong inducement for "dumping."

In general, the United States is likely to face increased competition for both international and domestic markets. Japan and Western Europe are intent on challenging America's lead where it still exists—in aircraft, computers and some other high-technology areas. And competition certainly will not lessen in the area of consumer goods and the more traditional manufactures such as steel, particularly where there is excess capacity in the world. Future competition, of course, includes that to be expected from the newly industrializing or "middle income" developing countries.

U.S. Policy Choices

These changes do not undermine the traditional merits of freer trade—enhanced competition at home, benefits for consumers in wider choice, improvements in the general welfare from international specialization. But they do make policy choices for the United States somewhat different from what they used to be.

One choice . . . goes under the name of "fair" trade and amounts to a decision that the United States will be prepared to act firmly against imports that are subsidized or dumped, provided only that these reports can be shown to injure domestic producers. Subsidies in particular now take a wide variety of forms. Some of them . . . ostensibly are designed to achieve only domestic purposes in the home country rather than to help exports as such. Thus, subjective judgments are unavoidably involved in each specific case of requested relief, but there is no longer a presumption that imports are to be encouraged, and import restraints foregone, under any and all circumstances. . . .

Another policy issue raised by the new world trading situation is ironic, in the light of history. One of the chief reasons for establishment of the International Monetary Fund and a set of rules for the world monetary system—chiefly exchange rate rules—was the fear of "competitive depreciation" of currencies, such as had been practiced in the years of the Great Depression of the 1930's. Now, in an age of inflation, that no longer is the problem. Nations are reluctant to devalue—even if such a move helps exports—because a downward change in the exchange rate makes domestic inflation worse. Today's problem is different, though analogous. The typical international "sinner" today is the nation that refused to let its exchange rate rise, for fear of harming its export industries. To the extent that a nation—through intervention on the foreign exchange markets or controls on incoming flows of capital—prevents appreciation of its exchange rate that otherwise would occur, it is in a real sense subsidizing its exports and penalizing imports, and thus hurting other nations.... [T]he problem of exchange rate manipulation will be a continuing one in the years ahead, and it is as much a problem of trade policy as of international monetary policy.

Agricultural Trade
One trade policy problem has not changed, but a kind of resignation has settled in about dealing with it. Practically every nation in the world has treated agriculture as a special case in trade policy, maintaining many kinds of instruments such as variable levies and outright quotas to protect domestic farmers against cheaper imports. With the possible exception of New Zealand, the United States has been the greatest sufferer from this stubborn refusal of the world to risk agricultural free trade, simply because the United States is the most efficient producer of a wide range of agricultural products, particularly grains. However, the United States does not have completely clean hands because it, too, has rigid protection in some items, such as dairy products.

American negotiators have fought a long, and only partially successful, battle in a series of trade negotiations lasting for three decades to improve access for U.S. farm products in foreign markets, particularly the markets of Europe and Japan. But while foreign barriers remain, U.S. agricultural exports have risen impressively all the same, as noted earlier. This is because of sharply improved U.S. productivity in agriculture, which holds down U.S. costs, and because the rest of the world needs more food. Even if domestic farmers in foreign countries are guaranteed the opportunity to sell their products first, making the United States a kind of residual supplier, demand growth has been so great that U.S. exports have continued to increase.

The welfare of the world's consumers of food has not been well served by the combination of domestic support prices and import barriers that is the farm policy in most of the world. In theory and in practice, agricultural free trade would mean cheaper food nearly everywhere. But there are powerful social and political reasons for the present state of affairs, and a major change cannot be regarded as probable.

Imports from Developing Countries
Probably the most difficult trade policy issue in the years ahead . . . will involve imports of manufactured goods from the "middle income" (and a few "low income") developing countries. . . . [T]he single greatest contribu-

tion the United States can make to the economic advancement of these countries—far greater than "foreign aid"—is to maintain and increase U.S. imports from them.

Furthermore, the U.S. record has been good to date, despite some import restraints such as those on textiles from nearly all countries and on televisions from South Korea and Taiwan. Excluding oil, imports from the developing countries have approximately quintupled in the last decade, reaching almost $45 billion in 1979.

The problem has arisen when the volume and variety of these imports begin to have a larger impact across U.S. industry. While many elements enter into the cost of foreign goods, there is no doubt that labor costs in these countries will continue indefinitely to be far lower than those at home or in other industrial countries. . . . If current practice is followed, it is clear the export volume to the United States from the poorer countries will continue to grow. . . .

Trade with Communist Countries

Two other trade policy issues are not new but are likely to provoke continued attention. The first involves trade with the Communist countries, where the price and availability of any product are not fixed by the market, or even by costs, but by the state. Political factors have taken precedence over economic factors in determining trade decisions with Communist countries. . . . This is as it should be and must be. Moreover, for the foreseeable future—even apart from political factors such as the state of U.S. relations with the Soviet Union—there will be limits on the volume of this trade that are set by the ability of the Communist countries to sell desirable goods in the U.S. market; that is, given the general desire of these countries for "balanced" trade, U.S. exports cannot for long exceed, in a major way, its imports; and imports are limited more by what is offered than by special trade barriers applied to goods from these countries. It would be poor policy—and is unlikely in any event—for the United States to depend on Communist sources for a substantial portion of its supply of any product, though exceptions may have to be made in the case of a few raw materials. Furthermore, while there have been few cases thus far, U.S. law properly provides special remedies against injury to domestic producers caused by imports from those countries, where the price may be set independently of the cost of production. Trade with Communist countries in the years ahead no doubt will continue to pose a series of specific policy choices (grain embargoes, most-favored-nation tariff treatment, exports of goods embodying high technology), but it seems safe to say, figuratively speaking, that the volume of headlines will exceed the volume of trade. . . .

General Agreement on Tariffs and Trade

. . . U.S. trade policy in the years since World War II has been dominated by a series of "rounds" of general international trade negotiations, conducted under the auspices of the General Agreement on Tariffs and Trade (GATT) in Geneva. . . .

The most recent Tokyo round was concluded in 1978. . . . Along with a further reduction of tariffs (which are now in general quite low in all the industrial countries), the latest round produced agreement on a new set of trading codes in such areas as subsidies, custom valuation procedures, and government procurement, though it did not solve all problems in the area of nontariff barriers to trade. It seems probable that the years ahead will see a focus on the gradual development of "case law" under these codes, including numerous individual points of friction, rather than any new effort at a general trade negotiations.

It is possible that if sluggish growth and rising unemployment persist among the industrial countries in the years ahead, there could emerge a fundamental change in trade policy around the world in the direction of protectionism. Despite many fears, and a few publicized cases of new trade barriers, this has not been the case so far, as the continued strong growth of world trade testifies. The interest of the United States continues to lie in a generally open trading world. . . .

THE CHANGING WORLD OF INTERNATIONAL FINANCE

At the end of World War II, the major financial powers, particularly the United States and the United Kingdom, established a new kind of gold standard. Under the Bretton Woods Agreement of 1944, the value of other currencies was stated in terms of dollars, and dollars were in turn linked to a fixed quantity of gold at $35 an ounce. Under this system the dollar became the principal source of international reserves.

The Dollar as a Reserve Currency
The structure of the Bretton Woods system contained several serious flaws. Pressures for adjustment fell largely on countries experiencing balance of payments deficits rather than on those in a surplus position. Exchange rate changes, though permitted by the system, proved politically difficult, even when clearly needed. It was particularly difficult for the key currency country, in this case the United States, to react effectively to a persistent payment imbalance, and it was almost impossible to devalue the dollar.

A steady expansion of international reserves was needed to finance a rapidly growing volume of international transactions. Persistent deficits could supply a steady stream of dollars, but also acted to reduce the durability of the dollar as a financial asset.

The Bretton Woods system was under attack throughout the 1960's. The demise of the system came when dollar convertibility into gold was abruptly terminated in August 1971. By 1973, the principal financial powers had abandoned the relatively fixed rate system of Bretton Woods for one of flexible or freely floating rates with currencies moving in response to supply and demand for each currency.

There had been some expectation that the need for international reserves would be greatly reduced under the flexible exchange rate system, but that has not been the case. Part of the reason is that nations have continued to feel the need to intervene in foreign exchange market trading which requires reserves.

The dollar is still the world's principal reserve asset and is likely to remain so through the [1980s], chiefly because the alternatives to dollar assets appear quite limited. At the same time, the world appears to be moving hesitantly in the direction of a multi-reserve currency system. The movement to flexible exchange rates has made it desirable for central banks as well as private corporations to reduce their exchange rate risk by holding a portfolio of currencies. Next to the dollar, the largest "reserve currency"— private and public—is probably the pound sterling, but the United Kingdom, understandably, does not want to play a major role. Germany, Japan, and Switzerland, the only other major candidates for shared reserve responsibilities, have been reluctant to accept the limitations that come with managing a reserve currency. . . .

The world may also turn again to the IMF to provide a managed increase in world reserves. Dollar instability in the late 1970's had spawned discussion of a new IMF facility where official holders of dollars could exchange them for an updated version of Special Drawing Rights (SDRs). The proposal for this substitution account stalled over questions of how liquid the SDRs would be, what interest rate they would carry and who would bear the risk of loss should the dollar depreciate relative to the SDR. Dollar recovery and American financial restraint in 1979 and 1980 reduced the pressure for movement away from the dollar, but the proposal could be renewed at a later date.

Flexible Exchange Rate Policy

The purpose of exchange rate policy should be to facilitate international transactions at a level and composition which result in a desired balance of payments. The optimum balance may be in surplus or in deficit, depending upon the phase of the business cycle, special factors such as oil imports, or the state of the country's development and its need and attraction for imported capital.

There is an additional burden on the United States, as the dollar has a role beyond simply that of a national currency. Because the dollar is still the world's major reserve currency, and the vehicle by which many transactions by third countries are carried out, changes in the dollar exchange rate can have worldwide effect. Thus, the Canadian dollar was allowed to float from 1950 to 1962 without upsetting confidence in the world economy. A floating U.S. dollar, however, affects the purchasing power of persons and firms in every trading country. . . .

In its simplest form, there are two parts to an exchange rate policy: What the existing rate should be, and the conditions under which the existing rate should be allowed to change. Factors which affect an appropriate existing rate include the composition of trade flows, elasticities of demand for various products, and domestic conditions such as the unemployment rate and inflation rate. However, this "appropriate" rate would be the same whether one operated under a fixed or a floating rate regime. What is new about floating rates, therefore, is that they change under different conditions than do fixed rates.

During the 28 years of the Bretton Woods system, "fundamental disequilibrium" was the term used to describe the conditions under which changes in exchange rates were permissible. Members of the International Monetary Fund were to refrain from changing the par value of their currency except to correct a fundamental disequilibrium. Under a floating rate regime, changes in exchange rates are generally determined by market perceptions about underlying economic trends, or about the intentions of government either in correcting those trends or in intervening in the exchange markets.

The important difference in the two systems is that they pose a different set of constraints for domestic economic policy. Under fixed rates, international economic events posed constraints on domestic economic policy largely through two related channels: Balance of payments developments and gains/losses in monetary reserves. In other words, domestic policy remained relatively free from international pressures, so long as these pressures did not exceed the ability of a nation's central bank to keep its currency within its allowable margin of exchange rate fluctuation.

In the U.S. case, the ultimate constraint was the level of the gold reserves.

The hope of those who supported a floating rate regime was that domestic policy would be free of these kinds of constraints. The floating rate system was theoretically designed to yield automatically a value for each currency which would ultimately result in balance-of-payments equilibrium. Policymakers have come to learn, however, that exchange rate appreciation or depreciation do constitute a major restraint on domestic policy. Furthermore, since exchange rates are the link between prices and costs in the United States and in other countries, a floating system means that the link is more immediate, and that the connection between domestic and international policy is more direct. This means that domestic monetary policy changes—especially changes which affect interest rate levels—show up rapidly in the form of exchange rate changes.

Fiscal policy, too, is closely linked to the dollar exchange rate. Under flexible rates, domestic expansion led by fiscal policy changes directly affects exchange rate expectations, which in turn erode the value of the dollar in the foreign exchange markets. This depreciation can take place even before the fiscal policy changes have had a measurable effect on aggregate demand. Thus, import prices, and the prices of domestically produced goods competing with those imports, can influence the rate of inflation before domestic fiscal policy has had a chance to spur employment. In this sense . . . the inflation/unemployment tradeoff is worsened under a flexible exchange rate system.

Exchange rate policy for the United States, then, encompasses elements of domestic as well as international policy. The present system demands greater attention to price stability than previously.

Despite this problem virtually all economists agree that the major changes in the international economy since the OPEC oil price hikes in 1973–74 could have been accommodated only with a floating exchange rate system. There is no way that IMF member governments could have arrived at realistic fixed exchange rates in a setting where the composition and volume of trade flows, and the prices of individual products, were changing so rapidly from month to month. What was necessary at that time was an international exchange rate system where changes in domestic economic conditions could be translated rapidly and efficiently into exchange rate changes. The death of the Bretton Woods came not a year too soon.

In its administration, the system of flexible exchange rates has not been ideal. The economist's model of a system where changes in underlying conditions are translated efficiently into exchange rate changes is obviously not taking place in the real world. Most economists predicted that rate changes would ordinarily be gradual, and approximately equal to differences in inflation rates between the United States and its major trading partners. But equilibrating forces have not been as automatic as had been hoped and there have been some unexpected turns. For example, between March 1973 and September 1975, there were six occasions when the dollar exchange rates for most of the major currencies rose or fell sharply in the course of a few months, sometimes by 20 percent or more. At the end of the 30-month period, the dollar exchange rates for these currencies were not substantially different from what they had been in the beginning. Underlying economic conditions do not change so much so quickly, nor do they reverse themselves so completely. It is probable that the exchange rate gyrations served simply to clear markets dominated by speculative expectations.

In addition, many third world countries have linked their currencies to the currency of a major industrial country which is a major trading partner in order to avoid the inevitable price distortions which would result if the link were not so direct. This means, however, that changes in the dollar exchange rate could affect the value of the Pakistani rupee and the Venezuelan bolivar against European currencies and the yen even if Pakistan and Venezuela were not experiencing major shifts in underlying economic conditions.

Another assumption by economists was that trade flows—the major evidence of international competitiveness—would follow changes in exchange rates and thus adjust a country's balance of payments at an equilibrium level more or less automatically. This assumption, also, was mistaken. A sharp depreciation of the dollar via-à-vis other major currencies could show up in domestic price changes as much as trade flows, as domestic producers who compete with foreign manufacturers simply raise their prices rather than attempt to gain additional market shares. This inflationary effect of currency depreciation has been shown, as a practical matter, to be the more dominant one over the short term. What this means is that many imports—which should become more expensive and thus less attractive with depreciation—instead become no less price competitive than the domestically produced product, but still are more expensive. This results in a worsening of the balance of payments over the short term, even though exchange rate depreciation is probably helpful over the long term. This effect is a practical reality which must be taken into account by policymakers. It complicates the balance of payments picture, since foreign exchange markets will respond to these short-term phenomena. For example, the sharp depreciation of the dollar in 1977–78 aggravated rather than helped the U.S. balance of payments during that period.

It was also assumed that government intervention or nonintervention in the foreign exchange markets would be accurately interpreted by the market participants, thus reinforcing exchange rate stability and helping to adjust automatically these countries' balance of payments. However, the enormous fall of the foreign exchange value of the dollar between the end of September 1977 and the end of October 1978 was proof that the passive exchange rate policy of the U.S. monetary authorities was being wrongly interpreted. It took a set of major changes in U.S. policy—beginning on November 1, 1978—to bring about exchange market conditions which more closely reflected the true value of the dollar vis-à-vis other important currencies. Apart from the sometimes perverse effects of intervention or nonintervention, there is also the enormous impact of capital flows that can occur for a variety of reasons, of which interest rate differentials are an important one. As another example of why capital can move, a sharp increase in political risk in Europe could lead to large flows of investment into the United States which in turn would increase the international value of the dollar; U.S. exports would then become somewhat less competitive. The fact is that capital flows, whatever their underlying motivation, can have a sharp impact on exchange rates and thus competitiveness, regardless of trade or current account balances.

Three major conclusions can be drawn from the evidence:

First, a pragmatic foreign exchange rate policy will demand greater exchange rate oversight by U.S. monetary authorities under the present system than under any system of fixed or partially fixed rates. . . . The evidence suggests that widely fluctuating exchange rates have an inflationary effect on the domestic economy; therefore, exchange rate stability is as much a matter of domestic as of international policy. . . .

Second, the link between U.S. inflation and world economic instability is now more direct. This places an extra burden on domestic policymakers to pursue a road of reducing price inflation even at the expense of the more immediate attainment of some other policy goals. . . . In this respect, the aims of domestic and international policy are roughly coincident.

Third, the world is still a long way from an ideal monetary system in which world aggregate demand and supply—and, thus, worldwide inflation—can be controlled through some form of international monetary cooperation or supranational monetary authority. For perhaps the next several decades or more, the world must depend on an imperfect system while getting used to the fact that the freedom of domestic economic policies of every country is constrained under the present system of flexible exchange rates, possibly even more than previously.

The Eurocurrency Markets

Closely linked to the issues of the efficiency of flexible exchange rates and the role of reserve currencies is the growth of Eurocurrency markets during the 1970's. Of the many changes in international finance, none is as widely visible and as little understood as the Eurocurrency market. It is an important wild card added to the international financial game that has ramifications for policy implementation confusing to companies and countries alike as well as to central and multinational banks. It is no wonder that some of the old rules of thumb are no longer dependable. There is a new type of international money flowing freely around the world which is unresponsive to many of the old policy tools, including exchange controls. . . .

Basically, the common denominator of all Eurocurrencies is that they are deposited outside of their country of issue. Dollars deposited in London, marks deposited in France, or yen deposited in the Bahamas are all conventionally referred to as Eurocurrency deposits. These funds have become a source of borrowed reserves for deficit countries, as well as an investment outlet for the central bank reserves of small countries and the investable surplus of OPEC countries. Thus, in the last decade, these markets and the multinational banks have become increasingly involved in financial and foreign exchange operations which were traditionally the province of central banks and international financial institutions, such as the IMF. This is a significant development quite apart from the extraordinary growth of the Eurocurrency markets and their increasingly central role in financing private trade and investment transactions around the world.

The implications for national economic policy are cloudy but of potentially great importance. Many of the conventional instruments of economic stabilization, taxation, and regulatory oversight cannot reach some of the operations of global banks and non-financial corporations. Indeed, they often choose the multinational route as much to evade regulation and policy restraint as to enhance their corporate efficiency. . . .

The international financial system is yet another realm of economic life where America is now closely tied to the vagaries of the world economy. The weak financial ties and limited trade dependence were the fences that created the good economic neighbors of the past. They no longer exist. . . .

11

THE THIRD WORLD
Exploring U.S. Interests

JOHN W. SEWELL
JOHN A. MATHIESON

At the beginning of the 1980s, relations between the United States and the developing countries seem to have come full circle. Over the preceding three decades, U.S. policy toward the nations that comprise the third world had gone through several phases. First there was a concern with alliances and aid designed to "contain" the Soviet Union. In the 1960s the emphasis shifted toward "nation-building" and winning the "hearts and minds" of people in the third world. The 1970s was a period of relative retreat, as the United States reacted to the Vietnam experience. The preoccupation with domestic problems was tempered only by a dawning awareness of America's dependence on certain developing countries—most notably for petroleum. The realities of dependence strengthened the links between developed and developing countries; at the same time they made the conduct of American foreign policy more difficult.

With the Reagan Administration, which came to office committed to restoring America's economic health and rebuilding its military power, came another shift in emphasis. The Administration tends to view the developing countries primarily as an arena for East-West competition, a drain on scarce U.S. budgetary resources, and potentially unstable sources of key materials that are needed by the United States.

Today's world is very different from the bipolar world of the 1950s and 1960s, when the United States was the preeminent economic, political and military power. The U.S. position in the world economy is no longer unrivaled. Other major industrial countries, notably Japan, West Germany and the other members of the Organization for Economic Cooperation and Development (OECD) have greatly increased their economic competitive-

Reprinted from Headline Series No. 259 (May/June 1982), "The Third World: Exploring U.S. Interests," by John W. Sewell and John A. Mathieson. Copyright 1982 by the Foreign Policy Association. Reprinted with permission. The essay is adapted from a chapter contributed by the authors to a volume entitled *Rich Country Interests and Third World Development* published by Croom Helm Ltd., in Great Britain in 1982. The book is available in the United States from the Overseas Development Council in a limited paperback edition by special arrangement with Croom Helm.

ness. So have a number of developing countries—not only the oil exporters, but such countries as Brazil, South Korea and Taiwan. Consequently, the United States today is far more vulnerable to external economic shocks. Floating exchange rates, competition from imports, increasing reliance on raw materials from abroad and runaway oil prices have all signaled the end of the relative economic independence of the United States. These develop- ments are making many Americans uneasy, and have added to concerns over the domestic performance of the U.S. economy.

Moreover, the United States and most other industrial nations are now beset with a combination of slow growth, high unemployment, and steep inflation. Most economists anticipate only marginal improvements in the economic outlook, and agree that a return to the spectacular growth rates experienced by much of the world in the 1950s and 1960s is unlikely before the mid-1980s, if then. The prospects are for slower growth in international trade (along with increasing pressures for restrictions), continued financial imbalances, and uncertainties in the supply and price of major commodi- ties, such as food and oil.

The international system is far more complex today, in part because of the increased number of nations that are asserting economic and political weight. As recently as 1959 there were only 92 independent countries. By the beginning of the 1980s, the number had grown to 172. All of the new entrants were developing countries which—in some cases individually, and certainly collectively—can affect the interests of the United States in signifi- cant ways.

These countries make up the so-called third world. The "first world" represents the industrial market economies; the "second," the industrial nonmarket economies of the U.S.S.R. and Eastern Europe. The third-world nations are widely diverse in history and culture, economic structure and political orientation. They actually fall into at least four groups, and even within the groups there are notable differences. The 13 members of the Organization of Petroleum Exporting Countries (OPEC) have used their rising oil revenues to expand their economies and gain political leverage. A small number of advanced developing countries, such as Brazil, Mexico and South Korea, have achieved high growth rates and export levels that put them almost in the ranks of the industrial countries. A large number of middle-income developing countries have attained some economic pro- gress, but face many more hurdles on the way to further development. Finally, the poorest nations of South Asia and sub-Saharan Africa, some- times referred to as the "fourth world," have seen little change in their econ- omies over the past few decades. Their prospects are the bleakest in the third world.

Despite their varying needs and potential, the developing countries have exhibited a remarkable degree of unity vis-à-vis the industrial nations in international negotiations. In this "dialogue," the developing countries have become known collectively as the South, since most (but not all) of them lie in the Southern Hemisphere. The industrial countries have been collectively termed the North, since most (but again not all) are in the Northern Hemisphere.

For the past two decades the developing countries have been calling for reform of an international economic system they contend is inequitable. Their proposals—first formally presented at the United Nations in 1974—call for a New International Economic Order (NIEO). The demand is for comprehensive changes in rules governing trade and investment and in financial institutions like the International Monetary Fund (IMF). The rationale lies in the third world's dissatisfaction with the distribution of power, wealth and income among developed and developing countries. These gaps were first attributed to colonialism, but when political independence did not yield rapid economic gains, third-world leaders began to focus on inequities in the international economic system itself. The NIEO proposals cover a wide range: commodity-price-stabilization mechanisms; increased access to industrial-country markets for third-world exports; international monetary reform; cancellation or rescheduling of debt on a case-by-case basis; codes of conduct for multinational corporations; and, in general, greater third-world representation and voting power in international institutions.

The third world's quest for reform has met with mixed success. Positive steps have been overshadowed by frustrations on the part of both industrial and developing countries. By the end of the 1970s, the Group of 77, the caucus of developing countries within the UN that now numbers about 120, stepped up its demands for global negotiations on a wide range of topics. Simultaneously, the Independent Commission on International Development Issues, a private group of leaders from both North and South, popularly known as the Brandt Commission after its chairman, former West German Chancellor Willy Brandt, proposed sweeping reforms in the international system and high-level discussions on world economic problems. This led to the North-South summit meeting of 22 heads of state from developed and developing countries at Cancún, Mexico, in October 1981.

The U.S. decision to participate in the Cancún summit brought a number of basic policy questions to the fore: What are this country's economic, political and strategic interests in the development of third-world nations? What kind of relations do we want with them? How will the changes that have taken place over the last three decades, both in the developing world and elsewhere, affect those relations? . . .

POLITICAL AND STRATEGIC INTERESTS

American interests in the developing countries in a very general sense are a reflection of the global interests that have shaped U.S. foreign policy since World War II. Briefly stated, the broad goals have included the following:

1. To maintain world peace and to avoid a repetition of the world wars

experienced in this century, particularly the outbreak of a nuclear war which would threaten human existence itself. To this end the United States maintains a large military establishment and promotes the peaceful settlement of disputes.

2. To contain the influence of those nations seen as fundamentally opposed to the American system of values. This goal, most marked in regard to the Soviet bloc, implies the need to maintain or strengthen the economic and political stability of U.S. allies.

3. To maintain an open world economy and protect U.S. access to foreign markets and sources of critical supplies.

4. To encourage the adoption by other nations of such principles as self-determination, the right of individuals to have a voice in decisions that affect them, and basic political and social rights, which are the foundation of America's political system.

Although these objectives are shared by the overwhelming majority of the American people, there are broad differences of opinion on their relative merits and the best way to achieve them. Is maintaining stability in a country which is considered an ally best served by providing arms, or by assisting its economic development? The answer frequently is not clear-cut.

The pursuit of U.S. strategic goals is complicated by several important factors. In general, U.S. relations with the developing countries are far less predictable than those with either industrial-country allies or even the Soviet Union. In general, the countries of North America, Western Europe and Japan are not threatened by serious instability. A number of developing countries, on the other hand, are afflicted by both internal problems and vulnerability to outside forces—an explosive combination that often makes for unexpected change and complicates policy formulation. Iran, Libya and El Salvador are all clear examples. Finally, much more attention in Washington has been focused on North Atlantic and East-West relations than on America's relations with the developing countries. As a result there is less understanding and knowledge of third-world countries. They tend to be neglected until a crisis erupts, as in Central America, or they gain economic leverage, as did the oil exporters.

As *The New York Times* correspondent Leslie Gelb noted after the Ottawa economic summit in July 1981, "The most serious difficulties for leaders of the Atlantic alliance have usually been not in Europe but in the gray areas of the third world—Korea in 1950, Dienbienphu [French Indochina] in 1954, Suez in 1956, the Cuban missile crisis of 1962, the Vietnam war, and, more recently, Iran and Afghanistan. This is where the fighting has been, and where the danger of conflict with the Soviet Union has been greatest." The rivalry between East and West will continue to be played out on the soil of developing countries.

While no developing country threatens the sanctity of American borders in a military sense, the United States has historically viewed the security and stability of Mexico, Central America, and certain Caribbean nations as essential to its own security. Expropriations of U.S. firms, terrorism and the seizure of U.S. hostages in Iran have confirmed that even relatively powerless nations can determine the security of Americans abroad.

In addition, certain third-world nations control or border on major sea-lanes (the Panama and Suez canals, the Strait of Malacca, Cape Horn and the Cape of Good Hope, etc.) and other transportation routes, such as oil pipelines which cross their borders or are contiguous to them. Developing countries are of growing importance to international economic stability, and to the U.S. economy in particular. They are inextricably involved in the entire range of U.S. strategic and political interests, even at a time when the latter are dominated by America's relations with the Soviet Union.

U.S. Expansionism

The United States first became actively involved in the third world in the late 19th and early 20th centuries when America emerged from relative isolation and began acting as a global power, intervening in the affairs of other countries when it suited its purposes. There were many reasons for the shift from insular to expansionist power: a desire to emulate the Europeans, who had colonized Africa and Asia; the transformation of the economy from agriculture to manufacturing; the end of the seemingly limitless open frontier; the increasing acceptance of Darwin's theory of evolution, with its supposedly biological evidence of Anglo-Saxon supremacy. The growing concept that sea power was essential to world power had prompted the United States to build a large modern navy. It planted the flag first in Alaska, Hawaii and Samoa, and then, as a result of the Spanish-American War, in Cuba, Puerto Rico and the Philippines. Successive American governments asserted an active claim to hegemony in Latin America (thereby extending the Monroe Doctrine), particularly in the Caribbean, where U.S. military interventions in Haiti, Nicaragua, Panama and the Dominican Republic became commonplace. In the Pacific, the United States was determined not to be shut out of the China market by the great powers—England, France, Russia, Germany—and to maintain an Open Door policy. It also sought to expand relations with Japan. In comparison, little attention was paid to Africa, South Asia and Southeast Asia, all of which were under colonial rule.

Americans were not wholly supportive of U.S. expansionism. Certain groups vigorously opposed the existence of U.S. colonies, both on moral grounds and in the belief that foreign commitments were dangerous. In the 1920s and 1930s the country resumed its traditional isolationism, which was shattered only by World War II. The war and the postwar concern with containing the Soviet Union led to the extension of American military power throughout the developing world. Worries over the Communist threat strongly influenced U.S.-third world relations—economic, technical and military. Still today the United States has defense alliances and treaties with 26 different third-world countries, mainly in Asia and Latin America.

Retrenchment

American strategic thinking about the developing countries began to change in the late 1960s, influenced strongly by the long and fruitless American involvement in Vietnam. The emphasis shifted from the direct use of U.S. troops to an increased reliance on friendly governments and local forces. This new policy—the so-called Nixon Doctrine—had a corollary: the United States would continue to supply the arms, equipment and other forms of support necessary to help developing-country allies counter external aggression or internal subversion, led or inspired, presumably, by the U.S.S.R. or China. One of the direct results of this shift in strategy was that the United States became one of the largest suppliers of arms to the world: between 1969 and 1978 U.S. arms transfers grew in constant dollars from $5.7 billion to $6.2 billion. Over three fourths of world arms transfers in 1978 went to the developing countries, primarily in Asia and the Middle East.

During much of the postwar period there was a consensus concerning American interests in the third world. The policy of containing the Soviet Union and China meant denying them political or ideological influence in the newly independent states. The U.S. mission was to stimulate the economic development of the poor countries and to encourage liberal economic and democratic systems to take root. In the late 1960s, however, this consensus evaporated, and by the early 1970s, many Americans felt there was little reason for deeper involvement in the third world. In 1971 the U.S. Senate even temporarily voted to end the U.S. foreign assistance program.

Détente was in the air. By 1972 U.S.-Soviet relations had thawed to the point where a continued reduction of tensions and broader economic and cultural relations seemed assured. From the American perspective, one of the implicit ground rules of détente was an acceptance of the status quo in the third world. Consequently, it was assumed that the Soviet threat to U.S. interests in the Middle East, Africa or elsewhere would recede.

By late 1973, though, U.S. attention was once more riveted on the developing countries. The immediate concern was not the Soviet Union but the oil embargo, followed by a fourfold increase in the price of oil by OPEC, and the growing world food crisis caused by drought and production shortfalls. For the first time many Americans realized, as they waited in line to fill their gas tanks, that developing countries could directly and immediately affect their well-being by controlling access to critical raw materials. The third world's political and strategic influence, previously discounted as relatively insignificant, had made itself felt at a time when U.S. worries about the role and intentions of the Soviet Union were beginning to rise dramatically. Part of the disenchantment with détente in the late 1970s stemmed from growing concern over Soviet activities in Ethiopia and South Yemen and Soviet support for Cuban troops in Angola and Mozambique. The Vietnamese invasion of Cambodia and the Soviet invasion of Afghanistan, the "discovery" of a Soviet brigade in Cuba and the ouster of Somoza in Nicaragua, the loss of U.S. influence in Iran and civil war in El Salvador strengthened those concerns. The Soviet Union, it appeared to many Americans, was once again aggressively seeking to extend its influence.

ECONOMIC INTERESTS

Before 1900 American economic involvement in the developing countries was insignificant. The United States itself was a developing country: it traded raw materials and food to Europe for manufactured goods. In most years before the turn of the century, the U.S. balance of payments showed current account deficits being offset by net capital inflows. The latter helped finance America's development. Not until after World War I did the United States record net investment outflows.

As the economy matured, American business became more active in developing countries. By 1929, almost half of the total U.S. foreign direct investment was located in Latin America, not quite three times as much as investment in Western Europe. In the same year, nearly one fifth of total U.S. exports were sold to Latin America, and Latin America supplied a quarter of U.S. imports. Following the Great Depression of the 1930s, U.S. economic relations with other developing countries, especially the Middle East and Far East, grew in intensity. It was during the 1970s, however, that economic links between the United States and developing countries expanded rapidly to create significant levels of interdependence.

Despite the growing importance of these economic relations, the United States has always had a hard time in setting policy toward the third world. First, the importance of those relations is largely ignored due to the historical insulation of the U.S. economy and the primary concern with economic ties with the industrial countries. Second, the level and forms of transactions with the third world and their impact on U.S. interests tend to be underestimated. Finally, and perhaps most importantly, different domestic economic sectors disagree over individual policy issues, and as a result difficult decisions tend to be postponed or compromised.

Trade

The third world as a whole represents the largest market for U.S. goods. Developing countries purchased about 38 percent of total U.S. exports in 1980, a share greater than that sold to the European Community, Eastern Europe, the Soviet Union and China combined. Developing countries purchase an average of 23 percent of industrial-country exports—a significantly smaller share than the 38 percent they buy from the United States.

While the composition of U.S. trade with individual developing countries varies enormously, as a whole it follows a predictable pattern. The United States sells machinery, trucks, aircraft and other transport equipment, relatively sophisticated manufactures such as computers and communications systems and agricultural products to the developing countries.

It buys oil, raw materials, tropical foodstuffs and labor-intensive consumer goods such as clothing and shoes. Predictably, trade has developed broadly according to comparative advantage. The United States has a relative abundance of land, capital and technology whereas some developing countries have a relative abundance of natural resources and labor. Because of the great discrepancy in comparative advantage, U.S. trade with developing countries probably creates more economic gains than trade with other developed countries. The latter tend to exchange similar products.

Since the United States buys more than it sells, it runs a significant merchandise trade deficit with the third world—a deficit which amounted to some $34 billion in 1979 and which by 1980 had climbed to $36 billion. These deficits have raised complaints that the United States is "exporting jobs," particularly in such visible and highly sensitive industries as textiles, shoes and consumer electronics. The aggregate figure, however, is deceiving. Of the total $116 billion in U.S. imports from developing countries in 1980, some 58 percent—$67 billion—was accounted for by gas, oil and petroleum products. In terms of manufactured goods, the United States continues to record large surpluses with the third world: some $26 billion in 1980. The third world buys some 40 percent of total U.S. exports of manufactures as well as large amounts of agricultural products. These exports probably account for one out of every 20 jobs in manufacturing in this country.

U.S. imports of manufactured goods from the third world, on the other hand, are growing so rapidly that they now amount to over one fourth of total manufactured imports. Over the 1970–79 period they grew at an average rate of 27 percent per year compared to an average growth rate of 19 percent for U.S. imports of manufactures from all sources. In 1980 the United States bought 27 percent of its manufactured goods from the developing countries, compared to 16 percent in 1965. Many of these imports require labor-intensive production and compete with relatively stagnant sectors in the U.S. economy. This type of trade leads directly to the classical case of increased efficiency in the economy as a whole and welfare gains to consumers, but loss of jobs in declining industries.

Many of these imports are less expensive than domestic products of equal quality. A 1979 analysis, carried out by economist William Cline and based on a survey of actual U.S. retail sales, found that imports from developing countries were as much as 16.3 percent cheaper than their domestically produced counterparts of comparable quality. By comparison, imports from developed areas were only marginally less expensive (0.4 percent) than comparable U.S. goods. Overall, American consumers were estimated to save more than $2 billion per year as a direct result of purchasing less-expensive imports. This is particularly important for low-income consumers. According to the study, they save as much as 13.1 percent on the purchase of imported goods rather than domestic goods.

The savings to consumers are dispersed widely throughout the economy, while the loss of jobs is concentrated in a relatively few slow-growth industries. Therefore imports from the third world have become a highly politicized issue, overshadowing such other causes of job displacement as automation and shifts in demand. Even though the overall employment effects of these imports are negligible (affecting perhaps one tenth of one percent of employment per year), the fact that they are highly visible has led unions and firms to focus a large amount of attention on them.

In response to these conflicting interests, the U.S. government has adopted a policy of keeping domestic markets relatively open to manufac-tured imports from developing countries, but at the same time placing con-trols on those imports like textiles, footwear and television sets which have been growing at above-normal rates. Sensitive products have been excluded from the U.S. general system of preferences, which permits certain developing-country products to come in duty-free. The United States has also taken the lead among industrialized countries in urging the advanced developing countries (ADCs) such as Brazil, Mexico and South Korea to "graduate," that is, to receive less preferential treatment and open their own markets to both developed and other developing countries. This policy of maintaining modified access to third-world goods and applying pressure for ADC trade liberalization is not likely to be altered in the foreseeable future.

Commodities

Though a major commodity producer in its own right, the United States depends heavily on the third world for many strategic materials. For example, in 1978, U.S. net imports from developing-market economies accounted for 93 percent of domestic consumption of tin, 88 percent of columbium, 56 percent of aluminum and 35 percent of manganese. Liter-ally all such items as rubber, coffee, cocoa, hard fibers and jute come from the third world. On the other hand, the United States produces large quanti-ties of minerals such as iron, lead, copper and phosphates, but it consumes most of these domestically.

Concern over the supply of key industrial raw materials, particularly those produced by South Africa and the U.S.S.R., has prompted a debate on the possibility of future "resource wars." Most analysts have concluded that these fears are exaggerated. Producer-governments, such as South Africa and Zimbabwe (formerly Rhodesia), which have 96 percent of the known deposits of chromium, will continue to sell resources because they need foreign exchange, and importing countries can buffer any possible short-term disruptions by such measures as building stockpiles.

Despite America's demonstrable interest in world trade of commodities—including access to supplies at reasonable prices; expansion of sales of U.S. commodities, again at remunerative prices; assuring that world demand is largely met—for humanitarian reasons as well as avoiding the disruptions caused by shortages; damping major fluctuations in com-modity prices; and promoting sufficient investment in raw material industries to satisfy growth in demand—its policy does not conform to the general notion of the U.S. interest. The United States has consistently rejected an integrated approach for dealing with all major commodities at the same time, preferring instead a case-by-case approach where specific U.S. producer and consumer interests can be identified and balanced. It has also actively resisted the growth and questioned the efficacy of producer cartels. OPEC's success in unilaterally raising the price of petroleum has only hardened U.S. opposition. Finally, the United States perhaps more than any other country has been ambivalent in its attitude toward market intervention. On the one hand, it extols the virtues of market mechanisms and castigates the evils of administered prices. On the other hand, it has a long history of market interventions—subsidies, price floors (for wages and agricultural products) and price ceilings (on oil).

Ironically, while it has been the developing countries that have pressed for commodity agreements, the largest measurable economic benefits from commodity price stabilization would accrue to the United States and the other industrial countries in the form of reduced inflationary pressures, according to an econometric analysis carried out in the late 1970s by economist Jere R. Behrman.

American ambiguity on commodity issues is reflected in a series of wide-ranging policy decisions. Historically, the United States has participated in commodity agreements on sugar and coffee. But when the UN Conference on Trade and Development (UNCTAD) in 1974 proposed an Integrated Program for Commodities (IPC), the United States initially opposed it, probably for fear of new cartels. In recent years, however, Congress approved implementing legislation for participation in the International Sugar and Coffee Agreements. The United States has joined an International Rubber Agreement and participates in the current tin agreement, but will not join the new tin agreement scheduled to begin in mid-1982. The United States also participated in the recently concluded negotiations on a new International Cocoa Agreement, but has yet to join.

Initially a strong opponent of the proposal for a Common Fund, a new international institution designed to finance commodity agreements, the United States eventually agreed to its formation in 1978, but succeeded in limiting the amount of direct government contributions to the fund. It has also declined thus far to contribute to the "second window," a mechanism within the Common Fund to finance third-world efforts at diversification, market promotion and research and development.

On a separate but related issue, the United States participated in the negotiation of an International Wheat Agreement which failed to reach a consensus on reserve stock levels or price bands among major producers and consumers. The agreement finally collapsed due to developing-country disagreement over stockpile release prices and maintenance costs.

In sum, the United States appears to have taken a gradualist approach. It has done some tough bargaining in an attempt to meet the current interests of domestic producers and consumers, but in so doing may have sacrificed long-term objectives to short-term concerns.

The Food Issue

One commodity of particular importance to the United States is cereal grains—wheat, maize and rice—of which it is the world's largest exporter, accounting for some 60 percent of total world trade in 1980–81. The 40 percent of these exports that go to the developing countries constitute nearly two thirds of the latter's imports. If control of a vital resource is a mark of national strength, then food is surely one important element of U.S. strength—especially vis-à-vis the third world.

Besides meeting domestic consumption requirements, U.S. agricultural production brought in more than $41 billion in export earnings in 1980, a significant contribution to the balance of payments. With a population of only 5 percent of the world total, the United States produces 15 percent of the world's wheat (the major food grain traded), 27 percent of the world's coarse grains (mainly maize), and 60 percent of the world's soybeans. Though a small producer, the United States is the world's leading rice exporter. U.S. corporations, operating in the relatively unregulated U.S. market, dominate international grain trade.

One out of three U.S. farm acres produces for export, and about one out of five for export to developing countries. U.S. farmers depend on developing countries for about two fifths of their export market. Developing-country net grain imports increased fourfold between 1960 and 1980, and the bulk of this increase came from the United States. The $20 billion of U.S. food imports, chiefly from developing countries, included mainly coffee, tea, cocoa, sugar and tropical fruits and vegetables.

In addition to its leadership in production and trade, the United States holds a major share of world stocks of such basic food commodities as wheat, coarse grains and oilseeds (mainly soybeans). These stocks are vital for providing food aid and emergency assistance to refugees and for responding to harvest shortfalls and natural disasters. Not only regular U.S. food exports, but also the large proportion of food stocks held in the United States, are important factors in the U.S. pursuit of its interests in the third world.

The growing demand for U.S. grain in the developing countries has raised questions about America's ability to continue indefinitely "feeding the world." Competition for agricultural land, rising production costs, reduction in soil productivity, growing energy dependence, lowering of underground water tables, environmental deterioration, crop vulnerability due to monoculture (especially of grains), leveling off of research activity and climatic changes have all hurt U.S. agricultural output. Although dramatic scientific and technological breakthroughs might possibly produce another Green Revolution, a gradually declining production growth rate is more likely for the next decade or two.

As the dominant world food producer, the United States has an opportunity to play a leadership role in improving global food security and the international food system. It is in the U.S. self-interest to do so. Unless worldwide production patterns change, the United States will find it steadily more difficult to meet the rising international demand for cereals, especially in the third world, without a sharp escalation in prices. It is to the U.S. advantage, therefore, to encourage developing countries to increase investments in agriculture; to adopt appropriate incentives, especially price incentives, to encourage their farmers to produce; and to help them increase their food production and improve its distribution. Food aid buys time and can assist development, but it cannot over the long term make up for food deficits in the developing countries.

Energy

The United States consumes more energy than it produces. It seeks sufficient supplies of energy at predictable prices (which is not necessarily the same as low or unchanging prices) for adequate but prudent use by industry and individuals. Historically, U.S. consumption has been less than prudent. Decades of abundant supplies and declining real prices led to wasteful consumption. In 1979, per capita consumption of energy in the United States, about 12,350 kilograms of coal equivalent, was more than 56 percent higher than the average consumption of industrialized countries (7,892 kilograms), and nearly 100 times that of low-income countries other than China and India (129 kilograms). The reduced supply of oil and price rises of the 1970s only recently began to alter the pattern. The delay was due largely to domestic policy. Because the price of domestic output was regulated, the cost to consumers was well below the level of other countries. Consumption relative to output began to decrease sharply only as prices rose and sharpened the incentives to conserve. The decision in 1981 to decontrol domestic oil prices entirely should accelerate the trend to conservation.

The problem of high U.S. consumption of energy has hurt nearly all other areas of economic relations with both developing and developed countries. U.S. imports of gas, oil and petroleum products, totaling $79 billion in 1980, have been primarily responsible for U.S. trade deficits. These deficits in turn have at times reinforced protectionist sentiments toward nonoil imports. Consumption patterns cannot be changed overnight, but reduced U.S. demand for energy is clearly in the best interest of the United States, other industrialized countries and developing countries. This point has been made by officials from OPEC and other OECD countries with increasing frequency and decreasing subtlety over the past several years. The current oil glut and price softening may be only a temporary phenomenon, but it already appears to be undermining the long-term objective of energy conservation.

Increased U.S. dependence on OPEC energy supplies has led the United States to alter its strategy in the Middle East and Persian Gulf and to

attempt to improve its often-neglected relations with such other major producers as Mexico and Nigeria, currently the second largest supplier of oil to
the United States.

In the longer run, energy shortages, whether in terms of physical supplies or in the form of high production costs, have the potential to dampen
the growth prospects and welfare of all countries. The United States, like
other countries, therefore has an interest in the expansion of world energy
production, the attainment of greater energy self-sufficiency by the developing countries, and the implementation of necessary domestic conservation measures. This implies the need for much greater emphasis on
investment in—and research and development of—conventional and alternative sources of energy.

International Investments

U.S. investments in the third world are large, highly visible, and important to both host and home countries. These investments provide the
United States with significant levels of raw materials, manufactures and
income. They provide the host country with capital and technology needed
to create employment opportunities.

In 1978 over 23 percent of cumulative U.S. foreign direct investment
was in developing countries—about $38 billion out of a total of $163 billion.
Two years later, 25 percent of foreign direct investment, valued at some $53
billion—an increase of 39 percent—was in developing countries. In the
1970–79 period, U.S. investments (excluding investments in petroleum)
grew at an average annual rate of 29 percent in developing countries, while
the figure for developed countries was 16 percent.

In 1980 almost 32 percent of total U.S. direct investment income came
from developing countries. The third world provided by far the bulk of net
U.S. service transaction earnings (i.e., income on foreign investment, plus
revenues from royalties, shipping, insurance and other services)—some
$23.2 billion or 64 percent of the total. Direct and other private investment
income accounted for a large proportion.

U.S. private bank lending to developing countries has also been
expanding rapidly. U.S. banks account for some 60 percent of total commercial bank claims on non-oil middle-income countries. U.S. bank claims on
developing countries amounted to $128.6 billion in mid-1980 and had been
growing at an average rate of about 30 percent per year following the oil
crisis. Interest from these loans constitutes a large and growing share of U.S.
banks' overall revenue.

Investment in the third world by U.S. firms, and its costs and benefits
both to the United States and to the host country, has been the subject of
intense debate over the past decade. Those who contend that foreign investment promotes American interests hold that capital flows encourage both
exports and imports. Besides, they give U.S. investors a "piece of the action"
that would go elsewhere if capital outflows were restricted. According to

these advocates, foreign investment further benefits the United States by encouraging efficiency, raising the quantity and quality of employment and providing access to needed raw materials. However, opponents of this view argue that foreign investment actually undermines American interests. The multinational corporations, they contend, export capital and technology and thereby "displace" domestic investment and employment.

Official policies, with few exceptions, have favored the free flow of capital and technology. The government facilitates U.S. investment in the third world both as a means of achieving "positive" U.S. gains and as a means of inducing capital formation in developing countries.

Though its overall approach has been laissez-faire, the U.S. government has not hesitated to intervene when American economic or strategic interests appeared threatened. The 1962 Hickenlooper Amendment, which provides the legal basis for suspending bilateral assistance to countries which expropriate U.S. property without prompt and adequate compensation, has been used only twice (in Ceylon, now Sri Lanka, and Ethiopia), but political and economic pressures have been applied in other cases where U.S. investments were seized. As an added protection to U.S. investors, the Overseas Private Investment Corporation (OPIC), an independent government organization, provides insurance for certain noncommercial risks. Finally, the United States affects trade and investment policies by the ways in which it pursues foreign policy goals and ethical concerns. Examples include anticorruption rules, restrictions on trade and investment in "unfriendly" nations, and antiboycott legislation.

Foreign Assistance

Foreign assistance has two major aims: promoting the general U.S. interest in world development and stability, and advancing specific U.S. interests (including security interests) in the third world. In the regional breakdown of the flow of U.S. economic assistance—including security support assistance, development assistance, Public Law 480 (Food for Peace) and other programs such as the Peace Corps—the Middle East is by far the largest recipient. Egypt and Israel alone accounted for over one fourth of total U.S. economic aid commitments in fiscal year 1980. This is a direct result of U.S. strategic interest in the Middle East and the Persian Gulf. South Asia, with India, Pakistan and Bangladesh among the 15 top recipients of U.S. aid, is another major recipient, with assistance primarily aimed at promoting development. The Philippines and Indonesia receive large amounts of American aid, the former because of historical ties and as compensation for U.S. military bases. Direct domestic benefits from the U.S. aid program are ensured by the fact that three fourths of the budget of the Agency for International Development (AID) is spent in the United States to purchase American goods and services. The food assistance program, administered under P.L. 480, also is of direct benefit to U.S. agriculture.

In addition to these and other related interests, the United States benefits indirectly from economic growth and progress in developing countries through trade with them. Finally, and not insignificantly, the United States has a humanitarian interest in eliminating the worst aspects of global poverty, meeting the basic human needs of the world's poor, and improving political and economic conditions and human rights worldwide.

Despite the positive interests that aid serves, Americans tend to see only the costs and ignore the benefits. This is particularly true in the current climate of budgetary stringency. Some opponents of aid claim that it does not fulfill humanitarian needs and that aid recipients demonstrate little goodwill toward the United States. Besides, the argument continues, pressing domestic problems deserve prior attention. Those who hold these views have attempted to limit overall assistance and to place conditions on aid disbursements. Allocating only 0.27 percent of its gross national product to official development assistance, the United States ranked very low compared to other donor countries in 1980.

Conflicting claims often leave the agencies interested in foreign assistance at odds over objectives. Should aid be used primarily for economic development or to promote U.S. security interests? The answer affects the functional and geographic allocation of funds. There are also differences over short-term, specific U.S. interests versus broader, long-term interests which frequently result in more efficient use of capital transfers. Administrators must also cope with such issues as aid flows to authoritarian regimes or countries ideologically opposed to the United States. These conflicts result in a rather eclectic U.S. policy, frequently unsatisfactory to both developing countries and American constituencies.

International Institutions and Systems

The United States played a leading role in the establishment of post-World War II institutions involved with international economic and political relations and security. Many systems and organizations dealing with economic matters (particularly those which emerged from the Bretton Woods agreement of 1945 governing international economic transactions) and strategic concerns (e.g., the North Atlantic Treaty Organization, the Southeast Asia Treaty Organization, etc.) were largely of U.S. design, and the creation of the UN system in 1945 received a strong U.S. endorsement.

Some of these institutions have been more successful than others in advancing U.S. interests. All have evolved over time, some to the liking of the United States, others not. The U.S. Administration or Congress has often reacted strongly when it saw American interests being threatened. For example, the United States temporarily withdrew from the International Labor Organization (ILO); it has attempted to block multilateral bank loans to countries it disapproved of—for example, Vietnam; and it has tried to withhold or restrict funding for the UN and its operations.

Specific conflicts aside, America's three principal postwar interests—

the avoidance of another major world war, the prevention of another major depression, and the reconstruction of the economies of the World War II combatants—have been well served by the institutions it helped create. The conflicts and crises of recent years have not been inconsequential, but they pale against the possibilities of major war or economic collapse. Indeed that is part of the reason why the United States on the whole resists changes in these institutions.

Over the last few decades, the United States has added two more goals to its list of priorities. The first is improving the prospects of the world's poorest people so that they can overcome the certainty of hunger, malnutrition and disease. This goal is clearly in the interest of the United States: unless it is achieved, a large portion of the world's population will permanently face conditions akin to those of war and depression.

The second objective, based on the growing recognition of a set of common problems that require cooperative action, is to deal with serious difficulties of "global-systems maintenance." Needed are solutions to environmental degradation, population growth, imbalances in food needs and supplies, the depletion of nonrenewable resources and problems eroding the viability of the world's trading and financial systems. These are "development" issues in the broad sense of the term because they affect rich and poor countries alike.

International institutions have helped third-world development efforts to varying degrees, but most of these countries consider their progress insufficient and that an overhaul of the international economic and political institutions is necessary. The United States has resisted the NIEO proposals primarily on the ground that they will not promote development, but it also does not consider them in the U.S. interest.

The United States, however, is not totally opposed to institutional reform. For example, it did support recent changes in the structures and operations of the General Agreement on Tariffs and Trade (GATT) and the IMF, and many of these changes have been aimed at benefiting the developing countries. But the United States favors gradual reform implemented in such a fashion as to minimize or avoid altogether any reductions in the level of American influence. Thus the United States has been loath to dilute the significant power it exercises in the IMF, GATT and the International Bank for Reconstruction and Development (World Bank). The U.S. reaction to the increasing militancy and perceived "anti-Americanism" of the developing countries in forums such as the UN system has been to retreat to organizations which are viewed as less hostile. Finally, the decline of U.S. economic hegemony and reduced confidence in the dollar and the role it plays in international finance have placed the United States in a defensive position vis-à-vis both developed and developing countries. The natural strategy for a country with a defensive posture is to maintain as much control as possible, avoid sweeping systemic change, and limit actions which might further damage its position. . . .

NEEDED: A DEVELOPMENT STRATEGY

The complex admixture of interests, tangible and intangible, that comes into play on any specific U.S.-third world issue makes it very difficult to assess the extent to which the general philosophy of any U.S. Administration (which theoretically defines and pursues the collective U.S. interest) is translated into policy. Indeed, one would be hard put to name an Administration that had both a comprehensive view of the third world and a consistent set of policies to match that view.

The first year of the Reagan Administration was marked by a renewed emphasis on the overriding importance of military security and on the need to restore American power. Its focus therefore has been on the intentions and capabilities of the Soviet Union, including its activities in the developing countries. This has been joined by an equal preoccupation with radical governments, such as Cuba and Libya, which are seen to be acting contrary to U.S. interests in the third world. In the economic sphere, the Administration has shown a clear preference for bilateral relations rather than working with multilateral institutions in which the United States has been a leader since World War II. It has put a heavy emphasis on private enterprise and market forces in economic development. . . .

Defining Interests

. . . A marked disparity exists between U.S. interests in the developing countries and the low priority U.S. policy-makers still assign them. The longer the disparity continues, the more opportunities will be missed, the higher the costs to this country, and the greater the risk of permanently losing the leadership role the United States has played for so long in encouraging international development cooperation.

There is of course no one overarching U.S. interest in the third world but rather a multiplicity of interests—complex, overlapping, often even conflicting. The United States needs to develop a broad definition of those interests—one that encompasses and balances its own political, security, economic and humanitarian objectives and is sensitive to those of other nations.

. . . No one can dispute the fact that what transpires between the United States and the Soviet Union will ultimately determine whether or not the world stays at peace, at least in the foreseeable future. There have, however, been countless trends and events affecting North-South interests (wars, famines, embargoes and the positive aspects of commercial relations) that have *not* involved the Soviet Union. There are times and areas where the actions of the Soviet Union may be important, but there are others where they may not. For example, there are certain places in the third world where Western interests are paramount and where actual or potential Soviet influence is a very serious question indeed—the Persian Gulf, for example. There are other areas, such as Central America or southern Africa, where the problems are more complex and Soviet influence far more tenuous. Approaching all issues and areas through the "East-West prism" can in many cases damage U.S. interests.

. . . [O]ne cannot disagree with the U.S. need to be prepared to defend its key interests if these are challenged, but the use of military power to achieve America's objectives in the developing countries does not always pass the test of either efficacy or morality. A classic example is the U.S. involvement in Vietnam, for which the United States received no benefits and bore high costs. The debate over American military involvement in Central America is a current illustration. A Brookings Institution study has identified 215 incidents since the end of World War II (185 of which were in developing countries) where U.S. forces were used for political purposes, and concluded that the use of military force has only a short-term effect and is no substitute for long-term diplomacy. [The Blechman and Kaplan article in Part I of this book is based on the Brookings Institution study cited here—*eds.*] Political scientist Stanley Hoffmann has observed that "Military power is of little use, either when the objectives we try to achieve are economic or when the threat to our economic security could be worsened by sending in the Marines." In sum, there is a range of other nonmilitary elements of national power—primarily strong economic and diplomatic relations—that can be much more effective than military force and need to be emphasized if peace is the ultimate objective.

Change may be destabilizing, but it is inevitable in a rapidly evolving world and does not necessarily work against longer-term U.S. interests. One of the great strengths of the American system is its adaptability and capacity to absorb change. This strength needs to be translated into the international system. Former Secretary of State Cyrus R. Vance declared in a commencement address at Harvard University in 1980 that the United States faces a "world undergoing rapid change, with growing expectations, better education, quickened communications; a world in which neither the United States nor any other country commands a preponderance of power or a monopoly of wisdom. It is a world of conflicts, among nations and values, among social systems and emerging new interests. It is a world in which competitive superpowers hold in their hands our common survival, yet paradoxically find it beyond their power to order events." In such a world, change should be managed and channeled as peacefully as possible. The peaceful transition to majority rule in Zimbabwe and the negotiation and ratification of a new agreement with Panama over the governance of the Panama Canal provide recent examples of successful accommodations to change.

Finally, the importance of the developing countries to America's economic well-being should be acknowledged and an appropriate response made to their proposals for change. Many Americans feel that the current international economic system is working fairly well, not only for the rich countries but also for the poor—and that what is needed is not a new order but rather some gradual reforms in the existing order. This assessment may have held true until recently, but there are enough strains building now— trade stagnation, large current account imbalances, increasing debt-servicing problems—to indicate that the current system does not have sufficient capacity to manage the overload indefinitely. It is not alarmist to recognize the need for reforms, whether arrived at in some form of global economic negotiations or carried out within existing institutional structures.

Global Problems, Multilateral Solutions

A balance must be struck between the need to achieve global cooperation to deal with major international problems on the one hand and to accommodate legitimate U.S. military security concerns on the other. The ability or inability to balance these two agendas may mark the success or failure of American foreign policy in the 1980s.

The fact that all nations—East and West, North and South—face a set of political, economic, social and environmental problems which cannot be resolved without extraordinary cooperative measures has become increasingly apparent over the past decade. Overcoming many of these problems is beyond the ability of any single nation-state. Many of them do not lend themselves to bilateral approaches—the spread of ocean pollutants, for example, or the depletion of the earth's protective ozone shield. Because of the complexity of dealing with such issues as nuclear proliferation, the environment, outer space, energy and food, multilateral action is imperative, and the role of the developing world has become vital. Unless solutions are found, the *Global 2000 Report to the President* warned, "The world in 2000 will be much more crowded, more polluted, less stable ecologically, and more vulnerable to disruption than the world we live in now. . . . Barring revolutionary advances in technology, life for most people on earth will be more precarious in 2000 than it is now—unless the nations of the world act decisively to alter current trends." [A summary of the *Global 2000 Report* is contained in Part VII of this book—*eds.*]

A Malthusian type of global apocalypse—when the world's population has outstripped its means of subsistence—may not be inevitable, but the events of the 1970s and early 1980s provide enough evidence that greater international efforts are required to reduce even the slightest chance of such an outcome. The national interest in such efforts may be difficult to calculate precisely, but is nevertheless obvious.

Perhaps the most important U.S. interest to be pursued, one which deals with the world as it now is and as it could be, is to help build a world with greater human dignity, well-being and freedom. Americans have been fortunate to be blessed with greater amounts of these "assets" than most other nations, and it has been abhorrent to many—though not all—sectors of American opinion that U.S. relative prosperity should coexist with the extremes of poverty in the third world. Hence there is a fundamental moral obligation to assist in the removal of poverty's worst aspects at least, if not poverty itself.

The United States still has the ability to calculate its own needs and implement policies that advance its own interests even at the expense of others. Unique among the industrial countries, the United States probably could benefit from a self-serving approach, at least in the short run, even if this meant running the risk of further dividing the international system and alienating the developing countries. Alternatively, the United States could take a long-run view of its relations with the third world and consider improvements as investments which will bring future returns, even at short-term cost. To do so, however, American attitudes, policies and governmental structures, fashioned in an era of abundance and relative isolation from the outside world, will have to be changed to fit an era of limits.

If the United States and other countries do not begin now to seek solutions to common problems, they will all face slower growth, higher prices and a world system more vulnerable to disruption. On the other hand, by concerted attention to these problems, it is possible to restore growth and stability and measurably increase the well-being of people everywhere. Favorable outcomes are possible, with benefits accruing to all, if national interests are defined and sought appropriately. Herein lies the real U.S. interest.

Part Three

SOCIETAL SOURCES OF AMERICAN FOREIGN POLICY

Many people think that the making of foreign policy is somehow "above politics." According to this belief, national interests are put ahead of partisan and personal interests in the formulation of the nation's foreign relations. The international strategic situation, not domestic considerations, is what matters. Politics, in short, stops at the water's edge.

Compelling as the "water's edge" view may be, it fails to take into account the fact that multiple motivations affect decision makers in the choices they make in foreign policy. And, in fact, many of their choices are often the result of internal, not international, considerations: the necessity of maintaining a power base, the pragmatic desire to preserve the freedom to maneuver in the future, the political need to remain popular with voters—all are examples of the influence of domestic concerns on the making of America's foreign policy. Thus, societal factors, whether they are stimuli or constraints, are important inputs into the foreign policy-making process.

The societal category of foreign policy sources, like the external environment discussed in Part II, encompasses a broad array of variables. James N. Rosenau defines societal sources as

> those nongovernmental aspects of a society which influence its external behavior. The major value orientations of a society, its degree of national unity, and the extent of its industrialization are but a few of the societal variables which can contribute to the contents of a nation's external aspirations and policies.[1]

In other words, nongovernmental national attributes—those general features of American society that define the kind of nation it is and differentiate it from other nations—partially determine American foreign policy.

Discussions of American foreign policy that locate its origins in domestic factors are commonplace. It was once popular, for example, to explain the nineteenth-century expansion of the United States, both within the continent and abroad, by references to "manifest destiny," a rationale that maintained that Americans were a chosen people with a divine right to expand. More recently, some observers, concentrating on the natural resources and size of the United States, have contended that these attributes drove the nation toward an active internationalist policy that reflected the superpower status nature assigned to it. Others have focused on the relationship between public opinion and foreign policy and have suggested that the former limits the range of permissible foreign policy options from which decision makers can choose. Related to these ideas are others that emphasize the potential power of the mass media to shape public preferences on particular policy issues.

Another view of the societal forces that shape American foreign policy focuses on the activities of special-interest groups. This perspective includes various power-elite theories that see the making of American foreign policy as the preserve of an "establishment"; and the "establishment's" policy is designed to serve its own special interests. Some revisionist views of American foreign policy, especially those emphasizing neo-Marxist ideas, locate the origins of that policy in the presumed needs of America's capitalist economy. A variant of this theme, which has gained renewed popularity in the 1980s, is the one associated with President Eisenhower's warning in 1961 about the "unwarranted influence" that the "military-industrial complex" could acquire and exert.

The essays which follow touch on many of these ideas. From among the complex array of interlocked domestic factors that could be examined, the essays focus in particular on the beliefs and preferences of Americans in leadership positions and of the American people in general regarding the appropriate role of the United States in world affairs. They also examine some of the mechanisms whereby those beliefs and preferences are translated into foreign policy making.

PERSPECTIVES ON SOCIETAL SOURCES OF AMERICAN FOREIGN POLICY: AN OVERVIEW

Is there a distinctive American "national character" that explains how the United States behaves in world affairs? Are there particular national attributes and shared life experiences among the American people which explain the choices made by American leaders? Does the political culture of the United States—the beliefs that Americans hold about their political system and the way it should operate—define the goals the nation seeks to attain abroad and explain the means that leaders choose to realize them?

Analysts differ in their answers to these questions. Yet, despite the differences, there remains a certain compelling logic to the argument that somehow the experiences of the American nation and its people over two centuries have had an important bearing on the nation's self-image, which in turn conditions perceptions of the world and America's place within it. "The frontier in American experience," "people of plenty," and "the exceptional American experience" are among the phrases associated with popular views that have been advanced to capture the essence of America's uniqueness among the world's nations,[2] and are linked to the belief that this uniqueness requires that America play a special role in world affairs.

Americans may inherit distinctive historical experiences and share certain widespread beliefs rooted in the seventeenth-century liberal philosophy of the English thinker John Locke—namely, that government's role should be a limited one designed to protect the individual's life, liberty, and property through popular consent, established laws, impartial judges, and effective executives whose power is balanced by other branches of government. But not all share in governance. In the realm of foreign policy, it is widely believed that political elites—the foreign policy "establishment"—run the show. Carl Gershman's article, "The Rise and Fall of the New Foreign-Policy Establishment" provides important insight into the concept of an "establishment"—who comprises it, what their ideas are, how those ideas are circulated, and how they become translated into foreign policy.

The essay is provocative as well as informative, for it argues that the election of Jimmy Carter, coming on the heels of the Vietnam debacle, represented the displacement of the "old establishment," for whom anti-Sovietism and containment were key foreign policy principles, with a "new establishment" that not only condemned the war in Vietnam but also concluded "that the containment of Communism by the United States was neither possible, nor necessary, nor even desirable." Without suggesting that the internationalist establishment of the Cold War era would be resurrected with the defeat of Jimmy Carter, Gershman clearly implies (even though he was writing before the 1980 presidential election) that Ronald Reagan's victory would be a defeat for the individuals and ideals associated with the new foreign policy establishment, which, according to Gershman, never spoke for the country as a whole but only for a narrow if influential sector of the elite which had ceased to believe in America after Vietnam, and which despite its proclaimed optimism [seemed] to have resigned itself to the forward momentum of political forces in the world committed to America's ultimate defeat.

Gershman's argument that Vietnam was the event that forced the "new establishment" to challenge the premises and promises of containment is consistent with the findings of public opinion analysts, who have concluded that only a "dramatic event" causes individuals to revise their images of international "reality," images that are typically formed early in life and normally remain the lenses through which people continue to interpret subsequent international events during adulthood. Many analysts have also argued that the Soviet invasion of Afghanistan in December 1979 was a similar dramatic event that restructured individual beliefs and images of international politics and caused many Americans to embrace a malevolent and aggressive view of Soviet intentions. As President Carter himself revealed at the time of the invasion (which is the statement alluded to in the opening sentence of Gershman's article), "my opinion of the Russians has changed more drastically in the last week than even the previous two-and-a-half years."

Ole R. Holsti and James N. Rosenau agree that Vietnam was a dramatic event that fundamentally altered the beliefs and images of the most influential segment of the American populace. Their article, "A Leadership Divided: The Foreign Policy Beliefs of American Leaders, 1976–1980," describes three distinct strands of thinking that emerged among American leaders in the wake of Vietnam. Holsti and Rosenau's empirical studies of the foreign policy beliefs of American leaders reveal, however, that the Afghan invasion did *not* produce another realignment in leaders' foreign policy images. Vietnam may have been responsible for a fundamental restructuring of the postwar foreign policy consensus that had been based on a broad agreement among American leaders about the nature of the Soviet threat, about the appropriateness of the containment foreign policy strategy, and, more generally, about the globalist role of the United States in world affairs; Afghanistan did not rekindle that consensus. Accordingly, the authors' findings shed light on the reasons underlying the often bitter debates that have taken place on many foreign policy issues in recent years, and they illustrate vividly that politics do *not* stop at the water's edge.

"Internationalism Comes of Age . . . Again," by Lloyd Free and William Watts, also deals with changes in foreign policy opinions in the context of Vietnam and Afghanistan. But in this case the focus is on the impact of those events on American opinions generally and not exclusively on the opinions of leaders. The authors corroborate that skepticism among large segments of the American public about the internationalist role of the United States since the end of World War II was greatest during the mid-

1970s. But they also point out that a new, more cautious vision of the country's role in the world has been developing since then. Hence, they challenge the view, popular in the spring of 1980 when their article first appeared, "that the Soviet invasion of Afghanistan, coming on top of the seizure of American hostages in Iran [in 1979], . . . brought about a sea of change in the attitudes of the American people toward the world around them." The data examined by the authors do not permit conclusions to be drawn about whether the majority of the American people are divided along lines that Holsti and Rosenau describe concerning American leaders; nonetheless, in developing their argument, Free and Watts do provide much useful information about the foreign policy attitudes of various socioeconomic groups within American society.

How are public preferences translated into policy outcomes? One view, noted earlier, is that public opinion sets the boundaries of permissible behavior within which decision makers must operate. These boundaries are typically so elastic, however, that they are perhaps better thought of as postponing rather than limiting factors. Moreover, while on occasion public opinion appears to be ahead of official thinking and thus able to stimulate policy innovations, more often governmental officials decide first and then use their considerable resources to mold public opinion to support the choices made. Even the electoral process has shown itself to be inadequate to the task of converting public preferences into particular policies. At best, it is a blunt instrument that citizens may use to support or oppose existing policies. Even then, however, it is rarely clear what policies motivate voter sentiments. The problem is especially acute in matters involving foreign policy, in which many Americans are often uninterested and about which they are frequently uninformed, since the issues normally appear far removed from their daily lives.

The elitist model of foreign policy making, which underlies Gershman's analysis of the rise and fall of the "new establishment" and implicitly motivates Holsti and Rosenau's inquiry, is one perspective on the opinion-policy linkage that, in barest form, suggests a select few govern America without any form of direction from the general public. The system allows the public to have participation (for example, through elections) without power, involvement without influence, while a small set of elites, acting both openly and behind closed doors, makes all the important decisions. As noted earlier, the thesis that a military-industrial complex dictates American foreign policy is a variant of the elitist perspective.

In contrast to elitism, the pluralist model of policy making sees public preferences channeled into the policy-making process through the interaction of private interest groups, each pursuing its own particular interests and each petitioning the government on behalf of the shared interests and values of its members. The public good is served much as Adam Smith theorized it would be served in the economic sphere, where the invisible hand of the marketplace supposedly translates the pursuit of private interests into the general welfare. The potential abuse of power is controlled by competition among countervailing centers of power. Public preferences therefore find expression through bargaining among interest-group elites. The product is government *for* the people, but not necessarily *by* them in an immediate or direct sense. Even the mass media can be viewed as a kind of interest group, since they seek to articulate and aggregate the views and concerns of the diverse elements of America's heterogeneous society.

Bernard C. Cohen, a scholar well-known for his study of the role of nongovernmental groups in the foreign policy-making process, discusses both the process and the product of interest-group and media involvement in foreign policy in his article, "The Influence of Special-Interest Groups and Mass Media on Security Policy in the United States." Eschewing simplistic single-factor and often conspiratorial models that either exaggerate the power of interest groups and the media or dismiss them altogether, Cohen chooses a middle path from which to explore alternative hypotheses that have been advanced to explain the impact—or lack of it—of these nongovernmental groups on the policy process. Cohen supplements the theoretical arguments in his essay with an exploration of the influence of the media and interest groups in four specific security policy cases: SALT II, general nuclear weapons policy, the sale of AWACS planes to Saudi Arabia, and U.S. policy in El Salvador. He concludes with the interesting observation that the media often play a critical role in creating the kind of environment conducive to interest-group influence in shaping policy outcomes.

NOTES

1. "Pre-theories and Theories of Foreign Policy," in R. Barry Farrell, ed., *Approaches to Comparative and International Politics* (Evanston, Ill.: Northwestern University Press, 1966), p. 43.
2. The phrases are attributed, respectively, to Frederick Jackson Turner, *The Frontier in American History* (New York: Henry Holt & Company, 1920); David M. Potter, *People of Plenty* (Chicago: The University of Chicago Press, 1952); and Louis Hartz, *The Liberal Tradition in America* (New York: Harcourt Brace & World, 1955).

12

THE RISE AND FALL OF THE NEW FOREIGN-POLICY ESTABLISHMENT

CARL GERSHMAN

When President Carter said that the Soviet invasion of Afghanistan had caused him "drastically" to alter his perception of Soviet intentions, many people wondered how a great power like the United States could have as its leader a man who, by his own admission, did not understand the most important strategic and military issue facing the country. The answer, at once simple and dismaying, is that the President's pre-Afghanistan "perception" of the Soviet Union was not at all exceptional or a product of his own naiveté but rather reflected the conventional wisdom of most government officials, academic experts, and others specializing in foreign affairs. No less a figure than former Secretary of State Cyrus Vance, a man who epitomizes urbane sophistication in foreign affairs, had observed in an interview with *Time* Magazine in 1978 that President Carter and Soviet President Brezhnev had "similar dreams and aspirations" about the future of the world. Views of this kind had not gained widespread acceptance in the country as a whole, since most Americans remained distrustful of the Soviet Union. But by the time Jimmy Carter assumed office, such ideas had become the stock-in-trade of the relatively small group of specialists constituting what is often called the foreign-policy establishment.

The foreign-policy establishment associated with the administration of Jimmy Carter may be viewed as the natural successor to the old internationalist establishment which presided over American policy during the era of the cold war and which collapsed as a result of America's defeat in Vietnam. The demise of the old establishment occurred about a decade ago and is not talked about much today, except as a subject of historical interest (it is, for example, an important underlying theme of Henry Kissinger's *White House Years*, which deals with the period in question). Nonetheless, it was a turning point in recent American history, for with the passing of this establishment, the bipartisan consensus which had sustained U.S. foreign policy and defined its purposes for a generation disappeared, leaving a paralyzing residuum of division and demoralization. Moreover, its passing was the occasion for the emergence of a new establishment dedicated to the transformation of American foreign policy in light of the experience in Vietnam.

It is perhaps misleading to distinguish between an old and a new establishment, since we are really speaking of a single group. The Council on Foreign Relations, the preeminent institution of the old establishment, did not fold up, nor was its leadership usurped by a dissident tendency. But it emerged from the trauma of Vietnam a very different institution from what it had been before and with a new political character.

It was not merely that the Council's reputation had been tarnished by the role its leading members had played in shaping American policy in Vietnam, a role amply documented in David Halberstam's book, *The Best and the Brightest,* or that it was increasingly opening its membership, as well as the pages of its journal, *Foreign Affairs,* to younger people who were bitter critics of that policy. Nor was it simply the fact that its influence over American foreign policy had significantly diminished in consequence of the unprecedented antagonism between the Council and the White House, whose new occupant, Richard Nixon, had never been accepted by the establishment and refused to acknowledge its authority. The principal way the Council had changed was that its leading members had ceased to believe in the world outlook they had espoused since the end of World War II.

In 1970, writing in *Foreign Affairs,* Townsend Hoopes, who had been Deputy Assistant Secretary of Defense and Under Secretary of the Air Force during the Johnson administration, asked how "so many intelligent, experienced, and humane men in government"—the establishment, in other words—could have failed to understand the "immorality" of the Vietnam intervention and the "cancerous division" it had created in America. His answer, which was fast becoming the prevailing view of these "intelligent, experienced, and humane men" themselves, was that they were products of a period dominated by the "cold-war syndrome and its ramified legacy." No one, Hoopes wrote, certainly no one *within* the establishment, could deny that these were "men of good conscience." But this was precisely why they had been so "vulnerable to the developing *hubris.*" Having embraced too fervently the Wilsonian "legacy of America's democratizing mission," they were "impelled by the iron logic of a messianic ideology" to take "actions beyond the rational requirements of our national security." Concluding that "the highest test of character is to learn from the past, to admit one's mistakes, and to act on that admission," Hoopes urged unilateral withdrawal from Vietnam and the rejection of the cold-war mentality that had led us into the war in the first place.

But it was not enough for the establishment to condemn the war in Vietnam. To restore its political authority, it had to undo its own historical link with the conflict. This was accomplished by transferring responsibility for the war to the Nixon administration, which remained, as Hoopes wrote, "residually hooked on the cold-war syndrome." Thus in 1972 the then editor of *Foreign Affairs,* the late Hamilton Fish Armstrong, wrote an article blaming the Nixon administration as well as the American public—but not the establishment—for the war in Vietnam and the sad decline of America's prestige in the world. Armstrong reiterated a thesis put forth fifty years earlier in *Foreign Affairs* by Elihu Root, to the effect that in a democracy the people are responsible for the conduct of foreign policy, and that only a well-informed public can curb the irresponsible acts of political leaders. In this respect, the American intervention in Vietnam, like the Senate's rejection in Root's time of U.S. participation in the League of Nations, could be traced ultimately to the "mistaken beliefs" of the public and thus constituted a failure of American democracy. The establishment, it seemed, had nothing whatever to do with this failure, though it would have an important role to play, according to Armstrong, in curing America's ills and "re-humanizing" the culture.

It was still not enough, however, merely to create the myth that the establishment had played no part in the Vietnam disaster. It was also necessary, as Hoopes had observed, to break with the "cold-war syndrome." Here the senior members of the establishment faced a difficult dilemma, for they could not repudiate the beliefs of a lifetime without destroying—not just in the eyes of others but, more critically, in their own as well—their legitimacy as a source of political authority. The containment of Communism was not, after all, a tactic which could be lightly abandoned in the course of a prudent retreat from a position of "overcommitment." It was the strategic core of the establishment's world view, the "basic organizing principle," as Zbigniew Brzezinski called it, which had for twenty-five years given coherence, continuity, and purpose to its stewardship of American foreign policy. Containment was as much a part of the identity of the establishment's senior members as was the memory of Munich and of the Soviet Union's seizure of Eastern Europe after the war—critical experiences which taught that totalitarianism could not be appeased.

Containment was, in a word, the establishment's creed. And since, as George Lichtheim once observed, "No ruling class can function without a creed," the establishment could regain its authority only if it fashioned a new creed, taking account of the failure in Vietnam and offering a new direction for American foreign policy in the post-Vietnam era.

Here the leading figures associated with the old establishment—men like McGeorge Bundy, William Bundy, Cyrus Vance, and Clark Clifford—were at something of a disadvantage, for they were too tied to the past to make a clean break with it, and their confidence had been too visibly shaken for them to chart a new course with the boldness that would be required. Still, they were distinguished and experienced men, and their support for the effort to reconstitute a functioning establishment would be valuable. Their conversion to a revised world view would suggest the emergence of a new consensus, while their steadfast presence would preserve the appearance of continuity, stability, and moderation—essential features of any establishment. Moreover, they still possessed considerable influence, if not with the Nixon White House then at least among its powerful critics in

Congress, the media, and the academic community. They could not be the architects of a new establishment, but their role could be something more than merely honorific.

The task of ideological reconstruction fell primarily to a group of specialists associated with *Foreign Policy,* a journal founded in 1970 "to stimulate rational discussion of the new directions required in American foreign policy" after Vietnam. Its two editors, Samuel P. Huntington and Warren Demian Manshel, felt that a magazine with "no institutional memory" was needed to redefine the "basic purposes" of America in the world "with a keener awareness that an era in American foreign policy, which began in the late 1940's, had ended." As it happened, the political outlook that *Foreign Policy* adopted was quite consistent with the one beginning to be developed in *Foreign Affairs,* and many of the same people wrote for both publications. But in the new journal one could discern a more systematic attempt to revise American policy and to formulate a new post-Vietnam world view.

The specialists who contributed most to this revision were not a monolithic group. Among them were some members of the old elite such as Townsend Hoopes, Paul C. Warnke, and Thomas L. Hughes. A larger element consisted of younger government officials of the "Vietnam generation" such as Leslie Gelb, Richard Holbrooke, and Anthony Lake, and academics like Richard H. Ullman of Princeton, who could reasonably think of themselves as future leaders of a revived establishment. They were joined by a small group of radical intellectuals, among them Richard J. Barnet of the Institute for Policy Studies and Richard A. Falk of Princeton, who saw the need for basic changes in American society if the country's foreign policy was to be set aright.

In addition to these different tendencies, several individuals who are not so easily categorized made important contributions to the effort to revise U.S. foreign policy. One of them was George F. Kennan, formerly a foreign-service officer and now at Princeton, who was best known as the author of the famous "Mr. X" article of 1947 in *Foreign Affairs* setting forth the containment doctrine, though he had broken with this policy even before it became fashionable to do so in the late 1960's. Another was Zbigniew Brzezinski of Columbia, who did not break until the early 1970's, and then did so very suddenly and with an elaborate theoretical justification. A third important figure was Stanley Hoffmann of Harvard, a consistent critic of U.S. foreign policy, whose Gaullist opposition to U.S. leadership in the world merged in the 1970's with the post-Vietnam denigration of American global power.

Writers like Kennan, Brzezinski, and Hoffmann differed with one another on significant points and in the emphasis they gave to various issues. But such differences (regarding U.S. relations with allies and with the Third World and the relative importance of transnational forces as opposed to the prerogatives of the nation-state) were much less important than their agreement that containment was no longer a valid basis for American foreign policy. In fact, opposition to containment was the principle that united all the writers who participated in the redefinition of an establishment perspective on foreign affairs. It was the starting point for any discussion of the U.S. world role, the basic assumption that all shared and none questioned. Opposition to containment could not by itself serve as a new creed, since it pointed in no positive direction. But the reaction to the Vietnam war was such that it was possible to bring people together merely on the basis of what they were against. And what everyone was against—at least everyone who aspired to a place in a new foreign-policy establishment—was American resistance to the advance of Communism in the world.

Thus during the first half of the 1970's, an elaborate intellectual structure was built in defense of the idea that the containment of Communism by the United States was neither possible, nor necessary, nor even desirable. This idea, above all others, was the "lesson of Vietnam," and the overriding purpose of the aspiring establishment was to make it the guiding principle of American foreign policy as a whole.

The argument that the containment of Communism was no longer possible began with an acknowledgement that the old establishment had ceased to function in any meaningful sense. Whether its passing was attributed to the Vietnam war, as by the British journalist Godfrey Hodgson in *Foreign Policy*, or to fundamental social changes which had displaced the "Wasp elite" from its position of unchallenged power, a view set forth by Brzezinski, the result was that no confident, cohesive leadership group which believed in containment and could command authority now existed in the United States.

The departure from the scene of this old establishment was accompanied by the arrival of what an article in *Foreign Affairs* called "the new generation of isolationists." This article, along with similar pieces that appeared in *Foreign Policy*, defended the attitudes of educated young Americans who were revolted by the war in Vietnam, profoundly disillusioned with American society, irritated by the "simplistic" distinction between the "free world" (a term never used without quotation marks around it) and the Communist world, and opposed to any form of military intervention, even where it was not dictated by the imperatives of containment. In a word, according to the *Foreign Affairs* piece, "they see no country for whose security they would fight."

But it was not only young people who felt this way. Americans in general, the journalist Ronald Steel declared in *Foreign Policy*, "are tired of the violence that has been committed in the name of peace, . . . of the numerous interventions conducted in the tired vocabulary of anti-Communism, of the sacrifice of their own unmet needs to an insatiable war machine, and of the deliberate deceit practiced by their leaders." Taking his own reading of the public mood, Bayless Manning, the then President of the Council on Foreign Relations, concluded that "the domestic atmosphere at this time of post-Vietnam and post-U.S. *imperium* is not propitious for a remobilization of the moral energies of the nation for a major overseas initiative." Watergate was still another factor undermining support in the country for a policy of containment, for as Leslie Gelb and Anthony Lake wrote in *Foreign Policy*, it had done for the concept of "national security" what Vietnam had done for "commitment," namely, to make it "an object for derisive satire." "For those who have been waging the fight to reduce defense expenditures these past five years," they added, "the demise of the concept of national security will come as a godsend."

Beyond the political atmosphere in the country and the attitudes of particular groups, American society was systemically incapable of sustaining a policy of containment. In the first place, as Adam Yarmolinsky (formerly of the Pentagon, now an academic) argued, American society simply could not afford to pursue a containment policy that would tie up resources and energies needed to deal with such critical matters as the plight of the cities, the needs of blacks and the poor, the restlessness of students, and the pollution of the environment.

Nor could we continue to tolerate the kind of political abuses that seemed to be the unavoidable consequences of containment. In competing with totalitarian states, Columbia's Marshall Shulman wrote in *Foreign Affairs*, democratic systems may be tempted to adopt the undemocratic methods of their adversaries, the example cited being the behavior of the CIA. Anthony Lake identified a parallel problem: "the psychology of the cold war" had encouraged government officials to lie to the public in the interest of national security, thus undermining the credibility of the government and causing educated people to regard official statements "with the same suspicion as a cigarette commercial." Ironically, in Richard Ullman's view, there was much more reason to believe that containment threatened American democracy than that it was necessary for our democracy's survival.

George Kennan shared these concerns about the effects of containment on the health of American democracy, but he went further in concluding that the United States was not "well constituted . . . to play a very active role in world affairs." The immense size and diversity of the country and the competing pressures of numerous political and ethnic groups and organized lobbies had made it impossible to conduct a coherent foreign policy, let alone one with ambitious objectives. The wisest course, according to Kennan, would be for the United States to recognize its limitations and "follow a policy of minding its own business to the extent that it can."

These various domestic constraints on the exercise of American power abroad, involving both political attitudes and structural features of the American system, were thought to present a formidable and probably insuperable obstacle to the continued pursuit of the containment policy. But even if none of them existed, the opponents of containment still felt that the United States had no choice but to abandon the use or even the threat of military force to oppose Communist advances in the world. "Perhaps the principal lesson of the past decade," Warnke and Gelb wrote, "is that military force is a singularly inept instrument of foreign policy." In a world dominated by nationalism and rising demands for economic equality, one could not emphasize enough, in Stanley Hoffmann's opinion, "the increasingly obvious irrelevance of military power to most of the goals pursued by states." In such a world, the United States, as "the biggest fly on the flypaper," would have to accommodate to the new forces and seek influence through the use of economic inducements rather than through the futile reliance on military power.

Since it followed from this line of reasoning that the Soviet Union was stuck on the same "flypaper" as the United States, containment, even if it were not also unfeasible, was in any case unnecessary.

"No nation," Hoffmann declared, "however mighty, can now pretend to shape or manage world order along the lines of its own preferences; any nation that tries will stagger from arbitrariness—the choice of the wrong track—to confusion—the attempt to run on all tracks at once." According to Richard J. Barnet, not only had it become much more difficult for both major powers to extend control over other countries, but recent history had shown that even "the entry of new countries into the Communist bloc involves heavy costs as well as benefits for the Soviet Union." The obvious conclusion, as stated by Charles Gati of Columbia (who imputed the view to the Nixon administration as well), was that "the possible future extension of Soviet influence (outside of Europe) might represent such acute problems for the Soviet Union as the extension of American influence has for the United States, and for this reason the United States should be attentive to but not overly anxious about such possibilities."

In fact, the whole notion that the outcome of conflicts like the one in Vietnam mattered any longer in world politics was based on a concept of security that had been rendered obsolete by advances in military technology. With both powers having acquired the capability to strike quickly anywhere in the world with missiles or conventional military forces dispatched from their own territory, the need to rely on local defense arrangements or to deny each other "strategic real estate" had greatly diminished. Paradoxically, therefore, wrote Barnet, "the arms race has reduced the tactical incentive of both major powers to resort to territorial aggression."

Advances in military technology had altered international relations in even more fundamental ways, virtually ruling out future confrontations between the great powers and opening the way for new forms of nonmilitary competition. According to Brzezinski, the "balance of terror" had rendered the power of the United States and the Soviet Union "largely non-usable." With both countries constrained by a "paralysis of power," containment was no longer relevant, and secondary powers such as China, Europe, and Japan would play an enhanced role in international diplomacy. Because the risks of confrontation were prohibitive, Robert E. Hunter of Johns Hopkins concluded that "the only real competitions that the United States and the Soviet Union will be able to permit themselves later in this decade will be in the economic realm." Indeed, he saw the world moving to "an era in which war between major states may virtually disappear."

Still another factor making containment irrelevant was the revolution in technology and communications which was thought to have created a more interrelated world order. Brzezinski, the leading exponent of this point of view, said that "an emerging global consciousness is forcing the abandonment of preoccupations with national supremacy and accentuating global interdependence." The ideological rivalry of the past had grown out of a need "for remaking a world that was both distant and largely unknown, but proximity and global congestion now dictate revolutionary diversity." He saw America becoming involved with "the less political and more basic problems" facing mankind, "emphasizing ecology rather than ideology" and encouraging the spread of "a more personalized rational humanist world outlook that would gradually replace the institutionalized religious, ideological, and intensely national perspectives that have dominated modern history."*

The transformation of international politics by new global forces was not the only reason given to explain why containment was no longer necessary. Even more significant was the idea that the Soviet Union had become a status-quo power and was now genuinely committed to détente with the United States. Marshall Shulman acknowledged that détente offered "tactical advantages" to the Soviet Union, but he felt that "more fundamental" factors—among them the Soviet Union's need for economic cooperation with the West, its desire to stabilize the arms race, and its fear of China— required Moscow to favor "a long-term commitment to a policy of low tension abroad."

George Kennan, whose views on this subject carried special weight because he had first enunciated the containment doctrine a quarter of a century earlier, now came to the conclusion that the military rivalry between the United States and the Soviet Union no longer had any "foundation in real interests." It was kept alive, he thought, by "irrational fear" and "institutionalized force of habit" which the military-industrial complex of each big power exploited to its own advantage. If the Soviets continued to espouse revolutionary doctrines and to support revolutionary movements in the Third World, this did not mean that they had any claims against the United States or posed any threat to American interests. The Soviet Union was motivated entirely by its rivalry with China and the fear that the loss of its image as the leader of the revolutionary forces in the world "would throw into question the legitimacy of its regime at home."

Indeed, said Kennan, the Soviet posture was everywhere defensive in character, born of a profound and unappreciated insecurity. The Soviet

*For a fuller discussion of these themes, see Brzezinski's book, *Between Two Ages: America's Role in the Technetronic Era* (1970).

Union was fearful of NATO, which had "ringed" it with missile bases. It was fearful, too, of West Germany, which resented the division of Germany and the Berlin Wall—positions Moscow was "obliged to cling to" if it was to preserve the status quo in Eastern Europe. It could not loosen its grip on Eastern Europe for fear that this would "set up liberationist ripples that would carry into the Soviet Union itself." Nor could it return the Kuriles to Japan for fear that it would "make itself vulnerable to similar demands for readjustment of borders in Europe." The Soviet Union's "sense of weakness" was such that it could not even tolerate the expression of dissent at home by "a relatively small and helpless band of intellectuals."*

Surely the worst thing one could do in dealing with such a country would be to increase its sense of insecurity by acts which it might construe as unfriendly and provocative. As Shulman pointed out, too much pressure for internal liberalization would only "reinforce" the regime's siege mentality, and make it take a harder line against the dissidents. And too much pressure on its external positions, in the name of containment, would only create the very danger which containment was supposed to defend against.

Kennan did not doubt, for example, that "we have taught the Soviet leadership something of our own obsession with military strength—have taught them, that is, to think in American-Pentagon terms—have caused them, too, to be hypnotized by the nuclear weapons race." This view was shared by Paul Warnke, who felt that America's "words and actions" were "admirably calculated to inspire the Soviet Union to spend its substance on military manpower and weaponry." Reviewing the history of containment, Richard J. Barnet noted how "ironical" it was that "the strategy chosen by the U.S. to deal with the limited Soviet challenge to American supremacy may well have helped to create a Soviet Union with global interests and commitments."

Containment, then, was counterproductive—and therefore undesirable—in addition to being unfeasible and unnecessary. This was true not only because it would provoke unfriendly Soviet behavior but also because it would draw the United States into situations harmful to its own best interests. As Shulman noted, the containment policy had led the United States to align itself in the Third World with conservative authoritarian regimes and to oppose "social protest movements" which were viewed as instruments of Communism. According to Bayless Manning, we had "wound up on the wrong side" of history and were held "in deep disfavor" by Third World countries which saw the United States "as the main external adversary opposing their national development, internal modernization, and economic advancement." The commitments undertaken in the name of containment on behalf of such hapless regimes led inevitably to protracted conflicts like Vietnam in which the United States sought vainly and at great cost to hold back the march of history.

*These positions are spelled out in Kennan's *The Cloud of Danger: Current Realities and American Foreign Policy* (1977).

The cruelest irony was that these commitments presumably had been made to help "free peoples" resist attempted subjugation, as the Truman Doctrine had pledged. In reality, of course, the peoples in question were not free, but rather subjugated by the very dictators propped up by *us*. And the help we offered, as one writer in *Foreign Policy* observed, ran the risk of destroying the very societies we hoped to save. We had embarked on these "bloody crusades" in the name of freedom, but as Brzezinski argued, the idea of equality—not liberty—was "increasingly the underlying mood and the felt aspiration in an increasingly congested world."

In this context, Manning pointed to the ultimate irony, which was that the "totalitarian regimes" we opposed were the unconscious agents of liberty in the developing world. They would "substitute a better, more efficient, more productive and widely sharing society" for what now existed, thereby making it possible at some future point for "new progressive elements . . . to build upon the social and economic gains made during the era of conscript modernization." At that point the United States might reclaim its "moral leadership" in the world, not through arms "but by virtue of its ideological example as a society of free men."

While the critique of containment was intended to dissociate the new establishment from the policies of the past, it suggested as well general guidelines for the policies of the future. The first such guideline was the adoption of an attitude of "equanimity," as one writer termed it, toward changes in the world which previously would have been considered injurious to American security. Since the United States was no longer engaged in a global struggle with Communism, it was possible to dispense with linkage, a "pernicious and destructive" concept, as Warren Demian Manshel called it, which had caused us to endow local events with a purely imaginary strategic significance. U.S. policy could henceforth be based on the understanding that "American physical security," in Richard Ullman's words, "would not in any immediate sense be affected by drastic changes in the internal political structure of any other state or states."

The doctrine of equanimity had many advantages for the United States, the most obvious one being that it would eliminate the prospect of a future Vietnam. And in a larger sense, it meant that the United States could now adopt an attitude of "benign neglect," as Warnke and Gelb put it, "toward international military involvements." It did not follow from this, however, that the United States should be indifferent to the fate and well-being of the peoples of the Third World. On the contrary—and this was another general guideline for American policy—it was necessary for the United States to identify with and actively assist "the forces of change" which we had opposed during the period of containment.

Toward this end, Ullman urged that "a central goal of American policy over the coming years" should be to terminate the support which had previously been extended to "repressive" regimes on "expediential grounds." It was also important, wrote Tom J. Farer of Rutgers, to "soften our image as an intractable opponent of change" by making "gestures" of accommodation on three issues of paramount concern to the Third World—Southern Africa, the Palestinians, and North-South economic relations.

Beyond this, Ullman added, we would have to demonstrate our concern with "the quality of political life in other countries" by opposing repression. Here, though, we would have to recognize that "human rights are relatively culture-bound in their applications." Societies like Tanzania and Yugoslavia, he cautioned, might lack democratic rights as we know them in the United States, but we were required to acknowledge that they had "achieved a certain degree of openness and tolerance, combined with genuine mass participation, within an all-embracing single-party structure."

Above all, Brzezinski wrote, American policy would have to be "sympathetically sensitive to the significant shift in global emphasis" toward equality. This would not necessarily be very costly for the United States, said Farer, since only the authoritarian elites in the Third World were demanding equality—for states, not individuals—and therefore "the overall number of people who have to be given a stake in the essential structures of the existing international economic system is relatively small." But even if one allowed that it might be costly, and many writers were of this opinion, it was still necessary for political reasons to respond sympathetically to demands for a "new international economic order."

For these same reasons, it was imperative that the United States eschew the kind of "democratic crusade" that had marred American policy during the period of containment and which Ambassador Daniel P. Moynihan had launched once again at the United Nations. Brzezinski warned that "for Americans to inject into American external relations the ideological claim that the contemporary world struggle is between liberal democracy and various forms of despotic statism" would "create a doctrinal coalition against the United States" and accelerate the country's "global isolation." Moynihan's criticism of Communist and Third World despotisms appealed to many Americans because it offered "a welcome escape from complexity, even if in the guise of isolated self-righteousness." But it encouraged a "siege mentality" which could destroy the "optimism and universalism" which were "the underlying basis of legitimacy of the American system as a whole." At any rate, America would be "compelled gradually to accommodate itself" to the international realities. The only real question was "how long it will take . . . to absorb and internalize a reasonably coherent yet necessarily flexible conceptual understanding of the emerging new world."

For Stanley Hoffmann, "a vindictive defense of our system of freedom," which was how he characterized Moynihan's "democratic crusade," was dangerous not just because of what it would do to America but because "it would wreck any chances for world order." Therefore America had to "curb" its own "aggressive nationalism," even as it sought to accommodate itself to hostile foreign nationalisms. To promote world order, it was necessary to "stress what is minimally objectionable," to smooth down "the cutting edge of one's own ideology," and not to put forward "proposals that will certainly arouse the hostility of all those who do not share America's preference for liberal democratic regimes." Moreover, "in the realm of conflict par excellence we must seek the cooperation of our rivals, and be ready to oppose our allies and clients when they pursue policies that run counter to the interests of world order."

Hoffmann recommended that the United States follow a general "rule of non-collision." As a guideline for American policy in the post-Vietnam period, such a rule had great appeal even to those who did not fully appreciate the subtleties of Hoffmann's "world-order" approach. This was especially true with respect to relations with the Soviet Union, where the risk of nuclear confrontation was a factor that had to be considered. Here the doctrine of equanimity was particularly useful, for it allowed one to support a "strategy of conflict-avoidance," as one writer called it, without any apparent strategic cost. Thus, articles in both *Foreign Affairs* and *Foreign Policy* argued that the placement of Soviet offensive missiles in Cuba in 1962 and the construction there of a submarine base in 1970 had only "symbolic" significance, and that the United States could have avoided dangerous crises over these Soviet initiatives by "showing rational or even naive unconcern" and simply dismissing "the issue of resolve." Both articles, in fact, maintained that the United States should have welcomed the construction of the Soviet submarine base, since this would have stabilized the strategic balance by allowing Moscow to complete its sea-launched deterrent.

On the whole, though, major difficulties with the Soviet Union were not anticipated. Ullman, for example, did not even mention U.S.-Soviet relations in the eight guidelines for American policy he published in 1976. Zygmunt Nagorski, Jr., then on the staff of the Council on Foreign Relations, looked forward to "a gradual converging of commercial and developmental interests between East and West" taking place beneath "the umbrella of parity of strength." If America did nothing to arouse Soviet fear and animosity, cooperation between the two superpowers seemed assured. "How to deal with the Communist world," Brzezinski wrote, "remains a key problem for U.S. foreign policy but it may no longer represent the central problem."

Beyond improving relations with the Third World, the new priority for American policy was "trilateralism," by which was meant the deepening of cooperation among the United States, Europe, and Japan in order to create what Brzezinski termed "a stable core for global politics." Marina v. N. Whitman, then at the University of Pittsburgh, called for "the replacement of leadership based on hegemony with leadership based on persuasion and compromise," a statement that was widely quoted because it summed up so succinctly the new approach that was needed. This approach also had to generate support at home, which was why it could not be, as Brzezinski described Kissinger's policy, "covert, manipulative, and deceptive in style ... committed to a largely static view of the world, based on a traditional balance of power." American policy had to become more open, compassionate, and committed to reform, for only in this way would it be capable of "tapping the moral resources of the American people."

Writing in *Foreign Policy* in 1973, Godfrey Hodgson had concluded his reflections on the demise of the old establishment by raising the possibility that "in time a new establishment will form from among those who are able to take as their starting point that the Vietnam war was a disaster." Were such a new establishment to emerge, its "essential moral" would be "that it is much more difficult and dangerous to use force in support of foreign-policy objectives than you might suppose."

In fact, by 1975 this very establishment had come into existence, constituting what Hoffmann called "a kind of expectant establishment in exile." It had conceived and enunciated an elaborate perspective on American foreign policy. And it was in possession of an organizing principle every bit as compelling after Vietnam as containment had been after Munich and the lowering of the Iron Curtain in Europe. This principle was anti-containment, or the non-use of force in world affairs.

A distinctive feature of this new establishment was its optimism, which stood out in such vivid contrast to the pessimism of those, like Henry Kissinger and Daniel P. Moynihan, who were troubled over what they perceived as the retreat of American power and the loss of political will throughout the West. For Richard Holbrooke, then managing editor of *Foreign Policy*, this pessimism was based on nothing more than the willful defeatism of those who regretted the loss of American "hegemony" and failed to appreciate the growing opportunities for American leadership in a changing world. America had no "need to dominate the world in order to live safely in it," he wrote, and anyway the United States was "still the most powerful nation on earth." It was true that the world's perception of American retreat was a problem, but this was the work of those who promoted a defeatist view and then confirmed their own conclusions by trying to get us involved in a futile and strategically irrelevant war in Angola. The country was strong and its world position secure. It could "survive everything but its own defeatism."

The pessimism decried by Holbrooke could be traced to America's defeat in Vietnam. But for Manshel, the end of the war was a source of hope. Writing in the immediate aftermath of the Communist takeover of Saigon, he saw America "entering a new era, free at last of the drain of overinvolvement and overcommitment to a cause never winnable (and never worth winning) in an area marginal to the strategic interests of the United States." America could now look to the future with renewed confidence, for "with the quixotic lance [of Vietnam] broken, the shield of the republic is stronger today than it was when the Vietnam debacle began a decade and a half ago."

This optimism, and the perspective underlying it, was in danger of being engulfed by the alarm which swept the country following the collapse of Indochina in 1975. According to Gelb and Lake, congressional liberals who should have known better had succumbed to administration arguments that the Mayaguez affair was "a test case of American resolve around the world" and that "the size of the defense budget is a vital signal of American will." These liberals were too "uncertain of themselves on foreign policy" and felt too vulnerable to "the charge of isolationism" to offer any meaningful alternative to the administration's policies. Thus the only hope was to "wait till next year for broad movement toward a sensible foreign policy."

Here the prospects were indeed bright. Recent poll data, Brzezinski reported, showed "a public opinion that is ambivalent but constructively malleable." This "heightened the need for national leadership that was capable of defining politically and morally compelling directions to which the public might then respond."

Thomas L. Hughes, the president of the Carnegie Endowment for International Peace, which published *Foreign Policy*, was "positively euphoric." The moment had arrived, he announced, for the emergence of a new "liberal-populist" governing coalition which looked "inward to the traditional pursuit of redistributing the affluence of an inequitable America" and "outward to . . . a constructive new American accommodation with mankind." Like "the Truman-Acheson arrangement" of a generation earlier, it would unite the foreign-policy elite with "the plain people," the chief difference being that the new coalition would be disposed "toward global as well as domestic accommodations." In foreign policy, such a new coalition would confirm and enlarge the "new East-West strategic bargains" and strike "new North-South bargains." It would rescue the country from the morally corrosive domestic effects of Kissinger's *Realpolitik* and the dangerously defeatist international consequences of Moynihan's "opposition to the world." It would succeed in "restoring our own self-confidence and the confidence of others in us" and in "re-establishing the steadiness of policy by moderating the crisis of authority within the American government." Such a coalition, in short, would "rise to the global occasion on the ashes of an unhappy decade of American history."

Hughes's article, which appeared in *Foreign Policy* in the fall of 1975, correctly anticipated the results of the forthcoming election. The victory of Jimmy Carter produced *exactly* the kind of "liberal-populist" governing coalition which Hughes had foreseen. It was exemplified, as it were, in the "Carter-Vance arrangement," wherein a Southern President who campaigned as a populist staffed his foreign-policy bureaucracy with members of the Eastern foreign-policy establishment, or, more precisely, the *new* foreign-policy establishment.

In addition to Vance, who shared the new outlook on foreign policy even if he had not publicly expounded it, those receiving high appointments in the Carter administration included Brzezinski, who became the President's national security adviser; Warnke, who was made both the director of the Arms Control and Disarmament Agency and the chief negotiator for SALT; Shulman, who was appointed the State Department's chief adviser on Soviet policy; and Gelb, Lake, and Holbrooke, who became, respectively, the director of the Bureau of Politico-Military Affairs at the State Department, the director of policy planning, and the Assistant Secretary for East Asian Affairs. There were many other key appointments of this kind, among them Andrew Young as United Nations Ambassador, Richard Moose as Assistant Secretary for African Affairs, and David Aaron and Robert Hunter as members of the National Security Council. These were only a representative handful of the appointments which brought members of the new foreign-policy establishment into the Carter administration.

Not only did the President turn to the new establishment to manage his foreign policy as earlier Presidents had turned to the old establishment, but he adopted in every important respect its political perspective and even its rhetoric. The President's famous Notre Dame speech of May 1977, in which he first described his administration's foreign policy, was a perfect synthesis of the ideas propounded by the new establishment during the preceding years. The speech began with the core idea of the new establishment, the rejection of containment. It was this policy, flowing from an "inordinate fear of Communism," that had led us "to embrace any dictator who joined us in our fear" and "to adopt the flawed principles and tactics of our adversaries." The result was a "sapping of worldwide faith in our policy" and "a crisis of confidence, made even more grave by the covert pessimism of some of our leaders."

Such pessimism, Carter explained, was based on an outdated view of the world—the "belief that Soviet expansion must be contained." But now "The unifying threat of conflict with the Soviet Union ha[d] become less intensive," and "new global questions of justice, equity, and human rights" had come to the fore. "It is a new world," the President said, "but America should not fear it." We now had "a new foreign policy" capable of responding "to the new reality of a politically awakening world." Rather than "expect that the other 150 nations will follow the dictates of the powerful," we would now try "to inspire and to persuade and to lead." Our policy would be one of "constructive global involvement," committed to human rights, détente, cooperation among the industrial democracies, and a new relationship with the nations of the Third World, with whom we would work closely "in a common effort as the structure of world power changes." We would "encourage all countries to rise above narrow national interests and work together to solve such formidable global problems" as hunger, racial hatred, and the arms race, patiently attempting "to create a wider framework of international cooperation suited to the new historical circumstances."

If there had been any doubt that the new foreign-policy establishment was now in power, the Notre Dame speech made it official. Thus while Carter as President must of course be held accountable for his own administration, this new establishment must take at least an equal share of responsibility for the course of American foreign policy under its conceptual guidance and practical management. Indeed, the new establishment's responsibility is all the heavier for its having broken so unequivocally with thirty years of historical experience. Had the new establishment claimed at least some continuity with the past, it might now be in a position to argue that its ideas and policies were not the only ones being tested but also the ideas and policies of its predecessors. But it claimed no such continuity. It rejected everything that had gone before, even including the conduct, if not the concept, of détente. By holding others so harshly to account, the new establishment invited strict accountability for itself.

What such an accounting reveals after a test of more than three years is an appalling deterioration in every area in which the new establishment so brashly predicted dramatic progress—in our relations with the Third World, in our relations with our allies, and most serious of all in our relations with the Soviet Union.

That our relations with the countries of the Third World are significantly worse today than they were when the new establishment took power is clear from the vehement anti-Americanism of the "nonaligned" conference in Havana last year [1979–eds.] and the mobs in the streets of Teheran. An equally vivid indication of the declining American position in the Third World is the growing anxiety of many countries that once considered the U.S. a trustworthy friend. The comment in the *New York Times* by a high Pakistani official that "you Americans don't seem to understand the world any more" reflects the thinking of many pro-Western leaders in the Third World who are losing faith in the capacity or even willingness of the United States to resist Soviet expansion. Such thinking explains the increasing tendency among these countries to keep a safe distance between themselves and Washington and to move toward an accommodation with Moscow.

U.S. relations with our "trilateral" partners, Europe and Japan, have deteriorated just as badly. The specter of neutralism now hangs over Europe as West Germany moves steadily closer to a separate accommodation with Moscow. As for Japan, before leaving on a visit to the United States in early May [1980], Prime Minister Ohira said that "the U.S. has become one of the powers and not a superpower any more. The days are gone when we were able to rely on America's [nuclear] deterrent." Such anxieties have not been expressed publicly until now, though they are known to represent the thinking of many leaders in Europe as well as Japan. They indicate an increased distrust of the U.S. which threatens the very survival of the postwar Western alliance.

Finally, relations between the United States and the Soviet Union are as bad as they were at any point during the cold war and far more dangerous, considering the disarray in the Western camp, the collapsing American position in the world, our new strategic vulnerability, the shift in the military balance toward the Soviet Union, and its consequently growing readiness to achieve its objectives through the decisive use of force. The application of the doctrine of equanimity to the 1978 Communist coup in Afghanistan did not prevent the Soviet invasion a year-and-a-half later. The unilateral cancellation of U.S. weapons programs did not have any noticeable effect on the Soviet military build-up. "Getting on the side of change" in Africa did not stop the Soviet Union and its proxies from intervening in Ethiopia. And following the rule of non-collision in the case of the Soviet brigade in Cuba, or the earlier installation there of Soviet MIG-23 attack planes, did not encourage Cuba to restrain its subversive and terrorist activities in Central America and the Caribbean.

An administration that began by assuming it could improve relations with the Soviet Union if only it downplayed East-West issues is now obsessed with such concerns. Having repudiated an illusory American hegemony, it now faces the real danger of Soviet hegemony—a prospect it is trying desperately to elude by restoring a balance of power, something it once considered outdated and "Machiavellian" and whose workings it still does not seem to understand. And though it founded its entire foreign policy—its very conception of America's world role, in fact—on the rejection of containment, it has discovered to its dismay that the Soviet Union has not abandoned that ambition for conquest which made containment necessary in the first place. If anything, Moscow's policies are much more clearly threatening now than during the cold war, for the Soviets have been emboldened by the change in the balance of power to proclaim that henceforth the Brezhnev Doctrine will be extended to countries (like Chile under Allende and perhaps Nicaragua under the Sandinistas) where Communists are trying to consolidate power, not merely to retain power already established.

Though the foreign-policy perspective of the new establishment has been thoroughly discredited by events, it has not yet been honestly reevaluated or clearly repudiated by any of its proponents, including the President.

In his State of the Union Address in 1979, Carter assured the nation that "our military defenses are strong" and that no superpower—by which he meant the Soviet Union—could or would "dominate the world." He added: "We have no desire to be the world's policeman, but America does want to be the world's peacemaker." It was a classic evocation of the post-Vietnam mentality, stunningly out of touch with the times. Yet, later that same year, in a speech calling for an increase in military spending, the President said that the postwar consensus built "around the concept of an active role for America in preserving peace and security for ourselves and for others" had endured, "despite all the changes that have swept across the world in the past thirty years."

The vast intellectual gulf separating these two statements—one rejecting the role of "policeman," the other endorsing the policy of containment—can be bridged only by an admission of error. But except for Brzezinski's apparent rediscovery of the containment doctrine and the President's offhand comment that his view of Soviet intentions changed "drastically" after the invasion of Afghanistan, such an admission has not been forthcoming. The appointment as the new Secretary of State of Edmund

Muskie, a man identified with the first statement and not the second, indicates that, despite its claim to the contrary, the administration has still not overcome its "Vietnam complex."

It is perhaps understandable that a President running for reelection should not admit that the foreign policy of his administration has been profoundly mistaken and that the country's security is now in grave jeopardy. Yet not even among members of the new establishment who are not part of the Carter administration, or who have retired from it, has there been any discernible readiness to reevaluate their perspective. Their independence, in fact, has had quite the opposite effect. That is, it has freed them to shift the blame for the nation's predicament from their own ideas and policies to Carter's alleged incompetence—as if what is at issue were not a flawed conception of the world but rather the gifts of the technician charged with carrying it out.

This tactic began to be applied early on. For example, Hoffmann (who has held no office under Carter) attributed the administration's difficulties during 1977 to its lack of a "comprehensive plan" for the conduct of its policies. Its approach was too "nonpolitical" and "technocratic," meaning that it suffered from having no perspective rather than a mistaken one. Thomas L. Hughes (who has also remained outside) conceded that the administration had a perspective—a correct one, too—but lacked the skill to implement it. "The administration's foreign-policy failures to date," he wrote in mid-1978, "are not the result of an excess of liberalism. They are failures of the central organizing forces of the administration."

In addition to blaming Carter for inconsistency and ineptitude, the new establishment responded to Soviet advances by excusing Soviet behavior and blaming the United States for the impasse in relations. Thus, writing in Foreign Affairs, Robert Legvold, the director of the Soviet Project at the Council on Foreign Relations, saw little evidence to support the "impression of an emboldened Soviet leadership" which was "embarked on a vast alliance system in the Third World." From Moscow's point of view, it was the West which was "overwhelmingly ascendant" and on the attack throughout Africa and the Persian Gulf. The Soviet Union, in fact, had shown great restraint in staying out of internal conflicts in Iran, the Western Sahara, Nicaragua, and elsewhere, and by initially seeking to mediate the disputes in Angola and between Ethiopia and Somalia. Moreover, "where restraint has given way to active intervention," as in Angola and Ethiopia, "the Soviet Union has acted with caution," for it "checked to see that the coast was clear before proceeding." There was danger, to be sure, in the Soviet Union's "extemporaneous, unplotted entanglement" in the Third World, but no evidence that the Soviet leaders were "thinking systematically about these issues."

The great need, Legvold continued, was "to spell out the standards of behavior both sides expect of each other," and here the United States was at fault. We could not expect "the Soviet Union to give up the right to involve itself in troubled areas, if we are not prepared to give up this right ourselves."

Furthermore, it was one thing to want the Soviet Union to stay out of local conflicts, but quite another to say that it could "not go to the aid of governments established by insurgent movements once they are installed." A realistic policy would recognize that "neither side will readily yield the right to intervene in troubled areas." At the same time, however, the Soviet leaders want "to give the overall competition stability and predictability," and they "are ready to begin a serious discussion, provided our purpose is not simply to upbraid them."

If Legvold identified the one-sidedness of the United States as the source of the problem, Hoffmann narrowed it still further. In his opinion, the crucial factor in the deterioration of U.S.-Soviet relations was those elements in the United States which adhered to "a new orthodoxy that identified the present American plight as the result of a retreat before an ascending Soviet steamroller." The goal of Soviet policy was not "world domination" but only "achieving equality with the United States." While the Soviet Union might relentlessly seek to expand its power, it had not been nearly so successful as was imagined. In any event, both powers, despite the competitive aspects of their relationship, had "a joint interest in moderation" deriving from their "common concern for survival and for development and economic well-being." The paramount task facing both of them, therefore, was to "organize the coexistence of competitive strategies" by defining the "common rules" by which they would abide. Those committed to the "new orthodoxy," in their nostalgia for "lost supremacy," were undermining this effort to stabilize relations at every turn—by linking arms-control talks to extraneous political issues, by opposing expanded trade relations between the two countries, by interjecting the human-rights issue into U.S.-Soviet relations, and by creating opportunities for Soviet expansion through their support of weak anti-Communist regimes (whose inevitable collapse then reinforced the erroneous and dangerous view that America was in retreat). The effect of their obstructive behavior and anti-Soviet "grandstanding" was to feed "Soviet paranoia" and to make U.S.-Soviet confrontation more likely.

Hoffmann's argument, which was composed shortly before the invasion of Afghanistan, rested entirely upon the unexamined assumption that the Soviet leaders shared *his* understanding of *their* interests and intentions. The invasion may have forced the President to change his mind about Soviet intentions, but not Hoffmann—though it did shake his confidence a bit. An article he published shortly after the invasion was filled with "murky questions" (Was the invasion an offensive or a defensive move? Did the Soviets act out of a sense of *their* weakness or a perception of *our* weakness?), and desperate affirmations ("There is no substitute for peaceful coexistence; and it can only be obtained if the Soviet Union is not pushed into a corner or locked into a position of implacable hostility"), and concluded with the confession that his function was not to define policy but simply "to question, to wonder, and to warn."

But not even that degree of wavering has been apparent among other ideologues of the new establishment. Instead of reexamining their assumptions, they have insisted upon them more strongly than ever. Claiming that the crisis created by the invasion had increased "the urgency of arms control," Warnke criticized the administration's "emotional pursuit of security through military means" and called for the implementation of the SALT treaty without Senate ratification. Decrying the "self-generated hysteria" in the country, Gelb called upon the United States to initiate a "dialogue" with Moscow and to indicate our desire for "normal" relations by ratifying SALT. And Kennan, still faithful to his belief that insecurity is the key to Soviet behavior, promoted the idea that the invasion was a "defensive" move that was not nearly as worrisome as the "militarization of thought and discourse" in Washington.

If such statements gave the impression that the United States and not the Soviet Union had caused the crisis, this was not unintended, for it was an article of faith within the new establishment that the Soviet invasion was a natural consequence of the growing opposition to détente within America.

Arguments of this kind were dangerously deluding before the invasion of Afghanistan, but they were inexcusable—both morally and politically—in its aftermath. They were also completely unpersuasive to the vast majority of the American people, a point implicitly acknowledged by the new establishment's final argument—that the President's poor handling of Afghanistan (and Iran) could be explained by his capitulation to political pressures in an election year when he should have been taking the sober diplomatic advice of Cyrus Vance. Gelb perceived "a classic clash of philosophies" between a politicized White House looking for immediate results and a professional State Department patiently trying to work out "the knotty problems of international politics."

But it will not be so easy for the new establishment to disclaim responsibility for the fearful disarray of American foreign policy. If the President appears to be inept, it is because events have shattered his original interpretation of the world—which was not his alone but that of the new establishment as well—and he is now left without a fixed compass, guided by nothing save his reading of the public mood. And if he has attempted to manipulate this mood to his domestic political advantage, even at the expense of the national security—a pattern one sees in his handling of the hostage crisis, to which he has subordinated all strategic concerns, including Afghanistan—this too may be traced back to the new establishment. For it was the new establishment that devalued the importance of national-security concerns in the first place, saturating American foreign policy with defeatism masquerading as optimism and "maturity" and "restraint," cravenly following international political fashion even if this meant denigrating the interests and values of one's own country, and worrying less about American security than about Soviet insecurity, in the name of which virtually any Soviet action could be condoned or blamed upon the United States.

As all the polls reveal, the American people have now overwhelmingly rejected the ideas of the new establishment. Apart from having been exposed as mistaken in all its major judgments, the new establishment never spoke for the country as a whole but only for a narrow if influential sector of the elite which had ceased to believe in America after Vietnam, and which despite its proclaimed optimism seems to have resigned itself to the forward momentum of political forces in the world committed to America's ultimate defeat. We have already been given a foretaste of what this defeat will mean in the Communist holocaust in Indochina, the growing numbers of refugees fleeing from totalitarianism, the spreading violence in a world increasingly exposed to Soviet power, and the deepening isolation of the United States. This is not the kind of world in which Americans—or other peoples, for that matter—want to live. And it is because the new establishment has resigned itself to this fate that it no longer deserves to be listened to by anyone who still believes a better world is possible.

13

A LEADERSHIP DIVIDED
The Foreign Policy Beliefs
Of American Leaders,
1976–1980[1]

OLE R. HOLSTI
JAMES N. ROSENAU

During the two decades following the
end of World War II, most Americans accepted a number of basic principles
about foreign affairs and the role of the nation in the world, including the
following:

- The United States had the responsibility and capabilities to be actively
  involved in efforts to create a just and stable world order. There were,
  to be sure, some prominent isolationists—for example, former President Herbert Hoover—who argued that such efforts would ultimately
  bankrupt the country. Moreover, even the internationalists disagreed
  on priorities (Europe versus the Far East, for example) or on details of
  implementation. Nevertheless, a substantial majority of American
  leaders appeared to have become convinced that the 1930s had demonstrated the bankruptcy of isolationism.
- The United States should be actively involved in a broad range of
  international organizations. The fact that certain people hoped and
  believed that the United Nations might be the forerunner of some
  type of world federation (for example, the United World Federalists),

Copyright © 1982 by Ole R. Holsti and James N. Rosenau. **Ole R. Holsti** is George V. Allen
Professor of International Affairs and Chairman, Department of Political Science, at Duke
University. He has also taught at Stanford University, the University of British Columbia, and
the University of California at Davis. He served as President of the International Studies Asso-
ciation in 1979–1980. His research has focused on psychological and cognitive aspects of deci-
sion making. Among his articles and books are *Crisis Escalation War* and *Content Analysis for
Social Sciences and Humanities.* **James N. Rosenau** is a professor at the School of International
Relations at the University of Southern California, where he is Director of the Institute for
Transnational Studies. He has taught previously at Rutgers University and at Ohio State University. His many books and articles have focused on the comparative study of foreign policy.
Among them are *The Scientific Study of Foreign Policy* and *The Study of Global Interdepen-
dence.*

whereas others were much more skeptical (like former Secretary of State Dean Acheson), did not undermine the proposition.
- The United States should not only join, but it should take a lead in creating, peacetime alliances. Formation of NATO in 1949, followed by a flurry of alliance activity during the following decade, represented a sharp departure from practice during the first century and a half of U.S. independence. During the period between World War I and World War II many were persuaded that the nation would be dragged into unnecessary wars by reckless allies; after World War II, however, most leaders emphasized the deterrent and collective security benefits of alliances.
- Liberalization of foreign trade was necessary to avoid destructive trade wars that would not only hurt all nations but would also contribute to political instability. Once again, the dominant view appeared to have been drawn significantly from the "lessons of the 1930s," which witnessed trade wars, a worldwide depression, and the collapse of democratic government in Germany and other parts of Europe. The result was broad support for the Bretton Woods arrangements, the General Agreement on Tariffs and Trade, and the like.
- Foreign aid programs, both economic and military, were not only an obligation for the richest nation in the world, they were also a hard-headed expression of U.S. national interests.
- Containment, rather than "roll-back" or preventive war (or a retreat into isolation), represented the most effective means of meeting the challenge of Soviet expansion. There were differences of emphasis and detail even within the majority supporting containment. For example, George F. Kennan, the intellectual father of containment, had serious reservations about the open-ended quality of President Truman's address to the Congress on March 12, 1947, as he appeared to place few limits on possible American efforts to protect other nations from Soviet imperialism. John Foster Dulles engaged in some rhetorical excesses in condemning containment as a static rather than dynamic policy during the 1952 campaign and, in a symbolic effort to demonstrate a break with past policies, he forced Kennan into retirement in 1953. However, Dulles' policies were essentially a continuation of containment, and containment itself was widely accepted as the proper response to the Soviet challenge.

As a consequence of the widespread acceptance of these principles, the Truman, Eisenhower, and Kennedy administrations could generally count upon a favorable response from the Congress, the media, other leaders, and the informed public when they pursued policies based on the above premises.

The foreign policy consensus of the 1945–1965 period was shattered by the Vietnam War. The post-Vietnam period has been marked not merely by disagreements about specific applications of basic principles or details of implementation, but also by a lack of consensus on fundamental beliefs about the international system, the proper American role in it, and appropriate strategies for pursuing the national interest. At least three quite different ways of thinking about international affairs have emerged among American leaders.

THREE PERSPECTIVES ON FOREIGN AFFAIRS

Cold War Internationalism[2]

Cold War internationalists are oriented toward the state of relations between East and West, locating along that axis the most fundamental challenges to a just and stable international order. Without denying that the international system has undergone some change since the 1950s, they nevertheless see a fundamental continuity in the structure of the system, the sources of threats to peace and stability, the appropriate international role for the United States, and the most effective instruments of external policy. They perceive a world of conflict in which the primary cleavages are those dividing the United States and its allies from the Soviet empire and in which most, if not all, of the most salient issues and conflicts are closely linked to each other and to that fault line. A quintessential statement of this outlook on world affairs may be found in Ronald Reagan's assertion, "Let's not delude ourselves. The Soviet Union underlies all the unrest that is going on. If they weren't engaged in this game of dominoes, there wouldn't be any hot spots in the world" (House, 1980: 1). In a system thus structured, disturbances in one region will reverberate throughout the international arena, and the consequences of failures in one area will be not unlike those predicted by the "domino theory" that was so frequently invoked during the Vietnam period. Within that system the United States faces an ambitious, often aggressive, but always patient, coalition of adversaries led by Moscow. Cold War internationalists depict the Soviet Union as an expansionist power that, under the guise of "peaceful coexistence" or détente, is lulling and gulling the United States into policies that bear a disturbing resemblance to those of Britain and France during the 1930s.

Whatever delusions Americans may have had about détente, the Soviet Union has made it a continuation, often not even in a subtle fashion, of a relentless Cold War against the West. In that conflict the Soviet arsenal of methods ranges from terrorism and subversion to Third World interventions by Cuban proxies. The basic errors have been to assume that the Soviet Union has only sought acknowledgment of having reached a status of parity with the United States, and to believe that, having reached superpower status, the USSR is now a conservative, status quo force in world affairs. In fact, the Soviet Union is not just another great power whose goals and methods may at times bring it into conflict with its lesser neighbors or with other major powers. Moscow harbors quite different global aspirations.

The overarching reality of the global system, according to Cold War internationalists, remains the confrontation between an expansionist Soviet Union and its allies, on the one hand, and the noncommunist nations on the other. And with respect to this fundamental fact of international life, changes during the past two decades are the occasion for neither congratulations nor complacency. Citing trends in Soviet defense spending during the past decade and a half, as well as recent adventures in Angola, Ethiopia, Yemen, Afghanistan, Somalia, Vietnam, and elsewhere, the Cold War internationalists argue that the balance of power—or what Soviet theoreticians call "the correlation of forces"—has swung so far in favor of the USSR that at best the international system is unstable, and at worst it may be headed for war.

The dangerous military asymmetry between the two superpowers has two dimensions. One is the imbalance of strategic and conventional forces; the other is the sharp difference that characterizes American and Soviet thinking about the role of force. Whereas the former are concerned with containment and deterrence, the latter are also thinking about the political implications of strategic forces and with winning a war, should it break out. As a consequence, the Cold War internationalists fear that the Soviets may gain their expansionist goals through nuclear coercion and blackmail. To avoid being faced with a "surrender or suicide" choice, the United States must immediately come to grips with the gaps both in strategic hardware and in realistic thinking about how to win a nuclear war as well as how to avoid one.

The basic problem for the United States is, therefore, to maintain the territorial and political integrity of the noncommunist parts of the world in the face of a highly armed, expansionist power that harbors an unchanging commitment to achieving a position of global hegemony. Even if some Cold War internationalists accept the proposition that the contemporary international system is more complex than the world that faced Metternich or Bismarck, they do not agree that the prudent, time-tested axioms of international intercourse—the realpolitik "rules of the game"—have been rendered obsolete; one of the central myths of American foreign policy is that there is an alternative to realpolitik. Some may agree that the game is more complex than dominoes, but few are prepared to dismiss the metaphor of the chessboard, a game with a well-defined hierarchy based on power in which position is a critical factor and which is basically zero-sum (your gain is my loss, and vice versa) in nature. The prescription is thus clear and unequivocal: the United States must accept the responsibilities and burdens of its leadership position within the noncommunist sector and, at minimum, it must restore a balance of power sufficient to convince the Soviet leadership that aggrandizement will not pay. To charges that such policies will merely revive the Cold War, advocates of Cold War internationalism usually reply that it never ended; détente and arms control were merely ploys by which the Soviets continued the conflict while the United States slept.

Expressions of deep concern about recent trends in American foreign and defense policies abound among Cold War internationalists. As a source of danger to national survival, running a close second behind self-generated delusions about détente, is Washington's obsession with arms control, and especially with what they perceive as its most notorious product—the SALT II Treaty. To those who warn of an uncontrollable arms race in a SALT-free world, they reply that the United States long ago opted out of the competition, leaving the USSR as the lone entrant in the race.

Although Cold War internationalists may disagree among themselves on the fine details of how to cope with the "present danger," two shared themes unite them. First, the United States must undertake substantial increases in military spending. It is now clear many Cold War internationalists within and outside the Reagan administration believe that even projected defense expenditures of $1.5 trillion would be totally inadequate, and that far greater defense outlays are necessary to restore American credibility and the genuine war-fighting capability that they believe to be the only effective deterrent to the Soviet challenge. They tend to support preservation of the triad concept through deployment of the MX land-based mobile missile system, acceleration of the Trident II submarine-launched ballistic missile program, and revival of the B-1 bomber; and this is by no means a complete shopping list, for it touches only upon strategic forces.

But perhaps even more than imbalances in military capabilities, the Cold War internationalists emphasize a second point, what they diagnose as an imbalance in resolution and willingness to use power, if necessary, to preserve vital national interests. A number of them have already written off Western Europe as hopelessly caught in a web of neutralism, pacifism, and defeatism, and they regard the United States as only a few steps behind in the process. A typical diagnosis is that there has been a "collapse of Western will."

Post-Cold War Internationalism[3]

Post-Cold War internationalists are not unaware of East-West tensions, if only out of recognition that therein lies the major danger of nuclear holocaust, but their conceptual map is more strongly oriented toward issues that tend to divide the world along a North-South line. At the center of their worldview is a series of closely related propositions concerning the international system, key actors, and America's proper role within it. The growing list of serious threats to a stable and just world order have created an international system of such complexity and interdependence as to render totally obsolete the premises that formed American foreign policy during the two decades following the end of World War II. Whereas the Cold War internationalists perceive an essentially bipolar structure that dominates most critical issues, the post-Cold War internationalists see a far richer and more varied menu of both threats to, and opportunities for, creation of a viable world order. Dangers arising from strategic/military issues remain real, but the roots of future international conflict are to be located not merely in military imbalances—real or perceived—but also in problems arising from poverty, inequitable distribution of resources, unfulfilled demands for self-determination, regional antagonisms, population pressures, technology that outpaces the political means for controlling its consequences, and the like. Whereas the Cold War internationalists maintain that the chessboard remains a valid metaphor of the global system, the post-Cold War internationalists perceive a multidimensional game in which the logic of the situation will ultimately reward cooperation more handsomely, and in which outcomes are more often than not nonzero-sum.

Not only has the age of bipolarity passed (if, indeed, it ever existed), but it is both futile and dangerous to believe that it may be replaced by resurrecting a classical balance-of-power system. Put most simply, unprecedented changes relating to actors, objectives, values and, indeed, the very nature of power itself, have rendered the balance of power a wholly inadequate model for world order. The primary task, then, is to create, nurture, and sustain new structures and processes for dealing effectively and equitably with a range of issues that goes well beyond traditionally defined security concerns. At the core of this world view is the premise that one cannot effectively cope with the problems and opportunities arising from "complex interdependence" save by means of international cooperation on an unprecedented scale; a crucial lesson of Vietnam is that no nation, not even one as powerful as the United States, can alone shape a world order.

The post-Cold War internationalist image of the Soviet Union varies sharply from that of the Cold War internationalists. The latter emphasize that the monolithic nature of the Soviet system gives rise to a uniformity of foreign policy goals, whereas the former place stress on the complexity of both Soviet structures and external motivations; typically they regard the USSR as a traditional great power rather than as a revolutionary, inherently expansionist one. Soviet foreign policy motivations can thus be understood, if not admired, as a mixture of security concerns and aspirations for recognition as the equal of the United States. Thus, whereas Cold War internationalists interpret Soviet actions in Afghanistan and elsewhere as part of a master plan to gain control of strategic areas—for example, as stepping stones toward control of the Persian Gulf oil fields—the post-Cold War internationalists usually interpret such actions more benignly, as motivated by local conditions, defensive considerations, temptations to take advantage of low-risk gains that few major powers could resist, or as efforts to score points in the continuing conflict with China. Although they do not applaud such actions as the invasion of Afghanistan, they are likely to be at least as critical of American "overreactions" to these episodes as the Cold War internationalists are to condemn Washington's complacency.

Because the post-Cold War internationalists are less than awed by the

Soviet Union, they are prepared to explore various forms of accommodation with Moscow, and they acknowledge that success will require flexibility by both of the superpowers. For example, the *New York Times* editorialized that, "Like the United States, the Soviet Union is becoming a mostly conservative force in world affairs, restrained by the fear of nuclear war and burdened with defense of far-flung political and economic interests." As a consequence, "The central axiom of Soviet-American relations today is that the interests of the two nations will periodically coincide and produce collaboration to try to preserve stability in unstable lands and so to avert a superpower conflict" (*New York Times,* 1979: A20).

On no issue is there perceived to be a clearer conjunction of interests than on arms control. Whereas the Cold War internationalists see tight connections between SALT and other issues, the post-Cold War internationalists are skeptical of efforts to create linkages. They are especially critical of tying arms control negotiations to satisfactory Soviet-American relations on such issues as Third-World conflicts. Only by separating that inherently difficult relationship into its component parts is there any real prospect of achieving progress on any of them. The former regarded both the rate of growth in Soviet defense spending and external adventures in Africa and the Middle East, as well as terms of the agreement itself, as ample reason for rejection of the SALT II Treaty; the latter—many of whom have questioned whether the Soviet Union has even matched, much less surpassed, American force levels—almost uniformly supported the treaty as inherently equitable, as a barrier against even greater Soviet military spending, and as the centerpiece of any effort to stabilize relations between the superpowers. Moreover, not a few post-Cold War internationalists suggest that the alarmist claims of the Committee on the Present Danger and others are no more justified than were cries about a "missile gap" during the closing months of the Eisenhower Administration. And even if the claims of Soviet military superiority were valid, they question whether such capabilities can be translated into political advantage, especially in light of Soviet defense needs arising from the Sino-Soviet dispute, the probable unreliability of its Eastern European allies, and other difficulties.

Consistent with these interpretations, the post-Cold War internationalists believe that an active American role in creating an equitable and stable world order is indispensable, not only because mankind is denied the luxury of procrastination in dealing with many world order issues, but also because to do otherwise may be to leave the field to those whose goals and values may be less benign. This is not to say that they are uncritical of American policies or institutions. Indeed, some of them hold views—for example, "The disposition toward repression in American foreign policy is mainly a matter of structure, not will" (Falk, 1976: 99)—that are strikingly similar to the Cold War internationalists' Manichean image of the USSR. The United States has both the obligation, especially in relations with the less-developed nations, and the capabilities to contribute toward creation of the institutions and processes necessary to deal effectively and in a timely fashion with the broad agenda of critical international issues that is by no means limited to those that are purely geopolitical and strategic. Withdrawal from an active international role, as suggested by the isolationists, is neither morally acceptable nor, in any case, a realistic option for the United States.

As a result, some of the notable differences between the Cold War internationalists and post-Cold War internationalists revolve around their conceptions of the Third World. The former view the less-developed nations largely in strategic terms, as one of several sites of the ongoing East-West conflict. In contrast, the post-Cold War internationalists tend to view the Third World as the hapless victims of nature (the uneven distribution of such vital resources as oil or arable land, or unfavorable climatic conditions) or of their colonial heritages. Post-liberation exploitation by the rich industrial nations of the West and, above all, by the multinational corporations, are an added burden. These conditions are regarded as necessary, and usually sufficient, to explain everything from populations that grow faster than gross national products to highly repressive regimes. It thus follows that there are both prudential and moral reasons for the industrial democracies to undertake massive programs of resource transfers as part of a "New International Economic Order:" prudential because only such undertakings can promote international stability and ultimately avert a North-South conflict; moral because justice and retribution for past sins require a more equitable distribution of the globe's goods and services. If the Cold War internationalists rarely exhibit excessive sensitivity to repressive governments of the right, most post-Cold War internationalists are equally tolerant of the most authoritarian left-wing governments, for whose excesses blame can usually be assigned elsewhere.

It was noted earlier that the Cold War internationalists demand some significant changes in recent American foreign and defense policies. The post-Cold War internationalists are, for very different reasons, equally critical of those policies. A necessary, if not sufficient, condition for success in implementing their proposals is a dramatic reorientation of America's international role. Stanley Hoffmann (1978) poses the alternatives in the title of his recent book, *Primacy or World Order*. To opt for the former means a continuation of excessive concern for military/strategic concerns; interventions to support unworthy regimes in areas where vital interests are, at best, marginally at stake; and neglect of global problems that ultimately offer a far greater threat to American security than many of those that have recently obsessed Washington. That choice assures for this country, and the global community as well, a future of confrontation, conflict, crises, and chaos— and the certainty of ultimate failure to achieve either primacy or world order. To choose the course of world order, on the other hand, requires a significant reexamination of some deeply ingrained American pretentions, premises, patterns of thought, and policies. At minimum, the politics of negotiation, compromise, and cooperation—what Hoffmann calls "moderation plus"—must replace the politics of confrontation and crisis.

Isolationism[4]

Unlike the two internationalist schools of thought on contemporary international affairs, the isolationists are concerned primarily with domestic problems, arising at least in part from excessive, if not obsessive, concern with both East-West and North-South issues. Much of their criticism of recent diplomacy is directed at premises that an activist foreign policy can create, either through balance-of-power manipulations or through pursuit of utopian schemes, a world order that is more congenial to American security and interests. Viewing the international environment as fundamentally intractable, if not inherently anarchic, they regard the premise that this nation can create a just or stable world order as a dangerous, but typically American, exercise in hubris. At worst it leads to dangerous and futile crusades to "make the world safe for democracy" or some other equally elusive goal; at best it can only lead to cynicism and despair when, as is inevitable, the utopian plans are not fulfilled.

For the isolationists, the cardinal rules that should guide this nation's concerns are, "know thy limits" and "heal thyself first." George McGovern's plea, "Come home, America," although clearly not a formula upon which to ride into the White House in 1972, nevertheless struck a responsive chord among a not insignificant element in the United States. George Kennan's assertion, "I think that I am a semi-isolationist," (Kennan, 1978: 125) and George Meany's proclamation that "free trade is a sham," and the appeal of "project independence" to many once confirmed internationalists indicate that isolationism has achieved a degree of respectability and support unknown since before Pearl Harbor.

Isolationists share with the post-Cold War internationalists several key propositions about contemporary international relations. They agree that the era of bipolarity has passed, in large part because the Soviet Union has been transformed from an aggressive revolutionary state into a conservative great power, governed by an aging leadership whose memories of the destruction wrought by World War II far outstrip their zeal for high-risk international adventures. Thus, what the Cold War internationalists perceive as a military superpower, confident that a dramatic change in the "correlation of forces" is opening up an era of unprecedented opportunities for Soviet expansion, the isolationists diagnose as a great power beset with intractable domestic problems, ranging from rampant alcoholism and an inefficient agricultural sector to uncertainties of leadership succession and potential ethnic conflicts. Additionally, the Kremlin has a full agenda of international difficulties, including, but not confined to, the China problem and threats of nationalism within its Eastern European empire. And, whereas the Cold War internationalists see in the fast-rising Soviet arms budget a clear indication of ultimate Soviet intentions—and thus an unprecedented threat to Western civilization—the isolationists are inclined to attribute the Soviet side of the arms race to a mixture of genuine fears of a two-front war, bureaucratic momentum, and strategic irrationalities that are not the monopoly of the leadership in the Kremlin. Most importantly, the record of Soviet efforts must not be exaggerated by alarmists; it is one in which the abysmal failures in China, Yugoslavia, Egypt, Sudan, and elsewhere far outstrip the few successes in such lesser countries as Yemen, Angola, Ethiopia, and Vietnam.

In some respects the isolationist diagnosis of Soviet-American relations goes farther. With its emphasis on the fact that the real problems and threats faced by both of the superpowers are domestic in origin, the isolationists are inclined to deny that there are any genuine conflicts of interest between them. The danger, then, is not so much that either poses an insuperable threat to the vital interests of the other but, rather, that fear, miscalculation, and misperception will drive them into a conflict that can only result in their mutual destruction, if not that of all mankind. The arms race plays a central role in this dangerous situation. It denies both sides resources that could be used to deal with vital domestic issues. More dangerously, the propensity to adduce aggressive foreign policy motivations from arms budgets and deployments drives the arms race in an action-reaction cycle that can only lead to a disastrous outcome.

But the isolationists are not inclined to give much greater credence to either the direst fears or the fondest hopes of the post-Cold War internationalists. For starters, they tend to regard the term "complex interdependence" as descriptively inaccurate for the most part, and a fact to be deplored rather than celebrated where in fact it does exist. As Kennan has put it, "To what extent this interdependence really exists and constitutes a commanding reality of our time, I cannot say. I will only say that however much there is of it, as a feature of the situation of the United States, I wish there were less" (Kennan, 1977: 50). The hope and expectation that interdependence provides both the imperative and the opportunity for long-overdue structural changes in the international system are dismissed as chimeral and utopian. The progeny of interdependence are more likely to be intervention and conflict than cooperation and progress.

The isolationist diagnosis of the contemporary international situation thus differs radically from that of the other two internationalist viewpoints described earlier. Its primary elements may be summarized with a set of three propositions. First, the USSR does indeed possess the capabilities to rain great destruction on the United States and the other Western democracies, but it lacks the slightest intention of doing so.

Second, many Third World nations do indeed envy and oppose the industrial democracies—often successfully exploiting wholly irrational guilt complexes in the West—but save for a few isolated instances they lack totally the capabilities for threatening the vital interests of the United States. There are thus few, if any, compelling reasons for taking seriously some of the more strident demands from the Third World for "reparations" or other types of massive resource transfers. Where the power to threaten such national interests in fact exists, notably with respect to oil, it is largely the consequence of a short-sighted, mad rush to place America's head in the noose by failing to exercise sufficient discipline in the use of resources to avoid becoming the eager hostages of OPEC. There are stark differences between the post-Cold War internationalists and the isolationists on the Third World, for the former are often inclined to insist that the United States cannot, either morally or practically, be indifferent to the claims of the poor nations. The isolationist response rejects the moral argument and asserts that economic and political development can only arise from self-reliance; they cannot be imposed or implemented from abroad, and the effort to do so may, in fact, hinder rather than assist the development process.

Third, the real threats to a just and humane social order in this country are largely to be found within its own borders rather than abroad. Decaying cities, inflation, unemployment, cultural decadence, illiteracy, crime, unresolved racial issues, environmental deprivation, and other familiar problems pose, according to the isolationists, a far greater threat to the quality of American institutions and lives than do the ambitions of the men in the Kremlin or the strident and generally unjustified demands of Third World leaders for a new international order. Indeed, many isolationists share with their intellectual forefathers a conviction that an activist foreign policy is incompatible with a stable and progressive domestic order—and perhaps it is not even compatible with the maintenance of democratic institutions. The isolationist argument is thus sustained not only by a pessimistic estimate of Washington's ability to solve pressing international problems. It is perhaps even more fundamentally grounded in a fear that the United States will lose its soul by excessive international involvement, whether to play the realpolitik game prescribed by the Cold War internationalists, or the "complex interdependence" game favored by the post-Cold War internationalists. *"The inescapable lesson common to both Vietnam and Watergate is that the ultimate trade-off is between internationalist foreign policies and the integrity of our constitution. We cannot maintain both"* (Ravenal, 1975: 91. Italics in the original).

Consistent with these diagnoses, the isolationist "grand design" for American foreign policy differs sharply with those of both internationalist schools of thought. They recognize the existence of conflicts along both North-South and East-West axes, but they tend to dismiss as a dangerous delusion the notion, widely accepted in the United States during the decades following the end of World War II, that there is any compelling practical or ethical imperative for this nation to be centrally involved in the amelioration of the world's ills. Especially discriminating selectivity should be exercised in limiting defense commitments to an indispensable minimum. Most importantly, there must be an awareness that just as every international problem is not caused by America, so, too, does it not necessarily have a unique or effective American solution.

More specifically, the isolationist prescription includes several main points. The United States should place high priority on negotiating outstanding differences with the Soviet Union, with the minimal goals of slowing down or reversing the arms race and thereby reducing the threat of unintended or unwanted conflict. The isolationists differ sharply with both varieties of internationalism with respect to appropriate policies toward the Third World. The Cold War internationalists regard the less-developed nations as a crucial battleground between the two major blocs, and the post-Cold War internationalists view them as the victim of neglect, if not exploitation, by the rich nations. The isolationists reject both of these diagnoses, the first because it can only lead to endless American interventions in volatile areas that do not threaten or even seriously engage vital American interests, and the second because it fails to recognize that self-reliance rather than external assistance offers the only effective path to development. Hence the prescription that the United States should deal with the Third-World nations only on the basis of genuinely shared interests—which are likely to be quite limited in scope—rather than on the basis of guilt for conditions that are not of America's making, or of romantic visions about what those interests might be. For the isolationists, the central lesson of Vietnam is that the United States cannot provide security for those who are incapable or unwilling to make the necessary sacrifices; nor can it provide the means of material, political, or spiritual improvement for those who are indifferent to such problems.

Isolationists believe that the United States should also initiate a process of disengagement from external alliances and military commitments until the security perimeter has reached a clearly defensible position. Some would define such a position as including Western Europe, Japan, and Israel; others would support a perimeter that is even more circumscribed. The Soviets or Chinese might choose to take advantage of such a narrowly defined perimeter by embarking upon external adventures in the Third World. However, such actions would rarely infringe upon vital American interests.

Finally, if the United States is to have a salutary influence on the rest of the world, it will come about largely through a demonstrated capacity to solve its own pressing domestic problems. In a large sense, then, according to isolationists, America's ability to contribute to a solution of many global issues—be it human rights or democratic development—is limited to the power of example. It therefore behooves this nation to achieve a satisfactory resolution of these problems at home before turning its attention and energies to preaching to or materially helping others.

WHO ARE THE ADHERENTS OF THE THREE FOREIGN POLICY BELIEF SYSTEMS?

More systematic evidence, drawn from a nationwide leadership survey in 1976, demonstrated the existence of the three foreign policy belief systems described in the previous section. The 2,282 participants in the survey included military officers, business executives, Foreign Service officers, media leaders, clergy, labor leaders, public officials, and lawyers, among others. There has been a good deal of speculation about the sources of the foreign policy cleavages that arose in the post-Vietnam era. For example, according to some observers, the divisions were essentially generational in origin, pitting the "hard-line" views of the older "World War II" generation against the "dovish" and isolationist beliefs of those constituting the "Vietnam generation." The 1976 leadership survey provides an opportunity to assess the validity of these and other generalizations about societal divisions on international affairs. Leaders taking part in this survey were initially ranked by their adherence to each of the three foreign policy belief systems on the basis of their responses to thirty-two questions. Further analyses were then undertaken to identify characteristics that may be associated with the three perspectives (see Table 1).

The results may be summarized briefly. The continuing impact of the Vietnam War on leadership beliefs is demonstrated in the finding that a *Vietnam policy position* is the best predictor of foreign policy beliefs; leaders participating in this survey were classified according to their policy preferences (whether they sought complete victory, to withdraw completely, to follow a policy in between victory and withdrawal, or were not sure) in both the early and late stages of the war (Holsti and Rosenau, 1979). Those consistently seeking a victory were classified as supporters; critics favored a complete withdrawal at both times; and five other groups were formed on the basis of various combinations of responses. The category *ideology* shared with a Vietnam policy position the top rank as the most potent predictor of foreign policy beliefs; conservatives favored Cold War internationalism, and liberals were stronger advocates of the other two perspectives on international affairs. Differences between *occupations* were also quite pronounced; for example, media leaders, clergy, and educators tended to adhere to views labelled as post-Cold War internationalism, while military officers predominated among Cold War internationalists, and labor leaders were substantially more pronounced in their support for isolationism than any other occupational group. *Political party* preferences were also related to foreign policy beliefs, but those relationships largely disappeared if ideology was held constant; for example, liberal Republicans tended to respond like liberals rather than like members of the G.O.P., and conservative Democrats also shared more views with conservatives than with other Democrats. *Military service* proved to be a rather weak predictor of foreign policy beliefs; it was especially weak after controlling for occupation, thereby permitting a distinction between career military officers and leaders who had experienced

TABLE 1

WHO ARE THE ADHERENTS OF THREE FOREIGN POLICY BELIEF SYSTEMS?: THE RELATIONSHIP BETWEEN LEADER ATTRIBUTES AND FOREIGN POLICY BELIEF SYSTEMS IN THE 1976 SURVEY OF 2,282 AMERICAN LEADERS

Attributes of Leaders	Groups Highest on Cold War Internationalism	Percentage in top quintile*	Groups Highest on Post-Cold War Internationalism	Percentage in top quintile*	Groups Highest on Isolationism	Percentage in top quintile*
Vietnam Policy Position†	Supporters	61%	Critics	47%	Critics	55%
	Converted Supporters	33%	Ambivalent Critics	30%	Ambivalent Critics	48%
correlation††	C = .58		C = .40		C = .51	
Ideology	Far right and very conservative	60%	Far left and very liberal	60%	Far left and very liberal	55%
	Somewhat conservative	33%	Somewhat liberal	32%	Somewhat liberal	31%
correlation††	C = .55		C = .46		C = .42	
Occupation	Military officers	37%	Clergy	44%	Labor	43%
			Educators	32%	Media	32%
			Media	30%	Educators	31%
correlation††	C = .45		C = .37		C = .40	
Political party	Republicans	32%	Democrats	32%	Democrats	34%
correlation††	C = .39		C = .29		C = .31	
Generation	—		—		—	
correlation††	C = .21		C = .20		C = .22	
Military Service	—		—		Non-veterans	30%
correlation††	C = .20		C = .18		C = .23	
Level of Political Interest	Low & none	30%	—		—	
correlation††	C = .18		C = .16		C = .14	
Sex	—		—		Women	34%
correlation††	C = .12		C = .08		C = .16	

*Percentage of group (row labels) that is included in the top quintile of each foreign policy belief system (column labels). For example, 61% of Supporters (leaders favoring U.S. search for a complete victory in Vietnam both early and late in the war) were among the top quintile on Cold War internationalism. Only groups with 30% or more in top quintiles are listed here; a dash indicates that no group achieved the 30% cutoff.

†Leaders were classified into one of eight categories on the basis of policy preferences early and late in the Vietnam war.

††The C coefficient is a non-parametric measure of correlation, corresponding roughly to the Pearson product-moment coefficient. Leaders were grouped into quintiles for each of the foreign policy belief systems. The C coefficient thus measures the association between leaders' foreign policy beliefs and their attributes, where the number of attribute categories ranges from two (sex) to ten (occupation).

limited service in the armed forces. Finally, *age* and *gender* differences were especially weak explanatory factors; the most pronounced divisions cut within rather than across generations, and in most respects, women and men responded very similarly to a broad range of foreign policy issues.

In summary, the 1976 survey revealed an American leadership divided on some fundamental aspects of international affairs. The cleavages appear to have originated in the decade-long war in Vietnam and to have been reinforced by both psychological (ideology) and sociological (occupation) factors.

FOREIGN POLICY BELIEFS, 1976-1980: CONTINUITY OR CHANGE?

The previous section summarized data collected in 1976, within a year of the final American withdrawal from Vietnam. During the next several years, different foreign policy leaders, other issues, and new crises came to dominate America's external relations. Have these, combined with the passing of time, eroded the impact of Vietnam? Have they served to forge a new consensus, as Vietnam receded into the past, and as Americans found their newspapers, evening news, and political debates centering on the price and availability of imported oil, trade balances and the declining value of the dollar, the Panama Canal, human rights abroad, Cubans in Angola and Ethiopia, hostages in Iran, Russians in Afghanistan, civil wars in Central America, the Camp David accords, the intricacies of SALT, MX basing modes, and the deterioration of détente? As a consequence, have spokesmen for the Carter and Reagan administrations, who agree on little else, been correct in asserting that these events have erased the last traces of the "Vietnam syndrome," while bringing Americans together in a new, post-Vietnam consensus? In short, have the external features and internal structure of American leadership beliefs, circa 1976, been "overtaken by events?"

A second foreign policy leadership survey was conducted in 1980, a few weeks after the start of the hostage crisis in Iran and the Soviet invasion of Afghanistan. The second survey involved 2,502 American leaders and provided a substantial body of evidence about foreign policy beliefs in the wake of turmoil in and near the Persian Gulf area. A number of questions compared responses in the 1976 and 1980 surveys and assessed the degree of change in foreign policy beliefs during the intervening years. Each effort yielded similar and reinforcing results: changes were not wholly absent, but they represented a relatively minor theme in an overall pattern of striking continuity. Not only did the 1976 and 1980 samples of leaders respond in very similar ways to ninety-three foreign policy questions that appeared in both questionnaires, but the pattern of group responses summarized in Table 1 remained virtually intact. Deep cleavages on many fundamental issues persisted, and they tended to reflect differences on the Vietnam War, ideology, and occupation, rather than such other attributes as sex, generation, or military service.

Against a background of domestic and international stability, these results might not seem especially noteworthy, but on any list of adjectives that might be attached to the 1976–1980 period, "tranquil" is among the least appropriate. The earlier survey was initiated with a recently installed and popular Gerald Ford in the White House. Jimmy Carter was among the longer shots in a crowded list of Democratic presidential hopefuls, and Ronald Reagan's faltering campaign for the G.O.P. nomination appeared to be the last hurrah in his political career. The Shah of Iran, a pillar of American security policy in the Persian Gulf region, was firmly on the Peacock throne, and Afghanistan might as well have been located on the back side of the moon for all the interest or knowledge most Americans had in that obscure Southwest Asian nation.

Four years later, President Carter was waging a desperate battle to win his own party's presidential nomination, while Ronald Reagan, who would defeat Carter in the 1980 election, was well on his way to an easy victory in the Republican primaries. The Shah had gone into exile and was dying. His successors in Teheran triggered a 444-day crisis by invading the American Embassy and taking its personnel hostage. Soon thereafter, Afghanistan was the victim of a brutal invasion by the Soviets, casting a distinct chill in relations between Washington and Moscow if not an outright renewal of the Cold War. Even had the rest of the world remained free from conflict and change—evidence from virtually every region clearly proved that it had not—the period in question was undeniably characterized by tumult and turmoil. Against such a background, the major finding of the 1980 survey— the foreign policy beliefs of American leaders remained quite stable—is of more than passing interest, whether one's concern is with substantive, theoretical, or policy-oriented aspects of American foreign policy.[5]

NOTES

1. The first two sections of this article draw extensively upon Holsti (1979); the third and fourth draw in part on Holsti and Rosenau (forthcoming).
2. A representative sample of the literature of this genre includes: Schlesinger (1977), and Podhoretz (1980); most foreign policy articles in *Commentary* and *National Review*; editorials in the *Wall Street Journal*; columns by George Will, Roland Evans, and Robert Novak; publications of The Committee on the Present Danger, the National Strategy Information Center, the Heritage Foundation, The Ethics and Public Policy Center at Georgetown University, and The Committee for the Free World; and various writings of Paul Nitze, Walter Laqueur, Edward N. Luttwak, Ben J. Wattenberg, Carl Gershman, Eugene Rostow, W. W. Rostow, Fred Iklé, Colin Gray, Daniel O. Graham, Albert Wohlstetter, Herbert Stein, and Irving Kristol.
3. This viewpoint is effectively represented by Hoffmann (1978), Keohane and Nye (1976), and Brown (1974); articles in *Nation* and *Progressive*; columns by Arthur Schlesinger, Jr., Tom Wicker, and Anthony Lewis; editorials in the *New York Times* and *Washington Post*; and the foreign policy writings of James Chace, Harlan Cleveland, Elliott L. Richardson, Jean Meyer, Robert Levgold,

Richard Barnet, Richard Falk, Paul C. Warnke, Les Aspin, Morton Kondracke, Jan M. Lodal, Adam Yarmolinsky, Richard H. Ullman, and Thomas Hughes.

4. Among the most articulate statements of the isolationist position are Kennan (1977) and Ravenal (1975). Both of these prolific authors have also developed their positions in many other writings during the past half decade. Aspects of the isolationist viewpoint may also be found in materials from various labor leaders, some industrialists, and several spokesmen for the Libertarian party.

5. A further development of these points may be found in Holsti and Rosenau (forthcoming).

REFERENCES

Brown, Seyom. (1974) *New Forces in World Politics.* Washington: The Brookings Institution.

Falk, Richard A. (1976) "Beyond Internationalism," *Foreign Policy,* 24 (Fall): 65–113.

Hoffmann, Stanley. (1978) *Primacy or World Order.* New York: McGraw-Hill.

Holsti, Ole R. (1979) "The Three Headed Eagle: The United States and System Change," *International Studies Quarterly,* 23 (September): 339–359.

Holsti, Ole R. and James N. Rosenau. (1979) "Vietnam, Consensus, and the Belief Systems of American Leaders," *World Politics,* 23 (October): 1–56.

————. *Vietnam, Consensus, and The Beliefs of American Leaders: The "Lessons of Vietnam" and American Foreign Policy* (tentative title). Forthcoming.

House, Karen Elliott. (1980) "Reagan's World: Republican Policies Stress Arms Buildup, a Firm Line to Soviet," *Wall Street Journal* (June 3): 1, 25.

Kennan, George F. (1978) "An Appeal for Thought," *New York Times Magazine* (May 7): 43.

————. (1977) *The Cloud of Danger.* Boston: Little, Brown.

Keohane, Robert O. and Joseph Nye. (1976) *Power and Interdependence.* Boston: Little, Brown.

New York Times. (1979) "A Rhomboid of Rhetoric" (January 11): A20.

Podhoretz, Norman. (1980) *The Present Danger.* New York: Basic Books.

Ravenal, Earl C. (1975) "Who Needs It?" *Foreign Policy,* 18 (Spring): 80–91.

Schlesinger, James R., et al. (1977) *Defending America.* New York: Basic Books.

14

INTERNATIONALISM COMES OF AGE...AGAIN

LLOYD FREE
WILLIAM WATTS

Current conventional wisdom has it that the Soviet invasion of Afghanistan, coming on top of the seizure of American hostages in Iran, brought about a sea of change in the attitudes of the American people toward the world around them. Many observers point to what they see as a new stiffening of the international and defense attitudes of Americans and a turning away from the less aggressively internationalist patterns that presumably prevailed during the immediate post-Vietnam years.[1]

An ABC-Harris survey, for example, published in mid-February of [1980], showed that almost seven respondents out of ten (69 percent) supported President Carter's doctrine that "any use of outside force to try to gain control of the Persian Gulf oil area will be regarded as a assault on the vital interests of the United States and will be repelled by American military force."

In a related vein, Harris reached the conclusion in late January [1980] that "the events in Iran and Afghanistan have finally modified the reluctance of the American people to commit U.S. military power around the globe," citing the fact that more than six out of ten of those sampled (61 percent) favored "the establishment of U.S. military bases in Somalia, Oman, Kenya, and Egypt."

A Harris finding in early March [1980] showed that more than three Americans in four (76 percent) favored "President Carter's call for the registration of young people to be available for a military draft."

Similarly, a Gallup survey in mid-February [1980] reported that almost one-half of those interviewed (49 percent) felt we were spending "too little" on defense; only 14 percent thought the amount was "too much"; and 24 percent said it was "about right." Gallup summed things up in this way:

"Internationalism Comes of Age . . . Again," *Public Opinion* (April/May 1980), pp. 46–50.

"Reflecting widespread and growing concern over recent Soviet military actions in Afghanistan, public support for increased defense spending has soared to the highest point recorded in Gallup surveys in more than a decade."

Such findings as these, however, are geared primarily to the crises in Iran and Afghanistan and understate or even overlook the emergence of an important trend that began as early as 1974–1975. As long . . . ago [as 1976], it is now clear, the public started to take a new and more skeptical look at the world in which we live. In their own shrewd and intuitive fashion, Americans began to shape a revised vision of the role they saw for the United States in a far more complicated and less tractable international environment.

As we pointed out . . . in *Foreign Policy* ("Nationalism, Not Isolationism," Fall 1976), "The realities of détente—a policy that increasingly falls short of its earlier promise—appear to have been thoroughly digested. The American people express a diminished sense of progress in our dealings with the Soviet Union; a substantial increase in concern over the threat of war; renewed willingness to come to the defense of some of our allies—especially our friends in Europe—in the event they come under Communist attack; and a more pessimistic view . . . about the prospects for future relations with . . . the Soviet Union. All this has fostered a mood in the United States that reverses a long-term trend—there is a new desire to put an end to what is seen as a weakening U.S. role in the world, and to resume the position of being 'number one.' "

THE CIVIC SERVICE SURVEY

The results of a new survey of 1,611 respondents, conducted February 1–15, 1980, by Civic Service Incorporated (and at the request of *Public Opinion* magazine), present in dramatic fashion the crystallization of this changed national mood. Iran and Afghanistan have not altered this reality, nor have they given birth to a new public stance. What they have done is to make a harder foreign policy posture legitimate and provide the basis for a revised national consensus. Defense-oriented internationalism has come of age.

To demonstrate where we are and how far we have come, let us look at responses over time to a series of seven statements with which crosssections of Americans have been asked to agree or disagree. Five of the statements were originally devised in 1964 and 1968; all seven were included in Potomac Associates' surveys in 1972, 1974, 1975, and 1976; two were also included in Potomac Associates' surveys in 1978 and 1979; and all seven were included in the 1980 survey. To facilitate understanding and interpretation, responses to statements involving an isolationist or unilateralist approach are discussed first below, followed by those characteristic of an internationalist or multilateralist position.

Isolationist-Unilateralist Statements

A. *Since the United States is the most powerful nation in the world, we should go our own way in international matters, not worrying too much about whether other countries agree with us or not.*

	Agree	Disagree	Don't know
1964	19%	70%	11%
1968	23	72	5
1972	22	72	6
1974	32	57	11
1975	23	67	10
1976	29	62	9
1980	26	66	8

In 1980, two-thirds of the sample disagreed, a dissenting proportion higher than in 1974 and 1976, but not quite up to the level reached in the period from 1964 through 1972. The moment of greatest favor for this proposition came in 1974.

B. *The United States should mind its own business internationally and let other countries get along as best they can on their own.*

	Agree	Disagree	Don't know
1964	18%	70%	12%
1968	27	66	7
1972	35	56	9
1974	41	47	12
1975	36	52	12
1976	41	49	10
1980	30	61	9

Rejection of this position—even more tilted toward isolationism or unilateralism—is now higher than at any time since 1968.

C. *We shouldn't think so much in international terms but concentrate more on our own national problems and building up our strength and prosperity here at home.*

	Agree	Disagree	Don't know
1964	55%	32%	13%
1968	60	31	9
1972	73	20	7
1974	77	14	9
1975	71	18	11
1976	73	22	5
1980	61	30	9

Despite the economic problems currently facing the United States . . . it is highly significant that the proportion in 1980 agreeing with the unilateralist point of view was lower (slightly more than six out of ten), and the percentage disagreeing higher (30 percent) than at any time since 1963. As with Statement A above, 1974 turns out to be the year in which this proposition was most in favor.

Internationalist-Multinationalist Statements
D. The United States should cooperate fully with the United Nations.

	Agree	*Disagree*	*Don't know*
1964	72%	16%	12%
1968	72	21	7
1972	63	28	9
1974	66	20	14
1975	56	30	14
1976	46	41	13
1980	59	28	13

Sentiment in favor of cooperating with the United Nations reached a low point (46 percent) [in 1976]. A Gallup poll published in December 1975 pointed to the reason for this, reporting that "the public's rating of the United Nations' performance has declined to a 30-year low point following passage of a resolution condemning Zionism as a 'form of racism and racial discrimination.'" The significant rebound in 1980 (to 59 percent) can be attributed in part, no doubt, to broad-based support in the United Nations for resolutions condemning events in Iran and Afghanistan. Nevertheless, the proportion advocating full cooperation with the United Nations remained markedly lower than what it was from 1964 through 1974.

E. In deciding on its foreign policies, the United States should take into account the views of its major allies.

	Agree	*Disagree*	*Don't know*
1964	81%	7%	12%
1968	84	9	7
1972	80	12	8
1974	69	16	15
1975	74	16	10
1976	72	18	10
1980	79	13	8

As can be seen, support for consultation with allies climbed seven points over the past four years (from 72 percent in 1976 to 79 percent in 1980), bringing it back almost to the levels that it obtained from 1964 through 1972.

Perhaps most dramatic of all the responses to the 1980 survey are reactions to the following two statements on use of U.S. forces abroad (not asked in 1964 or 1968 but included in surveys in 1978 and 1979):

F. The United States should come to the defense of Japan with military force if it is attacked by Soviet Russia or Communist China.

	Agree	Disagree	Don't know
1972	43%	40%	17%
1974	37	42	21
1975	42	39	19
1976	45	37	18
1978	50	35	15
1979	54	35	11
1980	57	24	19

Following the steady upward trend from the low point in 1974 (once again!), support for coming to the defense of Japan reached a substantial majority of 54 percent in 1979 and 57 percent in 1980.

G. The United States should come to the defense of its major European allies with military force if any of them are attacked by the Soviet Union.

	Agree	Disagree	Don't know
1972	52%	32%	16%
1974	48	34	18
1975	48	34	18
1976	56	27	17
1978	62	26	12
1979	64	26	10
1980	70	17	13

Even more so than in the case of Japan, 1980 has brought the proportion of those supporting the defense of Western Europe to a strikingly high level—a remarkable seven out of ten—the highest number we have recorded in this entire question series. Whether these sentiments will remain firm if Japan and/or our European allies are seen as failing to support American sanctions in regard to Iran and Afghanistan remains, of course, an open question. Substantial slippage almost certainly will ensue, we suspect, if Americans come to believe that our allies are letting us down.

INTERNATIONAL PATTERNS

To provide an overview of the present situation in comparison to past surveys, we have again utilized a system of "International Patterns"[2] first employed by the Institute for International Social Research in 1964 and

1968 and subsequently from 1972 through 1976 by Potomac Associates. This scheme uses reactions to the statements outlined above to place members of the respective samples on an internationalist/isolationist continuum. To qualify as "completely internationalist," a respondent has to disagree with the notions that the United States should go its own way (A), mind its own business (B), and concentrate more on national problems (C), while agreeing that the United States should cooperate with the United Nations (D), take into account the views of its allies (E), come to the defense of Japan (F), and Western Europe (G). To be classified as "completely isolationist," a respondent must give precisely the opposite answers. Categories are also provided for "predominantly internationalist" and "predominantly isolationist" (meaning conformity to the "completely" patterns in most but not all respects) and "mixed" (meaning a relatively even mixture of internationalist and isolationist patterns).

Defined in this way, Americans in the 1980 sample line up as follows:

Completely internationalist	17%
Predominantly internationalist	44
Mixed	26
Predominantly isolationist	11
Completely isolationist	2
	100%

A substantial majority of respondents—more than six out of ten—thus qualified as internationalists, either completely or predominantly. In contrast, the isolationists accounted for only 13 percent in total, and the "mixed" category to slightly more than one-quarter.

DEMOGRAPHIC VARIATIONS

It is worth special note that in this new survey there were no meaningful differences between Republicans, Democrats, and independents; on the subjects covered at least, no strong partisan variations emerged. Those who classified themselves as "liberals," however, proved to be somewhat less internationalist (56 percent) than those who said they were "moderates" (63 percent) or "conservatives" (62 percent).

Conforming to a pattern noted regularly in earlier surveys, a smaller percentage of women (57 percent) qualified as internationalists than did men (64 percent). Similarly, the total number of internationalists among people sixty years of age or over (54 percent) was much below the national average of 61 percent. Perhaps surprising to some, the age group most subject to possible draft or military services (18-29 years old) proved every bit as internationalist (61 percent) as the national average—but, in fact, this has been the case in all of our surveys going back to 1964, once again dispelling a bit of conventional wisdom.

There were fewer internationalists among blue-collar (55 percent) than white-collar workers (64 percent), and particularly among professional and business people (68 percent). It will therefore come as no surprise that the total internationalist percentages tended to increase steadily with rising income:

Income Level	Total Internationalists
Under $5,000	40%
$5,000–$9,999	56
$10,000–$14,999	58
$15,000–$24,999	68
$25,000 and over	70

Differences on the basis of education are of sufficient interest to warrant presenting them as shown in full in Table 1. Even among the least educated, it should be noted, almost one-half (48 percent) qualified as internationalists. From there on up the education ladder, the total percentages of internationalists increased to the very impressive level of nearly eight out of ten (79 percent) among those with post graduate education, with almost one-half of these placing themselves in the "completely" category (39 percent).

The most marked demographic variation of all, however, was based on race. While 64 percent of whites turned up as internationalists, this proportion dropped to a minority of 39 percent among blacks. Six black Americans out of ten put themselves either under the isolationist rubric (20 percent) or into the "mixed" category (41 percent), somewhere between isolationism and internationalism. This is almost certainly due in large measure to the greater preoccupation many blacks have with issues here at home, as well as the skepticism many black Americans share about U.S. policies abroad in areas of particular interest to them, especially Africa.

TRENDS THROUGH THE YEARS

To give the foregoing figures fuller significance, we are fortunately able to relate them to the international patterns that emerged in former surveys. This is done in Figure 1.

It will be noted that there was a steady drop in the proportion of total internationalists from 1964 (65 percent), to 1968 (59 percent), to 1972 (56 percent) and finally to the low point in 1974 (41 percent). The reversal of that trend, already evident in 1976, has now lifted the percentage of total internationalists back to a clear majority (61 percent).

TABLE 1
INTERNATIONALIST/ISOLATIONIST VARIATIONS BY EDUCATION

	Grade School	High School	College	Post Graduate
Completely internationalist	7%	13%	22%	39%
Predominantly internationalist	41	43	46	40
Total internationalist	48	56	68	79
Mixed	38	29	21	14
Total isolationist	14	15	11	7
Predominantly isolationist	11	13	9	5
Completely isolationist	3	2	2	2

Conversely, while the number of total isolationists was slightly greater in 1980 than during the period from 1964 through 1972, it has dropped markedly below the 1974 and 1976 levels. The number of respondents in the mixed category was lower than in any of our former surveys.

All these results point consistently to the mid-seventies as a watershed period in the recent history of American attitudes. The principal answer may be found in the fundamentally sober assessment Americans made at that time about the world around them and especially the effects of the tragedy in Vietnam. Even before the war ended, we believe, the American people had come to the view that Vietnam was a mistake, and that either we could not, or would not, win that particular struggle. They seem to have concluded that we must be more careful about the range of our foreign commitments, that we must pay greater attention both to our own sources of strength (as demonstrated by the steady growth in backing for increased defense spending), and that the security of our key allies abroad must command ever greater support.

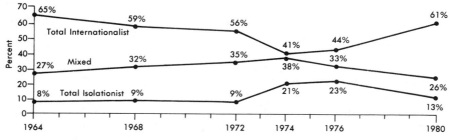

FIGURE 1 Internationalist/Isolationist Trends, 1964–1980

The recent emergence and solidification of this outlook on the world, carrying with it intertwined strands of both nationalism and internationalism, should give encouragement to our friends and send a warning to our adversaries. The American people do not show themselves as fickle and prone to sudden shifts in points of view, but rather as reasonably sensible and shrewd observers of the global environment. Our own leadership has much to build on in its efforts to forge a consistent foreign policy, and it can count on most Americans to view the world beyond our shores with considerable realism and maturity. Our friends can take comfort and assurance in the basic support they have achieved among our citizens, although that support must be reciprocated if it is to remain steady. And our adversaries should understand that Americans are quite ready to defend what they see as their fundamental interests, with the use of force to achieve that end fully acceptable.[4]

NOTES

1. See the review of recent findings in "The Hardening Mood toward Foreign Policy," by David R. Gergen, *Public Opinion*, February/March 1980.
2. This system was devised by Lloyd A. Free as president of the institute. The original results were reported in his book (with Hadley Cantril) *The Political Beliefs of Americans* (Rutgers University Press, 1967).
3. See the following Potomac Associates books by William Watts and Lloyd A. Free, *State of the Nation, 1972* (Universe Books, 1973); *State of the Nation, 1974* (Potomac Associates, 1974); and *State of the Nation III* (Lexington Books, 1978).
4. Willingness to use force against Iran was evidenced in a *Washington Post* poll of a national cross-section completed in mid-April. A majority of 55% versus 30% supported the proposition that "the United States should set a deadline for the return of the hostages, and take military action if they are not returned by then."

15

THE INFLUENCE OF SPECIAL-INTEREST GROUPS AND MASS MEDIA ON SECURITY POLICY IN THE UNITED STATES

BERNARD C. COHEN

A discussion of the influence of interest groups and the media of mass communication touches upon a number of issues of long-standing interest to students both of political science and of contemporary political and military affairs, and offers us an opportunity to try to test our general understandings and hypotheses about these influence patterns against the reality of contemporary affairs.

I will start by clarifying the question before us, in order to avoid misunderstandings, and false expectations.

I am uncomfortable with the concept of "influence," unless it is more precisely defined. I cannot differentiate between "influence" and "power"—they are different ways of describing a single relationship, that in which one party succeeds in getting another party to do, or not do, something other than that which the second party had originally intended. Clearly, such a relationship is difficult to uncover and to measure, even if one has good physical access to the persons involved. If we stand on this definition, we will get nowhere with our question. On the other hand, we will also get nowhere if we assume that the *efforts* to influence policy are the same as influences that in the end are *successful*. That is the burden of Milbrath's definition of influence as "the process by which a decision-maker considers the content of a message as he makes his decision" (Milbrath, 1967, p. 372). That grants too much to the many individuals and groups who get a "hearing" as they try to rearrange the public agenda, but who ultimately make no impact on that agenda. Unavoidably, we must start with

Bernard C. Cohen is Quincy Wright Professor of Political Science at the University of Wisconsin–Madison. Among his writings are *The Press in Foreign Policy* and *The Public's Impact on Foreign Policy*. This essay was adapted especially for this book from a paper originally prepared for a symposium on "Democracy and Foreign Policy," held at Noordwijkerhout, the Netherlands, March 25–26, 1982, under the auspices of the Netherlands Society for International Affairs. The author is grateful to Peter R. Baehr, Philip P. Everts, and C. Paulien van den Tempel for their suggestions and comments.

efforts to alter the intentions of others, yet we have to come to rest some-where short of definitive statements about the success of those efforts. I am afraid we may have to be satisfied with a concept of influence as an "appar-ent impact on the direction of policy"—rather nebulous, to be sure, but at least realistic as a first approximation.

I am also concerned with the paths or the routes that efforts to shape policy may take. To what extent are we dealing with a *direct* process—that is, from interest groups directly to policy makers—as distinguished from an *indirect* process, in which certain public groups or institutions may act as intermediaries? The ordinary formulation of the relationship suggests a direct process, with a limited number of participants and thus a focused and limited research effort. But reality is always more complex, and we are com-pelled in some small way at least to widen our scrutiny and thus enlarge the question before us: To answer it, we need to pay attention not only to inter-est groups and to the mass media, and to the makers of security policy, but also to some obvious intermediary institutions such as the American Con-gress, and even that most ambiguous of all institutions, "public opinion," since no one works entirely in a political vacuum.[1]

I

Let me start by asking what we might *expect* to discover about the influence of interest groups and the mass media on American security policy—an issue area that is marked by extraordinary technical complexity and diffi-culty; by massive uncertainty, both about the state of contemporary (often secret) affairs and about cause-and-effect relations; by high risks of great danger to large populations; and by high financial and opportunity (read: social) costs. What do we know about the roles of these two institutions in the American political system that we can apply specifically to the process of security-policy making? The answers are mixed and potentially even incon-sistent and contradictory.

For over twenty years now, the concept of a "military-industrial com-plex" has suggested untoward influence of American industrial power on weapons development and procurement, and, through them, on strategic doctrine and security policy. Coined by President Eisenhower in his fare-well address as president in 1961, the phrase reinforced a pervasive view—held by Marxists, neo-Marxists, and non-Marxists—that economic interest groups were the most influential in the foreign policy field (see, for example, Cohen, 1959). The question of precisely what drives the engine of weapons development and procurement remains a matter of current debate, in which arguments about the economic profits of corporations carry less weight than arguments about the structure of science and technology and about the institutional-bureaucratic needs of organizations in the science-technology business (see, for example, Brooks, 1976; Allison and Morris, 1976; Kurth, 1973). While the premises of the "military-industrial complex" argument are still shared by some—and indeed it would be imprudent for anyone to rule them out totally—the weight of current judgment is quite different: it is that interest groups of *all* kinds, including those that are economic in nature, have *little* influence on issues of security policy. Milbrath suggests three important reasons for this: (1) decisions having the characteristics of security policy (as I have described them above) are made more by intellective than by social processes and are thus less open to group influence; (2) issues that attract wide and/or intense public scrutiny—as security-policy issues do because of press attention—are less open to special-group influence; and (3) the greater the importance of the issue in the total scheme of things, the less the likelihood of group influence. In a contradictory vein, however, Milbrath argues that decisions that "gestate over a period of several months" (as security-policy issues generally do) are more open to group influence than decisions with a shorter decision time (Milbrath, 1967, pp. 248–57). Hughes, reviewing a larger body of literature than Milbrath, concludes along essentially the same lines that: "economic interest groups are most likely to be influential when there is decision making over a long period of time, when economic considerations are paramount, and when the issue has no major security component" (Hughes, 1978, p. 211). And noneconomic groups, he argues, are not particularly effective under circumstances that characterize security policy. But "in coalitions they can be influential, under the same circumstances in which the public is likely to be influential, and because they serve as an indicator of public sentiment to policy makers. This means that rapidly growing and large ad hoc groups can be especially effective" (p. 218).

These are but summaries of more complex judgments, yet two things seem to stand out clearly. One is that conditions of influence may cut across each other; thus we are left with little guidance as to which condition or principle takes precedence. Issues of security policy are frequently long in the making; does this fact enlarge the opportunities for interest groups to exert influence, or does the amount of public attention that such issues receive over a prolonged period diminish those opportunities? Indeed, what is the independent variable: the character of the issue, or of the interest group, or of such additional and circumstantial elements like "public attention"?

A second point that emerges clearly has to do with the apparent basis for the limited impact that interest groups are believed to have on security policy. The essence of interest-group activity is group advantage. But private-group advantage is difficult to calculate in the security-policy arena; we are all more or less advantaged or disadvantaged collectively. That is the kernel of truth in the otherwise misleading concept of "national interest." Private interest thus seems generally to yield to public—or national— interest when the latter is clearly formulated. The political question then turns more on the formulation of "national interest" in threatening circumstances than it does on the accommodation of private interests in non-threatening circumstances (which is the sphere of group activity in domestic politics). This is not to say that interest groups never see an identity between their own interests and a "national interest," but rather that the burden would appear to be on them to persuade those who govern of the validity or merit of their contribution to the national-security debate.[2] But because governments have an interest in consistent policies, there may be internal constraints on their capacity to be persuaded by external pressures if to do so means unstable, fluctuating policies.

These general remarks about the impact of interest groups on American security policy may apply more to some kinds of groups than to others. Just to indicate the possibilities, we might visualize a two-by-two matrix which on one axis distinguishes among groups according to their size, and on the other according to the particularism of their interests and concerns, as follows:

	Particular	General
Small	1	3
Large	2	4

Block 1 would be occupied by the narrowest of special-interest groups, those having few members and highly particularistic interests—for example, an organization of importers of Argentinian wine; at the other extreme, block 4 would be occupied by groups representing large political movements or objectives, for example, the large national committees which fought over the issue of American neutrality prior to our entry into World War II, or, in more recent times, the Vietnam Mobilization Committee, which represented most of the antiwar organizations in the United States. Hypotheses about the limited influence of interest groups *on security policy* (but not necessarily on other aspects of foreign policy) may have greater applicability to groups in blocks 1 and 2 than to those in blocks 3 and 4. The impact of groups in block 4 verges on electoral influence, or on what I have elsewhere referred to as the capacity of governments to govern (Cohen, 1973), and it needs to be understood in different terms. This extends the notion of interest-group influence beyond the decision-making process to the larger political process. This I presume is what Hughes (1978, p. 218) had in mind when he spoke of "coalitions . . . [which] serve as an indicator of public sentiment to policy makers," and which he judged to be "especially effective." I will return to these important general considerations after we have had a chance to look at some recent cases.

There are two additional hypotheses involving the influence of nongovernmental groups on security policy in the United States which deserve our attention at this point. These seem to be contradictory also, but in fact they are competitive. They are also rather more speculative in the sense that they have not yet been subjected to a great deal of research, although circumstantial evidence for them abounds. On the one hand, there is an often unspoken but nevertheless pervasive "fear of the right" on the part of many American officials, especially those not themselves on the right but even including some who are. Thirty years after the high point of "McCarthyism," many American politicians and government officials still are concerned lest they appear to be "too soft" on issues involving communism and the Soviet Union. Their behavior—and their public statements—are consistent with the recognition that Americans are deeply fearful of the Soviet Union and with the belief that substantial and uncontrollable ultraconservative/fundamentalist political forces lie in wait for those who "lose" anything—particularly other countries—to communism or to the USSR, or who seem to be indifferent to the issues of communist strength and Soviet domination. Better to play it safe—and hence to pay careful attention to the opinions and interests of conservative groups on such issues that have potential electoral or political significance. And issues of national-security policy are very high on that list. Even our more conservative presidents in recent times—who are less constrained by the right and thus freer to take steps such as the "opening to China" that more liberal presidents have been unwilling to risk—have nevertheless taken pains to establish their *bona fides* from time to time with the right-wing fringes of their party.

On the other hand, we have a new, post-Vietnam, phenomenon involving public participation in security affairs: what we might call a pervasive "fear of the left." Ten years after the end of American participation in the war in Vietnam, some American officials—not the least of them in the Department of Defense—are reluctant to advocate certain security measures involving the use of American combat troops for fear that they would thereby mobilize the old antiwar coalition from the Vietnam era, or create a new one just as effective in limiting the capacity of the United States to use its military force for any purpose less than obvious self-defense.

The classic attempt to define the competitive nature of these forces is the so-called "Ellsberg hypothesis:" Daniel Ellsberg argued that the causes of the American failure in Vietnam lay not in ignorance but in the political necessity to walk a fine line between these forces on the right and on the left. No administration, he said, could afford to "lose" Vietnam, nor could it afford to do what was required to win the war; all it could do was temporize and hope and, in the end, hand the problem on to its successor.[3] That these forces are still at work will be obvious in the evidence we have before us. Why and how they affect different people differently, however, is not yet so clear.

With respect to the role of the mass media, we might start by noting the difficulty of generalizing about so large a set of diverse institutions. But if we look at shared behavioral patterns, at the institutions that serve to "nationalize" the flow of information, and also at the media that pay particular attention to questions of public policy, there are a number of things we might expect to discover about the influence of the mass media on American security policy.

The media in the United States perform two roles: that of *active participant* in public debate affecting decision making, and that of *neutral observer* of these issues and events, to inform the participation of others in the body politic (Cohen, 1963). The doctrines that govern everyday behavior stress the neutral role and minimize the participatory role. In practice this does not mean that the media stay out of the political debate; on the contrary. But it does mean that there is limited opportunity and thus little incentive for individuals to try to create for themselves in the media positions of independent authority on national-security-policy concerns. That would mean specialization in the subject matter, a rather demanding task, whereas to be a reporter of events is not thought to require specific substantive skills. Security policy, like all other policy areas, has to make its way in the media on a competitive basis with all the other events of the day, and at the hands of people who for the most part have no special competence or even understanding of what we have termed an extraordinarily complex technical subject. It is a matter of some relevance here that the responsibilities of journalists—their so-called "beats"—tend to be defined institutionally rather than substantively; that is to say, they cover specific governmental agencies, such as the Department of Defense *or* the Department of State *or* the White House, but not, as a general rule, a *subject matter* (such as security policy) that might require them to go to all of those places, plus the Congress and a number of embassies in pursuit of any given question on any given day.

The implication is that the influence of the mass media on security policy can be expected to lie not in the substantive contributions of informed experts in their midst, but rather in the special role that the media play in tying together a very large and dispersed policy-making system. The functional substitutes for a specific "national press" in the United States are the wire services, which are heavily used by most daily newspapers and radio stations; the news services of the major television networks; and a handful of major newspapers having independent staffs of journalists and, often, offering their own mini news services to other papers. These institutions, together with the psychological and professional pressures on journalists to develop a convergent "news sense" in the absence of objective definitions of "news," serve to focus national attention, in and out of government, on the same issues, and thus to help set the policy agenda for public discussion. This is especially the case with issues that are not quickly resolved—that stay "in the news," so to speak, for extended periods of time. We should recall, in this connection, Milbrath's observations (1967, p. 249) that the level of public attention on any issue is a function of the level of press attention, and that issues that attract wide public attention are less open to group influence than issues attracting little public attention. In some ways Milbrath begs the question, because we are not told what accounts for the level of *press* attention to particular issues. Indeed, many journalists will defend their work by arguing that the level of press attention to any issue is a function of the level of public attention! ("We give people the news about things they are interested in.") The relationship is of course much more complicated than this, involving such things as prevailing judgments about "news," competing events, and the activities of government news sources (see, e.g., Abel, 1981; Gans, 1980). But the significance of Milbrath's observation is that media attention, whatever its origin, tends to lift persistent issues of national-security policy to levels of governmental decision making that are rather impervious to the pressures of special interests. At the same time, we should keep in mind Milbrath's contradictory hypothesis (1967, p. 250) that the longer issues stay in the public domain without decision, the more open they are to group influence. In either case, the media of mass communication may be said to be both an expression of public interest in security-policy issues and a shaper and transmitter of public opinions concerning those issues but not an indigenous source of important substantive analysis and ideas (Cohen, 1963; Epstein, 1973; Pool, 1976).

II

We can turn now to several recent and important issues that have affected the security policy of the United States and look at what has actually happened by way of interest-group and media participation and influence— after which we will be in a better position to assess the quality and usefulness of the hypotheses we have to work with. Four such issues that have stirred specific interest-groups and media activity are *SALT II*, general *nuclear weapons* policy, the sale of *AWACS* planes to Saudi Arabia, and U.S. policy in *El Salvador*. These issues represent American policy toward nuclear arms and arms control vis-à-vis the Soviet Union; toward the Middle East; and toward Central America—the latter two in the context of the possible extension of Soviet or communist political and military influence. Collectively they provide a good basis for empirical observation of the question at hand.

SALT II

SALT II—the second round of strategic-arms-limitation talks between the United States and the Soviet Union—has become a generic name for a set of negotiations, for an eventual proposed treaty, and for the overall arms-control process. The SALT II period is generally considered to extend from the conclusion of SALT I in 1971–72 to the end of 1980, but it mainly spans the years of the Carter administration (January 1977–January 1981). The SALT II issue was a field of combat both within the Carter administration

(Talbott, 1979, 1980) and on the outside, between what Elizabeth Drew (1977) has called the arms-control "liberals" (those who were very interested in reaching an agreement with the Soviet Union) and "conservatives" (those whose primary interest was not to confer any advantage on the Soviets in an arms-limitation treaty). The domestic political problem was set by the eventual need for a two-thirds vote of approval in the Senate for any treaty and by the announced intention of the "conservatives" in and out of the Senate to insist on "equality" in SALT II—SALT I having compensated for a then-existing Soviet technological inferiority by granting the Soviets a numerical advantage. The problem was additionally complicated by the inordinate complexity of the issues involved and by the necessity for a large measure of secrecy, both for military reasons and for the realities of bargaining seriously with the Soviets. Drew, writing at the beginning of the Carter administration's experience with SALT II, pointed out that this fight was different from others involving public policy because "in this instance, people are arguing from sincerely and deeply held opposing views of what is necessary for the nation's survival." She observed also that officials were concerned that they might be accused of being insufficiently alert to the communist threat (Drew, 1977, p. 99).

As a consequence of the exceedingly technical characteristics of the SALT II issue, the interest groups that became involved were composed rather heavily of "specialists"—many former officials, civilian and military, who had experience with military matters, scientists, and academic (civilian) strategists—joined by individuals and groups from the "old left" who were anti-Soviet and working with a few Congressmen and journalists. The major groups working on behalf of SALT II included the Arms Control Association, headed by Herbert Scoville, a former Deputy Director of the Arms Control and Disarmament Agency; the Federation of American Scientists; the Council for a Livable World, founded by Leo Szilard, one of the early atomic scientists; the Center for Defense Information, an independent source of information on strategic questions directed by retired Admiral Gene R. LaRocque; New Directions, an international-affairs organization modeled after Common Cause, which had been visibly effective in the domestic-politics and governmental-process areas; Americans for SALT, a coalition of a number of pro-SALT groups; and several university and quasiacademic research institutes having arms-control programs, including Harvard, M.I.T., and The Brookings Institution (Drew, 1977, pp. 106–7; Jensen, 1982, p. 139).

The major groups working against SALT II—the arms-control conservatives—were of two kinds: On the one hand there were the old conservatives, the right-wing anti-Soviet organizations like the American Security Council, which includes some retired military officers and ambassadors; the Emergency Coalition Against Unilateral Disarmament, whose constituent organizations included the American Conservative Union, Young Americans for Freedom, the Committee for the Survival of a Free Congress, as well as the American Security Council; the National Strategic Information Center, which is a promilitary lobby; and the Center for Strategic and International Studies, a research institute at Georgetown University. On the other hand there were two relatively new groups made up chiefly of old liberals—anticommunist trade unionists, intellectuals, and dissident conservative Democrats: the Coalition for a Democratic Majority, which was formed in 1972 after Senator McGovern won the Democratic nomination for the presidency, and which took no more joy in the Carter candidacy; and the Committee on the Present Danger, established in 1976 although bearing the name of a bipartisan, proadministration organization of the early 1950s. The new committee was founded by a group of former officials, including Paul Nitze, Eugene Rostow, and Henry Fowler, who were in opposition first to President Ford and Secretary of State Kissinger on their policy of détente and subsequently to some of the policies and appointments of President Carter (Drew, 1977, pp. 107–8; Talbott, 1979, 1980; Barnet, 1981). The committee quickly picked up support from unionists like Lane Kirkland, from intellectuals and critics like Norman Podhoretz and Richard Pipes, and from many members of the Coalition for a Democratic Majority.[4]

Both the pro-SALT and the anti-SALT groups were extremely active, and both established good working relations with individuals within the bureaucracy and with members of the Senate and their staffs. The White House, the Arms Control and Disarmament Agency, and the State Department worked closely with the pro-SALT groups: "Literature, spokespersons, mailing lists, and the like were shared with these groups in an effort to gain acceptance for the treaty" (Jensen, 1982, p. 139). The anti-SALT organizations forged an alliance with Senator Henry Jackson, Democrat of Washington, and one of his aides, Richard Perle (later an Assistant Secretary of Defense), who was widely acknowledged to be one of the most well-informed individuals on national security matters then working in or for the Senate. Talbott says that Jackson and one of the subcommittees he chaired were apparently sources of leaks of information to Paul Nitze, who was the most visible spokesman for the Committee on the Present Danger, and to Evans and Novak, a team of Washington-based, nationally syndicated columnists who kept up a running attack on the administration during the SALT II negotiations (Talbott, 1979, 1980, p. 142). By the time the negotiations were concluded and the treaty was ready for Senate consideration, it began to receive heavy coverage in the media of communication. Barnet reports that during the hearings, members of the Committee on the Present Danger testified on seventeen different occasions, participated in nearly 500 television and radio programs, and distributed over 200,000 pamphlets (Barnet, 1981, pp. 102–3). In the end, the Senate conservatives began to wring "hawkish" concessions from the Carter administration, including promises to increase defense spending by 5% a year. But even then the fate of SALT II in the Senate was highly uncertain, and President Carter almost gratefully seized the opportunity to withdraw the treaty before any vote was taken when the Soviet Union began (1979) its military intervention in Afghanistan.

In this as in other cases, it is not easy to isolate the specific contributions made by the interest groups and the media to the ultimate outcome. The opposition won on SALT II, but that opposition was strategically located in the Congress and elsewhere in the body politic and not only in interest groups. But arms-control conservatives, feeding the Congressional opposition as well as being fed by it, were politically experienced, got excellent media coverage, and obviously helped sustain the initiative of those opposed to the treaty. Among the members of the Committee on the Present Danger at that time was former California Governor Ronald Reagan, and ten months into the Reagan presidency, thirty-two of the 182 members of the Committee had been given positions in the Reagan administration, many of them in the national-security area (Shribman, 1981).

Nuclear Weapons

Pressure on behalf of a NATO build-up of medium-range rockets and cruise missiles to neutralize a growing Soviet medium-range missile capability picked up support during the SALT II debate, when the opposition to SALT II used it as one of its "bargaining chips" in return for their vote for the treaty. Concern over the growing imbalance of forces in Europe, both nuclear and conventional, was a part of a wider concern for security vis-à-vis the USSR; and while the arms-control conservatives were the ones who pressed for the deployment of new missiles in Europe, this was not initially a contentious or a divisive issue. Given the state of general public opinion at the time (Russett and Deluca, 1981), it may even have been a rather popular position.

But the Reagan administration's careless talk about limited nuclear war in Europe, and about nuclear "demonstration shots" across the Soviet bow, so to speak, was a powerful stimulus to a long-dormant American antinuclear movement already deeply disturbed by the administration's nuclear-rearmament efforts. And the European response to these events— massive and well-organized demonstrations in major European cities in the fall of 1981 against nuclear weapons—suddenly breathed new life into this nascent American movement. Groups that had been struggling to be heard—Physicians for Social Responsibility, the Federation of American Scientists and the Union of Concerned Scientists, the National Conference of Catholic Bishops, the Council of Churches, and countless community and church-related disarmament organizations—found themselves overnight the object of media attention, and they rapidly forged a collective identity in the Nuclear Weapons Freeze Campaign, a national coalition of over eighty organizations which was quickly joined by members of Congress (see Butterfield, 1982).

While it is premature to draw firm conclusions about the influence of this movement, its extraordinarily rapid growth suggests that it is likely to have some visible impact on the development of American nuclear-weapons policy in the future. There is at least circumstantial evidence that the START negotiations with the Soviet Union may have been influenced both in their substance and timing by the political pressures generated by the anti-nuclear movement. The endorsement of the freeze by a large number of prominent political figures, including Senator Edward M. Kennedy, Democrat of Massachusetts, certainly suggests that they believe it has significant political potential.

AWACS

Under current American law—which is coming under scrutiny in the federal courts for its possible unconstitutionality—presidential agreements to sell weapons over a certain dollar value to other countries may be nullified by the Congress within thirty days after it has received formal notification from the president. The security-policy question at issue here concerned congressional approval of President Reagan's proposed sale of five AWACS (Airborne Warning and Control System) electronic-surveillance planes and other military equipment (including fuel tanks for F-15 fighters) to Saudi Arabia, in pursuit of a security policy that attempted to subordinate the Arab-Israeli conflict to the needs of what Secretary of State Alexander M. Haig, Jr., called an anti-Soviet "strategic consensus." The president's intention to sell the planes was announced on April 21, 1981, after some months of internal debate and external pressure, both domestic and foreign. The Congress became officially involved on October 1, 1981, and had until the end of October to block the sale by adopting in both houses a resolution of disapproval. Members of Congress had already begun to feel the pressure of lobbying in April. In the second week of October, after six months of such lobbying, the House of Representatives voted by a large margin to disapprove the sale, and the Senate Foreign Relations Committee voted to disapprove by a margin of one vote. The full Senate was expected to disapprove also, by a very close vote. But on October 28, after strenuous White House efforts to influence uncommitted senators, the senate *rejected* the resolution of disapproval by a vote of 52 to 48, thus allowing the sale to take place.

The AWACS issue had many elements which are the "bread and butter" of American journalism: a new president, a close vote in a politically delicate area (delicate both abroad and at home), and the transfer of sensitive military equipment. The media gave their attention very substantially to those who were seeking to block the sale and thereby hand the president a defeat on his first major foreign-policy initiative. Nevertheless, the resolution of disapproval did have its opponents outside the Congress: the international oil companies were reported to be backing the administration, with Mobil Oil having conducted two major advertising campaigns; and the many companies who hold the AWACS contracts (Boeing being the prime contractor) mounted what *The New York Times* (October 24, 1981) called "one of the most intense lobbying campaigns in years: a campaign for the arms sale to Saudi Arabia that includes a blizzard of mail to undecided or opposition senators." The campaign also included intensive visits to the offices of such senators. One senator reported having been "inundated" by contractors from within his state, while another—a Republican from a state with few contracts—"has indicated that pressure tactics for the sale have been heavy-handed to the point of being counter-productive." But the center of the opposition to the resolution of disapproval was the government itself and the president's party, and they counted on such things as party loyalty and support for the president personally and for the credibility of his foreign policy.

Supporters of the resolution to disapprove—that is, opponents of the president's policy—have generally been described collectively as the "Jewish lobby" or the "Israeli lobby." (The Israeli government, arguing that AWACS planes in the hands of the Saudis were a threat to Israel, was an active participant in this process, as was the Saudi government on the other side; after some reflection I have excluded them both from further consideration because they fall outside the framework of "interest groups," even though they may well have been a resource as well as an inspiration to domestic interest groups.) For reasons on which one can only speculate, neither the recipients of pressure from Jewish groups nor the media that reported so extensively on the issue have identified the organizations that comprise what a journalist has called "one of Washington's most potent groups, the Israel lobby" (Smith, 1981). In a study of interest-group activity in American foreign policy in the Middle East between 1966 and 1971, Robert Trice (1974) identifies approximately 150 Jewish groups that engaged in public activity, but only twenty-five initiated an average of one or more actions per year. Twelve groups generated 25% of the total actions during those years, setting the tone of the debate, defining alternatives, and forming and leading coalitions. The major group, and the first to reach the administration after the April announcement, appears to have been the Conference of Presidents of Major American Jewish Organizations, which is at one time both an organization and a coalition of organizations (and this very ambiguity may contribute to the difficulty of precise identification.)[5] The Anti-Defamation League, which is concerned most of the time with combating anti-Semitism, took out nearly a full-page advertisement in *The New York Times* portraying segments of editorials in eight newspapers across the country opposing the AWACS sale. Beyond the activities of these groups, there were no doubt many Jewish organizations at the community and the state level that sought to bring electoral pressure to bear on individual members of Congress. In a statement issued on October 4, 1981, former President Richard Nixon referred to "the intense opposition by . . . parts of the American Jewish community." And Representative Dan Rostenkowski, a Democrat from Illinois, was quoted as saying that voting for the sale of AWACS "would have been the right vote but I didn't want Jewish groups coming down on me."

Senator Henry Jackson, who was so crucial a figure in the opposition to

SALT II a year earlier, presents an interesting case here of a senator who was heavily cross-pressured—and probably as much by his convictions as by interest groups. Senator Jackson long ago made his intellectual and political commitments to the state of Israel and has been one of its strongest supporters in Democratic political circles. But the Boeing company, the prime AWACS contractor, is located in Washington, and Senator Jackson's staunch support of it over the years, as well as his strong prodefense posture, have led some people to refer to him as "the senator from Boeing." Jackson announced early that he would support the sale of AWACS only in the framework of a regional security arrangement, with the planes owned by the United States but under binational command. Those conditions proving to be unacceptable to the Saudis, Senator Jackson was free to join the supporters of the resolution to disapprove the sale.

To sum up: In the end, as expected in the beginning, the vote on the AWACS sale was very close. But the outcome (refusal of the Senate to disapprove the sale) was different from that which had been expected, thus supporting the conclusion of Trice (1974, p. 413) that interest groups do not necessarily control American Middle East policy, even though they may have a strong impact on the views of some of the participants.

El Salvador

The question of American policy toward El Salvador concerns the extent, character, and openness of American support for the Duarte regime prior to the national election there in March 1982, as well as the American effort to cut off support for the guerrillas, which the United States claimed comes from Cuba and the Soviet Union, chiefly via Nicaragua.

Events in El Salvador evoked two divergent historical analogies: To some, they were seen as the forerunners of another "Cuba," that is, the founding of a new Soviet-oriented regime in the Western Hemisphere which would soon support other communist guerrilla movements in Central and South America. To others, they were seen as the forerunners of another "Vietnam," a bloody, unwinnable guerrilla war into which the United States would be drawn further and further, in support of a repressive government that mishandled its own people and could not survive without outside help.

Support for a strong pro-Duarte, interventionist American policy came from groups who feared in El Salvador the makings of another Cuba: conservative, anti-Soviet, anticommunist, and anti-Castro groups, one example being the Council for Inter-American Security. This being the basic policy orientation of the Reagan administration, however, the burden of supporting the policy in public was on American officials (as well as on Salvadoran officials). Opposition to U.S. policy came chiefly from those who saw in El Salvador the makings of another Vietnam, and who wanted to stop it: This opposition was well-organized, drawing on the experiences of individuals in the anti-Vietnam War movement. Its organizational center, according to *The New York Times* (November 18, 1981), was the Coalition for a New Foreign and Military Policy, established in the mid-1970's. The Coalition had forty-nine member groups, many of which were especially intersted in Central America and divided amongst themselves the work of opposition. Among the important constituent organizations were the Washington Office on Latin America, which was founded in 1974 by church groups, and which provided knowledgeable witnesses for congressional hearings; the Council on Hemispheric Affairs, established in 1975 and supported both by labor and religious groups, which specialized in contacts with the news media; Amnesty International, which worked on human-rights cases; and the American Friends Service Committee, a long-established political-action arm of the Quakers, which had been organizing "grass-roots" opposition to American policy in El Salvador. The Council of Churches also spoke out against the maintenance of injustice in El Salvador, and Senator Charles Percy, Republican of Illinois, Chairman of the Senate Committee on Foreign Relations, publicly remarked on the growing pressure on the Senate from American churches and civil-rights organizations concerned about the violations of human rights in El Salvador.

The impact of the mass media on El Salvador quickly began to resemble their impact on Vietnam. Journalists defined their job as having two justifications, which drew on the two roles of the media I mentioned earlier, the neutral and the participatory. The first was to bring directly to the American people, both by television and by newspaper, graphic accounts of those events that are "newsworthy" by current standards (and by Vietnam war-coverage standards). The other was limited participation, but participation nonetheless: to fulfill their responsibility in a democratic society by acting as the people's representatives in challenging their government, in asking the questions that the people themselves would presumably have liked to ask but were in no position to ask. Both of these definitions of the job affected the search for news: journalists were looking for, and finding, evidence of arbitrary violence and violations of human rights on the part of the Salvadoran government and army, as well as violations of presidential restrictions on American military advisers in El Salvador. News accounts of assassinations in communities, of the deaths of American nuns and Dutch journalists, and television pictures of American advisers carrying M-16 rifles are examples of media participation in this issue.

The interest-group opponents of an interventionist policy had an obvious impact on American policy: They mobilized moral criticism from many diverse and respectable sources at a comparatively early stage in the development of the policy. In comparison, the American government was fully committed to substantial military participation in the Vietnam War before moral outrage against the war became a powerful political force (van der Zee, 1982). Interest-group opponents have also provided the American Congress and the American public with useful and credible information which was often different from that provided by official government sources. Such information was reported (Croisette, 1981) to be especially useful to the staff members of congressional committees and subcommittees. And they made manifest what I earlier called the "fear of the left," the specter that American policy would, as in Vietnam, create massive dissent, openly and severely dividing the country.

In an interesting reversal, the opposition from these groups openly divided the administration on Salvadoran policy. The secretary of state, on the one side, was bellicose on El Salvador, seeming to fear the latent power of the right on what might be called a Cuban-related matter, and in an interview with CBS in February 1982 he specifically rejected any policy-making role for opposition public opinion. On the other side, the secretary of defense (hardly a shrinking violet) was unwilling to risk having his overall anti-Soviet military posture undermined by the massive mobilization of left-liberal dissent that would have followed the dispatch of American combat troops to El Salvador (Gwertzman, 1982). The opposition also apparently sent the president looking for alternative antileft policies toward Central America which, while politically and economically aggressive, did not involve the possibility of direct military encounters involving American troops. Furthermore, the evidence from the media that American military advisers carried weapons in El Salvador was apparently instrumental in inducing a group of twenty-nine congressmen to initiate a court case against the president for having violated the War Powers Act of 1973 when he sent the advisers to El Salvador without officially informing the Congress, thereby depriving it of the opportunity to disapprove of the action and to bring it to an end.

III

Let me return now to the questions I raised at the beginning and ask whether these examples seem to conform, or fail to conform, to the expectations about the influence of interest groups and the media generated by existing literature. I shall try to draw an overall assessment and conclusions separately for the two kinds of public-opinion institutions.

With respect to the interest groups represented in these examples, it is clear that many of them have had an important impact on American security policy, although different people and different policies have been affected differently.

a. On SALT II, the administration lost to opposition forces within the Congress and outside; it was not a case of "interest groups" versus the government, but of alliances with outsiders on both sides of the issue. The alliance of the opponents was more effective than the alliance supporting the administration.

b. On AWACS, the administration carried the day, but barely. Here, too, there were alliances with outsiders on both sides, but the supposedly dominant group—"the most powerful lobby in Washington" (Israel)—lost to a coalition that was guided more by international-political and party-political considerations than by interest-group pressures. But where the positions and votes of so many different Congressmen are involved, it is not an easy matter to characterize the real patterns of influence. It is reasonable to assume that interest groups on both sides may have been decisive in a large number of individual cases—perhaps enough even to have made the crucial difference. Much more work needs to be done in this case.

c. On El Salvador, the administration experienced severe constraints at the hands of an alliance in which interest groups played a big role—the same situation as in SALT II but with the political alignments reversed.

d. On the future of nuclear weapons, it is really too early to tell, as I noted earlier. A serious confrontation between the United States and the Soviet Union could either overwhelm the antinuclear movement, or it could give it added support; much would depend on the circumstances and on how they were handled by the administration. The rapid growth of an anti-nuclear movement has apparently been a response to an administration that has been bellicose and careless in its political treatment of nuclear questions. A government that showed more sensitivity to the public's concern about nuclear war might see antinuclear groups lose ground—but such a sensitivity might itself be the result of political pressures from these groups.

In the United States, then, some interest groups have been instrumental in helping to steer security policy in specific—although different—directions. These groups have been most effective when in alliance with members of Congress and on issues that have come before the Congress. It may in fact *be* those alliances, or the imminent prospect of them, that makes the executive branch pay attention to interest groups on security issues. There is certainly less evidence that interest groups have played a significant role in dealing with the executive branch on issues where the Congress is not yet involved. These findings raise interesting questions about the general applicability of the hypotheses that prevail in the literature about the influence of interest groups on security policy. It is not at all clear that decisions on security policy are made more by intellective than by social processes, for example—witness SALT II; but to the extent that they are, they are not therefore less open to group influence somewhere in the policy process. Similarly, it is not at all clear that issues which attract wide or intense public scrutiny are less open *on that account* to group influence. Further, it is not at all clear whether it makes any sense to talk about circumstances that are or are not "open to group influence" in the first place, when the evidence suggests that *any* set of circumstances may somewhere be open to the influence of some groups but not of others. In retrospect, the contradictory elements in these hypotheses stand out as more interesting and as more revealing of how little we really know. Among other possibilities, it may be the case that the existing bundle of hypotheses are time- and situation-bound, and do not really hold for the kinds of issues that we are living with today. It is possible, as recent election studies have shown, to have broad secular changes in political behavior that compel us to modify what we thought were our bed-rock understandings (Campbell et al., 1960; Nie et al., 1976).

We need to be more sensitive to where we stand in the matrix that I sketched earlier: Are we dealing here, and now, with interest groups that represent special interests as we have traditionally conceived them, or are we dealing with groups of whatever size that are laying a competing claim to represent the general interest? In a political system where parties are weak and programmatic responsibility is muffled, at a time when no one can find a "consensus" on international affairs, and in a setting where foreign- and security-policy issues have a weak hold on the voters' attention at election time, interest groups may be an increasingly important means of creating and mobilizing significant public opinion with respect to specific and unforeseen issues of external policy that arise between elections and have threatening consequences for the whole society. Under such circumstances, one might well expect officials and representatives to accord them greater weight—even though they may not always be happy doing so.[6] Had McGovern been elected president in 1972, he would no doubt have absorbed the Vietnam Mobilization Committee into his administration. When Carter was elected in 1976, he brought into his administration many members of the Trilateral Commission, an interest group of "notables" who were opposed to the economic unilateralism of the Nixon period. When Reagan was elected in 1980, he took into his administration a significant part of the leadership of the Committee on the Present Danger. These events compel us to rethink the concept of interest group as a phenomenon for the advancement chiefly of private (and implicitly selfish or self-serving) interest. Our thinking in the past may well have been too much dominated by the organized pursuit of private economic advantage and too little concerned with the very different phenomena of group activity at critical periods in our history when there has been no "dominant foreign policy paradigm"— when the nation and its leaders have not found a standard around which a clear and stable majority could rally.

With respect to the media of mass communication, it is important to keep in mind that "the media" is an abstraction rather than a collectivity. It includes very many, very diverse institutions with no organization or connection except for some convergence each day on what is news that day. To that extent, the media will have some focusing effect but not to any predetermined or planned or necessarily consistent purpose. Quite the contrary: The most important generalization we can make about the media is that in each of these cases they have focused attention on the *opposition* to declared government policy. That is so clear a pattern that one wonders whether it has become an operational definition of "news." During these same months there were other security matters of comparable import on which there was no significant organized opposition—for example, the proposed American decision to sell a new jet fighter to Taiwan—and only fleeting media attention. And when the opponents of U.S. policy in El Salvador quieted down after the March 1982 elections in that country, media attention diminished—although the struggle there did not.

Note, however, that the *actual* substantive focus of the media on these four issues has had quite divergent practical effects. On SALT II and AWACS, the effect of the media focus on the opposition was to highlight anti-Soviet, promilitary postures and policies. On El Salvador and on the nuclear-weapons questions, on the other hand, the effect of the media focus has been to play up critical attacks on the nation's military posture and policies. The media certainly played an important part in keeping El Salvador in the framework of the "Vietnam analogy" rather than the "Cuban analogy." This is an instructive finding, especially in view of the tendency of people on all sides to attribute unified political purpose or political effect to media coverage of foreign affairs.

Overall, to conclude, these cases seem to me to support the earlier hypotheses about the media, including one of Milbrath's conflicting hypotheses, to wit: The longer that issues stay in the public domain prior to decisions being taken, the more open these issues are to group participation and thus to the possibility of group influence. It is the media that have effectively placed these four issues in the public domain and kept them up front long enough for interests to be fully mobilized in response to them. There may even be an interactive effect between the public debate that thereafter takes place among interest groups and the length of time necessary to reach a decision. Indeed, these institutions work their ways in a highly interconnected fashion, and it may be unrealistic for us to believe that we can ever really untangle them.

NOTES

1. Cf. Milbrath (1967), who initially treats interest groups as themselves intermediaries between citizens and government but subsequently discusses interest groups' use of intermediaries.
2. A recent textbook on foreign policy sums up interest-group influence as follows: "The impact of interest groups on foreign-policy decision-making is extremely limited, since such groups have no authoritative position in the foreign policy process. They must be able to persuade government officials of the appropriateness of their viewpoints. This is often difficult to do, particularly with respect to general political and military policy, for interest groups cannot demonstrate that they as a group have an overriding interest in an issue apart from that of the nation as a whole" (Jensen, 1982, pp. 137–38).
3. One could update Ellsberg's hypothesis by arguing that Nixon's ultimate solution to the Vietnam problem was the same kind of balancing act: yielding to the forces on the left while appeasing the right by aggressive actions—the Cambodian invasion, the Christmas bombing—and by the verbal promise of a "peace with honor."
4. That this conservative coalition persists is illustrated by the following: In June, 1981, the chairman of the U.S. delegation to the Helsinki Review Conference in Madrid, Max Kampelman, a former member of the Committee on the Present

Danger, accused the Soviet Union in a speech at the conference of having unleashed an arms race and of representing a military threat to peace and security. That speech was published by the Department of International Affairs of the AFL-CIO in the *Free Trade Union News,* 36, 9, September 1981, under the title "Whose Arms Race?" Copies of it were subsequently distributed by the Wisconsin chapter of the Young Americans for Freedom.

5. The following account of the AWACS debate draws on articles in *The New York Times* of April 22 and October 4, 18, and 28, 1981.

6. Recall, in this connection, Hughes' observation (1978, p. 218) about coalitions serving "as an indicator of public sentiment to policy-makers."

REFERENCES

Abel, Elie. 1981, ed. *What's News: The Media in American Society.* San Franciso: Institute for Contemporary Studies.

Allison, Graham and Morris, Frederic. 1976. "Armaments and Arms Control: Exploring the Determinants of Military Weapons," in F. A. Long and G. W. Rathjens, eds., *Arms, Defense Policy, and Arms Control.* New York: W. W. Norton.

Barnet, Richard J. 1981. "A Reporter at Large: The Search for National Security," *The New Yorker,* April 27, pp. 96–103.

Brooks, Harvey. 1976. "The Military Innovation System and the Qualitative Arms Race," in F. A. Long and G. W. Rathjens, eds., *Arms, Defense Policy, and Arms Control.* New York: W. W. Norton.

Butterfield, Fox. 1982. "Anatomy of the Nuclear Protest." *The New York Times Magazine,* July 11, pp. 14 ff.

Campbell, A., Converse, P., Miller, W., and Stokes, D. 1960. *The American Voter.* New York: John Wiley & Son.

Cohen, Bernard C. 1959. *The Influence of Non-Governmental Groups on Foreign Policy-Making.* Studies in Citizen Participation in International Relations, Vol. II. Boston: World Peace Foundation.

———. 1963. *The Press and Foreign Policy.* Princeton: Princeton University Press.

———. 1973. *The Public's Impact on Foreign Policy.* Boston: Little, Brown.

Croisette, Barbara. 1981. "Groups Trying to Sway Latin-America Policy," *The New York Times,* November 18.

Drew, Elizabeth. 1977. "A Reporter at Large: An Argument over Survival," *The New Yorker,* April 4, pp. 99–117.

Ellsberg, Daniel. 1971. "The Quagmire Myth and the Stalemate Machine," *Public Policy,* 19, 2, pp. 217–74. (A revised version appears under the same title in Ellsberg, *Papers on the War,* New York: Pocket Books, 1972.)

Epstein, Edward J. 1973. *News From Nowhere: Television and the News.* New York: Random House.

Gans, Herbert J. 1980. *Deciding What's News: A Study of CBS Evening News, NBC Nightly News, Newsweek, and Time.* New York: Random House (Vintage Books).

Gwertzman, Bernard. 1982. *International Herald Tribune,* February 16.

Hughes, Barry B. 1978. *The Domestic Context of American Foreign Policy.* San Francisco: W. H. Freeman.

Jensen, Lloyd. 1982. *Explaining Foreign Policy.* Englewood Cliffs, N. J.: Prentice-Hall.

Kurth, James R. 1973. "Why We Buy the Weapons We Do." *Foreign Policy,* 11 (Summer), pp. 33–56.

Milbrath, Lester W. 1967. "Interest Groups and Foreign Policy," in James N. Rosenau, ed., *Domestic Sources of Foreign Policy.* New York: The Free Press.

The New York Times. 1981: April 22, October 4, 18, 24, 28.

Nie, N., Verba, S., and Petrocik, J. 1976. *The Changing American Voter.* Cambridge, Mass.: Harvard University Press.

Pool, Ithiel deSola. 1976. "Government and the Media," *American Political Science Review,* 70, 4 (December), pp. 1234–41.

Russett, Bruce, and Deluca, Donald R. 1981. " 'Don't Tread on Me': Public Opinion and Foreign Policy in the Eighties," *Political Science Quarterly,* 96, 3 (Fall).

Shribman, David. 1981. "Group Goes From Exile to Influence," *The New York Times,* November 23.

Smith, Hedrick. 1981. "Reagan's Day: Fortunes Soar at Home and Abroad," *The New York Times,* October 29.

Talbott, Strobe. 1979, 1980. *Endgame: The Inside Story of SALT II.* New York: Harper Colophon Books.

Trice, Robert H., Jr. 1974. *Domestic Political Interests and American Policy in the Middle East: Pro-Israel, Pro-Arab and Corporate Non-Governmental Actors and the Making of American Foreign Policy, 1966–1971.* Unpub. Ph.D. Diss., University of Wisconsin—Madison.

van der Zee, Sytze. 1982. " 'Stop US War in El Salvador.' " *NRC Handelsblad* (Saturday Supplement), February 20.

Part Four

GOVERNMENTAL SOURCES OF AMERICAN FOREIGN POLICY

Because foreign policy is a product of the actions officials make on behalf of the state they lead, it can be argued that the way the government is *structured* will affect the conduct and content of foreign affairs as well. In other words, we can hypothesize that a relationship exists between the substance of policy and the kind of government that makes it. The proposition is particularly compelling if we focus attention, not on the kinds of foreign policy *goals* the nation's leaders select, but on the *means* they choose to satisfy particular objectives.

Perhaps the best example of the way the structure of the American presidential form of government serves as a source of American foreign policy is found in the periodic struggles that emerge between the president and Congress over the shaping of U.S. relations with other nations. More generally, American foreign policy is influenced by such institutional features as (1) the Constitution, which divides authority for making and implementing foreign policy among the different branches of government; (2) the rise in the twentieth century of executive dominance in foreign policy making, culminating in what has been described as the "imperial presidencies" of Lyndon Johnson and Richard Nixon; and (3) the vast array of Cabinet-level departments and other organizations and agencies that have come to assume prominence in foreign policy making and have developed an organizational stake in the choices that are made.

Governmental variables undoubtedly constrain what the United States can do abroad and the speed with which it can do it and have thus contributed to the persistence and continuity of postwar American foreign policy. The enormous size and complexity of the federal bureaucracy, for example, militate against policy reversals. The constitutional division of power between the executive and legislative branches of government also promotes policy by compromise through incremental adaptation. Thus governmental variables limit the nation's ability to change its course in world affairs.

In some instances, however, elements of the government machinery have facilitated, rather than diminished, innovative shifts in policy. State Department formulation of the Marshall Plan for European economic recovery in 1947 and White House initiatives in constructing the new international economic policies announced in August 1971 (which radically altered the nature of the international economic order that had existed since the closing days of World War II) stand out as cases in point. Thus, whether in promoting change or inhibiting it, the structure of the American government, in combination with the other sources of American foreign policy, is an important influence on the nation's external conduct.

PERSPECTIVES ON GOVERNMENTAL SOURCES OF AMERICAN FOREIGN POLICY: AN OVERVIEW

The president and the institutionalized presidency—the latter consisting of the president's personal staff and the Executive Office of the President—are preeminent in the foreign policy-making process. This preeminence derives in part from the authority granted the president in the Constitution and in part from the combination of judicial interpretation, legislative acquiescence, personal assertiveness, and custom and tradition that has transformed one branch of the U.S. federal government into the most powerful office in the world. The very nature of the postwar world could be added to the list, for the crisis-ridden atmosphere that has pervaded most of the post-World War II period contributed to the enhancement of presidential authority by encouraging the president to act energetically and decisively when dealing with global challenges. The widely shared consensus that existed among American leaders and the majority of the American people (at least until the Vietnam War)—a recognition that the international environment demanded an active American world role—also contributed to the feeling that strong presidential leadership in foreign policy was needed.

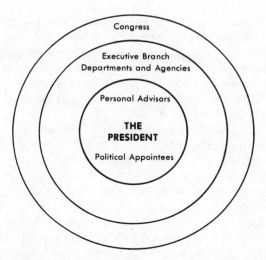

FIGURE 1 The Institutional Setting: The Concentric Circles of Policy Making

Although some (notably in Congress) questioned this proposition in the immediate aftermath of Vietnam, the need for strong presidential leadership in foreign affairs appears to have been a widely accepted viewpoint throughout most of the postwar period.

Because of the president's key role in foreign policy making, it is useful to consider the institutional arrangements as a series of concentric circles which in effect alter the standard government organization chart so as to draw attention to the core, or source, of the action. Thus the innermost circle in the policy-making process consists of the president, his immediate personal advisers, and such important political appointees as the secretaries of state and defense, the director of central intelligence, and various under and assistant secretaries who bear responsibility for carrying out policy decisions. The most important decisions involving the fate of the nation are made, in principle, at this level.

The second concentric circle contains the various departments and agencies of the executive branch. If we exclude from that circle the politically appointed heads of agencies and their immediate subordinates, whom we have already placed in the innermost circle, we can think of the individuals within the second circle as the career bureaucrats who provide continuity in the implementation of policy from one administration to the next. Their primary tasks—in theory—are to provide top-level policy makers with the information necessary for making decisions and to then carry out those decisions when they are reached.

Finally, the third concentric circle consists of Congress. A single institutional entity, Congress often appears to embrace many different centers of power and authority—ranging from the House and Senate leadership to the various coalitions operative in the legislative branch, and from the various committees and subcommittees in which the real work of Congress is done to the individual senators and congressmen who often vie with one another for publicity as well as power. Placing Congress in the outermost circle underscores the fact that, of all the institutions involved in foreign policy making, it is least involved in the day-to-day conduct of the nation's foreign relations.

The conceptualization described above was suggested some years ago in *To Move a Nation* by Roger Hilsman, who is both a perceptive student of American foreign relations as well as a former participant in the policy-making process. In his essay, "Policy-Making is Politics," drawn from that book, Hilsman provides an insightful summary of the activities and the linkages that exist among the various participants involved in making American foreign policy. He suggests that while governmental variables may affect the form and flow of policy making, the politicking inherent in the process—a feature often unrecognized by the casual observer—by no means conforms to neatly compartmentalized paths. Moreover, by noting that the policy-making process is affected not only by institutional structures but also by the policy-making roles occupied by decision makers and by the characteristics of the individuals who act out those roles, the essay conveniently introduces the subjects that are covered in more depth in the next two parts of his book. Hilsman lucidly argues that what the nation chooses to do abroad is the product of an often intense political struggle among all the pertinent players in the policy-making process, a perspective often unappreciated by most people.

Among the struggles is one that seems to have become endemic to the policy-making process—that between the head of the National Security Council staff, the president's assistant for national security affairs, and other key participants in the process, notably the secretary of state. The struggle grows out of a basic decision every new president must make: whether to give his secretary of state the primary role in the foreign policy-making system or to centralize and manage that system from the White House, often with the aid of an assertive assistant for national security affairs. The record of the past several administrations shows a clear preference for White House dominance. Henry Kissinger's rise to prominence during the Nixon and Ford presidencies began from his White House base. Similarly, Zbigniew Brzezinski, Jimmy Carter's national security assistant, eventually emerged as a key figure in the Carter administration's foreign policy-making apparatus. And Alexander Haig's resignation as Ronald Reagan's first secretary of state appears to have been caused at least in part by a conflict between the secretary and his own former assistant, William P. Clark, whom Reagan had appointed as national security adviser in early 1982.

The reasons underlying the emergence of the national security adviser as an important actor in the White House's domination of the making and implementation of the nation's foreign policy are perceptively analyzed in

I. M. Destler's article, "The Rise of the National Security Assistant, 1961–1981." Beginning with a description of the ideal role that the special assistant should play, the article contains important prescriptions for the future as well as an insightful, detailed analysis of the past. Among them is the admonition that "we need a more realistic conception of presidential leadership, . . . one of a leader who uses his personal leverage to nourish policy conceptions and policy coalitions that will further his goals, and who employs his staff to link him to these broader political-institutional realities rather than to shield him from them."

Destler concludes with a commentary on the early phases of the Reagan administration, in which he observes that even before the end of Reagan's first year in office, "The Reagan foreign policy process . . . was generating the same sorts of criticisms that Carter's began to sustain in mid-1978. If anything, the bad reviews were more numerous." Why, then, do presidents persist in their efforts to control policy analysis and implementation from the White House, with the national security adviser, operating under the aegis of the National Security Council, as the principal institutional as well as personal instrument for doing so? Specifically, why do presidents not choose the alternative of giving the secretary of state and the Department of State primary responsibility for managing American foreign policy?

In part the answer to these questions, as Destler notes in his analysis, is that historically the State Department has often been viewed as "the problem." The nature of "the problem" and the other factors that militate against a greater State Department role are examined by Leslie H. Gelb in his essay, "Why Not the State Department?" Among the important points he makes is that the State Department is far less conscious of presidential stakes and interests in particular issues than are members of the White House staff. Such insensitivity to politics in an environment where policy making *is* politics breeds irrelevance. At the same time, Gelb argues that conflict between the secretary of state and the national security adviser, which has become so pervasive a part of the question of who should be responsible for policy analysis and coordination, is as much a matter of personality as it is one of organization.

Despite this latter observation, organizational factors remain important. Principal among them is the fact that the State Department's major clients are other countries. "From a White House perspective," writes Gelb, "efforts to accommodate the legitimate concerns of other countries are often viewed as coming at the expense of American interests, and the accommodationists are viewed as not being tough enough. Presidents usually do not have much patience with this kind of advice, find they cannot change State's penchant for it, and soon stop listening."

Analogous considerations affect the State Department's relations with other executive branch organizations. Unlike the Department of Defense and unlike other primarily domestically oriented organizations such as the Agriculture, Commerce, Treasury, and Labor departments, the State Department has few domestic clientele groups (supporters of bureaucratic agencies who are served by or receive benefits from the organizations) to defend and support it. Because its principal focus is on foreign countries, it speaks by definition to a broad but weak *national* constituency rather than to particular, specialized interests. In contrast, the other departments and agencies have linkages with domestic political groups that give them important political influence in an environment where policy-making is politics. Furthermore, because of its relatively small size, the State Department often lacks bureaucratic muscle in dealing with other organizations and thus finds itself bargaining from a position of weakness rather than strength.

The Central Intelligence Agency, and the intelligence community more generally, are usually perceived as strong contenders in Washington's bureaucratic in-fighting and at the same time as comparatively immune from domestic politics. The secrecy shrouding intelligence activities and the historically important role that the CIA has played in combating communism appear to have largely insulated intelligence activities from domestic political scrutiny.

Harry Howe Ransom challenges appearances with the reality of the cyclical record of domestic scrutiny (notably from Congress) to which the CIA has periodically been subjected. His essay is built on the concept of *intermestic politics*, a term that refers to foreign policy issues that are domestic as well as international in nature. Ransom argues that the CIA has largely been immune from domestic political pressures during periods when top-level decision makers have thought the Soviet threat to be significant. Conversely, in periods when perceptions of the Soviet threat have been muted, criticism and scrutiny of the CIA have increased. The thesis is both original and provocative, since it offers an unusual perspective by simultaneously placing the CIA's role in promoting the persistent patterns of postwar American foreign policy in the context not only of what happens abroad but also at home. The implication is that the nation's conduct abroad is affected significantly by the ebb and flow of those domestic and international influences which have an impact on the government organizations responsible for implementing foreign policy decisions.

Ransom explains why the CIA was subjected to intense domestic criticism during the first half of the 1970s. It was during this time that détente with the Soviet Union became the official policy of the United States. At the same time, the nation was grappling with the meaning of the Vietnam war as it affected America's future role in the world. As we have seen in Part III, the debate was punctuated with questions about the wisdom of the objectives of globalism, anticommunism, and containment and about military might and interventionism as means for achieving them.

Congress was a focal point of the introspection of the 1970s. As noted above, in large measure it was responding to the "imperial presidencies" of Johnson and Nixon. In his essay, "A Resurgent Congress and the Imperial

Presidency," Thomas E. Cronin describes the factors underlying the "imperial" epithet and the responses it evoked in Congress. The issues discussed are intimately related to the larger question of the relative balance between Congress and the president in determining the nation's foreign policy. The political tug-of-war is played out when such matters are decided as whether to go to war with other countries, whether to conclude agreements with them, whether to spend money from the public coffers, and how to regulate the CIA. Cronin includes an examination of the arguments advanced by proponents of a strong presidency, who came to the fore in the late 1970s as the memories of the Vietnam and Watergate traumas faded. He concludes with the observation that "the responsibilities of the presidency these days, coupled with the complexities of foreign and economic policy, do not really permit any serious weakening of the office. Congress has regained some of its own lost power and it has very correctly tried to curb the misuse and abuse of power—but it has not weakened the presidency."

16

POLICY-MAKING
IS POLITICS

ROGER HILSMAN

. . . . "**W**ashington," I remember Secretary
of State Dean Rusk saying when one of our colleagues was cruelly and
unfairly attacked in the press, "is an *evil* town." It is, but not because the
people who inhabit it are evil by nature, but because of the struggle that is
inherent in the fact that the capital of a nation is the nerve center of the
nation's power. Where power is, there also are conflict and turmoil. Thus
the reasons that Washington is the way it is lie deep in the heart of both the
nature of the business of Washington and of the political and governmental
process by which that business is carried out.

DECISIONS

The business of Washington is making decisions that move a nation, decisions about the direction American society should go and decisions about
how and where and for what purposes the awesome power—economic,
political, and military—of this, the world's most powerful nation, shall be
used. The decisions are about social security and medicare and labor laws
and the rules for conducting business and manufacture. Or they are about
moving a nation toward war or peace—a test ban treaty, intervening in Vietnam, the UN in the Congo, or Soviet nuclear missiles in Cuba. Where the
power to move a nation is, there also are the great decisions.

What is decided is policy. It is policy about problems and issues that
may make or break powerful interests in our society—organized labor or the
medical profession or the massive interests represented by the "military-
industrial complex" that President Eisenhower warned about in his farewell
address. Or it is policy that will cost American lives in some foreign jungle
and result either in our continued survival and success as a nation or, conceivably, in our downfall in a nuclear holocaust that takes much of the rest of
the world with us. In the business of Washington, the stakes are high.

THE PROCESS OF POLICY-MAKING

The nature and importance of the business done in Washington are obvious. The process by which that business is done and the nation is moved is more obscure.

As Americans, with our flair for the mechanical and love of efficiency combined with a moralistic Puritan heritage, we would like to think not only that policy-making is a conscious and deliberate act, one of analyzing problems and systematically examining grand alternatives in all their implications, but also that the alternative chosen is aimed at achieving overarching ends that serve a high moral purpose. Evidence that there is confusion about goals or evidence that the goals themselves may be competing or mutually incompatible is disquieting, and we hear repeated calls for a renewed national purpose, for a unifying ideology with an appeal abroad that will rival Communism, or for a national strategy that will fill both functions and set the guidelines for all of policy. As Americans, we think it only reasonable that the procedures for making national decisions should be orderly, with clear lines of responsibility and authority. We assume that what we call the "decisions" of government are in fact decisions—discrete acts, with recognizable beginnings and sharp, decisive endings. We like to think of policy as rationalized, in the economist's sense of the word, with each step leading logically and economically to the next. We want to be able to find out who makes decisions, to feel that they are the proper, official, and authorized persons, and to know that the really big decisions will be made at the top, by the President and his principal advisers in the formal assemblage of the Cabinet or the National Security Council and with the Congress exercising its full and formal powers. And we feel that the entire decision-making process ought to be a dignified, even majestic progression, with each of the participants having roles and powers so well and precisely defined that they can be held accountable for their actions by their superiors and eventually by the electorate.

The reality, of course, is quite different. Put dramatically, it could be argued that few, if any, of the decisions of government are either decisive or final. Very often policy is the sum of a congeries of separate or only vaguely related actions. On other occasions, it is an uneasy, even internally inconsistent compromise among competing goals or an incompatible mixture of alternative means for achieving a single goal. There is no systematic and comprehensive study of all the implications of the grand alternatives—nor can there be. A government does not decide to inaugurate the nuclear age, but only to try to build an atomic bomb before its enemy does. It does not make a formal decision to become a welfare state, but only to take each of a series of steps—to experiment with an income tax at some safely innocuous level like 3 per cent, to alleviate the hardship of men who have lost their jobs in a depression with a few weeks of unemployment compensation, or to lighten the old age of industrial workers with a tentative program of social security benefits. Rather than through grand decisions on grand alternatives, policy changes seem to come through a series of slight modifications of existing policy, with the new policy emerging slowly and haltingly by small and usually tentative steps, a process of trial and error in which policy zigs and zags, reverses itself, and then moves forward in a series of incremental steps.[1] Sometimes policies are formulated and duly ratified only to be skewed to an entirely different direction and purpose by those carrying them out—or they are never carried out at all. And sometimes issues are endlessly debated with nothing at all being resolved until both the problem and the debaters disappear under the relentless pyramiding of events.

THE POWER OF THE PRESIDENT

One result of all this is that in spite of the great power they wield, presidents can very rarely command, even within what is supposedly their most nearly absolute domain, the Executive Branch itself. President Truman, as he contemplated turning the presidency over to Eisenhower, used to say, "He'll sit here and he'll say, 'Do this! Do that!' And nothing will happen. Poor Ike—it won't be a bit like the Army."[2]

Presidents, being human, sometimes find the system frustrating. Once at a press conference, President Kennedy surprised us all by answering a question about allied trade with Cuba with a promise to take certain measures that were still under discussion. "Well!" he said afterward with some exasperation. "Today I actually made a little policy." But mainly, presidents maneuver, persuade, and pressure—using all the levers, powers, and influences they can muster. And most presidents recognize that this is what they must do. On another occasion, for example, mid-way in the Vietnam crisis, there had been a morning meeting of the National Security Council in the Cabinet room of the White House at which several decisions that seemed to mark a watershed had finally been taken. After the meeting, Secretary of Defense Robert S. McNamara, the Chairman of the Joint Chiefs of Staff, Maxwell D. Taylor, Presidential Assistants McGeorge Bundy and Michael V. Forrestal and I repaired to the Situation Room just off Bundy's office in the basement of the White House to draft a cable reflecting the decisions. We were finished by early afternoon, but by that time the President was involved with thirty or forty congressmen in a bill-signing ceremony and a pile of other work he had to move, and only Bundy, Forrestal, and I waited until he was free to get his final okay. The three of us trooped into his oval office through the curved side door from the room his private secretary, Mrs. Lincoln, occupied and found the President rocking away in his chair before the fireplace, reading and signing the last of a pile of letters. He looked up and grinned. "And now," he said, "we have the 'inner club.'"

After he had cleared the cable and the three of us were walking down the hall, I asked Bundy if what the President had meant was that we now had in one room the people who were *really* familiar with the problem. "Yes," said Bundy, "but also something more. It's a private joke of his: he meant that, but also that now we had together the people who had known all along what we would do about the problem, and who had been pulling and hauling, debating and discussing for no other purpose than to keep the government together, to get all the others to come around. . . ."

On some occasions, the President clearly makes the decision, even if he cannot make it exactly as he might wish. On other occasions, the decision is just as clearly made by Congress. But in action after action, responsibility for decision is as fluid and restless as quicksilver, and there seems to be neither a person nor an organization on whom it can be fixed. At times the point of decision seems to have escaped into the labyrinth of governmental machinery, beyond layers and layers of bureaucracy. Other times it seems never to have reached the government, but remained in either the wider domain of a public opinion created by the press or in the narrower domain dominated by the maneuverings of special interests.

TURMOIL

Just as our desire to know who makes a decision is frustrated, so is our hope that the process of policy-making will be dignified. A decision, in fact, may be little more than a signal that starts a public brawl by people who want to reverse it. President Eisenhower's "New Look" decision to concentrate on air power at the expense of ground forces, for example, had no visible result for the first year except semipublic fights with the Joint Chiefs of Staff, an eruption of the so-called "Colonels' revolt," and frequent leaks of top secret information. The whole strategy was completely reversed when the Kennedy administration came into responsibility in 1961, and the reversal was fought by the same technique of leaks, but this time it was Air Force rather than Army partisans doing the leaking. . . .

Leaks, of course, are the first and most blatant signs of battle, and they are endemic in the policy process. When it became clear, for example, that the report of the Gaither Committee, set up by Eisenhower in 1957 to study civil defense in terms of the whole of nuclear strategy, would be critical of the "New Look" and the entire Eisenhower defense policy, the crucial battle between the different factions within the administration took place, not on the substance of the report, but on the issue of whether there would be two hundred top secret copies of the report or only two. For everyone knew without saying so that if the President did not accept the Gaither Committee's recommendations, it might be possible to keep the report from leaking to the press if there were only two copies, but never if there were two hundred. The committee won the battle, and two hundred top secret copies were distributed within the Executive Branch. The President did not accept the recommendations; and, sure enough, within a few days Chalmers Roberts of the *Washington Post* was able to write a story, covering almost two newspaper pages, that contained an accurate and comprehensive version of both the top secret report and its recommendations.

Not surprisingly, it was these continual leaks that especially puzzled and angered Eisenhower. In 1955, he said, "For some two years and three months I have been plagued by inexplicable undiscovered leaks in this Government." But so are all presidents, before and after Eisenhower. Not only are there leaks of secret information, but leaks that distort secret information so as to present a special view that is often totally false. There flows out of Washington a continuous stream of rumor, tales of bickering, speculation, stories of selfish interest, charges and countercharges. Abusive rivalries arise between the government agencies engaged in making policy, and even within a single agency different factions battle, each seeking allies in other agencies, among the members of Congress, from interest associations, and among the press. Officialdom, whether civil or military, is hardly neutral. It speaks, and inevitably it speaks as an advocate. The Army battles for ground forces, the Air Force for bombers; the "Europe faction" in the State Department for policy benefiting NATO, and the "Africa faction" for anticolonialist policies unsettling to our relations with Europe. All of these many interests, organizations, and institutions—inside and outside the government—are joined in a struggle over the goals of governmental policy and over the means by which these goals shall be achieved. Instead of unity, there is conflict. Instead of a majestic progression, there are erratic zigs and zags. Instead of clarity and decisiveness, there are tangle and turmoil, instead of order, confusion.

SOURCES OF THE TURMOIL

But even though we deplore the disorder and confusion, the seeming disloyalty of leaks, the noise and untidiness, and all the rest, it would be well to look more deeply into the nature of the process before condemning it.

Partly, of course, the turbulence derives from the nature of our constitution itself. As Richard E. Neustadt has pointed out, the constitutional convention of 1787 did not really create a government of "separated powers" as we have been taught, but a government of separated institutions sharing powers.[3] The Executive, for example, is clearly part of the legislative process—almost all major bills today are drafted and put forward by the Executive department concerned, and the President still has the veto. The courts, too, legislate. . . . And the Congress is equally involved in administration, in both its investigative function and its appropriation of money and oversight of spending. To the head of a department or agency, the Congress, with its power to reward and punish, is as much his boss as is the President. And some agency heads can build enough power on the Hill to put themselves beyond the reach of a President even to fire them—as J. Edgar Hoover succeeded in doing with his job as director of the FBI. Different institutions sharing powers, getting involved in each others' business, provide the checks and balances sought by the founding fathers and many other benefits besides. But they also contribute to the phenomenon of turbulence.

THE MULTIPLICITY OF ACTORS

Still another dimension is the now familiar fact that many more people are involved in the process of government than merely those who hold the duly constituted official positions. It is no accident that the press, for example, is so often called the "fourth branch of government." The press plays a role in the process of governance. It performs functions which are a necessary part of the process and which it sometimes performs well and sometimes badly.

There are also lobbies, the spokesmen of special interests of every kind and description from oil producers and farmers to the Navy League and Women Strike for Peace. Their efforts on Capitol Hill are more familiar, but the lobbies work just as hard to influence the Executive, although in different ways. In any case, they play a role in the process of governance and perform necessary functions, often for good but sometimes for evil.

And there are others who play a role. The academic world, the world of research in the universities, has an influence and participates in the process, both formally and informally. In the presidential campaigns of 1960 and 1964, for example, no candidate could be without his own team of university advisers—Kennedy and Nixon each had such a team, and so did both Johnson and Goldwater. Most of the more effective senators on Capitol Hill have academic friends, experts in the universities, whom they regularly consult. And there is a whole new set of institutions doing research of all kinds on contract with the government, organizations staffed with people who have governmental clearances for secret work but who are neither in the armed services nor the civil service—quasi-governmental organizations such as the RAND Corporation, in Santa Monica, California, the Institute of Defense Analyses, in Washington, and the Hudson Institute, just outside New York. All of these people and organizations influence policy. Although not accountable to the electorate, they have power and they are as much a part of the governmental process as the traditional legislative, judicial, and executive branches of government. There are many more people involved in making policy than those who hold official positions, in sum, and they have more subtle ways for shaping policy.

POLICY CONVICTIONS

But all this is only the beginning. . . . Most men find it easier to go against their own pecuniary interests than they do to go against a deep conviction on policy. As we have said, in the business of Washington, the stakes are high and the issues fundamental, both to our society and to the question of war and peace for the entire world. In such circumstances it is not surprising that passions run strong and full. It is not even surprising that men occasionaly feel so deeply that they take matters into their own hands, leaking secret materials to the Congress or the press in an attempt to force the President to adopt what they are convinced is the only right path, the salvation of the nation. When in the late 1950s, for example, intelligence officials leaked secret information foreshadowing an upcoming "missile gap' to Democratic senators and sympathetic members of the press, it was not because they were disloyal, but because they were deeply convinced that the nation was in peril. They had tried and failed to convince the top levels of the Eisenhower administration of the validity of their projections, and they felt completely justified in taking matters into their own hands by going over the President's head to Congress, the press, and the public. Colonel Billy Mitchell was doing the same in the 1920s when he provoked a court-martial so he could present the case for air power to the nation at large. But none of this is new. Throughout history, the motive for such deeds—for mankind's greatest achievements, but also, unhappily, for mankind's greatest crimes—has rarely been to benefit the individual, but for the glory of something the individual thinks of as bigger than himself, for his God, his nation, or his ideology.

There is nothing in this to nullify the point that selfish interests are also involved in these decisions, and that the decisions affect such powerful interests as labor, the farmers, the medical profession, and the "military-industrial complex." But society is made up of its different parts, and it is not merely a rationalization when farmers, for example, argue that a healthy nation depends on a healthy agriculture. There is nothing wrong in the people of a democracy expressing their interests, their values, hopes, and fears through "interest" organizations. How else, save through some such hierarchy of representative organizations, can the needs and desires of so many millions of people be aggregated?

Nor is there anything wrong in the fact that the bureaucracy itself is divided, that it represents special interests, and that its parts speak as advocates, fighting hard for their constituencies. The Department of Labor is inevitably and rightly more oriented toward workingmen than management; the Bureau of Mines more toward extractive industry than the industrial users of minerals; the Children's Bureau more toward restrictions on employers than permissiveness. Indeed some segments of society that are poorly organized for exercising leverage on either public opinion or the Congress would have a much smaller voice if the bureaucracy of the federal government did not represent their interests, and many of the long-range, more general interests of society as a whole have no other spokesman at all. But all this also contributes to the turbulence of the Washington scene.

INADEQUACY OF KNOWLEDGE

Still another dimension of the confusion and turbulence of the policy-making process is the complexity of the problems and the inadequacy of our knowledge of how and why things work in the social affairs of men, our limited capacity to foresee developments that bring problems or to predict the consequences of whatever action we do take. Partly this is because in the field of foreign affairs, especially, there are so many other people and nations involved, friends and enemies, with goals of their own and tactics of their own. But it is more than this. More and better understanding will not always or necessarily lead to sure solutions to knotty problems, but it sometimes does. If our understanding of the workings of a modern industrial economy had been better in the 1920s, the Great Depression could very probably have been avoided; and if our knowledge had been only slightly greater in the 1930s than it was, the measures to meet the Depression would probably have been more effective and quicker-acting. Winston Churchill called World War II the "unnecessary war," by which he meant that if we had better understood what Hitler and Nazism were really about and particularly their compelling dynamism leading toward war, it would have been politically possible to take the necessary preventive measures—which however hard and costly, would have been better than the horror of what actually occurred.

When knowledge is inadequate, when problems are complex, and especially when they are also new—presenting a challenge with which there has been no experience—there is in such circumstances room to spare for disagreement, conflict, and turmoil. It is not the only cause of disagreement, much less the central cause, but it is one of them. McGeorge Bundy once said that policy in Vietnam was "the most divisive issue in the Kennedy administration." He meant *inside* the administration, and he was right. And the cause of the dissension was precisely inadequate understanding and a failure of analysis. Modern guerrilla warfare, as the Communists practice it, is *internal* war, an ambiguous aggression that avoids direct and open attack violating international frontiers but combines terror, subversion, and political action with hit-and-run guerrilla raids and ambush. It is new to the Western world, and not yet fully understood. In the Kennedy administration there were those who saw it as a modified form of traditional war, but war nevertheless to be fought primarily with traditional military measures. Others saw guerrilla warfare as essentially political in nature, aimed at winning the people while terrorizing the government, and they believed that in fighting against a guerrilla insurgency military measures should be subordinated to political action. But there was simply not enough knowledge and experience with such matters to prove who was right, and the struggle within the administration became increasingly bitter.

POLICY-MAKING IS POLITICS

These are some of the facets of policy-making and the decisions that move nations—separate institutions sharing powers, the press, experts, and others who influence policy without holding formal power, selfish and unselfish interest groups that exert a different kind of power, the difficulties and complexities of analysis, prediction, and judgment. These many facets help to explain the turmoil, and they flag a warning to those who would be cynical about Washington and the hurly-burly that is disquieting or even repugnant to so many. But they do not completely explain even the surface phenomena of Washington, nor is what explanation they do give completely satisfying. As Americans, we aspire to a rationalized system of government and policy-making. This implies that a nation can pursue a single set of clearly perceived and generally agreed-to goals, as a business organization is supposed to pursue profits. Yet is this realistic? Is the problem of making policy in a highly diversified mass society really one of relating the different steps in making a decision to a single set of goals or is it precisely one of choosing goals—of choosing goals not in the abstract but in the convoluted context of ongoing events, with inadequate information, incomplete knowledge and understanding, and insufficient power—and doing so, in all probability, while we are pitted against opposition both at home and abroad? If so, the making of national decisions is not a problem for the efficiency expert, or of assembling different pieces of policy logically as if the product were an automobile. Policy faces inward as much as outward, seeking to reconcile conflicting goals, to adjust aspirations to available means, and to accommodate the different advocates of these competing goals and aspirations to one another. It is here that the essence of policy-making seems to lie, in a process that is in its deepest sense political.

Recognizing the political nature of policy-making might help us to a better understanding of the diversity and seeming inconsistency of the goals that national policy must serve. It might also help us to understand the powerful but sometimes hidden forces through which these competing goals are reconciled, why the pushes and pulls of these crosscurrents are sometimes dampened or obscured, and why they are sometimes so fiercely public. Even the roles of such "unrational" procedures as bargaining and power might also become more clear.

President Kennedy once said, "There will always be the dark and tangled stretches in the decision-making process—mysterious even to those who may be most intimately involved. . . ."[4] Yet it is equally true that we can understand better than we now do how a nation is moved and that better understanding can lead to more effective policy and perhaps even to improvements in the policy-making process itself. Understanding comes in looking at the vital stuff of events themselves, in the interaction of the President, the Congress, the press, and special interests and in the rivalries of the great Executive departments, State, Defense, and the Central Intelligence Agency, as they clash in the actual making of policy, in the crucible of events. . . .

NOTES

1. See Charles E. Lindblom, "The Science of 'Muddling Through,'" *Public Administration Review*, XIX, 1959, and his book *The Intelligence of Democracy*, 1965.

2. Richard E. Neustadt, *Presidential Power*, 1960, p. 9.
3. Richard E. Neustadt, *op. cit.*, p. 33.
4. In his foreword to Theodore C. Sorensen's *Decision-Making in the White House,* Columbia University Press, 1963.

17

THE RISE OF THE NATIONAL SECURITY ASSISTANT, 1961–1981

I. M. DESTLER

In the sixties and seventies, the major institutional development in the foreign affairs presidency was the increased influence—and prominence—of the assistant for national security affairs. The "National Security Council" became in practice not the powerful senior advisory forum envisioned at its creation, but the senior aide and staff instituted under the Council name. Presidents employed this aide and staff not just as a link to the permanent government but also as an alternative to it, at least for certain issues they deemed particularly important.

This development is particularly notable because, throughout this period, the foreign policy community was generally in favor of a very different sort of foreign policymaking system, one where the secretary of state had clear primacy (short of the president) and the White House foreign policy aide stuck to a low-profile, coordinating role. By the time of the 1980 presidential campaign, criticism of recent practice had become nearly universal. In a major television speech, candidate Ronald Reagan made "reorganizing the policy-making structure" the first of "nine specific steps that I will take to put American on a sound, secure footing in the international arena."

> The present Administration has been unable to speak with one voice in foreign policy. This must change. My administration will restore leadership to U.S. foreign policy by organizing it in a more coherent way.

This essay is adapted and updated from an analysis prepared originally for the Presidential Management Project, National Academy of Public Administration and published in Hugh Heclo and Lester Salamon, eds., *The Illusion of Presidential Government*, Westview Press, 1981, pp. 263–85. Reprinted with permission of the Academy. Copyright © 1981, National Academy of Public Administration. **I. M. Destler** is a senior associate at the Carnegie Endowment for International Peace, where he directs the research project on executive-congressional relations. His books include *Presidents, Bureaucrats, and Foreign Policy,* and *Coping with U.S.-Japanese Economic Conflicts* (co-edited with Hideo Sato).

An early priority will be to make structural changes in the foreign policy-making machinery so that the Secretary of State will be the President's principal spokesman and adviser.

The National Security Council will once again be the coordinator of the policy process. Its mission will be to assure that the President receives an orderly, balanced flow of information and analysis. The National Security Adviser will work closely in teamwork with the Secretary of State and the other members of the Council.[1]

In the months following his resounding election victory, Reagan took a number of steps consistent with this pledge, including the choice of a strong, assertive man as secretary of state, Alexander Haig, and reduction of the national security assistant's visibility and power. Yet within a year Reagan seemed to reverse himself, bringing longtime intimate William Clark into the White House as national security assistant to strengthen central policy management. The secretary of state, meanwhile, seemed in continuous combat with the secretary of defense and White House political aides—a situation that ultimately contributed to Haig's resignation in June 1982 and his replacement by George P. Shultz.

This raised serious questions about whether the president and his chief advisers could resist the broader forces that had brought the national security assistant to foreign policy prominence, and sometimes dominance, notwithstanding the expressed intention of Reagan and most of his predecessors. Recent experience suggests the existence of a serious, undernoticed tension between the operational needs of presidents, as they perceive them, and the requirements of careful, constructive U.S. participation in world affairs. The assistant's role has grown because presidents come to see it as responsive to them—even though, over the long run, it has tended to make their overall foreign policy less coherent and less effective.

This essay deals mainly with the sixties and seventies. The concluding section, however, addresses the Reagan experience as of late 1982.

THE CONSENSUS PRESCRIPTION: LOW-PROFILE FACILITATOR

For each of the five presidents of the sixties and seventies, the primary manager of foreign policy issues was the assistant ("special assistant" until 1969) for national security affairs. Under the formal aegis of the National Security Council, this aide has headed a staff of foreign policy analysts and operators which has varied in size—no more than twelve under McGeorge Bundy (1961–66), rising to eighteen under Walt Rostow (1966–69) and to a peak of over fifty under Henry Kissinger (1969–75) before dropping into the forties under Brent Scowcroft (1975–77) and the thirties under Zbigniew Brzezinski (1977–81).[2] The staff has been a mix of "in-and-outers" and agency officials on temporary assignment, and its members characteristically have been foreign policy professionals rather than political appointees

in the partisan sense. But they have been "political" in one crucial way—
they have departed, to be succeeded by a new staff, when the party affiliation of the president has changed.[3]

Over this twenty-year period, there developed a semi-articulated consensus among practitioners, scholars, and public observers as to what the
national security adviser should—and should not—be doing.[4] This consensus, originating in the sixties, was further developed and reinforced by reaction to the first Kissinger regime (1969–73) and Watergate. Its basic thrust
was that the national security assistant and staff should play at least part of
the linking and constraining role originally envisaged by the Council. To
this end, they should concentrate on certain types of activities and avoid
others:

TABLE 1
THE NATIONAL SECURITY ASSISTANT: THE PROFESSIONALS' JOB DESCRIPTION

YES ("Inside Management")	OK In Moderation	NO ("Outside Leadership")
Briefing the President, handling his foreign policy in-box	Discreet advice/ advocacy	Conducting particular diplomatic negotiations
Analyzing issues and choices:	Encouraging advocacy by NSC staff subordinates	Fixed operational assignments
a. Ordering information/ intelligence	Information and "background" communicating with press, Congress, foreign officials	Public spokesman Strong, visible internal advocacy (except of already established presidential priorities)
b. Managing inter-agency studies		Making policy decisions
Managing presidential decision processes		
Communicating presi-dential decisions and monitoring their implementation		
General interagency brokering, circuit-connecting, crisis management		

The basic argument for this job description was essentially two-fold. First,
the assistant's performance of "outside leadership" activities preempts or
undercuts other senior presidential advisers and the formally responsible
institutions, particularly the State Department and its secretary. Second, it
compromises the "honest broker" reputation for balance necessary to performance of the "inside management" functions, most of which (unlike the

functions in the right-hand column) are best handled from within the White House. As Bromley Smith put it in 1969:

> The theory was that the special assistant's greatest usefulness to the President is to be absolutely neutral so that the principals have full confidence that their views will be presented to the President, and that the assistant is not taking advantage of his position by introducing his own views. Once uncertainty develops, than it's a very difficult situation.[5]

No one would expect that any real-life system would follow such guidelines completely, despite the tendency of presidents to stress the inside, low-profile role whenever an assistant is newly designated. But even when allowances are made for personal idiosyncracies, the divergence has been impressive. National security assistants have frequently moved into the "outside leadership" tasks in the right-hand column of the table, becoming (1) prominent public spokesmen; (2) diplomatic operators, and (3) advocates pushing their own policy lines. And the Bundy-Rostow-Kissinger-Brzezinski sequence has identified the job, in the mind of the press and the informed public, as "president's intellectual" much more than staff facilitator. In fact, one can infer from recent practice an alternative role conception, far less confining than that of facilitator—that of a most senior aide serving the president personally and flexibly as the institutionally encumbered secretary of state no longer can. One result is congressional complaints of lack of access to the assistant and demands that he be subject to Senate confirmation and available for testimony to Congress. As Senator Edward Zorinsky puts it, "It's clear that we have two secretaries of state . . . and it's time we made the other one accountable, too."[6]

This divergence from the consensus prescription did not come about all at once. And it began with a president who wanted stronger State Department leadership and seems to have regarded his national security process reforms as means to this end. John F. Kennedy began by dismantling Eisenhower's network of formal interagency committees, with the avowed aim of giving greater initiative to senior department officials, above all the secretary of state. But Kennedy also, through the day-to-day handling of policy, redefined the role of the assistant. This provided the basis for his moving into more visible and operational activities if he were so inclined, and if his president allowed or encouraged it.

THE POSITION IN PRACTICE: A SECOND SECRETARY OF STATE

As Kennedy prepared to assume office, Senator Henry Jackson's Subcommittee on National Policy Machinery was beginning to issue reports highly critical of the Eisenhower NSC process: it was a cumbersome papermill; the new president should "deinstitutionalize" and "humanize" it.[7] The primary responsibility of Eisenhower's national security assistants had been to manage this process. Hence in his transition "Memorandum on Staffing the President Elect," Professor Richard Neustadt, a Jackson subcommittee consultant, listed that job as one "on which to defer decision." He warned, "This post should be avoided by all means until you have sized up your needs *and* got a feel for your new secretaries of state and defense."[8]

Kennedy did not avoid the post, but he did transform it. He invited McGeorge Bundy, dean of the faculty at Harvard, to assume the position. Bundy's job description was initially rather unclear: in some fashion he was to serve as the president's personal aide on national security issues. And Bundy was admirably suited, by temperament and experience, to operating within the type of open, informal, free-wheeling operation that Kennedy clearly preferred, developing staff and processes *ad hoc* to meet emerging needs. Numerous formal interagency committees were abolished. Formal NSC meetings were replaced, to a substantial degree, by issue-specific gatherings.

The dismantling of formal procedures, combined with Bundy's role as personal aide to Kennedy, meant that he was performing, in practice, the national security job handled under Eisenhower by staff secretary Andrew Goodpaster: staffing the president's day-to-day foreign and defense business. The system that emerged, in Bundy's words, "rubbed out the distinction between planning and operation."[9] With the position now tied to the day-to-day activities of an activist president, it now had enormous potential for engagement and influence—since it combined the formerly separate responsibilities of staffing the president and coordinating interagency decision-making. Bundy remained basically a facilitator, more oriented toward making the system work than toward monopolizing the action himself and excluding others. But his personal strength and broad competence attracted much business. So did his recruitment of a small number of particularly talented senior aides to carry the president's flag in interagency battles. In a 1964 interview, Robert Komer, one of the most aggressive of them, conveys much of the flavor of the operation:

> [The NSC label was] merely a budgetary device. Since NSC already had its own budget, it was sacrosanct. So instead of adding people to the White House staff, Bundy carried them all over here. But, in fact, Kennedy made very clear we were his men, we operated for him, we had direct contact with him. This gave us the power to command the kind of results that he wanted—a fascinating exercise in a presidential staff technique, which, insofar as I know, has been unique in the history of the presidency.

As Komer described it further, the staff acted as "eyes and ears" of the president, who wanted "a complete flow of raw information over here." It was also a "shadow network which clued the president on what bidding was before a formal, interdepartmentally cleared recommendation got to him." Thus "the president had sources of independent judgment and recommendation on what each issue was all about, what ought to be done about it, from a little group of people in whom he had confidence—in other words, sort of a double check." Finally, it provided "follow-through," working "to keep tabs on things and see that the cables went out and the responses were satisfactory, and that when the policy wasn't being executed, the president knew about it and he could give another prod."[10]

This type of staff could not help but put the slower moving State Department (or *any* established organization) somewhat in the shade. And though an internal memo stressed that the staff was "*not*—though this is a hard rule—a place meant for men trying to peddle their own remedies without presidential backing,"[11] particular members of the staff, like Komer and Bundy's deputy Carl Kaysen, did become identified with strong policy preferences which they worked to advance. But these were preferences generally encouraged by the president even when he felt unable fully to support them.

The activities of the Bundy operation generally conformed to the consensus job description. But the vigor and activism with which they were conducted nonetheless pulled power to the White House staff. As Bromley Smith put it:

It is true that, although State officers had the authority, they did not exercise it. They did not exert leadership at the various levels. Therefore, when the President had to have something done, it was almost easier for McGeorge Bundy to call a meeting in the Situation Room, bang all the heads together and get things going. The tendency was to do it that way.[12]

Bundy stayed on as national security assistant under Lyndon B. Johnson. The basic job remained the same, and Johnson shared Kennedy's preference for informal procedures. But he was far less comfortable with foreign policy than his predecessor; thus he initiated fewer issues himself and spoke with fewer officials personally. For Bundy, this meant both greater visibility and pressure to assume new roles—Johnson felt he needed him more than Kennedy had, yet simultaneously resented this need. Bundy went on a crucial "fact-finding" mission to South Vietnam in early 1965 and led a diplomatic mission to the Dominican Republic later that same year. As the Vietnam issue heated up domestically, Johnson pressed Bundy into service as "my debater," urging him to go on "Meet the Press" and other prestige forums to defend U.S. policy. Such activities foreshadowed greater involvement in negotiations and public advocacy by certain of Bundy's successors.[13]

By the time Bundy was succeeded in early 1966 by Walt Whitman

Rostow, Vietnam had of course become the administration's overriding foreign preoccupation. Rostow had strong, quasi-ideological convictions about the war, which tended to disqualify him as an honest broker on this issue. He also lacked Bundy's strong orientation toward process, being more an "idea man" interested in personally generating new policy formulations. Moreover, Rostow entered office under a handicap—Johnson, apparently determined to demonstrate he didn't need "another Bundy" to help him conduct foreign policy, denied him Bundy's full title—Rostow was designated simply "special assistant to the President," with "national security affairs" deleted. Nonetheless there was basic continuity in the day-to-day functions performed, as Rostow acted as staff focal point for the president's personal foreign policy business and for interagency coordination.

In terms of institutional development, then, the Rostow period was a holding action. It was left to Richard Nixon and Henry Kissinger to demonstrate the potential of the assistant position for foreign policy dominance, at least on the issues most important to the president himself.

Nixon clearly intended, from the start, to establish a highly centralized system of foreign policymaking, and his national security assistant, Henry Kissinger, was both his personal and institutional instrument to this end. Kissinger's appointment was announced a week before that of Secretary of State William P. Rogers, and Nixon declared also that his new aide was "setting up . . . a very exciting new procedure"[14] for presidential review of foreign policy issues. By December 27, Kissinger had ready for Nixon a comprehensive "Proposal for a New National Security Council System," a seventeen-page memorandum proposing means "to combine the best features" of the formal Eisenhower and informal Johnson decisionmaking systems.[15] Nixon approved it in almost every detail. It created a new system of interagency policy studies and committees to coordinate them, with a key role to be played by a new "NSC Review Group" which Kissinger himself would chair. The system was represented, not without sincerity it appears, as an alternative to "catch-as-catch-can" Kennedy-Johnson policymaking. The agencies would be able, it was said, to weigh in when an issue was being considered and to know what the president decided. But the system nonetheless cast Kissinger as the initiator and screener of a large number of studies designed to generate options for presidential decision.

This formal system continued through the Nixon administration (and through the Ford administration). But before two years had passed, it had been clearly supplanted by the Nixon-Kissinger taste for secret management of public issues. Kissinger became the prime negotiator on Vietnam, China, and SALT. "Back channels" were employed to an unprecedented extent to exclude the normally responsible officials at the State Department from key communications with foreign powers. Gerard Smith, Director of the Arms Control and Disarmament Agency, who was formally in charge of the SALT I negotiations with the Soviet Union, learned from Kissinger at a May 1971 breakfast that the latter had just achieved a "breakthrough"

SALT agreement after months of negotiating through a presidential channel of which Smith was unaware. Smith's only consolation was that Nixon "was just then advising the Secretary of State," and Secretary of Defense Melvin Laird would not learn anything until one in the afternoon![16] As Kissinger notes in his memoirs, such procedures also produced the opening to China, a Berlin agreement, and a Vietnam cease-fire; they also required progressively more egregious deception of the bureaucracy and corruption of the carefully designed policy studies system. In Kissinger's words:

> ... My staff was too small to backstop two complex simultaneous negotiations. The control of interdepartmental machinery served as a substitute. It enabled me to use the bureaucracy without revealing our purposes. I would introduce as planning topics issues that were actually being secretly negotiated. In this manner I could learn the views of the agencies (as well as the necessary background) without formally "clearing" my position with them. . . .
>
> These extraordinary procedures were essentially made necessary by a President who neither trusted his Cabinet nor was willing to give them direct orders. Nixon feared leaks and shrank from imposing discipline. But he was determined to achieve his purpose. . . .[17]

In the process of developing and dominating these procedures, Kissinger made many specific policy decisions himself. He ended up chairing three major interdepartmental committees and three important specialized groups.[18] He became a strong advocate of particular policy courses inside the government. And last of all, mainly as a product of his obvious de facto role as Nixon's senior foreign policy subordinate, he became, in 1972, the administration's prime public foreign policy spokesman. In short, Nixon-Kissinger practice obliterated all the old distinctions between what a White House assistant did and what a strong secretary of state would have done. The staff man became the key line operator in every important respect.

This use of the assistant gave Nixon considerable control and flexibility on those issues which he handled from the White House. On matters where State, Defense, or other established institutions inescapably had a major operating role, or those to which the assistant could give only limited personal time, the outcome was less salutary. As Kissinger later described it, referring particularly to the India-Pakistan crisis of 1971, "the result was a bureaucratic stalemate in which White House and State Department representatives dealt with each other as competing sovereign entities, not members of the same team."[19]

This pattern changed, of course, with Kissinger's appointment as Secretary of State and Gerald Ford's ascension to the presidency a year later. Kissinger took his strong policy role with him and used the new public platform to cement his position. Brent Scowcroft, first as deputy assistant and then as assistant to the president for national security affairs, played that role as the consensus description says it should be played. One reason was that Scowcroft's professional convictions supported this role conception. A second was that Kissinger's predominance kept the role from growing— Scowcroft never appeared, for example, on "Meet the Press" or "Face the Nation." A third was that President Ford tended to accept the advisory arrangements he inherited or those that his aides developed for him, rather than to assert any strong preferences.[20]

Jimmy Carter came to power publicly committed to cabinet government, openness, and decentralization. He and those who influenced him were reacting, in the main, to Kissinger's one-man show, particularly the 1969–1973 White House years. Unlike Nixon, Carter appointed his secretary of state well before his national security assistant and his designee, Cyrus Vance, was an experienced foreign policy professional with overwhelming establishment support. Unlike Kennedy, Carter designated his secretary before making any subordinate State appointments, and he allowed Vance considerable leeway in filling these positions. Vance moved quickly to capitalize on this leeway. Carter seemed to be reinforcing him when he abolished the network of formal interagency committees which Kissinger had chaired from the White House.[21]

But Carter also saw himself personally as a policy initiator and manager who would make the decisions himself, from the range of views provided by his senior advisers. This "spokes of the wheel" operating style would make it difficult for Vance (or any other senior Cabinet member) to establish and maintain a broad policy mandate, since there was no assurance the president would support him on crucial decisions. And the man Carter designated for national security assistant, Zbigniew Brzezinski, was an ambitious, assertive intellectual who had been a valuable counselor from early in the presidential quest. At the Plains, Georgia, press conference where Carter announced his appointment, Brzezinski deferred to the consensus prescription in describing the position.

> I don't envisage my job as a policymaking job. I see my job essentially as heading the operational staff of the president, helping him integrate policy, but above all, helping to facilitate the process of decision-making in which he will consult closely with his principal cabinet members.[22]

But as *New York Times* correspondent Leslie Gelb noted, Brzezinski did not hesitate to answer substantive questions, though Vance had hesitated at a similar press conference. Perhaps most revealing, when Brzezinski was asked, "Is Secretary Kissinger going to be a tough act to follow?", he did not reject this standard as inappropriate. Instead he replied: "I will let you make that judgment a number of years from now."[23]

Brzezinski began by maintaining a relatively low profile and cutting the NSC staff (though the number of substantive professionals remained double the Bundy-Rostow period). But in staff recruitment he gave priority at the outset to "idea people" to support him in supplying the presidential market, at the cost of professional policy management competence and experience.[24] And though he spoke insistently of his collegiality with "Cy" and "Harold" Brown, Secretary of Defense, Brzezinski was active from the start in pressing his personal policy views—particularly on relations with the Soviet Union and the SALT II negotiations. By 1978, a serious Brzezinski-Vance split was publicly visible. A major Carter speech on dealing with Russia compounded the problem, since it was apparently a splicing together of Vance and Brzezinski passages, with no serious effort at reconciling contradictions. At one peak of public confusion, fourteen members of the House International Relations Committee sent the president a letter in June 1978 formally asking him to clarify just "what is U.S. policy on such issues as Soviet-American relations and Africa."[25]

Thus the Carter foreign policymaking system never developed a clear, coherent pattern. At times, especially early in the administration, Secretary Vance seemed to speak more reliably for the president; later Brzezinski seemed more often ascendant, though other White House aides had foreign policy influence also. But the pervasive impression was incoherence in both process and content. Carter was not without foreign policy accomplishments—the Panama Canal treaties, normalization of relations with China, and above all the Camp David accords between Israel and Egypt. By Carter's fourth year, however, Russian troops were in Afghanistan, fifty-three American diplomats were hostage in Iran, and Carter's laboriously negotiated SALT II treaty was stymied in the Senate. Yet visible administration divisions continued.

In April, Carter sought to recoup his fortunes, and those of his nation, by ordering a secret raid to rescue the hostages held captive in Teheran. The mission failed. Secretary of State Vance—who had been out of Washington when Carter decided to proceed and was unable to reverse the decision—resigned in protest. U.S. allies were further shaken: they had just agreed to economic measures against Iran on the understanding that military force would not be employed. At home, Carter got considerable initial credit for trying, and his choice of Senator Edmund Muskie as Vance's replacement was widely applauded. But by summer Muskie was complaining openly about his exclusion from deliberation on a major presidential directive on U.S. nuclear strategy. By early fall, he "let it be known that he wants major changes in the way foreign policy is managed if he stays on in a second Carter Administration." Specifically, he said, "If I were President, I would appoint somebody as Secretary of State and make sure that the N.S.C. role is that of coordinating and not anything else."[26]

Muskie was not alone in zeroing in on Brzezinski—indeed, criticism of Carter's national security assistant had become nearly universal. Some of it addressed his policy positions, above all his "tough," combative line toward Moscow. Some of it focused on his style, a certain impulsiveness, a tendency to press for action without full thought as to consequences. But there was an important process critique also. It focused on the badly needed management job that Brzezinski was *neglecting*—bringing order and reliability to the policy process. (For example, Carter issued a new directive on the targeting of nuclear weapons that Muskie didn't even know about!) And it focused on the roles Brzezinski was *playing* which undercut the assistant's credibility and objectivity for the management task.

Unlike Kissinger, Brzezinski did not conduct most major negotiations himself, though China normalization was an important partial exception. But he was, more than any of his predecessors, identified as an advocate of particular policy directions; his reported efforts to intervene in Iran's revolution, in fact, seem to have reflected his own impulses rather than any clear presidentially determined policy.[27]

Brzezinski also became a highly visible policy spokesman. And while Kissinger's visibility tended to follow his attainment of influence and policy success, Brzezinski's seemed more independently generated—by his own flair for public expression, by Carter's readiness to have him play this role,[28] and by the press's natural interest in a newsworthy incumbent once Bundy and Kissinger demonstrated the job's potential. In any case Brzezinski continued a trend—interrupted by Scowcroft—the emergence of the assistant as a major, visible foreign policy figure in his own right.

Interestingly, most of the assistants themselves have expressed strong misgivings about the inflation of the assistant's role. Kissinger by 1979 had "become convinced that a president should make the secretary of state his principal adviser and use the national security adviser primarily as a senior administrator and coordinator to make certain that each significant point of view is heard."[29] Rostow in 1980 was "inclined to deplore the radical expansion of the NSC staff that occurred in the Nixon Administration and the failure of the two subsequent administrations to perform an act of radical deflation."[30] Scowcroft that same year described the position as "very much a substantive job," but a "private" one, giving priority to coordination, adding that "by and large it is wrong for the national security adviser to be a negotiator."[31] Bundy wrote in November 1980 that President-elect Reagan was "entitled to the comfort of knowing that there is one place where less would be more—in the job of Assistant for National Security Affairs."[32] Even Brzezinski, as earlier noted, declared on his appointment that he did not see the position "as a policy-making job," but rather as "helping to facilitate the process of decision."[33]

CONCLUSIONS

Consensus eludes us on the content of current American foreign policy, but several propositions may perhaps command broad agreement:

- The relative power of the United States is less than it once was—militarily, economically, politically.

- The United States remains, for most world issues, the most important single nation; it is certainly the leading power in the West.
- The world is less orderly, with power diffused, international regimes under stress, dependence on unstable sources of oil, etc.
- Effective coping within this world requires careful, continuous, consultative leadership by the United States in our dealings with allies and adversaries, linked to programs—defense, economic, energy—which support this leadership.

This suggests that our foreign policy problems are both *long-term* and *cross-cutting*. We therefore need foreign policy institutions that provide *continuity*—strong, permanent repositories of expertise, initiative, and operational competence within the executive branch—and promote *integration*—the linking of U.S. actions to one another and to broader purposes.

In the best of institutional circumstances, there would be tension between these two goals. In practice neither seems well served, and one important reason is how the foreign policy presidency has evolved since 1960, particularly the rise of the assistant for national security affairs. Why has this happened? Dean Rusk provided part of the answer when he observed:

> The real organization of government at higher echelons is not what you find in textbooks or organization charts. It is how confidence flows down from the President.[34]

For though presidents inherit certain structures and institutions they also create their own: through how they operate, who they work with, what they demand. Their day-to-day signals condition, over time, their senior officials' responses, the relative power of these officials and their agencies, how these senior officials deal with *their* subordinates, etc. It is unlikely that presidents calculate many of these effects in advance, or even that they understand very much about them as they are occurring. Nonetheless, it is the president's operating style and personal relationships as they evolve that structure U.S. policymaking on the most important issues.

This is particularly true for national security policymaking. International issues (together with economic issues) are where presidents feel most accountable, more so than ever in the nuclear age, and where they may see the greatest opportunity for historic impact. Partly for these reasons, presidents are major foreign policy actors in an operational sense. They make foreign policy statements, epochal and trivial, in carefully prepared speeches and impromptu press conferences. They decide many issues personally. They consult and negotiate with foreign counterparts.

Such daily personal policy engagement has a decisive effect on presidentially generated foreign policymaking systems. In responding to the president's immediate needs, these systems tend to undercut the senior officials and the established institutions which the president also needs, over the longer run, to make his administration's foreign policy coherent and effective. In extreme form, this produces split-level government, as under Nixon and Kissinger in 1969–1973. Or it can produce chronic discontinuity in policy, as during the Carter administration. But these de facto foreign policymaking systems do tend to provide certain things that presidents value very highly, at least in the short-run, day-to-day world within which they must operate.

They favor *innovation* (visible if sometimes transient) over continuity within an administration and *connection* between its efforts and those of its predecessors. Rather than serving as a bridge between administrations, presidential staffing widens the gulf. The personal tendency of Carter (and Defense Secretary Harold Brown) to go beyond Ford's Vladivostok formula on SALT II was reinforced by the simultaneous arrival of committed aides with strong SALT views—not just Brzezinski but also his deputy, David Aaron. The case for building on the past was heard but overridden, and Secretary of State Cyrus Vance was dispatched to Moscow with the egregiously unsuccessful "comprehensive proposal" of March 1977. This episode sowed the seeds of serious future SALT difficulty at home and abroad, with Carter one of the principal losers. But at the time, the system gave Carter what he wanted—*his own* SALT proposal, not Gerald Ford's.[35]

Staff-dominated policymaking provides the president a *responsive personal environment* (*his* senior experts, just down the hall, a minute's walk away) while *reducing the degree he works personally with senior statutory aides* who have competing institutional loyalties—the secretaries of state and defense, the joint chiefs of staff—and thus shielding him somewhat from the political-institutional realities of the world outside 1600 Pennsylvania Avenue. The senior military early in the Carter administration were apparently unhappy not just with the substance of some early Carter decisions but with the way he made them. They felt excluded from serious advisory contact. Their frustration reinforced the argument of Carter critics that he was soft on national security, something which (again) cost him dearly. Yet in the short run, a president who has trouble developing new personal relationships will find it much easier to work with and through staff men both closer to him and more completely his subordinates.

While maximizing a president's capacity to *pull specific decisions into his own hands*, a staff-heavy system weakens a president's capacity to *multiply his ultimate leverage* through delegating relationships of personal confidence with senior line subordinates. If issues are repeatedly appealed to him, and he supports one adviser sometimes, another at other times, the adviser charged with exercising day-to-day bureaucratic, congressional, and international leadership is undercut, because he is perceived as not speaking for the president in any consistent, continuing way. And effective policy execution may prove impossible. Contrast, for example, Carter's delegation of the successful multilateral trade negotiations to Robert Strauss with his continuous, detailed immersion in the SALT II treaty. Yet Carter almost certainly saw himself as increasing his control when he decided and re-decided such questions as how to limit encryption of telemetric transmission of missile performance data.

Heavy reliance on the national security staff *seems to serve the goal of policy integration*—its purview is, after all, broader than that of any foreign policy agency, State included. But in practice, *integration is usually achieved only selectively and sporadically* as aides give priority to serving the president's personal needs (and sometimes to seizing particular issues themselves).[36] In fact, not only is comprehensive integration seldom attained, but national security advisers and their staffs have tended above all to focus on State Department business and political-strategic relationships—paying considerably less attention to defense and foreign economic questions. This too may reflect presidential inclinations, but it also means that the staff *coordinates less,* and *competes more* with State and its secretary.

In sum, the evolution of White House policy staffing between 1961 and 1980 responded to presidents' immediate needs and catered to their personal convenience but did not serve their broader, long-term need to lead a strong, loyal and responsive government. It served the illusion of presidential power more than its reality. It reinforced an exaggerated sense of the importance of specific presidential decisions—even on third- and fourth-order issues—while neglecting the officials and institutions, empowered by statute and ongoing engagement, that must carry weight for policy on most issues, most of the time. And it changed the role of staff from *mediating between the president and senior officialdom* to that of *substituting for officialdom,* reducing the president's perceived need to work with and through established institutions at all.

A better system would be one which both reinforces the ongoing departments and agencies and broadens their outlook by linking them. The logical prescription for this is the traditional one: strong agency heads (above all the secretary of state) with close ties to the president, and low-profile White House staffs which facilitate communication and questioning up, down, and across.

There is only one problem. The president, whoever he is, has to agree. Not that he must endorse such a system formally—this would be useful but not necessary and certainly not sufficient. Rather, he has to behave in a way which reinforces such a system rather than undercuts it. Organizational change will be durable only if linked to a viable pattern of presidential engagement in foreign policy, one which meets the president's needs as well as the broader needs of the nation.

Can presidents be brought to accept constraint on themselves in their day-to-day flexibility? Can they, as a result, impose or accept constraint on their staff aides, to the end of reinforcing and regularizing the larger policy-making system? The U.S. tradition is against such constraints. Institutionally, the American people are quite permissive to presidents. A British or Japanese prime minister is quickly supplied with "private secretaries" from the career service, men astute in serving politicians but within established broader traditions of governing. By contrast, a U.S. president-elect is generally advised that there are few firm rules, that he should structure his policy staffs to meet his particular needs, that anything is legitimate if it serves him as he perceives things.

But once a president is in office, Americans tend to expect far more from him than any human being could conceivably deliver. After the Iran rescue mission, for example, Hugh Sidey wrote in *Time:*

> It is a season for new resolve, for a display of determination that this White House has never reached before. These days cry out for daring, defiance . . . How [Carter] puts this all together will decide if he survives as President, if the U.S. marches ahead or cringes.[37]

It was as if, through sheer personal will, Carter could somehow transcend the excruciating limits of U.S. options that the real world had imposed and that the mission had so starkly illuminated!

If the United States is to move toward greater continuity in executive policy institutions, this will require a more realistic conception of presidential leadership, one which both presidents and president-watchers can find attractive; one which deemphasizes the president's role as a decider of specific issues and elevates his role as leader-executive in the broadest political sense; one of a president who works his will not just by great decisions but also by choosing, supporting, and influencing strong subordinates with broad policy mandates; one of a leader who uses his personal leverage to nourish policy conceptions and policy coalitions that will further his goals and who employs his staff to link him to these broader political-institutional realities rather than to shield him from them. In the end, his staff aides need to serve his subordinates' needs as well as his own. Only then will the broad policymaking "system" a president generates conform more closely to what many analysts have prescribed.

THE REAGAN EPILOGUE

Measured against this experience and these prescriptions, what was the shape of the early Reagan administration? The president-elect followed up on his promise to make the secretary of state his "principal [foreign policy] spokesman and adviser" by choosing for the post an assertive veteran of previous policy wars—General Alexander Haig—who had sharpened his bureaucratic skills through service as Henry Kissinger's NSC deputy and Richard Nixon's chief of staff.

Haig moved quickly to exploit and expand his authority by speaking out publicly, by taking interagency leadership on a range of issues, and by moving quickly to place his own people in subordinate State positions. By contrast, Reagan's national security assistant, Richard Allen, was performing the "disappearing act" he promised when his designation was announced in December 1980. Like Brzezinski before him, he came to this post through campaign advisory service, a role that had afforded him considerable public exposure. But he consistently endorsed the low-profile, facilitator conception of the job, telling the *New York Times* two weeks after the election that "the policy-formulation function of the national security adviser should be offloaded to the Secretary of State."[38] And unlike Brzezinski, his base was not academia but Washington, where he had served twice in the Nixon White House and then mixed international consulting with involvement in the 1976 and 1980 Reagan campaigns.

To underscore the administration's determination to cut the national security post down to size, White House organization charts placed Allen (and domestic policy assistant Martin Anderson) not directly under the president but under senior assistant Edwin Meese, a long-time Reagan associate. And it was Meese who moved into the symbolically important White House corner office that Brzezinski had occupied, with Allen located in the White House basement where Bundy and Rostow had served.

Where Haig ran quickly into difficulty, however, was in relations with the senior White House staff generally, as well as with his Cabinet colleagues—Secretary of Defense Caspar Weinberger in particular. Not content with his early de facto primacy, Haig sought to pin it down by seeking, on inauguration day, a formal grant of presidential authority much more sweeping than Nixon had given Kissinger twelve years before. The White House resisted, as did the secretary of defense, and Meese ended up brokering a compromise in February in which State, Defense, and CIA each chaired policy coordination committees for their respective spheres. Then, a month later, Haig objected to a pending proposal to establish an interagency crisis coordination committee chaired by Vice President George Bush. When Haig went public with his reservations, Reagan quickly approved the proposal; the White House released a terse explanation that "management of crises has traditionally—and appropriately—been done within the White House."[39]

This was a serious blow to Haig's claim to leadership, made worse by the public impression that it was at least partly self-inflicted. Thereafter, the secretary came across not as the self-proclaimed "vicar" of Reagan foreign policy, but rather as a struggling, wounded protagonist whose demise was widely anticipated. His individualistic, assertive approach clearly clashed with the collegial way that Reagan and his long-time associates preferred to make policy (a problem that presaged his ultimate departure from the administration).

Yet though the new administration had trouble doing *with* Haig, it also had difficulty doing *without* him, and certain of the threats to his authority were more apparent than real. The Bush-chaired committee was largely cosmetic—how could an intermittent policy player suddenly assume command when an issue became a "crisis" and then retire from the leadership when it ceased to be one? Nor was Allen, whose personal coolness toward Haig dated from the early Nixon administration, the sort of threat suggested in the media. The press highlighted their rivalry, and one peculiar incident led Reagan to summon the two men to the White House in November 1981 for a lecture on the need to avoid fighting in public. But in fact Allen was among the lesser of Haig's problems: Allen lacked the mandate and the stature within the White House that he would have needed to challenge the Secretary. And Haig's resistance, combined with the operational weaknesses of Allen and his staff, made it hard for the NSC staff to play the invisible, inside coordinating role that it had been assigned.

Haig did face, however, more formidable rivals, men possessing the established presidential ties he personally lacked. Secretary of Defense Caspar Weinberger was a close Reagan associate who had been budget director in California before heading the Office of Management and Budget and the Department of Health, Education and Welfare under Nixon. Presidential Counselor Meese was also a Reagan intimate of long standing. Both Weinberger and Meese found Haig difficult to work with and each found ways to use the presidential connection to thwart him. Yet neither had Haig's foreign policy background or credibility with U.S. allies. So neither could—at least initially—reasonably aspire to broad international leadership, though Weinberger was more active diplomatically than any defense secretary since Robert McNamara. And President Reagan seemed strikingly detached from day-to-day policy engagement, because his preferred style was one of delegation, and because he was giving priority to winning approval of his economic program. (In fact, Reagan's major foreign policy accomplishment of 1981 was to rescue, through his adroit one-on-one lobbying of senators, his administration's mismanaged proposal to sell advanced radar warning aircraft to Saudi Arabia.)[40]

Well before the close of 1981, the Reagan foreign policy process thus was generating the same sorts of criticisms that Carter's began to receive in mid-1978. If anything, the bad reviews were more numerous. Even Brzezinski, in a year-end interview, could label Reagan's foreign policy-making system "the worst ever."[41] Haig and the State Department had the lead on most issues but were stalemated on the most important: relations with NATO, Middle East policy, and arms control. Infighting was highly visible, and no one seemed to be coordinating things. Then, an unlikely pseudo-scandal broke in mid-November, involving Allen's alleged acceptance of $1,000 from Japanese journalists for his role in setting up an interview with Nancy Reagan. The issue became inflated far beyond its intrinsic importance through a combination of media hyperbole, inconsistent administration accounts of the facts, and the opportunity the matter afforded to those who felt Allen should be replaced on policy management grounds. Allen spent December on leave-of-absence, during which he embarked on a major media campaign defending his good name. In early January 1982, the president asked for and received his resignation.

Taking Allen's place was William Clark, who had served as deputy secretary of state during Reagan's first year in office. Clark, once chief of Reagan's gubernatorial staff and thereafter a California judge, had originally joined the administration over the objections of both Haig and numerous senators, who protested what many saw as Clark's complete lack of foreign policy qualifications. But he quickly won Haig's confidence and proved a much-needed broker and connector between the secretary and the White House. A pragmatist who personally shunned the limelight, Clark had at one time or another worked with or for all of the protagonists—Haig, Meese, Weinberger, and of course Reagan himself. They trusted and respected him. With his appointment the national security post was re-elevated in the White House hierarchy. Clark would report not through Meese but directly to Reagan.

The change symbolized what was crucial, for Clark from the start was perceived to have the sort of personal presidential mandate which Allen had lacked. Speculation was immediate that he would soon become a rival to his former boss at State. But Clark played his role in early 1982 both forcefully and quietly, following the consensus prescription of low-profile facilitator. He was constraining Haig but also helping him in the White House, where the secretary was weakest. And when a Weinberger trip to the Mideast generated careless statements from the defense secretary about tilting U.S. policy away from Israel, the national security assistant took steps, personal and organizational, to reduce the chances of this occurring again. Thus Clark was doing an invaluable job: that of president policy broker and enforcer.

But the leverage of a national security assistant tends to be limited in an administration where the chief executive himself is not playing an active, energizing, initiating role. For a staff man must build his influence primarily around the transactions of his boss, and under Reagan there seemed to be less presidential foreign policy business than at any time in the last fifty years. This means that, barring a reversal of Reagan's operating style, any constructive foreign policy leadership would almost have to come from a secretary of state with strong presidential confidence and at least tolerable relations with his Cabinet peers.

Haig reached for this leadership role, but was unable to form the personal relationships which were its necessary precondition. Finally, after seventeen stormy months, he lost the confidence of Clark, his last senior ally. This, combined with crises over Lebanon and U.S.-European relations, led to Reagan's acceptance of Haig's resignation on June 25, 1982. George P. Shultz, immediately named as his replacement, was expeditiously and unanimously confirmed by the Senate.

In style Shultz was Haig's polar opposite—low-key, collegial, deferential to the president and eager to establish smooth relations with his cabinet peers. This approach required that he publicly downplay his personal influence. Nonetheless, Shultz moved quickly into the lead in developing, for presidential presentation, a more active and explicit Reagan stance on the central issue of Arab-Israeli peace terms.

Performance and style problems, then, had led Reagan to replace both his national security assistant and his secretary of state. The new duo of Shultz and Clark seemed, on its initial performance, a clear improvement. There was even the possibility that Reagan might achieve a combination that had eluded most of his predecessors—an effective secretary of state working in harmony with the president and a strong (but low-profile) White House national security aide.

Only time would tell, of course, whether this pattern would emerge and endure. But the early Reagan experience clearly underscored, once again, the critical importance of the president's preferred operating style, and those of his key officials, to the functioning of the American government. For the president is both solution and problem. He is the only available source for central foreign policy leadership. Yet in practice, presidents often bring idiosyncracy and discontinuity to foreign policymaking. If policymaking processes cater above all to short-run presidential needs, to his day-to-day flexibility and even whim, they will compound the problem. Yet without clear and visible presidential confidence, no subordinate official or institution can amass the leverage necessary to pursue coherent, effective United States foreign policy in the president's name.

NOTES

1. Address of October 19, 1980, reprinted in *New York Times*, October 20, 1980.
2. The numbers refer to substantive professionals, mid-career level and up, not to support or communications personnel. Most have been in actual NSC slots, but a substantial minority have been "detailees" from State and other national security agencies.

    Kissinger held two positions—Secretary of State and National Security Assistant—from September 1973 to November 1975. Scowcroft, as deputy assistant, generally managed the national security staff and process during this period and his elevation to the assistant position in 1975 essentially formalized an arrangement that already existed in practice.
3. Bromley Smith, a senior NSC staff member under Eisenhower, stayed on under Bundy and Rostow, becoming NSC Executive Secretary. Kissinger insisted on changing all the substantive aides except Harold Saunders (Middle East) and Roger Morris (Africa). William Hyland, Deputy Assistant to Scowcroft, stayed on the staff through most of 1977 to provide some continuity, and perhaps four other senior staff members under Ford stayed on for at least a year. These are, to the author's knowledge, the only significant exceptions to the rule of discontinuity in 1961, 1969, and 1977.
4. I have in mind a consensus among former senior officials like McGeorge Bundy, Henry Kissinger, Brent Scowcroft, Andrew Goodpaster, Francis Bator, and Bromley Smith, and political scientists like Richard Neustadt, Graham Allison, Peter Szanton, Alexander George, David K. Hall, Robert H. Johnson (a former

NSC aide), and myself. This view is also reflected in the Heineman Task Force Report to Lyndon Johnson in 1967, some of the analyses done for the Carter transition staff in 1976, the general philosophy of the EOP (Executive Office of the President) reorganization report presented to President Carter in June 1977, and most recently on the National Academy of Public Administration panel report, "A Presidency for the 1980s." Obviously there are variations in views among those named, and none bears any responsibility for the way this consensus is characterized here.

For recent statements of former senior officials, see "The National Security Adviser: Role and Accountability," Hearing before the Committee on Foreign Relations, United States Senate, April 17, 1980, pp. 139–50.

5. Oral History for Lyndon B. Johnson Library, Austin, Texas, Tape #1, July 29, 1969, p. 35.
6. *Washington Post*, May 11, 1979. See also Senate Foreign Relations Committee, "The National Security Adviser."
7. "The National Security Council," Report of the Subcommittee on National Policy Machinery, Committee on Government Operations, U.S. Senate (henceforth referred to as the "Jackson subcommittee") in *Organizing for National Security*, Vol. III, 1961, p. 38. For an argument that the Eisenhower policy process was much more humanized than the Kennedy people thought, see I. M. Destler, "A Lost Legacy? The President and National Security Organization 1945–1960," paper delivered at U.S. Military Academy Symposium, April 22, 1982.
8. "Memorandum on Staffing the President-Elect," October 30, 1960, John F. Kennedy Library, transition files, p. 20 (emphasis in original).
9. Bundy letter of September 1961 to Senator Henry Jackson, reprinted in Jackson subcommittee, *Organizing for National Security*, Vol I., pp. 1337–38.
10. Oral history interview with Robert W. Komer, John F. Kennedy Library, Part 4, October 31, 1964, pp. 20–22. Quoted with permission.
11. "Memorandum for the President: Current Organization of the White House and National Security Council for Dealing with International Matters," June 22, 1961, National Security File, No. 283/15, Kennedy Library, unsigned.
12. Oral History Tape #1, Johnson Library, p. 18.
13. See David K. Hall, "The National Security Assistant as Policy Spokesman 1947–1981," paper delivered at annual meeting of American Political Science Association, September 3, 1981.
14. Henry A. Kissinger, *White House Years*, Little, Brown and Company, 1979, p. 38.
15. Memorandum for the President-Elect, "Subject: Proposal for a New National Security Council System." The author's copy, obtained from an unofficial source, is consistent with Kissinger's report of the document in *White House Years*. The language quoted is from page 2 of the memorandum.
16. Gerard Smith, *Doubletalk: The Story of SALT I*, Doubleday and Company, 1980, pp. 222–25; Kissinger, *White House Years*, p. 819.
17. Kissinger, *White House Years*, pp. 805–806.
18. See I. M. Destler, *Presidents, Bureaucrats, and Foreign Policy*, Princeton University Press, 1972, pp. 127–28.
19. Kissinger, *White House Years*, p. 887.
20. Ford's adaptability on this score is illustrated by the fact that he employed very different advisory systems for differing policy areas: on foreign policy he

depended on one predominant aide; on economic policy he worked with and reinforced a formal, participatory policy review system based on a cabinet committee (the Economic Policy Board); and on domestic policy he worked with unstructured "ad hoc-racy."

21. Carter replaced them with two committees, both at Cabinet level: the Policy Review Committee (PRC) and the Special Coordinating Committee (SCC). The distinction between the two was never entirely clear, at least to the outsider, but in general terms the former, chaired by the appropriate Cabinet member, handled those issues where one department had clear lead responsibility; the latter, chaired by the national security assistant, handled other issues, as well as crisis coordination. Interestingly, the SCC handled SALT from the outset, even though Vance and ACDA Director Paul Warnke had lead negotiating responsibility.

22. *New York Times,* December 17, 1976.

23. *Ibid.*

24. See Philip Odeen, "National Security Policy Integration," Report to the President under the auspices of the President's Reorganization Project, September 1979, reprinted in Senate Foreign Relations Committee, "The National Security Adviser," pp. 106–28.

25. Letter of June 7, 1978, released by the Committee.

26. *New York Times,* October 6, 1980.

27. See William H. Sullivan, "Dateline Iran: The Road Not Taken," *Foreign Policy* 40, Fall 1980, pp. 175–86, and Michael A. Ledeen and William H. Lewis, "Carter and the Fall of the Shah: The Inside Story," *The Washington Quarterly,* Spring 1980, pp. 3–40.

28. By one account, "When President Carter took his new secretary of state . . . and his national security advisor . . . to Camp David to work out ground rules for the delicate relationship between the two, several key aides tried to persuade Carter to silence Brzezinski completely. They wanted Carter to make it clear that foreign policy speeches, television appearances and negotiations with foreign governments would be off-limits to all but the secretary of state. Carter flatly refused." See Alison Muscatine, "Brzezinski is 'Closer' Among Policy Equals," *Washington Star,* June 18, 1980.

29. *White House Years,* p. 30.

30. Statement in Senate Foreign Relations Committee, "The National Security Adviser," p. 150.

31. Personal interview, February 5, 1980.

32. "Mr. Reagan's Security Aide," *New York Times* (op-ed page), November 16, 1980.

33. For Brzezinski's retrospective description of the Carter system, with himself squarely at its center, see "The Best National Security System," in *Washington Quarterly,* Winter 1982, pp. 71–82.

34. Quoted in *Life,* January 17, 1969, p. 62b.

35. See Strobe Talbott, *Endgame,* Harper and Row, 1979, Chapter 3.

36. Thus in 1963, Neustadt noted that "the 'personal aide' [of Kennedy's foreign policy staffing] seems firm enough, but not the other side, the 'institutional side.'" And in September 1979 Philip Odeen's report for Carter sounded a similarly understated warning that "despite this stress on the personal advisory role, the [NSC] staff's institutional role must not be neglected." Jackson subcommit-

tee, *Administration of National Security*, 1965, p. 81, and Odeen, "National Security Policy Integration," p. 109.

37. "Days That Call for Daring," *Time*, May 5, 1980, p. 25.
38. *New York Times*, November 19, 1980.
39. *New York Times*, March 25, 1981.
40. See I. M. Destler, "Reagan and Congress—Lessons of 1981," in *The Washington Quarterly*, Spring 1982.
41. "The Best National Security System," p. 77.

18

WHY NOT THE STATE DEPARTMENT?

LESLIE H. GELB

. . . For the last twenty years or so most public commissions, organization experts, and foreign policy commentators who have addressed the problem of how to organize the foreign policy apparatus of the executive branch have consistently recommended that the authority to make policy should be clearly and firmly lodged in the Department of State.[1] Every recent president has echoed this recommendation at the beginning of his term; yet none ever followed through and did it. Why is it that every president from Kennedy to Carter began by looking toward the State Department only to look back soon thereafter to the White House itself? Is the State Department the right place to make policy and have these presidents simply been shortsighted and wrong, or is the State Department incapable of playing the leading role? If the State Department is incapable of making policy to satisfy the White House, is the best alternative to give that power to the president's national security adviser, with all the well-known problems that entails? Is there another alternative? More disturbing, what ever happened to "policy," and can organization really be of any help in developing it?

I. M. Destler makes the case for a State Department-centered organizational strategy in its purest form in his book, *Presidents, Bureaucrats, and Foreign Policy*.[2] Always thoughtful and often incisive, Destler argues that the "president must want [the secretary of state] to be his preeminent foreign policy official," and that he must make this clear and give the secretary the necessary powers to coordinate and focus policy under the president. Destler acknowledges that the Department has not had the requisite expertise and outlook to perform this central role in the recent past, but he maintains that these qualities can be developed. Indeed, he argues they must be

Reprinted with permission from *The Washington Quarterly: A Review of Strategic and International Studies*, White Paper, Special Supplement to the Autumn 1980 issue. Copyright © 1980 by the Center for Strategic and International Studies, Georgetown University, Washington, D.C. 20006.

developed, for there is no other place short of the presidency where coherence and purposefulness can be provided for policy.

The steady drumbeat of support for the primacy of the secretary of state and his department derives from historical nostalgia, pure logic, and the necessity on the part of some organizational experts to find clean and clear solutions. The nostalgia rests on what almost everyone regards as the halcyon days of the State Department and of genuine creativity in U.S. foreign policy, when President Truman gave full support to Secretaries of State George Marshall and Dean Acheson. These men, in turn, pressed their subordinates to frame a whole series of imaginative and coherent policies toward the Soviet Union, European reconstruction, and the colonial world. Moreover, by pure logic, the State Department is the only place that has purview over the full range of foreign relations. Where else could one allot responsibility under the president? And for the organizational expert, any other solution is messy. To the expert, State may well be parochial and overly concerned with pleasing client countries, but it is the only department in the executive branch capable of giving the long view of national interests and security, relatively free from short-run domestic political considerations.

Henry Kissinger may have surprised some in his recent and excellent memoir in writing: "Though I did not think so at the time, I have become convinced that a president should make the secretary of state his principal adviser and use the national security adviser primarily as a senior administrator and coordinator to make certain that each significant point of view is heard." But a closer look seems to reveal that his heart is not in this judgment—the two arguments he makes are weak. The first is nominalistic: "If the security adviser becomes active in the development and articulation of policy he must inevitably diminish the secretary of state and reduce his effectiveness." The second, more serious, is that foreign governments would be confused by the competition and play one off against the other.[3]

Moreover, as Kissinger warms to his discussion of organization, the views he expressed more than twenty years ago in his book, *Nuclear Weapons and Foreign Policy*,[4] reappear and he once again seems to be arguing for a White House-centered structure. In rapid fire, he writes that presidents cannot leave the presentation of options to one department; they always narrow the scope for presidential decision, not expand it. They think in terms of a preferred option, not a range. They fear being overruled by the president, so the departments come together to work out a vacuous consensus. They are parochial, not national, in their perspectives.[5]

What counted, as Kissinger candidly ends up saying, was being there. "My role would almost surely have been roughly the same if the Johnson system had been continued. Propinquity counts for much; the opportunity to confer with the president several times a day is often of decisive importance, much more so than the chairmanship of committees or the right to present options." And then another curious twist: "For reasons that must be

left to students of psychology, every president since Kennedy seems to have
trusted his White House aides more than his cabinet."[6] What is at stake, as
Kissinger has always understood, are matters of domestic and bureaucratic
politics.

Here, in an ironic way, the argument for a State Department-centered
system begins to undrape its own real weakness. It also becomes clear why
presidents look to their immediate aides and not to the cabinet, as Kissinger
tells us. Foreign policy cannot be freed from short-run domestic political
considerations. This is not to say that presidents make policy simply or even
principally for their political advantage. Contrary to endemic Washington
cynicism about such matters, my experience has been that the presidents
are quite high-minded about the national interest and often are prepared to
take political lumps for what is right. But what is right has to be supportable,
and presidents soon find that the State Department—with some exceptions
from time to time—does a poor job of framing its proposals in terms that will
elicit political support, and it does not think about potential costs to the
president. It is, of course, possible that foreign service officers—and certainly the outside political appointees—could learn to do this, but doubtful.
The irrepressible ethos of the building is to look outside the United States,
not inward.

It has been my experience that the same staffer behaves very differently in the White House than in the State Department, Defense Department, or CIA; one is far more conscious of presidential stakes and interests
when in residence in Pennsylvania Avenue. It is not a question of learning
politics, but a matter of being there and knowing specifically what politicians in the White House are thinking of at a particular time. But more to
the point, a president is not going to wait for the State Department to
learn—he soons discovers that he can have his decisions framed in more
politically acceptable ways by his own staff. Once a president comes to
believe that Foggy Bottom is not attuned to politics, they are doomed to
being ignored. Once he concludes that his staff has political savvy, that staff
is on its way to dominating policymaking.

The divergence of views between the White House and NSC staffs on
the one hand and the State Department on the other on how to handle the
situation of the American hostages in Iran is a good example of this. In the
first few months, all of the key participants accepted the need for a period of
private exchanges with the Iranian leaders without increasing the sanctions
or public rhetoric. But as the months wore on and presidential candidates
and editorial writers began to exclaim against "Carter's do-nothing policy,"
the perspectives of the two different buildings began to pull policy in conflicting directions. The State Department tried to define the issue from a
long-term perspective. Its advice was not to back Iranian authorities into a
corner with further sanctions or tougher public rhetoric, arguing that if we
did not alienate the new regime, there would be a reasonable chance that
the hostages would be released and Iran would eventually gravitate back

toward the U.S. orbit. The White House and NSC people began to define the problem as American impotence and argued that unless the president took firm action like a naval blockade, U.S. credibility in the world would suffer, as would the president's electoral chances. In order simply to maintain some fraction of President Carter's attention, the State Department had to go along with much of what the White House staff was proposing.

Which approach was better is irrelevant for the purposes of this article. What is important is that the approach of the White House staff was hard and seemed realistic and was political in the broadest sense of the word. It is very difficult to compete with that.

The divergent perspectives reached fateful proportions when Secretary Vance stood alone against Mr. Brzezinski (and all of the president's other top advisers, to be sure) in opposing the commando mission to rescue the hostages, and felt compelled to resign. On one level, the Vance resignation was simply directed against the idea that the hostages could be freed without making new hostages of other Americans in Teheran and of the captured commandos. This was a practical objection. On another level, Vance was making a statement that force was not the way to solve a problem created and sustained by a national nervous breakdown in Iran, and that threats to use force or the use of force would lead to Iranian calls for Soviet help. On a third level, Vance was implicitly calling attention to the seeming ascendancy of domestic political concerns, i.e., the president's need in an election year to show that he is tough and decisive over the diplomatic and long-term interests of the nation. My guess is that even had Henry Kissinger been Secretary of State, the department would have given him the same advice as Vance gave the president.

The record indicates that in the beginning of each administration, presidents often do turn to the State Department—just as they traditionally start off making visible use of their cabinets and vice presidents. Typically, the president discovers that State usually stresses bilateral and long-term interests with a country or region. From a White House perspective, efforts to accommodate the legitimate concerns of other countries are often viewed as coming at the expense of American interests, and the accommodationists are viewed as not being tough enough. Presidents usually do not have much patience with this kind of advice, find they cannot change State's penchant for it, and soon stop listening.

The different approaches of State and the NSC are demonstrated by the diverging advice they have given over the years on West European policy. The European bureau is at the very heart of the State Department in prestige and influence, and the Europeanists often find reasons for the United States not to take issue with their clients on economic matters, security questions, or East-West relations. The National Security Council staff often argues that the department is "babying" the Europeans. These different thrusts were brought to a head recently over the issue of what Washington should expect of its European allies and Japan in placing economic sanctions against Iran and taking action against the Soviet Union as reprisal to the invasion of Afghanistan. The NSC staff tended to see West European reluctance to follow White House policy as a sign of economic greed and cravenness toward Soviet power. They argued that unless the president could bring our major allies into line with his policies, he would appear weak. State Department Europeanists tended to argue that the West Europeans were somewhat justified in their hesitations because they could not rely on our policy being consistent and because their interests were not identical to ours. While the Europeanists wanted the allies to help, they did not want to compel them to do so in a public showdown. However, Carter opted for the public showdown. The Europeanists felt this was causing a crisis in the NATO alliance, while the NSC staffers and White House political people felt that it was precisely the lack of support from NATO and Japan that would constitute the crisis.

Recent presidents have probably concluded some time during their first year that they cannot trust anyone in the State Department below the secretary—and perhaps one or two others. Presidents Carter, Ford, and Nixon very rarely discussed policy with assistant secretaries of state, who are actually responsible for making the connection between policy and action in the machinery. This puts the secretary in a horrendous position. Either he can disassociate himself from his own department to preserve his standing with the president, thereby letting his institution flounder, or he can become an advocate for his department and end up being suspect himself. John Foster Dulles and Dean Rusk came close to doing the former, and William Rogers pretty much did the latter. Cyrus Vance fell between the two stools. Either way, it was not a happy position for any of the secretaries.

Another reason presidents find they cannot look to the State Department and its secretary for the formulation of policy is that State simply is not sufficiently informed or well situated to make economic tradeoffs for international economic policy. As many organizational experts have observed, foreign policy is increasingly concerned and consumed with international economic, and therefore, domestic political considerations. Neither the Treasury nor the Commerce Departments, for example, will take direction from the State Department on issues these departments deem vital. But beyond that, no White House is going to let the secretary of state decide which domestic constituency is going to gain and lose in a trade negotiation or in commodity arrangements with the Third World.[7] Nor will the Pentagon take orders from State on military or arms control issues. All of these issues can be adjudicated only through the interagency system headed by the NSC staff.

Also not to be forgotten or dismissed, presidents and their staffs soon start to search for opportunities for leadership, areas to demonstrate that the president is on top of things and making policy. When this game is played, the loser is almost invariably the State Department and not the Pentagon. It is difficult for the president and his NSC and Office of Management and

Budget (OMB) staffs to really get on top of the defense budget. It is made up of thousands of detailed programs put together by thousands of staffers, and it is boring. To do more than scratch the surface of a few front page military issues would require a much larger White House staff than any president would want to contemplate and a lot of political risk. Policy, on the other hand, is words, and the president and his staffers can step in at any time and put the words together themselves.

The temptations for the president and his staff to short circuit the process and make policy themselves—and to make it quickly—is often irresistible. Despite the well-deserved reputation of foreign service officers as people of exceptional ability, neither by training nor by disposition are many of them gifted or even interested in the formulation of policy. The ethos of maintaining flexibility is exceptionally strong in the diplomatic profession, and the more flexibility one seeks, the more vacuous the policy. Policy is purposeful behavior, something specific is to be achieved and certain maneuvers and sacrifices to be made in order to achieve it. Flexibility— sought almost as an end in itself—means to ride the waves and make the best of whatever happens. While most politicians also stress flexibility, presidents are not most politicians. They are seeking accomplishments in their terms of office. And behind the last five presidents I have observed, there has been an NSC and White House staff constantly reminding the president that the State Department does not help much in policymaking.

Thus for a host of powerful reasons—mainly that the State Department cannot be the place where tough political decisions and economic trade-offs are made, and because of State's difficulty in formulating policy— presidents soon turn away from the State Department as the crucible for making policy. But does this mean that the secretary of state and his department are not the appropriate place for this responsibility? Does it mean that the national security adviser to the president and the NSC staff is a better place, or indeed the only place?

From the standpoint of organizational theory, there are strikes against both the secretary and the NSC adviser. The major shortcomings of the State Department were just discussed, but one more merits mention. Precisely because the secretary and the departments are engaged in and have primary responsibility for the conduct of foreign policy, i.e., the day-to-day business of diplomacy and congressional appearances, as a practical matter there is little time to make policy. It seems inconceivable that such day-to-day tasks should even take precedence over policymaking, but they must be done; there is no choice. By and large, this is true of the State Department's policy planning staff as well.

Even if it were possible to free the secretary of state from many of the duties of running his department, and if the president were to grant the secretary an unambiguous and paramount organizational role in the formulation of policy, it is doubtful this could be sustained. This has really worked only once, from 1947 to 1961, under special circumstances. In general, the position of the secretary of state was aided by a consensus about what foreign policy should be and by virtue of a less complex environment. Also in those years, the secretary of state had little or no competition. There had been no secretary of defense (just secretaries for the army and navy) before the National Security Act of 1947. The first defense secretary, James Forrestal, tried to be a major formulator of policy, but failed, and his proximate successors confined themselves largely to military hardware, doctrinal, and budget issues. The NSC was established in 1948, but it was not until 1953 that the post of NSC adviser was created. The names of these early NSC advisers never became household words even in Washington[8]—they were simply *hautes clerques*. Thus, George Marshall, Dean Acheson, and John Foster Dulles had a clear field.

Purists in the State Department and elsewhere maintain that the president can come close to recreating the conditions of the past, when secretaries of state were dominant, by enhancing the power of the secretary and specifically limiting the activities of the adviser. The list of limitations would include: no chairing of interagency meetings, no contact with the press, no foreign travel; no NSC channels and dialogues with foreign counterparts or with ambassadors in Washington; and no contacts with Congress. Such restrictions, it is argued, would not constrain the adviser's input on policy matters given his close personal relationship with the president; but if they were put into effect, the secretary would enjoy greater public stature which could reinforce his standing with the president as well. What president, however, would be prepared to exclude his adviser from these activities? It is too easy to think of exigencies where the president specifically would want his NSC adviser to have certain dealings with the press, Congress, and foreign diplomats. It is also easy to recite all of the issues where departmental interests overlap and instances when there is little alternative to the NSC adviser's serving as chairman of interagency meetings.

However, it is reasonable to insist that the NSC adviser not make public speeches, appear on radio and television broadcast interviews, or even be quoted by name. To permit such public statements and exposure is to invite comparisons of personality and words with the secretary of state. Diplomats and journalists will look for conflicts between the two, perhaps where none actually exists. Here again, however, presidents may insist on seeing the situation otherwise, as Nixon did with Kissinger and Rogers and as Carter, with Brzezinski and Vance, and there is not much that can be done about it.

Would it be better or easier to give the policymaking mantle to the NSC adviser? It is difficult to argue how this would not be efficient. Being a few steps from the president and being in the thick of the political concerns of the White House are tremendous advantages, because matters can be dealt with quickly and in person. There is a good case that this would be a better arrangement as well: the White House is best situated to give an overall strategic view in which departmental parochialism is subordinated to broader presidential concerns. It also stands to reason that presidents will believe that the NSC staff will provide a fairer accounting of each department's views than the State Department, which is—in the president's eyes—just another advocate. Moreover, since it is generally assumed that the NSC adviser speaks for the president, his words are bound to be considered more authoritative than anyone outside the White House. But better in some respects and easier does not necessarily make it wise or right.

There are serious problems to formally expanding the role of the NSC adviser, whatever the informal arrangements might be. His staff provides all breadth and little depth, unlike the State Department. It is dangerous to make policy from a questionable basis of knowledge. Moreover, it is difficult enough now for the State Department to make the case for long-term interest; it would be impossible if State's role were formally reduced. Also, to give the NSC adviser formal policymaking authority would necessitate his being available to Congress on at least the same terms as the secretary of state. That would not only raise real problems for the confidentiality of his working relationship with the president, but it would consume a substantial amount of time, leaving less time for policymaking and reducing his comparative advantage over the secretary of state. Finally, and most important, it would destroy any semblance of order. The value of organization may be limited, but certain elementary notions of organization can be disregarded only at great peril. To anoint the NSC adviser as secretary of state for policy would render the secretary powerless to run the State Department; he would not be regarded as authoritative by his own people. It would also have a deadening effect on all diplomatic contacts.

By the same token, there is nothing to be gained by trying to turn the prince back into a frog and make the current-day NSC adviser back into the good old high-priced clerk he was in the 1950s. Presidents certainly should not deny themselves a top-flight, policy-oriented NSC adviser in order to protect some enfeebled secretary of state; the president surely needs another voice or two when dealing with the secretaries of state and defense. For all the reasons Destler[9] and others cite, the adviser must be able to run an efficient operation that is perceived to be fair to various points of view. But this has never meant that presidents will limit the adviser's role.

Much of the discussion over the secretary of state versus the NSC adviser is actually a debate over policy and personality, not organizational virtues. To begin with, if proper organization were in fact the vital issue, the debate could have begun after McGeorge Bundy in 1965 or to a lesser extent, after Walt Rostow in 1968. The job under these two men already had changed complexion substantially. However, the organizers and other experts held their powder dry for Kissinger and Brzezinski.[10]

Most of the criticism of the Nixon system of White House control and the call for a stronger secretary of state was in truth an attack on the person and policies of Kissinger, and it continued even after Kissinger moved over to the State Department and began to have great influence on policy from there—as critics had been saying a secretary of state should. The real concern was not where decisions were being made, but what decisions were being made and by whom.

The Commission on the Organization of the Government for the Conduct of Foreign Policy, better known as the Murphy Commission, is the most recent case in point, emphasizing two important points: First, the executive branch is not well structured to deal with the most important policy problem of the future, namely foreign economic policy. Second, never again should a president invest one man with the two responsibilities of secretary of state and national security adviser. The two points were not unrelated; Kissinger was seen as notoriously indifferent to foreign economic policy.

While President Carter lost no opportunity before his inauguration and for many months thereafter to emphasize that Cyrus Vance would be his principal foreign adviser and that Brzezinski would simply be the "coordinator," Carter's system was actually as oriented toward making decisions in the White House as Nixon's—perhaps even more so. Carter . . . insisted on making the most minute action decisions, as well as the policy decisions. One of many examples of this was the procedure he established for approving each and every government-to-government arms sale reported to Congress. This aside, the point is that Carter, like all of his immediate predecessors except Presidents Truman and Eisenhower, did not want to leave matters entirely up to the state department.[11] As the evidence mounted that decisions were being made in the White House, Brzezinski's power grew beyond being a coordinator. (It would have for other reasons as well, but these are not relevant here.)

On one level, the debate in Washington proceeded as if Brzezinski had usurped Vance's role without Carter's knowing it or wishing it. The argument was that Brzezinski's position had become so powerful that he could interfere without presidential sanction. There is some truth to this. But on a deeper level, what really troubled many in Congress, the media, and the executive branch about Brzezinski were his views and his person. Many of Vance's future subordinates deeply mistrusted Brzezinski for his views on the Soviet Union well before his first day in office. The Kissinger crowd bowed to no one in their dislike of Brzezinski, for they felt that he was setting out to attack Kissinger just for spite and to be different.

Graham Allison and Peter Szanton took these considerations into account in offering an alternative to both the secretary of state and the NSC adviser with their idea of a floating system of policymaking. In their distinguished book, *Remaking Foreign Policy: The Organizational Connection,* they conclude that "the instinct of new administrations to choose a single new system—more formal or more fixed, regular or ad hoc—is mistaken. Instead, the problem is how to use several systems selectively and in parallel ways that exploit the advantages of each."[12] From this prudent judgment, they go on to make some astute observations about the limitations of the State Department as a focal point for policymaking. They recommend that

State's role be one of "advocacy" for the long-run perspective. They define this as arguing that "the interests of the United States are most reliably advanced by policies and actions that meet the legitimate requirements of all nations."[13]

With the State Department thus stereotyped as representing the long-term view, the authors then have to divine how to integrate this with the short-term views. Here the force of their book languishes as they put forward the idea of an executive committee of the cabinet (EXCAB) to replace the national security council. Other than the name change and adding a few new members (like the secretary of the treasury and the secretary of HEW to represent domestic matters), I am at a loss to discover how this would be much different from standard operating procedure for many years. Moreover, they remain silent on who under the president will run EXCAB.[14]

In their silence resides the one stark truth about organization of the foreign policy apparatus—that personalities and abilities are far more important than structure and process, and that these factors will determine who will make policy and decisions under the president. The sad fact is that virtually everyone who writes on organization asserts this point, then ignores it. Rarely are conclusions or recommendations or devices or systems built to take it into account. In fact, the traditional organizational experts consciously attempt to work around it.

There is only one conclusion on this subject that holds up—simply that the policymaking role under the president went to the dominant personality who had a policy-mind in each administration. Initially, neither Secretary of State James F. Byrnes nor anyone else emerged under President Truman. But thereafter, Marshall and Acheson were clearly the dominant figures. Under President Eisenhower, Dulles had obvious sway. In the last two years of the Eisenhower administration, with Christian Herter at State and Thomas Gates at Defense, no strong figure emerged and the president determined policy himself. President Kennedy wanted his principal advisers to revolve around him, but Defense Secretary Robert McNamara nevertheless stood out for his dynamism and strong point of view. Dean Rusk's role was never anything near paramount, even after President Johnson structured the system to give him and the State Department the organizational reins. Kissinger against William P. Rogers was no contest, but Kissinger against Defense Secretary Melvin Laird was, and he knew enough to avoid trying to tangle with Laird. Nonetheless, Kissinger was the dominant man while in his NSC job, and only somewhat less so as secretary of state.

The only safe prediction on organization is that however the formal system is constructed, actual power will gravitate to the person whose policy views and style prevail with the president. This is not to argue that the policies that resulted from this law of nature were good or effective. But recommendations on organization should never stray far from this reality.

There are some crucial points to keep in mind about the relationship between organization, and personalities and abilities. First, the tone of the administration, the public perception of administration policies, and bureaucratic rivalries will flow in large measure from relations between the top three presidential aides—the secretaries of state and defense and the NSC adviser. If a president wants to create a decision-making system that encourages competing views over which he presides and decides, he can do that. Similarly, if he wants to stress the image and the fact of harmony or professionalism or division of labor, he can do that as well. If relations do not develop as the president had anticipated, the errant personalities should be asked to leave; if the president does not remove the odd man, he will pay dearly. It will appear that he did not know what he was doing in the first place, or worse, that he is not now in charge.

Jimmy Carter stressed that his top three national security positions would be filled by men who were compatible with him and with each other. Judging from the positions take by Vance, Brzezinski, and Brown before they entered his administration, Carter had every reason to believe that all of their views were quite similar, and the history of their personal relations with one another also boded well. It soon became apparent, however, that the three were to varying degrees to the right of Carter on most matters.

The gap between the president and his senior advisers was visible to all of those who attended cabinet-level meetings in the White House during the first year of the administration. For example, all of the president's cabinet-level appointments and almost all of the appointees on the second and third tiers opposed Carter's decision to withdraw U.S. troops from South Korea, favored increasing defense spending by 3 percent in real terms as opposed to Carter's desire to make cuts, were stunned by Carter's announcement at a press conference that he would seek demilitarization of the Indian Ocean, and worked toward getting the president to backpeddle on this by making demilitarization an ultimate goal and a freeze on Soviet and American forces the proximate goal. Even on the issue of human rights, Vance felt compelled to give a speech some months into the administration defining that policy in very practical and limited terms, as distinguished from the more absolutist rhetoric of the president.[15]

At first, the situation was manageable because Brzezinski indicated his views were still close to Carter's, particularly in the areas of arms sales, human rights, and nonproliferation. Vance was skeptical but accommodating, and Brown was to the right of Vance but still went along, having signalled early on that he would not engage in any intramural infighting. After several months went by, Brzezinski jumped well to the right of Brown, especially on matters with any relevance to U.S.-Soviet relations. While Vance did everything he could to downplay the rivalry, Brzezinski and some of Vance's aides began squaring off. President Carter proved unable either to make a choice between the two or to blend the two views into one coherent approach. From then on, there was tension between state and the NSC on most issues that transcended organizational questions.

By the end of his first year, suspicions began to spread that Carter was not in control, despite all of the denials about a Vance-Brzezinski clash. At that point, Carter should have decided whether to keep both men and emphasize his organizational setup—i.e., to have conflicting viewpoints—or to fire one or both of them. A year or so later, it would be impossible to do anything but let the situation ride. The president chose to do nothing, and his administration fell into obvious disarray.

A second point for presidents to keep in mind about personality and organization is that the one place in the organization apparatus where personality matters most is the national security adviser's position. An NSC adviser inclined toward mischief and personal aggrandizement with the president at the expense of the departments will not find much resistance. The staff responsibility to "cover" a memorandum from a cabinet officer in order to provide other points of view, missing facts, etc. is crushingly influential—even to an alert president. This power to prejudice the prince has always inhered in household staff, and it gives the person in the NSC job an unmatchable advantage. He can spread more gossip to the news media and Congress with impunity because most will presume that he is speaking for the president or simply repeating what the president said. Also, given the scale of transactions in the American government, the power of special assistant jobs has become so pivotal and tempting that one is tempted to elaborate on Lord Acton's famous axiom as follows: Propinquity to power corrupts, and the greater the propinquity, the greater the impulse to corruption.

A good case can be made that the NSC position is now more inherently powerful than that of the secretary of state. Perhaps the best way to make the case is to take the one example of a man who held both jobs and evaluate where he was more powerful. Henry Kissinger in the White House rarely lost a policy battle; Kissinger as secretary of state had to make a great many more compromises. For example, Defense Secretaries James Schlesinger and Donald Rumsfeld were politically savvy and had broad policy concerns. They resisted all of Kissinger's policies toward the Soviet Union, détente and SALT in particular, and often got their half of the loaf from President Ford. Treasury Secretary William Simon also did not fare badly against Kissinger in the range of energy and economic questions Kissinger delved into at the end of his tenure. The inroads on Kissinger's power, it should be underlined, were all accomplished without the collusion of Brent Scowcroft. Had Scowcroft been a less restrained NSC adviser and less sympathetic to Kissinger, his power at the State Department would have been even more circumscribed.

Putting aside major policy issues, the NSC job still has a decisive vote on day-to-day issues because of the bureaucratic constellation of interests. The defense department is not going to take orders from the state department and vice versa, and this is true for the other departments as well. Each has enough power, if only the power of being the one to implement the decision, to resist the other. But under most circumstances, each will accept the arbitration of the NSC staff because that staff is presumed to know what the president really wants. The decision-making system would break down totally if these second and third order decisions could not be made by the NSC system and had to be elevated to cabinet or presidential levels.

A third point for the president to keep in mind when fashioning his national security apparatus is that he will not be able to make an accurate forecast of how his three leading personalities will interact and how his NSC adviser will behave. Because of this, presidents should consider making some of the formal decisions about the organization of their administrations after several months in office, not before.

Deferring formal decisions on organization is intended to prevent the traditional pattern—informal systems rising to correct the miscalculations of the formal. What happens is that presidents will misjudge personalities but then be inclined to live with a dud or a mistake rather than incur the messiness of a dismissal. Presidents and cabinet officers are reluctant to fire someone who does not live up to expectations, which means everyone then develops an informal system to work around the dud. To be sure, decisions do get made and implemented through such informal systems, but without much reliability. Those who do not participate in the informal system usually will not accept the validity of decisions it produces. It is also easier for anyone who disagrees with the decision to oppose or ignore the implementation. The probability of mistakes is very high because there is no staff present to record the decision and reasons, and the participants invariably have conflicting accounts of what was decided. The acid test of the efficacy of any organization is whether the informal system closely approximates the formal one.

A president need not forbear entirely. Short of simply extending the system of his predecessor, he could make a few changes that still would leave some flexibility. He then could see how things were working and ask others to make evaluations as well. The most useful organizational reports in recent years have been by Philip Odeen and Richard Steadman, and they were both done in the second and third years of the Carter administration.[16] Both authors studied the existing system and personalities, saw what was falling through the cracks, and made their recommendations accordingly. The fact of the matter is that it is unusual to make wholesale changes in an organization immediately upon changing leadership. Like many other notably poor organizational practices, such practice occurs only in the federal government.

This discussion does not answer the question of where policymaking authority under the president should be lodged, because my point is that such an issue cannot be decided in the abstract, apart from the top three personalities under him. However, this analysis can serve to remind the president of a few elementary factors:

- While the secretary of state, as head of the senior agency with expertise would be the logical foreign policy leader, it is "natural" for reasons of propinquity and politics for the NSC adviser to play such a role as well.
- Since the NSC adviser has so many natural advantages, a president who truly wants his secretary of state to be in charge will have to be extremely careful in choosing his top three personalities and constructing a system to ensure that the secretary has control.
- If the president wants his secretary of state to be the clearly paramount figure under him, he also must go out of his way to help the secretary sustain such a role. If, however, the president is leaning toward his NSC adviser as his primary policy formulator, the president must go out of his way to put himself forward as the man-in-charge. If the NSC adviser has too public a role, it becomes increasingly difficult to conduct orderly business and to understand whose policy is authoritative. The president has to provide "cover" by being more active himself.
- Since there may be a fifty-fifty chance of misjudging the personalities and the mechanism to fit them, a president should consider forgoing the temptation of instant reorganization and wait several months to evaluate the personalities and abilities at work before calling forth a new system for making policy.

PROBLEMS OF ANTIPOLICY

There are two tendencies endemic to modern government that run strongly counter to effective policymaking: allowing policy considerations to be subsumed by operations and coordination, and making decisions by committee. Together, these tendencies conspire to make the system antipolicy, and they are reinforced by the general trend in Washington towards the fragmentation and decentralization of power.

If there are iron laws of American bureaucracy, they are first, that operations drive out policy; and second, that administering, regulating, and coordinating drives out operations. President Eisenhower organized his administration to make a sharp distinction between policy and operations. Overreacting to this, President Kennedy transformed the two into one. From then on, any impulse to entertain separate policy discussions generally has been subordinated to the requirements of solving the immediate problem; the assumption being that real policy is made by doing. That is true, but it is also true that this variety of policymaking tends to become more tactical and less oriented to accomplishing basic goals. Without policy, there is no structure and direction for action.

The history of the State Department's policy planning staff is a good example. By all accounts, the last time this staff really did policy planning was during the Truman administration. Thereafter, either the staff became operational or it was irrelevant. At least more recently, the fault has not been with the directors of this staff. Winston Lord for Kissinger and Anthony Lake for Vance were ideally suited by virtue of their personal relationships with their bosses and their own abilities and dispositions toward policymaking to fulfill the true function of their staffs. But precisely because they were so trusted and so able, their secretaries dragged them into operations and speech writing. Yet, even if they had been provided the leisure to think about policy, it is far from clear that their thoughts could have influenced anyone beyond the secretary of state. There is at present no mechanism to orchestrate policy. Trying to do more would summon all of the problems—and more—that the secretary himself encounters in trying to assert his policy views in the system.

This desire to participate, almost as an end in itself, is a less important but even more maddening antipolicy tendency in the bureaucracy. It is difficult to escape the feeling that most civil servants and political appointees are satisfied when their views have been solicited and when they have been invited to the meetings. This is an absolute fetish with the military services and the foreign service. If they are not consulted, the president can expect them to continue questioning his policies.

The committee system of making decisions that results from trying to include all parties produces antipolicy. At best, committees can produce either limited responses to specific situations or legal contracts whereby the parties each agree to do what they want. There are innumerable reasons for this but four are of particular importance. First, senior officials tend to shy away from policy discussions out of concern that their policy will not be accepted. If they lose a policy decision, all would be lost; if they lose a decision on a specific action, they can fight another day. Second, it is difficult to discuss policy because it is so abstract. Third, high-level decision makers often act as if policy discussions are a waste of time, that if they are to come together with their peers, it should be to agree on taking concrete actions. Fourth, talking policy often reveals more about their true beliefs than senior officials are inclined to reveal.

This disdain for and fear of policy virtually guarantees that the president and his principal advisers will be glorified action officers. It also ensures that governmental actions will be tactical rather than strategic and random rather than purposeful. There are no easy organizational solutions to this problem. About the only thing one can do is to hold interagency meetings expressly for the purpose of discussing policy. The Carter administration went almost entirely in the other direction. Virtually every high-level White House meeting consisted of making recommendations to the president on actions to be taken on four or five specific issues with three or four options for each issue, and the principals would vote for their preferred opinion.

Policymaking, as distinguished from coordinating action and the word games committees play, is an intensely personal process. It is essentially the outpouring and coherence that can derive from only one mind at a time. Others can help to do some contouring and fixing of mistakes and oversights. But if they do more than that, it is at the price of direction and coherence.

Organization is something very personal and very political. It is like a suit of clothes. Formal organization like formal wear does not allow for much choice, and it is only worn occasionally. Informal organization—how business actually is conducted—is like everyday clothes, rich in variety. And yet, the instinct to be a salesman of the formal suit is irrepressible. This is ironical but realistic. It is ironical because the organizational expert knows that the formal organization will not be used for most important matters. It is realistic because this expert knows one cannot hope to influence the informal workings.

NOTES

1. Such studies include: (1) The Hoover Commission report ("Foreign Affairs," A Report to the Congress by the Commission on Organization of the Executive Branch of the Government, February 1949); (2) the first Brookings Study (*The Administration of Foreign Affairs and Overseas Operations*, A Report Prepared for the Bureau of the Budget, Executive Office of the President, Brookings, 1951); (3) the Woodrow Wilson Foundation study (William Yandell Elliott et al., *United States Foreign Policy: Its Organization and Control*, Columbia University Press, 1952); (4) the second Brookings study (H. Field Haviland, Jr., et al., *The Formulation and Administration of United States Foreign Policy*, A Report for the Committee on Foreign Relations of the United States Senate, Brookings, 1960); (5) the Rockefeller proposal (presented in U.S. Senate, Committee on Government Operations, Subcommittee on National Policy Machinery [henceforth "Jackson Subcommittee"], *Organizing for National Security*, Vol. I [Hearings], pp. 942–1001); (6) The Jackson Subcommittee staff report ("Basic Issues," reprinted in *Administration of National Security*, Staff Reports, pp. 7–26); (7) the Herter Committee report (*Personnel for the New Diplomacy*, Report of the Committee on Foreign Affairs Personnel, Carnegie Endowment for International Peace, December 1962); (8) the Sapin study (Burton M. Sapin, *The Making of United States Foreign Policy*, Praeger [for The Brookings Institution], 1966); (9) the Heineman task force report (unpublished, submitted to President Johnson by the President's Task Force on Government Organization on October 1, 1967); (10) the American Foreign Service Association (AFSA) report (*Toward a Modern Diplomacy*, A Report to the American Foreign Service Association by its Committee on Career Principles, AFSA, 1968); and (11) the Institute for Defense Analyses (IDA) study (published as Keith C. Clark and Laurence J. Legere, *The President and the Management of National Security*, Praeger, 1969).
2. I. M. Destler, *Presidents, Bureaucrats, and Foreign Policy*, Princeton, New Jersey: Princeton University Press, 1972, 261.
3. Henry Kissinger, *The White House Years*, Boston: Little, Brown and Company, 1979, 30. It is true that as you read the rest of the Kissinger book, he does talk about troubles that develop between State and the NSC and it could be construed that he feels he lacked authority at the State Department. Kissinger's preference for State, however, may be colored by envisioning himself on the job.
4. Henry Kissinger, *Nuclear Weapons and Foreign Policy*, New York: Council on Foreign Relations and Harper Brothers, 1957, 403–436.

5. Kissinger, *The White House Years*, 48.

6. Ibid., 47.

7. Destler, op. cit.; Graham Allison and Peter Szanton, *Remaking Foreign Policy: The Organizational Connection*, New York: Basic Books, 1976.

8. Early NSC advisers: 1953–55, Robert Cutler; 1955–56, Dillon Anderson; 1956, William Jackson (Acting); 1957–58, Robert Cutler; 1958–61, Gordon Grey; 1961–66, McGeorge Bundy; 1966–69, Walt Rostow. From 1954 to 1961, General Andrew Goodpaster served as defense liaison to the NSC.

9. I. M. Destler, "A Job That Doesn't Work," *Foreign Policy*, 38 (Spring 1980), 80–88.

10. There were some stirrings about McGeorge Bundy in the Heineman Commission Report and, of course, some personal animosity towards Rostow because of Vietnam, but these criticisms fell well short of the Kissinger and Brzezinski phenomenon.

11. Perhaps Eisenhower played a stronger role in policymaking than has been thought in the past. For a persuasive argument see: Fred I. Greenstein, "Eisenhower as an Activist President: A Look at New Evidence," *Political Science Quarterly*, 94:4 (Winter 1979–80), 575–599.

12. Allison and Szanton, op. cit., 74.

13. Ibid., 123–124.

14. Allison and Szanton, op. cit., 78–80.

15. Address by Secretary of State Cyrus R. Vance, "Human Rights and Foreign Policy." Made at Law Day ceremonies at the University of Georgia School of Law, Athens, Georgia, April 30, 1977.

16. Report of a study requested by the president under the auspices of the President's Reorganization Project: *National Security Policy Integration*, September 1977. Report of a study requested by the president and conducted in the Department of Defense: *The National Military Command Structure*, July 1978.

19

STRATEGIC INTELLIGENCE AND INTERMESTIC POLITICS

HARRY HOWE RANSOM

A permanent, secret intelligence system within the American constitutional framework creates special policy dilemmas. The record of efforts to solve them offers insights into the interactions of foreign and domestic policy. What have been the major political influences shaping the policy choices between operational permissiveness and secrecy and accountability for the Central Intelligence Agency?

The United States is unique among the world's nations in that its secret intelligence apparatus has not been isolated from the public political process. Other nations barely acknowledge the existence of their intelligence agencies. Although the intelligence function is as old as international relations, the United States considered a central intelligence system a necessity only in wartime. It was not until 1947 that Congress created the CIA, thus setting up a permanent intelligence system.

Immediately after World War II, however, controversy had abounded regarding the purpose, functions, and organization of central intelligence. While much internal bureaucratic conflict occurred over the structure of the postwar national security system, little detailed Congressional debate was recorded on intelligence issues. Congress was assured at the outset that the CIA would have no domestic investigative role and understood that its principal mission, in serving the presidency, would be to coordinate information gathered primarily by the State Department and the armed services. Nothing was said publicly at the time about the CIA as an instrument for covert political intervention overseas.

This essay argues that America's relationship with the Soviet Union, and the impact of that relationship on domestic politics, are keys to an

Harry Howe Ransom, "Strategic Intelligence and Intermestic Politics." This chapter was written specially for this book. Harry Howe Ransom is Professor of Political Science at Vanderbilt University. He is author of *The Intelligence Establishment* and *Can American Democracy Survive Cold War?* as well as many other works. He was a Congressional Fellow of the American Political Science Association (1953–1954) and a fellow of the Woodrow Wilson International Center for Scholars (1975).

understanding of public policy regulating the intelligence agencies. More specifically, the state of relations with the Soviet Union determines the degree of accountability imposed upon intelligence operations. The greater the hostility between the U.S. and the U.S.S.R., and the stronger the consensus about threats to national security, the fewer the restrictions, audits, and controls that will be imposed upon the CIA. And when cooperation or détente with the U.S.S.R. is at a high level, the more likely that CIA operations will be circumscribed and the more demanding the oversight mechanisms. Thus the rules of the game for intelligence agencies are determined in the context of what may be called *intermestic politics*.

The terms *strategic intelligence* and *intermestic politics* need definition. Strategic intelligence has a specific meaning: it refers to evaluated foreign information useful for national foreign and defense policy decisions. In common usage, however, the term refers not only to its informing function but also to a variety of secret operations, including espionage, counterintelligence, and covert intervention overseas. The argument here is that each of these functions has been regulated in a fluctuating domestic and international political milieu that determines the degree of oversight and public accountability—hence the term *intermestic politics*. This term was coined by Bayless Manning with reference to foreign policy issues that he sees as "simultaneously, profoundly and inseparably both domestic and international" (Manning, 1977: 309). Domestic influences on foreign policy are most commonly assumed to be economic (although sometimes ethnic or ideological) and here intermestic influences are most visible. But there are also liberal, democratic domestic values which stress First Amendment rights and their status is also affected by international relations and events.

In original conception the CIA was to serve the presidency in a nonpartisan way by supplying coordinated foreign information. The slogan of the agency, initially, was "we supply the facts only, we do not recommend policy." But from its original clearinghouse assignment the CIA quickly came to have operational functions around the globe, including espionage, psychological warfare, paramilitary operations, and political intervention. In the process, the agency tended to lose its objectivity, raising problems of policy, organization, and oversight. Originally conceived to be above politics, the agency inevitably became enmeshed in intermestic politics.

The United States is the only great power that attempts to operate an intelligence system within a constitutional framework that separates executive and legislative authority into two distinct and often competing branches that share decision-making power. Separation of presidential-congressional powers is not the only complicating factor. The basic constitutional rights of free speech and press in a political culture suspicious of government secrecy complicate the management of secret intelligence services. An illustration of the democracy-intelligence secrecy dilemma is inherent in the remarks of William J. Casey to the 1981 Senate hearing on his confirmation as Director of Central Intelligence: "There is a point in intelligence operations at which rigid accountability, detailed accountability can impair performance" (U.S. Senate, *Hearing*, 1981: 43). Secret services inevitably must also sometimes deceive and undertake illegal operations. How to accommodate this reality to a constitutional government with a high expectation of public accountability becomes periodically a major political issue.

The following pages will analyze the historical evolution of the CIA in its intermestic context. Visible in this analysis will be patterns suggesting that intelligence issues—centering on questions of restrictions and accountability—were most importantly influenced by the state of United States relations with the Soviet Union. Periods of détente were accompanied by movements for intelligence "reform," limitations on secret activity, and demands for more accountability, while periods of superpower hostility coincided with intelligence agency secrecy, permissiveness, or calls for "unleashing" the CIA.

THE EARLY YEARS

The CIA and the Cold War were born in the same year. President Harry S. Truman told Congress in his 1947 message requesting aid for Greece and Turkey, both seen as threatened by Communism, that the United States must resist Communist expansion everywhere in the world. But even in an atmosphere of Cold War, the functions of the CIA were nonetheless circumscribed by the originating legislation. As suggested earlier, Congress understood that the CIA was to be primarily an information clearinghouse. No major operational functions were assigned and certainly no domestic spying or internal covert operations were envisioned. Some congressional concern for civil liberties was evident, but there was perhaps greater bureaucratic and congressional concern for protecting the jurisdictional turf of existing departments. Furthermore, although its legislative charter was written in ambiguous terms, the CIA was not seen initially to have covert operational functions overseas. The armed services, the State Department, and the Federal Bureau of Investigation had waged bitter internal struggles to maintain their domestic and foreign intelligence mandates.

The CIA's principal advantage from the start was as an arm of the presidency, answerable only to the National Security Council, over which the president presided. After 1947, relations between the United States and the Soviet Union became more and more hostile. Indeed, 1948 was the year of the "war scare," when some military advisers were openly suggesting the possibility of a war with the Soviet Union. In February 1948 the Communists had brutally seized control in Czechoslovakia; simultaneously the governments of France and Italy were threatened by Communist electoral gains; and in the United States the Army intelligence chief had received a cable from the commander in chief of the European Command, General Lucius Clay, suggesting that war with the Soviet Union might come at any time. Shortly thereafter, the CIA was secretly launched into a massive program of covert operations to stem the perceived Red tide. The National

Security Council approved NSC 10/2, a secret paper that dramatically increased the scope and range of covert actions aimed at the Soviet Union, including political, economic, and psychological warfare, and even paramilitary operations.

In this state of heightened hostility toward the Soviets, Congress in 1949 amended the National Security Act and granted the CIA an extraordinary degree of secrecy. The director was made responsible for protecting the sources and methods of the agency from disclosure, if need be even from Congress; he was exempt from requirements that he disclose, even to Congress, the size and budget of the agency; and he was authorized to spend money for secret operations on his own personnel voucher. A few members of Congress had protested the blank-check quality of these amendments but were only able to get assurances that all CIA operations would be overseas; fears of a domestic *Gestapo*, they were assured, were groundless, and restraints on CIA domestic operations remained unchanged in the statutory charter. The year 1949 being a time of great international tension, few questions were asked about accountability, but the degree of secrecy granted the agency at the time would make future Congressional oversight difficult.

The CIA had, in fact, been granted exemption from normal accountability in the year that most top officials were "studying" the possibility of war and had persuaded the public of a clear and present danger from communism. Within a few months the North Atlantic Treaty was signed, the Soviet Union exploded its first atomic bomb, and China came under communist control. Top security planners were feverishly at work on NSC-68, a scheme to remobilize American resources for aggressively fighting a cold, and perhaps a hot, war with the Soviet Union. The secret plan proposed a major espionage role for the CIA, psychological warfare, covert political action overseas, and paramilitary operations. At the same time, an intense anticommunism, verging on hysteria, gripped America. Congressional committees began to make daily headlines about subversion and espionage in America, from Hollywood to the Department of State.

Meanwhile, in the midst of this period of high political tension, the CIA received its initial NSC directive for foreign covert action. In the year and a half after the "war scare" in March 1948, the CIA was assigned its secret missions against the Soviet Union. Included, in the words of a major participant, were assignments:

> 1. To collect secret intelligence on the Soviet Union itself. . . . 2. To place American agents within the Soviet intelligence services. . . . 3. To carry out covert actions designed to weaken Soviet control over its own population and the peoples of Eastern Europe. . . . (Rositzke, 1977: 17)

Pressures increased in policy planning circles to mobilize American resources not only to "contain" the Soviet Union but to defeat it. The CIA set out to defeat the Communists in the Italian elections in 1948 and came away with a sense of success. In some of its other more difficult assignments, such as arming anti-communist guerrillas and carrying out sabotage operations behind the Iron Curtain, the going was rougher and the results often counter-productive. But all of this had a profound effect upon the CIA's future. The agency came to be dominated by the covert operators, and the intelligence function received second priority. The cost of this change was high.

For example, the North Korean attack on the South that began the Korean War in 1950 came as a surprise to the United States. American leaders had not been forewarned by the intelligence system; in fact, the net intelligence estimate at the time was that a war on the Korean peninsula was unlikely. As a result of the invasion, not only did President Truman decide to intervene with American troops, but America began to remobilize on a major scale. Resistance by Congress to the defense build-up implications of NSC-68 faded, and the CIA entered a period of enormous expansion, in personnel, in funds, and in missions.

The period, 1946–52, then, were the formative years of the CIA. Other than the strict prohibition against domestic spying, the agency operated with minimum executive controls and with little congressional oversight. Most striking was the growth in size of the agency. By 1953 the CIA had grown to six times its 1947 size. The deputy directorate for operations, at that time called "Plans," the division responsible for espionage and covert operations, also came to command the major share of the agency's budget, personnel and resources. Three-fourths of the agency's budget in 1952 was spent on espionage and covert action (U.S. Senate, *Final Report Book IV*, pp. 40–41). Almost two-thirds of CIA's employees by the end of 1952 could be accurately described as "secret agents." While part of agency activity was in pursuit of information, most was devoted to various forms of political intervention. The policy of the United States was worldwide containment of the Soviet Union; the CIA was on the front lines attempting to implement this policy. Few questions were asked by responsible political authority because a foreign policy consensus supporting containment had emerged.

THE DULLES ERA (1953–1961)

Hostility toward the Soviets continued throughout the directorship of Allen W. Dulles, who joined the agency in 1951 as chief of covert operations, was named director in 1953 by President Eisenhower, and served until 1961. The Dulles era may best be characterized by the phrase "trust in honorable men." Accountability procedures normal for most government functions were waived in the CIA's case.

During the Eisenhower years, the primary foreign policy objective was an aggressive containment of communism around the world. During the campaign of 1952, Republicans were highly critical of the Democratic administration's "passive" containment, and Eisenhower spoke of the need for a more aggressive foreign policy. He cited the Communist victory in China, Soviet control of Eastern Europe, and the stalemated Korean War as examples of U.S. timidity. Some of his associates, such as John Foster Dulles, named secretary of state following Eisenhower's victorious campaign, spoke of "rolling back" Communism, of the "liberation" of Eastern Europe, and of the need for programs not only to contain but to defeat the Communists. Containment was to be expanded from Central Europe to other parts of the globe, not only in the Middle East, Africa, and Southeast Asia, but East Asia and Latin America as well. The CIA was seen as the tool to maintain the status quo in many parts of the world threatened by revolution. The scope and scale of secret operations grew enormously during the Allen Dulles period and went forward secretly, with few external controls. When external controls, and limited accountability, began to be suggested in the mid-1950s, they were reactions to domestic political pressures and came when tensions with the Soviet Union were temporarily relaxed.

Throughout the 1950s the Central Intelligence Agency was, if not a "rogue elephant," at least a major instrument of foreign policy operating in semi-independence. Rather than being an adjunct of the State or Defense departments, the CIA, in the words of one of its most authoritative historians, "assumed the initiative in defining the ways covert operations could advance U.S. policy objectives and in determining what kinds of operations were suited to particular policy needs" (U.S. Senate, *Final Report Book IV*, p. 42). The CIA staged major covert operations in Iran and Guatemala in 1953 and 1954 in which it managed to remove, with surgical skill, two allegedly communist-leaning governments, one in Central America and the other in the Middle East. While details of these operations were not publicly disclosed at the time, they were later skillfully leaked to the media, leaving the impression that the CIA was a foreign policy instrument of cool, bloodless efficiency.

The effect was to strengthen even further the Clandestine Service (as the deputy directorate for operations came to be known) within the CIA. The information or intelligence function of the agency came to be neglected. More seriously, the absence of Congressional controls and monitoring procedures caused mistakes, bad political judgment, and invited dangers that covert operators detached from intelligence analysts and responsible elected officials could be self-defeating. An "anything goes" atmosphere pervaded the Clandestine Service.

The clandestine mentality led to excesses. A prime example is the agency's drug testing program, details of which did not become public knowledge until 1975, when it was disclosed that the CIA had tested a number of potentially dangerous drugs on unsuspecting individuals. Drugs were given to individuals without prior medical screening and without the participation of medical and scientific personnel. One person is known to have died as a result. The drug testing program is an example of a CIA operation that at the time was exempt from accountability and control procedures.

Most striking of all in this period, however, is the fact that until 1955 covert action projects went forward without any formal approval at the diplomatic or at the National Security Council level. When covert action was first authorized by the President in 1948, it was assumed that the State and Defense departments would provide policy guidance. As covert operations expanded in the 1950s, general guidance from political authorities outside the agency rather than any specific review of projects became the practice. Detailed accountability did not exist. In 1955 the National Security Council issued two policy directives that formalized control procedures for approving proposed covert actions. Even so, until 1959 approval procedures remained highly irregular. It was not until after the Bay of Pigs fiasco in 1961 that a vigorous, inter-agency formal review mechanism for covert operations was enacted. Congressional oversight was equally casual through most of the 1950s.

In March, 1953, Joseph Stalin died. Within a few months the posture of the Soviet Union was perceived to have changed. Within the next two years, the tone in the relations between the United States and U.S.S.R. became somewhat less hostile. Clearly, internal debate about U.S.-Soviet relations was occurring in both Washington and Moscow. Most important from the perspective of this essay was the fact that the Democrats recaptured the House and the Senate in the 1954 elections, and the new Democratic leadership urged Eisenhower to make efforts toward better relations with the Soviet Union. A Soviet-American summit meeting was proposed to discuss possible disarmament schemes and to attempt to resolve other major East-West conflicts. By the spring of 1955 a summit meeting became inevitable, although Eisenhower's principal advisers were wary.

In spite of a foreign policy consensus, and the appearance of smooth relations between the CIA and the congressional leadership, there were rumblings of discontent within the intelligence community about Allen Dulles' lack of administrative efficiency and among liberal Democrats about the "invisible government" aspects of the intelligence system. Domestic values were accorded a higher priority with changed perceptions of the external world. Some felt that accountability and control were underlying problems with inherent long-term dangers. A Commission on the Organization of the Executive Branch of Government, with Herbert Hoover as chairman, was organized in 1954, and as a part of its investigation, a small task force under General Mark Clark was assigned to study the intelligence system. The Clark task force was critical of the administration of the CIA, expressing concern about the absence of external controls and oversight. It recommended to the full Hoover commission the establishment of an oversight group composed of members of Congress and distinguished citizens. The commission rejected this idea, proposing instead a joint Congressional oversight committee and an independent group composed of private citizens to monitor intelligence operations for the president.

Senator Mike Mansfield introduced a resolution in January 1955 calling for a joint congressional oversight committee. The resolution was debated for over a year in Congress—it was the year of the "Spirit of Geneva," referring to Eisenhower's meeting with the Soviet leadership—and was backed by 35 co-sponsors in the Senate.

In response to the Mansfield proposal, the CIA mounted a powerful counter-attack on proposals to widen the circle of knowledge and control of secret operations. Dulles quietly lobbied the president as well as congressional leaders by suggesting the possibly damaging consequences of a Joint Congressional committee with full access to CIA secrets.

More significant was opposition by the "inner club" of the Senate, particularly senators like Richard Russell, Carl Hayden, and Leverett Saltonstall—who were already privy to secret CIA information. They were joined by Senator Alben Barkley, a former vice-president (1949–1953) and NSC member, and Senator Stuart Symington, former Air Force secretary, who strongly opposed the bill. In April, 1956, the measure was defeated by a vote of 59 to 27, with more than a dozen original co-sponsors abandoning the proposal. As the "Spirit of Geneva" faded and U.S.-Soviet relations veered again toward hostility, the desire for intelligence oversight reform dimmed in Congress. National security concerns returned to a dominating position; liberal domestic values were accorded lower priority.

Nonetheless, it was during the period 1956–57 that Congress regularized its intelligence oversight mechanisms. Formal oversight subcommittees of the Armed Services and the Appropriations committees were established in the Senate. The House Armed Services Committee also created an intelligence oversight subcommittee. In the Appropriations Committee, an informal group with oversight responsibilities was designated by Chairman Clarence Cannon, but its membership remained secret. Even with these arrangements, however, little permanent staff time was assigned to this oversight function. The committees met irregularly for some years afterwards. "Oversight windowdressing" might be an appropriate label to apply to these efforts, but they do illustrate the proposition that relations with the Soviet Union interacting with partisan domestic values had measurable impact upon intelligence policy, organization, and control.

THE KENNEDY-JOHNSON YEARS (1961–1969)

Secret intelligence operations under the Kennedy and Johnson administrations went forward in a period characterized by extreme hostility between the United States and the Soviet Union, at least at the outset. Consequently, it was not a period of agitation for substantial intelligence reform. During this perod, the intelligence system evolved into a massive bureaucracy, essentially unfettered by external monitoring, legislative oversight, or detailed accountability. One major exception to this generalization occurred after the failure of the Bay of Pigs invasion in 1961, for which the leadership of the CIA was held accountable. Within six months after the

Bay of Pigs, Allen Dulles and his principal deputies were gone from the agency.

But the Bay of Pigs did not lead to significant internal reorganization or to more effective forms of external oversight. While John F. Kennedy was disillusioned about the professionalism of the intelligence system as a result of the abortive Cuban expedition, he nonetheless saw the nation to be in danger of losing to Communism and Communist-backed movements in various parts of the world. The intelligence system in all of its components continued to be perceived as a vital instrument of American foreign policy, and secrecy and limited accountability were assumed to be required. As a senator, Kennedy had favored the creation of a congressional joint committee on intelligence. As president he opposed the idea. The construction of the Berlin wall, the Vienna summit meeting with Khrushchev, the continuing unrest in Laos, Vietnam, and the Congo, and the Cuban missile crisis of 1962, all combined to produce an atmosphere in which the intelligence apparatus remained virtually immune from questioning. This was so even though the Bay of Pigs, the Berlin wall, and the Cuban missile crisis had all revealed basic flaws in the intelligence system, both in its informational and operational features. But the Kennedy administration had reaffirmed the Truman Doctrine and expressed intentions of pushing forward with programs for military superiority, flexible response, and support of regimes fighting indigenous communist-supported revolutionary movements. Khrushchev's statements in support of wars of national liberation and Soviet efforts to put strategic missiles in Cuba left small constituencies for the relatively small group of intellectuals and liberal (or neoisolationist) members of Congress who remained concerned about the dangers of a freewheeling secret intelligence system.

When Kennedy was murdered in Dallas, one of Lyndon Johnson's first questions was whether it had been the work of the communists. As president, Johnson continued the basic Cold War assumptions about containment and the need for the United States to oppose communist-inspired revolution lest the "domino theory" become a reality. Consequently, little concern was apparent at the highest levels of the Johnson administration about problems of intelligence agency policy, organization, or controls. With a growing U.S. involvement in Southeast Asia, particularly after 1965, voices of concern about the "intelligence problem" were drowned out by a political consensus supporting a necessary, if limited, war in Southeast Asia.

But there were voices of protest. Throughout most of the Cold War years, some 10 percent of the House membership and perhaps 20 percent of the Senate held deep reservations about the intelligence system's freedom from accountability. During the 1960s there were many proposals for reform, usually taking the form of calls for more detailed congressional oversight. In 1963, Representative John Lindsay, a liberal Republican from New York, proposed a thorough investigation of the CIA. His effort failed. In the Senate an effort was made by Eugene McCarthy in 1966 to have the Foreign

Relations Committee conduct an investigation of CIA effects on foreign policy. Substantial debate was generated, but the Senate's "inner club" prevailed, McCarthy's proposal was defeated, and the Foreign Relations Committee remained excluded from a role in intelligence policy or oversight.

Such efforts at reform occurred roughly in the period between the limited test ban treaty with the Soviet Union (1963) and the so-called "Spirit of Glassboro" (1967) when President Johnson met with Soviet Premier Alexei Kosygin in New Jersey. This period also was marked by the beginning of the collapse of the Cold War consensus. Opposition to the Vietnam War started the evaporation of secrecy from a number of major and questionable CIA covert operations. And the number of proposals—and support for them—to make the CIA more accountable began to rise.

It was in the context of opposition to the war that *Ramparts* magazine disclosed in February 1967 the CIA's extensive program of secretly subsidizing scores of American private, voluntary organizations. Among them were student, religious, labor, journalistic, literary, academic research, and publishing organizations, and almost any group with overseas programs. The CIA's subsidies, which secretly supplied millions of dollars to these groups, were designed to counter Soviet efforts overseas. American private organizations by the score—often unknowingly to their rank and file members—had become tools of American foreign policy. The most widely publicized example of this program involved the National Student Association, a student-managed organization made up of some 300 member colleges in the United States. Between 1952 and 1967, NSA secretly received more than $3 million in CIA funds for international programs. Money was provided as an expedient so that the United States could be represented by college students at international youth conferences abroad, where the communist youth movements were strongly present.

The fact that the CIA had covertly invaded the American private sector pervasively for Cold War purposes produced a strong negative outcry. There was a storm of congressional, editorial, and public criticism. In response, President Johnson ordered an end to CIA financing of the NSA and appointed a three-man committee to review the secret subsidy program. Undersecretary of State Nicholas Katzenbach headed the committee which recommended that no federal agency provide secret financial assistance to any of the nation's educational or private voluntary organizations. The president accepted this recommendation, and the storm subsided. The important point is that all of this controversy boiled up in conjunction with growing opposition to the Vietnam War.

On January 30, 1968, North Vietnam and Vietcong military forces launched a massive offensive during the Vietnamese Tet holiday against major bases and urban centers in South Vietnam. This massive military offensive was ultimately a military defeat for the north, yet they won a psychological victory of sorts, for they were able to knock over the "essential domino"—American public opinion. The shock of the Tet offensive—during which the Vietcong penetrated the U.S. embassy compound—

coming after American leaders had said the war was going well, was the beginning of the end of the Cold War consensus. These events ended Lyndon Johnson's political career, and marked the beginning of the end of the Vietnam War for the United States. The objective of military victory in Vietnam was, in effect, renounced, and America entered the long negotiations that would end with complete American withdrawal and a North Vietnamese victory in 1975. In the process, liberal democratic values began to compete more vigorously with national security requirements.

THE END OF CIA IMMUNITY AND LEGITIMACY (1970–1974)

In his first major foreign policy statement, President Nixon said that the postwar era in international relations had ended. What did this mean? It meant the bipolar world, one dominated by the United States and the Soviet Union, had ended. It meant that China had become the number one foe of the Soviet Union. And it meant that the Soviets had achieved military power roughly equal to that of the United States. It also suggested that a spiraling arms race endangered both superpowers. In this context the "Nixon Doctrine" was proclaimed, suggesting vaguely a new foreign policy of negotiation, reduced American interventionism abroad, and greater burden-sharing by U.S. allies. Containment of the Soviet Union was not abandoned; it was expressed with less strident rhetoric and was eventually to be transformed into an even vaguer concept of détente.

One consequence of this altered perspective was that the CIA lost its immunity from unrestrained probing and criticism by the media and Congress. Disclosures about a variety of CIA covert operations confronted the agency with a legitimacy crisis. The crisis was heightened with the release of the *Pentagon Papers* in 1971. This document, among its other effects, engendered widespread distrust of the government's secret decision-making structure. Covert operations in Southeast Asia were seen by some as a major cause of America's entrapment in Vietnam. Nixon faced a Congress that was aggressively reasserting itself, first with the National Commitments Resolution in the Senate in 1969, which sought to limit presidential power, and followed by the repeal of the Gulf of Tonkin Resolution in 1970. The War Powers Act, passed over presidential veto in November 1973, was a major example of the congressional challenge to the "imperial" presidency.

President Nixon's trips to China and to the Soviet Union in 1972, and the first round of the SALT agreements that year, set the stage for major shifts in the public view of the Soviet threat. Relations between the United States and the U.S.S.R. were moving sharply in the direction of greater cooperation on a variety of issues throughout the early 1970s. Covert actions overseas had begun to diminish in the late 1960s, clearly a by-product of the atmosphere of détente. This was also in keeping with an overall retrenchment in American foreign policy that stemmed from a disillusionment over the Vietnam War. Despite some setbacks, it can now be seen that the climate was right at this time for challenging presidential power, of which covert operations shrouded in secrecy were major instruments.

Two major events of CIA covert activity, when brought to public light, contributed to the ending of CIA anonymity and its privileged secrecy. One was the disclosure that the CIA had played a role in attempts to distort the electoral process in Chile in the early 1960s, ending with crude attempts to undo the election of the socialist Salvador Allende as president in 1970 and, perhaps, with complicity in his ultimate overthrow and death three years later. The other was the disclosure that the CIA had been engaged in domestic spying on anti-Vietnam War dissidents in violation of its legislative charter. If U.S. relations with the Soviet Union had been at a high level of hostility in the early 1970s, or had the United States been engaged in a war with more substantial popular support, either of these covert activities would not have been disclosed in such detail, or, had they been, there would have been greater congressional and public tolerance of them.

Disclosures of CIA intervention in Chile received widespread, bipartisan condemnation, and the CIA's engagement in domestic spying and its indirect complicity with some aspects of the Watergate scandal were judged by many to be grave mistakes. One should hasten to add that these uses and abuses of the CIA were at presidential command; they did not originate within the CIA. The vulnerability of the CIA in the face of these disclosures was a reflection of a redefinition of foreign policy, the breakdown of consensus, but more important, the evaporation of some of the basic assumptions about the Cold War. In the five-year period between 1973 and 1978, détente was at its height, with American leaders and leaders of the Soviet Union and China engaged in a wide-ranging redefinition of relations. Summit meetings in Washington, Moscow, and Peking, international agreements at Vladovostok and Helsinki, trade agreements, cultural exchanges, and a panoply of communications characterized this period. But it was also characterized by deep suspicions within the United States about the activities of the CIA and about the adequacy of arrangements for oversight, accountability, and evaluation of performance of secret operations. The ground was fertile for major intelligence reform.

THE REFORM ERA (1975–1980)

The era of intelligence agency reform began in 1974, when Congress, reacting to disclosures about U.S. intervention in Chile and to revelations about a secret war in Laos, circumscribed CIA foreign operations by imposing statutory restrictions. These came in the form of an amendment to the Foreign Assistance Act of 1974 (Section 622, 75 Stat. 424) known as the Hughes-Ryan Amendment. Congress stipulated that in the future the CIA was to be used overseas for intelligence collection only. Covert actions were to be limited to those cases in which the president certified to Congress that vital national interests were involved and reported details of the operations in a timely fashion to appropriate Congressional committees. This requirement would later come to mean that covert actions were to be reported to eight committees, including House and Senate committees on foreign affairs, armed services, appropriations, and intelligence. The Hughes-Ryan Amendment constituted the first serious Congressional oversight of covert operations.

Meanwhile other groups began to probe the CIA. A Commission on the Organization of the Government for the Conduct of Foreign Policy, known as the Murphy Commission, sponsored detailed studies and concluded that "firmer direction and oversight of the intelligence community are essential" (*Final Report,* 1975). Disclosures of domestic spying by the CIA prompted President Ford to appoint a commission under Vice President Rockefeller. Former Governor Ronald Reagan of California and other well-known leaders were members. Their report concluded that CIA had violated its charter in some of its domestic activities and recommended new congressional and executive oversight mechanisms. Major organizational reforms were called for, including a joint congressional oversight committee (*Report to the President,* June 6, 1975).

But the focal point of attention in 1975 and 1976 were the major investigations undertaken by select committees in the House and Senate. The Senate committee, under Frank Church, held many hearings and issued a great number of reports that suggested scores of reforms. The major emphasis was on the need to prevent future abuses and to reform and reorganize the intelligence system. More effective congressional oversight and a sharpened internal accountability were especially recommended. The report's most important suggestion was for a new statutory intelligence charter specifying the roles and restrictions for all of the national intelligence agencies.

The House investigation, under Otis Pike, was a stormy affair, bringing the committee into confrontation with President Ford, Secretary of State Kissinger, and the CIA. But the House committee, like its Senate counterpart, created a substantial record. It became so embroiled in controversy that its final report was suppressed by the full House; nonetheless its contents leaked to the press, and its recommendations were published. Like the Senate, the House committee called for major reforms, including a new legislative charter for the intelligence agencies and the creation of a permanent House select committee for intelligence oversight. These recommendations reflected the domestic political reaction to new interpretations of international conditions. With foreign threats seen to be somewhat diminished, liberal domestic values were gaining ground on perceived security needs.

REFORMS UNDER FORD AND CARTER (1975–1980)

CIA reform was a major plank in Jimmy Carter's program when campaigning for the presidency in 1975–76. His campaign rhetoric frequently mentioned "CIA abuses," which he promised to curb as president. In campaign speeches he frequently referred to "Watergate, Vietnam, CIA." His choice for Vice-President, Senator Walter F. Mondale, had been a leading liberal member of Frank Church's select intelligence committee. Together they promised the American people to work for an intelligence community that would be more effective in providing accurate information and in being more accountable. These objectives were to be achieved by executive orders and support for a revised legislative charter in which Congress would spell out what the intelligence agencies were supposed to do and not do. Congress would have full access to information about secret operations as well as control over all intelligence legislation and appropriations.

President Ford, responding to major criticisms that had emerged from the various Congressional investigations and special studies, had tried to neutralize intelligence as a partisan issue by an executive order, promulgated on February 18, 1976 (Executive Order No. 11905). Reforms in Ford's order dealt mainly with internal organization, particularly the authority of the director of central intelligence, which was greatly strengthened. Accountability was strengthened and the president had to approve major future covert operations. "Plausible deniability," in which former presidents could disclaim knowledge of covert operations that were exposed, was now ruled out. Many critics felt that Ford's reforms did not adequately circumscribe intelligence agency actions. Standards for accountability and responsibility and for limits on covert operators were still thought to be too loose.

By the end of 1975 the CIA had become a political football, but the pendulum began to swing in the opposite direction. Two days before Christmas, Richard Welch, the CIA station chief in Athens, Greece, was murdered by unknown assailants after he had been mentioned as a CIA operative in an Athens newspaper. Earlier, Philip Agee, an ex-CIA officer, published a book, *Inside the Company: CIA Diary* (1975), one feature of which was to expose a substantial number of individuals who were secret CIA agents. This began an epidemic of disclosing the names of many CIA agents in sensitive posts overseas. The effect was to strengthen counter-reform activity.

President Ford dismissed William Colby as CIA director in late 1975, implying that he thought Colby had been too cooperative with the media and with congressional investigators. Colby was replaced in January 1976, by George Bush, a former congressman and chairman of the Republican National Committee and a man with presidential ambitions. Bush's main assignments were to improve the morale of CIA personnel, improve the agency's public image, and strengthen CIA support in Congress. Apparently it was thought that an effective politician was needed to "turn around" the CIA issue, to limit the damage that was assumed would result from some reforms supported in Congress, and to take advantage of the growing feeling that perhaps the CIA had been subjected to too much exposure and was endangered by some reform proposals and the antics of disaffected CIA personnel.

Given the context—national and international—perhaps it was inevitable that the CIA had become more and more politicized. From its origins after World War II the CIA, of course, had never been detached from the intermestic political process. What had changed after the evaporation of the Cold War consensus beginning in 1968 was that intelligence politics had become publicly visible.

EFFORTS AT CHARTER REFORM

The primary intelligence objective of the Carter administration was to guide Congress in the formulation of an omnibus charter for all of the major intelligence organizations, particularly the CIA and FBI. Such a charter would codify existing statutes and executive orders, rationalize the organization of the intelligence system, and, most important, place limits on the permissible behavior of secret agencies and establish accountability.

Visible politicization of intelligence, however, was first evidenced in the Carter administration when the president decided to appoint a new director of central intelligence. It had been previous practice that the CIA head would *not* change with each new administration. In all earlier changes of administration, the incumbent CIA chief had continued in office, and no fixed term had existed for the office. President Carter nominated Theodore Sorenson, who had been one of President Kennedy's principal White House aides and was later active in New York politics. Powerful forces in the Senate, aided by elements of the intelligence establishment, opposed the nomination. It was eventually withdrawn and the president turned to a more acceptable nominee, Admiral Stansfield Turner. For the first time a president had been denied his initial choice for CIA director.

In addition to working closely with the Senate Intelligence Committee on a new intelligence charter, the president's staff drew up an executive order on intelligence. Issued on January 24, 1978, the president's order (Executive Order No. 12036) reflected many of the recommendations of the Church Committee. Eight of its twenty-six pages dealt with prohibited activities. Accountability was sharpened and detailed provisions for presidential and congressional oversight were prescribed. While the order strengthened control and oversight mechanisms, ultimate legitimacy was to come from a carefully drawn congressional charter.

But public and congressional opinion about the intelligence agencies was soon to be affected by a growing consensus that previous projections concerning the growth of Soviet military power had been seriously underestimated. Soviet military power, particularly in long-range missiles and bombers, suddenly appeared to be greater than had been anticipated. Furthermore, developments in certain volatile areas of the world—particularly Angola, South Yemen, and Ethiopia—conveyed a picture of a Soviet Union on the move, aided by Cuban soldiers, against an increasingly ineffective United States. The fall of the Shah in Iran and the subsequent hostage crisis, which found the United States both misinformed and powerless, capped by the Soviet invasion of Afghanistan, created an entirely new atmosphere that demonstrated once again the powerful influence of international events on domestic values.

By the late 1970s it had become clear that intelligence reformers were on the defensive. The intelligence establishment had managed to manipulate the many interests in a pluralistic decision-making system to foil any major attempts at radical reform. It now seemed likely that the concerns of security rather than of individual liberty would take precedence. Fewer voices were heard expressing support for reform of the CIA while more called for beefing up both intelligence and covert action capabilities. Relations with the Soviet Union turned sour and a spirit of permissiveness returned to the intelligence debate.

Despite this changing atmosphere, an omnibus intelligence charter in the form of a 263-page bill was introduced in the Senate with bipartisan support in early 1978. The bill was the result of several years of executive-legislative negotiations and represented an attempt to deal with all the major problems of the various intelligence agencies. By 1978, however, times had changed, and the apparent consensus favoring a reform charter had faded. The bill died in the 95th Congress. A less complex bill was introduced in the next Congress, but this more modest effort at intelligence charter reform also failed.

Soon it was clear that while charter reform maintained substantial support among the leadership of the House and Senate intelligence committees, the president and the intelligence community were no longer behind these reforms. As one astute senator quipped: "Carter has now discovered that it is *his* CIA!" And while Stansfield Turner continued to express support for a wide-ranging intelligence charter, he was adamant—presumably with administration support—on a number of points: he opposed prior notification of Congress regarding covert operations, objected to prohibited use of the media, academics, and the clergy as "cover," stressed the need for stiff sanctions on those disclosing the names of agents, and favored restrictive amendments to the Freedom of Information Act. On the international scene, relations with the Soviet Union had turned decidedly hostile, and prospects for ratification of the SALT II treaty were rapidly fading. In this atmosphere, calls for restrictions on intelligence agencies began to lose political popularity. A striking harbinger of the new mood could be seen in President Carter's 1980 State of the Union address. Remember that Carter had campaigned for the presidency in 1976 promising to curb CIA abuses. In January 1980 he was still calling for "quick passage" of a new charter to define legal authority and accountability for the intelligence agencies and to guarantee that "abuses do not recur." But he added, "we must tighten our controls on sensitive government information and we need to remove unwarranted restraints on America's ability to collect intelligence."

Election year politics in 1980 soon rapidly overtook the intelligence reform movement. The Senate committee worked diligently, and its staff remained committed to reform, but after numerous revisions and shortening of the bill, and after many sessions of open and closed testimony, it became clear that no version of the bill was acceptable to the major interested parties. As is often the case, forces supporting the status quo gained the stronger position in the face of rumblings of a new Cold War with the Soviet Union. But Congress was not going to drop the matter without asserting its own prerogatives. A consensus was strong for a higher and more systematic degree of congressional oversight. A sufficiently bitter aftertaste of Watergate and associated CIA scandals persuaded a majority of the members that it was good politics as well as good policy to assert a congressional claim for a role in intelligence decision making.

And so the Senate Intelligence Committee dropped all efforts at charter reform in 1980 and focused on the question of oversight. This took the form, ultimately, of repeal of the Hughes-Ryan amendment, limiting the reporting of the intelligence agencies to two instead of eight congressional committees, expanding the oversight coverage to other intelligence agencies, including the CIA, and giving the House and Senate intelligence committees access to all intelligence information, including the right to be notified in advance (except in special situations) of covert operations. If the president should decide to limit prior notice of a covert action because of "extraordinary circumstances affecting vital interests of the United States," then he must at least inform the ranking members of the House and Senate intelligence committees, the speaker and the minority leaders of the House, and the majority and minority leaders in the Senate. At long last, Congress was by statute made an informational if not decision-making partner with the executive on covert action.

On the partisan political front the Republican National Committee, in the late summer of 1979, issued a twelve-page intelligence broadside, condemning the Democratic administration for its intelligence policy, blaming Democrats for weakening and politicizing the intelligence system, and charging that the Democratic Congress had fostered debilitating intelligence policies in the name of reform. The Republican position advocated return to the National Security Act of 1947, with its absence of a clear delineation of what the CIA was to do or not do. Better to amend the original act than to adopt a grandiose charter filled with do's and don'ts. At any rate the Republicans had determined that intelligence was to be a major campaign issue. The Democratic party platform in 1980 avoided the issue. In a general plank on defense it merely stated "we will act to further improve intelligence gathering and analysis."

The Republican platform for 1980 had a detailed intelligence plank. It decried the weakening of the intelligence system under Carter, cited the existence of a "strong national consensus" to strengthen it, and set forth a number of specific recommendations that carried the flavor of "unleashing" the CIA by repealing some of the restrictions the Democrats had placed on secret operations. In fact, little choice on intelligence policy was offered by the two major parties in the 1980 campaign. The third-party candidate, John Anderson, however, was the intelligence-reform candidate. The Anderson approach to intelligence policy was clearly the one that would restrict secret intelligence. He strongly supported congressional oversight and advocated prior notification of Congress on covert operations. Anderson also wanted to prohibit the covert use of journalists, academics, and clergy, and suggested that punishing journalists who had never been intelligence employees would violate the First Amendment.

During Reagan's first year as president, none of his campaign promises on intelligence that required legislation was fulfilled. The administration pressed for amendments to the Freedom of Information Act, legislation to protect the identities of secret agents, and a roughly 15 percent increase in intelligence budgetary resources. But Congress, with the exception of increased budgets, had not resolved these issues by the end of Reagan's first year.[1] The administration had returned to essentially a Cold War stance with regard to relations with the U.S.S.R. The imposition of martial law in Poland as well as the earlier events in Afghanistan were seen as proof of Soviet imperialism. Other events in Reagan's first year, including much talk of growing Soviet military power and the menace of the Soviet secret service (KGB) within the United States, created an atmosphere in which secret intelligence agencies were permitted to operate in a much wider circle of permissibility.

That this would be the tenor of the Reagan administration was first evidenced by the nomination of William J. Casey to be director of central intelligence. Casey had been Reagan's political campaign manager, had served with high rank in the Office of Strategic Services (OSS) in World War II, and had pursued a varied and controversial business and government career. Within a few months, the CIA was again embroiled in controversy stemming not only from Casey's freewheeling style but also from the appointment of Max Hugel to head the CIA's covert operations branch. Allegations of irregular business dealing led to Hugel's quick resignation, and for many months Casey's own business background was under detailed Senate scrutiny. Casey was finally cleared by a Senate committee, which issued an unenthusiastic report that he was "not unfit" to continue in office. Thus the first year of the Reagan administration had produced anything but stability or a favorable new image for the agency.

Meanwhile, Reagan's intelligence advisers spent much of the first year drafting an executive order delineating organization, roles, functions, and limits for the intelligence system. Several drafts were circulated during this period, the initial versions of which removed many of the restraints on CIA actions that had been imposed earlier by Presidents Ford and Carter. Although earlier drafts of the proposed new executive order were never released, leaks indicated that they proposed to authorize the use of "intrusive techniques" including searches, physical surveillance, and infiltration of domestic organizations. In essence, security was given higher priority in some cases than civil liberties. The Reagan administration approach seemed to be driven by 1950s' Cold War assumptions and by a concern to control terrorist activities and the international flow of narcotics as well as espionage efforts within the United States by foreign intelligence services.[2]

It was not until December 4, 1981, that President Reagan's intelligence executive order was released in its final form (Executive Order No. 12333). The major change from earlier executive orders by Presidents Ford and Carter was that it broadened the authority of intelligence agencies to collect information from Americans at home and abroad. Liberals and civil libertarians were disturbed by the order but many acknowledged that it was not as bad as expected. Conservatives hailed the new order, but some thought that it did not go far enough in "unleashing" the CIA. President Reagan candidly admitted that the new order was "consistent with my promise in the [political] campaign to revitalize our nation's intelligence system" ("Text of Reagan Statement on Order," *The New York Times*, December 5, 1981, p. 11).

In sum, international tensions between the United States and the U.S.S.R. in 1981 produced a political climate within the United States more tolerant of the intelligence agencies and of the national defense establishment in general. What had been gained by the "other side" in this debate (those wishing to strictly limit secret intelligence operations) was a redressing of the executive-legislative imbalance. What had been gained in the five years of effort at reform was primarily a legal and political expectation that members of the legislative branch would have *some* say in formulating rules of the game in intelligence. The legislature, through a relatively small number of bipartisan watchdogs, managed to force a right-wing administration on to a middle ground in intelligence policy. Congress exerted its classic function of setting limits on the executive. What were seen by reformers in 1975–76 as unacceptable "abuses" were, however, now authorized by Reagan's executive order: CIA investigations and covert operations within the United States, surveillance of Americans abroad, the opening of mail in the United States, and CIA cooperation with local law enforcement agencies. The executive order did, however, prohibit even worse abuses: the unlicensed infiltration of private American organizations, the inherent authority of the president to order wiretaps, the unlimited authority to investigate "leaks," and the waiving of the responsibility of intelligence agency heads to report possible Federal crimes by their employees.

Thus, reviewing the evolution of policy regarding the CIA since 1947, we find the following highlights:

1947: The onset of the Cold War; the CIA is created by Congress.

1949: U.S. relations with the U.S.S.R. worsen; Congress grants the CIA authority to operate with increased secrecy.

1955: Temporary easing of U.S. relations with the U.S.S.R.; tighter executive accountability instituted for CIA covert actions and serious efforts (ultimately unsuccessful) for more effective Congressional oversight of the CIA.

1963–66: Limited test ban treaty with the U.S.S.R.; "Spirit of Glassboro"; major Congressional efforts to strengthen CIA oversight procedures.

1966–68: Rise of Vietnam War protests; media disclosures of secret subsidies to private U.S. organizations; criticism of CIA secret subsidies and their abolition by president.

1970–75: Era of détente; CIA secrecy damaged and legitimacy questioned after disclosure of its intervention in Chile and its spying on Americans; major reforms in process.

1976–80: Gradual increase in U.S.-U.S.S.R. hostility, capped by Soviet invasion of Afghanistan; declaration of "Carter Doctrine" and failure of major CIA reform efforts.

1980–82: Intensification of Cold War; Reagan issues executive order "unleashing" the CIA.

It seems likely that if the United States in the years ahead should return to a wide-ranging policy of détente with the Soviet Union, should Cold War policies be replaced with those of cooperation, and should tangible arms control or disarmament agreements result, support will grow in Congress for tighter restrictions on intelligence agencies. The day might come when the superpowers will enter into intelligence sharing agreements and a mutual, if partial disbanding, of their vast intelligence apparatuses. Alternatively, should we move closer to the brink of war, one could expect a further "unleashing" of the secret intelligence arms of government—a return to the concept of "the president knows best" or "trust in honorable men." Intelligence agencies may represent the most delicate of all areas of public policy, an area where liberty and authority must always be balanced. That balancing has occurred and probably will continue to occur in the context of shifting priorities. At some times policies will be influenced by perceptions of foreign threats to national security. At other times of lessened international tensions, liberal democratic values will prevail. Day in and day out this delicate balancing act will reflect intermestic politics.

NOTES

1. On June 23, 1982, the President signed a bill making it a crime to disclose the name of a secret government intelligence agent in some circumstances, even if the information is obtained from public records.

2. In April, 1982, Admiral Bobby R. Inman resigned as Deputy Director of Central Intelligence in apparent disagreement with the CIA's return to some of its earlier Cold War tactics, including some forms of domestic surveillance.

REFERENCES

Agee, Philip. (1975) *Inside the Company: CIA Diary*. London: Stonehill.

Commission on CIA Activities Within the United States. (1975) Nelson A. Rockefeller, chairman. *Report to the President*. Washington, D.C.: Government Printing Office. June 6.

Commission on the Organization of the Government for the Conduct of Foreign Policy. (1975) Robert D. Murphy, chairman. *Final Report*. Washington, D.C.: Government Printing Office. June 28.

Manning, Bayless. (1977) "The Congress, the Executive and Intermestic Affairs: Three Proposals," *Foreign Affairs*, 55 (January) 306–324.

Reagan, Ronald. (1981) "Text of Reagan Statement on Order," *The New York Times*, December 5, p.11.

Rositzke, Harry. (1977) *The CIA's Secret Operations*. New York: Reader's Digest Press.

U.S. Senate, Select Committee on Intelligence. (1976) *Final Report Book IV*, "History of the Central Intelligence Agency," by Anne Karalekas. Senate Report No. 94-755. 94th Congress, 2nd Session. Washington, D.C.: Government Printing Office. 1–102.

U.S. Senate, Select Committee on Intelligence. (1981) *Hearing*, "Nomination of William J. Casey." 97th Congress, 1st Session. Washington, D.C.: Government Printing Office, January 13.

20

A RESURGENT CONGRESS AND THE IMPERIAL PRESIDENCY

THOMAS E. CRONIN

Back in the early 1970s the "imperial presidency" meant many things to many people. But it especially suggested the abuse and misuse of presidential powers. By 1973 it became an accepted term to describe presidential deceptions, lying, and transgressions against cherished notions of separation of powers. A deep-seated skepticism set in as an increasing number of Americans lost confidence in President Nixon.

As a general proposition, citizen trust in the president had been high during and after the New Deal. Historians, political scientists, and journalists had generally held that a strong presidency was a necessity.[1] Indeed, many observers of American politics added that the United States's leaders needed a free hand. Too many checks and balances would paralyze presidents. In a way, they were saying that the absence of power can also corrupt.

But then came Watergate. It was a subversion and corruption of the political process. Nixon did not invent the tactics so much as extend and refine them. For he inherited most of the short cuts, the growing reliance on secrecy and deceit, from several of his predecessors. But unlike them, he was caught. In the wake of Watergate we witnessed the disappearance of the easy optimism that once characterized popular attitudes toward presidents.

During the early and mid-1970s, the American public's attitudes toward the government took on a deep cynicism. This loss of faith was doubtless caused by a variety of events, among which were political assassinations, civil disorders, rising crime rates, racial strife, recession, soaring inflation, and high unemployment—and especially the deep divisions in the country over U.S. involvement in the Vietnam War and over Watergate.

Reaction to Watergate and the Vietnam War took at least two forms.

Revised and adapted from Thomas E. Cronin, "A Resurgent Congress and the Imperial Presidency," *Political Science Quarterly*, 95 (Summer 1980), 209–237. Copyright Thomas E. Cronin. Thomas E. Cronin is professor of political science at Colorado College. He is the author or co-author of several books on American government and the American presidency, the most recent of which is *Rethinking the Presidency*. He is a former White House Fellow and White House aide.

Critics claimed irrefutable evidence that the presidency was isolated, autocratic, and imperial. They charged too that the deceptions during Vietnam and the corruptions of Watergate occurred because our checks and balances were inadequate and that too much power had been given to the presidency.

Defenders of the presidency argued that Vietnam and Watergate exemplified not so much the *excess* of power as the *abuse* of power. Moreover, supporters of the American system of dispersed powers saw at least some evidence that the system was working—that is, they felt the courts, the press, and even Congress did assert themselves when put to a critical test.

The Watergate disclosures and the first forced resignation of a president in U.S. history aroused public concern about the role of Congress. Certainly in the mid-1970s the public wanted Congress to become a more coequal branch of government, more assertive and alert, more jealous of its own powers.

The change in public attitudes is well documented by polls taken before and after Vietnam and Watergate. In 1959, social scientists at the University of Michigan asked: "Some people say the President is in the best position to see what the country needs. Other people think the President may have good ideas about what the country needs, but it is up to the Congress to decide what ought to be done. How do you feel about this?" Sixty-one percent chose the president and 17 percent chose Congress (the remainder said about equal or were undecided).[2] In 1977 the *New York Times* asked virtually the same question: "In general, who do you think *should* have the most to say in the way our government is run, the Congress or the President?" Fifty-eight percent chose Congress and only 26 percent chose the president (the remainder said about equal or were undecided).[3]

In the late 1970s, the general sentiment had shifted back in the direction of the presidency, but the public still plainly wanted the Congress to play a significant role in overall policymaking. By 1980, the American public wanted both Congress to play a more significant role *and* a stronger, more effective problem-solving presidency. And Reagan was elected and Carter rejected in part because the shift back in favor of a more vigorous president had grown even greater.

What form did the congressional reassertion of the 1970s take? Did Congress effectively address the charges made against the "imperial presidency"? Has the new array of checks and balances crippled the presidency and undermined its potential for creative leadership?

THE IMPERIAL PRESIDENCY

In his provocative book *The Imperial Presidency,* historian Arthur M. Schlesinger, Jr., contends that presidential power became so expanded and abused by 1972 that it threatened our constitutional system. This imperial presidency, he said, was created primarily as a result of America's wars, particularly Vietnam.[4] Schlesinger explores two critical instruments that gave rise to the abuse of power by presidents: the war power and secrecy. In discussing the evolution of the war power, he points out the troubling constitutional ambiguity in the president's power as commander in chief: it is an undefined *office*, not a *function*—the only constitutional office a president is given. Schlesinger makes what he believes to be a critical distinction between the *abuse* and the *usurpation* of power. Abraham Lincoln, Franklin Delano Roosevelt, and Harry Truman temporarily *usurped* power in wartime, knowing they would be held accountable after the wartime emergency ended. Lyndon Johnson and Richard Nixon, however, *abused* power, even in peacetime, claiming a near absolute power to be the permanent prerogative of the presidency.

Schlesinger's second theme is the evolution of secrecy as a weapon to protect and preserve the president's national security power. He notes that until President Eisenhower, the presumption was that Congress would get the information it sought from the executive branch and that instances of secrecy were to be rare exceptions.

Schlesinger says that the notion of a bipartisan foreign policy was a bad one. It had the effect, the longer it ran, of stifling debate. "And it gave the Presidency a powerful new peacetime weapon by refurbishing the wartime theory of 'national security' as the end to which other values could be properly sacrificed in times of crisis."[5]

Schlesinger devotes much of his attention to the Nixon presidency, arguing that under Nixon the office became not only fully imperial, but also revolutionary. That is, Nixon in effect tried to carry out a revolution against the separation of powers and the American Constitution. For instance, in authorizing the "plumbers" group, Nixon became the first president in our history to establish an extralegal investigative force, subsidized by the taxpayers but unknown to Congress and accountable to no one but himself. Other misuses of intelligence agencies and authorized breaking and entering meant that Nixon became the only American president in peacetime who was publicly known to have supervised blatantly lawless actions. Moreover, the White House ignored, lied to, and spied on the Congress.

Schlesinger's book is a useful point of departure for a review of the general charges of a too powerful presidency. Over the years, it had become obvious that the presidency needed the power to respond to sudden attacks and to protect the rights and property of American citizens. But just how much power did a president have to conduct undeclared war?

The Department of State in a 1966 legal memorandum summed up some of this enlarged mandate this way:

> In the twentieth century the world has grown much smaller. An attack on a country far from its shores can impinge directly on the nation's security. . . . The Constitution leaves to the President the judgment to

determine whether the circumstances of a particular armed attack are so urgent and the potential consequences so threatening to the security of the U.S. that he should act without formally consulting the Congress.[6]

Legal advisers to Presidents Johnson and Nixon insisted that while the framers of the Constitution rejected the traditional power of kings to commit unwilling nations to war, they recognized the need for quick executive response to rapidly developing international situations. This apparently encouraged Johnson and Nixon to become exceedingly inventive in circumventing the congressional war-making power.

Congress became especially upset at President Johnson because in 1964 he succeeded in getting the Gulf of Tonkin Resolution passed on information that was later proved to be highly misleading. (Congress in 1971 repealed that resolution.) Later, a secret air war in Cambodia was waged in 1969 and 1970 with no formal congressional authorization or knowledge. Also, the U.S. military operated in Laos without formally notifying the Congress.

The framers of the Constitution, in giving to Congress, and not to the president, the power to declare war, intended to prevent just such occurrences as these. They sought to create a permanent institutional safeguard against unilateral presidential war-making. What happened in Indochina was the result, many members of Congress believed, of a disregard by the White House of the Constitution. But many members of Congress agreed too that presidential excess in these matters came about because Congress either agreed with presidential policies or silently did nothing to stop them.

Since the Great Depression in the early 1930s, Congress has passed about 500 federal statutes that give a president extraordinary powers. Once a state of emergency is declared, for example, a president may seize property, organize and control the means of production, seize commodities, assign military forces abroad, institute martial law, control all transportation and communications, restrict travel, regulate the operations of private enterprise, call up all the military reserves, and in countless other ways control all aspects of our lives.[7]

Abuses of presidential power under these vast emergency laws included the detention of American citizens of Japanese descent during World War II and the suspension of federal law requiring the publishing of official documents in the *Federal Register*. This latter practice allowed President Nixon to cover up the bombings in Cambodia and also his directives to the FBI for domestic surveillance and intelligence work. "If the President were to make use of all of the power available to him under the emergency statutes on the books, he could conduct a government without reference to usual constitutional processes," declared Senator Frank Church (D-Idaho). "These powers taken together could form a basis for one-man rule."[8]

Treaty ratification procedures require that diplomatic agreements receive the consent of two-thirds of the Senate, but executive agreements permit a president to enter into secret and highly sensitive arrangements with a foreign nation without congressional approval. Many members of Congress believed the subversion of the treaty ratification process of the Constitution was an important element in the growth of the imperial presidency.

Executive agreements have been recognized as distinct from treaties since George Washington's days, and their use by the executive has been upheld by the courts. But what irked Congress in the 1960s and 1970s was that while the Senate was asked to ratify international accords on trivial matters, the White House arranged critically important mutual-aid and military-base agreements without even informing Congress. Walter F. Mondale, while still a senator, put the complaint this way:

> During the 1960's and 1970's, the Senate disposed by treaty of such "crucial" issues as the preservation of archeological artifacts in Mexico, a protocol relating to an amendment to the International Civil Aviation agreement, the Locarno Agreement establishing an international classification of goods and services to which trademarks are applied, revisions of international radio regulations, and an international agreement regarding maintenance of certain lights in the Red Sea.
>
> Yet Congress was not informed about the secret agreements or understandings pledging American assistance that President Nixon apparently entered into with former South Vietnamese President Thieu in 1973, at the time of the signing of the Paris Peace Accords. And the Senate subcommittee involved with such matters had no knowledge of vital executive agreements in 1960 with Ethiopia, in 1963 with Laos, in 1964 with Thailand, in 1966 with Korea, and in 1967 with Thailand.[9]

It was argued that these practices were an insult to the Congress and a violation of the Constitution's clear intent that Congress share in the making of foreign policy. Members of Congress began to probe for ways to limit the president's authority to make executive agreements.

The founding politicians did not intend that the president should decide what information Congress and the American people needed to know. They were aware of the maxim that he who controls the flow of information rules our destinies. Moreover, without information, Congress cannot oversee the execution of its laws, and if it cannot do that, it is scarcely in a position to legislate at all.

The difficulty arises because constitutional scholars, the courts, and Congress concede that a president does have the right to withhold certain diplomatic and military information when it is vital to the national security. Thus during World War II, the executive properly kept secret the time and place of the Normandy Beach invasion.

THOMAS E. CRONIN **325**

Several presidents have invoked a prerogative that has come to be called "executive privilege," a claim based on the constitutional separation of powers, to the effect that the executive branch may withhold information from Congress. It was invoked about thirty-four times prior to the Nixon presidency. During Nixon's first term, executive privilege was invoked three times on matters that included military assistance and five-year plans and foreign aid for Cambodia.

It was only with the spectacular Watergate disclosures after the 1972 election, when the Senate investigating committee began to request documents, tapes, and testimony, that executive privilege became a really celebrated issue. It was then that Nixon and his lawyers, in a brief before Judge John Sirica, claimed that executive privilege was an inherent and absolute power and that while Congress and the courts may request information from a president, the separation of powers meant that disclosure could not be forced on him.[10]

Legal historian Raoul Berger, on the other hand, contends that executive privilege is "a myth, without constitutional basis, and the best evidence that can be mustered for it is a series of self-serving presidential assertions of power to withhold information."[11]

Most people, and most members of Congress, felt that the truth seemed to lie somewhere between the views of Richard Nixon and those of Raoul Berger. Senator Sam J. Ervin, Jr., accused the executive branch of "contempt of Congress" for refusing to cooperate by sharing information. In fact, Ervin supervised a study of refusals by the executive branch to provide information to Congress, and he found there were nearly 300 instances of withheld information during the 1964–73 period.

The extraconstitutional power of impoundment allows the executive to refuse to spend funds that have been appropriated by Congress. Impoundment is a complicated practice because it can take—and has taken—so many forms. Refusals to spend have occurred in the past to effect savings either because of a change in events (for example, a war is over and funds are no longer needed) or for managerial reasons (for example, a project can be carried out in a more efficient way).

Before President Nixon, impoundments were rather infrequent, usually temporary, and generally involved insignificant amounts of money. Only occasionally were earlier impoundments controversial. Still, the precedent was set for the future. Nixon stretched the use of impoundments to limits previously not attained. Altogether he impounded about $18 billion of funds appropriated by Congress, far above the amounts withheld by any previous president.

What bothered Congress about Nixon's impoundments of funds for water pollution control, urban aid, the emergency loan program of the Farmers Home Administration, and others, was that he used impoundment to set policy and reorder the nation's domestic policy priorities. Congress felt it was one thing for a president to delay funds for purposes of efficiency, but quite another for him to use impoundment to engage in extensive policymaking or priority setting.

CONGRESS REASSERTS ITSELF: 1972–1979

The role of Congress in helping to end the war in Vietnam and then in the impeachment hearings against President Nixon gave the legislative branch some much-needed new vigor. The public looked to Congress for leadership. Congress set out to recover lost authority and discover new ways to participate more fully in national policymaking. In doing so it clearly tried to reassert itself. But even the most ardent supporter of Congress realizes that many of the so-called post-Watergate reforms are provisional. It is one thing to enact new curbs; it is quite another to put them into practice and enforce them rigorously. Moreover, while presidential powers are somewhat constrained by what Congress has done since 1973, it is not really the case that the presidency has been seriously weakened. Congress is doubtless in a better position to participate in policymaking, but improvements in Congress are not the same as reverses for the presidency. A few examples of congressional reassertion are discussed below to illustrate the ambiguity of the enterprise.

In an attempt to redress the imbalance, Congress in 1973 took an unprecedented step when it enacted the War Powers Resolution. Nixon vetoed the resolution, calling it an unconstitutional intrusion into the president's constitutional authority and an action that seriously undermined the nation's ability to act decisively and convincingly in times of international crisis. Congress overrode the veto, however, and by law declared that henceforth the president could commit the armed forces of the United States in three circumstances only: pursuant to a declaration of war by Congress; by specific statutory authorizations; or in a national emergency created by an attack on the United States or its armed forces. After committing the armed forces under this third condition, the president must report immediately to Congress; and within sixty days, unless Congress has declared war, the troop commitment is to be terminated, with the proviso that the president may be allowed another thirty days if he certifies to Congress that unavoidable military necessity for the safety of U.S. forces requires their continued use. Ninety days having elapsed, the resolution then permits Congress, by concurrent resolution not subject to a presidential veto, to direct the president to disengage the troops. A president is also obligated by this resolution to consult Congress "in every possible instance" before committing troops to battle.

Not everyone was pleased by the passage of the War Powers Resolution. Some members of Congress supported President Nixon's stand. Still another group in Congress, and many scholars as well, felt that the resolution granted a president *more power* than he already had, perhaps even to the extent of encouraging short-term interventions. Whether or not this resolution will make any difference, it may reflect a new determination in the Congress to try to control a president's formerly unlimited discretion to decide when, where, and under what conditions American troops might be engaged. Any future president who remembers the reaction of Congress and the nation to the Vietnam War and who remembers the 1973 War Powers Resolution will know that a commitment of American troops to foreign combat is subject to the approval of Congress.

Whether the intensity of this reaction will last much longer than the disenchantment over Indochina remains an open question. Congress certainly has the constitutional authority to intervene whenever it has the will to do so. But will it have the courage to resist being stampeded into granting power whenever a president waves the flag and says there is an urgent crisis? This emphasis on will or courage strikes some observers as naive or hazy. They feel that, under most circumstances, whenever a president takes a foreign-policy initiative, he is likely to have most of the country behind him, including influential business leaders, the communications media, and the bulk of the public. The history of presidential actions in wartime suggests that presidents in the future will not have much difficulty in doing pretty much what they please. The Constitution, as Chief Justice Hughes once said, is a "fighting Constitution."[12] Nothing in it will ever be permitted to prevent a president from winning a war that is truly vital to our national survival. Legal niceties will be given little attention. The Lincoln example will doubtless be followed, for national survival will always be the ultimate value. Only after the initiative is shown "not to work"—that is, after the death tolls and inflation become unbearable—will popular support begin to flag and the Congress begin to reflect the popular feeling.

The Case Act of 1972, sponsored by Senator Clifford P. Case (R-N.J.), requires the secretary of state to submit to the Senate within sixty days the final text of any international agreement made by executive agreement. Executive agreements having sensitive national security implications may be submitted to the Senate Foreign Relations Committee and the House International Relations Committee on a classified basis. Presidents still negotiate executive agreements, however, and sometimes fail to comply with the Case Act's relatively mild provisions. Recent presidents and their aides have responded to the Case Act provisions by simply negotiating fewer international agreements and have used other titles or names for certain non-treaty negotiations.

Even when executive agreements are reported to the appropriate committees of Congress, there is no provision for any congressional response. Some efforts were made in the mid-1970s to enact a stronger law that would permit Congress an opportunity to review and disapprove executive agreements. In 1974 the Senate actually passed such a measure, but the House failed to act on it. Later attempts have also failed, but the following initiatives have won congressional support.

- A Senate-sponsored bill requiring executive agreements to be submitted only to the Senate, with such agreements to take effect at the end of sixty days unless the Senate disapproves them by simple resolution.

- A House-sponsored bill requiring executive agreements to be submitted to Congress, with such agreements to take effect in sixty days unless both houses adopt a concurrent resolution disapproving them.
- Another Senate-sponsored bill providing that if either house decides that an international agreement is sufficiently important to require congressional approval, it must be approved through regular legislative procedures or as a treaty.[13]

Abuse of the intelligence and spying agencies was also a central contention of the imperial presidency argument. The Central Intelligence Agency was established in 1947 at a time when the perceived threat of "world communism" encouraged a vast arsenal of national security instruments, including covert overseas political operations and espionage. When the CIA was established, Congress recognized the dangers to a free society inherent in a secret organization not accountable in the ordinary way for what it does. Hence it was stipulated that the CIA was *not to engage in any police work or to perform operations within the United States.*

But from 1947 to the mid-1970s, no aspect of national policymaking was more removed from congressional involvement than CIA operations. In many instances Congress acted as if it really did not want to know what was going on. Said one senator: "It is not a question of reluctance on the part of CIA officials to speak to us. Instead it is a question of our reluctance, if you will, to seek information and knowledge on subjects which I personally, as a Member of Congress and a citizen, would rather not have."[14] The evidence is substantial that Congress declined to use its resources to participate in intelligence policymaking.

Congress has tried in recent years to amend this. In 1974 Congress enacted the so-called Hughes-Ryan Amendment which requires the administration to advise eight congressional committees of its plans for clandestine operations. This same measure forbids such clandestine operations unless they are specifically approved by the president. In 1975 the Senate established a temporary committee of inquiry chaired by Senator Frank Church. This committee found widespread abuses of power and violations of the rights of American citizens in the conduct of both foreign and domestic intelligence operations. The Church committee recommended that Congress bring all the intelligence operations within the framework of congressional oversight.

The Senate then voted to create a permanent Select Committee on Intelligence, with legislative and budgetary authority over the CIA and other intelligence agencies. Subsequently, the House voted to set up a similar panel. But since we now know that even presidents have had difficulty getting a handle on the CIA, there is some doubt about whether Congress will have any better luck. Yet in an unprecedented exercise of its power over the intelligence budget, Congress in 1976 amended the Defense Appropriations Bill to terminate American covert intervention in Angola. "The inevitable public disclosure of a secret operation served, in this instance, the will of Congress; and in the short run the Angola controversy was a warning that the Executive should proceed with caution."[15]

How likely is it that Congress will be effective in regulating the CIA? People differ widely in their answers to this question. Halperin et al. conclude their study by saying: "To date, only a few patchwork elements of reform have been put into effect. At every turn the executive branch continues to fight any major changes and, instead, offers 'reforms' that end up authorizing for the future the abuses of the past."[16] Some critics say the Senate committee should spell out a charter that would limit the CIA to foreign operations, severely restrict and control all covert activities, require written approval for any major field operations, and shut down the political intelligence work of the FBI. Others feel the full disclosure of the intelligence community's budget is necessary.

A longer-range view suggests that the intensity and direction of congressional interest in these matters depend on the movement of larger political forces. That is, when a national consensus supports a president and his foreign-policy initiatives, as it plainly did in the early part of the cold war, Congress is likely to go along. But in the absence of such a consensus, a more assertive Congress may try to find a more realistic system of accountability for the CIA and related activities as a substitute for the public scrutiny that normally is given major governmental operations. It is worth recalling that we have already had committees in the Congress to oversee the intelligence agencies, but those simply did not do their job.

Ford, Carter, and Reagan have all criticized Congress for weakening the CIA. They felt that Congress went too far and that Congress should ease the restrictions on covert operations by the CIA. The Carter administration especially pressed this case in early 1980, as the Iranian and Afghan crises loomed large in the background. Officials in the Carter White House said that the administration was deterred from going ahead on certain overseas operations for fear that their disclosure to the eight congressional committees might result in leaks to the press. The Carter White House also favored tightening up provisions of the Freedom of Information Act, which gives individuals and foreign governments access to large amounts of official data that used to be classified information. Carter aides pointed out, for example, that Communist bloc countries had become a major consumer of certain foreign and national security records. And time and again in the 1980 presidential primaries, candidates such as George Bush, himself a former director of the CIA, and Ronald Reagan condemned the restrictions that Congress in the mid-1970s had placed upon overseas intelligence operations.

Another area in which Congress attempted to reassert its authority was the budget. Congress had become too dependent on the president's budget proposals and had no budget system of its own—only a lot of separate actions and decisions coming at various intervals throughout the year with little or no connection among them. "Congress has seen its control over the federal pursestrings ebb away over the past fifty years because of its inability to get a grip on the overall budget, while the Office of Management and Budget in the executive branch has increased its power and influence," said Senator Edmund S. Muskie (D-Maine) in 1974.[17]

Muskie was one of the chief authors of the 1974 Congressional Budget and Impoundment Control Act. That act was designed to encourage Congress to evaluate the nation's fiscal situation and program-spending priorities in a comprehensive way. It was also hoped that in a period of high inflation Congress could help put a lid on unnecessary spending. An increasing number of members of Congress began to take seriously the aphorism: he who controls the stream of budget making controls policymaking.

Within recent years Congress has turned the so-called legislative veto into an instrument of policymaking. The Constitution stipulates that every bill, order, resolution, or vote to which the concurrence of the Senate and House may be necessary shall be presented to the president for his approval or veto. But "concurrent resolutions," in contrast to "joint resolutions," by convention do not have to be submitted to the president. In the past this made little difference, since concurrent resolutions were used merely to express congressional sentiments and had no force of law.

Then in 1932 Congress passed a joint resolution allowing President Hoover to reorganize the executive agencies but stipulated that his proposed reorganizations would not take effect for ninety days, during which time either house of Congress by a simple resolution could veto the regulation. Since then the legislative veto (sometimes also called the congressional veto) has come to be a frequently used statutory provision through which Congress authorizes a federal program to be administered by the executive branch but retains the authority to approve or disapprove part of the program before final implementation. Usually, Congress either may disapprove a measure by vetoing it or must approve it by affirmative action. This must take place within a specified period of time, generally sixty or ninety days. The legislative veto may take the form of a concurrent resolution, a simple resolution passed by either house, or a committee veto.

Since 1932 more than 300 pieces of legislation have carried some form of legislative veto; more than half have been enacted since 1970, and most of those since 1974. Significant statutes with legislative-veto provisions include the Budget and Impoundment Control Act of 1974, the Trade Act of 1974, and the Energy Policy and Conservation Act of 1975.

Congressional spokesmen favor the legislative veto and contend that it is the most effective device Congress has to insure that the president and the federal bureaucrats issue regulations that conform to the intent of Congress. They also argue that without the use of the veto, when Congress delegates powers to the president, he could use his veto to prevent Congress from terminating the delegation. Representative Elliott Levitas (D-Georgia) reflects the sentiment in Congress in favor of a veto on administrative rules and regulations when he complains that the bureaucracy is infringing on Congress's right to make laws by putting out "a thick tangle of regulations that carry the force of law without benefit of legislative consideration." To back up his point he cited statistics showing that in 1974 Congress passed 404 public laws, while sixty-seven agencies adopted 7,496 regulations.[18]

Most supporters of the presidency consider the legislative veto a violation of the doctrine of separation of powers and an unconstitutional intrusion into the executive branch. President Carter said in 1978 that he accepts only one form of legislative veto as constitutional, the one-House veto used to disapprove presidential plans to reorganize the executive branch. He also warned that excessive use of legislative vetoes impedes the United States's ability to respond to rapidly changing world conditions.[19] Advocates of a strong presidency also argue that the legislative veto gives lobbyists more influence on government. John Bolton, a Washington lawyer, writes that the legislative veto

> eliminates the president from the law-making function by not presenting him with "legislation" that he can veto. It allows Congress to change its mind an unlimited number of times about what a statute is intended to do after passage of the statute—in effect, amending the statute. . . . The President's administrative authority—his duty to "take care that the laws be faithfully executed"—is impinged because he is prevented from implementing regulations he deems suitable and consistent with the enabling legislation.[20]

Testifying before a congressional committee in late 1975 a Ford Justice Department official opposed the expanded and new use of the legislative veto as follows:

> As our system operates Congress makes the laws, in as much detail as it desires; the President executes those laws, with due regard for the congressional intent; and the judiciary determines the President's execution, including issuance of regulations, to be of no effect when it is inconsistent with the laws or the Constitution.
> This rough division of government power is what the doctrine of separation of powers is all about.
> Both of the present bills [under discussion before the House Committee on the Judiciary] disrupt this system in one way or another, depending upon how the ambiguities discussed earlier are resolved. If they envision Congress setting regulations aside on the basis of its own notions as to what constitutes desirable enforcement policy, they intrude upon the executive's functions.
> If, on the other hand, they mean only to permit congressional review of the executive's compliance with statutory intent, they intrude upon the province of the judiciary. Either way, they carry Congress beyond its proper function of making laws under Article I of the Constitution.[21]

Congress surely used the legislative veto to reassert itself. The House of Representatives, through its Subcommittee on the Rules of the House, issued in February 1980 a comprehensive survey of legislative vetoes and their use. These studies suggest an impressively broad range of positions on both the practicality and legality of legislative vetoes. A political scientist who coordinated these studies for the House, concludes there are three rather different categories of legislative vetoes. His distinctions and reasoning are worth noting.

> First, legislative vetoes originate as a condition attached to authority that Congress had exercised in the past. In delegating to the President or executive officials the authority to reorganize executive agencies, suspend deportations, and adjust federal salaries, Congress relinquishes power only with the assurance of a legislative veto. The authority and the legislative veto are inseparable, the Administration could not have had the authority without the condition. . . .
>
> Second, legislative vetoes are sometimes added as a restraint on authority previously delegated. Here Congress tries to recapture power that had drifted too far from legislative control. In this category are the legislative vetoes applied to arms sales, trade authority, regulatory agencies, and the General Services Administration.
>
> Third, some of the legislative vetoes do not concern power delegated by Congress. Instead, the problem is how the legislative and executive branches can share a responsibility that combines elements of congressional and presidential power. Unable to define by statute the precise boundary between the branches, Congress relied on a legislative veto as a procedural link between rival and conflicting constitutional interpretations. Included within this category are the legislative vetoes in the War Powers Resolution, and national emergency legislation.[22]

Thus the matter of legislative vetoes is hardly a simple, easy-to-resolve tension between the two branches. Federal courts have begun to refine or define anew the extent to which legislative vetoes are constitutional. Doubtless various accommodations will generally be worked out between specific administrations and the Congress with whom they must deal.

Congress has also become more involved in foreign-policy making, increasingly imposing its own goals on the executive. Shaking off years of inertia, Congress imposed a cutoff of aid to Vietnam, called a halt to bombing in Cambodia, and restrained the Ford administration from getting involved in Portugal and Angola. Led by Senator Henry Jackson (D-Washington), Congress refused to permit the White House to grant the Soviet Union the "most-favored nation" treatment allowed for in the Trade Reform Act of 1974. Congress has also demanded and won a greater role in arms sales abroad and in determining U.S. aid to Turkey.[23]

The maintenance of democratic controls over foreign and military policy has become increasingly difficult in the cold war and the nuclear age. Secrecy is at the heart of the problem. All of our recent presidents have said that you cannot have successful diplomacy without secrecy.

But executive secrecy is subject to abuses, as Watergate has dramatically illustrated. People could understand, even if they might oppose, the use of secrecy in the president's negotiations with China or in his diplomatic initiatives with Middle Eastern nations. But most people found it difficult to understand the need for secrecy in dealing with congressional leaders. Tapping telephones to prevent security leaks and breaking into offices—these are the tactics not of politics, but of war. These practices may be appropriate in dealing with enemies, but they are inappropriate when dealing with domestic political opponents.

How is it possible to prevent the use of secrecy to cover up obstructions of justice while permitting its legitimate use for diplomatic purposes? Some Americans feel that even at the risk of a less effective foreign policy, what is needed is a greater sharing of power with Congress over foreign policy. And some indeed have doubts whether the exclusive power of the president is more likely to produce good policy than sharing power with Congress.

Some congressional proposals to reassert authority have failed to gain approval. Among them was former Senator Sam Ervin's suggestion that the Department of Justice be removed from the executive branch. He felt that was necessary to separate the vital justice and prosecution functions from the contamination of partisan politics and undue White House influence; but he failed to persuade many members of Congress. Representative Henry Reuss (D-Wisconsin) championed a constitutional amendment providing a vote of no-confidence that would permit Congress to call for new elections when it believed a president had become incompetent or had lost the support needed to govern effectively. Others proposed a constitutional amendment to limit the president to a single six-year term. Another proposal provided for an American "question hour" in which cabinet members or even the president would regularly go before the Congress to respond to questions and participate in a dialogue on major policy questions. Finally, some members of Congress wanted to establish ceilings on the number of White House aides and involve the Congress in overseeing the policymaking powers of the unconfirmed White House staff. None of these measures got beyond committee hearings.

"I do not want a honeymoon with you. I want a good marriage," said Ford to Congress as he started his presidency. "As President I intend to listen," he continued. Ford said his relations with Congress would be characterized not by confrontation but by "communication, conciliation, compromise and cooperation."[24] But his hoped-for holy wedlock soured and an unholy deadlock set in as he proceeded to veto sixty-nine legislative measures.

Congress did give Ford a hard time. Having shaken off years of inertia,

Congress took advantage of an appointed president to regain some of its own lost authority. Thus they rejected some of his nominations; they took four months to confirm Nelson Rockefeller; they rejected Ford's foreign-aid bill, trimmed his defense appropriations, curtailed military aid to Turkey, denied him the means to conduct open or covert operations in Angola, and so on.

Some of Ford's aides warned of a new period of congressional government. Ford himself said:

> Frankly, I believe that Congress recently has gone too far in trying to take over the powers that belong to the President and the executive branch.
>
> This probably is a natural reaction to the steady growth of executive branch power over the past forty years. I'm sure it is a reaction to Watergate and Vietnam. And the fact that I came to this office through a Constitutional process and not by election also may have something to do with current efforts by the Democratic Congress to take away some of the power of the President.
>
> As a member of Congress for twenty-five years, I clearly understand the powers and obligations of the Senate and House under our Constitution. But as President for eighteen months, I also understand that Congress is trying to go too far in some areas.[25]

Why did Ford have such troubled relations with Congress? Reaction to the Vietnam War and Watergate obviously played a role in his difficulties. Congress had reorganized itself in several ways. It was a more democratic institution now, with power more noticeably dispersed among its members. It had streamlined some of its procedures, and it was more conscious of its responsibility to the people. But there were additional factors that help explain Ford's difficulties. Perhaps the major problem was that he was decidedly more conservative than Congress. That should have come as no surprise to those who had looked at his voting record in Congress. He had voted against Medicare, opposed the creation of the Office of Economic Opportunity, opposed aid to education, and opposed federal help for state water pollution control projects. He had, however, always been a strong supporter of Defense Department spending.

Moreover, Ford was an appointed president. As the United States's first president to be appointed under the Twenty-fifth Amendment, he also bore the stigma of illegitimacy. He had absolutely no mandate from the people. He had to deal with a Congress controlled by Democrats. He came to office right in the midst of a mid-term congressional election. At the State Department he had the always secretive Henry Kissinger who had by then acquired strong opponents in both parties. And he had to contend with a strong attack from the right wing of his own minority party. The Ford presidency experienced additional troubles because it came during the seventh and eighth years of the Nixon-Ford administrations. The top people were tired and had run out of imaginative ideas and solutions. Finally, Ford suffered from the disillusionment that invariably sets in toward the end of an eight-year hold on the presidency. The same thing had happened in 1960 and 1968.

In fact, the Ford presidency was not as weak and constrained as it wanted people to believe. (The White House liked to convey the impression that the press, the courts, and the Congress were literally undermining presidential powers.) Ford himself may have been vulnerable, but the presidency was not weakened during this period. The major powers of the office were still available to presidents. Of course, the effective use of those powers required shrewd use and clear communication of intent.

PRESIDENT CARTER AND CONGRESS

Carter's relations with Congress were turbulent. He suffered setbacks on his energy package, his proposed SALT II agreement, election reform, his Korean strategy, the proposed consumer protection agency, and countless other measures. He scored victories, too (for example, on the B-1 bomber and the Panama Canal), but these often seemed to be the exception to the rule. And even his victories seemed to anger the Congress.

Carter's initial difficulties with Congress were partially due to the post-Watergate efforts to constrain the American presidency. But *only partially*. To be sure, Congress did not want to become a rubber stamp for a Democratic president. And Congress was enjoying its struggle to reassert itself. Also, the dispersion of influence (that is, power to the subcommittees and subcommittee chairmen) in the House of Representatives made it more difficult for a president to deal with the Congress. Gone were the days when the White House could deal with a handful of "whales" who really ran the show. But Carter's difficulties stemmed from a number of other factors as well.

Carter ran for the White House as a Mr. Clean, a Mr. Integrity, and a Mr. Outsider. He sold himself almost like a detergent who would go to Washington and clean things up. That only bred resentment. His campaign slogans were seen as a "put down" to Congress. He talked too much of the mess in Washington to win friends there. He said Congress was inherently incapable of leadership, and added that in the absence of strong presidential leadership there is no leadership.

His personal style of campaigning stressed confrontation more than negotiation. He seemed righteous and almost too good to be true. He implied that his administration would be guided by only the highest moral standards. So when the Bert Lance affair occurred, he was judged all the more critically. Congress resented his pious style and that plainly made the honeymoon shorter.

Much was made of the idea that most of the problems in presidential-congressional relations could be overcome if only both branches were held by the Democrats. That came to pass in January 1977, but the promised harmony never came about.

Part of the reason is that the Democratic party is in many ways two parties in one. Any party with both a Ron Dellums and a James Eastland is a party either very split or very strained. Moreover, Carter really had no substantive political base within the Democratic party. He was not really a Southern old-boy conservative. Some have suggested that he was more of a Yankee puritan. In many ways, the mere fact that he was a Southerner in the White House made him a novelty. Ironically, although Carter enjoyed his highest popularity in the southeastern section of the nation, the members of Congress from that same region gave him just about the lowest rates of support for his programs in Congress.

Carter, moreover, ran well behind the Democrats running for Congress and for the state houses in 1976. His election seemed to be due more to the public's lack of confidence in Gerald Ford than to any program Carter put forth.

Some of Carter's difficulties came about because he did not enjoy the politics of dealing with members of Congress. He gave the impression that he was the rational man and that Congress should deal with him and his programs completely on their merits. The idea that deals will be made and favors dispensed appeared alien to Carter. Thus he gladly sold the presidential yacht, the *Sequoia,* an action many congressmen said, in retrospect, was a big mistake. It was on that pleasure boat that Lyndon Johnson and his cabinet did some of their most effective congressional-relations lobbying.

Members of Congress complained too that Carter did not consult enough. Unlike Lyndon Johnson before him or Ronald Reagan after him, he did not invite them in to go over the drafts of prospective bills; he often seemed to prefer a government by surprise. He also had a penchant for bypassing Congress and going to the country. Of course, all presidents do that, but his style of doing it coupled with his reputation as an "outsider" came back to weaken his ties to Congress.

One scholar who has studied Carter's legislative-relations staffs offers the additional explanation that because Carter won the nomination and then the presidency itself largely without having to build coalitions with the left, right, and center of the Democratic party, so also his congressional relations teams, both at the White House and in the departments, did not build the coalitions needed to get things passed.[26]

In 1960 the mood of the country embodied a seemingly boundless confidence in itself and in what its government could achieve. We could go anywhere and do anything—from conquering outer space to effecting land reform in Latin America and political reforms in Indochina. Poverty in America could be ended once and for all. John Kennedy became president during this era of good feelings, this era of confident adventuresomeness. Optimism and idealism aided both him and Lyndon Johnson in their efforts to deal with Congress.

But that era is over. Today we dwell on the scarcity of resources and the interdependency of the U.S. economy with those of several other nations. Americans acknowledge that the United States overextended itself abroad. Americans salute the slogan "small is beautiful," and they read study after study predicting the limits to growth.

President Carter wanted to provide leadership of the Roosevelt, Wilson, and Kennedy kind, but he did not have the appropriate climate of expectations. He could draw on neither the trauma of a depression nor the crusading spirit of a world war nor the buoyant national optimism of the early 1960s. The Carter presidency was obviously constrained by a national mood of conservatism and hostility to many governmental programs and regulations. Carter's difficulties with the Congress arose in no small measure from his desire to offer leadership to a nation that has turned introspective and anti-Washington.

A NEW IMPATIENCE: RESTRENGTHEN THE PRESIDENCY

Even as the presidency was being soundly criticized for abuses of power in the late 1960s and early 1970s, it was simultaneously portrayed by many people as alarmingly battered by the Vietnam War and Watergate. The ranks of the defenders of presidential government may have been temporarily thinned in 1973 and 1974, but at least by 1980 the cult of the presidency was alive and well. As several analysts observed, the Right worried about the imperial presidency at home and the Left worried about the imperial presidency abroad. What is not pointed out is that the Right doubtless wants a near-imperial Teddy Roosevelt kind of presidency abroad and the Left often wants something approaching an imperial, super-planning presidency at home.

The American public may have lost confidence in its leaders, but it has not lost hope in the efficacy of strong, purposive leadership. The Gallup organization in 1976 asked a national sample: "Do you think what the country needs is really strong leadership that would try to solve problems directly without worrying about how Congress or the Supreme Court might feel or do you think that such leadership might be dangerous?" By a 49 to 44 percent margin the respondents indicated a preference for a strong government over a constitutional one. By late 1979 this same question received a 63 to 30 percent response in favor of strong presidential leadership.[27]

Fears of another Watergate presidency seemed to disappear. Perhaps all the revelations about the crimes of Watergate and the dramatic resignation of a president have lulled most people into believing that "the system worked"—that the checks checked and the balances balanced. Perhaps the very cataloging of the misuses of presidential powers seemed to solve the problem.

In the wake of the wounded or imperiled presidency of the Watergate era, could Congress furnish the leadership necessary to govern the country?

Most scholars and writers say no. The conventional answer heard in the early eighties is that the United States will need a presidency of substantial power if it is to get on top of economic problems and maintain its position in foreign affairs. The major 1980 presidential challengers—Reagan, Bush, and Kennedy—all called for stronger, more effective presidential leadership.

The president's primacy, they would add, has been founded in the necessities of the American condition. Today, the federal government has become committed to burdens of administration that demand vigorous, positive leadership. We live too in a continuous state of emergency, where instant nuclear warfare could destroy the country in a matter of minutes and where global competition of almost every sort highlights the need for swiftness, efficiency, and unity in our government. Further, Reagan to the contrary notwithstanding, today's social and urban and environmental problems require persistent creative presidential leadership. Any reduction in the powers of the president might leave us naked to our enemies, to the forces of inflation and depression at home, and to the forces of unrest and aggression abroad.

Former President Gerald Ford scoffed in 1977 at the idea that Congress had improved things in recent years. Speaking for the repeal of the War Powers Resolution of 1973, Ford said, "When a crisis breaks out, it is impossible to draw the Congress into the decisionmaking process in an effective way." Ford cited these reasons for this claim:

- Legislators have too many other concerns to be abreast of foreign policy situations.
- It is impossible to wait for a consensus among scattered and perhaps disagreeing congressional leaders.
- Sensitive information supplied to legislators, particularly via the telephone, might be disclosed.
- Waiting for consultation could risk penalties for the President "as severe as impeachment."
- Consultations with congressional leaders might not bind the rank and file, particularly independent younger members.[28]

Such defenders of a powerful presidency as Samuel Huntington and columnist Robert Novak wondered how a government could conduct a coherent foreign policy if legislative ascendancy really meant the development of a Congress into a second United States government. Could the United States afford to have two foreign policies? A nation cannot long retain a leadership role in the world unless its own leadership is both clear and decisive. They argued, too, that congressional decisions—including foreign-policy decisions—must be based almost entirely on domestic politics, which is why Congress cannot conduct foreign policy.[29]

More specifically, critics charged, Congress, by its headline-hunting investigations, had destroyed the Central Intelligence Agency as an effective means of national policy for the United States. Thus in the Angola episode Congress in effect served notice that the president cannot conduct the foreign policy of his country to confront brush fire occurrences or to confront Soviet expansionism.[30]

Huntington urges readers to recognize the legitimacy and the necessity "of hierarchy, coercion, discipline, secrecy, and deception—all of which are, in some measure, inescapable attributes of the process of government. . . . When the President is unable to exercise authority, no one else has been able to supply comparable purpose and initiative. To the extent that the United States has been governed on a national basis, it has been governed by the President."[31]

The same verdict is heard from those who yearn for strong, creative leadership in domestic or economic matters. Thus Arthur Schlesinger, Jr.— even as he condemns the imperial presidency—says that "history has shown the presidency to be the most effective instrumentality for justice and progress."[32] Supporters of a strong, powerful presidency worry that a president has too little power today to tackle economic and energy resource problems effectively. For example, he has little influence over the Federal Reserve Board's policies on credit and money. He has few tools for effective, long-range economic planning. And, as President Carter learned, his authority over government reorganizations was puny compared to our expectations of him as the official "chief executive."

Without vigorous presidential leadership, the parochialism in Congress, advocates of a strong presidency contend, is profound, insidious, and unremitting. Advocates of national planning are especially fond of looking to the White House for leadership because they believe that only the president has the national perspective to plan coherently, to plan comprehensively. Sure, they say, Congress has its role. But Congress, rather than balancing presidential powers, has often simply blocked needed presidential actions because of localized self-interests.

Thus, as almost always during the twentieth century, advocates of a strong presidency lament that presidential powers are not stronger. For the presidency is America's strongest weapon against those banes of progress: sectionalism, selfish or over-concentrated corporate power, and totalitarianism abroad.

Americans still long for dynamic, reassuring, and strong leadership. Watergate notwithstanding, Americans still celebrate the gutsy, aggressive presidents, even if many of them did violate the legal and constitutional niceties of the separation of powers. It is still the Jeffersons, Jacksons, Lincolns, and Roosevelts that get placed on the top of the lists of great presidents. What the country often wants most—more than laws and programs—is a few courageous, tireless, assertive leaders in whom the people can put their faith; the type, by the way, who will undoubtedly dominate Congress. In the words of Theodore Sorensen, "a supine presidency has no more to recommend it in the foreign affairs area than an imperial presidency."[33]

In sum, more and more people think the nation in the mid-1970s entered a period of overreaction to Watergate, the Vietnam War, and the Nixon presidency. Some rebalancing was needed, but many in the Congress and elsewhere embarked upon a course that endangered the effectiveness of the presidency. Those who hold to this overreaction thesis say the White House today is enmeshed in a complex web of constraints that hobbles presidents and that would have prevented an FDR or a Lincoln from providing vital leadership. Fears of presidential dictatorship, they say, are much exaggerated. It is unfortunate that people dwell so much on Richard Nixon and his abuse of office. The Nixon presidency, they contend, was one of a kind, and it was dealt with effectively by the impeachment provisions of the Constitution. The central challenge, then, is not to reduce the president's power to lead, to govern, or to persuade, but to check the president's power to mislead and corrupt.

Defenders of the presidency argue that Congress and the reformers have overreacted to Watergate, and they call for the repeal of the War Powers Resolution of 1973, further restrictions on the use of legislative vetoes, restraints on the oversight of the intelligence agencies, independence for the executive's use of executive agreements, and in general a word of caution to Congress not to interfere too much in executive branch negotiations in foreign policy and security matters.

There are, however, still many, though clearly a minority, who insist that the reassertion of congressional power is a much-needed corrective that did not go far enough. Supporters of a truly tenacious Congress question the depth, sincerity, and staying power of congressional assertiveness. They point to President Ford's failure to comply with the War Powers Resolution of 1973 when he ordered military action and bombings in connection with the 1975 rescue of the merchant ship *Mayaguez*. They note that the Defense Department's budgets continue to grow and to pass through the Congress with minimum changes. They point to Carter and Reagan and their penchant for surprising the Congress or for bypassing it entirely with appeals to the public. They contend too that despite all the talk about more and better program oversight, most members of Congress find this type of work the least glamorous, least appealing, and least rewarding—especially in terms of winning reelection. Hence they wonder whether Congress will really maintain its interest in this vital work. They suggest also that despite much talk about strengthening the confirmation process, Congress all too easily lapses back to its traditional "rubber stamp" habits.

Those who want more reform point out that the imperial presidency was at least as much the product of an unassertive Congress as it was of power-hungry presidents. They argue, too, that although Congress may have asserted itself in response to the events of Watergate, the more distant those events become, the less motivated Congress will be to challenge the presidency. This reasoning leads them to note that it is the Congress after Watergate that bears watching, and it is the Congress that needs to develop a leadership strength of its own.

There is also the view that the presidency is an indestructible office, tough and resilient. It readily survived, and Watergate may have actually strengthened it. That is, Watergate had a kind of purifying effect on the office, for after the trauma of 1973–74, many people found a false comfort in the claim that "the system worked." Once Nixon was removed, the problems of the office were assumed to have been eliminated. But to those who still worry about a too strong presidency, this attitude is very dangerous. Americans, they warn, should have been more alarmed than they were, or than they are. The seeds of the imperial presidency are still there.

But the period of post-Watergate reforming has just about run its course. Few new reform ideas are being heard these days. The call for strengthening the presidency is dominant now and likely to be so for the next few years. Fears of another era of congressional government are unfounded. Plainly, the pendulum has already swung back in the other direction, although how far it will swing and what consequences will follow cannot yet be determined.

CONCLUSION

Relations between Congress and the president are not merely constitutional questions but also struggles for the support of public opinion. People may be more attentive to presidents than to Congress, yet most Americans have reacted to Watergate and the Vietnam War by hoping that Congress will play a more significant role in shaping public policy. Americans cherish the ideal of the separation of powers. But in practice the presidency has become the dominant branch, especially in foreign policy. The president must work with the Congress, but there is still wide latitude granted a president in an era of emergencies. As Larry Tribe has put it, "We are, and must remain, a society led by three equal branches with one permanently 'more equal' than the others: as the Supreme Court and Congress are preeminent in constitutional theory, so the President is preeminent in constitutional fact."[34]

Our system of checks and balances must be strong enough for effective leadership, while dispersing power enough to insure liberty. It is when the "national security" is at stake that uncertainties and confusion arise. Justice Robert Jackson warned us that "security is like liberty in that many crimes are committed in its name."[35] Certainly that was so in the recent past.

The balance is delicate, and rebalancing efforts such as the congressional reassertion of the 1970s will often be necessary. The reaction to the imperial or Watergate presidency has been significant even if not lasting. There is a healthy skepticism toward presidents. There is less glorification of presidents and their policies. We have both bigger and better staffed houses of Congress than ever in the past. There is a new spirit of independence among members of the Congress, who say: "We want a strong and intelligent president, but he has to bear one thing in mind—we got elected, too"; or "The people have not chosen to be governed by one branch of government alone."[36]

There have been campaign finance reforms, open meetings on sunshine laws, a special prosecutor act, and congressional committee restructuring. There is also a new emphasis on accountable and responsible leadership. Strength in the White House these days is judged less on intimidation strategies and more on the quality of solutions, on the president's integrity, know-how, and negotiating skills, and on the quality of the staff he can assemble to help him shape and implement his policies.

Nearly everyone agrees that Congress is likely to remain a more important force in domestic, economic, and foreign-policy making as a result of these new tools and the new restrictions placed on the president. If many of the reforms of the 1970s were symbolic in nature, others did have the effect of permitting Congress to gain the information it needs to play a more responsible role in policymaking activities.

How long will Congress remain an activist influence in policymaking? How long will the American public support the Congress in its more assertive activities? Much will depend, understandably, on how Congress exercises its regained and new influence.

However much the public may want Congress to be a major partner with the president and a major check on the president, the public's support for Congress will always be subject to deterioration. Power is much dispersed in Congress. Its deliberations and quarrels are very public. After a while, the public begins to view Congress as "the bickering branch" or the policy-thwarting branch, especially if there is a vigorous activist in the White House.

Polls show that people think Congress pays more attention to public views than does the president. Assuredly the Congress is a splendid forum that represents and registers the diversity of America. But that very virtue makes it difficult for Congress to provide leadership and difficult for it to challenge and bargain effectively with presidents. Not surprisingly, a wary public, dissatisfied with programs that do not work and policies that do not measure up to the urgencies of the moment, will look elsewhere—which will often be the president, or an aspiring presidential candidate offering himself as an alternative to the president.

How one stands on the question of a strong presidency depends in part on what policies one favors and how those policies are advanced or hampered by the president or Congress.

A theory of cyclical relations between the president and Congress has long been fashionable. It holds that there will be periods of presidential ascendancy followed by periods of congressional ascendancy. Usually these periods have been a decade or more, and sometimes a generation, in length. The analysis suggests that a moderate but brief congressional resurgence took place in the immediate post-Watergate years. But the responsibilities of the presidency these days, coupled with the complexities of foreign and economic policy, do not really permit any serious weakening of the office. Congress has regained some of its own lost power and it has very correctly tried to curb the misuse and abuse of power—but it has not weakened the presidency.

Many will continue to worry about future imperial presidents and about the possible alienation of the people from their leaders as complex issues continue to centralize responsibilities in the hands of the national government and in the executive. Those who are concerned about these matters will not content themselves, nor should they, with the existing safeguards against the future misuse of presidential powers. The difficulty is that so few of the additional safeguards suggested seem to be politically or practically acceptable. It is not easy to contrive devices that will check the president who would misuse powers without hamstringing the president who would use those same powers for purposive and democratically acceptable ends.[37]

In the end, both the president and Congress have to recognize they are not two sides out to "win" but two parts of the same government, both elected to pursue together the interests of the American people.

NOTES

1. See Thomas E. Cronin, *The State of the Presidency* (Boston, Mass.: Little, Brown and Co., 1980), chap. 3.
2. These figures are from Roberta S. Sigel, "Image of the American Presidency: Part II of an Exploration into Popular Views of Presidential Power," in *The Presidency*, ed. Aaron Wildavsky (Boston, Mass.: Little, Brown and Co., 1969), p. 300.
3. *New York Times*/CBS Poll, April 1977.
4. Arthur M. Schlesinger, Jr., *The Imperial Presidency* (Boston, Mass.: Houghton Mifflin Co., 1973).
5. Ibid., pp. 129–30.
6. See Leonard C. Meeker, "The Legality of U.S. Participation in the Defense of Vietnam," *Department of State Bulletin*, 28 March 1966, pp. 484–85.
7. See J. Malcolm Smith and Cornelius P. Cotter, *Powers of the President during Crisis* (Washington, D.C.: Public Affairs Press, 1960). See also Harold C. Relyea, "Declaring and Terminating a State of Emergency," *Presidential Studies Quarterly* 6 (Fall 1976): 36–42.
8. Quoted in "The President Versus Congress: Special Report," *National Journal*, 29 May 1976, p. 736. See also U.S., Congress, Senate, *Emergency Powers Statutes, Report of the Special Committee on the Termination of the National Emergency*, 93rd Cong., 1st sess., 19 November 1973.
9. Walter F. Mondale, *The Accountability of Power* (New York: David McKay, 1975), pp. 114–15.
10. See his own account in Richard Nixon, *RN: Memoirs of Richard Nixon* (New York: Grosset and Dunlap, 1978), pp. 896–910. See also Leon Jaworski, *The Right and the Power* (New York: Pocket Books, 1977), chap. 10.
11. Raoul Berger, "The Grand Inquest of the Nation," *Harper's*, October 1973, p. 12. See also idem., *Executive Privilege: A Constitutional Myth* (Cambridge: Harvard University Press, 1974).
12. Charles Evans Hughes, "War Powers Under the Constitution," *American Bar*

Association Reports 42 (1917), p. 238. See also *Home Building and Loan Association* v. *Blaisdell*, 290 U.S. 398, 426 (1934).

13. See Senate Subcommittee on Separation of Powers, *Congressional Oversight of Executive Agreements–1975.*

14. Leverett Saltonstall (R-Mass.) quoted in Harry Howe Ransom, *The Intelligence Establishment* (Cambridge: Harvard University Press, 1970), p. 169.

15. John T. Elliff, "Congress and the Intelligence Community," in *Congress Reconsidered,* eds. Lawrence C. Dodd and Bruce I. Oppenheimer (New York: Praeger, 1977), pp. 193–206.

16. Morton H. Halperin et al., *The Lawless State: The Crimes of the U.S. Intelligence Agencies* (New York: Penguin Books, 1976), p. 279. For general background on this question, see Tyrus G. Gain et. al., eds., *The Intelligence Community: History, Organization and Issues* (New York: R. R. Bowker Company, 1977).

17. Quoted in *National Journal,* 29 May 1976, p. 742. See also James P. Pfiffner, *The President, the Budget, and Congress: Impoundment and the 1974 Budget Act* (Boulder, Colo.: Westview Press, 1979).

18. Quoted in Mary Russell, "Bill to Give Congress Veto Power Is Defeated," *Washington Post,* 22 September 1976.

19. For President Jimmy Carter's message on his opposition to most forms of legislative veto, see "Legislative Vetoes: Message to Congress, June 21, 1978," in *Weekly Compilation of Presidential Documents,* week of 26 June 1978, p. 1146.

20. John R. Bolton, *The Legislative Veto: Unseparating the Powers* (Washington, D.C.: American Enterprise Institute, 1977), pp. 31–32. For a different view, see Louis Fisher, "A Political Context for Legislative Vetoes," *Political Science Quarterly* 93 (Summer 1978): 241–53.

21. Antonin Scalia, assistant attorney general, testimony in U.S., Congress, House, Subcommittee on Administrative Law and Government Relations, *Hearings,* 94th Cong., 1st sess., October and November 1975, p. 377. See also Scalia's "The Legislative Veto: A False Remedy for System Overload," *Regulation* (November-December 1979): 19–26.

22. Louis Fisher, Introduction, *Studies on the Legislative Veto,* prepared by the Congressional Research Service for the Subcommittee on Rules of the House, Committee on Rules, U.S. House of Representatives, 96th Cong., 2d sess., February 1980, pp. 14–15.

23. William J. Lanouette, "Who's Setting Foreign Policy—Carter or Congress?" *National Journal,* 15 July 1978, pp. 1116–23.

24. Statements made in summer of 1974, quoted in Gerald R. Ford, *A Time to Heal* (New York: Harper & Row, 1979), p. 134.

25. Ford, in written reply to a *New York Times* query, quoted in Philip Shabecoff, "Appraising Presidential Power," in *The Presidency Reappraised,* 2nd ed., eds. Thomas E. Cronin and Rexford G. Tugwell (New York: Praeger, 1977), p. 37.

26. Eric L. Davis, "Legislative Liaison in the Carter Administration," *Political Science Quarterly* 94 (Summer 1979): 301.

27. *Newsweek,* 12 April 1976, p. 31, and Gallup Poll for WHYY/PBS (Philadelphia-Wilmington), October 1979, p. 21.

28. Ford, quoted in Don Oberdorfer, "Ford: War Powers Act Not Practical," *Washington Post,* 12 April 1977. See also Gerald R. Ford, "The War Powers Resolution: Striking a Balance between the Executive and Legislative Branches" (speech delivered 11 April 1977 at the University of Kentucky, Louisville, and reprinted by American Enterprise Institute, Reprint 69, June 1977, pp. 1–7).

29. This is a point made by U.S. Senator John G. Tower, "Congress Versus the President," *Foreign Affairs* 60 (Winter, 1981–82): 229–246.

30. See, for example, Robert Novak's views in John Hoy and Melvin Bernstein, eds., *The Effective Presidency* (Pacific Palisades, Calif.: Palisades Press, 1976).

31. Samuel Huntington, "The Democratic Distemper," in *The American Commonwealth*, eds. Nathan Glazer and Irving Kristol (New York: Basic Books, 1976), p. 24.

32. Schlesinger, *Imperial Presidency*, p. 404. See also a similar theme in Theodore Sorensen, *Watchmen in the Night: Presidential Accountability after Watergate* (Cambridge, Mass.: MIT Press, 1975). For a different view, however, see Philip B. Kurland, *Watergate and the Constitution* (Chicago, Ill.: University of Chicago Press, 1978).

33. Theodore C. Sorenson, "Political Perspective: Who Speaks for the National Interest?", in Thomas M. Franck, ed., *The Tethered Presidency: Congressional Restraint on Executive Power* (New York University Press, 1981), p. 14.

34. Larry Tribe, *American Constitutional Law* (Mineola, N.Y.: Foundation Press, 1978), p. 157.

35. Justice Robert Jackson, *United States ex. rel. Knauff v. Shaughnessy*, 338 U.S. 537, 551 (1950).

36. "The President Versus Congress: Special Report," *National Journal*, 29 May 1976, p. 730.

37. For discussions of presidential accountability, see William S. Livingston, "Britain and America: The Institutionalization of Accountability," *Journal of Politics* 38, no. 4 (1976): 879–94; Louis Fisher, *The Constitution between Friends* (New York: St. Martin's Press, 1978), and Cronin, *State of the Presidency*, chap. 10.

Part Five

POLICY-MAKER ROLES AS SOURCES OF AMERICAN FOREIGN POLICY

Many different people, widely dispersed throughout the government, contribute to the making of foreign policy. Some of the departments, offices, and other elements of government concerned with foreign policy were examined in the previous part of this book. In Part V we are concerned with the process of decision making and with how the roles established by the way the government is organized for the conduct of foreign policy influence the behavior of the policy makers occupying those roles, and, ultimately, American foreign policy itself. Our working assumption is that the roles and the process, rather than the characteristics of either the individuals making the decisions or the structures within which they are made, influence the course of action the United States pursues abroad. Furthermore, any changes in policy are assumed to result from changes in the processes through which decisions are reached rather than from changes in individuals or in structures.

The concept of a foreign policy "role" is difficult to grasp intuitively.

The role source category, for example, includes the consideration of the impact of the *nature* of the office on the behavior of its occupants. That is, decision makers' actions are influenced significantly by the socially pre-scribed behaviors and legally sanctioned norms that are attached to a given position.

To suggest that the role one occupies influences one's thoughts and behavior should not be disturbing. All people play roles in life, and unless they are hermits they find themselves on occasion in unprecedented social situations. They respond to new circumstances by changing their attitudes and behavior in accordance with what they think is conduct appropriate to the role they are in. Witness the changes, for example, as shifts are made from the role of student to that of employee, or to that of new parent or even politician; individuals will act, perhaps subconsciously, in the manner they think is expected of them. Their vocabulary and attire change, impor-tant ideas will undergo subtle but meaningful fluctuations, and the way the world is viewed as well as one's place within it will shift in accordance with the new role. Each of us plays a variety of roles in our life, and these roles, evidence suggests, explain and predict our attitudes and behavior.

The positions policy makers hold also substantially affect their behav-ior. Consequently, ultimate policy outcomes are influenced by the kinds of roles existing in the policy-making arena more than by the particular individ-uals who happen to be in authority at any given moment. Role theory goes far, its proponents claim, in explaining why, for example, each recent Ameri-can president has acted, once in office, so much like his predecessor, and why each has come to view American interests and goals in such similar terms. Correspondingly, so the reasoning continues, merely changing the person sitting behind the desk in the Oval Office will not bring about funda-mental alterations in the nation's policies. Nor, for that matter, would mas-sive changes of personnel within the foreign affairs bureaucracies bring about policy innovations. Roles, it seems, determine behavior more than do the qualities of individuals.

Because foreign policy decisions are made by large-scale organi-zations—as, indeed, they must be in order to meet the varied demands faced by a great power—it is necessary to delve into the effects of collec-tive decision making on the kinds of decisions reached and to explore the typical thinking and behavior patterns of individuals who occupy bureau-cratic roles. Indeed, role theory is particularly useful in explaining the kinds of policy decisions routinely made by and within the large bureaucratic organizations that bear responsibility for the implementation of foreign policy, for it seeks to explain not just individual behavior, but group be-havior as well.

Roles attached to bureaucratic positions in the decision-making machinery carry with them certain expectations, obligations, rights, and images of appropriate behavior, and they produce pressures that influence policy performance and policy outcomes. Role pressures may lead, for instance, to inertial respect for the orthodox views of an agency. Such tendencies are clearly more conducive to policy continuity than to innovation or radical revision. In addition, role factors help account for the inability of presidents to get policies implemented by entrenched bureaucratic agencies acting (as role theory suggests they will) in terms of their own parochial needs and preferences rather than in terms of the needs of the president or the nation.

To develop these ideas, the essays assembled in this part explore various ways in which the decision-making roles occupied by individuals and the policy-making roles embraced by entire bureaucracies influence the foreign policy of the United States. In this context the selections address such questions as "What consequences result from the president's dependence on the bureaucratic organizations created to serve him?" and "Are bureaucracies 'ruling servants' in control of policy by virtue of their power to impede?" If so, is a "rational" foreign policy—dictated by the national interests of the country rather than by the parochial interests of the foreign affairs establishment—possible?

PERSPECTIVES ON ROLES AS SOURCES OF AMERICAN FOREIGN POLICY: AN OVERVIEW

What is the most meaningful way to conceptualize the process by which foreign policy decisions are reached? The conventional view maintains that policy makers—notably the president and his principal advisers—devise strategies and implement designs to realize objectives "rationally," that is, in terms of calculations regarding national interests defined by the relative costs and benefits associated with alternative goals and means. However, many scholars have questioned the accuracy of this popular model. Much of the evidence drawn from particular case studies points in another direction: to the strong likelihood that foreign policy making is shaped more fundamentally by bargaining among competing actors within the foreign affairs establishment. Correspondingly, what has come to be known as the "bureaucratic politics model" of decision making has gained popularity as a description of the actual processes through which policy making unfolds. Stressing the roles within large-scale organizations that lead, inevitably, to policy making by negotiated compromise between and among many organizational actors, proponents of the bureaucratic politics model claim it captures the essence of the highly politicized foreign policy decision-making process more completely and accurately than does the model of rational behavior.

The bureaucratic politics model is illustrated by Stephen D. Cohen in the selection entitled "The Impact of Organization on U.S. International Economic Policy." The essay details the institutional setting within which international economic policy is made and demonstrates how the organizational context itself affects the kinds of decisions that are ultimately reached. In the process, Cohen illustrates how decisional procedures and the policy-making process—not simply the foreign policy issue at stake—

often determine the substance of policy. This linkage, suggesting as it does, in the language of George W. Ball, that the process can be the author of the policy, is not altogether comforting because, as Cohen notes, the policy product may be less than satisfactory. But in bringing into focus the extent to which U.S. international economic policy is shaped by the role of politics among bureaucracies within the institutional machinery, Cohen injects a useful dose of realism into the idealized image of rational foreign policy making that most citizens tend to harbor. Incorporating the organizational setting of policy making into the picture also enables us to understand better why bureaucracies seem so preoccupied with such things as their budgets, the morale and loyalty of their staffs, their autonomy, and the protection of their domain of operation from invasion by competing organizations—often, it seems, to the exclusion of concern for the substance of policy. These tendencies, Cohen points out, can be made understandable only by reference to the roles and norms that organizational structures create.

Extending this orientation and the reasoning that underlies it, Jerel A. Rosati demonstrates the utility of explanations of American foreign policy that rest on characteristics of bureaucratic organizations and their operating procedures. His essay, "Explaining SALT from a Bureaucratic Politics Perspective," identifies the central propositions of the bureaucratic politics model. It then shows how these found expression in the decision-making process regarding strategic arms negotiations with the Soviet Union during both the Johnson and Nixon administrations. The study illustrates vividly how decisional roles and decisional contexts influence the course of policy development while also contributing to an understanding of the SALT process as it unfolded within the U.S. government.

For a variety of often incompatible reasons, most observers regard America's involvement in the Vietnam war as an unfortunate, even tragic, event. The protracted series of decisions that took the United States into Indochina and, eventually, after years of fighting and the loss of thousands of lives, out of it on unsatisfactory terms, raises serious questions about the manner in which American foreign policy is conducted. "How Could Vietnam Happen?" asks James C. Thomson, Jr., almost rhetorically. His answer—that the tragedy was rooted in the roles and bureaucratic processes embedded in the way the United States government organizes itself for the making of foreign policy—illustrates vividly the dysfunctional consequences that may emanate from a system characterized by bureaucratic policy making. Thomson's case study thus documents the thesis implicit in role theory and the bureaucratic politics model, namely, that some of the most catastrophic of America's foreign policy initiatives were the result, not of evil or stupid men, but of misdirected behaviors that were encouraged by the nature of the policy-making system. The failure of Vietnam, Thomson contends, was the failure of America's policy-making process, not of its leadership. His argument, however disturbing, adds insight into the milieu of decision making and introduces a large number of concepts crucial to understanding how the roles created by the organizational setting of decision making influences the kinds of decisions that leaders make and that bureaucracies implement.

In principle, bureaucracies and the roles embodied within them are designed to make American foreign policy making more rational and efficient. Bureaucratic organizations are not created by accident—they are created to perform essential functions; without them, the globalist foreign policy posture of the United States could not be maintained. But in practice, the norms and roles of foreign affairs bureaucracies often operate as obstacles to the adaptive reorientation of American foreign policy. In his essay, "Bureaucratic Constraints on Innovation in American Foreign Policy," Charles F. Hermann provides a probing discussion of the ways that the operating procedures of bureaucratic organizations may interfere with the nation's ability to confront successfully emergent challenges from abroad. His broad-ranging treatment of the way agendas are set and problems detected (or *not* detected) provides a perceptive diagnosis of the effects of organizational behavior on successive stages of the policy-making process. The essay asks whether the organizational procedures associated with the worldview of the Cold War era will be able to cope with the issues of the 1980s. The tasks implied in the question are highlighted by Hermann's conclusion that "more than hope is needed to make certain that the interaction of new situations and old organizational routines does not obstruct the recognition and definition of problems that need to get on the American national agenda and on the agenda of other governments and world actors as well."

Finally, we include a thoughtful critique of bureaucratic politics focused on the 1962 Cuban missile crisis, and in particular of perhaps the most famous bureaucratic treatment of that critical juncture in Soviet-American relations, Graham Allison's *Essence of Decision*. Stephen D. Krasner's "Are Bureaucracies Important?" finds Allison's interpretation wanting. Krasner argues that the picture Allison and others provide of foreign policy making, which emphasizes bureaucratic roles as all-powerful determinants of policy outcomes, is greatly exaggerated. Indeed, Krasner's reexamination of the facts surrounding the Cuban missile crisis reveals overwhelming evidence that, while bureaucracies do exert an impact on foreign policy, decision makers nonetheless have a capacity for rational choice, and that the choices they make—rather than those made by bureaucratic organizations—ultimately matter most. Hence, individuals elected by and responsible to the people they represent, *do* matter, and how they define their decision-making roles can prove decisive. In essence, Krasner's essay poses a challenge to those whose explanations of American foreign policy rest almost exclusively on bureaucratic roles. In so doing, his article sets the stage for a consideration of the impact that leaders' personal predispositions exert on the content of American foreign policy, the topic of the subsequent section of this book.

21

THE IMPACT OF ORGANIZATION ON U.S. INTERNATIONAL ECONOMIC POLICY

STEPHEN D. COHEN

The international economic policies of the United States are the out-growth of four basic trends: the values, ideologies, and personalities of the president and his senior political-economic advisers; the sentiment of Congress; trends and events overseas; and the organization in the executive branch by which policy is constructed. The first two factors reflect the preferences of U.S. voters. The third is largely beyond the control of any one country. The final variable, organization, is the easiest to control and the subject of this [essay]. It is therefore deserving of intensive analysis.

Organizational variants and bureaucratic behavior patterns are important, if not critical, variables in determining policy substance. U.S. international economic policy is frequently a reflection of organizational dynamics, namely the procedures for reconciling values and goals. Individuals articulate and defend these values and goals, but there is a high correlation between the positions taken by individuals and their bureaucratic affiliation. In effect, role playing becomes the first stage of policy formulation. The second stage is the efficiency with which organizational processes reconcile competing intrabureaucratic concerns and perspectives.

THE RELATIONSHIP OF THE ORGANIZATIONAL PROCESS TO POLICY SUBSTANCE

The procedures by which international economic policy is formulated are one factor in determining the nature of the final product—policy substance. Bureaucratic actors are charged with worrying about different dimensions of international economic policy, and it is in their interest to have as much influence as possible in enhancing their viewpoint and con-

Originally published in Stephen D. Cohen, *The Making of United States International Economic Policy*, Second Edition, Praeger Publishers, 1981. © 1981 by Praeger Publishers. Reprinted with permission.

taining opposing positions. Each bureaucratic actor considers its dimension—and the values and constituents involved therein—to be very important. Each will pursue a relatively consistent set of perspectives and priorities commensurate with its perceived mission and self-interests under any conventional arrangement. The success or failure of its drive to maximize certain values will be a function of the extent to which the government's decision-making process listens to and takes seriously the various bureaucratic inputs. An overall organization that is biased in favor of, or against, certain agencies probably will tilt policy priorities in certain directions. Assuming the bureaucratic political process is operating within an efficient overall process and in a democratic environment, a balanced policy is more probable than in a situation where the environment is controlled by a "benevolent despot" operating with a clear presidential mandate and an equally clear policy orientation. The policymaking process is a political process.

The impact of organization on the substance of policy cannot be described or predicted with precision. Furthermore, economics, being more an art than a science, would present limitations on policy prognosis under any type of organization. The reasons for the importance of government organization and procedures in general were well summarized by the Murphy Commission and are relevant here:

> Good organization does not insure successful policy. Nor does poor organization preclude successful policy. But steadily and powerfully, organizational patterns influence the effectiveness of government.
>
> Policymaking on any subject of importance requires adequate consultation with the various parties legitimately concerned, and balanced assessment of the alternative courses of action. Once a decision is made, it must be clearly communicated to those responsible or affected by it, carefully monitored in its implementation, and evaluated for its actual effects. . . .
>
> But organization affects more than the efficiency of government; it can affect the outcome of decisions. Organizational patterns determine the probabilities that a decision will be taken at one level rather than another, or in one agency instead of another.[1]

The question of the impact of organization in this case should be divided into two reasonably distinct processes. The primary one is how the different goals, perspectives, self-interests, and ideas of the participating bureaucracies are to be introduced and assigned weights and priorities. The existence or nonexistence of particular departments and offices, the distribution of powers, procedures for concurrence or consultation, and staffing patterns are organizational arrangements that present advantages and disadvantages to competing interests. Therefore, the key question in organizing is, specifically: Which perspectives are introduced, when, and with what weights in the processes of decision and action? The key is to assure that before the government embraces a given policy, all important interests will be represented, and that the weights accorded to competing considerations will be appropriately balanced and reviewed in a timely fashion.

The struggle to maximize the impact of one's own values in the weighting process is the heart of bureaucratic politics. Energetic bureaucracies seek to do this by protecting their domain and autonomy and by enhancing their budget. Sheer size can be an effective tool in the bureaucratic struggle by assuring that a pool of talent is available, first to provide an agency position, and then to overwhelm competing agencies with a barrage of expertise and argumentation. An agency's having the chairman of an interagency working group can be turned to its advantage if it is possible to dominate the setting of the agenda or the selection of participating organizations. The control of communications from overseas embassies and delegations, or of data reported by the private sector (for example, crop forecasts and harvests) are powers that, if used selectively, can affect the delicate balancing of the weighting process. Recourse can be made to the power and influence of constituents or allies in the private sector and in the Congress as an aid to the intrabureaucratic struggle.

Access to the president's Oval Office is another organizational means of affecting policy. This can be done by being the last official to talk with the president before he decides a delicate issue, or by being able to add a cover note commenting on the memoranda submitted by the responsible departments on a given matter; or, it may be the power to write the memorandum to the president on behalf of the departments and agencies involved in policy formulation; finally, it may be the method itself by which the bureaucracy makes policy recommendations to the president. President Eisenhower's wanting a unified recommendation from his advisers often led to a watered-down consensus being the standard procedure. In contrast, President Nixon's wanting to see all of the options allowed the extreme range of viewpoints to be brought before the president's attention. In one documented case (Nixon's renunciation of U.S. chemical and biological warfare capabilities), the difference in presidential memo styles affected the substance of policy by impelling the president to upset the long standing status quo.

The second and lesser process normally precedes the weighting process—it may be broadly categorized as the support function. Included here would be personnel training and practices; lines of communication and authority; liaison with groups outside the executive branch; and information—intelligence, analysis, and planning. In terms of the stages of policymaking, this category would emphasize problem identification, data collection, and evaluation stages. The viewpoint weighting category would emphasize the enunciation of options and actual decision stages.

Organizational issues, in sum, are much more than academic ponderings as to where to move boxes on a chart. They involve struggles for position and power. By making it easier for some officials than for others to have access to the most senior ranks, by providing for the accumulation of one kind of information and not another, or by following procedures that let some problems rise to the top of the government's agenda before others, some organizational procedures facilitate certain kinds of policy while other procedures facilitate other kinds of policy.[2]

The focus, chairmanship, and membership of the various groups comprising the interagency coordination process, discussed in detail below, can affect the outcome of a specific policy formulation process. Different international economic policy-related coordinating groups have different mandates, and departments seeking approval (or rejection) of a policy proposal will prefer to utilize a group with a comparable perspective. This was the reason for the State and Treasury departments' each adopting a preference during the Ford administration for different White House coordinating bodies (the National Security Council and the Economic Policy Board, respectively). This explains the ploy by certain agencies to use the White House's Economic Policy Group (chaired by the secretary of the treasury) rather than the Trade Policy Committee (chaired by the U.S. trade representative) in 1980 to consider the possible reinstitution of the Trigger Price Mechanism to provide a floor price for steel imports. Given its opposition to this proposal on the grounds that it was unacceptably inflationary, the Treasury Department naturally opted to have interagency deliberations and articulation of policy recommendations to the president emanate from a forum whose focus was macroeconomic policy, not the area of trade relations (where a good case could be made for the steel import proposal).

A good deal of international economic policy consists of outgoing instructions to U.S. negotiating delegations and embassies overseas. The absence or presence of a given agency, or bureau within an agency, in the process that clears outgoing communications from Washington, D.C. could make the difference in part of the contents and in the overall nuance of the policy position being transmitted to the field.

Departments are seldom successful in realizing their deep-rooted ambitions to achieve unequivocal domination over sectors of international economic policy. In most cases, the decision-making process must function with the premise that different, and sometimes opposing, viewpoints must be accommodated and integrated into policy substance. The basic issue is how diversity of bureaucratic actors and diversity of goals are to be managed.

THE BUREAUCRATIC POLITICS OF INTERNATIONAL ECONOMIC POLICY

There is no single answer to the question of what is the ultimate overriding objective of U.S. international economic policy. Is it to prevent international chaos and warfare? Is it to contribute to the domestic political base of the Democratic or Republican parties? Is it to increase the relative wealth and comfort of U.S. citizens? Is it to contribute to a better distribution of the world's income? Or is it to serve as an external outlet to increase the profits of those sectors of U.S. industry venturing into international business transactions? To resort to cliche, honorable people can differ. To use logic, the answer includes all of the above. There cannot be one answer for overall policy for any extended period of time. International economic policy on a day-to-day basis requires the constant reconciliation between ever-changing priorities in domestic politics and economics and overseas politics and economics. These competing interests cannot be quantified and assigned fixed weights over an extended time period.

As a consequence, there can be no unambiguous, self-apparent strategy or tactics in U.S. international economic policy on a permanent basis. Trade-offs are required in the policy formulation process. Strategy becomes a series of variations on a number of themes. Even when general agreement existed that national security concerns were dominant, there was no unanimity as to exactly which tactics would best serve national security priorities. The current coequal status of national security and domestic economic concerns serves to multiply the need to reconcile competing interests within the federal bureaucracy. Rather than a methodical process of determining what is in the overall national interest under such circumstances, inexact shortcuts are more likely to be used. The policy search seeks out the acceptable, not necessarily the excellent.

The study of U.S. foreign policy has undergone a major shift in emphasis. No longer is policy attributed simply to the construction of a national interest-related, power-seeking response by a unitary, rational actor—that is, the federal government. The bureaucratic politics model dismisses grand theories of policy, be they pragmatism or imperialism. The model doubts that events in international politics consist essentially of deliberate, purposive acts of unified national governments or that their behavior can be understood as being analogous to the intelligent, coordinated acts of individual human beings. Devil theories, conspiracies, and the gross incompetence of the bureaucracy are all discarded as determinants of policy.

What the bureaucratic politics model does suggest is that, in most instances, government policy can best be understood in terms of the outcome of bargaining among participants in various parts of the bureaucracy. Policy emanates not from a centralized, objective decision maker, but from a conglomerate of large organizations and political actors with different missions, different perceptions, and different priorities. Frequently disagreeing among themselves about what their government should do on a particular issue, bureaucracies compete against each other in attempting to determine both governmental policies and actions.[3]

Bureaucratic units having jurisdiction in a policy sector negotiate among themselves when considering the formulation of U.S. policy. Each unit has a reasonably predictable visceral reaction to policy issues, which determines the departmental position to be presented and defended in interagency groups. These reactions are directly related to bureaucratic "essence"—the dominant view held in each organization concerning its mission and needs. The actual technique of bargaining is affected by existing organizational arrangements. So, too, are the outcomes of the negotiations. In any event, the individual positions of the bureaucratic players in international economic policy could generally be predicted in specific instances if one knows merely how each organization perceives its own overall self-interest. Bureaucratic officials seldom have an a priori vision of a common approach to an issue. They seldom are venal or stupid. Rather, they are all searching, but from different angles.

In point of fact, few situations suggest a response or course of action that is unambiguously, unequivocally correct and consonant with everyone's priorities and preferences. More often than not, policy is determined by a committee-bred consensus that everyone can live with; that is, a line of least resistance, not a font of dynamism. The need to pursue bureaucratic consensus means that the policymaking process more often than not is a pragmatic search for a mutually acceptable course of conduct than an idealistic pursuit of optimal policy.

Shared perceptions of broad principles held by all in the bureaucracy can render the normal bargaining process unnecessary. In the case of international economic relations, the desirability of promoting essentially free-market oriented trade and investment systems is universally accepted within the U.S. government as being good policy. It is thus a shared perception, as is the need in principle for the rich countries to financially assist the poorer countries. However, conflicting "microactions" and "micropolicies" can, and do, fall within the broad limits set by these perceptions. When the virtue of an action or policy is ambiguous and uncertain, as is generally the case, a quick consensus is rare, despite a few shared images.

At any given moment, divergent viewpoints can exist on the precise means of proceeding towards a stable, growing, and equitable market-oriented world economy. In studying international economic policy or foreign policy, it is insufficient to say that the United States seeks global prosperity in the former and seeks to protect and enhance its security in the latter policy area. Such generalizations afford very little predictive power concerning policy specifics. Similarly, they ignore the fact that if these two objectives prove to be mutually exclusive vis-à-vis a specific issue, priority weights will have to be apportioned on a case-by-case basis. If we are to explain and anticipate a nation's international economic policy decisions and actions, we must first identify the various participants of the bureaucracy, discover the sources of their particular perceptions of the national good, and seek to understand the process of interaction that yields decisions and actions. This process of identification would be of enormous value in determining how U.S. interests are measured and what resources could be utilized to pursue these interests.

Given the imprecision of the social sciences, the form of international economic policy is subjective in nature. To those who argue that "good policy is good policy," the question that must be asked is: Who is to determine exactly what is good policy at a given moment? In the case of U.S. international economic relations, the answer is that it must be a joint or group effort among dozens of executive branch departments, agencies, and offices. The system is not built to allow major decisions by one department in callous disregard for the views of others. Indirectly, this effort includes congressional preferences and the viewpoint of organized public opinion as expressed by corporations, trade associations, labor unions, and consumer and environmental groups.

The interaction of these groups is the raw material of U.S. international economic policy, just as it is in the case of traditional national security-related foreign policy. Certain principles of the bureaucratic politics model are applicable to economic policy interaction: government officials will examine any policy proposal, at least in part, to determine whether it will increase the effectiveness with which the mission of their particular organization can be carried out. Their organizational responsibilities will help to define for these officials the nature of the issue as they see it.[4]

Policy officials' viewpoints (at least on the record) typically become identified closely with those of their agency, which is where their careers, reputations, and professional self-esteem are made or broken. In the course of his duties, the typical public servant seldom perceives any major conflicts either between his personal views and those of his organization, or between his organization's attitude and his view of the national welfare. In the first place, persons are not likely to be attracted to, or to flourish in, organizations whose missions are antithetical to their personal values. Few persons who are antagonistic to utilizing negotiations as a means of pursuing international harmony would be attracted to the foreign service. An antagonism toward big business would discourage career employment with the Commerce or Treasury departments. Furthermore, barring crass hypocrisy, most bureaucrats who have developed a philosophic difference of opinion would seek transfer to another agency.

The image of the U.S. government employing a unitary strategy over a long period of time to march lockstep toward an international economic grand design is a chimera. In many instances, individual actions and policies are better understood—and are predictable—as the end products of ceaseless bureaucratic maneuvers, which only occasionally are dominated by the objective intellectual merits of the issue. In the abstract, countries do pursue broad national interests. But bureaucracies play politics. They pursue individual values and goals in a milieu of differing opinions. They seek to maximize these values by using their own resources and capabilities to determine what exactly is "good policy." Each bureaucracy is created to perform a specified function. Bureaucrats are paid to worry about a relatively narrow aspect of overall U.S. interests. "All organizations seek *influence*;

many also have a specific *mission* to perform; and some organizations need to maintain expensive *capabilities* in order to perform their mission effectively."[5]

An insider's perspective on this process was revealed by W. Michael Blumenthal in 1979, after he had resigned as secretary of the treasury. The focus of the interview was the reflections of a businessman on his public service in Washington, D.C.; i.e., how management styles differ between the public and private sectors and how the frustrations and rewards differ. "The people who come to Washington to work at the top level of government do so because they want to influence policy," he said. The bureaucracies that these people lead are in a sense their instruments for exerting this influence. In a later passage, Blumenthal advised people assuming senior roles in government that "you should recognize that you lose your anonymity for a while, you lose your freedom in many ways, you work harder than you ever did before, the level of frustrations will rise inordinately, and you'll take great risks of being portrayed as something you're not." (He discreetly omitted mention of a large reduction in salary, as well.) Nevertheless, argued Blumenthal, government service is worthwhile; his experience as treasury secretary provided him with "the satisfaction, the thrill of participating at the center of the decision-making process and helping to make the kind of system of government work that I believe to be the best."[6]

Alexander M. Haig, Jr.'s resignation of his corporate presidency to return to Washington in 1981 to become secretary of state exemplified Mr. Blumenthal's criteria for public service fulfillment. General Haig made it immediately clear that he would be no figurehead. Among his earliest efforts at his job was the (unsuccessful) attempt to gain White House approval for expanded State Department policymaking authority. Even without the requested directives, he convened several interagency meetings on a host of foreign policy issues, a prerogative usually assumed by the National Security Council. "Other agencies sent representatives, lest they be left out of the action. Their attendance ratified the authority of the State Department to create and preside over the policy groups on an interim basis."[7] Images of authority are important. Although none of this assured the State Department that it would expand its bureaucratic control and power, it shifted the odds somewhat in its favor.

Nevertheless, there are also many instances when direct presidential intervention or perfectly shared perceptions in the bureaucracy have negated the effects of bureaucratic politics on international economic policy. An example of the first situation was the crude bullying of Japan between 1969 and 1971 by the Nixon White House to restrict that country's textile exports to our market. Not only did this policy violate the basic U.S. preference for market forces over governmental intervention, it excluded any meaningful participation by the line departments. On the question of whether to limit new foreign direct investment abroad or within the United

States, there is a bureaucratic consensus that the national interest requires an essentially "open-door" approach. Similarly, a consensus exists on the merits of flexible exchange rates over fixed ones.

The majority of efforts at international economic policymaking, however, must follow from a basic dilemma: Is a strong, stable domestic economy the prerequisite for an effective, domestically popular U.S. involvement in the world order in general and in international economic relations in particular? Or is an accommodating, flexible international economic policy the means of assuring national security in a favorable world environment at the tolerable cost of occasional, limited financial losses to certain sectors of the domestic economy? International economic policy is simultaneously subtle and complex. This situation encourages bureaucratic participants to regularly argue different, predictable points of view.

The general principles of bureaucratic politics are similar in the cases of both national security and international economic policies. The presence of bureaucratic disagreement is assured in the latter area for three reasons: the larger number of bureaucratic participants involved; the pervasively unclear lines of jurisdiction, or domain; and the imprecision of economics, wherein economists continually differ on both technical analyses and policy prescriptions. On questions of defense and military operations, a pattern of shared responsibilities has developed between the National Security Council (NSC), the Pentagon, the State Department, and the Joint Chiefs of Staff. But a far messier, overlapping pattern exists in the international economic area. Not only does primary jurisdiction vary according to the sector involved (trade, investment, and so on), but even within the same sector, considerable confusion and overlap exist. This pattern of fragmentation unfortunately is repeated in the corresponding jurisdictions of the congressional committee system.

The jurisdictional arguments that arise frequently in international economic policy formulation are surrogates to a significant degree for deeprooted cleavages of basic objectives, perspectives, and self-interests. Discussions of jurisdictional and coordinating problems often mask what are really conflicts over the priorities of the two fundamental approaches to the subject. International economic policy can be viewed as being *primarily* an extension of domestic economic policy management, or as *primarily* the economic aspect of foreign regulations. The resolutions of these conflicts indicate which bureaucratic players have the most power and influence in translating their objectives into actual policy. This is a very healthy exercise if reasonably controlled to prevent prolonged or excessive argumentation. It must be remembered that right answers are elusive, and by definition, a number of factors must be inserted into a valid calculation of the national interest in international economic relations.

Bureaucratic politics in this area reaches its zenith in the rivalry between the State and Treasury departments. This is no coincidence. The former is the most important department in the conduct of U.S. foreign policy; the latter is the most important department in the conduct of domestic economic policy. Each department has extensive interests and resources, and each has a very different perception of its mission. The key to most policy formulation is the reconciliation of their two missions; that is, pursuit of a harmonious world order versus pursuit of a stable, prosperous domestic economy. In matters of food policy, the U.S. Department of Agriculture (USDA) substitutes for Treasury, in name only, to pursue domestic values, sometimes against State's foreign priorities.

A compromise or a common position between State and Treasury normally is tantamount to the establishment of U.S. international economic policy, except when extraordinary congressional pressures are applied. There are many instances when their perspectives and goals coincide, such as the need for a hardline American attitude to the oil price increases by the OPEC cartel and a disinclination to impose quotas on specialty steel or footwear imports in response to escape clause recommendations by the International Trade Commission (ITC) in 1976. In other cases, there are only minor nuances in their policy recommendations. Disagreements stemming from their dissimilar missions, values, and internal structures are innumerable but not inevitable.

The Department of State has overall charge of the design and conduct of American foreign policy. Other things being equal, that organization's perspective will emphasize the needs and sensitivities of other countries as well as their responses to U.S. policies. The department will argue the need to prevent the isolation of the U.S. position on international issues, and it will defend the utility of give-and-take negotiations to promote agreement and international harmony. Given the role of world leadership assumed by the United States, the State Department is not happy when other countries are unhappy with U.S. indifference to their legitimate economic interests.

Although the attitudes and actions of other countries are legitimate, necessary factors in policy formulation, the perception of the State Department as a knee-jerk spokesman for foreigners has grown so extensively that it is more relevant than whatever is the real situation. This perception has weakened the department's credibility in the policymaking process, especially in Congress. State is also disadvantaged by having no natural domestic constituency (as do the Treasury, Commerce, Agriculture, and Labor departments) from which to gain additional support from outside the bureaucratic system.

Prior to the 1970s, foreign service traditions inspired an indifference toward the need for maximizing the department's competence in international economic matters. Before the belated discovery that economic issues were here to stay, and that the foreign service was losing clout because of its lack of economic expertise, an actual career disincentive existed for foreign-service officers specializing in economics rather than political affairs. Changes in recruiting and promotion techniques have eased this situation. Nevertheless, the hiring of senior economists on a lateral entry basis is all but unknown in the department at the present time. Overall, the approach of State to international economic policy today is still influenced by the inevitable priorities of bright, career-oriented people who are being paid to be responsive to a foreign viewpoint and who are usually looking ahead to their next overseas assignment.

The erasure of the demarcation line between foreign and domestic concerns means that the Treasury Department has demonstrated a continuing and significant leadership role in the international sphere since the 1950s. A profound effect on the policymaking process has resulted from the different values and missions that are associated with the Treasury. Whereas State has been active in the foreign arena since the founding of the Republic, Treasury's continuing involvement has been both relatively recent and sudden. It has relatively little tradition or experience, therefore, in dealing with and accommodating the policies of other sovereign countries. It judges friendly countries not so much on a military basis as in terms of their impact on the American economy. Whereas State's values are rooted in international political cooperation, Treasury's values are rooted in the pursuit of a healthy U.S. economy and preservation of such basic capitalistic principles as the market mechanism. This fosters an insular approach based on economic orthodoxy.

Just as businessmen look for profits, Treasury and Commerce look to the advancement of American domestic economic interests and values as the indicator of sound international policy. These departments, unlike the State Department, exist to worry about U.S. economic security, not traditional national security. Countries are judged to be friendly or hostile mainly in terms of their impact on the U.S. economy, not on the more traditional basis of political orientation and military strength.

A major implication of this situation is that the Treasury Department tends to have a "nondifferentiated-adversary attitude" toward international relations. Allies deserve no special economic favors at the cost of the domestic economy. Unlike State, which primarily deals with and worries about foreign governments, and Defense, which worries about foreign military bases, the Treasury Department has relatively little dependency on the goodwill of other countries.

The Treasury Department as an organization has capitalized on the fact that the performance of the economy has become critically important to the fortunes of the incumbent president and his party. Aided by a succession of strong secretaries in the 1971–76 period, a large, influential organization has been built. No other line department has Treasury's number of professionally trained international economists. No other department has established such an extensive series of links with congressmen and business and financial leaders. These outsiders generally are more knowledgeable and have greater personal stakes in international economic relations than in foreign political questions. In general, their domestic orientation and emphasis on fiscal soundness coincide with the Treasury's approach.

It now takes a very strong secretary of state to neutralize the greater domestic political appeal and stronger alliances of the Treasury Department. . . .

NOTES

1. [Report of the] *Commission on the Organization of the Government for the Conduct of Foreign Policy* (Washington, D.C.: U.S. Government Printing Office, 1975), p. 21.
2. Roger Hilsman, *The Politics of Policy Making in Defense and Foreign Affairs* (New York: Harper and Row, 1971), p. 152.
3. Graham Allison and Morton Halperin, *Bureaucratic Politics: A Paradigm and Some Policy Implications*, Reprint 246 (Washington, D.C.: Brookings Institution, 1972), p. 42.
4. Morton Halperin and Arnold Kanter, *Readings in American Foreign Policy* (Boston: Little, Brown, 1973), p. 10.
5. Ibid.
6. "Candid Reflections of a Businessman in Washington," *Fortune*, January 29, 1979, p. 49.
7. Don Oberdorfer, "Haig Starts Fast and Strong," *Washington Post*, February 8, 1981.

22

EXPLAINING SALT FROM A BUREAUCRATIC POLITICS PERSPECTIVE

JEREL A. ROSATI

In *Presidential Power: The Politics of Leadership,* Richard Neustadt's recurring theme is that "Presidential power is the power to persuade."[1] A President, in order to be more than just a clerk—a leader—must make use of his influence. According to Neustadt, the efficacy of a President's influence is derived from three related sources: the bargaining advantages inherent in the job, his professional reputation, and his public prestige. Thus, power does not automatically exude from a President; he must work to promote his influence. *Presidential Power* was one of the earliest works of significance to describe the governmental process as one of inherent bargaining.[2]

Since 1960, many researchers have described the bargaining nature of the governmental decision-making process. Studies have been particularly concerned with the intricacies of making foreign policy decisions. Samuel P. Huntington, Warner Schilling, and Roger Hilsman have depicted policy as a result of negotiating and bargaining among the major participants.[3] However, it was Graham Allison who solidified the bargaining nature of governmental policy into a decision-making model.

Using the Cuban missile crisis as a case study, Allison formalized three decision-making paradigms.[4] Two of these—organizational process and governmental politics—have popularly become known as the "bureaucratic politics" model of decision making. Allison's formulations have been further complemented by the work of Morton Halperin. . . .[5]

The bureaucratic politics model has achieved great popularity since its initial presentation. According to Robert P. Haffa, Jr., "Allison's analytic approach to decision-making theory has recently become one of the most

Jerel A. Rosati, "Developing a Systematic Decision-Making Framework: Bureaucratic Politics in Perspective," *World Politics*, Vol. 33, No. 2 (January, 1981): pp. 234–251. This selection has been abridged and the footnotes renumbered to appear in consecutive order, with the permission of the author and publisher. Reproduced by permission of Princeton University Press.

widely disseminated concepts in all of social science."[6] Numerous works, particularly those concerned with U.S. foreign policy, have utilized the bureaucratic politics approach in their description and explanation of the policy process.[7]

As is typical of a popular concept, much criticism has been leveled at the model [See especially Stephen Krasner's essay in this volume—*eds.*]. A great deal of debate concerning the applicability of bureaucratic politics to policy-making behavior has resulted. In this [essay], I intend to clarify some of the assertions and corresponding confusion regarding the controversy.[8] First, I will define the foundation of the bureaucratic politics model. Second, the policy-making behavior for SALT I under the Johnson and Nixon administrations is presented to serve as an illustration of the model's decision-making relevance. . . .[9]

THE BUREAUCRATIC POLITICS MODEL

The bureaucratic politics model describes decision making only as it occurs in the executive branch. Allison and Halperin are not concerned with decisions involving the legislative branch or other external institutions: "Here we focus only on part of this process—that involving the bureaucracy and the President as he deals with the bureaucracy."[10]

The primary sources of the bureaucratic politics model are Allison's "Conceptual Models and the Cuban Missile Crisis" (fn. 4) and *Essence of Decision,*[11] Allison and Halperin's "Bureaucratic Politics," and Halperin's *Bureaucratic Politics and Foreign Policy* (both fn. 5). From these four sources, I have extracted four propositions that express the essential ingredients of the bureaucratic politics model, without some of the model's limiting rigidity.[12]

Proposition I. For any single issue, the executive branch of the government is composed of numerous individuals and organizations, with various differences in goals and objectives. Any one issue will draw the concern and involvement of a number of diverse individuals and organizations in the executive branch. The divergent goals of the interested parties result in conflict over the issue; at a minimum, the participants are not in agreement regarding methods:

> The "maker" of government policy is not a single calculating decision-maker, but rather a conglomerate of large organizations and political actors who differ substantially about what their government should do on any particular issue and who compete in attempting to affect both governmental decisions and the actions of their government.[13]

> Each government consists of numerous individuals, many of them working in large organizations. Constrained, to be sure, by the shared images of their society, these individuals nevertheless have very different interests, very different priorities, and are concerned with very different questions.[14]

Proposition 2. No preponderant individual or organization exists; the President, if involved, is merely one participant, although his influence may be the most powerful. In the bureaucratic politics perspective, the President is far from omnipotent in influence. Allison believes that in the United States government, the President is only one of many chiefs: "the President, the Secretaries of State, Defense, and Treasury, the Director of the Central Intelligence Agency, the Joint Chiefs of Staff, and, since 1961, the Special Assistant for National Security Affairs." Furthermore, even if the President were to exercise his authority, a Presidential decision is not necessarily binding: "When a governmental or Presidential decision is reached, the larger game is not over. Decisions can be reversed or ignored."[15] Therefore for any single issue, no participant involved is dominant, including the President.

Proposition 3. The final decision is a "political resultant"—the outcome of bargaining and compromise among the various participants. Since no one participant is powerful enough to force a decision through when disagreement exists among the participants, the eventual decision is a result of consensus. Policies are

> resultants in the sense that what happens is not chosen as a solution to the problem but rather results from compromise, conflict, and confusion of officials with diverse interests and unequal influence; political in the sense that the activity from which decisions and actions emerge is best characterized as bargaining along regularized channels among individual members of the government.[16]

A decision is the result of the "pulling and hauling" among the various participants as they attempt to advance their concepts of personal, group, organizational, and national interests.

Proposition 4. A considerable gap usually exists between the formulated decision and its implementation. Once a decision has been reached, the decision-making process does not come to an end; the decision must still be implemented.[17] Due to the lack of central direction and control, considerable slippage can occur between the formulation and the implementation of a decision: "What is done will be heavily influenced by the standard operating procedures and interests of the implementers."[18] Allison and Halperin maintain that deviation occurs because "decisions are rarely tailored to facilitate monitoring. As a result, senior players have great difficulty in checking on the faithful implementation of a decision."[19] The implementation of a decision, consequently, will usually produce some unintended variation.

These four propositions comprise the essential elements of the bureaucratic politics model of decision making. The first two form the "structure" of the decision-making model: numerous individuals and organizations, with varying interests, are involved for any single issue, without the predominance of any participant. The latter two propositions comprise the decision-making "process": the decision is formulated through bargaining and compromise, and considerable slippage occurs during implementation. The bureaucratic politics model, hence, focuses on the decision-making structure and process in describing and explaining foreign policy behavior. A description of decision-making behavior during the first Strategic Arms Limitation Talks (SALT I) in the Johnson and Nixon administrations will serve as an illustration of the model's applicability in policy making.[20]

SALT I AND THE JOHNSON ADMINISTRATION[21]

During the Johnson administration, numerous individuals and organizations with contrary viewpoints were involved in making decisions concerning SALT I. President Johnson, however, played only a minor role; he rarely took an active part in the decision-making process. The resultant SALT I proposal was presented by an *ad hoc* group that incorporated the views of the various participants, and thus anticipated the bargaining and compromise that would be required.

Most of the major organizations concerned with foreign policy issues in general were involved in the formulation of the U.S. government's position on SALT—the Defense Department, State Department, the Arms Control and Disarmament Agency (ACDA), and the Central Intelligence Agency.[22] The latter was particularly concerned with force postures and capabilities, and with the issue of verification. Arms limitations were the principal concern of ACDA and the State Department. Within the Defense Department, a conglomeration of organizations became involved: the military was represented by the Joint Chiefs of Staff (JCS) and by the individual services—Army, Navy, and Air Force. On the civilian side, there were International Security Affairs (ISA), Systems Analysis, Defense Department Research and Engineering (DDR&E), and the Defense Intelligence Agency (DIA).

As a result of the variety of the participants, the SALT decision-making process produced severe intragovernmental conflicts. "Narrow organizational interests aside, much of the conflict proceeds from two attitudes driven far apart by some SALT-related issues, less so by others."[23] One side favored restricting the development and deployment of strategic weaponry. The other side—normally considered more "hard line"—feared that any arms limitation would undermine security due to cheating and accelerated development by the Soviet Union in areas not covered by any agreement. "In the broadest sense, the order of battle pits the State Department and ACDA against the Pentagon."[24] In general, the former were sympathetic to arms negotiations while the latter was skeptical. For the most part, the CIA was in agreement with the views of the State Department and ACDA. The White House was rarely involved in the decision-making process beyond the actual initiation of the SALT talks.

During 1966 and 1967, the Johnson administration had made a number of overtures to the Soviet Union concerning the possibility of a discussion on arms limitations, but Moscow had not responded favorably. However, in a speech before the United Nations on May 20, 1968, the Russians signaled that they were now interested in taking steps to reach an agreement on arms limitations. Johnson reacted soon afterwards: while signing the Non-Proliferation Treaty, he acknowledged that the United States was willing to meet with the Soviet Union in the near future to discuss limitations on strategic weapons.[25]

Once the talks had been agreed upon, a U.S. negotiating position had to be developed. President Johnson refused to become involved in the decision-making process. He wanted to present a consensus position to the U.S.S.R:

> Neither Johnson nor his staff would take part in bureaucracy's epic struggle to produce not just a simple, clear proposal, but one that would actually make a serious matter of SALT. In Johnson's day there was no Henry Kissinger to hold the bureaucracy in line and to force up Presidential options, as distinct from the preferences of the various parts of the government. Unlike Nixon, Johnson—as everyone in government knew—wanted agreement, not options. This meant that the Joint Chiefs had to be on board.[26]

While Johnson sought consensus, he also insisted that the U.S. SALT position be ready by late summer—which left very little time for the bargaining process to develop within the bureaucracy.

The initiative to present a SALT position was taken by Morton Halperin, the Deputy Assistant Secretary of Defense for Policy Planning and Arms Control. He ignored the staff of military and civilian arms control specialists directly assigned to him; instead, he organized an *ad hoc* working group, recruiting his own personnel from within and outside the government. This group—which became known as "the SALT committee"—consisted of middle-level bureaucrats:

> The tiny ISA Halperin unit became the nucleus of a Pentagon committee that controlled the SALT process. . . . This little *ad hoc* band identified the issues, analyzed them, and solicited estimates, often independently, from various parts of the intelligence community.[27]

Since the State Department and ACDA were sympathetic toward SALT, the Halperin group had little trouble in getting them to approve the bypass procedure. The Joint Chiefs, however, were suspicious of the arms negotiations. Thus, the SALT committee was very deliberate in meeting the minimum demands of the JCS.[28]

> Pressed to implement the President's directive for a consensus position, the Defense participants joined in a fruitful prenegotiation of disputed points. Questions were not presented formally to JCS until they could be framed in a manner calculated to elicit concurrence.[29]

Thus, before making a formal presentation to the Joint Chiefs, the Halperin group solicited support for the proposal among the lower-level personnel of the Pentagon. In this way, the "pulling and hauling" needed to reach consensus was circumvented.

The proposal was sent to the JCS only one week before it would be presented to the Committee of Principals, the group who would directly pass the proposal on to the President.[30] The essence of the proposal was a broad permissiveness in the development of antiballistic missiles (ABM) and a freeze on long-range offensive missiles—both land (ICBM) and sea (SLBM)—at existing levels.[31] After one week of deliberation, the Joint Chiefs agreed to the proposal: they only suggested minor revisions, which were quickly incorporated by the Halperin group.[32] President Johnson received and approved the entire package in late August. The talks between Washington and Moscow were scheduled to begin on September 30.

Newhouse points out that "little of preparation for SALT had much reference to Moscow's attitudes; Washington did not know what these were. The concern was, not what might be negotiable with Moscow, but what could be negotiated within the Pentagon."[33] Regardless of the viability of the U.S. SALT package, the talks were called off when Soviet military units intervened in Czechoslovakia.

SALT I AND THE NIXON ADMINISTRATION[34]

Although evidence of the bureaucratic politics model was occasionally visible, a totally different decision-making pattern for SALT emerged during the Nixon administration. The White House became actively involved in the strategic arms limitation talks.

Nixon came to the Presidency with a strong interest in foreign affairs. He preferred to consider a variety of information and options himself, which enabled him to analyze all facets of an issue before arriving at a decision. The White House was to be the major instrument of foreign policy making:

> He arrived in power determined not to endorse decisions largely shaped by bureaucracy's talent for narrowing choice; instead, he sought to extend the range of choice and to make independent decisions. He would not be, like some Presidents, one of a number of players, albeit the key player. Instead, working through Kissinger, he would make of the White House the fountainhead of initiative and the solitary instrument for decision.[35]

This centralized structure was accomplished by the rejuvenation of the National Security Council, and especially its staff, under the direction of Henry Kissinger.

The White House activated the bureaucracy by issuing a National Security Study Memorandum (NSSM), which instigated rigorous study of a topic in order to promote various policy options. Once the study had been completed and transmitted to the President, he would decide on a particular course of action. At this point, a National Security Decision Memorandum (NSDM) would be issued, which formulated the President's decision and instructed the bureaucracy as to the procedure of implementation. This process was coordinated and directed by Henry Kissinger through use of the National Security Council staff. In 1969, the White House utilized this method to gain control of the foreign policy process.

In the first few months of the new administration, Nixon and Kissinger allowed the bureaucracy to administer the study on SALT. NSSM 28 was issued, licensing ACDA to launch an elaborate and comprehensive study focusing on all facets of arms limitation.[36] It soon became evident that the decentralized bureaucracy was not capable of meeting Nixon's demand for a variety of information and policy alternatives.

Debate ensued over the completed study after its formal presentation to the National Security Council. The Joint Chiefs disagreed with the treatment of verification. The main issue concerned the Soviet SS-9 missiles. ACDA, relying on CIA estimates, argued that the SS-9 had only a MIRV (Multiple Re-entry Vehicle) capability for the near future. The Joint Chiefs disputed this point, asserting the SS-9's MIRV capability.[37] An *ad hoc* committee, chaired by Henry Kissinger, was set up to examine the SS-9 verification issue.

This committee became known as the Verification Panel. "Very quickly, the style of the MIRV panel convinced Kissinger and his staff that they had hit on the right device for handling SALT." The panel functioned through lower-level working groups chaired by senior Kissinger aides, and drew on the technical skills of the bureaucracy. According to Newhouse, "these new groups would establish the central White House control of SALT that had been lacking."[38]

Once the centralization of the process had been established by the Verification Panel and its various working groups, exhaustive studies began on SALT. Eventually, nine options were presented to the President as a result of this decision-making procedure. They spanned a spectrum of positions for the arms talks—from no ABMs to unlimited ABMs, from a ban on MIRVs to no ban, and from a freeze on strategic offensive missiles to unlimited deployment.[39] These options became known as "building blocks."

No single option was to be presented to the Soviet Union. Instead, all the elements of each option could be combined in a variety of ways, thereby allowing a multitude of possible negotiating packages. "The building blocks, in short, would permit swift reaction to the Soviets, while minimizing bureaucratic conflict in Washington. The building blocks were, moreover, yet another device by which White House control of SALT would be assured."[40]

Eventually, the nine options were narrowed down to four—titled A, B, C, and D—and then further reduced to two—C and D. Since the White House was not completely satisfied with these two, a new alternative, E, emerged: "Whereas the other options had been methodically shaped and honed by the entire SALT apparatus; Kissinger, consulting closely with the President and one or two members of his staff, was the architect."[41] The bureaucracy was circumvented when option E became the negotiating position of the U.S. SALT delegation.[42]

Seven SALT negotiating sessions were held, alternating between Helsinki and Vienna, beginning in November of 1969. The composition of the U.S. delegation replicated the SALT bureaucracy, consisting of five members representing the Office of the Secretary of Defense, the JCS, the State Department, the scientific community, and ACDA; the Arms Control and Disarmament Agency Director was the designated chairman. The U.S. delegation was authorized to discuss all Soviet proposals, but all decisions were to be made by the President.[43]

The principal method used by President Nixon for controlling the implementation process was "the back channel." While the American and Soviet delegations met formally ("the front channel"), Henry Kissinger would quite often be meeting with Soviet Ambassador Anatoly Dobrynin in secret. In this way, President Nixon was able to communicate his position more directly to the Soviet leaders. The use of the back channel resulted in a breakthrough in the talks in 1971, and was instrumental in setting up Nixon's summit trip to Moscow.[44]

When Nixon arrived in Moscow in May of 1972, there were still a number of points of contention concerning SALT. The remaining problems involved ABM radars, land-based offensive missile limitations, submarine-based missile limitations, and the question of a "trade-in" of old ICBMs for new SLBMs. None of them were resolved until the final day of the summit; the direct participation of President Nixon and General Secretary Brezhnev was necessary before the first strategic arms limitations agreements could officially be signed.[45]

APPRAISAL

As we have seen, two different decision-making patterns occurred with regard to the strategic arms limitation talks. During the Johnson administration, the bureaucratic politics model was representative of the decision-making structure and process. During the Nixon administration, once the White House achieved control of SALT, the bureaucratic politics model lost its applicability. It appears evident, therefore, that the President's level of involvement is the critical factor accounting for the difference in decision-making behavior.

The Decision Structure. Most of the critiques of bureaucratic politics are concerned with Presidential attention.[46] The President appoints the higher-level personnel within the executive branch: he selects the men who head the large bureaucracies. He also sets the rules of the game, determining which participants will have access to him and the decision-making process. Furthermore, the bureaucracy must always be aware of the President's point of view, for he is capable of suppressing most plans. In other words, a President can be an omnipotent player if he so desires. "The ability of bureaucracies to independently establish policies is a function of Presidential attention. Presidential attention is a function of Presidential values."[47]

During the SALT I negotiations, two different Presidential styles were prevalent. Johnson was heavily interested in SALT, but did not want to dominate the decision-making process: he wanted consensus among the bureaucracy in arriving at a U.S. negotiating position. Nixon wanted options: the bureaucracy was used to provide the necessary information and alternatives. In this way, the ultimate decision would rest with the President: he would determine the U.S. position. The different manners in which these Presidents approached decision making are described by Newhouse:

> The White House normally likes to keep options open, but what it does depends on the style of the President. Under Lyndon Johnson, the tendency was to stand aloof and let the bureaucracy thrash out most SALT-related issues, even if this sometimes risked stalemate—a no-decision contest. Under Richard Nixon, the fondness for options runs much deeper, and the tendency is to exploit existing divisions the better to exercise control.[48]

The President's style—his level of attention and involvement—is the most critical factor in determining the decision-making structure. A second factor of less importance is the level of individual and organizational involvement.

Not all issues necessitate involvement by the same individuals and organizations. As the issue varies, so do the number and type of participants. For instance, a minor issue is likely to draw the attention of only a minimum number of participants—the issue does not cross over the jurisdiction of numerous organizations, nor are the stakes high enough for many individuals to become concerned. Much of the day-to-day policy that is set by the executive branch involves only a few persons from one or two organizations. In such cases, the structure proposed by the bureaucratic politics model does not apply. When only a few participants are involved and Presidential attention is at a minimum, the decision-making structure becomes "localized."

In sum, two factors are principally responsible for the structure of decision making that occurs within the executive branch: the level of Presidential attention and involvement, and the level of individual and organizational attention and involvement. . . .

The Decision Context. The external setting or environment can have important consequences on the decision-making structure. "The situation not only determines, in part, who will participate in a decision, and thus, whose images count, but also affects the selection and formation of images."[49] Therefore, the context can be a major determinant of decision-making behavior, and particularly of the decision structure.

The type of the decision structure depends largely on the critical or noncritical nature of the issue.[50] The contextual variables include the level of prior planning for reaching a decision, the time available for deliberation and choice, and the importance of values as perceived by the decision makers. Charles Hermann has hypothesized that during a time of crisis—involving surprise, little time, and threat—"the highest level of government officials will make the decision(s)."[51] Thus, when the issue is extremely critical, the President and his closest advisors are likely to become heavily involved. Likewise, for noncritical issues—routine situations—the President and his advisors will be least involved. "The bureaucracy plays its largest role in routine day-to-day affairs, its smallest during crises."[52]. . .

The Decision Process. The bureaucratic politics model is dependent upon a simple, two-step, linear relationship between decision structure, decision process, and foreign behavior. In other words, the structure of the decisional unit determines the decision-making process; thereafter, the process determines the decision outcome. However, the existence of a decision-making structure does not solely determine the exact nature of the decision process.

For instance, the decision-making process corresponding to the "Presidential Dominance" structure [i.e., when presidential involvement is high—*eds.*] may be highly analytical (or rational), as it was in the case of SALT I under President Nixon, when a wide range of information and alternatives was brought to the President so he could maximize his choice.[53] On the other hand, U.S. policy in Vietnam was anything but analytical. President Johnson was the dominant player after the United States became heavily involved in the war in Vietnam. Although decisions were made, a variety of information and alternatives was constantly lacking. As noted above, Johnson wanted consensus; therefore degrees of escalation were the only options. Irving Janis argues that "groupthink," rather than an analytical appraisal of all the options, best describes the decision-making process that occurred.[54] Thus, although a dominant decision-making structure may exist, the actual process can vary enormously. . . .

Furthermore, the participants involved are bound to have diverse personalities and belief systems which may have a substantial impact on their behavior. The result is a decision-making structure with a variety of possible processes.

In sum, to actually determine the nature of the decision-making process, knowledge beyond the decision structure must be considered. The beliefs, personalities, and modes of thinking of the participants will have a direct effect on the decision-making process. In addition, external forces will have an influence on the perceptions of the participants. These two clusters of variables—decision context and decision participants—must be analyzed for each decision structure in order to determine the exact nature of the decision-making process.[55] Since these factors have a different impact within the decision structure, the resultant decision process will vary. . . .

NOTES

1. Neustadt, *Presidential Power: The Politics of Leadership* (New York: Wiley, 1960), 10.
2. Although earlier studies had also been concerned with the nature of intragovernmental politics, it was not until *Presidential Power* that the notion of intragovernmental bargaining began to gain popularity. See Gabriel Almond, *The American People and Foreign Policy* (New York: Praeger, 1950), and Charles E. Lindblom, "The Science of Muddling Through," *Public Administration Review*, xix (Spring 1959), 79–88.
3. Huntington, *The Common Defense* (New York: Columbia University Press, 1961); Schilling, "The Politics of National Defense: Fiscal 1950," in Schilling, Hammond, and Snyder, eds., *Strategy, Politics, and Defense Budgets* (New York: Columbia University Press, 1962); Hilsman, *To Move a Nation* (New York: Doubleday, 1967).
4. Allison, "Conceptual Models and the Cuban Missile Crisis," *American Political Science Review*, Vol. 63 (September 1969), 689–718.
5. Allison and Halperin combine Model II (organizational process) and Model III (governmental politics) in their formulation of bureaucratic politics. See their "Bureaucratic Politics: A Paradigm and Some Policy Implications," in Raymond Tanter and Richard H. Ullman, eds., *Theory and Policy in International Relations* (Princeton: Princeton University Press, 1972), 40. See also Halperin, *Bureaucratic Politics and Foreign Policy* (Washington, D.C.: Brookings, 1974).
6. Haffa, "Allison's Models: An Analytic Approach to Bureaucratic Politics," in John E. Endicott and Roy W. Stafford, eds., *American Defense Policy*, 4th ed. (Baltimore: The Johns Hopkins Press, 1977), 224.
7. See I. M. Destler, *Presidents, Bureaucrats, and Foreign Policy: The Politics of Organization Reform* (Princeton: Princeton University Press, 1974); William I. Bacchus, *Foreign Policy and the Bureaucratic Process: The State Department's Country Director System* (Princeton: Princeton University Press, 1974); Francis E. Rourke, ed., *Bureaucratic Power in National Politics* (Boston: Little, Brown, 1978); John Spanier and Eric M. Uslaner, *How American Foreign Policy is Made* (New York: Holt, Rinehart & Winston, 1978); Stephen D. Cohen, *The Making of United States International Economic Policy* (New York: Praeger, 1977); Chris L. Jeffries, "Defense Decision-making in the Organizational-Bureaucratic Context," in Endicott and Stafford (fn. 6), 227–39; Graham Allison and Peter Szanton, *Remaking Foreign Policy: The Organizational Connection* (New York: Basic Books, 1976); and Charles W. Kegley, Jr., and Eugene R. Wittkopf, *American Foreign Policy: Pattern and Process* (New York: St. Martin's Press, 1979). Although the latter two works never formally mention the bureaucratic politics model, they do utilize a bureaucratic politics approach.
8. Some attempts have been made to determine the applicability of the bureaucratic politics model by comparing it with other decision-making models. However, further confusion has been the result, for the models were not presented

and analyzed in a clear, systematic fashion. See Wilfred L. Kohl, "The Nixon-Kissinger Foreign Policy System and U.S.-European Relations: Patterns of Policy Making," *World Politics*, XXVIII (October 1975), 1–43; John C. Donovan, *The Cold Warriors: A Policy-Making Elite* (Lexington, Mass.: D. C. Heath, 1974); Barry B. Hughes, *The Domestic Context of American Foreign Policy* (San Francisco: W. H. Freeman, 1978); Cohen (fn. 7), 78–102; and William B. Quandt, *Decade of Decisions: American Policy Toward the Arab-Israeli Conflict, 1967–1976* (Berkeley: University of California Press, 1977).

9. In the initial development of the decision-making approach during the 1950s and early 1960s, the primary emphasis was on the development of a comprehensive conceptual framework. The earlier works attempted to locate the principal components of the system—clusters of variables—that influenced foreign policy behavior. Although the 1970s have witnessed advancement in the development of decision-making models and theoretical formulations, scholars have focused only on one or two clusters of decision variables. This lack of comprehensiveness in the recent literature has resulted in an oversimplification of policy-making behavior. See Richard C. Snyder, H. W. Bruck, and Burton Sapin, "Decision-Making as an Approach to the Study of International Politics," in Snyder and others, *Foreign Policy Decision-Making: An Approach to the Study of International Politics* (New York: Free Press of Glencoe, 1962), 14–185; James A. Robinson and R. Roger Majak, "The Theory of Decision-Making," and James N. Rosenau, "The Premises and Promises of Decision-Making Analysis," in James C. Charlesworth, ed., *Contemporary Political Analysis* (New York: Free Press, 1967), 175–88, 189–211.

10. Halperin (fn. 5), 5.

11. Graham T. Allison, *Essence of Decision: Explaining the Cuban Missile Crisis* (Boston: Little, Brown, 1971).

12. I am attempting to allow as much flexibility as possible for the bureaucratic politics model. For instance, none of my propositions contain the notion "where you stand depends on where you sit"—which is a definite constraint for the model. In this way the applicability of the model is maximized.

13. Allison and Halperin (fn. 5), 42.

14. Halperin (fn. 5), 311.

15. Allison (fn. 11), 164, 172.

16. *Ibid.*, 162.

17. Unless, of course, it is a "negative" decision—one in which no action or implementation is required.

18. Halperin (fn. 5), 313.

19. Allison and Halperin (fn. 5), 53.

20. The bureaucratic politics model has been principally supported through the use of defense policy case studies. (On this basis I chose SALT I as a case study.) See Kenneth N. Ciboski, "The Bureaucratic Connection: Explaining the Skybolt Decision," in Endicott and Stafford (fn. 6), 374–88; Graham T. Allison, "Questions About the Arms Race: Who's Racing Whom? A Bureaucratic Perspective," in Robert L. Pfaltzgraf, Jr., ed., *Contrasting Approaches to Strategic Arms Control* (Lexington, Mass.: D. C. Heath, 1974); Morton H. Halperin, "The Decision to Deploy the ABM: Bureaucratic and Domestic Politics in the Johnson Administration," *World Politics*, XXV (October 1972), 62–95; Michael H. Armacost, *The Politics of Weapons Innovation: The Thor-Jupiter Controversy* (New

York: Columbia University Press, 1969); and Edmund Beard, *Developing the ICBM: A Study in Bureaucratic Politics* (New York: Columbia University Press, 1976).

21. Sources for the decision-making behavior concerning SALT I during the Johnson administration are: John Newhouse, *Cold Dawn: The Story of SALT* (New York: Holt, Rinehart & Winston, 1973); Alton Frye, "U.S. Decision-Making for SALT," in Mason Willrich and John B. Rhinelander, eds., *SALT: The Moscow Agreements and Beyond* (New York: Free Press, 1974), 66–100; Lyndon Baines Johnson, *The Vantage Point: Perspectives of the Presidency, 1963–1969* (New York: Popular Library, 1971); U.S., Congress, Senate, Committee on Foreign Relations, *Soviet Diplomacy and Negotiating Behavior: Emerging New Context for U.S. Diplomacy*, Committee Print (Washington, D.C.: U.S. Government Printing Office, 1979); Jerome H. Kahan, *Security in the Nuclear Age: Developing U.S. Strategic Arms Policy* (Washington, D.C.: Brookings, 1975); Burton R. Rosenthal, "Formulating Negotiating Positions for SALT: 1968, 1969–1972," in *Commission on the Organization of the Government for the Conduct of Foreign Policy*, IV, Appendices (Washington, D.C.: U.S. Government Printing Office, 1975), 325–43; and Thomas W. Wolfe, *The SALT Experience* (Cambridge, Mass.: Ballinger, 1979).

22. Newhouse (fn. 21), 36; Wolfe (fn. 21), 24.

23. Newhouse (fn. 21), 35.

24. *Ibid.*

25. Johnson (fn. 21), 483–89.

26. Newhouse (fn. 21), 108. For an in-depth discussion of Johnson's foreign policy machinery, see Destler (fn. 7), chap. 4; Henry Graff, *The Tuesday Cabinet: Deliberation and Decision on Peace and War under Lyndon B. Johnson* (Englewood Cliffs, N.J.: Prentice-Hall, 1970); Fred Geyelin, *Lyndon B. Johnson and the World* (New York: Praeger, 1966); and Keith C. Clark and Laurence J. Legere, *The President and the Management of National Security* (New York: Praeger, 1969).

27. Newhouse (fn. 21), 120.

28. Actually, the process was considerably more complex. ACDA was the agency that had formal jurisdiction for presenting the initial proposal. However, the members of the Halperin group were able to convince members of ACDA and the State Department that their method of formulating the proposal was preferable. The problem was that the Pentagon perceived ACDA as the "super-dove" agency. Adrian Fisher, Deputy Director of ACDA, played a crucial role in reconciling these positions. Nevertheless, in the end, it was ACDA which formally presented the proposal to the JCS. See Rosenthal (fn. 21), 329, and Newhouse (fn. 21), 114–16.

29. Frye (fn. 21), 77.

30. The Committee of Principals was chaired by Secretary of State Dean Rusk. It also included the Director of ACDA, William Foster; the Secretary of Defense, Clark Clifford; the Chairman of the JCS, General Wheeler; and the President's Special Assistant for National Security, Walt Rostow. The Committee had been created to supervise work on the Non-Proliferation Treaty. According to Newhouse, the Committee of Principals was not the forum for SALT I because of the recent departure of Secretary of Defense McNamara, without whom Rusk was not capable of managing the Joint Chiefs. Furthermore, ACDA was constrained by the suspicions of the JCS toward it. Halperin and his group filled the void. Newhouse (fn. 21), 110–11.

31. Kahan (fn. 21), 126; Rosenthal (fn. 21), 331.
32. It is Newhouse's belief that the Joint Chiefs bought the proposal at the price of excluding both a MIRV (Multiple Independently Targeted Re-entry Vehicle) ban and an ABM limit. Newhouse (fn. 21), 12; see also Wolfe (fn. 21), 25.
33. Newhouse (fn. 21), 125.
34. In addition to the sources cited in fn. 21, others for the decision-making behavior during the Nixon administration include: Marvin and Bernard Kalb, *Kissinger* (New York: Dell, 1974); Henry Brandon, *The Retreat of American Power* (Garden City, N.Y.: Doubleday, 1973); Roger Morris, *Uncertain Greatness: Henry Kissinger and American Foreign Policy* (New York : Harper & Row, 1977); John P. Leacacos, "Kissinger's Apparat," and I. M. Destler, "What Can One Man Do?" *Foreign Policy*, No. 5 (Winter 1971–72), 3–27 and 28–40; Samuel C. Orr, "Defense Report/National Security Council Network Gives White House Tight Rein over SALT Strategy," *National Journal*, III (April 24, 1971), 877–86; Raymond Garthoff, "Negotiating SALT," *The Wilson Quarterly*, I (Autumn 1977), 76–85, and "Negotiating with the Russians," *International Security*, I (Spring 1977), 3–24; Richard Nixon, *The Memoirs of Richard Nixon* (New York: Warner, 1978); William Safire, *Before the Fall: An Inside View of the Pre-Watergate White House* (Garden City, N.Y.: Doubleday, 1975); Tad Szulc, *The Illusion of Peace: Foreign Policy in the Nixon Years* (New York: Viking, 1978); and Henry Kissinger, *White House Years* (Boston: Little, Brown, 1979).
35. Newhouse (fn. 21), 144. . . .
36. Rosenthal (fn. 21), 333.
37. The Joint Chiefs argued that each warhead on the missile could be independently targeted (unlike MRVS), thereby making the SS-9 a more devastating weapon. Frye (fn. 21), 81; Rosenthal (fn. 21), 334.
38. Newhouse (fn. 21), 161, 162. See also Rosenthal (fn. 21), 334.
39. Brandon (fn. 34), 310–11.
40. Newhouse (fn. 21), 171.
41. *Ibid.*, 186.
42. Option E set a limit of 1900 offensive missiles; either 100 ABMs for the capital or no ABMs at all; MIRV was completely excluded; land mobile missiles, the modification of silos, and new hardened silos were forbidden. Brandon (fn. 34), 311.
43. Garthoff (fn. 34), 76–79; Wolfe (fn. 21), 33–34.
44. The agreement between the U.S. and the U.S.S.R. stipulated that limitations in both offensive and defensive weapons would be discussed in one package; that the ABM site would not be limited strictly to the capital city; that U.S. Forward-Based Systems in Europe would not be discussed; and that there would be no quantity equivalence in missiles, simply a freeze. Kissinger (fn. 34), 820; Garthoff, "Negotiating SALT" (fn. 34), 80–81.
45. Kalb (fn. 34), 358–78; Kissinger (fn. 34), 1202–57.
46. See Robert Art, "Bureaucratic Politics and American Foreign Policy: A Critique," *Policy Sciences*, IV (December 1973), 467–90; Stephen D. Krasner, "Are Bureaucracies Important (Or Allison Wonderland)," *Foreign Policy*, No. 7 (Summer 1972), 159–79; D. J. Ball," "The Blind Men and the Elephant: A Critique of Bureaucratic Politics Theory," *Australian Outlook*, XXVIII (April 1974), 71–92; Amos Perlmutter, "The Presidential Political Center and Foreign Policy: A Critique of the Revisionist and Bureaucratic-Political Orientations," *World Politics*, XXVII (October 1974), 87–106; Miriam Steiner, "The Elusive

Essence of Decision: A Critical Comparison of Allison's and Snyder's Decision-Making Approaches," *International Studies Quarterly*, XXI (June 1977), 389–422; and James H. Nathan and James K. Oliver, "Bureaucratic Politics: Academic Windfalls and Intellectual Pitfalls," *Journal of Political and Military Sociology*, VI (Spring 1978), 81–91.

47. Krasner (fn. 46), 168. This fact is occasionally acknowledged even by bureaucratic politics theorists:

The President stands at the center of the foreign policy process in the United States. His role and influence over decisions are qualitatively different than those of any other participants. In any foreign policy decision widely perceived at the time to be important, the President will be a principal if not the principal figure determining the general direction of actions.

However, in these instances the decision-making pattern is not considered to be bureaucratic politics. Morton Halperin and Arnold Kanter, "The Bureaucratic Perspective: A Preliminary Perspective," in Halperin and Kanter, eds., *Readings in American Foreign Policy: A Bureaucratic Perspective* (Boston: Little, Brown, 1973), 6.

48. Newhouse (fn. 21), 36.

49. James A. Robinson and Richard C. Snyder, "Decision-making in International Politics," in Herbert C. Kelman, ed., *International Behavior: A Social-Psychological Analysis* (New York: Holt, Rinehart, & Winston, 1965), 456.

50. For other potentially fruitful uses of the concept "issue area," see William C. Potter's review of the literature in "Issue Area and Foreign Policy Analysis," *International Organization*, XXXIV (Summer 1980), 405–27.

51. Hermann, "International Crisis as a Situational Variable," in James N. Rosenau, ed., *International Politics and Foreign Policy* (New York: Free Press, 1969), 416.

52. John Spanier, *Games Nations Play: Analyzing International Politics* (New York: Praeger, 1975), 410.

53. See Allison (fn. 11), for a discussion of the "rational-actor" model, and John D. Steinbruner, *The Cybernetic Theory of Decision: New Dimensions of Political Analysis* (Princeton: Princeton University Press, 1974), for a description of the "analytic" paradigm.

54. Janis, *Victims of Groupthink* (Boston: Houghton-Mifflin, 1972), 101–35.

55. A detailed discussion of these variables and their impact on the decision process is beyond the scope of this paper. For a work on the decision context as a situational variable and its effect on the decision process, see Linda P. Brady, "The Situation and Foreign Policy," in East and others (fn. 54), 173–90. Also see Margaret G. Hermann, "Effects of Personal Characteristics of Political Leaders on Foreign Policy," in East and others (fn. 54), 49–68, for a general discussion of the importance of decision participants' attributes.

23

HOW COULD VIETNAM HAPPEN?
An Autopsy

JAMES C. THOMSON, JR.

$\mathbf{A}$s a case study in the making of foreign policy, the Vietnam War will fascinate historians and social scientists for many decades to come. One question that will certainly be asked: How did men of superior ability, sound training, and high ideals—American policy-makers of the 1960s—create such a costly and divisive policy?

As one who watched the decision-making process in Washington from 1961 to 1966 under Presidents Kennedy and Johnson, I can suggest a preliminary answer. I can do so by briefly listing some of the factors that seemed to me to shape our Vietnam policy during my years as an East Asia specialist at the State Department and the White House. I shall deal largely with Washington as I saw or sensed it, and not with Saigon, where I . . . spent but a scant three days, in the entourage of the Vice President, or with other decision centers, the capitals of interested parties. Nor will I deal with other important parts of the record: Vietnam's history prior to 1961, for instance, or the overall course of America's relations with Vietnam.

Yet a first and central ingredient in these years of Vietnam decisions does involve history. The ingredient was *the legacy of the 1950s*—by which I mean the so-called "loss of China," the Korean War, and the Far East policy of Secretary of State Dulles.

This legacy had an institutional by-product for the Kennedy Administration: in 1961 the U.S. government's East Asian establishment was undoubtedly the most rigid and doctrinaire of Washington's regional divisions in foreign affairs. This was especially true at the Department of State, where the incoming Administration found the Bureau of Far Eastern Affairs the hardest nut to crack. It was a bureau that had been purged of its best China expertise, and of farsighted, dispassionate men, as a result of McCarthyism. Its members were generally committed to one policy line: the

James C. Thomson, Jr., "How Could Vietnam Happen? An Autopsy," *The Atlantic*, April, 1968, pp. 47–53. Copyright © by James C. Thomson, Jr.

close containment and isolation of mainland China, the harassment of "neutralist" nations which sought to avoid alignment with either Washington or Peking, and the maintenance of a network of alliances with anti-Communist client states on China's periphery.

Another aspect of the legacy was the special vulnerability and sensitivity of the new Democratic Administration on Far East policy issues. The memory of the McCarthy era was still very sharp, and Kennedy's margin of victory was too thin. The 1960 Offshore Islands TV debate between Kennedy and Nixon had shown the President-elect the perils of "fresh thinking." The Administration was inherently leery of moving too fast on Asia. As a result, the Far East Bureau (now the Bureau of East Asian and Pacific Affairs) was the last one to be overhauled. Not until Averell Harriman was brought in as Assistant Secretary in December, 1961, were significant personnel changes attempted, and it took Harriman several months to make a deep imprint on the bureau because of his necessary preoccupation with the Laos settlement. Once he did so, there was virtually no effort to bring back the purged or exiled East Asia experts.

There were other important by-products of this "legacy of the fifties":

The new Administration inherited and somewhat shared a *general perception of China-on-the-march*—a sense of China's vastness, its numbers, its belligerence; a revived sense, perhaps, of the Golden Horde. This was a perception fed by Chinese intervention in the Korean War (an intervention actually based on appallingly bad communications and mutual miscalculation on the part of Washington and Peking; but the careful unraveling of that tragedy, which scholars have accomplished, had not yet become part of the conventional wisdom).

The new Administration inherited and briefly accepted *a monolithic conception of the Communist bloc.* Despite much earlier predictions and reports by outside analysts, policy-makers did not begin to accept the reality and possible finality of the Sino-Soviet split until the first weeks of 1962. The inevitably corrosive impact of competing nationalisms on Communism was largely ignored.

The new Administration inherited and to some extent shared *the "domino theory" about Asia.* This theory resulted from profound ignorance of Asian history and hence ignorance of the radical differences among Asian nations and societies. It resulted from a blindness to the power and resilience of Asian nationalisms. (It may also have resulted from a subconscious sense that, since "all Asians look alike," all Asian nations will act alike.) As a theory, the domino fallacy was not merely inaccurate but also insulting to Asian nations; yet it has continued to this day to beguile men who should know better.

Finally, the legacy of the fifties was apparently compounded by an uneasy sense of a worldwide Communist challenge to the new Administration after the Bay of Pigs fiasco. A first manifestation was the President's traumatic Vienna meeting with Khrushchev in June, 1961; then came the

Berlin crisis of the summer. All this created an atmosphere in which President Kennedy undoubtedly felt under special pressure to show his nation's mettle in Vietnam—if the Vietnamese, unlike the people of Laos, were willing to fight.

In general, the legacy of the fifties shaped such early moves of the new Administration as the decisions to maintain a high-visibility SEATO (by sending the Secretary of State himself instead of some underling to its first meeting in 1961), to back away from diplomatic recognition of Mongolia in the summer of 1961, and most important, to expand U.S. military assistance to South Vietnam that winter on the basis of the much more tentative Eisenhower commitment. It should be added that the increased commitment to Vietnam was also fueled by a new breed of military strategists and academic social scientists (some of whom had entered the new Administration) who had developed theories of counterguerrilla warfare and were eager to see them put to the test. To some, "counterinsurgency" seemed a new panacea for coping with the world's instability.

So much for the legacy and the history. Any new Administration inherits both complicated problems and simplistic views of the world. But surely among the policy-makers of the Kennedy and Johnson Administrations there were men who would warn of the dangers of an open-ended commitment to the Vietnam quagmire?

This raises a central question, at the heart of the policy process: Where were the experts, the doubters, and the dissenters? Were they there at all, and if so, what happened to them?

The answer is complex but instructive.

In the first place, the American government was sorely *lacking in real Vietnam or Indochina expertise*. Originally treated as an adjunct of Embassy Paris, our Saigon embassy and the Vietnam Desk at State were largely staffed from 1954 onward by French-speaking Foreign Service personnel of narrowly European experience. Such diplomats were even more closely restricted than the normal embassy officer—by cast of mind as well as language—to contacts with Vietnam's French-speaking urban elites. For instance, Foreign Service linguists in Portugal are able to speak with the peasantry if they get out of Lisbon and choose to do so; not so the French speakers of Embassy Saigon.

In addition, the *shadow of the "loss of China"* distorted Vietnam reporting. Career officers in the Department, and especially those in the field, had not forgotten the fate of their World War II colleagues who wrote in frankness from China and were later pilloried by Senate committees for critical comments on the Chinese Nationalists. Candid reporting on the strengths of the Viet Cong and the weaknesses of the Diem government was inhibited by the memory. It was also inhibited by some higher officials, notably Ambassador Nolting in Saigon, who refused to sign off on such cables.

In due course, to be sure, some Vietnam talent was discovered or developed. But a recurrent and increasingly important factor in the decision-making process was *the banishment of real expertise.* Here the underlying cause was the "closed politics" of policy-making as issues become hot: the more sensitive the issue, and the higher it rises in the bureaucracy, the more completely the experts are excluded while the harassed senior generalists take over (that is, the Secretaries, Undersecretaries, and Presidential Assistants). The frantic skimming of briefing papers in the back seats of limousines is no substitute for the presence of specialists; furthermore, in times of crisis such papers are deemed "too sensitive" even for review by the specialists. Another underlying cause of this banishment, as Vietnam became more critical, was the replacement of the experts, who were generally and increasingly pessimistic, by men described as "can-do guys," loyal and energetic fixers unsoured by expertise. In early 1965, when I confided my growing policy doubts to an older colleague on the NSC staff, he assured me that the smartest thing both of us could do was to "steer clear of the whole Vietnam mess"; the gentleman in question had the misfortune to be a "can-do guy," however, and [was subsequently] highly placed in Vietnam, under orders to solve the mess.

Despite the banishment of the experts, internal doubters and dissenters did indeed appear and persist. Yet as I watched the process, such men were effectively neutralized by a subtle dynamic: *the domestication of dissenters.* Such "domestication" arose out of a twofold clubbish need: on the one hand, the dissenter's desire to stay aboard; and on the other hand, the nondissenter's conscience. Simply stated, dissent, when recognized, was made to feel at home. On the lowest possible scale of importance, I must confess my own considerable sense of dignity and acceptance (both vital) when my senior White House employer would refer to me as his "favorite dove." Far more significant was the case of the former Undersecretary of State, George Ball. Once Mr. Ball began to express doubts, he was warmly institutionalized: he was encouraged to become the inhouse devil's advocate on Vietnam. The upshot was inevitable: the process of escalation allowed for periodic requests to Mr. Ball to speak his piece; Ball felt good, I assume (he had fought for righteousness); the others felt good (they had given a full hearing to the dovish option); and there was minimal unpleasantness. The club remained intact; and it is of course possible that matters would have gotten worse faster if Mr. Ball had kept silent, or left before his final departure in the fall of 1966. There was also, of course, the case of the last institutionalized doubter, Bill Moyers. The President is said to have greeted his arrival at meetings with an affectionate, "Well, here comes Mr. Stop-the-Bombing . . ." Here again the dynamics of domesticated dissent sustained the relationship for a while.

A related point—and crucial, I suppose, to government at all times— was *the "effectiveness" trap,* the trap that keeps men from speaking out, as clearly or often as they might, within the government. And it is the trap that keeps men from resigning in protest and airing their dissent outside the government. The most important asset that a man brings to bureaucratic life is his "effectiveness," a mysterious combination of training, style, and connections. The most ominous complaint that can be whispered of a bureaucrat is: "I'm afraid Charlie's beginning to lose his effectiveness." To preserve your effectiveness, you must decide where and when to fight the mainstream of policy; the opportunities range from pillow talk with your wife, to private drinks with your friends, to meetings with the Secretary of State or the President. The inclination to remain silent or to acquiesce in the presence of the great men—to live to fight another day, to give on this issue so that you can be "effective" on later issues—is overwhelming. Nor is it the tendency of youth alone; some of our most senior officials, men of wealth and fame, whose place in history is secure, have remained silent lest their connection with power be terminated. As for the disinclination to resign in protest: while not necessarily a Washington or even American specialty, it seems more true of a government in which ministers have no parliamentary back-bench to which to retreat. In the absence of such a refuge, it is easy to rationalize the decision to stay aboard. By doing so, one may be able to prevent a few bad things from happening and perhaps even make a few good things happen. To exit is to lose even those marginal chances for "effectiveness."

Another factor must be noted: as the Vietnam controversy escalated at home, there developed *a preoccupation with Vietnam public relations as opposed to Vietnam policy-making.* And here, ironically, internal doubters and dissenters were heavily employed. For such men, by virtue of their own doubts, were often deemed best able to "massage" the doubting intelligentsia. My senior East Asia colleague at the White House, a brilliant and humane doubter who had dealt with Indochina since 1954, spent three quarters of his working days on Vietnam public relations: drafting presidential responses to letters from important critics, writing conciliatory language for presidential speeches, and meeting quite interminably with delegations of outraged Quakers, clergymen, academics, and housewives. His regular callers were the late A. J. Muste and Norman Thomas; mine were members of the Women's Strike for Peace. Our orders from above: keep them off the backs of busy policy-makers (who usually happened to be nondoubters). Incidentally, my most discouraging assignment in the realm of public relations was the preparation of a White House pamphlet entitled *Why Vietnam,* in September, 1965; in a gesture toward my conscience, I fought—and lost—a battle to have the title followed by a question mark.

Through a variety of procedures, both institutional and personal, doubt, dissent, and expertise were effectively neutralized in the making of policy. But what can be said of the men "in charge"? It is patently absurd to suggest that they produced such tragedy by intention and calculation. But it is neither absurd nor difficult to discern certain forces at work that caused decent and honorable men to do great harm.

Here I would stress the paramount role of *executive fatigue.* No factor seems to me more crucial and underrated in the making of foreign policy.

The physical and emotional toll of executive responsibility in State, the Pentagon, the White House, and other executive agencies is enormous; that toll is of course compounded by extended service. Many . . . Vietnam policy-makers [had] been on the job for from four to seven years. Complaints may be few, and physical health may remain unimpaired, though emotional health is far harder to gauge. But what is most seriously eroded in the deadening process of fatigue is freshness of thought, imagination, a sense of possibility, a sense of priorities and perspective—those rare assets of a new Administration in its first year or two of office. The tired policy-maker becomes a prisoner of his own narrowed view of the world and his own clichéd rhetoric. He becomes irritable and defensive—short on sleep, short on family ties, short on patience. Such men make bad policy and then compound it. They have neither the time nor the temperament for new ideas or preventive diplomacy.

Below the level of the fatigued executives in the making of Vietnam policy was a widespread phenomenon: *the curator mentality* in the Department of State. By this I mean the collective inertia produced by the bureaucrat's view of his job. At State, the average "desk officer" inherits from his predecessor our policy toward Country X; he regards it as his function to keep that policy intact—under glass, untampered with, and dusted—so that he may pass it on in two to four years to his successor. And such curatorial service generally merits promotion within the system. (Maintain the status quo, and you will stay out of trouble.) In some circumstances, the inertia bred by such an outlook can act as a brake against rash innovation. But on many issues, this inertia sustains the momentum of bad policy and unwise commitments—momentum that might otherwise have been resisted within the ranks. Clearly, Vietnam [was] such an issue.

To fatigue and inertia must be added the factor of internal confusion. Even among the "architects" of our Vietnam commitment, there [was] persistent *confusion as to what type of war we were fighting* and, as a direct consequence, *confusion as to how to end that war.* (The "credibility gap" [was], in part, a reflection of such internal confusion.) Was it, for instance, a civil war, in which case counterinsurgency might suffice? Or was it a war of international aggression? (This might invoke SEATO or UN commitment.) Who was the aggressor—and the "real enemy"? The Viet Cong? Hanoi? Peking? Moscow? International Communism? Or maybe "Asian Communism"? Differing enemies dictated differing strategies and tactics. And confused throughout, in like fashion, was the question of American objectives; your objectives depended on whom you were fighting and why. I shall not forget my assignment from an Assistant Secretary of State in March, 1964: to draft a speech for Secretary McNamara which would, *inter alia*, once and for all dispose of the canard that the Vietnam conflict was a civil war. "But in some ways, of course," I mused, "It *is* a civil war." "Don't play word games with me!" snapped the Assistant Secretary.

Similar confusion beset the concept of "negotiations"—anathema to much of official Washington from 1961 to 1965. Not until April, 1965, did "unconditional discussions" become respectable, via a presidential speech; even then the Secretary of State stressed privately to newsmen that nothing had changed, since "discussions" were by no means the same as "negotiations." Months later that issue was resolved. But it took even longer to obtain a fragile internal agreement that negotiations might include the Viet Cong as something other than an appendage to Hanoi's delegation. Given such confusion as to the whos and whys of our Vietnam commitment, it is not surprising, as Theodore Draper has written, that policy-makers [found] it so difficult to agree on how to end the war.

Of course, one force—a constant in the vortex of commitment—was that of *wishful thinking*. I partook of it myself at many times. I did so especially during Washington's struggle with Diem in the autumn of 1963 when some of us at State believed that for once, in dealing with a difficult client state, the U.S. government could use the leverage of our economic and military assistance to make good things happen, instead of being led around by the nose by [foreign dictators]. If we could prove that point, I thought, and move into a new day, with or without Diem, then Vietnam was well worth the effort. Later came the wishful thinking of the air-strike planners in the late autumn of 1964; there were those who actually thought that after six weeks of air strikes, the North Vietnamese would come crawling to us to ask for peace talks. And what, someone asked in one of the meetings of the time, if they don't? The answer was that we would bomb for another four weeks, and that would do the trick. And a few weeks later came one instance of wishful thinking that was symptomatic of good men misled: in January, 1965, I encountered one of the very highest figures in the Administration at a dinner, drew him aside, and told him of my worries about the air-strike option. He told me that I really shouldn't worry; it was his conviction that before any such plans could be put into effect, a neutralist government would come to power in Saigon that would politely invite us out. And finally, there was the recurrent wishful thinking that sustained many of us through the trying months of 1965–1966 after the air strikes had begun: that surely, somehow, one way or another, we would "be in a conference in six months," and the escalatory spiral would be suspended. The basis of our hope: "It simply can't go on."

As a further influence on policy-makers I would cite the factor of *bureaucratic detachment*. By this I mean what at best might be termed the professional callousness of the surgeon (and indeed, medical lingo—the "surgical strike" for instance—seemed to crop up in the euphemisms of the times). In Washington the semantics of the military muted the reality of war for the civilian policy-makers. In quiet, air-conditioned, thick-carpeted rooms, such terms as "systematic pressure," "armed reconnaissance," "targets of opportunity," and even "body count" seemed to breed a sort of games-theory detachment. Most memorable to me was a moment in the late 1964 target planning when the question under discussion was how heavy our bombing should be, and how extensive our strafing, at some midpoint in the projected pattern of systematic pressure. An Assistant Secretary of State resolved the point in the following words: "It seems to me that our orchestration should be mainly violins, but with periodic touches of brass." Perhaps the biggest shock of my return to Cambridge, Massachusetts, was the realization that the young men, the flesh and blood I taught and saw on these university streets, were potentially some of the numbers on the charts of those faraway planners. In a curious sense, Cambridge [was] closer to this war than Washington.

There is an unprovable factor that relates to bureaucratic detachment: the ingredient of *cryptoracism*. I do not mean to imply any conscious contempt for Asian loss of life on the part of Washington officials. But I do mean to imply that bureaucratic detachment may well be compounded by a traditional Western sense that there are so many Asians, after all; that Asians have a fatalism about life and a disregard for its loss; that they are cruel and barbaric to their own people; and that they are very different from us (and all look alike?). And I *do* mean to imply that the upshot of such subliminal views is a subliminal question whether Asians, and particularly Asian peasants, and most particularly Asian Communists, are really people—like you and me. To put the matter another way: would we have pursued quite such policies—and quite such military tactics—if the Vietnamese were white?

It is impossible to write of Vietnam decision-making without writing about language. Throughout the conflict, words [were] of paramount importance. I refer here to the impact of *rhetorical escalation* and to the *problem of oversell*. In an important sense, Vietnam [became] of crucial significance to us *because we . . . said that it [was] of crucial significance.* (The issue obviously relates to the public relations preoccupation described earlier.)

The key here is domestic politics: the need to sell the American people, press, and Congress on support for an unpopular and costly war in which the objectives themselves [were] in flux. To sell means to persuade, and to persuade means rhetoric. As the difficulties and costs . . . mounted, so [did] the definition of the stakes. This is not to say that rhetorical escalation is an orderly process; executive prose is the product of many writers, and some concepts—North Vietnamese infiltration, America's "national honor," Red China as the chief enemy—. . . entered the rhetoric only gradually and even sporadically. But there [was] an upward spiral nonetheless. And once you have *said* that the American Experiment itself stands or falls on the Vietnam outcome, you have thereby created a national stake far beyond any earlier stakes.

Crucial throughout the process of Vietnam decision-making was a conviction among many policy-makers: that Vietnam posed a *fundamental test of America's national will*. Time and again I was told by men reared in the tradition of Henry L. Stimson that all we needed was the will, and we would then prevail. Implicit in such a view, it seemed to me, was a curious assumption that Asians lacked will, or at least that in a contest between Asian and Anglo-Saxon wills, the non-Asians must prevail. A corollary to the persistent belief in will was a *fascination with power* and an awe in the face of the power America possessed as no nation or civilization ever before. Those who doubted our role in Vietnam were said to shrink from the burdens of power, the obligations of power, the uses of power, the responsibility of power. By implication, such men were soft-headed and effete.

Finally, no discussion of the factors and forces at work on Vietnam policy-makers can ignore the central fact of *human ego investment*. Men who have participated in a decision develop a stake in that decision. As they participate in further, related decisions, their stake increases. It might have been possible to dissuade a man of strong self-confidence at an early stage of the ladder of decision; but it is infinitely harder at later stages since a change of mind there usually involves implicit or explicit repudiation of a chain of previous decisions.

To put it bluntly: at the heart of the Vietnam calamity [was] a group of able, dedicated men who [were] regularly and repeatedly wrong—and whose standing with their contemporaries, and more important, with history, depended, as they [saw] it, on being proven right. These [were] not men who [could] be asked to extricate themselves from error.

The various ingredients I have cited in the making of Vietnam policy ... created a variety of results, most of them fairly obvious. Here are some that seem to me most central:

Throughout the conflict, there [was] *persistent and repeated miscalculation* by virtually all the actors, in high echelons and low, whether dove, hawk, or something else. To cite one simple example among many: in late 1964 and early 1965, some peace-seeking planners at State who strongly opposed the projected bombing of the North urged that, instead, American ground forces be sent to South Vietnam; this would, they said, increase our bargaining leverage against the North—our "chips"—and would give us something to negotiate about (the withdrawal of our forces) at an early peace conference. Simultaneously, the air-strike option was urged by many in the military who were dead set against American participation in "another land war in Asia"; they were joined by other civilian peace-seekers who wanted to bomb Hanoi into early negotiations. By late 1965, we had ended up with the worst of all worlds: ineffective and costly air strikes against the North, spiraling ground forces in the South, and no negotiations in sight.

Throughout the conflict as well, there [was] *a steady give-in to pressures for a military solution* and only minimal and sporadic efforts at a diplomatic and political solution. In part this resulted from the confusion (earlier cited) among the civilians—confusion regarding objectives and strategy. And in part this resulted from the self-enlarging nature of military investment. Once air strikes and particularly ground forces were introduced, our investment itself had transformed the original stakes. More air power was needed to protect the ground forces; and then more ground forces to protect the ground forces. And needless to say, the military mind develops its own momentum in the absence of clear guidelines from the civilians. Once asked to save South Vietnam, rather than to "advise" it, the American military could not but press for escalation. In addition, sad to report, assorted military constituencies, once involved in Vietnam, . . . had a series of cases to prove: for instance, the utility not only of air power (the Air Force) but of supercarrier-based air power (the Navy). Also, Vietnam policy . . . suffered from one ironic by-product of Secretary McNamara's establishment of civilian control at the Pentagon: in the face of such control, interservice rivalry [gave] way to a united front among the military—reflected in the new but recurrent phenomenon of JCS unanimity. In conjunction with traditional congressional allies (mostly Southern senators and representatives) such a united front would pose a formidable problem for any President.

Throughout the conflict, there [were] *missed opportunities, large and small, to disengage ourselves from Vietnam on increasingly unpleasant but still acceptable terms.* Of the many moments from 1961 onward, I shall cite only one, the last and most important opportunity that was lost: in the summer of 1964 the President instructed his chief advisers to prepare for him as wide a range of Vietnam options as possible for postelection consideration and decision. He explicitly asked that all options be laid out. What happened next was, in effect, Lyndon Johnson's slow-motion Bay of Pigs. For the advisers so effectively converged on one single option—juxtaposed against two other, phony options (in effect, blowing up the world, or scuttle-and-run)—that the President was confronted with unanimity for bombing the North from all his trusted counselors. Had he been more confident in foreign affairs, had he been deeply informed on Vietnam and Southeast Asia, and had he raised some hard questions that unanimity had submerged, this President could have used the largest electoral mandate in history to de-escalate in Vietnam, in the clear expectation that at the worst a neutralist government would come to power in Saigon and politely invite us out. . . .

In the course of these years, another result of Vietnam decision-making [was] *the abuse and distortion of history.* Vietnamese, Southeast Asian, and Far Eastern history [was] rewritten by our policy-makers, and their spokesmen, to conform with the alleged necessity of our presence in Vietnam. Highly dubious analogies from our experience elsewhere—the "Munich" sellout and "containment" from Europe, the Malayan insurgency and the Korean War from Asia— [were] imported in order to justify our actions. And [later] events [were] fitted to the Procrustean bed of Vietnam. Most notably, the change of power in Indonesia in 1965–1966 has been ascribed to our Vietnam presence; and virtually all progress in the Pacific region—the rise of regionalism, new forms of cooperation, and mounting growth rates—has been similarly explained. The Indonesian allegation is undoubtedly false (I tried to prove it, during six months of careful investigation at the White House, and had to confess failure); the regional allegation is patently unprovable in either direction (except, of course, for the clear fact that the economies of both Japan and Korea . . . profited enormously from our Vietnam-related procurement in these countries; but that is a costly and highly dubious form of foreign aid).

There is a final result of Vietnam policy I would cite that holds potential danger for the future of American foreign policy: *the rise of a new breed of American ideologues who saw Vietnam as the ultimate test of their doctrine.* I have in mind those men in Washington who have given a new life to the missionary impulse in American foreign relations: who believe that this nation, in this era, has received a threefold endowment that can transform the world. As they see it, that endowment is composed of, first, our unsurpassed military might; second, our clear technological supremacy; and third, our allegedly invincible benevolence (our "altruism," our affluence, our lack of territorial aspirations). Together, it is argued, this threefold endowment provides us with the opportunity and the obligation to ease the nations of the earth toward modernization and stability: toward a full-fledged *Pax Americana Technocratica.* In reaching toward this goal, Vietnam [was] viewed as the last and crucial test. Once we . . . succeeded there, the road ahead [was seen to be] clear. In a sense, these men [were] our counterpart to the visionaries of Communism's radical left: they are technocracy's own Maoists. . . .

Long before I went into government, I was told a story about Henry L. Stimson that seemed to me pertinent during the years that I watched the Vietnam tragedy unfold—and participated in that tragedy. It seems to me more pertinent than ever . . .

In his waning years Stimson was asked by an anxious questioner, "Mr. Secretary, how on earth can we ever bring peace to the world?" Stimson is said to have answered: "You begin by bringing to Washington a small handful of able men who believe that the achievement of peace is possible.

"You work them to the bone until they no longer believe that it is possible.

"And then you throw them out—and bring in a new bunch who believe that it is possible."

24

BUREAUCRATIC CONSTRAINTS ON INNOVATION IN AMERICAN FOREIGN POLICY

CHARLES F. HERMANN

Shortly before five o'clock in the afternoon on April 24, 1980, President Jimmy Carter conferred by telephone with his Secretary of Defense, Harold Brown. Half way around the world in the moonless darkness of the Iranian desert a situation required an urgent presidential decision. A critical problem emerged at the secret refueling rendezvous of the military team attempting to rescue the American hostages held in Teheran. One of the remaining six helicopters had just experienced mechanical failure. The carefully rehearsed plan called for a minimum of six helicopters—the two extra helicopters that had been included to provide a margin of redundancy already were down. The president faced a lonely decision. Should he risk going ahead with the mission with less than the planned number of helicopters or should the operation be aborted? In the White House office with President Carter was a single adviser, Dr. Zbigniew Brzezinski, his assistant for national security affairs. Only the president, however, could make the decision. Carter canceled the mission.

At first glance such a decision appears to have been the epitomy of the individual acting in virtual isolation. In fact, Carter's decision, similar to most in contemporary American foreign policy, depended upon the involvement of complex governmental organizations. In reality the president had

Charles F. Hermann is Director of the Mershon Center at the Ohio State University. He taught at Princeton University and served for a year on the U.S. National Security Council staff as an International Affairs Fellow of the Council on Foreign Relations of New York. His major research interests include American and comparative foreign policy, national security policy, international crisis, and event data analysis. Hermann is the author or editor of a number of books and journal articles dealing with these topics, including *International Crises* (Free Press, 1972) and *Why Nations Act* (Sage, 1978). He is currently on the Governing Council of the International Studies Association which he has also served as Vice-President. An earlier and somewhat different version of this essay appeared in Charles W. Kegley, Jr., and Pat McGowan, eds., *Challenges to America* (Beverly Hills, Cal.: Sage, 1979), pp. 269–292.

simply ratified an option that had been established after extensive study and dress rehearsals of the rescue involving many people—if six helicopters were not available for the final leg of the operation, it could not proceed.

The hostage crisis in Iran, including the attempted rescue, shares a number of basic characteristics with many foreign policy matters the United States will confront in the years ahead. The decision to attempt a rescue required attention to a time, in a place, and in a manner that was difficult and awkward for the United States. As noted, it required complex, interorganizational coordination within the government. It depended upon blending human talents with sophisticated technology. It created a severe tension between diplomatic and military modes of dealing with the world. It generated in its wake new problems, some of which were unforeseen. Perhaps, most fundamentally, it shared with every other instance of American foreign policymaking the prior recognition by American decision makers that a problem existed.

The thesis of this essay is that governments—all governments—act only in response to recognized problems. Furthermore, it is argued that governments of complex contemporary societies such as the United States approach foreign policy problems through the use of multiple specialized organizations. In these respects the hostage issue was no exception. Yet in other ways, it was extremely unusual. First, the problem received the full and extended attention of the top levels of government for many months. For each such problem as the hostage crisis which the leadership of the government considers, many more problems are ignored or postponed. The more time and energy spent with one issue, the less is available for others. Given the range of American interests and the diversity of actors in the world, many potential problems inevitably cannot receive careful examination. The hostage issue and rescue attempt were different from most issues in a second way. The failure of the rescue mission—and especially the tragic collision of a refueling plane and a helicopter as the team started to withdraw—became known quickly. Policy makers knew that additional decisions would be required to explain what happened and to pursue the release of the hostages. A clear, prompt outcome with recognizable consequences is frequently missing in foreign policy. For many foreign policy problems, whether attended to or ignored, the outcomes unfold gradually or in an unexpected and sometimes unnoticed fashion. Thus, the consequences of government action or inaction (and the possible secondary and tertiary effects that result) may also go unrecognized for a considerable period of time. The need to recognize the consequences of decisions or nondecisions becomes a variation of the need to recognize the existence of an important problem in the first place. In short, the outcome of the rescue mission was clear, but for many other problems this important kind of information—what happened and with what effect—may be missing.

Such observations lead to fundamental questions about the making of foreign policy. How do foreign problems get the attention of authoritative policy makers? Why do some problems appear to be quickly addressed whereas others are ignored, receive consideration after much delay, or are even misunderstood? How might the structures and processes established to handle foreign policy problems actually contribute to the ignoring of what may turn out to be critically important problems?

For any problem-solving entity—whether it be an individual, a nation, or a civilization—the failure to address a major problem in time could mean severe deprivation for those who face the problem and even their destruction. In the early post-World War II years some in the United States government believed that the Soviet Union posed a deadly military threat to our European and Asian allies and ultimately to America. They feared that the American democracy, lacking a strong tradition of a large and expensive peacetime military establishment, would fail to take adequate precautions and neglect to respond to the problem in time. Debates within the government over the Marshall Plan, the Truman Doctrine, and NCS-68 reflected this profound concern on the part of these individuals and their efforts to mobilize the government and society to respond to the alleged threat.[1]

More recently others have examined with alarm the vast U.S. military defense and its theoretical justification (particularly the doctrine of strategic nuclear deterrence) and have argued that we have generated a problem of awesome proportions that could destroy civilization. Jonathan Schell (1982: 217) is one spokesman of this concern:

> In the decades since nuclear arms first appeared in the world, the doctrine of nuclear deterrence has commanded the sincere respect and adherence of many people of good will. . . . Its deceptive claim that only by building nuclear weapons can we save ourselves from nuclear weapons lent the doomsday machine a veneer of reason and of respectability—almost of benevolence—that it should never have been given. For to build this machine at all was a mistake of the hugest proportions ever known—without question the greatest ever made by our species. The only conceivable worse mistake would be to put the machine to use. Now deterrence, having rationalized the construction of the machine, weds us to it, and, at best, offers us, if we are lucky, a slightly extended term of residence on earth before the inevitable human or mechanical mistake occurs and we are annihilated.

In both cases—those individuals and groups who either advocate or decry a certain course of action—fear that the government will fail to confront the problems and will fail to put the matters on their agenda in time. These illustrations dramatize the need for understanding the foreign policy monitoring system and its relationship to the agenda-setting process.

Of course, the foreign policy problems competing for the attention of the United States government vary greatly in magnitude. The severity of their potential consequences, however, does not necessarily determine whether a problem will be recognized and addressed. Among the factors that influence the attention a problem receives is the nature of the organizations designed to deal with emergent foreign policy problems. After offering several basic definitions, this essay will examine these organizational features and discuss their implications for American foreign policy in the 1980s.

BASIC DEFINITIONS

Problem

Three basic concepts need clarification: they are *problem, problem recognition,* and *problem definition.* A problem exists when there is a recognized discrepancy or imbalance between a preferred state of affairs and the present or possible future state of affairs. A number of corollaries follow from this definition. First, a problem requires that the actor be aware of one or more goals. If a government's foreign policy goals are poorly defined, then so are any problems that might arise from them. Most governments share certain basic goals—national physical survival, protection of citizens and their property abroad, continuation of the government in office, and so on. Beyond such basic national goals, however, governments differ in the degree to which goals pertaining to other foreign policy goals are defined.

Consider the attempted rescue of the American hostages in Iran. Was the primary goal to get the American hostages out safely? If the mission had proceeded to the American embassy in Teheran, where the hostages were being held, could they all have escaped their captives unharmed? That was uncertain and therefore raises questions about whether the safe release was the primary goal. Most of the officials that planned the rescue effort expected some casualties among both hostages and the rescue team. Was the main goal to terminate the hostage issue one way or the other, thus erasing the perception of many in the United States and abroad that America was being humiliated by a small group of revolutionaries? Was the goal to punish Iran and inflict harm on those who had supported this action against Americans so as to discourage others from trying such ventures? Were these all goals, and, if so, which were primary and which were secondary? Unless the goals are clearly defined and ordered—and this is often a difficult task for governments—the problem cannot be fully recognized and the appropriate government response determined.

It should be noted that goals may be identified and refined in an interactive process. As an analogy, consider a small child who may not attach much value to a toy until another child shows interest in playing with it. Suddenly maintaining possession of the toy becomes an important goal and the interest displayed in that object by the other child becomes the problem. After asserting ownership over the object, the first child may lose interest in it entirely and even forget its whereabouts. In a more complex fashion, the analogy can reveal something about the behaviors of collective entities such as governments. Conditions or objects that are the subjects of goals need not be continuously valued at the same level of importance. The importance and the attainment of a foreign-policy goal may emerge more or less suddenly in response to developing circumstances.

A second result of stipulating that the concept of problem depends on an entity's goals is that problems are relative. Whenever individuals or organizations have different goals or have assigned significantly different priorities to the same goal, then the possibility exists that what is seen as a problem for one will not necessarily be a problem for another. The same circumstances in different countries may create very different problems. For example, the size of the Turkish or Mexican poppy crop may not in and of itself be a problem for the United States unless the U.S. government has the goal of controlling the heroin produced from these crops. Moreover, if the Turkish government does not share such a goal, then it may not be a problem for the Turks.

Somewhat less frequently acknowledged is the idea that different departments, agencies, or bureaus within a government may have different—even competing—goals and, hence, different problems. For example, the United States Commerce and Defense departments may have goals that are advanced by the sale of sophisticated arms to an ally, but the same arms sale may create a problem for the Arms Control and Disarmament Agency and the Department of State if they each have a goal that involves restricting the distribution of certain armaments and maintaining an equilibrium in regional arms supplies. Thus, one of the first tasks of those who set agendas within a government may be to convince other government agencies of the importance of adopting a particular goal.

A third corollary of the proposed definition of a problem is that the government must have some knowledge of present conditions and possible trends. In other words, for a problem-solver in government to identify a discrepancy, he must be aware not only of his goals but also of the existing or emerging conditions that seem likely to affect those goals. This intelligence about the environment and the interpretation of what effect it may have on the government's goals need not necessarily be accurate to generate action. The foreign policy literature as well as research on other kinds of problem-solving contains numerous illustrations and evidence of misperception and erroneous estimates of cause and effect.[2] However, accuracy in the interpretation of the environment and changes within it is essential for effective responses.

A fourth corollary of the term problem involves the concept of discrepancy. Often one thinks of discrepancies that result from negative circumstances such as punishment or threats of punishment. For example, the deployment of multiple or MIRV warheads on ballistic missiles, which makes more difficult (i.e., threatens) the goal of a verifiable arms agreement on strategic weapons, is a discrepancy between the goal of future arms control and an emerging state of affairs. Potential opportunities, which are positive circumstances, can also produce a discrepancy and, hence, a problem. Suppose the presence of an American military base in a foreign country is obstructing the goal of improving diplomatic relations with that country. If changing world conditions and improved military technology substantially reduce the importance of the base to the United States, the opportunity exists for moving toward a goal of the United States. Unless a given develop-ment will transpire automatically without any government action, it remains only a potential opportunity. Recognizing a potential opportunity and the need for action to bring about its realization creates a discrepancy and a problem for a government. Moreover, failure to realize the opportu-nity becomes a deprivation.

Problem Recognition

An individual with cancer may ultimately die from it if not successfully treated. Until the individual's condition is detected, however, the cancer is not a problem; an undetected disease is not a matter for concern nor is it treated, and hence no discrepancy exists between the individual's preferred state of health and present health. An equivalent situation can occur for governments. The requirement that a policy maker be aware of a discrepancy between a preferred and existing state introduces another basic concept in need of specification—problem recognition. The human characteristic of selective attention and perception is well established (e.g., Tajfel, 1969; Tagiuri, 1969). Both individuals and organizations normally operate in such rich environments that they cannot possibly attend to all stimuli, so they systematically screen out many signals—perhaps most—and select only a few to which they give conscious attention. Such selective recognition is the first analytical step necessary for coping with a problem.

For organizations, problem recognition is more demanding than for individuals. The individual has the capacity for both problem recognition and problem coping, although the latter may be inadequate under some circumstances. By contrast, the specialization and division of labor in large, complex organizations or set of organizations (such as those that normally deal with foreign affairs) separate the functions of problem recognition from those of decision and policy implementation. It is at the lower "working level" of the State and Defense departments, Agency for International Devel-opment, and C.I.A., for example, that most of an organization's interaction with, and monitoring of, its environment occurs. It is the political officer in an embassy, the military assistance officer in the field, the intelligence ana-lyst, or the arms control negotiator that often is the first member of the government to become aware of a problem. In most cases, however, such an official will not have the authority to resolve the problem and must confine his role to reporting to his organizational superiors. The studies of foreign policy are full of problems identified at the periphery of an organization only to be lost, discounted, or simply set aside until later.[3] Nowhere has this organizational difficulty been more clearly highlighted than in the classic by Ogburn (1961) who relates the hypothetical case of the overthrow of a Western-oriented government in the Middle East. The coup is postulated to have occurred weeks after U.S. embassy personnel and the responsible desk officer at the State Department had observed that the government was in trouble and recommended supportive measures. Their proposals simply were not attended to at the higher decision making level, which was plagued by a myriad of seemingly more urgent problems. The conclusion is clear. From the perspective of problem solving, organizational problem recognition occurs only when awareness of the problem reaches those within the organization with sufficient authority to decide whether any action is appropriate and, if so, to implement the policy decided on.

Problem Definition

Analytically it is useful to distinguish problem recognition from problem definition. Problem definition means the *interpretation* of a problem by policy makers. Snyder, Bruck and Sapin (1962) have referred to this as the "definition of the situation." In the practical world, it seems clear that an interpretation must be at least tentatively made at the time a problem is recognized. Thus, the question might arise as to why *definition* should be analytically separated from *recognition*. At least two reasons can be offered. Because meaning is subjective, the same problem may be defined quite differently by different observers. Furthermore, the interpretation of the problem, that is, its definition, is dynamic and can change dramatically across a period of months, weeks, days, or even hours. Such change in the definition of a problem can result either because the actual problem is evolving or because the policymakers' perceptions of the problem are changing.

We know that the same problem may be defined differently by different individuals, organizations, and nations. The matter of a shared definition of a problem is particularly acute in foreign affairs because of cross-cultural differences, governmental motivations for keeping signals ambiguous or deceptive, and conflicting messages sent from different parts of one government to another (e.g., Jervis, 1976). For example, what meaning should the United States attach to the discovery that the Soviet Union is enlarging certain intercontinental ballistic missile (ICBM) silos? Is the move simply the expression of a long standing cultural need to build ever-larger weapons systems? Or is it a provocative attempt to create a first-strike capability by deploying missiles capable of destroying American land-based missiles?

Not only must one contend with multiple interpretations by different individuals, agencies, and governments, but the same group's definition of the problem may vary through time. Paige (1968) illustrates the rapidity with which the interpretation of a problem can undergo change in his study of the Truman administration's decision to enter the Korean War. At first, the president and his advisers believed the South Koreans could stop the invasion by themselves. Within less than a week, their interpretation of the Korean situation had changed substantially and American ground forces were committed. In contrast to the Korean example, sometimes problems are re-defined out of existence. For example, the American concern in the 1970s over the need for alternative sources of energy virtually disappeared in the early 1980s after the Reagan administration concluded that the problem should be handled by the private sector, even though the energy companies found development too expensive.

Considerable attention has been devoted here to definitions. This essay contends that the task of monitoring the external environment for potential foreign policy problems also requires careful attention to the multiple tasks implied by the concepts of problem recognition and definition. The implications that already have been drawn from these concepts should make the reader suspicious of simple proposals for improving the agenda-setting function of foreign policy organization for the 1980s. For example, it should now be possible to recognize as inadequate such hypothetical recommendations as: "Give me more diplomats, military officers, and intelligence analysts skilled in political reporting and who know the national interests, and I will provide you with an improved foreign policy monitoring and agenda-setting capability." If the proposal had the primary effect of overloading those with decision-making authority by producing more problems for them to cope with, the system could very well reduce the effectiveness of organizations' agenda-setting function. Further insights into the requirements for improving this capability can be acquired by examining the characteristics of governmental organizations.

ORGANIZATIONAL QUALITIES

As we saw in the case of President Carter's decision to abort the rescue mission in Iran, few American foreign policy problems are recognized and defined by individuals acting alone. Despite appearances to the contrary, Carter was responding to a problem identified and defined by several bureaucracies. If foreign policy officials are embedded in governmental organizations, it is not surprising that the qualities of those organizations can influence what problems are recognized and how they are defined. That is both good news and bad. When compared to individuals working alone or in small groups, those in large organizations are potentially better able to *recognize* a problem. The specialization of tasks and the usual procedures for information coordination enable one specialist to monitor a single area or type of issue and then to pool his observations with numerous others. Because of hierarchical structure and competing interests in an organization, however, bureaucracies may have greater difficulties than isolated individuals in *defining* a foreign policy problem. Furthermore, even though an organization should offer a favorable context for problem recognition, it can fail to do so if the problem is extremely unusual or if its effective treatment requires a radically different approach from those used previously. These strengths and weaknesses will become more evident by examining some particular qualities of governmental organizations.

Organizational Restructuring

Problems can emerge from perceived changes in the foreign environment or from internal restructuring within the foreign policy machinery of the government. By restructuring, we mean the new interpretation of existing information through reassessments often caused by the shift of organizational personnel. As a result of new assignments people who hold different interpretations of available information have new power to enable them to shape government action.

Of course, the major restructuring of American foreign policy personnel typically occurs when there is a change in presidential administration. The shift can be dramatic when the movement is between administrations with substantially different political outlooks. It could be argued that the actual foreign policy environment of the United States changed only slightly between the last months of the Carter administration and the first months of the Reagan administration, but the perception of problems and the perceived best means of treating them changed substantially. Everything from human rights to the basing of the MX missile was reinterpreted by the incoming Reagan appointees.

The reassignment or promotion of key personnel offers another form of restructuring. A military officer who has been a field commander may have recognized a foreign policy problem, but been unable to get support from those in a position to address the issue. Suppose his next assignment is on one of the specialized staffs of the Joint Chiefs of Staff, where he finds that his new position gives him the authority to mobilize those policy makers able to deal with the problem he had identified previously. Assuming that the authority required to make most nonroutine choices resides at the middle and upper levels of government, then the appointment of new individuals at these levels is apt to trigger new problem recognition through restructuring. With internal restructuring, changes in the foreign environment are not necessary to generate new problems for the policy agenda. The general conclusion is that the more foreign policy organizations reassign personnel—particularly across hierarchical levels of authority or through the recruitment of new personnel into the organization—the more likely are new problems to be recognized or old ones to be redefined. There is, however, an important exception. While the new personnel are learning the office routines and the information retrieval system as well as the substance of an unfamiliar foreign policy area, they may miss information or be less able to piece it together than would an "old hand." The subtle shift in a trend or a small change in a foreign position might be more likely to alert the more experienced person that a problem is developing. Thus, organizational restructuring can have short-run liabilities for problem recognition.

Selective and Differential Search

The alternative means by which policy problems emerge is by changes in the organization's external environment. Foreign policy organizations must establish search routines to monitor any such possible environmental changes. Organizations by their nature involve specialization and role differentiation. Thus, specialists develop who search for a particular kind of problem or monitor a certain source of information. These specialists establish routines or standard operating procedures by which they search or monitor their assigned domains. For example, in the Department of State, as in most other foreign policy agencies, specialization involves a mix of geographical and functional categories for defining search capabilities. Facilities can be developed for monitoring special types of situations (e.g., the Crisis Communication Center, the Berlin Task Force) and procedures for transmitting information can be made systematic (e.g., under specified conditions cables of only a certain priority are to be transmitted; or instructions are given the watch officer to awake key individuals during the night if certain occurrences transpire).

The difficulty arises because search routines, decision rules, and standard operating procedures by definition focus the search for potential foreign policy problems toward some cues or particular kinds of signals, but not others. The unavoidable question thus becomes: What about critical problems that do not have the characteristics established by the specialized search routines? Searching for the unexpected will always pose major challenges to foreign policy organizations, but they can at least avoid certain kinds of common biases. Pool and Kessler (1969: 669–670) provide a convenient list of selective attention patterns particularly applicable to bureaucratic specialists as well as isolated individuals:

1. People pay more attention to information that deals with them.
2. People pay less attention to facts that contradict their views.
3. People pay more attention to information from trusted, liked sources.
4. People pay more attention to information that they will have to act on or discuss because of the attention by others.
5. People pay more attention to information bearing on actions they have already taken, i.e., action creates commitment.[4]

Internal Communication

Another consequence of organizational role specialization and task differentiation is the separation of the individuals and units engaged in search and intelligence activities from those who ultimately make a decision as to whether action should be taken on a particular problem. As noted previously, this is the reason that problem recognition within a foreign policy organization cannot be usefully defined as the perception of a problem by *any* member of the organization, regardless of his position. The problem must be recognized by those individuals whose role specialization and level of authority enable them to mobilize the organization for action. Given the specialization of tasks, it is almost certain that the individual who first discovers a problem will *not* be the individual with authority to approve action. Furthermore, if the internal communication system between the initial perceiver of a problem and the occupant of the necessary authority role fails for any reason, then the organization's behavior will not reflect the discovery. In a meaningful sense the organization can be said not to have recognized the problem at all. Therefore, a critical feature of any organization is the internal communication system. How quickly and accurately can information be transferred from one unit to another? Regrettably, communication among parts of an organization can be inadequate.

Problem Load

The failure of problem recognition can result not only from weaknesses in the internal communication system of foreign policy organizations, but also because of the heavy decision load on the middle and political levels of the organization. Study after study (e.g., Kissinger, 1966; Hoffmann, 1968) has noted the decision overload on foreign policy makers at this level of government. Given the broad range of global activities that are assumed to pertain to American interests, many problems are stillborn because they fail to get out of the in-basket of the necessary policy maker. It is reasonable to speculate that the broader the base of an organization's authority structure and the greater the delegation of authority, the more likely are external problems to be recognized, provided internal communication is well maintained. The difficulty of such a configuration arises when the collected information and analysis is passed up through the organization and becomes part of the overload on top-level officials.

A word of caution is required about one of the consequences of overloading the agenda-setting process. In order to capture a position on the overcrowded agenda of senior policy makers, earnest subordinates may attempt to mobilize support from other parts of the government, the media, the public, and even from foreign nations. In the process of creating such support, the characterization of the problem may become distorted and, frequently, the consequences of failing to deal with the issue are exaggerated to promote attention. This matter deserves separate consideration.

Responsiveness to Public Pressure

Why do public campaigns to mobilize support for a problem lead to distortion in the perception of the problem? Two major reasons can be advanced. First, in order to motivate people to act it becomes necessary to persuade them that their vital interests are affected. To shape a foreign policy issue into an effective appeal for public support may require associating the issue with a greater issue—for example, the danger of war, severe economic loss, militant communism, increased taxes, or the need for a military draft. In the process of linking the issue to one of these basic concerns, the definition of the problem may become distorted. Second, to reach millions of people requires the use of the media—especially the electronic media of radio and television. Because news stories in the media must be short and easily grasped, mass media treatment can serve as another force acting to simplify and exaggerate aspects of an issue. The result is an increase in the constraints on the ability of the government to define the problem accurately. Compounding the problem of distortion is the prospect that public involvement may actually decrease the likelihood that quick agreement can be reached on any definition of a problem. As Thurow (1981) has argued in another context, the influence of domestic politics on many issues in the United States has created a zero-sum game in which many diverse interests have the ability to block action if they are threatened. Once a foreign policy issue becomes a subject of domestic debate, each interest group may try to prevent other groups from defining it as a problem in a way unfavorable to their concerns.

Organizational Goals

At the beginning of this essay, a problem was described as involving goals or preferred conditions. Goals are both formal and informal, and this brings us to a final organizational characteristic. The literature on bureaucratic organizations has made the point repeatedly that organizations and bureaus within organizations often have different missions and goals. If individuals see their promotions and careers dependent on how well they succeed in their particular bureau or organization, then it will be natural for them to promote the goals of their bureaucratic units. The result is that individuals in different bureaucracies will have a built-in disposition to interpret problems in terms of their organization's goals and mission.

This process is at the heart of bureaucratic politics. It also makes the task of reaching consensus on problem definition within the government difficult unless other factors intervene (e.g., a strongly expressed presidential preference). Furthermore, once consensus on the definition of a problem has been reached within an organization, inertia sets in and works against any revision of that definition that may become necessary. The evolution of a problem definition thus tends to be more gradual for bureaucratic organizations than for individuals; exceptions might arise, however, when the top of an organization changes suddenly, when a new administration comes to power, or when a coalition collapses whose interpretation of a problem had prevailed previously.

IMPLICATIONS OF A SHIFT IN THE ARRAY OF PROBLEMS

In this final section we will examine how the characteristics of American bureaucratic organizations could prove to be constraints in recognizing and defining the foreign policy problems of the 1980s. Basic to the discussion is the contention that the types of major foreign affairs problems in need of attention are undergoing a profound change.

Post-Cold War Problems

For much of the period since the end of World War II, most American organizations concerned with monitoring foreign affairs problems were influenced greatly by the Cold War. The protracted and intense antagonism between the United States and the Soviet Union shaped the problems that were recognized and the ways in which they were defined. Anyone who became an adult after the late 1940s is undoubtedly familiar with the episodes, issues, and policies that reflected America's overriding concern with the Soviet Union—the fear of Soviet military expansion into an economically stagnant and politically uncertain Western Europe, North Korea's attack on South Korea in 1950, the fear of domestic infiltration of Communist sympathizers at its peak during the McCarthy era, the potential or actual emergence of Russian- or Chinese-oriented governments or ruling groups in Third World countries, and the more recent concerns about the qualitative and quantitative buildup in strategic armaments.

Even issues that in other periods might have been interpreted very differently were defined as Cold War problems—such as the end of colonialism, the emergence of nationalistic forces, the efforts at economic development, and innovations in science and technology.

Of course not every problem became an adjunct of the Cold War, but the budgets of major agencies, the time allocations of presidents and other officials, and the foreign policy debates in Congress and the media point to the prominence of the Cold War framework in foreign policy problem recognition and definition.

The political and military problems stemming from the conflict between the Communist and Western powers have not disappeared. In fact some of these problems may even become more acute in the future. There could be an accelerated tendency on the part of the U.S.S.R. to engage in conflicts that are far removed from its borders. Perhaps the most troubling aspect for the United States is its loss of clear superiority in many areas of conventional and nuclear forces relative to the Soviet Union. For most of the Cold War period, America enjoyed unquestioned predominance, at least with respect to nuclear weapons and military technology. However, with Soviet military advances and with changes in destructive capabilities that have robbed the concept of nuclear superiority of useful meaning, a fundamental transformation has occurred. Even if this loss of clear Western military superiority in certain areas does not create problems, and even if the Soviets exercise restraint, the American coalitions that developed as a result of the Cold War may continue to interpret problems in the framework of the Cold War. Such problem definitions would conform to needs and experiences, regardless of present reality.

Having noted this continuing Cold War legacy, we must nevertheless recognize that many individuals inside and outside the American foreign policy community are identifying and debating problems that cannot be understood by reference to Cold War antagonisms. Even if problems with the Soviet Union continue to be of major importance to the United States, they may dominate our foreign policy agenda only if we ignore other pressing and urgent challenges.

A study done for the Commission on the Organization of the Government for the Conduct of Foreign Policy (known for short as the Murphy Commission) identified eight global problem areas that could have major adverse effects on the United States and the rest of the world after the year

2000 if not effectively handled before then. These problems, which were drawn exclusively from the area of global environmental and resource interdependence, were ocean pollution, atmospheric pollution, weather modification, resource monitoring satellites, communication satellite jurisdiction, nuclear reactors, food, and population (Keohane and Nye, 1975). Given the environmental orientation of this list, it is perhaps understandable that energy did not surface as a more general problem than in its nuclear reactor form and that the entire range of economic problems was excluded. However, economic problems—ranging from trade deficits and widespread inflation to the calls for a new international economic order—illustrate the emergence of acute foreign policy problems that seem to have little or no direct relationship to the Cold War.

From a somewhat different perspective, Mesarovic and Pestel (1974) have noted a multiple set of unprecedented crises emerging in population, energy, raw materials, and pollution that are a result of undifferentiated growth and of rapidly increasing interdependence.

> The most outstanding lesson which can be drawn from these events is a realization of how strong the bonds among nations have become. A bureaucratic decision in one region . . . —not to increase the spring wheat acreage—resulted in a housewives' strike against soaring food prices in another part of the world and in tragic suffering in yet another part of the world. . . . The world is already interdependent to that extent, and interdependence is certain to increase (Mesarovic and Pestel, 1974: 19–20).

From yet another perspective, the shaping of the world economy in the next quarter century constitutes "the greatest challenge to industrial civilization since it began to take shape two centuries ago" (Rostow, 1978).

Only time will tell whether Keohane and Nye (1975), Mesarovic and Pestel (1974), Rostow (1978) or other forecasters (e.g., Platt, 1969; Schell, 1982) have enumerated accurately the most demanding set of foreign policy problems of the future. Because we are interested in the recognition and definition of new international challenges, the particular problems identified by various individuals are less important than the apparent shift away from what appear to be Cold War-type problems. If there are likely to be significantly different types of problems threatening the well-being of the United States in the 1980s, how will situational characteristics and organizational properties influence their successful recognition and definition?

INTERACTION OF SITUATIONAL AND ORGANIZATIONAL PROPERTIES

How well foreign policy organizations meet future challenges depends not only on the qualities of the organizations that were discussed above but also on the nature of the situations they encounter. Do they differ in any important respects from the situations foreign policy organizations have been dealing with over the past four decades? By considering such characteristics of situations as threats, opportunities, complexity, awareness, and decision time, the impression emerges that many future situations could be of a different nature from those of the past.

With respect to future threats, they may be directed not only at physical survival through possible war, but to a variety of social, political, and economic institutions and even to ecological systems as well. As in the Cold War, threats may involve painful tradeoffs (for example, between individual freedom versus public order). Both threats and opportunities may well emerge from sources other than those to which we have grown accustomed to dealing. Not only may they involve familiar antagonists, but they also may originate from nonstate actors—such as terrorists, multinational corporations, nonterritorial nations—and, in general, from human interaction with nature.

Complexity can be interpreted as an interaction between the requirements for solution posed by a problem and the capabilities of the problem solvers. The problem side of the equation might be expected to become more complex in several respects. First, the growth in interdependence between international social and economic systems may complicate attempts at resolution by requiring coordination of a multiplicity of units inside and outside the United States. Those units outside the United States may not be particularly susceptible to American governmental influences. Interdependence may increase the likelihood that "solutions" to problems have more unanticipated secondary and tertiary effects which trigger new problems or confound the treatment of the original one. What may confuse detection of such problems is a breakdown in any clear idea of cause and effect. A second source of complexity may result from an increased tendency for multiple, large, demanding problems to arise simultaneously. Platt (1969: 1116) refers to this difficulty when he notes: "What finally makes all of our crises more dangerous is that they are now coming on top of each other." The concentration on one may deflect attention from the presence of others.

Awareness of problems also affects the other side of the complexity equation—the ability of foreign policy agencies to cope with these problems. For example, as dangerous as the repeated crises over West Berlin were, the United States in time gained familiarity with some recurrent features of the problem and characteristics of the adversary. This general awareness might not have prevented the onset of a tactical surprise in any particular crisis, but it made it easier for American policymakers to recognize the problem and define it within the context of the Cold War whenever a critical situation suddenly arose. One of the difficulties facing policy makers in an era of emerging new foreign policy problems could be the absence of familiarity with these problems and with their associated indicators and danger signs.

Many of the problems of the Cold War—such as in the Cuban missile crisis or the invasion of South Korea—emerged as crises in which decision time was extremely short. Although one can envision some future nuclear confrontation in which decision time is reduced to something less than the 30 minutes required for ICBMs to reach their targets, the Cold War problems of the past may have established benchmarks for acutely short decision times that are unlikely to be surpassed in the vast majority of new challenges. In fact, some of the emerging problems could be just the reverse, in that they have long lead times before they become a major danger (an example would be the problem of ocean pollution). However, the time during which action must be initiated to avert or correct a dangerous problem may considerably precede the time when the full danger is actually experienced. (See Keohane and Nye [1975] for a discussion of problems that they believe need prompt attention if their adverse effects are to be avoided when they materialize sometime between 2001 and 2020.)

The previous paragraphs have tried to illustrate the possible nature of situational characteristics of problems different from those that have dominated American attention during the Cold War. Assuming that such different types of problems become more important for American foreign policy, how would the organizational characteristics identified previously affect recognition and identification of these new problems?

Perhaps the most critical organizational feature concerns the selective search processes of organizations. We have suggested that governmental organizations, just as individuals, must be selective in the domains they search. The Cold War provided a framework that for more than 35 years served as a structure that indicated to the foreign policy organizations of the United States government what situations to monitor and what meaning to attach to problems that arose. These highly established search routines and interpretative processes may now become increasingly dysfunctional by not directing monitoring activities to situations that could pose new kinds of dangers or opportunities or by imposing a Cold War definition on a detected problem that may be inappropriate for effective response.

The organizational restructuring that regularly marks foreign policy agencies as new people assume key positions could aid in the more rapid erosion of the Cold War framework. The arrival at top posts of individuals who have not had firsthand experience in policy making during the most extreme period of the Cold War could facilitate new patterns for monitoring international affairs. A darker side, however, also must be considered. If more of the foreign policy problems of the future demand extremely long lead times to avoid severe adverse effects, no leadership may find it desirable or politically feasible to attend to problems whose outcomes may not be experienced until long after they have left office. The turnover of political leadership also may make it more difficult to construct coalitions with a shared definition of the problem. For instance, an agreement on the nature of the problem that is presumably within grasp might be adversely affected by the defeat of the chairman of a key congressional committee or by the resignation of a needed deputy undersecretary or by the replacement of the entire executive administration.

Many agencies of the United States government participate in foreign policy decisions, but the Cold War gave certain agencies dominance— including the State and Defense departments, the Joint Chiefs of Staff, the C.I.A., the Agency for International Development and its precursors, and, increasingly, the National Security Council staff. Established channels of communication, clearance processes, and interagency working groups have gradually evolved. Faced with different types of problems these internal channels of communication may not be the most salient ones, nor may these agencies be the most appropriate. Indeed, no present agency may be charged with monitoring for a given set of future problems. Even if an agency does engage in such monitoring, it may be unclear who has responsibility for assessing and communicating whether or not a problem merits further attention on any agency's agenda. In other words, who should be alerted if a new problem is detected? Internal communications may need major revision.

What about problem overload? Any available organizational slack could be more than consumed in one of several ways. If problems are unfamiliar or seemingly more complex, it may take longer to agree on their definition and devise an acceptable response; thus other problems will have to be placed "on hold." Furthermore, if Platt (1969) is correct, the emerging challenge is not simply one of different kinds of problems but of more problems occurring concurrently.

Copying with a certain type of problem in foreign affairs has become part of the mission or goals of particular foreign policy organizations. The very names of some units indicate much about their assigned problems—for example, the Arms Control and Disarmament Agency, the Agency for International Development, and the International Communication Agency. The difficulty arises when *no* agency regards a certain problem as falling within the definition of its primary mission or goals. If several organizations regard themselves as having only secondary responsibility for a given type of problem, it may be that none is devoting significant resources to monitoring the problem. The real possibility exists that the present array of organizational goals of the various American foreign policy bureaucracies are such that any meaningful attention to some kinds of potential problems of the future is, in effect, not possible.

CONCLUSION

The hostage crisis in Iran may represent a kind of transition problem to the foreign policy issues of the 1980s. It differed from the past in that our Cold War framework did not apply. America was dealing with a fragmented regime whose outlook could not be understood in terms of a struggle between communism and western pluralistic societies. U.S. interests in Iran flowed from a concern with petroleum and with creating stability in the Middle East. At the same time, however, the situation posed an almost classic foreign policy problem—the protection of diplomats and citizens abroad. Such types of problems may not disappear in the future, but others of a very different nature may arise with greater frequency. Such problems will require organizational innovations in order simply to be recognized and defined in a timely fashion.

It can be argued that the picture sketched in this essay exaggerates the constraints and difficulties in problem management and response in foreign policymaking. The author hopes so, but perhaps more than hope is needed to make certain that the interaction of new situations and old organizational routines does not obstruct the recognition and definition of problems that need to get on the American national agenda and on the agenda of other governments and world actors as well. The avoidance of these pitfalls partially entails modifying organization capabilities to meet the requirements of foreign policy in the 1980s and beyond.

Some might be tempted initially to regard substitution or replacement as the approach. The government, it could be argued, should shift from an East-West framework to one focused on North-South conflicts; from agencies concerned with military capability to economic capability; from crisis management to long-range planning. All indications are that such attempts to "redistribute" responses would be most inadequate and inappropriate. Few careful observers would claim that many of the older type of problems have been resolved or have faded away. The U.S. government must still attend to such problems. Even though various sources seek to dramatize presently emerging issues, relatively few responsible individuals or groups claim to have a clear and certain vision of what the total array of future foreign policy problems will be. Thus, a greater sensitivity to the unusual in international affairs and its environment appears to be a watchword for monitoring rather than locking on a given alternative domain of new problems.

Going beyond the heightened attention to various forms of activity, those responsible for foreign policy—and the conduct of government generally—may need to invest more in the exploration of new forms of social organization for collective problem recognition and management. McNeill (1963) argues that civilizations began to emerge when humankind developed primitive administrative and bureaucratic skills. Perhaps if we are to avert unpleasant future deprivations not only to our society but also to our civilization, we should devote significantly more resources and energy to the design of, and experimentation with, new forms of collective problem recognition and management.

NOTES

1. The task of mobilizing support is well documented in the case of the Marshall Plan by Jones (1955), for the Truman Doctrine by Gaddis (1972), and for NSC-68 by Hammond (1962).

2. For a social psychological study of the mistaken belief in events and their anticipated effect, see Festinger, Riecken and Schachter (1956). In organizational
theory, Thompson (1967) has made activities done on the basis of collective
beliefs about cause and effect relationships an organization's core technology—
regardless of whether the beliefs are correct or not. Misperception in international politics has been a major concern of Jervis (1976).
3. This difficulty in problem recognition is illustrated by the "loss" in the system of
cues that might have alerted U.S. policy makers to the Pearl Harbor attack (see
Wohlstetter, 1962) and by the failure to consider intelligence about the location
of German Panzer divisions prior to the beginning of Operation Market-Garden
in 1944 (see Ryan, 1974).
4. It is possible to construct some plausible organizational parallels to the Pool and
Kessler (1969) statements about selective perception of individuals. Consider
these examples: (a) an organization pays more attention to information pertaining to itself or its mission; (b) an organization pays less attention to—or seeks to
deny or to alter—information that contradicts its objectives or that challenges
its prior behavior.

REFERENCES

Festinger, Leon, Riecken, Henry W., and Schachter, Stanley. (1956). *When Prophecy Fails*. Minneapolis, Minn.: University of Minnesota Press.

Gaddis, John Lewis. (1972). *The United States and the Origins of the Cold War*. New York: Columbia University Press.

Hammond, Paul Y. (1962). "NSC-68: Prologue to Rearmament." Pp. 267–378 in W. R. Schilling, Paul Y. Hammond, and Glenn H. Snyder, *Strategy, Politics, and Defense Budgets*. New York: Columbia University Press.

Hermann, Charles F. (1979). "Why New Foreign Policy Challenges Might Not be Met." Pp. 269–292 in Charles W. Kegley, Jr., and Pat McGowan (eds.), *Challenges to America*. Beverly Hills: Sage.

Hoffmann, Stanley. (1968). *Gulliver's Troubles, or the Setting of American Foreign Policy*. New York: McGraw-Hill.

Jervis, Robert. (1976). *Perception and Misperception in International Politics*. Princeton: Princeton University Press.

Jones, Joseph N. (1955). *The Fifteen Weeks*. New York: Harcourt, Brace and World.

Keohane, Robert O., and Nye, Joseph S. (1975). "Organizing for Global Environmental and Resource Interdependence." Pp. 43–64 in *Appendices for Commission on the Organization of the Government for the Conduct of Foreign Policy*, Vol. 1, Appendix B. Washington, D.C.: U.S. Government Printing Office.

Kissinger, Henry A. (1966). "Domestic Structure and Foreign Policy." *Daedalus*, 95 (2): 503–529.

McNeill, William. (1963). *The Rise of the West*. New York: Mentor.

Mesarovic, Mihajlo, and Pestel, Eduard. (1974). *Mankind at the Turning Point*. New York: Dutton.

Ogburn, Charlton. (1961). "The Flow of Policy-Making in the Department of State." Pp. 229–244 in James N. Rosenau (ed.), *International Politics and Foreign Policy*. First edition. New York: Free Press.

Paige, Glenn D. (1968). *The Korean Decision*. New York: Free Press.

Platt, John. (1969). "What We Must Do." *Science*, 166 (November 28): 1115–1120.

Pool, Ithiel de Sola, and Kessler, Allen. (1969). "The Kaiser, the Tsar and the Computer." Pp. 664–678 in James N. Rosenau (ed.), *International Politics and Foreign Policy*. Second edition. New York: Free Press.

Rostow, Walt W. (1978). *Getting From Here to There*. New York: McGraw-Hill.

Ryan, Cornelius. (1974). *A Bridge Too Far*. New York: Simon and Schuster.

Schell, Jonathan. (1982). *The Fate of the Earth*. New York: Knopf.

Snyder, Richard C., Bruck, H. W., and Sapin, Burton. (1962). *Foreign Policy Decision-Making*. New York: Free Press.

Tagiuri, Renato. (1969). "Person Perception." Pp. 395–449 in Gardner Lindzey and Elliot Aronson (eds.), *Handbook of Social Psychology*, Vol. 3. Reading, Mass.: Addison-Wesley.

Tajfel, Henri. (1969). "Social and Cultural Factors in Perception." Pp. 305–394 in Gardner Lindzey and Elliot Aronson (eds.), *Handbook of Social Psychology*, Vol. 3. Reading, Mass.: Addison-Wesley.

Thompson, James. (1967). *Organizations in Action*. New York: McGraw-Hill.

Thurow, Lester C. (1981). *The Zero-Sum Society*. New York: Penguin.

Wohlstetter, Roberta. (1962). *Pearl Harbor: Warning and Decision*. Stanford: Stanford University Press.

25

ARE BUREAUCRACIES IMPORTANT?

A Re-Examination of Accounts of the Cuban Missile Crisis

STEPHEN D. KRASNER

Who and what shapes foreign policy? In recent years, analyses have increasingly emphasized not rational calculations of the national interest or the political goals of national leaders but rather bureaucratic procedures and bureaucratic politics. Starting with Richard Neustadt's *Presidential Power,* a judicious study of leadership published in 1960, this approach has come to portray the American President as trapped by a permanent government more enemy than ally. Bureaucratic theorists imply that it is exceedingly difficult if not impossible for political leaders to control the organizational web which surrounds them. Important decisions result from numerous smaller actions taken by individuals at different levels in the bureaucracy who have partially incompatible national, bureaucratic, political, and personal objectives. They are not necessarily a reflection of the aims and values of high officials. . . .

Analyses of bureaucratic politics have been used to explain alliance behaviour during the 1956 Suez crisis and the [1962] Skybolt incident, Truman's relations with MacArthur, American policy in Vietnam, and now most thoroughly the Cuban missile crisis in Graham Allison's *Essence of Decision: Explaining the Cuban Missile Crisis,* published in 1971 (Little Brown & Company). Allison's volume is the elaboration of an earlier and influential article on this subject. With the publication of his book this approach to foreign policy now receives its definitive statement. The bureaucratic interpretation of foreign policy has become the conventional wisdom.

My argument here is that this vision is misleading, dangerous, and compelling: misleading because it obscures the power of the President; dangerous because it undermines the assumptions of democratic politics by relieving high officials of responsibility; and compelling because it offers

This chapter appeared originally as Stephen D. Krasner, "Are Bureaucracies Important? (Or Allison Wonderland)" *Foreign Policy,* 7 (Summer, 1972), pp. 159–179. Reprinted with permission from *Foreign Policy* magazine #7 (Summer, 1972).

leaders an excuse for their failures and scholars an opportunity for innumerable reinterpretations and publications.

The contention that the Chief Executive is trammelled by the permanent government has disturbing implications for any effort to impute responsibility to public officials. A democratic political philosophy assumes that responsibility for the acts of governments can be attributed to elected officials. The charges of these men are embodied in legal statutes. The electorate punishes an erring official by rejecting him at the polls. Punishment is senseless unless high officials are responsible for the acts of government. Elections have some impact only if government, that most complex of modern organizations, can be controlled. If the bureaucratic machine escapes manipulation and direction even by the highest officials, then punishment is illogical. Elections are a farce not because the people suffer from false consciousness, but because public officials are impotent, enmeshed in a bureaucracy so large that the actions of government are not responsive to their will. What sense to vote a man out of office when his successor, regardless of his values, will be trapped in the same web of only incrementally mutable standard operating procedures?

THE RATIONAL ACTOR MODEL

Conventional analyses that focus on the values and objectives of foreign policy, what Allison calls the Rational Actor Model, are perfectly coincident with the ethical assumptions of democratic politics. The state is viewed as a rational unified actor. The behaviour of states is the outcome of a rational decision-making process. This process has three steps. The options for a given situation are spelled out. The consequences of each option are projected. A choice is made which maximizes the values held by decision-makers. The analyst knows what the state did. His objective is to explain why by imputing to decision-makers a set of values which are maximized by observed behaviour. These values are his explanation of foreign policy.

The citizen, like the analyst, attributes error to either inappropriate values or lack of foresight. Ideally the electorate judges the officeholder by governmental performance which is assumed to reflect the objectives and perspicacity of political leaders. Poor policy is made by leaders who fail to foresee accurately the consequences of their decisions or attempt to maximize values not held by the electorate. Political appeals, couched in terms of aims and values, are an appropriate guide for voters. For both the analyst who adheres to the Rational Actor Model, and the citizen who decides elections, values are assumed to be the primary determinant of government behaviour.

The bureaucratic politics paradigm points to quite different determinants of policy. Political leaders can only with great difficulty overcome the inertia and self-serving interests of the permanent government. What counts is managerial skill. In *Essence of Decision*, Graham Allison maintains that "the central questions of policy analysis are quite different from the kinds of questions analysts have traditionally asked. Indeed, the crucial questions seem to be matters of planning for management." Administrative feasibility not substance becomes the central concern.

The paradoxical conclusion—that bureaucratic analysis with its emphasis on policy guidance implies political non-responsibility—has most clearly been brought out by discussions of American policy in Vietnam. Richard Neustadt on the concluding page of *Alliance Politics* . . . muses about a conversation he would have had with President Kennedy in the fall of 1963 had tragedy not intervened. "I considered asking whether, in the light of our machine's performance on a British problem, he conceived that it could cope with South Vietnam's. . . . [I]t was a good question, better than I knew. It haunts me still." For adherents of the bureaucratic politics paradigm, Vietnam was a failure of the "machine," a war in Arthur Schlesinger's words "which no President . . . desired or intended."[1] The machine dictated a policy which it could not successfully terminate. The machine not the cold war ideology and hubris of Kennedy and Johnson determined American behaviour in Vietnam. Vietnam could hardly be a tragedy for tragedies are made by choice and character, not fate. A knowing electorate would express sympathy not levy blame. Machines cannot be held responsible for what they do, nor can the men caught in their workings.

The strength of the bureaucratic web has been attributed to two sources: organizational necessity and bureaucratic interest. The costs of coordination and search procedures are so high that complex organizations *must* settle for satisfactory rather than optimal solutions. Bureaucracies have interests defined in terms of budget allocation, autonomy, morale, and scope which they defend in a game of political bargaining and compromise within the executive branch.

The imperatives of organizational behaviour limit flexibility. Without a division of labor and the establishment of standard operating procedures, it would be impossible for large organizations to begin to fulfill their statutory objectives, that is to perform tasks designed to meet societal needs rather than merely to perpetuate the organization. A division of labor among and within organizations reduces the job of each particular division to manageable proportions. Once this division is made, the complexity confronting an organization or one of its parts is further reduced through the establishment of standard operating procedures. To deal with each problem as if it were *sui generis* would be impossible given limited resources and information processing capacity, and would make intra-organizational coordination extremely difficult. Bureaucracies are then unavoidably rigid; but without the rigidity imposed by division of labor and standard operating procedures, they could hardly begin to function at all.

However, this rigidity inevitably introduces distortions. All of the options to a given problem will not be presented with equal lucidity and conviction unless by some happenstance the organization has worked out its scenarios for that particular problem in advance. It is more likely that the organization will have addressed itself to something *like* the problem with which it is confronted. It has a set of options for such a hypothetical problem and these options will be presented to deal with the actual issue at hand. Similarly, organizations cannot execute all policy suggestions with equal facility. The development of new standard operating procedures takes time. The procedures which would most faithfully execute a new policy are not likely to have been worked out. The clash between the rigidity of standard operating procedures which are absolutely necessary to achieve coordination among and within large organizations, and the flexibility needed to spell out the options and their consequences for a new problem and to execute new policies is inevitable. It cannot be avoided even with the best of intentions of bureaucratic chiefs anxious to faithfully execute the desires of their leaders.

THE COSTS OF COORDINATION

The limitations imposed by the need to simplify and coordinate indicate that the great increase in governmental power accompanying industrialization has not been achieved without some costs in terms of control. Bureaucratic organizations and the material and symbolic resources which they direct have enormously increased the ability of the American President to influence the international environment. He operates, however, within limits set by organizational procedures.

A recognition of the limits imposed by bureaucratic necessities is a useful qualification of the assumption that states always maximize their interest. This does not, however, imply that the analyst should abandon a focus on values or assumptions of rationality. Standard operating procedures are rational given the costs of search procedures and need for coordination. The behaviour of states is still determined by values although foreign policy may reflect satisfactory rather than optimal outcomes.

An emphasis on the procedural limits of large organizations cannot explain nonincremental change. If government policy is an outcome of standard operating procedures, then behaviour at time t is only incrementally different from behaviour at time t-1. The exceptions to this prediction leap out of [such] events . . . [as Nixon's] visit to China and [his] new economic policy. Focusing on the needs dictated by organizational complexity is adequate only during periods when policy is altered very little or not at all. To reduce policy-makers to nothing more than the caretakers and minor adjustors of standard operating procedures rings hollow in an era rife with debates and changes of the most fundamental kind in America's conception of its objectives and capabilities.

Bureaucratic analysts do not, however, place the burden of their argument on standard operating procedures, but on bureaucratic politics. The objectives of officials are dictated by their bureaucratic position. Each bureau has its own interests. The interests which bureaucratic analysts emphasize are not clientalistic ties between government departments and societal groups, or special relations with congressional committees. They are, rather, needs dictated by organizational survival and growth—budget allocations, internal morale, and autonomy. Conflicting objectives advocated by different bureau chiefs are reconciled by a political process. Policy results from compromises and bargaining. It does not necessarily reflect the values of the President, let alone of lesser actors.

The clearest expression of the motivational aspects of the bureaucratic politics approach is the by now well-known aphorism—where you stand depends upon where you sit. Decision-makers, however, often do not stand where they sit. Sometimes they are not sitting anywhere. This is clearly illustrated by the positions taken by members of the ExCom during the Cuban missile crisis, which Allison elucidates at some length. While the military, in Pavlovian fashion, urged the use of arms, the Secretary of Defense took a much more pacific position. The wise old men, such as Acheson, imported for the occasion, had no bureaucratic position to defend. Two of the most important members of the ExCom, Robert Kennedy and Theodore Sorensen, were loyal to the President, not to some bureaucratic barony. Similarly, in discussions of Vietnam in 1966 and 1967, it was the Secretary of Defense who advocated diplomacy and the Secretary of State who defended the prerogatives of the military. During Skybolt, McNamara was attuned to the President's budgetary concerns, not those of the Air Force.

Allison, the most recent expositor of the bureaucratic politics approach, realizes the problems which these facts present. In describing motivation, he backs off from an exclusive focus on bureaucratic position, arguing instead that decision-makers are motivated by national, organizational, group, and personal interests. While maintaining that the "propensities and priorities stemming from position are sufficient to allow analysts to make reliable predictions about a player's stand" (a proposition violated by his own presentation), he also notes that "these propensities are filtered through the baggage that players bring to positions." For both the missile crisis and Vietnam, it was the "baggage" of culture and values, not bureaucratic position, which determined the aims of high officials.

Bureaucratic analysis is also inadequate in its description of how policy is made. Its axiomatic assumption is that politics is a game with the preferences of players given and independent. This is not true. The President chooses most of the important players and sets the rules. He selects the men who head the large bureaucracies. These individuals must share his values. Certainly they identify with his beliefs to a greater extent than would a randomly chosen group of candidates. They also feel some personal fealty to the President who has elevated them from positions of corporate or legal to ones of historic significance. While bureau chiefs are undoubtedly torn by conflicting pressures arising either from their need to protect their own bureaucracies or from personal conviction, they must remain the President's men. At some point disagreement results in dismissal. The values which bureau chiefs assign to policy outcomes are not independent. They are related through a perspective shared with the President.

The President also structures the governmental environment in which he acts through his impact on what Allison calls "action-channels." These are decision-making processes which describe the participation of actors and their influence. The most important "action-channel" in the government is the President's ear. The President has a major role in determining who whispers into it. John Kennedy's reliance on his brother, whose bureaucratic position did not afford him any claim to a decision-making role in the missile crisis, is merely an extreme example. By allocating tasks, selecting the White House bureaucracy, and demonstrating special affections, the President also influences "action-channels" at lower levels of the government.

The President has an important impact on bureaucratic interests. Internal morale is partially determined by Presidential behaviour. The obscurity in which Secretary of State Rogers languished during the China trip affected both State Department morale and recruitment prospects. Through the budget the President has a direct impact on that most vital of bureaucratic interests. While a bureau may use its societal clients and congressional allies to secure desired allocations, it is surely easier with the President's support than without it. The President can delimit or redefine the scope of an organization's activities by transferring tasks or establishing new agencies. Through public statements he can affect attitudes towards members of a particular bureaucracy and their functions.

THE PRESIDENT AS "KING"

The success a bureau enjoys in furthering its interests depends on maintaining the support and affection of the President. The implicit assumption of the bureaucratic politics approach that departmental and Presidential behaviour are independent and comparably important is false. Allison, for instance, vacillates between describing the President as one "chief" among several and as a "king" standing above all other men. He describes in great detail the deliberations of the ExCom implying that Kennedy's decision was in large part determined by its recommendations and yet notes that during the crisis Kennedy vetoed an ExCom decision to bomb a SAM base after an American U-2 was shot down on October 27. In general, bureaucratic analysts ignore the critical effect which the President has in choosing his advisors, establishing their access to decision-making, and influencing bureaucratic interests.

All of this is not to deny that bureaucratic interests may sometimes be decisive in the formulation of foreign policy. Some policy options are never presented to the President. Others he deals with only cursorily, not going beyond options presented by the bureaucracy. This will only be the case if

Presidential interest and attention are absent. The failure of a Chief Executive to specify policy does not mean that the government takes no action. Individual bureaucracies may initiate policies which suit their own needs and objectives. The actions of different organizations may work at cross purposes. The behaviour of the state, that is of some of its official organizations, in the international system appears confused or even contradictory. This is a situation which develops, however, not because of the independent power of government organizations but because of failures by decision-makers to assert control.

The ability of bureaucracies to independently establish policies is a function of Presidential attention. Presidential attention is a function of Presidential values. The Chief Executive involves himself in those areas which he determines to be important. When the President does devote time and attention to an issue, he can compel the bureaucracy to present him with alternatives. He may do this, as Nixon apparently [did] by establishing an organization under his Special Assistant for National Security Affairs, whose only bureaucratic interest [was] maintaining the President's confidence. The President may also rely upon several bureaucracies to secure proposals. The President may even resort to his own knowledge and sense of history to find options which his bureaucracy fails to present. Even when Presidential attention is totally absent, bureaus are sensitive to his values. Policies which violate Presidential objectives may bring Presidential wrath.

While the President is undoubtedly constrained in the implementation of policy by existing bureaucratic procedures, he even has options in this area. As Allison points out, he can choose which agencies will perform what tasks. Programs are fungible and can be broken down into their individual standard operating procedures and recombined. Such exercises take time and effort but the expenditure of such energies by the President is ultimately a reflection of his own values and not those of the bureaucracy. Within the structure which he has partially created himself he can, if he chooses, further manipulate both the options presented to him and the organizational tools for implementing them.

Neither organizational necessity nor bureaucratic interests are the fundamental determinants of policy. The limits imposed by standard operating procedures as well as the direction of policy are a function of the values of decision-makers. The President creates much of the bureaucratic environment which surrounds him through his selection of bureau chiefs, determination of "action-channels," and statutory powers.

THE MISSILE CRISIS

Adherents of the bureaucratic politics framework have not relied exclusively on general argument. They have attempted to substantiate their contentions with detailed investigations of particular historical events. The most painstaking is Graham Allison's analysis of the Cuban missile crisis in his *Essence of Decision*. In a superlative heuristic exercise Allison attempts to show that critical facts and relationships are ignored by conventional analysis that assumes states are unified rational actors. Only by examining the missile crisis in terms of organizational necessity, and bureaucratic interests and politics, can the formulation and implementation of policy be understood.

The missile crisis, as Allison notes, is a situation in which conventional analysis would appear most appropriate. The President devoted large amounts of time to policy formulation and implementation. Regular bureaucratic channels were short-circuited by the creation of an Executive Committee which included representatives of the bipartisan foreign policy establishment, bureau chiefs, and the President's special aides. The President dealt with details which would normally be left to bureaucratic subordinates. If, under such circumstances, the President could not effectively control policy formulation and implementation, then the Rational Actor Model is gravely suspect.

In his analysis of the missile crisis, Allison deals with three issues: the American choice of a blockade, the Soviet decision to place MRBM's and IRBM's on Cuba, and the Soviet decision to withdraw the missiles from Cuba. The American decision is given the most detailed attention. Allison notes three ways in which bureaucratic procedures and interests influenced the formulation of American policy: first, in the elimination of the nonforcible alternatives; second, through the collection of information; third, through the standard operating procedures of the Air Force.

In formulating the U.S. response, the ExCom considered six alternatives. These were:
1. Do nothing
2. Diplomatic pressure
3. A secret approach to Castro
4. Invasion
5. A surgical air strike
6. A naval blockade

The approach to Castro was abandoned because he did not have direct control of the missiles. An invasion was eliminated as a first step because it would not have been precluded by any of the other options. Bureaucratic factors were not involved.

The two non-military options of doing nothing and lodging diplomatic protests were also abandoned from the outset because the President was not interested in them. In terms of both domestic and international politics this was the most important decision of the crisis. It was a decision which only the President had authority to make. Allison's case rests on proving that this decision was foreordained by bureaucratic roles. He lists several reasons for Kennedy's elimination of the nonforcible alternatives. Failure to act decisively would undermine the confidence of members of his Administration, convince the permanent government that his Administration lacked leadership, hurt the Democrats in the forthcoming election, destroy his reputation among members of Congress, create public distrust, encourage American allies and enemies to question American courage, invite a second Bay of Pigs, and feed his own doubts about himself. Allison quotes a statement by Kennedy that he feared impeachment and concludes that the "non-forcible paths—avoiding military measures, resorting instead to diplomacy—could not have been more irrelevant to *his* problems." Thus Allison argues that Kennedy had no choice.

Bureaucratic analysis, what Allison calls in his book the Governmental Politics Model, implies that any man in the same position would have had no choice. The elimination of passivity and diplomacy was ordained by the office and not by the man.

Such a judgment is essential to the Governmental Politics Model, for the resort to the "baggage" of values, culture, and psychology which the President carries with him undermines the explanatory and predictive power of the approach. To adopt, however, the view that the office determined Kennedy's action is both to underrate his power and to relieve him of responsibility. The President defines his own role. A different man could have chosen differently. Kennedy's *Profiles in Courage* had precisely dealt with men who had risked losing their political roles because of their "baggage" of values and culture.

Allison's use of the term "intra-governmental balance of power" to describe John Kennedy's elimination of diplomacy and passivity is misleading. The American government is not a balance of power system; at the very least it is a loose hierarchical one. Kennedy's judgments of the domestic, international, bureaucratic, and personal ramifications of his choice were determined by *who* he was, as well as *what* he was. The central mystery of the crisis remains why Kennedy chose to risk nuclear war over missile placements which he knew did not dramatically alter the strategic balance. The answer to this puzzle can only be found through an examination of values, the central concern of conventional analysis.

The impact of bureaucratic interests and standard operating procedures is reduced then to the choice of the blockade instead of the surgical air strike. Allison places considerable emphasis on intelligence-gathering in the determination of this choice. U-2 flights were the most important source of data about Cuba; their information was supplemented by refugee reports, analyses of shipping and other kinds of intelligence. The timing of the U-2 flights, which Allison argues was determined primarily by bureaucratic struggles, was instrumental in determining Kennedy's decision:

> Had a U-2 flown over the western end of Cuba three weeks earlier, it could have discovered the missiles, giving the administration more time to consider alternatives and to act before the danger of opera-

tional missiles in Cuba became a major factor in the equation. Had the missiles not been discovered until two weeks later, the blockade would have been irrelevant, since the Soviet missile shipments would have been completed . . . An explanation of the politics of the discovery is consequently a considerable piece of the explanation of the U.S. blockade.

The delay, however, from September 15 to October 14 when the missiles were discovered reflected Presidential values more than bureaucratic politics. The October 14 flight took place 10 days after COMOR, the interdepartmental committee which directed the activity of the U-2's, had decided the flights should be made. "This 10 day delay constitutes some form of 'failure,' " Allison contends. It was the result, he argues, of a struggle between the Central Intelligence Agency and the Air Force over who would control the flights. The Air Force maintained that the flights over Cuba were sufficiently dangerous to warrant military supervision; the Central Intelligence Agency, anxious to guard its own prerogatives, maintained that its U-2's were technically superior.

However, the 10-day delay after the decision to make a flight over western Cuba was not entirely attributable to bureaucratic bickering. Allison reports an attempt to make a flight on October 9 which failed because the U-2 flamed out. Further delays resulted from bad weather. Thus the inactivity caused by bureaucratic in-fighting amounted to only five days (October 4 to October 9) once the general decision to make the flight was taken. The other five days' delay caused by engine failure and the weather must be attributed to some higher source than the machinations of the American bureaucracy.

However, there was also a long period of hesitation before October 4. John McCone, Director of the Central Intelligence Agency, had indicated to the President on August 22 that he thought there was a strong possibility that the Soviets were preparing to put offensive missiles on Cuba. He did not have firm evidence, and his contentions were met with skepticism in the Administration.

INCREASED RISKS

On September 10, COMOR had decided to restrict further U-2 flights over western Cuba. This decision was based upon factors which closely fit the Rational Actor Model of foreign policy formulation. COMOR decided to halt the flights because the recent installation of SAM's in western Cuba coupled with the loss of a Nationalist Chinese U-2 increased the probability and costs of a U-2 loss over Cuba. International opinion might force the cancellation of the flights altogether. The absence of information from U-2's would be a national, not simply a bureaucratic, cost. The President had been forcefully attacking the critics of his Cuba policy arguing that patience and restraint were the best course of action. The loss of a U-2 over Cuba would tend to undermine the President's position. Thus, COMOR's decision on September 10 reflected a sensitivity to the needs and policies of the President rather than the parochial concerns of the permanent government.

The decision on October 4 to allow further flights was taken only after consultation with the President. The timing was determined largely by the wishes of the President. His actions were not circumscribed by decisions made at lower levels of the bureaucracy of which he was not aware. The flights were delayed because of conflicting pressures and risks confronting Kennedy. He was forced to weigh the potential benefits of additional knowledge against the possible losses if a U-2 were shot down.

What if the missiles had not been discovered until after October 14? Allison argues that had the missiles been discovered two weeks later the blockade would have been irrelevant since the missile shipments would have been completed. This is true but only to a limited extent. The blockade was irrelevant even when it was put in place for there were missiles already on the island. As Allison points out in his Rational Actor cut at explaining the crisis, the blockade was both an act preventing the shipment of additional missiles and a signal of American firmness. The missiles already on Cuba were removed because of what the blockade meant and not because of what it did.

An inescapable dilemma confronted the United States. It could not retaliate until the missiles were on the island. Military threats or action required definitive proof. The United States could only justify actions with photographic evidence. It could only take photos after the missiles were on Cuba. The blockade could only be a demonstration of American firmness. Even if the missiles had not been discovered until they were operational, the United States might still have begun its response with a blockade.

Aside from the timing of the discovery of the missiles, Allison argues that the standard operating procedures of the Air Force affected the decision to blockade rather than to launch a surgical air strike. When the missiles were first discovered, the Air Force had no specific contingency plans for dealing with such a situation. They did, however, have a plan for a large-scale air strike carried out in conjunction with an invasion of Cuba. The plan called for the air bombardment of many targets. This led to some confusion during the first week of the ExCom's considerations because the Air Force was talking in terms of an air strike of some 500 sorties while there were only some 40 known missile sites on Cuba. Before this confusion was clarified, a strong coalition of advisors was backing the blockade.

As a further example of the impact of standard operating procedures, Allison notes that the Air Force had classified the missiles as mobile. Because this classification assumed that the missiles might be moved immediately before an air strike, the commander of the Air Force would not guarantee that a surgical air strike would be completely effective. By the end of the first week of the ExCom's deliberations when Kennedy made his decision for a blockade, the surgical air strike was presented as a "null option." The examination of the strike was not reopened until the following week when civilian experts found that the missiles were not in fact mobile.

This incident suggests one caveat to Allison's assertion that the missile crisis is a case which discriminates against bureaucratic analysis. In crises when time is short the President may have to accept bureaucratic options which could be amended under more leisurely conditions.

NOT ANOTHER PEARL HARBOR

The impact of the Air Force's standard operating procedures on Kennedy's decision must, however, to some extent remain obscure. It is not likely that either McNamara who initially called for a diplomatic response, or Robert Kennedy who was partially concerned with the ethical implications of a surprise air strike, would have changed their recommendations even if the Air Force had estimated its capacities more optimistically. There were other reasons for choosing the blockade aside from the apparent infeasibility of the air strike. John Kennedy was not anxious to have the Pearl Harbor analogy applied to the United States. At one of the early meetings of the ExCom, his brother had passed a note saying, "I now know how Tojo felt when he was planning Pearl Harbor." The air strike could still be considered even if the blockade failed. A chief executive anxious to keep his options open would find a blockade a more prudent initial course of action.

Even if the Air Force had stated that a surgical air strike was feasible, this might have been discounted by the President. Kennedy had already experienced unrealistic military estimates. The Bay of Pigs was the most notable example. The United States did not use low flying photographic reconnaissance until after the President had made his public announcement of the blockade. Prior to the President's speech on October 22, 20 high altitude U-2 flights were made. After the speech there were 85 low level missions, indicating that the intelligence community was not entirely confident that U-2 flights alone would reveal all of the missile sites. The Soviets might have been camouflaging some missiles on Cuba. Thus, even if the immobility of the missiles had been correctly estimated, it would have been rash to assume that an air strike would have extirpated all of the missiles. There were several reasons, aside from the Air Force's estimate, for rejecting the surgical strike.

Thus, in terms of policy formulation, it is not clear that the examples offered by Allison concerning the timing of discovery of the missiles and the standard operating procedures of the Air Force had a decisive impact on the choice of a blockade over a surgical air strike. The ultimate decisions did rest with the President. The elimination of the nonforcible options was a reflection of Kennedy's values. An explanation of the Cuban missile crisis which fails to explain policy in terms of the values of the chief decision-maker must inevitably lose sight of the forest for the trees.

The most chilling passages in *Essence of Decision* are concerned not with the formulation of policy but with its implementation. In carrying out the blockade the limitations on the President's ability to control events become painfully clear. Kennedy did keep extraordinarily close tabs on the workings of the blockade. The first Russian ship to reach the blockade was allowed to pass through without being intercepted on direct orders from the President. Kennedy felt it would be wise to allow Khrushchev more time. The President overrode the ExCom's decision to fire on a Cuban SAM base after a U-2 was shot down on October 27. A spy ship similar to the Pueblo was patrolling perilously close to Cuba and was ordered to move further out to sea.

Despite concerted Presidential attention coupled with an awareness of the necessity of watching minute details which would normally be left to lower levels of the bureaucracy, the President still had exceptional difficulty in controlling events. Kennedy personally ordered the Navy to pull in the blockade from 800 miles to 500 miles to give Khrushchev additional time in which to make his decision. Allison suggests that the ships were not drawn in. The Navy being both anxious to guard its prerogatives and confronted with the difficulty of moving large numbers of ships over millions of square miles of ocean failed to promptly execute a Presidential directive.

There were several random events which might have changed the outcome of the crisis. The Navy used the blockade to test its antisubmarine operations. It was forcing Soviet submarines to surface at a time when the President and his advisors were unaware that contact with Russian ships had been made. A U-2 accidentally strayed over Siberia on October 22. Any one of these events, and perhaps others still unknown, could have triggered escalatory actions by the Russians.

Taken together, they strongly indicate how much caution is necessary when a random event may have costly consequences. A nation like a drunk staggering on a cliff should stay far from the edge. The only conclusion which can be drawn from the inability of the Chief Executive to fully control the implementation of a policy in which he was intensely interested and to which he devoted virtually all of his time for an extended period is that the risks were even greater than the President knew. Allison is more convincing on the problems concerned with policy implementation than on questions relating to policy formulation. Neither bureaucratic interests nor organizational procedures explain the positions taken by members of the ExCom, the elimination of passivity and diplomacy, or the choice of a blockade instead of an air strike.

CONCLUSION

A glimpse at almost any one of the major problems confronting American society indicates that a reformulation and clarification of objectives, not better control and direction of the bureaucracy, is critical. Conceptions of man and society long accepted are being undermined. The environmental-ists present a fundamental challenge to the assumption that man can con-trol and stand above nature, an assumption rooted both in the successes of technology and industrialization and Judeo-Christian assertions of man's exceptionalism. The nation's failure to formulate a consistent crime policy reflects in part an inability to decide whether criminals are freely willing rational men subject to determinations of guilt or innocence or the victims of socio-economic conditions, or psychological circumstances, over which they have no control. The economy manages to defy accepted economic precepts by sustaining relatively high inflation and unemployment at the same time. Public officials and economists question the wisdom of eco-nomic growth. Conflicts exist over what the objectives of the nation should be and what its capacities are. On a whole range of social issues the society is torn between attributing problems to individual inadequacies and social injustice.

None of these issues can be decided just by improving managerial techniques. Before the niceties of bureaucratic implementation are investi-gated, it is necessary to know what objectives are being sought. Objectives are ultimately a reflection of values, of beliefs concerning what man and society ought to be. The failure of the American government to take deci-sive action in a number of critical areas reflects not so much the inertia of a large bureaucratic machine as a confusion over values which afflicts the society in general and its leaders in particular. It is, in such circumstances, too comforting to attribute failure to organizational inertia, although noth-ing could be more convenient for political leaders who having either not formulated any policy or advocated bad policies can blame their failures on the governmental structure. Both psychologically and politically, leaders may find it advantageous to have others think of them as ineffectual rather than evil. But the facts are otherwise—particularly in foreign policy. There the choices—and the responsibility—rest squarely with the President.

NOTE

1. Quoted in Daniel Ellsberg, "The Quagmire Myth and the Stalemate Machine," *Public Policy*, Spring 1971, p. 218. [For an exemplary treatment of this thesis, see James C. Thomson's essay in this volume—*eds.*]

Part Six

INDIVIDUALS AS SOURCES OF AMERICAN FOREIGN POLICY

When asked "What factors most influence the direction of American foreign policy?" the answer that comes immediately to mind is "the people who are responsible for its formulation." The president figures prominently in such thinking, followed by those immediately surrounding the commander in chief.

The popularity of explanations that emphasize the impact political leaders have on foreign policy is easy to understand. Most people operate instinctively from a "great man" image of political leaders—one which equates policy actions with the preferences of the most highly placed officials—because it is both tempting and comforting to think in such terms. Most want to believe that elected and appointed officials are "leaders," just as they are inclined to ascribe to them power over the nation's destiny. In fact, the conviction that the individual who holds office makes a difference is one of the major premises underlying the electoral process in a democratic society, one which motivates citizens to express their political preferences through the ballot box.

The view that individuals matter is compelling for a variety of other reasons. In the realm of foreign policy, where decisions are often made by a remarkably small number of individuals, who the decision makers are is, axiomatically, crucial. The perspective is reinforced by the tendency to attach to policies the names of presidents (for example, the *Truman* Doctrine, the *Kennedy* Round, *Reagan*omics), a propensity that suggests that policies are synonymous with the people who first promulgated them and that national policies are determined exclusively by those presumed to be most responsible for their formulation. The widespread belief that in a democratic society leaders will make public policy in accordance with public preferences also strengthens the image of the importance of leaders, for they alone interpret what public preferences are. And the view that different leaders will inaugurate different policies is supported by the efforts of new administrations to distinguish themselves from their predecessors and to highlight policy departures in order to convey the impression that their policies are distinctive. From any of these perspectives, it would seem that all history is biography, and that the qualities of leaders play a fundamental role in determining America's posture toward the world beyond its borders.

Clearly, the characteristics unique to the individuals who make American foreign policy exert a potentially powerful influence on the nation's external behavior, and no account of the sources of American foreign policy would be complete without a discussion of them. But despite their importance, apparently confirmed in theory as well as fact, it would be misleading and simplistic to ascribe too much influence to the individuals responsible for the conduct of American foreign policy or to assume that influence is the same for all leaders in all circumstances. The question to be asked is not "Do individuals make a difference?" (for they obviously do in a variety of ways, ranging from the style and tone they set for the conduct of diplomacy to the important choices they often must make for the nation, including the decision of whether American soldiers must engage in battle and perhaps die for their country). Rather, the question to ask is "Under what circumstances do the idiosyncratic qualities of leaders exert their greatest impact?" and, secondarily, "What kinds of policy outcomes are likely to result from different *types* of officials?" Addressing these questions forces an examination of the mechanisms through which individual characteristics may find expression in foreign policy outcomes in ways that otherwise might not be anticipated, a consideration that in turn requires an appreciation of the more subtle manner in which idiosyncratic characteristics leave their imprint on foreign policy performance.

PERSPECTIVES ON INDIVIDUALS AS SOURCES OF AMERICAN FOREIGN POLICY: AN OVERVIEW

Margaret G. Hermann's essay, "Leaders, Leadership, and American Foreign Policy," introduces the complex analytical problems that necessarily surround the individual perspective on foreign policy making while simultaneously clarifying several key concepts that relate to the impact of individuals on American foreign policy. In particular, she argues that the multiple factors involved in assessing leaders' impact on foreign policy can usefully be analyzed in terms of leaders' characteristics (world view, political style, interest and training in foreign affairs, and political socialization), their constituencies (the American people, Congress, executive branch departments and agencies, their own staff aides and political appointees, and foreign leaders), and the functions they perform in relation to their constituencies (motivators, policy advocates, consensus builders, recruiters, and managers). These characteristics, Hermann argues, are the ones that ultimately determine how American leaders will respond to the contexts and situations they face as leaders. No one can read this broad-ranging overview without gaining keener awareness of the manner in which the human dimension of American diplomacy makes itself felt and the profound extent with which the response of a policy maker to a given situation may be affected by his or her own uniquely individual characteristics. The illustrative material provided in the essay also contributes to an understanding of how individuals' interpretations of the roles they occupy can influence their subsequent behavior (and, correspondingly, the degree to which individual behaviors can modify role factors that otherwise act as a potent source of American foreign policy).

The remaining selections in this part develop some of the key variables discussed in Hermann's essay on leaders and leadership. John G. Stoessinger's article, "Crusaders and Pragmatists: Two Types of Foreign Policy-Makers," elaborates on the function that leaders' world views play in shaping their responses to policy problems. The thesis advanced is that two types of leaders have occupied roles in the foreign affairs establishment of the United States: those with strongly held world views whose missionary zeal for abstract principles led them to crusade for the realization of their ideals (usually, Stoessinger contends, with catastrophic results), and those with less well-entrenched world views who by temperament were willing to experiment pragmatically with alternative foreign policies in order to accommodate the nation to emergent international exigencies (usually with the result that the nation was in a better position to deal with new challenges). Although Stoessinger's book-length treatment of his thesis covers the gamut of major foreign policy makers in the twentieth century, the abridged portion reprinted here is restricted to two examples: Lyndon B. Johnson, a crusader, and Henry A. Kissinger, a pragmatist. The account provides a lively illustration of the way in which the personality of foreign policy makers may leave an indelible stamp, for better or for worse, upon the kinds of foreign policies that are forged for the nation.

Alexander L. George discusses the interaction between individuals and institutions in his essay, "Presidential Management Styles and Models." Noting that "each president is likely to define his role in foreign-policy making somewhat differently and to approach it with a different decision making and management style," George describes three different approaches presidents have evolved for managing the tasks inherent in the positions they occupy: "formalistic," "competitive," and "collegial." What approach a president will choose and how it will be permitted to operate in practice will itself be shaped by the president's personality, that is, by his cognitive style (analogous to world view), by his sense of efficacy and competence, and by his general orientation to political conflict. By using these concepts, George is able to build an insightful portrait of the whys and hows of presidential approaches to control and coordination of policy analysis and implementation from Roosevelt to Reagan.

The final article in this part is an assessment by James David Barber of Ronald Reagan's character. In addition to illustrating Barber's well-known typology of presidential character, the essay provides insight into the important role that early experiences and political socialization play in shaping a leader's approach to subsequent contexts and situations. Although the article was first published on Ronald Reagan's inauguration day (January 20, 1981), it retains its pertinence even today by demonstrating the potential contribution that this kind of inquiry can make to an understanding of the personal factors that shape policy-making performance.

Collectively, these selections invite a critical probe of the often untested assumption that the characteristics of individual decision makers serve as a source of American foreign policy. Should the view that American foreign policy is the exclusive product of the leaders who formulate it, and that changes in foreign policy are caused by the innate differences among principal policy makers, be accepted unquestioningly? Indeed, do contrasts among decision makers make a difference in the content of policy as well as its style? Is the type of person selected to policy-making roles a fundamental factor determining the behavior of the country abroad? And do the particular personal qualities of the people who have held positions of power make a difference in the way the nation charts its course in world affairs? Finally, if we conclude that individuals do, indeed, matter, should other sources be incorporated into the equation to make the explanation of continuity and change in American foreign policy more complete?

26

LEADERS, LEADERSHIP, AND AMERICAN FOREIGN POLICY

MARGARET G. HERMANN

When we think about the leaders who have helped shape American foreign policy in the twentieth century, names like Woodrow Wilson, Harry Truman, Franklin Roosevelt, Henry Kissinger, John Foster Dulles, J. William Fulbright, Richard Helms, Clark Clifford, Douglas MacArthur, Robert McNamara, and George Marshall come to mind. Among these people are presidents, secretaries of state and defense, directors of the CIA, presidential advisers, senators, and generals. All were part of the foreign policy machinery of the United States; all led groups and organizations that have an input into American foreign policy decisions. Why do we remember these leaders? What is it about the quality of their leadership and their personalities that links their names to American foreign policy? In this chapter we will explore the aspects of leadership that are likely to influence the way foreign policy is made and the resulting policy itself. We will discover what it is about our political leaders we need to learn to determine if and how they will affect American foreign policy.

THE LEADERSHIP DILEMMA

Let us consider three images of leadership. The first might be called the "pied piper of Hamelin" image. Like the pied piper who led the mice out of Hamelin, this type of leader sets the goals and directions for his followers and with promises charms them into following him. The leader is in charge of what happens and how it happens.

Margaret G. Hermann is a Senior Research Associate at the Mershon Center, Ohio State University. She was a NIMH Postdoctoral Fellow at the Educational Testing Service and Lecturer at Princeton University before coming to Ohio State. Her major research interests include political leadership, political personality, and comparative foreign policy. Professor Hermann is the author or editor of a number of books and journal articles among which are A *Psychological Examination of Political Leaders* (Free Press, 1977) and *Describing Foreign Policy Behavior* (Sage, 1982). She has been Vice-President of the International Studies Association and has just completed a term as editor of *Political Psychology*, the journal of the International Society of Political Psychology.

The second image is that of the leader as salesman. Leadership involves being sensitive to what people want and offering to help them get it. Responsiveness to people's needs and desires is important as is being able to persuade people that you can help them. As Harry Truman (see Neustadt, 1960: 10) noted: "The principal power that the President has is to bring people in and try to persuade them to do what they ought to do without persuasion."

The third image is that of leader as puppet. In this image of leadership, the leader is given direction and strength by his followers who pull the strings and make him move. The leader is the agent of the group, reflecting the goals of the group and working in its behalf.

The dilemma of American leadership today is that we expect our political leaders to exhibit all three of these images. We want strong leaders who have vision but who at the same time are responsive to our wishes and able to persuade us of their convictions. As Cronin (1980: 3–22) has observed about the presidency, we want a decent and just leader who is also decisive and guileful, a leader with programmatic ideas who is also pragmatic, an innovative and inventive leader who is also responsive to the majority's wishes, an open and sharing leader who is also courageous and independent as well as a symbolic, ceremonial leader who is also a tough manager. There is little recognition of the contradictions inherent in our expectations and images. In effect, we seek supermen.

How can we make our expectations more realistic? One way is to consider the many different types of political leadership there are. Leadership involves more than one kind of behavior; it is an umbrella concept that has within it a number of different variables. Figure 1 suggests the ingredients in leadership. To understand leadership we need to know something about: (1) the leader's personality, background, and the recruitment process by which he became a leader; (2) what groups and individuals the leader is accountable to (that is, who the leader leads) and what they are like; (3) the nature of the relationship between the leader and those he leads; (4) the context or setting in which the leadership is taking place; and (5) what happens when the leader and those led interact in a specific situation. What kind of leadership we have depends on the nature and combination of these five ingredients. As in a recipe for food, these basic ingredients can be combined in different ways to produce a variety of results.

In examining the relationship between leadership and the formulation of American foreign policy, an important initial consideration is who are the leaders we should be studying. The positions that appear to afford their occupants an opportunity to influence American foreign policy and that provide for the exercise of control over others are president, secretary of state, secretary of defense, director of the Central Intelligence Agency, presidential adviser for national security affairs (at least since the Kennedy administration), chairman of the joint chiefs of staff, and, in some instances, chairman of a foreign policy-related congressional committee. As this list

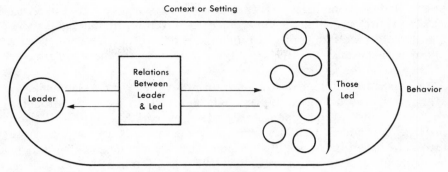

Context or Setting

Leader

Relations
Between
Leader
& Led

Those
Led

Behavior

FIGURE 1 The ingredients of leadership

suggests, the concept of "leader" is relative, since the president also has authority over the other leaders listed above, with the exception of the chairmen of congressional committees. With the exception of the latter, these leaders are appointed by the president and are accountable to him. For purposes of the present discussion, however, we will use as examples individuals who have held any of the seven roles listed above to illustrate our points.

Having established which leaders can affect American foreign policy, let us examine the various ingredients of leadership in order to see why certain people have more of an impact on foreign policy behavior than others and the nature of that leadership.

LEADER CHARACTERISTICS

What is the leader like? Specifically, what characteristics may influence leaders' proposals in the foreign policy arena? A search of writings by students of American foreign policy suggests five kinds of characteristics are important to learn about leaders. We want to know (1) what their world view is, (2) what their political style is like, (3) whether they are interested in and have any training in foreign affairs, (4) what the foreign policy climate was like when the leader was starting out his political career, and (5) how the leader was socialized into his present position. World view and political style tell us something about the leader's personality; the other characteristics give information about the leader's previous experiences and background.

View of the World
The most direct linkage between what a leader is like and American foreign policy behavior is through the leader's view of the world. View of the world shapes how the leader interprets the international environment and America's place in that environment. It helps the leader chart or map the foreign policy terrain in which the United States is operating as he perceives that terrain to be. A world view implies certain goals and strategies. For example, Reagan's push to increase the defense budget grew out of his

belief that the United States is currently losing the arms race to the Soviet Union. Carter's belief in the importance of confronting human rights issues led him to urge reductions in foreign aid to governments with flagrant human rights violations. In each of these cases a view of the world affected foreign policy behavior.

Recently a number of scholars have attempted to assess systematically the world views of American presidents and secretaries of state through a concept known as the "operational code" (see, e.g., Holsti, 1977; Walker, 1977; Stuart and Starr, 1982). The operational code is used to assess the rules and beliefs that guide the foreign-policy positions taken by a president or secretary of state (see George, 1969, 1979). By examining how presidents and secretaries of state have described such things as how aggressive they perceive the Soviet government to be, their own ability to shape international events, and their willingness to take risks in foreign policy, scholars have defined the operational codes (or views of the world) under which such leaders appeared to be operating. Elsewhere the author (Hermann, 1977, 1980a, 1980b) has discussed several kinds of world views that affect how cooperative or competitive heads of government will be in their foreign policy. These particular world views focus on how independent the leader wants his government to be in foreign policy, how influential the leader wants his government to be in the international arena, and how responsive the leader will let his government be to other governments.

We need to consider more than the substance of a leader's view of the world. Another important piece of information concerns how *important* the world view is to the leader. Is the leader so persuaded of the particular world view he espouses that it is a dominant force in his life, acting as a lens through which all external events are interpreted, or is the leader more responsive to the environment, letting events shape and change his beliefs? A leader's world view can have a more direct influence on American foreign policy the more resistant it is to outside influences. Like the crusader of old, the leader with a strong world view seeks to convince others of his position and is likely to see most international activity as relevant to his cause. Leaders whose world views are less firmly entrenched are more pragmatic. The nature of the situation will generally determine how firmly—and whether—such leaders press their case. An astute observer of American foreign policy (Stoessinger, 1979) has argued that this is a critical dimension in assessing the effectiveness of those responsible for making American foreign policy in the twentieth century and that recent American presidents and secretaries of state can be divided into "crusaders" and "pragmatists."

John Foster Dulles, Eisenhower's secretary of state, is an example of a leader who had a strongly held world view, particularly his beliefs about the nature and motivation of the Soviet leadership. Dulles believed that Communism was inherently bad and, thus, the Soviet government as an instrument of international Communism was inherently bad and out to further its own interests, which were in direct contradiction to those of the United States. The Soviet leadership could do nothing right in Dulles' eyes. Even such relatively tension-reducing steps on the Soviet government's part as the reopening of an East-West dialogue with the United States in Geneva in 1955 and the agreement with the United States on the Austrian treaty of statehood were interpreted by Dulles as events in which the Soviets had ulterior motives. Dulles' view led him to persist in urging on the American government a policy of brinkmanship with the Soviet Union backed by the threat of massive retaliation—according to Dulles, the United States should "roll-back" the Iron Curtain and rid the world of Communism.

Political Style

A leader's political style can also influence a government's foreign policy. The influence, however, is more indirect than that of world view. Political style has an effect by shaping how the government responds to foreign policy problems. Political style here refers to the techniques the leader prefers to use in dealing with other governments, the particular activities that the leader favors when it comes to interacting with other governments. For example, like Kissinger, does the leader emphasize personal diplomacy and face-to-face meetings with world leaders? Or, like Dulles, is the emphasis on political rhetoric and propaganda? Is there a flair for the dramatic like Nixon showed when he opened relations with China? Is there a willingness to work with leaders of other governments in solving problems or is the tendency to "go it alone"? Is there an interest, like Johnson had, in wanting to see information first hand—to talk, for example, to the ship captains in the Gulf of Tonkin off Vietnam—or is the leader content, as Nixon was, to examine summaries of events based on staff interpretations? Is secrecy essential? Each of these questions focuses on an element of political style.

The style characteristics of a leader can have the effect of limiting the choices of behavior available to those under the leader. Political style limits choice in at least two ways. First, there is a tendency on the part of subordinates, particularly at the highest levels of government, to cater to the stylistic preferences of the leader in order to keep open access to him. Thus, for example, it is said (see Safire, 1982) Reagan is perceived to prefer information presented in a visual format, and the bureaucracy is geared to producing material in a movie or television context. Here emphasis is given to one type of material, with its advantages and disadvantages, to the exclusion of other media and sources of information.

The second way in which political style can limit choice results from what Bennis (1973) calls the *doppelgänger* effect. Political leaders tend to choose staff and political appointees that are their doubles or *doppelgängers*; that is, the leader surrounds himself with people who have similar stylistic preferences or styles that are complementary. Thus, the leader's preferences may begin to permeate the bureaucracy.

Interest and Training in Foreign Affairs

In considerations of foreign policy, ascertaining a leader's interest and training in foreign affairs is critical to knowing how involved he will become in foreign policy issues and the extent of the repertoire of feasible behaviors he will have for dealing with foreign policy problems. Presidents, in particular, have differed in their interest in foreign policy. Franklin Roosevelt and John Kennedy were so interested in foreign affairs that they became, in effect, their own secretaries of state. Such a president "closely involves himself in major problems, sets high policy standards, intrudes upon routine, and engages heavily in diplomatic negotiations" (Koenig, 1981: 222). Not much will happen in the foreign policy arena that a president with a high interest in foreign affairs will not try to control. At the other extreme are presidents whose interest in foreign policy issues is not all consuming and who are willing to delegate much of the responsibility to others. Eisenhower and Ford are examples of presidents who appear to have granted much of the authority for foreign policymaking to their secretaries of state, Dulles and Kissinger, respectively. Former Senator Fulbright is quoted as saying: "Secretary Dulles seemed at times to be exercising those 'delicate, plenary, and exclusive powers' which are supposed to be vested in the President" (Koenig, 1981: 223). Although both Eisenhower and his aides indicated that major decisions were not made without consultation and prior approval, the question arises about where policy originated. With the highly interested president, policies and ideas are likely to be generated by his staff, whereas with the less intensely interested president, policies and ideas probably originate outside the White House.

Because intense interest in foreign affairs on the part of the president generally leads to concentration on foreign policy problems, it can have several pitfalls. The first is that foreign problems and policies can become internalized—the leader identifies with the policy and problem to such an extent that they are no longer just issues of American foreign policy but personal concerns. The leader's sense of self can become tied to the success or failure of a broad range of policies. The leader may try to repeat foreign policy successes but can experience severe stress when policies are failing (Hermann, 1979). A second pitfall centers around the president or leader becoming so involved in what is happening that he loses perspective. Information is sought from sources "on the scene" without being filtered or set into context through bureaucratic exchange. Thus, the president may talk with persons on the scene, as Lyndon Johnson did with the harried U.S. ambassador to the Dominican Republic whose embassy was under siege, and may act on this information. Often the leader's reaction and subsequent actions may be more extreme than the situation warrants.

Training in foreign affairs can temper interest in foreign affairs. Training here refers to the amount of time an individual has been responsible for dealing with foreign policy issues and problems before assuming a leadership position. In the latter part of the twentieth century, most American presidents have had little foreign policy experience at the time they assumed office. To compensate for this lack of experience these presidents have tended to choose secretaries of state or national security affairs advisers with previous experience and expertise. Experience provides the leader with an idea of what will and will not work and what protocol and precedent dictate. With little experience or training in foreign affairs, the leader may be unduly influenced by experts. Moreover, his view of the world and political style are more likely to affect what he proposes since he has little other background on which to rely (see Hermann, 1980a).

Examinations of the Kennedy and Carter presidencies offer examples of the effects of lack of experience. With Kennedy we note the difference between his handling of the Bay of Pigs situation in the early months of his administration and the Cuban missile crisis a year later. Accounts of the Bay of Pigs decision (George, 1980; Janis, 1972; Schlesinger, 1965; Sorensen, 1965) suggest that Kennedy was somewhat overwhelmed by the expert opinion around him, some of the important voices such as CIA Director Allen Dulles being carryovers from the Eisenhower administration. George (1980: 211) has commented:

> The lessons [Kennedy] and his close associates had drawn from his inept management of the policymaking group in the Bay of Pigs case were quickly put to use in improvising a quite different approach to crisis decisionmaking when they were suddenly confronted in October 1962 by Khrushchev's deployment of missiles into Cuba.

Kennedy understood better in the fall of 1962 than in the spring of 1961 the realities of the Cuban situation and the nature of the personnel in his own administration. In a similar vein, Koenig (1981: 242) has observed about Carter:

> Early in his administration, taking a benign view of the world, Carter called for the withdrawal of American troops from South Korea. After prickly maneuver, the Chiefs [Joint Chiefs of Staff] induced the President to qualify his decision with three conditions: to effect the withdrawal in a manner not destabilizing to the delicate situation in Korea; to pledge to uphold American defense obligations to South Korea; and to affirm American intent to remain a Pacific power. As his administration wore on and his view of Asian realities hardened, Carter shelved his plan to reduce American forces.

Table 1 suggests how interest and training in foreign affairs interrelate in determining the leader's involvement and focus on foreign policy issues. When interest is low the leader tends to delegate. The choice of who is given authority will depend on the extent of the leader's experience—the leader with more experience will seek out persons with foreign policy outlooks and experiences similar to his own. The leader with less experience will tend to

TABLE 1
EFFECTS OF INTEREST AND TRAINING IN FOREIGN AFFAIRS

| | | Extent of Interest in Foreign Affairs | |
		LOW	HIGH
	Low	Will rely on experts for advice; will probably delegate foreign policymaking to others.	Will want to be involved in foreign policymaking; leader's view of world and political style will dominate policy proposals.
Extent of Training in Foreign Affairs	High	Will rely on historical precedents in making foreign policy; will choose foreign policy advisers to delegate responsibilities to whose interests and experiences match leader's.	Will want to be involved in all facets of foreign policymaking; will want to personally interact with other world leaders; will be interested in the particulars of foreign policy situations and problems.

choose those with a reputation in the foreign policy arena but with little control for similarity of outlook. When the leader's interest is high, he insists on being part of the foreign policymaking process. With training the leader has a better sense of where to intervene to have an impact. Also with training the leader tends to focus on what is happening in the particular situation. The leader with less experience will base his decision more on his own predilections than on nuances in the situation.

Effects of Political Socialization

American leaders do not come "full blown from the head of Zeus." In many ways they are the product of their experiences and the times in which they live. Stewart (1977) has argued that even birth order helps mold our leaders' political skills. According to Stewart's data, first-born sons and only children who have early been given authority over others and have generally dealt with adults or "higher authorities" have been elected president during periods in American history of international and domestic crisis. Franklin Roosevelt, who was an only child, is an example. It is younger sons who have had to learn from early childhood the political tools of persuasion, coalition building, and consensus formation in order to get their way who have become president during times of relative peace and consolidation. Andrew Jackson, a third-born son, who was elected president at the beginning of a period of domestic consolidation, is an example of a younger son president.

What kinds of backgrounds have our leaders had that might affect their foreign policy positions? One piece of background information that has proven relevant in studying foreign policymakers in other countries is travel and study abroad (see, for example, Welsh, 1977). Has the leader had many encounters with other cultures, enough to build an understanding of what these other peoples are like? Were these experiences primarily in one part of the world or were they more general? We note that General Douglas MacArthur, who was central in shaping American policy during the reconstruction of Japan, took an extensive tour of the Far East during his mid-twenties. MacArthur (1964: 32) has noted

> [This trip] was without a doubt the most important factor of preparation in my entire life. . . . It was crystal clear to me that the future and, indeed, the very existence of America, were irrevocably entwined with Asia and its island outposts. It was to be sixteen years before I returned to the Far East, but always was its mystic hold upon me.

Kennedy, who had a certain charisma with Europeans as well as Americans, spent a summer at the London School of Economics during his college years as well as a semester traveling extensively in Europe.

Barber (1972) has observed that another important piece of background information is learning about the first political position a leader has held. The experiences enabling the leader to gain and hold this first position often shape political style and world view. A leader will tend on future occasions to fall back on the rhetoric and practices which helped him succeed the first time. Moreover, early experiences, because they are first, are often vivid and given extra significance in memory. Reagan's views on Communism appear to have been shaped by his first political position, president of the Screen Actors Guild. As he noted in an interview with Barrett (1980: 19–20):

> [I was] unaware that certain labor unions had been infiltrated by the American Communist Party. I was unbelieving until they made their big effort in a jurisdictional strike to gain control of the picture business. Then I discovered firsthand the cynicism, the brutality, the complete lack of morality of their positions and the cold-bloodedness of their attempt, at any cost, to gain control of that industry. . . . [Communists] have one course and one course only. They are dedicated to the belief that they are going to take over the world.

Johnson (1977) has examined the early and later beliefs of Senator Frank Church about international relations and American foreign policy. He found that the former chairman of the Senate foreign relations' committee held ten of the thirteen basic beliefs in 1972 that he had held in 1956, when he was first elected a senator in a surprising defeat of an incumbent.

In addition to our own experiences, we are also products of our times.

What was going on in the United States and the world when the leader was growing up, seeking his first job, and assuming responsibility? What were the events and ideas shaping young people during the time the leader was moving from adolescence through early adulthood? Surveying America's future leaders, Broder (1981: 11) has commented:

> America is changing hands. In the 1980s the custody of the nation's leadership will be transferred from the World War II veterans, who have held sway for a generation, to a new set of men and women. These newcomers . . . are the products of a set of experiences different from those which shaped the dominant American personalities of the past quarter-century. They do not carry the memories or the scars of the Great Depression. They were not part of the victory over totalitarianism in Italy, Germany, and Japan. The next ones who will take power . . . were shaped in a very different time. Theirs has been a time of affluence and inflation, of extraordinary education advance, and of wrenching social change and domestic discord. . . . [T]heir wars were fought in Korea and Vietnam, and if fewer of them returned as casualties, none returned as victors.

Broder's observations suggest the common generational experiences that can have an effect on those who become leaders. If not imbued themselves with the ideas that have shaped their generation, leaders will have to deal with these ideas to stay in power.

LEADERS' CONSTITUENCIES

To understand the relationship between leadership and American foreign policy, we also need to know something about the expectations of the leader's various constituencies. What do they want the leader to do or help them to do? And we need to determine how the leader is viewed by these constituencies. What images do the constituencies hold of the leader? Let us, for example, consider the constituencies that a president must deal with. To be effective in shaping foreign policy, presidents must work with the people who elected them, the Congress, the agencies and departments of the executive branch of government, their own staffs and cabinets, and foreign leaders. What kinds of expectations and images do these various groups have of the president?

If foreign policy becomes an important campaign issue for the presidency, there is an expectation on the part of the public that something will happen. In both the elections of Eisenhower in 1952 and Nixon in 1968, getting out of an unpopular war was an important campaign issue, and the public wanted action. Special interest groups within the public can also have foreign policy expectations that presidents must consider in dealing with specific foreign policy problems. We note the so-called Jewish lobby that becomes quite active when questions of Israel are under consideration.

At times there can be a ground swell of public opinion for or against a particular policy that demands attention—the increased public dissatisfaction
with the Vietnam War in the late 60s and the concern for a freeze on the
level of nuclear arms in the 80s are examples. Most of the time, though, the
American public is something like the crowds at the gladiator games in
ancient Rome who indicated thumbs up when they approved of what was
going on and thumbs down when they disapproved or wanted more action.
Like these ancient Romans and their emotional response to the games, the
American public's response to foreign policy issues is generally more emotional than rational, felt but not always carefully thought through. And the
response is highly time specific, changing as the situation changes. By such
responses the public appears to indicate what the outer boundaries are on
what a president can do in the foreign policy arena at a particular point in
time. The fickleness of the public, however, enables the president to consider molding public opinion. Sorensen (1963), a Kennedy speechwriter, has
observed that the president can use public opinion as a sword as well as a
compass.

Turning to Congress as a constituent, we note that in most instances
Congress enacts what the president proposes with regard to foreign policy.
But since Watergate and the Vietnam War, this process has not been as
automatic as it once was. In fact, since the mid-1970s an adversarial relationship has developed between Congress and the president. Congressmen
are asking to be told the facts and convinced of why a particular foreign
policy activity is appropriate. Congressmen are interested in exercising
more influence over foreign policy than they perceive they have had in the
past. They are interested, at the least, as former Senator Fulbright (1979) has
observed, in advising on broad policy directions.

The image that congressmen have of the president is determined by
several factors: the amount of attention the president pays to winning their
support, the president's popularity with the people, and the president's popularity with foreign leaders. Koenig (1981) suggests that congressmen are
more responsive to a president who becomes involved in gaining their support for policies, one who courts their favor. On foreign policy issues this
courting often must cut across party lines. Carter's problems with Congress
were often attributed to his aloofness in dealing with the Senate and the
House (Cronin, 1980). Congress also responds like a barometer to the president's popularity at home and abroad. Congressmen become more assertive
and less supportive of the president's policies when his popularity is low,
particularly if it is an election year.

When we examine the expectations and images of the president that
are held in departments and agencies of the executive branch, we assume
that there will be a similarity between the president's view of foreign policy
and those held within the bureaucracy. Such is not necessarily the case,
however. Presidents come and go, many are only in office four years (since
World War II, only two of eight presidents have been elected twice). Career

bureaucrats, on the other hand, expect to spend their professional lives in a particular department, bureau, or agency. Their loyalty is to their organization and not necessarily to the president. There is often a resistance on the part of career bureaucrats to policies they perceive are not in the best interests of the United States. Moreover, each department tends to define problems from its own perspective and to seek support for options that further its view of what American foreign policy should be.

The image career bureaucrats have of the president varies with the president's skill at involving such officials in the foreign policymaking process. Conflict tends to arise when departments and agencies think they are being by-passed. But as a Kennedy aide observed, it is much easier to give an order than to try to win cooperation (Cronin, 1980: 233).

Among the president's various constituencies, the group most likely to share his views on foreign policy are his staff and cabinet appointees. All owe their positions to the president and serve at his request. Cabinet appointees, however, can quickly become caught up in departmental issues and constrained by the fact that they are accountable to Congress as well as to the president.

> Every power a cabinet officer exercises is derived from some Act of Congress; every penny he or she expends must be appropriated by the Congress; every new statutory change the Cabinet officer desires must be submitted to the Congress and defended there. A Cabinet officer's every act is subject to oversight by one or more regular or special Congressional Committees. . . (Patterson, 1976: 17–18).

Thus, cabinet members are often caught between the wishes of the Congress and the president. The images cabinet members have of the president, in turn, result from the latitude given them to perform their functions and from the support for their decisions they receive from the president.

Of his various constituencies, the president's staff members are generally the most supportive—loyalty is a prerequisite for the job. Moreover, many staff members are chosen because they have served the president well in previous positions—in other political roles or on the campaign trail. The key presidential staff position in the foreign policy area since the Kennedy administration has become the adviser for national security affairs. McGeorge Bundy, W. W. Rostow, Henry Kissinger, and Zbigniew Brzezinski are among those who have held this role from the Kennedy to the Carter administrations. Because of the difficulties in controlling their other constituencies, presidents have increasingly turned to their national security affairs advisers and these advisers' staffs for the development of foreign policy and oversight of the foreign policymaking process. Information on foreign policy issues is filtered from the various departments and agencies through the adviser for national security affairs; thus he can shape the expectations of the president and, in turn, the image others hold of the foreign policymaking skills of the president.

One last constituency is important in considering American foreign policy: foreign leaders. To be effective in international relations, the president must convince foreign leaders as well as American policymakers that a particular course of action is appropriate. Moreover, foreign leaders often have certain expectations concerning the president's behavior. Leaders of countries allied with the United States—for example, leaders of the NATO countries—expect to be consulted before the United States endorses an action that has implications for their country. Soviet leaders have expectations regarding what Americans will do in foreign policy, as do leaders of Third World countries. Foreign leaders' images of the president are built on how well he meets these expectations. They are interested in how much they can count on the American president and how predictable his behavior is.

A LEADER'S RELATIONS WITH CONSTITUENCIES

How does a leader like the president relate to the constituencies we have just described in order that at least some of their expectations are met and that his own world view has a chance of becoming part of American foreign policy? How does the leader mobilize these constituencies to deal effectively with foreign policy issues? In other words, how does the leader exercise leadership? Continuing with our example of the president, we note that how effectively he relates to his various constituencies depends on how well he carries out certain functions or activities. These functions are those of motivator, policy advocate, consensus builder, recruiter, and manager.

Journalist James Reston has proposed that the White House is the "pulpit of the nation and the president the chaplain." The motivator function grows out of this perception of the presidency. In serving as motivator, the president provides inspiration for the people, builds morale, and gives the nation a sense of mission. For example, Franklin Roosevelt, with his "fireside chats" provided inspiration to the American people. He was able to arouse confidence in the listener and a sense of pride in the country as well as hope for the future. Nixon's flare for the dramatic, as seen in his trip to China, and his enthusiastic support of Kissinger's shuttle diplomacy in the Mideast, as well as Carter's unabashed pleasure in the Camp David accords between Israel and Egypt, also captured the imagination of the people and made them proud of what their country was doing in the world. In performing the function of motivator, however, the president must beware of the fleeting quality of inspiration and learn not to count on what was said or done to inspire for long. Motivation is in constant demand.

To ensure that their own ideas about American foreign policy influence and shape government actions, presidents become policy advocates for issues they perceive are particularly important. Like Reagan with his firm stand on the need for increased defense spending, Carter with his advocacy of the Panama Canal treaties, and Kennedy championing a nuclear test ban treaty, the president turns into a salesman for a particular foreign policy position and, in effect, lobbies both the Congress and the people for support. Such policy advocacy can also extend to the international arena and involve making specific proposals to the United Nations and other international organizations or to another country. Carter's advocacy of human rights throughout the world is an example of such behavior. Being a policy advocate, however, does not mean automatic success, and presidents often have to settle for some compromise. The classic pitfall of the policy advocate is an unwillingness to give even an inch and to stake one's political reputation on the outcome. This is a situation ripe for disaster, as Woodrow Wilson experienced when he was unwilling to compromise in 1919 with Congress on the proposed Versailles treaty, which, if ratified by the Senate, would have meant U.S. entry into the League of Nations.

Neustadt (1960) defined the major tools of the president as those of persuasion and bargaining. These are, indeed, the tools of the consensus-building function of the presidency. Consensus building involves arranging compromises among people or groups with disparate points of view as well as building support for a particular policy among people and groups previously uncommitted. Consensus building requires being sensitive to what people want and how much they want it. And consensus building requires being willing to "twist arms" as well as "butter" people up. Generally it is done behind the scenes and, thus, is as likely to occur in a summit conference or international negotiations as in Congress or in the State Department. Carter's personal diplomacy with Egyptian and Israeli leaders in hammering out a peace settlement, for example, involved much consensus building. Consensus building often involves promises to one side or the other in order to encourage them to compromise or change their position. One negative outcome of the consensus building process is that the leader promises too much and cannot deliver. To remain credible the leader needs to rely on rewards that can be delivered or, at least, are perceived within his power to deliver.

Theodore Roosevelt once remarked that the best executive was one who had sense enough to pick good men to do what he wanted and the self-restraint to keep from meddling with them while they did it. Presidents themselves cannot do everything required of them. They must delegate some responsibilities; thus the importance of the recruiter function in leadership. The trick for the leader is to pick people to whom he is willing to delegate responsibility. This task becomes all the more important in the foreign policy area because the president often knows less about foreign issues and problems initially than he does about domestic affairs. It is helpful, at the outset, at least, to have someone with experience or knowledge in the foreign policy arena. Thus, presidents have selected people like Kissinger and Brzezinski, both academic experts in international relations, to become their advisers for national security affairs and have sought skilled secretaries of state like Vance and Haig, who had previous foreign policy-making experience.

In addition to selecting skilled people the recruiter activity involves using one's appointees effectively. Here presidential style enters in to affect how the relationship is structured. Some presidents (Eisenhower with Dulles, Nixon with Kissinger) have delegated authority and depended on the secretary of state or national security affairs adviser to act as an intermediary for them with the bureaucracy and other countries. Other presidents (Kennedy with Rusk) have preferred a more collegial relationship, with the president involved in day-to-day policymaking and using the secretary of state as a source of, and a sounding board for, ideas.

One problem that may arise as a result of the recruitment of highly qualified individuals is a difference of opinion or competition for power between them. In one foreign policy arena such a rivalry has developed between the secretary of state and the president's adviser for national security affairs. For example, a difference of perspective on the nature of U.S.-Soviet relations between Secretary of State Vance and National Security Affairs Adviser Brzezinski during Carter's administration led to much behind-the-scenes maneuvering for the president's ear. Until the Soviet invasion of Afghanistan, Carter tolerated the clashing perspectives and the vigorous debate within the government over the nature of American policy toward the Soviet Union. Most presidents, however, have been unable to tolerate for long such open conflict within their inner circle and have eventually given more authority to either the secretary of state or the national security affairs adviser. The choice of which one gets more authority depends on the president's political style and on the similarity of world views between the president and the occupants of these positions. The president, however, retains more control over foreign policymaking if his national security affairs adviser is predominant, and, indeed, since Kennedy's presidency the power of the national security adviser has increased.

The policy process is not over when a decision is made. There is also the need to implement the policy, to see that it is carried out. Presidents, therefore, also have to function as managers to see that things get done. They have to oversee and push the bureaucracy to ensure that policies are translated into actions. This function can be particularly frustrating for a president because it must coexist with the need to be making other decisions. Kennedy's frustration during the Cuban missile crisis at discovering that the U.S. missiles he had earlier ordered out of Turkey were still there and could become a quid pro quo for the removal of the Soviet missiles from Cuba is a case in point. Some attention must be paid to monitoring what is happening after a presidential decision is made. However, foreign policy decisions are difficult to monitor because what happens often occurs in another country and often requires an initial action on the part of the leadership of the other country before anything can start. Like the childhood game where a word is whispered around a circle and checked at the end to see if it is anything like what was started at the beginning, a foreign policy decision is passed through various departments, bureaus, military commands, embassies, and even at times clandestine personnel that need to operate on it. And, like the usual result of the game, the decision may change somewhat in form if not substance before it is implemented—if, indeed, it is implemented at all. As Cronin (1980: 177) observes:

> What is needed is a White House strategy that consciously recognizes presidential dependency on the federal bureaus and field operations and takes into account the fact that presidential policy objectives will lose clarity between the stages of legislation and implementation. What is also needed are innovative outreach and feedback strategies designed to keep organizations well informed of presidential intent, motivated to carry out such intents, and accountable for performance. These are, of course, far easier to talk about than to achieve.

The management function presents a real challenge to presidents.

We have described five different functions a president can perform in working on foreign policy. It is important to note that presidents do not necessarily perform all five functions equally well nor do they emphasize all five functions equally. Indeed, the characteristics of the president and the nature of the various constituencies that the particular president is accountable to often help to determine the emphasis and how well any are performed. For example, the president with a fixed world view who is relatively insensitive to other's opinions may focus more activity on policy advocacy than the president whose view is less fixed and, thus, more open to the input of others. The latter type of president may find the consensus building function more palatable. Part of the stress presidents can experience results when there is an incompatibility between the functions they as presidents feel comfortable performing and the desires and expectations of their important constituencies. Lyndon Johnson's interest and skills in consensus building included much behind-the-scenes activity, which led the public to perceive him as a "wheeler-dealer" and to become suspicious of the nature of the private promises he was making. Johnson was never able to understand this reaction and, particularly as his troubles with the public over Vietnam mounted, lashed out at those people he thought were responsible for his problems—the press, liberals, and intellectuals.

THE CONTEXT AND LEADERSHIP

What leadership functions are relevant as well as what constituents are likely to be expecting is in large part determined by the situation of the moment. What kind of foreign policy problem is the leadership of the country facing? For example, are leaders such as the president faced with an international crisis (a war, the seizure of hostages, an embargo of Middle East oil), the need to replace an ambassador, an attempt by Congress to reassert itself in the foreign policy arena, or discontent among the people about a particular foreign policy issue? In each of these instances the president would need to emphasize different functions to deal effectively with the problem. Showing that he has a possible solution to the problem or has a way of working on the problem (policy advocacy) is important for a president during times of international crisis. Groups turn to the president for guidance. Selection of an ambassador involves the recruiting function and the need to choose someone who will both serve the president's interests and work well with the leadership of the country to which he or she will be assigned. The selection can also involve patronage and reward to someone for past service. Building a working coalition in Congress or acting as a consensus builder is needed when Congress poses threats to the president's programs. When the public becomes overly disgruntled with a particular policy (or lack of a particular policy), the president can benefit by becoming a motivator, trying to show why the country needs to do what it is doing but also listening to the leaders of the disaffected groups and seeking to mold their opinions.

Whether leaders pick up the cues from the situation and fit their behavior to the context depends on their personalities and backgrounds. How adaptable leaders can be and how easily they can learn once in office depends in some measure on their personalities and on their previous experiences. World view, style, training in foreign affairs, and how their earliest political successes and failures have structured their behavior will affect their malleability.

Two other types of situations that presidents face merit comment. One is the honeymoon period following an election; the other is the election itself. Every president appears to enjoy a period early in his term, generally within the first 100 days of taking office, when both Congress and the people lend their support and hold back criticism. Bipartisanship runs strong in the Congress and an air of expectancy and optimism pervades the country. Even foreign leaders will often refrain from criticism. Within this period, presidents, if organized, can shape what happens in foreign policy more almost than at any other time during their presidency. They have the opportunity to set the foreign policy agenda for their administration. The opposite, however, is true of election periods. With politicians nowadays starting to run for the presidency several years before an election, politics becomes an important part of most presidential policymaking by the end of the third year of a president's term and may be pivotal at the mid-term elections if public support for the president has declined. Unless forced by international events, presidents become careful at election times (whether the mid-term or presidential election) not to embroil themselves in foreign policy debate that might prove costly politically.

SUMMARY

To understand the relevance of leadership to the examination of American foreign policy, we have argued that it is important to learn not only what the leaders involved are like but also what the expectations are of those they lead, how the leaders relate to their various constituents, and the nature of the current situation. Leadership can change as these ingredients change, with possible consequences for foreign policy. We have indicated the kinds of personality characteristics and experiences of American foreign policy leaders that can influence foreign policy behavior as well as the expectations that various players in the foreign policymaking process are likely to have of their leader. Moreover, we have suggested the kinds of functions a leader, particularly a president, will have to perform to meet what is expected of him. The situation helps determine which foreign policy leaders and which constituencies are relevant. American foreign policy results from the interaction of the particular leader with his characteristics and the relevant constituencies with their expectations. In effect, American foreign policy is made by people and what those people are like helps determine what happens.

REFERENCES

Barber, James David (1972) *The Presidential Character.* Englewood Cliffs, N.J.: Prentice-Hall.

Barrett, Laurence I. (1980) "Meet the Real Ronald Reagan," *Time,* October 20.

Bennis, Warren (1973) "The Doppelgänger Effect," *Newsweek,* September 17, 13.

Broder, David S. (1981) *Changing of the Guard: Power and Leadership in America.* New York: Penguin, 1981.

Cronin, Thomas E. (1980) *The State of the Presidency.* 2nd ed. Boston: Little, Brown.

Fulbright, J. William (1979) "The Legislator as Educator," *Foreign Affairs,* 57, 719–732.

George, Alexander L. (1980) *Presidential Decisionmaking in Foreign Policy: The Effective Use of Information and Advice.* Boulder, Colo.: Westview Press.

George, Alexander L. (1979) "The Causal Nexus between Cognitive Beliefs and Decision-Making Behavior: The 'Operational Code,' " pp. 95–124 in Lawrence S. Falkowski (ed.), *Psychological Models in International Politics.* Boulder, Colo.: Westview Press.

George, Alexander L. (1969) "The Operational Code: A Neglected Approach to the Study of Political Leaders and Decision-Making," *International Studies Quarterly,* 13, 190–222.

Hermann, Margaret G. (1980a) "Explaining Foreign Policy Behavior Using the Personal Characteristics of Political Leaders," *International Studies Quarterly,* 24, 7–46.

Hermann, Margaret G. (1980b) "The Implications of Leaders' Foreign Policy Orientations for the Quality of Foreign Policy Decisions." Paper presented at the meeting of the International Studies Association, Los Angeles, Calif., March 19–22.

Hermann, Margaret G. (1979) "Indicators of Stress in Policymakers during Foreign Policy Crises," *Political Psychology,* 1, 27–46.

Hermann, Margaret, G. (ed.) (1977) *A Psychological Examination of Political Leaders.* New York: Free Press.

Holsti, Ole R. (1977) "The 'Operational Code' as an Approach to the Analysis of Belief Systems." Final Report to the National Science Foundation, Grant SOC75-15-368, Duke University.

Janis, Irving L. (1972) *Victims of Groupthink*. Boston: Houghton Mifflin.

Johnson, Loch K. (1977) "Operational Codes and the Prediction of Leadership Behavior: Senator Frank Church at Midcareer," pp. 82–119 in Margaret G. Hermann (ed.), *A Psychological Examination of Political Leaders*. New York: Free Press.

Koenig, Louis W. (1981) *The Chief Executive*. 4th ed. New York: Harcourt Brace Jovanovich.

MacArthur, Douglas (1964) *Reminiscences*. New York: McGraw-Hill.

Neustadt, Richard (1960) *Presidential Power*. New York: Wiley.

Patterson, Bradley H., Jr. (1976) *The President's Cabinet: Issues and Questions*. Washington, D.C.: American Society for Public Administration.

Safire, William (1982) "Is Castro Convertible?" *Columbus Citizen Journal*, April 27, 6.

Schlesinger, Arthur, Jr. (1965) *A Thousand Days: John F. Kennedy in the White House*. New York: Houghton Mifflin.

Sorensen, Theodore C. (1965) *Kennedy*. New York: Harper and Row.

Sorensen, Theodore C. (1963) *Decision-Making in the White House: The Olive Branch or the Arrows*. New York: Columbia University Press.

Stewart, Louis H. (1977) "Birth Order and Political Leadership," pp. 206–236 in Margaret G. Hermann (ed.), *A Psychological Examination of Political Leaders*. New York: Free Press.

Stoessinger, John E. (1979) *Crusaders and Pragmatists: Movers of Modern American Foreign Policy*. New York: Norton.

Stuart, Douglas, and Starr, Harvey (1982) "The 'Inherent Bad Faith Model' Reconsidered: Dulles, Kennedy, and Kissinger," *Political Psychology*, 3, 1–33.

Walker, Stephen G. (1977) "The Interface Between Beliefs and Behavior: Henry A. Kissinger's Operational Code and the Vietnam War," *Journal of Conflict Resolution*, 21, 129–168.

Welsh, William A. (1977) "Effect of Career and Party Affiliation on Revolutionary Behavior among Latin American Political Elites," pp. 276–308 in Margaret G. Hermann (ed.), *A Psychological Examination of Political Leaders*. New York: Free Press.

27

CRUSADERS AND PRAGMATISTS
Two Types of Foreign Policy Makers

JOHN G. STOESSINGER

In our time, we have been led to think of states almost as living actors on the world scene. How often we hear a phrase such as "the *United States* decided" or "the *United States* agreed." The question we must ask, however, is "*who* decided for the United States and *who* agreed." To speak of "actors," "powers," or of "systems" merely beclouds the basic truth that human beings, made of flesh and blood, make these decisions on behalf of collectivities called states. States have no existences apart from the lives of men and women. They are creatures of the human will.

While this chapter will focus on personalities, it is *not* meant to be a single-factor analysis. Clearly, personality does not explain everything. But like any effort at theoretical innovation, mine will emphasize *that* conceptual insight which is original and new. Unlike a photograph, the analysis will not attempt to reproduce every detail of the truth; more like a portrait, it will try to uncover a new truth. . . .

A leader's *personality* is a decisive element in the making of a foreign policy. Whether a leader uses his power for good or evil is secondary to the fact that this power exists as an objective reality. Such a leader is a historical *fact* at least as much as a state or "system." Differences in leaders' personalities thus may make or break a nation's foreign policy. It matters very much, in short, *who* is there at a given moment.

Two basic personality types have characterized decision makers in twentieth century America. First, there has been the *crusading* type whose hallmark is a missionary zeal to make the world better. The crusader tends to make decisions based on a preconceived idea rather than on the basis of experience. Even though there are alternatives, he usually does not see

Reprinted from *Crusaders and Pragmatists: Movers of Modern American Foreign Policy* by John G. Stoessinger (New York: W. W. Norton, 1979): pp. xiii, xv–xvi, 174–175, 177–183, 205–207, 237–245, 287–290. Reprinted by permission of the author and publisher. Footnotes have been renumbered to appear in consecutive order.

them. If the facts do not square with his philosophy, it is too bad for the facts. Thus, the crusader tends toward rigidity and finds it difficult, if not impossible, to extricate himself from a losing posture. He does not welcome dissent and advisers will tend to tell him what he wants to hear. He sets out to improve the world but all too often manages to leave it in worse shape than it was before.

The second basic type is the *pragmatic* one. The pragmatist is guided by the facts and his experience in a given situation, not by wishes or unexamined preconceptions. He is generally aware of the alternatives to his chosen course of action and explores the pros and cons of each as objectively as possible. He encourages advisers to tell him what he ought to know, not what they think he wants to hear. Always flexible, he does not get locked into a losing policy. He can change direction and try again, without inflicting damage to his self-esteem. Neither hope nor fear but evidence alone governs his decisions. And when there is no evidence as yet, there is always common sense.

Naturally, these two basic types are not to be considered as mutually exclusive. A pure crusader would be a saint or a fanatic, while a pure pragmatist would be an efficient machine. Usually both types are present to some degree in each personality, but one tends to *predominate*. Over the years, crusading and pragmatic leaders have tended to alternate in cycles. The crusading spirit has dominated American foreign policy in times of protracted crisis or prolonged national trauma while the pragmatic mode has been more in evidence during periods of relative calm and consolidation. Like a pendulum, America has tended to swing between two moods: Sunday evangelism and weekday realism. . . . [To illustrate this point, this chapter will focus on a single swing of the pendulum: on Lyndon Johnson, a crusader; and, on Henry Kissinger, a pragmatist.—*eds.*]

LYNDON BAINES JOHNSON

Lyndon Johnson was one of the most complex and most tragic figures in recent American history. His rise from obscurity in Texas is a Horatio Alger story. But his decline and fall is an American tragedy.

As a young boy, Johnson was very close to his grandfather. The old man liked to talk about the old days of the frontier. Fantasy mingled with memory, lifting ordinary events to the level of heroic legend. Extravagant claims were made for the courage and daring of the cowboy: the tall, strong he-man, ready for action in any situation. After his grandfather's death, young Lyndon began to idolize his father. But Sam Johnson had very definite ideas about manliness. He taught Lyndon how to hunt animals and, once, when the boy had thrown up after killing a rabbit, his father called him a coward. Later, as president, Johnson forced people around him to submit to *his* tests of manhood. Visitors to the LBJ ranch were handed rifles and expected to shoot an antelope or deer in Johnson's presence. From the boy's fear of being tested came the man's determination to *give*, rather than take the tests. Courage had become synonymous with machismo.

Very early, Johnson developed a strong tendency to manipulate those around him. When a student at San Marcos State Teachers College, he managed to work for the college president, because the powerful man's favor would have a multiplier effect with the faculty and student body. His mother, however, had taught him that power had value only when used to benefit people. Whether it was the student manipulating the college president or the president of the United States promising houses and jobs for the American people, Johnson always associated the delivery of "good works" with the attainment of power and position.

Lyndon Johnson always believed that America was the best of all possible worlds. This assumption of superiority imposed a moral obligation to share the American way with the world. He felt a sense of outrage at the slightest criticism of America. Lack of faith in the United States or its heroes was tantamount to treason. The problem was with the critic, not the country.

Johnson's manipulativeness soon made him into a consummate political animal. Politics became his passion. Every human contact had a purpose. He wanted to be liked by everyone he met, but defined friendship in terms of a willingness to accommodate to his ends. Relationships with other men were perceived by him in terms of domination or submission. Only with his wife, Lady Bird, did Johnson attain a deep and lasting human bond. Otherwise, he was a profoundly lonely man.

In his political campaigns, for the Congress and later for the Senate, Johnson was completely single-minded. He poured his massive energy into every political meeting. There emanated from him a torrential, tireless flow of labor and activity that no other candidate could match. He would visit every village, walk countless streets, and shake hands with everyone he met. Winning was essential to his emotional survival. Defeat was an unbearable humiliation.

When Lyndon Johnson became president of the United States, his political personality was clearly defined, immovable, and fixed. He was eager to be generous with those who acknowledged his mastery. Those who provoked him, he would fight relentlessly. Like a sheriff in a Western town, he would bring criminals to justice. And above all, he would manipulate so that those he would dominate would also learn to love him. In his virtues and his flaws, Lyndon Johnson was an American original. . . .

Lyndon Johnson's personality had a decisive impact on the course of the Vietnam war. To be fair to Johnson, we must admit that he inherited a world view, shared by most Americans in 1964, that Vietnam would have to be defended. It is entirely possible that Truman or Dulles might have reached similar decisions in the early stages of the war, including the bombings of North and South Vietnam. Dulles had in fact been prepared to commit ground troops to Indochina in 1954. But there were some aspects of

Johnson's handling of the war that bore the unmistakable stamp of his own extraordinary personality. The first of these was the degree of deception employed by Johnson vis-à-vis the American people around election time in 1964. Briefly stated, Johnson ran against Barry Goldwater on the pledge that he would not expand the war. In fact, in his campaign literature, Johnson specifically linked Goldwater to an escalation in Vietnam. At that very time, however, he asked the Congress for a virtual blank check over Vietnam policy. The Congress readily obliged with the Tonkin Gulf resolution, passed in response to an incident that never happened, except in the president's imagination. Lyndon Johnson misled Congress and the people, and through subterfuge was able to obtain congressional authorization for a war that he had decided on months before while he was promising the voters peace. The sequence of these events is worth examining.

During his campaign for reelection in 1964, Johnson tried to keep Vietnam out of the public view as much as possible. When later asked why, he answered: "If you have a mother-in-law with only one eye and she has it in the center of the forehead, you don't keep her in the living room."[1] As far as the voters were concerned, Johnson had disposed of the bothersome mother-in-law completely. As 1964 moved toward election day, he emphasized more and more the contrast between himself and his opponent, Senator Barry Goldwater, on the issue of Vietnam. Five examples will show this progression

On August 16, Johnson declared: "Some others are eager to enlarge the conflict. They call upon us to supply American boys to do the job that Asian boys should do."[2] Two weeks later, his accusations became more specific: "I have had advice to load our planes with bombs and to drop them on certain areas that I think would enlarge the war."[3] On September 25, for the first time, he took a clear stand against escalation: "We don't want our American boys to do the fighting for Asian boys."[4] And again, on October 21: "We seek no wider war."[5] On October 27, one week before the election, Johnson stated categorically, in a speech in Pittsburgh: "There can be and will be, as long as I am President, peace for all Americans."[6] He won the election by a landslide. Yet, all throughout 1964, the Joint Chiefs of Staff urged Johnson to increase the Vietnam commitment in order to win the war more quickly. As early as January 1964, they had addressed the following memorandum to the president: "The United States must be prepared to put aside many of the self-imposed restrictions which now limit our efforts, and to undertake bolder actions which may embody greater risks."[7] Specifically, the Joint Chiefs were of the opinion that aerial bombing would bring North Vietnam to its knees. Policy-planning chief Walt Rostow, in support of this recommendation, stated that "Ho Chi Minh has an industrial complex to protect; he is no longer a guerrilla fighter with nothing to lose."[8]

In the meantime, Robert Johnson, Rostow's deputy, undertook a careful study of the probable effects of bombing. The study concluded that the bombing would not work and predicted, prophetically, that it would imprison the American government. Economic growth was not a major Hanoi objective, the study said, challenging one of Rostow's favorite theses; rather, it was the unfinished business of throwing the foreigners out of the country. Hanoi had two formidable pillars of strength: the nationalist component of unity and the Communist component of control, which made for an organized, unified, modern state. Bombing would not affect such a regime. On the contrary, it might even strengthen it.

This remarkable study was ignored. Rostow, who was totally committed to bombing, never brought it to the president's attention. More and more, as 1964 drew to a close, the president's advisers, both civilian and military, moved toward a consensus on the bombing policy. Robert McNamara, McGeorge Bundy, Maxwell Taylor, and Dean Rusk—all of them perceived a chain of aggression emanating from China that urged on North Vietnam. Ho Chi Minh, in turn, was reported to be the source of the Vietcong aggression in the South. Thus, bombing would stop aggression at the source—in the North—and would convince China of American determination. No more dominoes would be permitted to fall to communism. In a revealing memorandum to McNamara, John McNaughton, former Harvard law professor and assistant secretary of defense in 1964, set forth American goals in South Vietnam in terms of the following priorities:

70 percent—To avoid a humiliating U.S. defeat
20 percent—To keep South Vietnamese territory from Chinese hands
10 percent—To permit the people of South Vietnam to enjoy a better, freer way of life.[9]

Thus, the official reason that was given to the American people for the intervention in Vietnam with air power and ground troops made up only one-tenth of the real reason.

Lyndon Johnson was in essential agreement with his advisers. Vietnam would have to be defended. If the Americans "turned tail" and got out, it would be Hitler all over again. As Johnson declared:

> Everything I knew about history told me that if I got out of Vietnam and let Ho Chi Minh run through the streets of Saigon, then I'd be doing exactly what Chamberlain did in World War II. I'd be giving a big fat reward to aggression. . . . And so would begin World III.[10]

Thus, Lyndon Johnson faced a dilemma: He was convinced that he would have to escalate the war in order to win, but his political instincts told him that such a course would jeopardize his reelection. Johnson's solution was to fashion himself an instrument whereby he could escalate by stealth. This instrument was the Tonkin Gulf resolution.

In the first days of August 1964, an American destroyer escorting South Vietnamese ships was approached by three North Vietnamese torpedo boats. The American skipper later said he fired the first shot, and then sank two of the PT boats. On August 4, the president went on television to talk about a second "unprovoked attack" on the destroyers *Maddox* and *C. Turner Joy*. "These acts of violence," Johnson warned, "must be met not only by alert defense, but with positive reply. That reply is being given as I speak to you." On that day American bombers destroyed twenty-five North Vietnamese PT boats and blew up the oil depot at Vinh in North Vietnam. Defense Secretary Robert McNamara reported to the president that, at Vinh, "the smoke was observed rising to 14,000 feet." Johnson was overheard to say to a reporter: "I didn't just screw Ho Chi Minh; I cut his pecker off."[11]

The North Vietnamese provocation, as was revealed much later, never really occurred. The North Vietnamese vessels were later dismissed by a *Maddox* officer as "nothing more than a flock of geese on radar screens."[12] The *Maddox*'s captain told reporters: "Evaluating everything that was going on, I was becoming less and less convinced that somebody was there."[13] And a *Maddox* lieutenant confessed: "I had nothing to shoot at.... We didn't have any targets."[14] "Hell," Johnson said later, "For all I know, our Navy was shooting at whales out there."[15]

Nonetheless, this fictitious episode in Tonkin Gulf became the pretext for the passage of one of the most momentous congressional resolutions in modern American history. On August 4, 1964, Lyndon Johnson called upon Congress "to approve and support the determination of the President, as Commander-in-Chief, to take all necessary measures to repel any armed attack against the forces of the United States and to prevent further aggression." Furthermore, the president asked the Congress for authority "to take all necessary measures, including the use of armed force, to assist any member or protocol state of SEATO requesting assistance in defense of its freedom."[16] In a political master stroke, Johnson asked his old friend, Senator J. William Fulbright, to serve as floor manager in the Senate for the Tonkin Gulf resolution.

As chairman of the Senate's Committee on Foreign Relations, Fulbright enjoyed considerable power and prestige. He feared Barry Goldwater and believed that Johnson would always consult him about the war. Thus, while he was aware of the dangers of the wording of the resolution, he was willing to take the risk. Besides, he did not seek the stigma of opposing the president on an issue of patriotism. Only two senators asked unfriendly questions during the discussion on the Senate floor: Ernest Gruening and Wayne Morse. Both men believed that the resolution was so open-ended that it gave the president the power to take the nation into war without a congressional declaration. Nonetheless, on August 7, the Senate approved the resolution by a vote of eighty-eight to two. Senator Morse, explaining his negative vote, declared:

> I believe that history will record that we have made a great mistake in subverting the Constitution of the United States . . . by means of this

resolution. We are in effect giving the President . . . warmaking powers in the absence of a declaration of war. I believe that to be a historic mistake.[17]

He was right, of course. Johnson had it both ways. Congress gave him a blank check without really declaring war. Both Gruening and Morse lost their next elections, largely because of their opposition to Lyndon Johnson. In 1966, Fulbright was to remember Tonkin Gulf with deep regret and bitterness. Like so many people, he had been used by Lyndon Johnson. And when American combat troops were committed to Vietnam and the debate over the war intensified, lawmakers began to ask who had given the president authority for such drastic measures. *You* did, Lyndon Johnson was pleased to be able to reply.

What is the explanation for this incredible duplicity? The answer must be found in Johnson's second major goal: The Great Society.

Johnson deeply admired FDR. He went back past Kennedy's New Frontier all the way to the New Deal. He was determined to get legislation through the Congress that would dwarf even Roosevelt's initiatives. The Great Society, he hoped, would spell an end to poverty and squalor in America. But the war, too, had to be fought. And, fatefully, he did not believe that he would have to make a choice. As Johnson confessed:

> I was determined to keep the war from shattering that dream, which meant I simply had no choice but to keep my foreign policy in the wings. I knew the Congress as well as I know Lady Bird, and I knew that the day it exploded into a major debate on the war, that day would be the beginning of the end of the Great Society. . . . I was determined to be a leader of peace. . . . I wanted both, I believed in both. . . . After all, our country was built by pioneers who had a rifle in one hand to kill their enemies and an ax in the other to build their homes and provide for their families.[18]

A full-scale public commitment to Vietnam would have forced Johnson to make choices and accept limits. This he was not prepared to do. Instead, he hoped that he could conduct a major war in virtual secrecy while simultaneously summoning the American people toward the Great Society. He did not feel it necessary to make full disclosure. In the Senate, Johnson had been able to keep his dealings with one group a secret from the next. He had developed manipulation into a fine art form. Now, as president, he would manipulate the American people for their own good. As a result, they would be able to "pull off" both the war in Vietnam and the Great Society at home. Specifically, he would conceal the costs of the war so that he might receive the Great Society appropriations before the truth came out. In short, he would accomplish the impossible.

In 1970, two years after he left office, Lyndon Johnson appeared to have some insight into his own folly. "If I left the woman I really loved, the

Great Society," he said, "in order to get involved with that bitch of a war on the other side of the world, then I would lose everything at home. All my programs. All my hopes and all my dreams. . . ."[19]

HENRY A. KISSINGER

Henry Kissinger has written history as a scholar and made history as a statesman. His diplomacy was deeply rooted in the insights of the young doctoral student at Harvard of a quarter century before. It was, in fact, a virtual transplant from the world of thought into the world of power. Hence, if we are to understand the statesman, we must first understand the philosopher-historian.

Kissinger's favorite book in his early student days at Harvard was Oswald Spengler's *The Decline of the West*. The deep strain of pessimism that permeated every page of Spengler's classic struck a responsive chord in Kissinger. It was reflected in a concluding passage of his undergraduate honors thesis where he observed that "life involves suffering and transitoriness," and that "the generation of Buchenwald and the Siberian labor-camps [could] not talk with the same optimism as its fathers."

Kissinger regarded history as the memory of states. As the knowledge of a person's past gives us some clues about his future, history provides us with clues about a nation's future. It never repeats itself exactly. If it can teach us anything at all, it teaches through analogy, not through identity. Like the Oracle at Delphi, a particular historical event may be open to several interpretations. The supreme challenge of the statesman is to make the correct analogy. In this undertaking, he may be given only a single opportunity, for he is his own subject. In effect, he performs the experiment upon himself and his own nation. He may not have a second chance.

Kissinger's choice of a subject for his doctoral dissertation was deeply influenced by these considerations. He stated these reasons in his preface with perfect clarity:

> The success of physical science depends on the selection of one crucial experiment; that of political science in the field of international affairs, on the selection of the crucial period. I have chosen for my topic the period between 1812 and 1822, partly, I am frank to say, because its problems seem to me analogous to those of our own day.

Thus, Kissinger's interest in the diplomacy of the early nineteenth century was not academic in the usual sense. He wanted to know how these statemen in the distant past had managed to erect such a durable structure of peace; and he wanted to find out whether their insights could be transplanted into the modern world. For most students pursuing a Ph.D. degree, the dissertation is viewed as a gateway into the academic world. This was only partially true of Henry Kissinger. He hoped that the knowledge he would derive from his research would prepare him for action on a larger stage. The title of his doctoral dissertation was *A World Restored*. In it, he explored how Austria, England, Russia, and Prussia restored the peace of Europe after Napoleon's defeat in 1815. His later diplomacy was deeply rooted in the intellectual insights of this dissertation.

Henry Kissinger differed from most American statesmen in the sense that his policies were based on doctrine and deliberate design rather than on the more day-to-day approach that has often characterized the conduct of American diplomacy. This doctrine, which rested on three main pillars, emerged very clearly in *A World Restored*. First, to be secure, a peace must be based on a negotiated settlement, with all sides in equilibrium, rather than on a victor's peace. Everybody is a little bit unhappy, but no one is completely unhappy. Thus, no one will try to overthrow the settlement through yet another war, and the relative insecurity of each guarantees the relative security of all. Second, a victorious power, in order to have peace, will not attempt to annihilate the vanquished but will co-opt it into the established order by giving it something of its own substance. Thus, the victor decontaminates the defeated of his revolutionary ardor and transforms him subtly from a "have-not" into a "have" nation. Third, in the absence of a globally controlled system, the best guarantor of peace is balance and, hence, a balancer is essential. This balancer will seldom ask the question, "Who is right and who is wrong?" but rather, "Who is weak and who is strong?" He will throw his weight on the weaker side whenever an imbalance occurs and by so doing restore the equilibrium and maintain the peace. Hence, peace, to Henry Kissinger, was a bonus of a successful balance policy. . . . [The problem, then, for Kissinger as a statesman was how to translate his doctrine for peace into effective diplomacy. And our concern is with how his personality shaped that diplomacy.—*eds.*]

A great deal has been written about Henry Kissinger's personal diplomacy. His insistence on conducting important negotiations personally and his habit of establishing close relationships with adversary leaders are well-known characteristics of his statecraft. His low opinion of the bureaucracy has also been widely commented upon. This penchant for the solo performance has been variously attributed to Kissinger's "enormous ego," his "obsessive secrecy," or to his "elemental need for power and glory."[20]

There is another interpretation. In order for Kissinger to succeed in his most historic diplomatic initiatives, he *had* to establish personal dominance over the bureaucracy. To establish such control moreover, he had to act decisively, often secretly, and, at times, alone.

Kissinger had never had much patience with bureaucracy. When a professor at Harvard, he had reserved his most acid comments for university administrators. His tolerance for bureaucracy in government was not much greater. After having studied the American "foreign policy-making apparatus," he had come to the conclusion that it was a kind of feudal network of competing agencies and interests, in which there was a "powerful tendency to think that a compromise among administrative proposals [was] the same thing as a policy." The bureaucratic model for making a decision, in Kissinger's opinion, was a policy proposal with three choices: the present policy bracketed by two absurd alternatives.

Kissinger had been a consultant to both the Kennedy and Johnson administrations. While he never said so publicly, he had been deeply disappointed. So much had been promised, so much less had been attempted, and, in his judgment, so little had been done. He had had the opportunity to observe government decision making from a fairly close perspective. What impressed him most was that the foreign policy bureaucracy had a way of smothering initiative by advocating a path of least resistance. The lawyers, businessmen, and former academics who ran the hierarchy generally seemed to place a premium on safety and acceptance rather than on creativity and vision. The result was that any innovative statesmanship tended to expire in the feudal fiefs of the bureaucracy or come to grief on the rocks of organizational inertia.

There was ample basis for Kissinger's impatience. SALT might have been initiated at the Glassboro summit in 1967, between Lyndon Johnson and the Soviet leaders, but there had been no decisive leadership. Nor had there been a clear-cut stand on the possible limitation of strategic arms. Instead, there were endless arguments among the Joint Chiefs of Staff, the Pentagon, the State Department, and academic experts in the field of arms control. Similarly, the Arab-Israeli war of 1967 had presented opportunities for American diplomacy and mediation, but there had been no one with a plan, let alone the courage to place himself between competing claims. Instead, there emerged from the bowels of the bureaucracy countless position papers by learned academic experts. There was no agreement on an overall strategy for mediation in the Middle East, only an almost fatalistic sense of hopelessness and drift.

This was the reason why Kissinger decided, immediately after January 20, 1969, to establish personal control over the bureaucracy. Those whom he could not dominate, he would manipulate. And those whom he could not manipulate, he would try to bypass. He embarked on this course of action as a result of a rational decision. He simply feared that *unless* he dominated, bypassed, or manipulated, nothing would get done. He, too, would ultimately be submerged in a long twilight struggle of modern feudal baronies. This he was simply not prepared to accept.

In his position as assistant for national security affairs, Kissinger came to dominate the bureaucracy as no other figure before him had done, and as no other is likely to do for a very long time to come. He promptly established his control through the establishment of a few small committees, each of which he personally chaired. There were a number of interdepartmental groups: a review group, a verification panel for SALT, a Vietnam special studies group, the Washington Special Actions Group for Crisis Control, and the Forty Committee, which dealt with covert intelligence operations.

It was out of these committees that Kissinger forged the great initiatives that have assured his place in history: SALT I in 1969, the opening to China after his secret trip to Peking in 1971, and the diplomatic mediation in the Middle East after the October war in 1973. It is true, of course, that some of the more dubious decisions also had their genesis in this small elitist structure, particularly in the Forty Committee. The "destabilization" of the Allende government in Chile in 1971, alleged payments to Italian neo-Fascists in 1972, and the denouement in Indochina are some of the more disturbing examples. Only history can provide the necessary distance for a balanced assessment of these various initiatives. But what can already be asserted with a fair amount of certainty is that Kissinger was right in his assumption that, in order to put into effect a coherent global policy, he would have to concentrate as much power in his hands as possible.

Kissinger's pursuit of power had a very clear-cut purpose. During two decades of reflection he had evolved a theory of global order that, in his judgment, would bring the world a few steps closer to stability and peace. Nothing was more important to him in 1969 than the chance to test that theory. He believed with the most absolute conviction that he was the one best qualified. On one occasion, in 1968, when Nelson Rockefeller's speech writers had made some changes in a Kissinger position paper, the author exclaimed furiously: "If Rockefeller buys a Picasso, he doesn't hire four housepainters to improve on it." In Kissinger's own view, this was not an arrogant statement. It was merely the reflection of an enormous, though quite genuine, intellectual self-confidence. He believed, quite matter of factly, that he was the Picasso of modern American foreign policy.

The drawing up of any balance sheet on the centerpiece of Kissinger's foreign policy—détente with the Soviet Union—must remain a highly personal business on which thoughtful people may have widely differing opinions. Any such analysis must enter in the realm of competing values, since in creating that centerpiece, choices had to be made and a price had to be paid. Hence, it is only fair that, as we enter this discussion, the author should reveal the basis of his judgment and share his values and prejudices with the reader.

It seems that Henry Kissinger was right when he declared that the overriding reason for détente with Russia was the avoidance of a nuclear catastrophe. It also appears that if such a world cataclysm has become less likely, this is in no small measure to be credited to Kissinger. This is not to deny that the American relationship with Russia leaves a great deal to be desired. But there is no question that the danger of nuclear war has substantially receded. It no longer intrudes into our daily lives the way it did when Kissinger was a professor. Mothers then worried about radioactive waste and strontium-90 in their children's milk and John F. Kennedy almost went to nuclear war with Khrushchev over missiles in Cuba. Today, we argue with the Soviet Union about strategic arms control, trade, and human rights, but we no longer live in daily terror of a nuclear exchange. The fearful scenarios that were conjured up in Herman Kahn's *Thinking About the Unthinkable* today read almost like horrible anachronisms. In addition to the elements of luck and timing, it was also Kissinger's design and courage that made détente possible at all.

Clearly, the price that Kissinger has paid on behalf of the United States has been enormous. But, to be fair, we must ask ourselves whether the alternatives would have yielded better results. In strategic arms control, Kissinger's accusers have blamed him for his acceptance in SALT I of Soviet superiority in missile numbers. They have also been suspicious of his lack of interest in alleged evidence that the Soviet Union had violated the spirit and perhaps even the letter of SALT I. Critics have also taken umbrage at his reported willingness—during the SALT II negotiations—to exclude the Soviet Backfire bomber from an overall ceiling while including the American cruise missile.

But the critics, in my judgment, have never given a convincing answer to Kissinger's own questions: "What in God's name," he asked in 1974, "is strategic superiority? What is the significance of it, politically, militarily, operationally, at these levels of numbers? What do you do with it?" Kissinger simply did not believe that a marginal "overkill" capacity on either side could be translated into a meaningful strategic or political advantage. It does not appear that there is conclusive evidence that such a translation can in fact be made.

The great paradox of Kissinger's conception of détente is in his relative tolerance vis-à-vis the Soviet Union, still the fountainhead of communism, and his combativeness toward local Communist movements in peripheral areas. How can Kissinger proclaim détente with the Soviet Union, the supporter of Communist causes everywhere, and yet fight communism to the death in Indochina, warn Western European heads of state against coalition governments with Communists, and demand action against the Communists in Angola?

The key to this riddle is to be found in Kissinger's primary commitment to stability. In the central relationship between the superpowers, there can be no decisive change in the power balance, short of nuclear war. The balance could be changed dramatically, however, if a minor nation shifted its allegiance from one side to the other and thus added appreciably to the strength of one of the two main contenders. The direct jockeying for mutual advantage between Russia and the United States was not likely to affect the global balance. But Communist advances elsewhere could, at least cumulatively, affect the balance of power in the world: hence, Kissinger's concern with stemming Communist advances in peripheral areas.

This logic, however, runs into serious difficulties. It may stand up in an area such as Angola where thousands of Cuban troops were imported to do battle for the Communist cause. In such a case, there was at least good circumstantial evidence for direct Soviet-sponsored intervention. But there was little, if any, evidence that the Soviet Union was very active in helping the Communists in Portugal, Italy, France, or Chile. The growth of the Italian Communist movement in Italy under Enrico Berlinguer might be attributable more to that Italian's "historic compromise" with democratic socialism than to subversion by the Soviet Union. Yet, Kissinger accused the Portuguese foreign minister of being a "Kerensky," quarantined Portugal from NATO, had secret payments made to a neo-Facist Italian general, and helped in the overthrow of the Allende government in Chile. In such cases, a good argument can be made that, by his indiscriminate opposition to all local forms of communism, Kissinger might force breakaway groups back into Moscow's arms and thus bring about the very developments he was so eager to prevent.

On the deeper level, Hans Morgenthau has made the most telling criticism:

> Since the causes and effects of instability persist, a policy committed to stability and identifying instability with communism is compelled by the logic of its interpretation of reality to suppress in the name of anticommunism all manifestations of popular discontent and stifle the aspirations for reform. Thus, in an essentially unstable world, tyranny becomes the last resort of a policy committed to stability as its ultimate standard.[21]

This is how, in Morgenthau's opinion, Kissinger, despite his extraordinary brilliance, often failed. He tended to place his great gifts at the service of lost causes, and thus, in the name of preserving stability and order, aligned the United States on the wrong side of the great historic issues.

Morgenthau may be a little harsh in such a judgment. What if the Italian Communists renounced their "historic compromise," made common cause with Moscow, and other European countries followed suit? The result could well be a catastrophe for the United States. Morgenthau, as critic, does not have to make that awesome choice. But can a statesman dare to take such risks at a moment when he must base his decisions on conjecture rather than on facts? Here the scholar, it appears, owes the statesman a measure of empathy and tolerance.

There may be a psychological interpretation of Kissinger's paradoxical approach to communism. It may be found in his profound suspicion of the revolutionary as the greatest threat to a stable world order. In theory, it made little difference to him whether a revolutionary was "red" or "white." But in practice, he always feared the "red" revolutionary infinitely more. It is not that he approved of a Greek or Chilean junta, but he simply did not believe that it posed the kind of threat to international stability as that presented by an Allende, a Castro, or a Ho Chi Minh. These were the types of leaders, rather than a Brezhnev or a Mao Tse-tung, who were most likely to upset the global balance. They still retained that messianic revolutionary quality that had a vast potential for dislocation and contagion. In relation to the Soviet

Union and China, one could afford to take some chances without risk to equilibrium. But when it came to the smaller revolutionaries, Kissinger believed that the warmaker still made the most effective peacemaker.

The opening of China was probably Kissinger's most uncontaminated triumph in his tenure as a statesman. It was also his greatest diplomatic adventure. Once he perceived the depth of the rift between China and the Soviet Union, he became convinced that rapprochement with China might make the Soviet Union more receptive to a genuine détente. In short, China, in his view, had become the key to Russia. In addition to establishing this triangular linkage, Kissinger's secret trip to Peking in 1971 had made him the first messenger of reconciliation. Furthermore, to discover that beyond the Himalayas, there were men who elicited his admiration and respect only added to his elation. One of the few times that Kissinger happily admitted that he had been wrong was an occasion when he discussed his change of heart about Mao Tse-tung and Chou En-lai. In 1966, during the Cultural Revolution, he had perceived the Chinese leaders as the two most dangerous men on earth. Five years later, he had come to regard them as rational statesmen who pursued China's national interest in a manner not altogether inconsistent with the rules of international stability. But then it was Henry Kissinger who had once said about himself that while he had a first-rate mind, he had third-rate intuition about people. In the case of China, fortunately, the reality turned out to be more pleasant than the fantasy.

Perhaps the most haunting questions about Kissinger's foreign policy are of a philosophical nature. What is the role of ethics in Kissinger's world of stability and power? What is the relationship between personal and political morality? What room does Kissinger's pursuit of a stable world order leave for justice? What should be our criterion for judging his success—his intentions or the consequences of his actions? In short, what must concern us is the problem of statesmanship and moral choice.

As the German philosopher Immanuel Kant might have put it, Kissinger made the pursuit of a stable world order the categorical imperative of his foreign policy. If, in the process, the human element had to be sacrificed at times on the altar of stability or of a larger strategic vision, so be it, since without stability, peace could not be born at all and justice, too, would be extinguished. He felt that in a tragic world, a statesman was not able to choose between good and evil, but only among different forms of evil. Indeed, whatever decision he made, *some* evil consequences were bound to flow from it. All that a realistic statesman could do in such a world was to choose the lesser evil.[22]

Was Kissinger's conceptual approach to foreign policy closer to the crusading or the pragmatic mode? It appears that Kissinger was a pragmatist who exposed possibilities, but *only* those that fitted into his conceptual design. Thus, the initiative to open China and the pursuit of détente with the Soviet Union stemmed from Kissinger's personal conviction that his design for a stable global order was the best hope for world peace. The key to this design was balance. Whenever the conditions for balance *objectively* existed, as in the relations between Russia and America, China and America, and the Arab states and Israel, Kissinger pushed his opportunities with remarkable success. But he would also try to squeeze the facts into his conceptual design even when they did not fit. At such times, he came close to being a crusader. Thus, he believed that a fifty-fifty compromise between North and South Vietnam would achieve a balance that would be acceptable to all when, in fact, the North Vietnamese were determined to throw out *all* Americans. A mind more open to the unique historical experience of the Indochinese people might not have superimposed a nineteenth-century intellectual design on a twentieth-century Asian reality. Thus, when doctrine coincided with reality, Kissinger was successful. But when, as in Vietnam, the reality principle was abandoned, failure was the consequence.

Finally, there does remain the question: What was Nixon's share and what was Kissinger's between 1969 and August 1974? There is little doubt that, until Nixon became mired down in Watergate in 1973, he took a leading role in foreign policy. He and Kissinger reached similar conclusions on fundamentals, such as the openings to Russia and China, though for somewhat different reasons. Kissinger thought primarily in terms of global strategy while Nixon was more concerned with political support at home. For example, both men agreed that a rapprochement with China was overdue, but Kissinger saw the move primarily as leverage over the Soviet Union while Nixon already had an eye on the 1972 election. Watergate, of course, had a decisive impact on Kissinger's career. During the early years, Kissinger's relationship with Nixon had resembled that of Acheson to Truman. At the end, however, the secretary of state had completely eclipsed the president. *During the last year of Richard Nixon's presidency and the two years of Gerald Ford's, Henry Kissinger became virtually the sole architect of American foreign policy.*

Timing thus plays a crucial role in an individual's power over policy. Henry Kissinger, with all his brilliance, could not have opened China in 1950 or 1960; the country simply was not ready yet for reconciliation with the United States. In 1970, it *was* ready, and Kissinger grasped the opportunity. A crusading moralist, such as John Foster Dulles, might have let the moment pass. It took the right man at the right time to seize the day and change direction. Luck, too, may be crucial. Without Watergate, would Kissinger have enjoyed such a free hand? Would he have been allowed to bypass the bureaucracy so completely if Nixon had survived as president? Would he have become a solo performer on the stage of history? . . .

THE "MIGHT-HAVE-BEENS" OF HISTORY

[In concluding we must note that] a basic assumption has been made: It makes a difference *who* is there at a given moment. This is particularly true when high threat, surprise, and short decision time combine to form a crisis situation. Under such conditions, a leader's personality—his character and values—may even be decisive. Stated in another way, if the decision maker had been a different person, the course of events might have taken a different turn. This premise raises an important question: What about the "ifs" and "might-have-beens" of history?

It is true that we shall never know the road not taken. History does not reveal its alternatives. "Ifs" and "might-have-beens" are not scientifically provable. By definition, they must always remain hypothetical. They are based on analogies that, by their very nature, are imprecise comparisons. History never repeats itself exactly.

But it does not follow from these arguments that only nonhypothetical questions are meaningful. The attitude behind such an approach seems to be that what has been has been and we need to know no more. But if we seek understanding from history's vast tapestry, we must pay attention to the "might-have-beens." Some of them may be as relevant to the chances of the future as a recognized mistake is to the successful action that follows it. These "might-have-beens" are not just ghostly echoes, but, in many instances they were *objective possibilities* that were missed. They might have been missed for a variety of reasons but, most of the time, they were missed for want of a *free intelligence*, prepared to explore alternatives. Hence, it is our responsibility not to ignore these "ifs" and "might-have-beens" for they *could have been*.

In this context, our distinction between "crusading" and "pragmatic" personalities becomes most meaningful. The crusader usually blinds himself to policy alternatives while the pragmatic leader will tend to be open to a variety of options. *Hence, the most tragic "ifs" and "might-have-beens" of history tend to apply more to crusaders than to pragmatists.*

One cannot say, of course, with certitude that a greater openness to alternatives would definitely have prevented a specific alternative that did in fact occur. But one *can* say that, in the law of averages, a more open mind would probably have helped.

How can the foreign policy decision maker maximize his understanding? Clearly, he must guard against the mentality of the crusader: the tendency to see what he wants to see and to respond to situations not on the basis of evidence, but on the basis of his needs or wishes; the tendency to rationalize decisions and to surround himself with people who will tell him what he wants to hear rather than what he ought to know; the tendency to personalize an issue and link it to his ego; and above all, the tendency to confuse morality with moralism, to preach and judge rather than to listen and try to understand. In the postatomic era leaders must decontaminate their policies of shopworn slogans that only narrow possibilities. They must be open to new concepts and new facts, not offer up their people's bodies in defense of shadows. . . .

How often have we heard that a particular tragedy in world politics was "inevitable"? Crusaders are particularly fond of making such assertions. In truth, *no* event in the affairs of states has *ever* been inevitable. History does not make history. Men and women make foreign policy decisions. They make them in wisdom and in folly, but they make them nonetheless. Often, after a war or other national calamity, historians look back and speak of fate or inevitability. But such *historical determinism merely becomes a metaphor for the evasion of responsibility.* There is, after all, in our lives, a measure of free will and self-determination.

We must, of course, remember that a statesman's lot is often hard and cruel. When faced with a decision, he cannot postpone it until all the facts are in and historical perspective has illuminated the situation. He must decide and act in the present and cannot but act on incomplete knowledge. Once all the facts are in, foreign policy has become history. In that sense, the stateman's burden is a heavy one. . . .

The future would look rather bright if the great movers of American foreign policy were pragmatists rather than crusaders. But unfortunately, the moralist mentality is embedded very deeply in America and seems to come in cycles. It is not likely that we have seen the last of the crusaders.

All this is not to say that pragmatists never make mistakes. They often do. But as a general rule, such mistakes are more easily reversible than those of the crusaders. It is also true that a pragmatist may lack an overall blueprint or design for American foreign policy. But this does not mean that the pragmatic mind is unable to conceive a general philosophy. The crucial difference is this: the pragmatist always tests his design against the facts of his experience. If the design does not hold up against the facts, the design will have to change. The crusader, on the other hand, tends to sacrifice unwelcome facts on the altar of a fixed idea. If the facts do not conform to his design, it may be too bad for the facts. A pragmatist may thus be an idealist, but he will be a *practical* idealist. In contrast, the crusader's idealism all too frequently congeals into an obsession. . . .

NOTES

1. David Halberstam, *The Best and the Brightest* (New York: Random House, 1972), p. 424.
2. *New York Times,* 17 August 1964.
3. Ibid., 30 August 1964.
4. Ibid., 26 September 1964.
5. Ibid., 22 October 1964.
6. Ibid., 28 October 1964.
7. Halberstam, op. cit., p. 350.
8. *The Pentagon Papers,* as published by the *New York Times* (New York: Bantam, 1971), p. 249.
9. Ibid., p. 263.
10. Doris Kearns, *Lyndon Johnson and the American Dream* (New York: Signet, 1977), pp. 264–265.
11. Halberstam, op. cit., p. 414.
12. Anthony Austin, *The President's War* (Philadelphia: Lippincott, 1971), *passim.*
13. Ibid.

14. Ibid.
15. Halberstam, op. cit., p. 414.
16. U.S. Foreign Relations Committee, Senate, *Vietnam: Policy and Prospects 1970.* Hearings 90th Congress, 2nd session, 1970.
17. Quoted in Halberstam, op. cit., p. 419.
18. Kearns, op. cit., p. 296.
19. Ibid., p. 263.
20. George W. Ball, *Diplomacy for a Crowded World: An American Foreign Policy* (Boston: Atlantic-Little, Brown, 1976), *passim.*
21. Hans J. Morgenthau, "The Kissinger Legacy," *Encounter,* November 1974, p. 57.
22. For a more detailed discussion of these dilemmas, see the author's *Henry Kissinger: The Anguish of Power* (New York: Norton, 1976), *passim.*

28

PRESIDENTIAL MANAGEMENT STYLES AND MODELS

ALEXANDER L. GEORGE

Every new president faces the task of deciding how to structure and manage high-level foreign-policymaking in his administration. The task is a formidable one since responsibility for different aspects of national security and foreign policy is distributed over a number of departments and agencies. Relevant information, competence, and influence over policy is widely dispersed within the executive branch as well as outside of it. This imposes on the president and his assistants the task of mobilizing available information, expertise, and analytical resources for effective policymaking. In addition, the president and his closest associates have the responsibility for providing policy initiative and coherence throughout the executive branch.

To discharge these tasks effectively requires internal coordination within the government. Those parts of the executive branch that have some responsibility for and/or contribution to make to a particular policy problem must be encouraged to interact with each other in appropriate ways. Left to themselves, these various agencies, of course, would interact voluntarily and achieve some measure of "lateral coordination" in formulating policy. But it is essential for the president (and each department or agency head) to ensure lateral coordination by institution of various procedures and mechanisms, such as ad hoc or standing interdepartmental committees, policy conferences, liaison arrangements, a system of clearances for policy or position papers, etc.

However important lateral coordination is, it cannot be counted upon to produce the caliber of policy analysis, the level of consensus, and the

Revised and adapted from *Presidential Decisionmaking in Foreign Policy: The Effective Use of Information and Advice* (Boulder, Colorado: Westview Press, 1980), pp. 145–168. Alexander L. George is Graham H. Stuart Professor of International Relations at Stanford University. He served as president of the International Studies Association in 1973–1974. Among his many articles and books are *Woodrow Wilson and Colonel House: A Personality Study* (with Juliette L. George); *Deterrence in American Foreign Policy* (with Richard Smoke), which won the Bancroft Prize in 1975; *Force and Statecraft: Diplomatic Problems of Our Time* (with Gordon Craig), and *Managing U.S.-Soviet Rivalry: Problems of Crisis Prevention.*

procedures for implementation required for an effective and coherent foreign policy.

Moreover, lateral coordination may be weakened and distorted by patterns of organizational behavior and the phenomenon of "bureaucratic politics" that create impediments to and malfunctions of the policymaking process. Accordingly, all presidents have found it necessary to impose mechanisms for control and coordination of policy analysis and implementation from above—either from the White House itself or from the NSC—or have fixed responsibility for achieving control and coordination with the State Department; or have adopted a combination of these mechanisms.

The traditional practice for seeking improvement in the performance of the foreign-policymaking system was to undertake *structural reorganization* of the agencies and the mechanisms for achieving their coordination and cooperation. Periodically—indeed, at least once in each presidential administration—the foreign-policymaking system was reorganized.[1] But the results of reorganizations have been so disappointing that the "organizational tinkering" approach has fallen into general disrepute. Instead, greater attention is being given to the *design and management of the processes* of policymaking.

Coupled with this shift in focus from organizational structure to process is a new awareness among specialists in organization and public administration that their past efforts to identify a single standardized model of policymaking that would be optimal for all presidents were misguided. Instead, it is now recognized that each president is likely to define his role in foreign-policymaking somewhat differently and to approach it with a different decisionmaking and management style. Hence, too, he will have a different notion as to the kind of policymaking system that he wishes to create around him, feels comfortable with, and can utilize. In brief, the present emphasis is on designing organizational structures to fit the operating styles of their key individuals rather than attempting to persuade each new top executive to accept and adapt to a standardized organizational model that is considered to be theoretically the best.

As this implies, the first and foremost task that a new president faces is to learn to define his own role in the policymaking system; only then can he structure and manage the roles and relationships within the policymaking system of his secretary of state, the special assistant for national security affairs, the secretary of defense, and other cabinet and agency heads with responsibilities for the formulation and implementation of foreign policy.

The president's basic choice is whether to give his secretary of state the primary role in the foreign-policymaking system or to centralize and manage that system from the White House itself. Still another model is that of a relatively decentralized system that is coordinated from the White House for the president by his special assistant for national security affairs.

A new president may receive advice on these matters from specialists in organization or in foreign policy, but in the last analysis his choices in these matters will be shaped by preferences of his own that stem from previous experience (if any) in executive roles and the extent to which he regards himself as knowledgeable and competent in foreign policy and national security matters. Finally, as all president-watchers have emphasized, the incumbent's personality will shape the formal structure of the policymaking system that he creates around himself and, even more, it will influence the ways in which he encourages and permits that formal structure to operate in practice. As a result, each president is likely to develop a policymaking system and a management style that contain distinctive and idiosyncratic elements.

Detailed comparison of past presidents from this standpoint suggests that a variety of personality characteristics are important, of which three can be briefly noted.[2] The first of these personality dimensions is *"cognitive style."* Cognitive psychologists have found it useful to view the human mind as a complex system for information processing. Every individual develops ways of storing, retrieving, evaluating, and using information. At the same time the individual develops a set of beliefs about the environment, about the attributes of other actors, and about various presumed causal relationships that help the person to explain and predict, as best he can (correctly or incorrectly), events of interest to him. Beliefs of this kind structure, order, and simplify the individual's world; they serve as models of "reality." Such mental constructs play an important role in the individual's perception of what is occurring in his environment, in the acquisition and interpretation of new information, and in the formulation and evaluation of responses to new situations.

At the same time, individuals differ in their approaches to processing and evaluating information, and this is generally what is meant by "cognitive style." There is as yet no standardized approach to characterizing the dimensions of cognitive style. For present purposes, the term is used to refer to the way in which an executive such as the president defines his informational needs for purposes of making decisions. "Cognitive style" also refers to his preferred ways of acquiring information from those around him and making use of that information, and to his preferences regarding advisers and ways of using them in making his decisions.

Defined in these terms, as we shall note, an individual's cognitive style plays an important role in his preference for one management model as against others. Cognitive styles do vary among presidents, and it simply will not work to try to impose on a new president a policymaking system or a management model that is uncongenial to his cognitive style.[3]

A second personality dimension that influences a president's choice of a policymaking system is *his sense of efficacy and competence* as it relates to management and decisionmaking tasks. In other words, the types of skills that he possesses and the types of tasks that he feels particularly adept at doing and those that he feels poorly equipped to do will influence the way in which he defines his executive role.

A third personality dimension that will influence the president's selection of a policymaking model is his general *orientation toward political conflict* and, related to this, toward interpersonal conflict over policy among his advisers. Individuals occupying the White House have varied on this personality dimension, too. Thus, we find that some chief executives have viewed politics as a necessary, useful, and perhaps even enjoyable game while other presidents have regarded it as a dirty business that must be discouraged or at least ignored. The personal attitude toward conflict that a president brings into office is likely to determine his orientation to the phenomena of "cabinet politics" and "bureaucratic politics" within his administration as well as to the larger, often interlinked, game of politics surrounding the executive branch. Individuals with a pronounced distaste for "dirty politics" and for being exposed to face-to-face disagreements among advisers are likely to favor policymaking systems that attempt to curb these phenomena or at least shield them from direct exposure. They also are likely to prefer staff and advisory systems in which teamwork or formal analytical procedures are emphasized in lieu of partisan advocacy and debate.

Cognitive style, sense of efficacy, and orientation toward conflict (and, of course, the nature of any prior experience in executive roles and the level of personal competence and interest in foreign policy and national security affairs)—all these combine to determine how a new president will structure the policymaking system around him and how he will define his own role and that of others in it.

Three management models have been identified that characterize at least in general terms the approaches displayed by different presidents in recent times.[4] These are the "formalistic," "competitive," and "collegial" models. The formalistic model is characterized by an orderly policymaking structure, one that provides well-defined procedures, hierarchical lines of communication, and a structured staff system. While the formalistic model seeks to benefit from the diverse views and judgments of participants in policymaking, it also discourages open conflict and bargaining among them.

The competitive model, in contrast, places a premium on encouraging a more open and uninhibited expression of diverse opinions, analysis, and advice. To this end the competitive model not only tolerates but may actually encourage organizational ambiguity, overlapping jurisdictions, and multiple channels of communication to and from the president.

The collegial model, in turn, attempts to achieve the essential advantages of each of the other two while avoiding their pitfalls. To this end, the president attempts to create a team of staff members and advisers who will work together to identify, analyze, and solve policy problems in ways that will incorporate and synthesize as much as possible divergent points of view. The collegial model attempts to benefit from diversity and competition within the policymaking system, but it also attempts to avoid narrow parochialism by encouraging cabinet officers and advisers to identify at least partly with the presidential perspective. And by encouraging collegial participation in group problem-solving efforts, this approach attempts to avoid the worst excesses of infighting, bargaining, and compromise associated with the competitive model.

Truman, Eisenhower, and Nixon employed one or another variant of the formalistic approach. Franklin D. Roosevelt employed the competitive model, and John F. Kennedy the collegial one. As for Lyndon B. Johnson, he began by trying to emulate Franklin Roosevelt's style and gradually moved toward a formalistic approach but one that exhibited idiosyncratic features.

Let us begin with Franklin D. Roosevelt, whose unusual policymaking system is the prototype for the competitive management model. A dominant feature of FDR's personality was his strong sense of political efficacy. He felt entirely at home in the presidency, acting in the belief that there was close to a perfect fit between his competence and skills and some of the most demanding role requirements of the office. Then, too, FDR viewed politics and the games that go with it as a useful and enjoyable game and not, as others before him (for example, Taft and Hoover) as an unsavory, distasteful business to be discouraged or avoided. FDR not only felt comfortable in the presence of conflict and disagreement around him; he saw that, properly managed, it could serve his informational and political needs. Instead of trying, as his predecessor had, to take the politics out of the policymaking process, Roosevelt deliberately exacerbated the competitive and conflicting aspects of cabinet politics and bureaucratic politics. He sought to increase both structural and functional ambiguities within the executive branch in order to better preside over it. For Roosevelt, exposure to conflict among advisers and cabinet heads did not stir up anxiety or depression; nor did he perceive it as threatening in a personal or political sense. Not only did he live comfortably with the political conflict and, at times, near-chaos around him, he manipulated the structure of relationships among subordinates in order to control and profit from their competition. What is noteworthy is that Roosevelt did not attempt to create a formal, centralized model of the policymaking process (as advocated, for example, in later Hoover Commission proposals for reorganization of governmental agencies); rather, he deliberately created "fuzzy lines of responsibility, no clear chains of command, overlapping jurisdictions" in order to promote " 'stimulating' interdepartmental conflict which could and did eventually land in his own lap."[5]

At the risk of simplification, it is possible to delineate some features of the distinctive communication network or patterns associated with FDR's competitive model[6] (see Figure 1).

The following are characteristic features of the competitive model (FDR): (1) the president deliberately encourages competition and conflict among advisers and cabinet heads by giving them overlapping assignments and ambiguous, conflicting jurisdictions in given policy areas; (2) there is relatively little communication or collaboration among advisers; (3) the president reaches down on occasion to communicate directly with subordinates of cabinet heads to get independent advice and information; (4) relevant

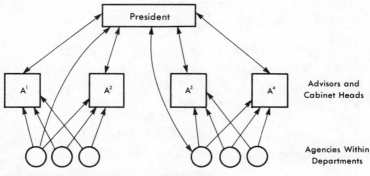

FIGURE 1 The Competitive Model (FDR)

information on important policy problems is forced up through the network to the president himself; competing advisers are forced to bring important policy problems to the president for resolution and decision; but (5) the president avoids the risk of becoming overloaded or involved by operating this system selectively; on occasions (not depicted on the chart), he encourages and insists that subordinate officials settle things themselves and refuses to become identified with their policies or pet projects.

Harry Truman adopted a different strategy for coping with the complex morass that governmental structure had become as a result of Roosevelt's style and administrative practices and the wartime expansion of agencies. Initially, Truman tried to tidy up the mess by clarifying and dividing up the jurisdictions. He also established the NSC in 1947 as a vehicle for providing orderly, balanced participation in foreign-policymaking deliberations. Truman tried to weaken the game of bureaucratic politics by strengthening each department head's control over his particular domain and by delegating presidential responsibility to him. New in the office, Truman took special pride in his ability to delegate responsibility and to back up those he trusted. He learned through experience, however, that to delegate too much or to delegate responsibility without providing clear guidance was to jeopardize the performance of his own responsibilities.

When faced with larger policy issues that required the participation of heads of several departments, Truman attempted to deal with them by playing the role of chairman of the board, hearing sundry expert opinions on each aspect of the problem, then making a synthesis of them and announcing the decision. Truman not only accepted the responsibility of making difficult decisions, he liked doing so for it enabled him to satisfy himself— and, he hoped, others—that he had the personal qualities needed in the presidency. His sense of efficacy expressed itself in a willingness to make difficult decisions without experiencing undue stress. A modest man in many ways, Truman adjusted to the awesome responsibilities of the presidency suddenly thrust upon him by respecting the office and determining to become a good role player. By honoring the office and doing credit to it,

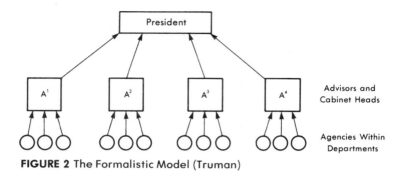

FIGURE 2 The Formalistic Model (Truman)

he would do credit to himself. Included in this role conception was Truman's desire to put aside personal and political considerations as much as possible in the search for quality decisions that were in the national interest. He was willing to accept the political costs both to himself and to his party entailed in making controversial decisions, such as his policy of disengaging the United States from the Chinese Nationalists in 1949, his refusal to escalate the Korean War after the Chinese Communist intervention, his firing of General MacArthur, and his refusal to dismiss his loyal secretary of state, Dean Acheson, when he came under continuing attack.

Truman's variant of the formalistic model may be depicted, again in simplified terms, as in Figure 2.

The following are characteristic features of the formalistic model (Truman): (1) specialized information and advice flows to the president from each of his cabinet heads and advisers; (2) the president tends to define the role of each cabinet head as a functional expert on some aspect of national security or foreign policy; each official briefs the president authoritatively on that aspect of a policy problem for which he has jurisdiction; (3) each adviser receives information and advice from his subordinate units; (4) the president does not encourage his advisers to communicate with each other or to engage in joint efforts at policy analysis and problem solving; (5) the president sticks to channels and seldom reaches down to bypass a cabinet head to get independent information or advice from one of his subordinates; and (6) the president takes responsibility for intellectual synthesis of specialized inputs on a policy problem received from his advisers.

Dwight D. Eisenhower avoided personal involvement as much as possible in the bureaucratic politics aspects of policymaking within the executive branch and in less savory aspects of politics generally. At the same time, however, Eisenhower recognized that conflict and politics are inevitable and adapted to them by defining his own role as that of someone who could stand "above politics," moderate conflict, and promote unity. In doing so, Eisenhower expressed his special sense of efficacy that led him (and others) to believe that he could make a distinctive and unique contribution by seeming to remain "above politics" and by emphasizing the shared values and virtues that should guide governmental affairs. This did not prevent Eisenhower, however, from engaging in political maneuvers of his own when he perceived that his interest required it.[7]

Eisenhower did not attempt (as Nixon was to later) to depoliticize and rationalize the formal policymaking process completely. Rather, Eisenhower's variant of the formalistic model encompassed advocacy and disagreement at lower levels of the policymaking system, even though he wanted subordinates eventually to achieve agreement, if possible, on recommendations for his consideration. Moreover, formal meetings of the large NSC were often preceded by less formal "warm-up" sessions with a smaller group of advisers that provided opportunities for genuine policy debate. The conventional depiction of Eisenhower's NSC system as an unimaginative, bureaucratic body laden with the preparation and presentation of cautiously formulated positions, therefore, is not justified.[8]

What these observations about Eisenhower's policy system reveal is that a formalistic management model need not be highly bureaucratized. Examples of the formalistic management model, which always seem bureaucratized on the surface, need to be examined much more closely in order to determine how they actually function. As is well known, policymaking in complex organizations usually proceeds on *two* tracks: the formal, visible, official track and the informal, less visible track. Even the most formalistic of policymaking systems is accompanied by some kind of informal track that is utilized by the participants—including sometimes the president himself—in an attempt to "work with" or "work around" the formal procedures.

In particular, a president's use of surrogates as "chiefs of staff" in a formalistic management model needs close examination to determine to what extent he actually restricts his own involvement in policymaking and remains unaware or disinterested in the important preliminaries of information processing. Thus, in Eisenhower's case, recent archival research reveals that two of his "chiefs of staff"—Governor Sherman Adams and Secretary of State John Foster Dulles—were by no means as powerful as has been thought. "Adams was not the all powerful domestic policy gate-guard he is said to have been. He did not keep important information from Eisenhower's attention, nor did he make important decisions solo. . . . In the case of Dulles . . . not even the most obsequious Lyndon Johnson courtier could have been more assiduous about testing the waters. . . . Dulles was in touch with the president daily, and was consistently responsive to Eisenhower's directives."[9]

With these important caveats in mind, we can proceed to examine how the visible structure of his formalistic model differed from Truman's. This can be seen by comparing the chart for Truman's system with that presented here of Eisenhower's (see Figure 3).

The following are characteristic features of the formalistic model (Eisenhower): it is similar to Truman's variant of the formalistic model with

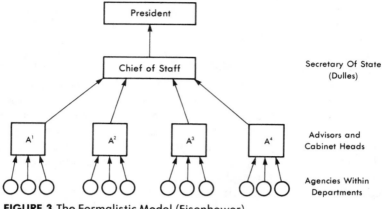

FIGURE 3 The Formalistic Model (Eisenhower)

two important exceptions: (1) a "chief of staff" position is created to be utilized, when the president wishes, as a buffer between himself and cabinet heads and to arrange for preparation of formal recommendations to the president (Sherman Adams performed this role for Eisenhower on domestic policy matters; in practice, Secretary of State John Foster Dulles came to assume a similar, though informal, role for Eisenhower in foreign policy, though not in defense matters); and (2) again, unlike Truman's version of the formalistic model, in this one the president attempts to protect himself from being overloaded by urging advisers and cabinet heads to analyze problems and resolve policy differences wherever possible at lower levels.

Richard Nixon, too, strongly favored a formalistic model. As a number of observers have noted, several of Nixon's well-defined personality characteristics shaped his management style and approach to decisionmaking. During his early years, Nixon had developed a cognitive style that enabled him to cope with deeply rooted personal insecurities by adopting an extremely conscientious approach to decisionmaking. As described so well in his book, *Six Crises*, the whole business of acquiring information, weighing alternatives, and deciding among them was experienced by him as extremely stressful, requiring great self-control, hard work, and reliance upon himself. Dealing with difficult situations posed the necessity but also offered an opportunity for Nixon to prove himself over and over again. He experienced his greatest sense of self and of his efficacy when he had to confront and master difficult situations in which a great deal was at stake.[10]

Nixon's pronounced sense of aloneness and privacy, his thin-skinned sensitivity and vulnerability were not conducive to developing the kind of interpersonal relationships associated with a collegial model of management. Rather, as Richard T. Johnson notes, "Nixon, the private man with a preference for working alone, wanted machinery to staff out the options but provide plenty of time for reflection. . . ." Similarly, "with his penchant for order," Nixon inevitably "favored men who offered order," who acceded to his demand for loyalty and shared his sense of banding together to help him cope with a hostile environment.[11]

Nixon's preference for a highly formalistic system was reinforced by other personality characteristics. He was an extreme "conflict avoider"; somewhat paradoxically, although quite at home with political conflict in the broader public arena, Nixon had a pronounced distaste for being exposed to it face-to-face. Early in his administration, Nixon tried a version of multiple advocacy in which leading advisers would debate issues in his presence. But he quickly abandoned the experiment and turned to structuring his staff to avoid overt manifestations of disagreement and to avoid being personally drawn into the squabbles of his staff,[12] hence, Nixon's need for a few staff aides immediately around him who were to serve as buffers and enable him to distance himself from the wear and tear of policymaking.

It is interesting that Eisenhower's "chief of staff" concept was carried much farther in Nixon's variant of the formalistic model. The foreign-policymaking system that Kissinger, the special assistant for national security affairs, developed during the first year of Nixon's administration is generally regarded as by far the most centralized and highly structured model yet employed by any president.[13] Nixon was determined even more than Eisenhower had been to abolish bureaucratic and cabinet politics as completely as possible; but, more so than Eisenhower, Nixon also wanted to enhance and protect his personal control over high policy. To this end, a novel system of six special committees was set up operating out of the NSC, each of which was chaired by Kissinger. These included the Vietnam Special Studies Group, the Washington Special Actions Group (to deal with international crises), the Defense Programs Review Committee, the Verification Panel (to deal with strategic arms talks), the 40 Committee (to deal with covert actions), and the Senior Review Group (which dealt with all other types of policy issues).

Reporting to the Senior Review Group were six lower-level interdepartmental groups that were set up on a regional basis (Middle East, Far East, Latin America, Africa, Europe, and Political-Military Affairs), each of which was headed by an assistant secretary of state. In addition, Kissinger could set up ad hoc working groups composed of specialists from various agencies and run by his own top staff aides.

Thus, not only did Kissinger's committee structure reach down into the departments and agencies, absorbing key personnel into various committees controlled by Kissinger or his staff aides, but other committees created on an interdepartmental basis, though chaired by assistant secretaries of state, were given their assignments by Kissinger and reported to the Senior Review Group chaired by Kissinger. As a result, a novel, unconventional policymaking structure was created and superimposed upon the departments and largely superseded the traditional hierarchical policymaking system. Striking differences with Eisenhower's formalistic model can be noted (see Figure 4).

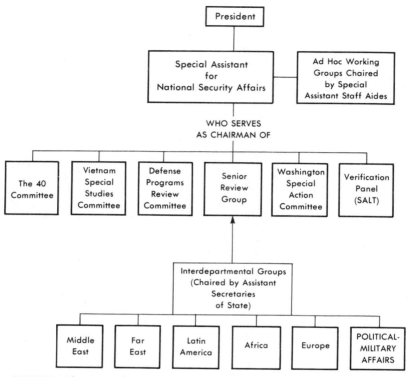

FIGURE 4 The Formalistic Model (Nixon)

John F. Kennedy felt much more at ease with the conflictual aspects of politics and policymaking than his predecessor Dwight Eisenhower; his sense of efficacy included confidence in his ability to manage and shape the interpersonal relations of those around him in a constructive fashion, and his cognitive style led him to participate much more actively and directly in the policymaking process than Eisenhower had or Nixon would later on. These personality characteristics contributed to forging a collegial style of policymaking based on teamwork and shared responsibility among talented advisers. Kennedy recognized the value of diversity and give-and-take among advisers, and he encouraged it. But Kennedy stopped well short of the extreme measures for stimulating competition that Roosevelt had employed. Rather than risk introducing disorder and strife into the policy-making system, Kennedy used other strategies for keeping himself informed, properly advised, and "on top." He did not find personally conge-nial the highly formal procedures, the large meetings, and the relatively aloof presidential role characteristic of Eisenhower's system. Particularly after the failure of the Bay of Pigs invasion of Cuba, Kennedy employed a variety of devices for counteracting the narrowness of perspective of leading members of individual departments and agencies and for protecting himself

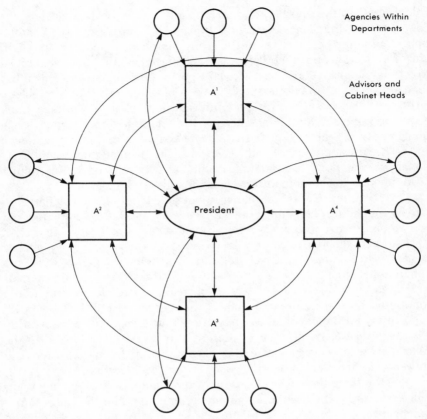

FIGURE 5 The Collegial Model (JFK)

from the risks of bureaucratic politics. Noteworthy is Kennedy's effort to restructure the roles and broaden the perspectives of top department and agency officials and to introduce a new set of norms to guide their participation in policymaking.

The kind of teamwork and group approach to problem solving that Kennedy strove to create—and achieved with notable success in the Cuban missile crisis (1962) at least—is often referred to as the "collegial" model to distinguish it both from the more competitive and more formal system of his predecessors. The sharp contrasts between Kennedy's collegial system and the competitive and formalistic models emerge by comparing Figure 5 with Figures 1–4.

The following are characteristic features of the collegial model (JFK): (1) president is at the center of a wheel with spokes connecting to individual advisers and cabinet heads; (2) advisers form a "collegial team" and engage in group problem-solving; (3) information flows into the collegial team from various points lower in the bureaucracy; (4) advisers do not perform as individual filters to the president; rather, the group of advisers functions as a "debate team" that considers information and policy options from the multiple, conflicting perspectives of the group members in an effort to obtain cross-fertilization and creative problem solving; (5) advisers are encouraged to act as generalists, concerned with all aspects of the policy problem, rather than as experts or functional specialists on only part of the policy problem; (6) discussion procedures are kept informal enough to encourage frank expression of views and judgments and to avoid impediments to information processing generated by status and power differences among members; and (7) the president occasionally gives overlapping assignments and occasionally reaches down to communicate directly with subordinates of cabinet heads in order to get more information and independent advice.

As for Jimmy Carter, his management style is perhaps aptly characterized as embracing elements of both the collegial and bureaucratic models. As one observer reported, Carter's national security policymaking system [was] "an amalgamation selectively drawn from the experiences of his predecessors."[14] As in Kennedy's case, Carter initially rejected a "chief of staff" system for organizing his work and contacts with others. (Hamilton Jordan was appointed chief of staff in mid-1979.) Instead, Carter clearly preferred a communications structure in which he was at the center of the wheel with opportunity for direct contact with a number of officials and advisers. Further, again like Kennedy, Carter preferred to be actively involved in the policymaking process and at earlier stages before the system produced options or a single recommended policy for his consideration.

At the same time, Carter differed from Kennedy in preferring a formally structured NSC system and retained elements of the "formal options" system developed by Kissinger for Nixon. Carter restored the prestige of the NSC staff following the brief eclipse that occurred during the Ford years (1974–1977) when Kissinger was secretary of state, and he relied on its studies for help in making decisions.[15] Carter's preference for underpinning the collegial features of his management model with formalistic structure and procedures was not surprising given his training and experience as an engineer. Carter brought with him to the White House a cognitive style and sense of personal efficacy that gave him confidence in the possibility of mastering difficult problems and of finding comprehensive "solutions" for them.[16] In his somewhat technocratic approach to policymaking, experts and orderly study procedures played an essential role, and so the features of the collegial model that Carter valued had necessarily to be blended somehow with features of a formalistic model.

In this mixed system, policymaking was not as highly centralized as in the Nixon administration. Carter not only allowed relatively liberal access to the Oval Office, he also had a more decentralized advisory system than did Nixon. This reflected not only his personality and management style, but also the lessons that he and others drew from the experience of his predecessors in that office. Carter's main concern was to set up his foreign-policy machinery in a way that would avoid the extreme centralization of power that Kissinger, as special assistant for national security affairs, had acquired during Nixon's first term and that led him to replace for all practical purposes the secretary of state. In Carter's administration, the special assistant (Brzezinski) was not as powerful as Kissinger. Carter wanted his secretary of state, Cyrus Vance, to be his leading foreign-policy adviser and the State Department to provide the major backup in policy preparation. In line with this concept, the number of committees in the NSC staff was reduced over what they had been in Nixon's administration and, moreover, Brzezinski did not chair all of the NSC committees as Kissinger had. Instead of allowing the special assistant to become the dominant actor in the system and a virtual "chief of staff," Carter tended to rely on collegiality among his principal national security advisers—the secretary of state, the secretary of defense, the special assistant, the vice-president—to achieve the necessary interaction and coordination. Accordingly, the NSC organization under Carter was more modest than Nixon's both in centrality, structure, and operations.[17]

Although Carter succeeded in avoiding a highly centralized, "closed" system of foreign-policymaking, it must also be said that he was much less successful in avoiding the potential difficulties of the mixed formalistic-collegial model that he preferred. A number of weaknesses became evident in the Carter system that seriously affected its performance. The collegial model requires close contact and continuing interaction between the president, his secretary of state, and the assistant for national security affairs. This they achieved, at least for a time, but their respective roles remained highly fluid and not well defined. There was, for example, no clear arrangement for policy specialization and division of labor among these three principals. (In contrast, the secretary of defense's role appears to have been well enough understood by all concerned so that his participation on policymaking was relatively free of serious ambiguities or conflicts with others.) In the absence of role definition and specialization, all three—the president, his secretary of state, and the national security assistant—can and do interest themselves in any important policy problem. A shared interest in all major policy problems is to be expected in a collegial system, but some understandings must also be developed to regulate initiative, consultation, the articulation of disagreements, and the formulation of collective judgment. Carter evidently counted on the fact that the three men knew and respected each other prior to his election to the presidency to make his collegial approach work. And, to be sure, on the surface it genuinely seemed to be the case that the three men got along well. More than cordiality, however, is needed for effective policymaking in a collegial system.

Collegiality entails certain risks, and its preservation may exact a price. Some evidence indicates that the preservation of cordiality was accompanied, at least in the first part of Carter's administration, with a perhaps partly unconscious tendency to subordinate disagreements over policy among the three men that should have been articulated, confronted, and dealt with in a timely fashion. One of the problems was Carter himself. He had a habit of suddenly taking the initiative or intervening in an important foreign-policy matter, as in the case of his human rights initiative, leaving Vance and Brzezinski with the embarrassing and difficult task of making the best of it or of trying to modify the policy.

Another weakness of Carter's system quickly developed and proved difficult to cope with. Foreign policy became badly fragmented in the first year of Carter's administration. It was characterized by (1) overactivism— the floating of many specific policy initiatives within a relatively short period of time; (2) a tendency to initiate attractive, desirable policies without sufficient attention to their feasibility; (3) poor conceptualization of overall foreign policy, and, related to this, a failure to recognize that individual policies conflicted with each other; (4) a poor sense of strategy and tactics; (5) a badly designed and managed policymaking system.[18]

These flaws cannot be attributed merely or even primarily to Carter's inexperience in foreign policy. After all, his administration included various high-level officials who were experts on foreign policy. Part of the explanation had to do with important aspects of his personality, which are attractive in and of themselves. Carter was a man of high moral principles, as exemplified by his sincere commitment to human rights. He wanted to imbue American foreign policy with renewed moral purpose; he was an activist in this respect, and therefore took genuine pleasure that his administration could launch so many worthwhile policy initiatives so quickly. He could see no harm in pushing ahead simultaneously with so many good initiatives.

What was needed to safeguard against an overloading of the foreign-policy agenda and the fragmentation of foreign policy was a strong policy planning and coordinating mechanism, one that would alert Carter to this problem and assist him in dealing with difficult trade-offs among conflicting policy initiatives by establishing priorities, and generally to better integrate the various strands of overall foreign policy. Such a policy planning and coordinating mechanism, however, was lacking. The need to develop it somehow fell between the two stools of Carter's mixed collegial-formalistic model. Thus, neither the formalistic nor the collegial components of Carter's system provided the necessary planning-coordinating mechanism and procedures. When criticism of Carter's foreign policy mounted, persons apparently close to Vance and Brzezinski let it be known, however discretely, that it wasn't always easy to curb Carter's tendency to take over important matters or to have an adequate opportunity to advise Carter beforehand. Whether determined efforts to do so were made by his principal advisers is not clear from the available record.

Another problem was that Vance and Brzezinski did have important disagreements over policy, particularly on matters having to do with assessment of Soviet intentions and the best strategy and tactics for dealing with the Soviet Union. The effort to preserve collegiality in the first eighteen months of the administration may have led both men to paper over their disagreements and to avoid the difficult but necessary task of coming to grips with these fundamental policy questions. But these matters could not be avoided indefinitely, and after jockeying and competing with each other to influence Carter's position on these issues, first one way and then the other, the controversy between Vance and Brzezinski spilled out into the open—with Brzezinski aggressively speaking out to undermine the positions taken by the secretary of state. Among other things, Brzezinski wanted the administration to exploit the Sino-Soviet conflict, "play the China card," in order to exert pressure on the Soviets. Vance opposed this effectively for some time. But Brzezinski continued his efforts and was successful in obtaining the president's approval for his trip to China. The national security assistant's outspoken disagreements with the secretary of state became so damaging that Vance finally went to the president in the summer of 1978 and prevailed upon him to restrain Brzezinski from airing his disagreements publicly. Ultimately, of course, Vance left the administration in 1980 because of his disagreement with Carter's decision, supported by Brzezinski, to attempt a military rescue of American diplomatic personnel held hostage in Iran.

But the roots of the problem lie deeper. It has to do with the question whether an expert on foreign policy, someone who wants to influence foreign policy, should be put into the position of assistant for national security affairs. The most important responsibility of the assistant ever since the NSC was created in 1947 has been to serve as the custodian-manager of the top-level policymaking process—i.e., to organize in an orderly, systematic way the flow of studies, papers—in other words, an administrator of the procedures that are needed to ensure that the president and his top foreign-policy advisers get high-quality information and analysis for a broad enough range of policy options before decisions are made, and then to communicate these policy decisions down the line and monitor their implementation. Until Kennedy became president, the person who served as assistant for national security affairs was not an adviser on policy; rather, he was supposed to confine himself exclusively to being a neutral, efficient, sophisticated manager of the process and the flow of work. Since then, the assistant, while retaining the role of custodian-manager of the process, has gradually acquired important new roles—that of a major policy adviser himself, that of public spokesman for and defender of the administration's foreign policy, and that of an operator actively engaged in the conduct of diplomacy.

This development came to a head with Kissinger, who as Nixon's national security assistant, acquired and tried to perform *all* of these roles. The result was not only that he was overloaded, but also that he experienced serious conflict among these various roles. The most important role conflict was that Kissinger's roles as the major policy adviser and operator undermined his incentive to serve as the *neutral* custodian-manager of the process. Instead, being only human and quite self-confident regarding his own judgment in foreign policy, Kissinger succumbed to the temptation of using his control of the many NSC committees and over the policymaking process in order to enhance his influence with Nixon at the expense of others in the system who may have had different views. It was predictable that Brzezinski would experience similar temptations.[19]

There were other weaknesses in the management of Carter's foreign-policy system. Under Brzezinski, and given the character of his staff, the NSC did not function effectively to help coordinate the various strands of foreign policy and to help Carter with his difficult task of managing the various contradictions and trade-offs between different foreign-policy objectives. Neither Brzezinski himself nor his deputy, David Aaron, earned a reputation in their positions for being good administrators or for defining their roles as high-level staff rather than as activists in making policy. In fact, both appear to have been much more interested in influencing policy rather than in managing the policymaking process in a neutral, efficient manner. Moreover, many of the people Brzezinski brought into the NSC staff to work with him were also eager to influence policy as best they could from the vantage point of the White House.

As a result, the fragmentation of foreign policy at the conceptual level, to which many critics called attention, was reinforced by the failure to develop an effective central coordinating mechanism for the organization and management of the policymaking process. Beginning in the second year of his administration, Carter turned increasingly to the creation of special task forces for each major policy issue in order to centralize authority in the White House and to improve coordination of agency and department officials on behalf of presidential policy. Following the successful use of ad hoc task forces to direct efforts to secure ratification of the Panama Canal Treaty and to deal with other major issues, in late 1978 Carter established an executive committee headed by Vice President Mondale to be responsible for dealing with the president's agenda and priorities. This committee endorsed a plan for forming task forces for all major presidential issues for 1979. Task forces were established on a dozen issues of high priority, including domestic as well as foreign-policy issues.[20]

• • •

Each of these three management models tends to have certain advantages and to incur certain risks. These are discussed in some detail by Richard T. Johnson with respect to each of the six presidents he studied (see Table 1).[21]

In addition, Johnson makes a number of useful suggestions for reducing the shortcomings and risks of each of these three management models:

> For example, a President who adopts the formalistic approach might choose [as Eisenhower did on occasion] to establish more fluid

TABLE 1
THREE MANAGEMENT METHODS

Formalistic Approach

BENEFITS	COSTS
Orderly decision process enforces more thorough analysis.	The hierarchy which screens information may also distort it. Tendency of the screening process to wash out or distort political pressures and public sentiments.
Conserves the decisionmaker's time and attention for the big decision.	
Emphasizes the optimal.	
	Tendency to respond slowly or inappropriately in crisis.

Competitive Approach

Places the decisionmaker in the mainstream of the information network.	Places large demands on decisionmaker's time and attention.
Tends to generate solutions that are politically feasible and bureaucratically doable.	Exposes decisionmaker to partial or biased information. Decision process may overly sacrifice optimality for doability.
Generates creative ideas, partially as a result of the "stimulus" of competition, but also because this unstructured kind of information network is more open to ideas from the outside.	Tendency to aggravate staff competition with the risk that aides may pursue their own interests at the expense of the decisionmaker.
	Wear and tear on aides fosters attrition and high turnover.

Collegial Approach

Seeks to achieve both optimality and doability.	Places substantial demands on the decisionmaker's time and attention.
Involves the decisionmaker in the information network but somewhat eases the demands upon him by stressing teamwork over competition.	Requires unusual interpersonal skill in dealing with subordinates, mediating differences, and maintaining teamwork among colleagues.
	Risk that "teamwork" will degenerate into a closed system of mutual support.

Source: Richard T. Johnson, *Managing the White House* (New York: Harper and Row, 1974). Reproduced with minor changes and additions in *The Stanford Business School Alumni Bulletin*, Fall 1973.

machinery or reach further down the information channels when facing a decision of particular importance to his Administration. [Similarly] a Chief Executive who adopts the competitive style might commission [as FDR did on occasion] formal study groups to ensure careful staff work on complex policy questions. . . . A President who chooses the collegial approach might utilize [as Kennedy did on occasion] a more formalistic structure for routine matters in order to concentrate his energies on the more sensitive policy areas.[22]

In concluding this discussion of the different management styles generally favored by different presidents, we should remind ourselves once again that our depiction of the communication structures associated with each of them necessarily oversimplifies the more complex reality and working of each system.[23] To some extent, elements of two or even all three models may be present in different mixes, with different emphases, in the policymaking system of each president.

Over the years, as the foreign-policy activities in which the U.S. government is engaged have multiplied, the organizational arrangements for dealing with them within the executive branch have proliferated. To some extent, the sheer magnitude and complexity of the foreign-policy enterprise forces every modern president to rely at least to some extent on formalistic procedures. It would be difficult in the modern era for even so gifted a politician and leader as Franklin Roosevelt to rely heavily on a competitive model. Of particular importance, therefore, are studies of variants of formalistic models that, in addition, attempt to make use of elements of the competitive and/or collegial models as well.

Finally, although each of these three management models has certain advantages and disadvantages, the effort to improve their performance by introducing modification of one kind or another encounters serious limits. The search for improvement in policymaking systems must go beyond general management models of this kind to more discriminating ways of improving information processing.

POSTSCRIPT: THE REAGAN ADMINISTRATION

Even before Ronald Reagan took office in January 1981 he indicated that he would reduce the scope and functions of the office of the assistant for national security affairs in order to avoid a repetition of the damaging competitive relationship that had developed between Brzezinski and Secretary of State Vance in the Carter administration. Reagan's determination to do so could only have been strengthened by the hearings held in the spring of 1980 by a subcommittee of the Senate Committee on Foreign Relations chaired by Senator Edward Zorinsky.

These hearings documented the fact that a substantial consensus existed among former national security assistants and many leading specialists on foreign policy organization that the assistant's role should be reduced to what it had been prior to President Nixon's elevation of Henry Kissinger to a level of importance that ultimately overshadowed that of the secretary of state.[24]

It was also evident, even before he appointed Alexander Haig as secretary of state, that President Reagan wished to create a foreign-policymaking system centered in the State Department rather than in the White House, and that he would select a strong, dominant specialist in foreign affairs for that position. The appointment of Richard Allen as assistant for national security affairs and the public characterization of the role he would play seemed entirely consistent with this objective. Although knowledgeable in foreign affairs, Allen did not enter office with the intellectual stature of Kissinger or Brzezinski. He gave no prior indication of harboring aspirations to play a leading role in determining the substance of foreign policy, and, once in office, he appeared content to exercise his administrative skills to enhance the efficiency of policymaking procedures. The basis for a renewal of conflict between the secretary of state and the assistant for national security affairs in the new administration seemed to have been removed both by the sharp downgrading of the special assistant's role and by the nature of the appointments made to fill the two positions.

However, for various reasons, many of them of a quite unexpected nature, Reagan's State Department-centered foreign policy system did not work as effectively and smoothly as expected. Secretary of State Haig formulated a directive, which he presented to the president on inauguration day, that would have institutionalized and solidified his control over policy. Reagan, however, withheld his approval, and this may have inadvertently encouraged other foreign policy officials to challenge or resist Haig's assertion of his primacy in foreign policymaking. Haig did have the confidence and respect of the president, but he lacked the close association and long-standing friendship that was enjoyed by such long-time Reagan advisers as Edwin Meese, who had been appointed to the key position of counselor to the president, and Michael Deaver, who was serving as assistant to the president and deputy chief of staff. Meese and Deaver, along with James Baker, stood closest to the president in the White House. (Baker, appointed as chief of staff, had joined Reagan's inner circle after working for George Bush in his 1980 presidential campaign.) Haig's undisguised presidential ambitions (he had tested the water in the early stages of the 1980 contest for the Republican nomination) could hardly have encouraged a sanguine view on the part of the Meese-Deaver-Baker troika concerning the wisdom of allowing the secretary to put himself squarely astride the foreign policymaking system in a way that might have overshadowed the White House. In the months that followed the inauguration, indications of conflict between Haig and Allen and their staffs began to appear in the media.

That conflict should develop among Reagan's foreign policy team was not surprising or unexpected. Reagan had entered the White House without a well-developed set of position papers on security matters and foreign policy, such as challengers for office usually prepare during their presidential campaigns. Indeed, his campaign advisers had decided not to attempt to articulate specific positions in order not to expose the latent disagreements among his supporters. While all his major foreign policy and security advisers shared the general view that a "tougher" posture toward the Soviet Union should be adopted and that U.S. military capabilities should be "strengthened," this so-called consensus was a shallow one that only thinly covered major disagreements concerning specific strategies and policies that should be adopted. Inevitably, therefore, intense competition set in among different factions within Reagan's administration to shape and control specific policies, a struggle that was to prove time-consuming and costly. Indeed the administration soon became vulnerable to criticism that it was slow in formulating policy on key defense and diplomatic issues and lacked a coherent, consistent foreign policy.

While Haig was anointed by Reagan as his leading foreign policy adviser—his "vicar of foreign policy," as Haig referred to himself—the secretary of state found it difficult to take firm hold of the fragmented foreign policy apparatus. And it was even more difficult to coordinate the development of military strategy and force posture, an activity centered in the Department of Defense, with foreign policy. Operating from the State Department, Haig lacked the advantages that a position in the White House would have provided, and he could not count on its firm, consistent support. Haig's own more moderate foreign policy views and some of his early appointments to positions of influence in the department marked him in the eyes of those who were to the right of him in the Reagan entourage, in Congress, and among attentive opinion leaders. This included the secretary of defense, Caspar Weinberger, one of Reagan's longstanding political friends, and a number of Weinberger's associates in the Defense Department.

Even if Allen had been neutral in the policy competition that increasingly developed between Weinberger and Haig, he was ill-equipped to play the role of a strong custodian-manager of the top-level foreign-policymaking system. Allen's office had been so downgraded in importance that he did not have direct access to the president as had his predecessors in previous administrations. Rather, Allen reported to Meese, a man who lacked any experience in foreign policy and security affairs and who, besides, was concerned with formulation of all policy—domestic and economic as well as foreign. With the passage of time it became increasingly evident that the task of coordinating the policymaking process at the White House level could not be managed effectively through the existing organizational pattern. Visible evidence of feuding among leading foreign policy advisers damaged Reagan at home and abroad.

A final component of the explanation for the disappointing performance of Reagan's foreign-policymaking system during his first year in office had to do with the president himself. Not only did Reagan bring to the White House the same preference for a formalistic chief of staff system and a management style of broad delegation of responsibility to subordinates that he had displayed as governor of California; in addition, he was relatively disinterested in foreign policy and gave higher priority in the first year and a half of his presidency to his economic policies. Reagan counted upon collegiality among his top-level advisers to smooth the workings of his administration. But while collegiality was preserved and indeed played an important role in the workings of the inner circle composed of Meese, Deaver, and Baker, it did not spread outward to lubricate the interactions of the principal advisers in the security and foreign-policymaking system—Haig, Weinberger, and Allen.

What emerged, therefore, was not a well-designed, smoothly working system which, while centered in a strong secretary of state, was complemented, as indeed it should have been, by additional high-level coordination and linkage to the president himself through the assistant for national security affairs. Rather, what emerged was a fragmented, competitive, inadequately managed system in which distrust was ever present and which gave rise repeatedly to damaging intra-administration conflicts over policy. Unlike Roosevelt's competitive *system*, which was designed to bring important issues up to the presidential level and to improve the quality of information and advice available to a president who was interested and actively involved in making the important decisions, the competitive-conflictful features of Reagan's foreign policy machinery were the consequences of a poorly structured and inadequately managed system, one that did not engage the president's attention except sporadically when international developments required him to act or intraadministration conflicts got completely out of hand and required his personal attention.

To his credit and that of his leading advisers, Reagan, well before the end of his first year in office, recognized that his foreign-policymaking system was not working and that it required reorganization and change of personnel. In response to questions raised about the propriety and legality of Allen's behavior in accepting certain gifts and honoraria, the president accepted his resignation at the beginning of 1982, appointing in his place William Clark, a close friend and a former supreme court justice in California who had been serving as undersecretary of state under Haig. In addition, Reagan now strengthened the position of assistant for national security affairs; Clark would henceforth deal directly with the president on a daily basis and no longer report to Meese. It was made clear, too, that Clark would play a stronger role in policy coordination between the State and Defense departments. In other words, a determined effort was made to enable Clark to discharge more effectively the traditional role of custodian-manager of the system.

The role evidently appealed to Clark. It drew upon his experience both as sometime chief of staff in Reagan's governorship and as a justice in the California Supreme Court. Clark himself referred to his new role as that of "honest broker." In his first six months as national security assistant he began cautiously to establish a new pattern of operation, one that would bring the president more intimately into the decisionmaking process, providing him with daily foreign policy and defense briefings and moving to reestablish the traditional National Security Council staff role of balancing and packaging the often conflicting views of different governmental departments in the form of well-considered options for the president's attention. As one commentator observed, it was Clark's duty "to determine the issues that require presidential attention and to govern the timing and format of the options presented for decision. . . . [and] it will be up to him to orchestrate the administration's foreign policy pronouncements."[25]

It would remain to be seen how effectively the secretary of state and the strengthened assistant for national security affairs could work together to reshape the policy machinery and to coordinate the search for viable foreign policies. During the first half of 1982 relations between Haig and Clark developed with a minimum of friction. In part this was because Clark moved slowly and cautiously in restructuring the system which, as mid-year approached, appeared to be operating relatively smoothly. Intra-administration disagreements that continued to arise over policy were ironed out without a renewal of feuding and open warfare, and Haig's influence over foreign policy appeared to be consolidated. This impression was widely shared. Less than a month before Haig's resignation in June 1982, the *New York Times* observed in an editorial that "the Reagan Presidency has finally found its 'single voice' in foreign affairs. . . . Whatever shenanigans may rage in the kitchen, the administration now speaks to the world with some rhetorical coherence." Continuing, the editorial took note approvingly of "the muzzling of the Secretary's critics at the Pentagon and White House and the quiet traffic management of the new national security adviser, William Clark"; further, the editorial complimented Haig on his "considerable achievement . . . the recapture, from inexperienced rivals, of the policy ground. . . . He has proved that his department's crew of professional analysts is best equipped to define the real choices abroad."[26]

Behind the scenes, however, lay still unresolved questions between the White House and State as to the direction and control of foreign policy, questions that were severely exacerbated by the clash of styles and personalities. With Secretary of State Haig's resignation, it became evident that the new policy machinery created by the strengthening of the role of the assistant for national security affairs had not stabilized itself sufficiently to cope with new stresses that developed in connection with the president's trip to Europe and the Israeli invasion of Lebanon, both in June 1982. Because Clark had acted so slowly and cautiously, it became evident only now that his move into a strengthened version of the assistant's position was intended not merely to moderate interdepartmental conflicts over policy but also to strengthen the president's involvement and ultimate control over foreign policy. It also became clear that the enhanced presidential role would mean, when Reagan's top White House advisers thought it necessary, the assertion of control over the secretary of state's conduct of policy and the overriding of his judgment.[27]

At first, new in his position, Clark had tended to remain neutral on policy issues, content to introduce an orderly, balanced process of policy-making and to play a moderating role. Haig was initially happy with Clark's performance at the National Security Council since, as one of his State Department associates recalled, the operation was improved and Haig had more control over policy matters; " 'Then in the last three months he [Haig] saw the process as an obstacle.' "[28] Clark gradually began to define policy-making procedures and to assert authority over the process. Viewed from the standpoint of the White House this was the traditional and fundamental role of the national security assistant and in implementing it Clark apparently had the full backing of the president and his closest advisers. But from Haig's standpoint such procedures could be and indeed were increasingly employed to weaken his authority and influence. He was sensitive, perhaps overly sensitive, because of what he believed it portended. For example, seemingly minor procedural steps were taken by Clark, such as a memorandum insisting that all foreign travel, even that of the secretary of state, would have to be approved by the White House, and the decision that the White House, not the State Department, should announce that Haig would attempt to mediate the Falkland Islands crisis.

Haig was even more disturbed at indications that Clark was beginning to define his own role not merely as that of custodian-manager of the process but more broadly as that of an adviser and operator in substantive foreign policy. Haig saw Clark as siding increasingly with his adversaries—in Reagan's decision to impose sanctions against the Soviet Union and to prevent the building of the West European-Soviet natural gas pipeline because of the Soviet role in the imposition of martial law in Poland in 1981, and in White House communications with Saudi Arabia during the Lebanon crisis, which were at variance with the strategy that Haig was pursuing at the time.[29]

It should be noted that the Israeli invasion of Lebanon in June 1982 exacerbated frictions between the White House and State because it brought to a head the long-simmering disagreement over responsibility for crisis management. Reagan's decision early in his administration to repose responsibility for crisis management with Vice President George Bush, while the secretary of state retained the primary policy role, left unsettled the necessity to integrate these two important dimensions of foreign policy. The fact of the matter is that policy and crisis management are inextricably related: existing foreign policy must guide the way some crises are handled while in other cases a crisis forces the shaping or reshaping of major foreign policies.

Thus, within less than a year and a half after his inauguration, President Reagan was forced to replace both his national security assistant and his secretary of state, an unprecedented admission of failure to develop an effective foreign-policymaking system. Insofar as personality clashes and differences of style had contributed to Haig's departure, there was every reason to expect that these impediments would disappear with the choice of George Shultz as his replacement. What was also clear by mid-1982 was that President Reagan had significantly modified his initial preference for a State-centered foreign-policymaking system. Such a model had worked effectively in past administrations and appealed to Reagan for reasons already noted. The viability of a State-centered system always depended not merely upon selecting a self-confident, competent, and experienced person as secretary of state but, even more, on developing a complementary role relationship between the president and his secretary and a working relationship based upon sufficient mutual respect, confidence, and trust to withstand the efforts of other policy advisers to undermine it.[30] Acheson had such a relationship with Truman; Dulles had such a relationship with Eisenhower; Kissinger (as secretary of state) had much the same type of relationship with Ford. Haig, in contrast, never developed such a relationship with Reagan.

The role of the assistant for national security affairs, in turn, can be defined in a stable, viable manner only in conjunction with the way in which the president chooses to define his own role, the role of the secretary of state, and the working relationship between them. It remained to be seen how these fundamental dimensions of Reagan's foreign-policymaking system would be defined. The moderation of intra-administration conflicts was a necessary step in this direction. But the fundamental intellectual—and political—tasks facing the Reagan administration in the foreign policy sphere remained, for it still had to formulate a well-conceptualized, reasonably coherent foreign policy that could be well enough understood and gain enough acceptance both within and outside the executive branch to enable the administration to conduct it in a consistent and effective manner.

NOTES

1. For a history and critical analysis of these efforts at reorganization, see I. M. Destler, *Presidents, Bureaucrats, and Foreign Policy* (Princeton, N.J.: Princeton University Press, 1972), chapter 2. Nonetheless, as Destler and other students of the problem recognize, organization design and structural parameters do affect foreign policy performance. For a sophisticated discussion, see Graham Allison and Peter Szanton, *Remaking Foreign Policy: The Organizational Connection* (New York: Basic Books, 1976); see particularly Chapter 1, "The Argument: Organization Matters." For a more general discussion applying not merely to foreign policy but the presidency as a whole, see Stephen Hess, *Organizing the Presidency* (Washington, D.C.: The Brookings Institution, 1976).
2. The following paragraphs draw upon A. L. George, "Adaptation to Stress in Political Decision-making," in George V. Coelho, David A. Hamburg, and John E. Adams, eds., *Coping and Adaptation* (New York: Basic Books, 1974).
3. This general point is emphasized repeatedly also by Graham Allison in his study for the Commission on the Organization of the Government for the Conduct of Foreign Policy. For example: "The critical variable affecting which mechanisms [of centralized management] are used is the president: his personal preferences and style. . . . It follows, therefore, that efforts to legislate structure for high-level centralized management cannot succeed." Graham T. Allison, ed., *Adequacy of Current Organization: Defense and Arms Control*, vol. 4, Appendices, Commission on the Organization of the Government for the Conduct of Foreign Policy, June 1975 (Washington, D.C.: U.S. Government Printing Office, 1976), p. 35; see also pp. 10, 58.

4. These three management styles are described and evaluated in Richard T. Johnson, *Managing the White House* (New York: Harper & Row, 1974). See particularly chapters 1 and 8. A useful discussion of the evolution of the modern presidency and of the styles of different presidents is provided by Stephen Hess, *Organizing the Presidency* (Washington, D.C.: The Brookings Institution, 1976).
5. Richard Fenno, *The President's Cabinet* (New York: Vintage Books, Knopf, 1959), pp. 44–46. See also Arthur Schlesinger, Jr., *The Age of Roosevelt*, vol. 2, *The Coming of the New Deal* (Boston: Houghton Mifflin, 1959), chapters 32–34; and Richard E. Neustadt, *Presidential Power* (New York: Wiley, 1960), chapter 7.
6. The figures in this selection (with the exception of the one describing Nixon's variant of the formalistic model) are taken directly, with minor adaptations, from John Q. Johnson, "Communication Structures Among Presidential Advisors" (seminar paper, Stanford University, September 1975). The seminal work on communication networks is that of Alex Bavelas, "Communication Patterns in Task-oriented Groups," *Journal of Acoustic Society of America* 22 (1950): 725–30. A summary of early work of this kind appears in Murray Glanzer and Robert Glaser, "Techniques for the Study of Group Structure and Behavior," *Psychological Bulletin* 58 (1961): 2–27.
7. Recently available archival materials at the Eisenhower Library evidently require a substantial revision of the conventional image of Eisenhower as an apolitical military man, one who was generally uninformed about and not very attentive to his executive responsibilities, one who was prone to overdelegate his responsibilities, and one who was naive about the art of governing. What emerges, rather, is a different executive style that Fred Greenstein refers to as Eisenhower's "invisible hand" mode of leadership in which he sought actively to secure his goals by indirection (Fred I. Greenstein, "Presidential Activism Eisenhower Style: A Reassessment Based on Archival Evidence," [paper delivered to the 1979 Meeting of the Midwest Political Science Association, January 1979]).
8. Ibid., p. 9. See also Douglas Kinnard, *President Eisenhower and Strategy Management: A Study in Defense Politics* (Lexington: University of Kentucky Press, 1977); and Murray Kempton, "The Underestimation of Dwight D. Eisenhower," *Esquire* (September 1967).
9. Greenstein, "Presidential Activism," p. 10.
10. See, for example, James David Barber, *The Presidential Character* (Englewood Cliffs, N.J.: Prentice-Hall, 1972) and Johnson, *Managing the White House*, pp. 199–229.
11. Johnson, *Managing the White House*, pp. 210–11.
12. Ibid.
13. For a particularly detailed account of the structure, evolution, and performance of Nixon's NSC, *see* Chester Crocker, "The Nixon-Kissinger National Security Council System, 1969–1972: A Study in Foreign Policy Management," vol. 6, Appendices, Commission on the Organization of the Government for the Conduct of Foreign Policy, June 1975 (Washington, D.C.: U.S. Government Printing Office, 1976), pp. 79–99.
14. Don Bonafede, "Brzezinski—Stepping Out of His Backstage Role," *National Journal* (15 October 1977): 1598. See also Elizabeth Drew, "A Reporter at Large: Brzezinski," *The New Yorker*, May 1978; and Marilyn Berger, "Vance and Brzezinski: Peaceful Coexistence or Guerrilla War?" *New York Times Magazine*, 13 February 1977.

15. Bonafede, "Brzezinski."

16. For a remarkably incisive set of observations regarding aspects of Carter's personality and outlook that adversely affected the organization of his advisory system and his performance generally, see the series of articles published by his former speech writer, James Fallows, "The Passionless Presidency," *The Atlantic Monthly*, May and June 1979. Some of these difficulties were anticipated earlier by two political scientists, Jack Knott and Aaron Wildavsky, "Jimmy Carter's Theory of Governing," *The Wilson Quarterly* 1 (Winter 1977). An in-depth, thoroughly researched critical appraisal of Carter's personality and career has been done by Professor Betty Glad of the Political Science Department, The University of Illinois (*Jimmy Carter: In Search of the Great White House* [New York: Norton, 1980]).

17. For a description of the NSC under Carter, see Bonafede, "Brzezinski"; and Lawrence J. Korb, "The Structure and Process of the National Security Council System in the First Year of the Carter Administration" (paper delivered at the annual meeting of the International Studies Association, Washington, D.C., 22–25 February 1978). On Brzezinski's role, see also chapter 11 in A. L. George, *Presidential Decisionmaking in Foreign Policy* (Boulder, Colorado: Westview Press, 1980).

18. *See*, for example, Stanley Hoffmann, "The Hell of Good Intentions," *Foreign Policy* 29 (winter 1977–78); and Thomas L. Hughes, "Carter and the Management of Contradictions," *Foreign Policy* 31 (summer 1978).

19. For a more detailed discussion of the evolution of the position of special assistant for national security affairs, *see* chapters 10 and 11 in George, *Presidential Decisionmaking in Foreign Policy*. [See also I. M. Destler's "The Rise of the National Security Assistant, 1961–1981" in this book—*eds.*]

20. Jack Nelson, "Task Forces Increase White House Efficiency," *Los Angeles Times*, 26 April 1979.

21. Johnson, *Managing the White House*, chapter 8; reproduced with minor changes and additions in *The Stanford Business School Alumni Bulletin*, fall 1973.

22. Ibid., pp. 237–39.

23. Important refinements in the description of each president's preferred executive work style are introduced by David K. Hall in his Ph.D. dissertation at Stanford University, "Implementing Multiple Advocacy in the National Security Council, 1947–1980" (1982).

24. *The National Security Adviser: Role and Accountability*, Hearing before the Committee on Foreign Relations, United States Senate, 96th Congress, 2nd Session, April 17, 1980 (Washington, D.C.: U.S. Government Printing Office, 1980).

25. Dick Kirschten, "Clark to the Rescue," *National Journal*, January 1, 1982, p. 76.

26. *New York Times* editorial, May 30, 1982. See also article by Hedrick Smith, *New York Times*, June 16, 1982.

27. It is also possible that high-level White House officials had for some months entertained the expectation of replacing Haig after the mid-term elections and were preparing the ground, and the president, for this eventuality when developments in June 1982 brought matters to a head prematurely and led the White House to force Haig's resignation. (See article by Lou Cannon, *Washington Post*, June 27, 1982, and interview of presidential aide Michael Deaver by Larry Liebert, *San Francisco Chronicle*, July 1, 1982.)

28. Article by Lou Cannon, *Washington Post*, June 26, 1982.

29. According to news accounts, several State Department sources attributed Haig's declining influence to the rise of Clark who, it was perceived, was beginning to side with Haig's policy opponents, such as Secretary of Defense Weinberger. " 'It was Clark who made the difference,' one senior State Department official said. . . ; 'Haig knew Clark was someone he couldn't beat, and he felt policy was drifting in ways he couldn't control.' " (Article by John Goshko, *Washington Post,* June 26, 1982.)

    According to several newspaper accounts Clark told the Saudis that Washington would achieve an Israeli pullback from Beirut while Haig was seeking to enhance pressure on the Palestine Liberation Organization to get out of West Beirut. (Article by Bernard Gwertzman, *New York Times,* June 27, 1982; see also article by Steven R. Weisman, *New York Times,* June 27, 1982; article by Don Oberdoster, *Washington Post,* June 27, 1982.)

30. For an insightful critical examination of the feasibility of a State-centered foreign-policymaking system, see Leslie H. Gelb, "Why Not the State Department?" *The Washington Quarterly,* Autumn 1980. [The Gelb article is reprinted in Part IV of this book—*eds.*]

29

PRESIDENT REAGAN'S CHARACTER
An Assessment

JAMES DAVID BARBER

. . .Like everyone else he ever met, I like Mr. Reagan. I'd like to have him over to watch "Little House on the Prairie" and tell stories. But he did not run for best friend.

As president, he will be dangerous, his dangers being very different from those we are familiar with in the cases of rigid, hard-driving presidents such as Johnson and Nixon, and very different from the main dangers his opponents were highlighting just a few months ago. For the benefit of next time, we ought to ponder how we picked him. And for the months ahead, those who back and oppose him ought to know what to watch for.

Reagan floated into the presidency on a recurrent tide that swells through politics with remarkable regularity—the tide of reaction against too long and hard a time of troubles, too much worry, too much tension and anxiety.

Sometimes people want a fighter in the White House and sometimes a saint. But the time comes when all we want is a friend, a pal, a guy to reassure us that the story is going to come out all right. In 1980, that need found just the right promise in Ronald Reagan, the smiling American.

Echoes of similar elections were everywhere in the Reagan repertoire. "Smile, honey, smile!" his wife would whisper as he got set for the cameras. It recalled that lovable Lub, William Howard Taft, with his motto for 1908, "smile, smile, smile," coming in to help the nation rest after Roosevelt who counseled him to "let the audience see you smile, *always*, because I feel that your nature shines out so transparently when you do smile—you big, generous, high-minded fellow."

Mike Deaver, Reagan's public relations man, announced after the 1980 election that "we'll have a return to normalcy," echoing that wonder of flatulent fellowship, Warren G. Harding, who invented the word.

An abridged version of "Reagan's Sheer Personal Likability Faces Its Sternest Test," *The Washington Post*, January 20, 1980, p. 8. Reprinted by permission of *The Washington Post* and James David Barber. Copyright © 1981 by *The Washington Post*.

Then there were Reagan's imitations of Franklin Roosevelt, the master reassurer and hoper of 1932, not only in such phrases as "the only thing the cause of peace has to fear is fear itself" but also in the manner of Reagan's fireside chats, aping FDR's folksy radio style:

"I'd like to speak to you for a few moments now not as a candidate for the presidency but as a citizen, a parent—in fact, a grandparent—who shares with you the deep and abiding hope for peace."

Reagan's sheer personal likability in 1980 conjured Ike in 1956, Mr. Likable himself, easing the nation through the throes of suburbanization. And as Reagan stood before his party convention in 1980, the slogan of the day was plastered in great white letters across the platform: "Together—A New Beginning," derived no doubt from memories of 1968, when another Republican won on the promise to "Bring Us Together."

So there we were again. The drama for 1972 had been the drama of combat, especially the shredding of the Democratic Party. Called for in 1976 were conscience and a revival of morals after a decade of political debacle; both Carter and Ford rang the bell for God and goodness.

By 1980, we were ready as a nation for a surcease of anxiety. We had had enough of bickering and preaching. After the shakedown to the nominations, the public had one choice among three—a moralist (Anderson), a fighter (Carter) and a reassurer (Reagan).

Reagan virtually had it from the start in his own party and in the nation after the cut-'em-up Democratic convention. John Connally, the hot fighter of the Republican Party, won exactly one delegate to his national convention.

Sen. Kennedy, after his Georgetown speech the fighter of the Democratic nomination phase, was swamped by Carter, who then adopted Kennedy's losing style. The president, whose approval rating had descended to sub-Nixonian levels, worst in the history of the question, had to apologize to Barbara Walters for his "meanness," which nevertheless kept popping up.

Reagan, guided by his ad man, Stuart Spencer, kept his comforting cool. Spencer said of Carter, "The harder he gets, the softer we're going to get."

When Carter and Reagan met, first at the Al Smith dinner in New York City and then in their face-to-face debate, Reagan managed to define himself as the apparent incumbent, outsmiling and condescending to his ill-tempered little pal Jimmy.

Reagan closed his debate with a question: "And, most importantly—quite simply—the basic question of our lives: Are you happier today than when Mr. Carter became president of the United States?"

Pat Caddell called the election "a referendum on unhappiness." His team's strategy—to hit Reagan and "make him less grandfatherly, less genial"—got nowhere, and Caddell's "fed-up vote" shaped what Elizabeth Drew called "a great national to-hell-with-'em."

In 1976, Carter won on a conviction that the White House ought to be swept clean of the trashy behavior Nixon exemplified. In 1980, Reagan won on an emotion, that happiness was down and needed restoring. Despite his defeat, Carter was able to keep people thinking he was a decent man, though flawed.

The Reagans, both privacy freaks, never had much use for reporters, a sentiment sure to be reciprocated.

It seems clear now that no "conservative revolution" lends force to what Reagan will achieve in the coming months. Only 11 percent of Reagan voters decided for him as a "real conservative," and the polls say the main reason was "it's time for a change."

Nor does the evidence show any long term mass slide of voters toward the right. In short, Reagan was elected primarily because he is not Carter, as Carter was voted for because he is not Reagan. Reagan, for all his campaign posturing, says he thinks "I'm kind of moderate."

He has surrounded himself with middling administrators from the Nixon and Ford administrations; there is not one certified red-hot radical rightist among them. He has been backing away from the libertarian theoreticians in the party for a good while.

Jesse Helms found the radical 1980 Republican platform a good one. Reagan's man Ed Meese quickly noted that "a platform represents the party. A presidential candidate represents his own policies and views." Since the election, the news has been thick with the oil of compromise, as the edgier campaign statements are reinterpreted into moderation.

Reagan's old friend, Tom Reed, says that for Reagan, "The reasonable periods come when he is in office." That was the case, at least comparatively, when he went from 33 years of show business into the California governorship. As is now well known, his record in office bore only a near-random relationship to his rhetoric in running for it.

Reagan never signed on with Ayn Rand or any other intellectual; his conservatism is an attitude, not a theory. Not even his litany of values—"family, work, neighborhood, freedom, peace"—connects clearly with either his personal or his public priorities.

He speculates that "maybe the people see themselves and that I'm one of them," but of course his round of life has long been unplugged from that of mainstream America.

Reagan's *operative* world view—the one he acts upon—seems clearer. He is a Republican millionaire and hangs around with those folks. Like them, he values "success"; like them, he has not much respect for the regular arts of politics.

Reagan now has a much tougher task, it seems. For he has staked his fortunes on popular satisfaction—on results, on actual improvements in the lives of citizens, not just on trying or hoping or posturing. He is supposed to make it well again. That is very likely to prove difficult, if not impossible. The structure of power stands in the way.

Reagan's best bet for popular support in darker months to come may well be the fury of the radical right, whose indignant disillusionment with Reagan will help him gain acceptance with moderates. But his initial popular support is thinner than his "landslide" in the electoral college makes it look.

Reagan won in an election with the lowest turnout in 32 years. Only about one-fourth of the eligible voters bothered to vote for him. He has a modest majority in the Senate, but Democrats control the House, through which his novel tax-cut strategy must be played.

The bureaucrats in what Reagan called "the puzzle palaces on the Potomac" have their own ways with victors from out of town, as Jimmy Carter eventually learned. Reagan's knottiest problem, inflation, has proved incredibly resistant to reform, here and elsewhere throughout the civilized world.

And Reagan has no terrible social disaster going for him, no clear-cut trauma, such as the collapse that brought in Franklin Roosevelt, to put steam behind a burst of effective legislation in his first 100 or 200 days.

So far, Reagan has charmed Washington. *Winning* Washington—and maintaining his fragile support with the press and public—will take a good deal more doing.

The press and television will be crucial for Reagan. Intrigued initially with his novelty (vs. four more years of The Carter Family), the press will write for a while about the opening ceremonies and the emerging plans.

Then will come the inevitable "performance gap" stories, featuring bobbles and corruptions on the road to Utopia. Reagan himself will do well with fireside chats and televised addresses, but unrehearsed interviews and press conferences threaten to reveal even more areas of vast ignorance and mistaken perception.

The hit-and-run rhetoric of the campaign has its challenges, but they are nothing like the sustained and fact-anchored scrutiny Reagan will face as president. The alternative—seclusion—threatens the journalist's bread and butter, stimulating his furious imagination.

He was drafted for the gubernatorial race by the group of rich, aging Californians who then became his friends, managing his trust, counseling him regularly.

Twentieth Century-Fox bought 236 acres of his for "nearly 30 times what he had paid for it only a few years before and twice what it was appraised at by Los Angeles County," according to *Atlantic* magazine. In 1974, nothing having been done with the land, it was sold to the state of California for about one-fifth of the original price.

The deal still waits explanation. What is clear on the record, though, is that Reagan's administration was, as he put it, "business oriented." During his administration, ruling after ruling paved the way for big gains by private corporations. Reagan would not release his income-tax returns, except for 1970 when, his aide said, he owed no tax.

A reasonable inference is that as long as Reagan's business friends are happy with moderation, he will be, too. He is unlikely to go off the deep end with Milton Friedman; already he has allowed that the Chrysler bailout is okay after all, and the New York City bailout and farm parity and maybe even the minimum wage and involuntary social security.

His domestic economic policies may indeed turn out to be too watered down to be effective, whatever their supposed ideological base. The foreign policy his business friends will press on him cannot be inferred from his California experience.

A reasonable guess would be: distract attention by waving the fist at the Soviet Union, while quieter and more profitable arrangements are worked out "realistically" in the Third World, unhampered by "Utopian" human rights considerations. As president, Reagan is as likely to be "business oriented" as ever, at home and abroad.

What makes it difficult to sort out Reagan's operative world view is his peculiar way with rhetoric. Obviously, it dominates his political style.

Reagan has little interest in homework on the issues; he gets his staff to reduce the information to one page per problem and usually takes the staff's recommendation. The charms of personal negotiation are also lost on him, particularly if they involve an element of disagreement or confrontation. The staff takes care of that, too.

Reagan himself is in charge of the speaking, composing from bits and pieces of information he discovers. His rhetorical output has been enormous. In 1960 alone, he gave about 200 speeches as a Democrat for Nixon.

The Carter-Mondale campaign collected a sizable pile of notebooks filled with Reagan's most egregious bloopers—not only outrageous recommendations, but also gross factual errors about important issues.

To Carter, these books proved Reagan "ridiculous," a man out of touch with the simplest realities of political life. To Reagan, they were just blown lines to be done again or passed over. He described his method of speech research: "Like any other speaker, I'd see something, and I'd say, 'Hey, that's great,' and use it."

The content of his speeches is for effect, composed to elicit a response from the audience at hand. Reagan often goes overboard when he adds some thrilling assertion for the audience present. But his style of speaking is far more closely studied—he has spent hours perfecting a toss of the head, a shrug of the shoulders, a crease of the brow. Reagan, after all, came to political rhetoric from acting, and acting reinforced his natural ability to pretend.

I think he experiences most of his own political speeches as if they were fiction. As a young boy, Reagan was extremely nearsighted and had to bluff his lessons in school. More pretending was necessary to hush up and conjure away from reality his father's drunkenness.

More again to play football without much weight and height and more to get through college exams without studying the material. He got his first radio job by demonstrating he could pretend to be watching what he was only imagining—a mythical football game. He went on to become expert in faking live broadcasts of ball games from wire-service reports.

His theatrical experience began long before that, at home listening to mother and dad declaim classic plays, then taking part. When suddenly Ronald began to read at age five, his surprised mother at once got the neighbors in to listen to him perform.

Acting in movies, the most hypnotic of pretend media, simply extended this fictional experience. "So much of our profession is taken up with pretending," he wrote, "with interpretation of never-never roles, that an actor must spend at least half his waking hours in fantasy."

He told his aide Stuart Spencer in 1966 that "politics is just like show business. You have a hell of an opening, coast for a while and then have a hell of a close."

As his brother Neil put it, "Ronnie always played Ronnie." He is a master at playing himself, and he achieved that mastery in its fullest flower in political speechmaking, first for General Electric and then in his own campaigns. He knows the power of narrative and timing and eye contact and even the technique of the apparent stumble.

But he has never given evidence of a mind that links what he says today to what he was yesterday or what he will do tomorrow. His rhetoric is essentially ahistorical and apolitical. He is bound to contribute to the ever-widening gap in American politics between speech and meaning, presaged in the isolation of the campaign from the presidency, preparing the way for the Orwellian absurdities.

Reagan's way of being a politician is held together by his character, his orientation toward his own experience. As Lou Cannon noted, he is "basically a passive person," a conserver of his energies, a take-it-easy type.

And, as everyone everywhere has noticed, he is an optimist, a booster, a smiler, a genial fellow. In my jargon, that combination makes Reagan a "passive-positive," that is, "the receptive, compliant, other-directed character whose life is a search for affection as a reward for being agreeable and cooperative rather than personally assertive."

The good of that is that Reagan is definitely no Nixon; as his party's cochairman Betty Heitman put it, "There is no hatred in him, no vindictiveness, no grudges, no desire to get back at anybody."

The worry of that is his type's tendency to drift, particularly with forces in the close-up environment. The danger is confusion, delay and then impulsiveness. If tragedy comes to Ronald Reagan, it will be because he wants to be liked too much.

There is no great mystery about the roots of Reagan's compliant, genial stance toward life. He was his mother's boy, named after her, appearing when she and his father expected a little girl.

The family tale is that at birth his father said that "For such a little Dutchman, he makes a hell of lot of noise," but his mother said, "I think he's perfectly wonderful."

His older brother became the outdoor type, bluff and hearty like their father. Ronald, very nearsighted and slight of build, played indoors, with the toys in the attic or "hidden in a corner downstairs in Uncle Jim's jewelry store, with its curious relics, faint lights from the gold and silver and bronze, lulled by the erratic ticking of a dozen clocks and the drone of customers who came in."

His huge black spectacles made him shy, but his mother showed him a way past that. She "had a conviction that everyone loved her just because she loved them."

Always cheery, she taught him not to condemn his father for his drinking, a disease, not a crime. Despite much instability and shifting about, Ronald learned to paper over the unpleasant side of life: "We never had a worry in the world that I can remember."

He learned to accentuate the positive, to smile and encourage and step aside from trouble. People came to like him. Eventually, he found a wife who, fleeing her own ghosts, clung to him like a ship-wrecked sailor to a floating spar, constantly reinforcing his courage, protecting and advancing him.

"Ronnie is the softest touch in the world," she said. "I'm always sorry when I read he's unfeeling. You know, he's the most sentimental, tender man I've ever known."

Having taken on a sentimental president, now we must live with him. The odds are small that, four years from now, he will emerge pleased at his presidential role. He is a nice guy who finished first, soon to discover that not everyone is a nice guy.

The best hope is that, like Gerald Ford and Jimmy Carter, Ronald Reagan will leave the Constitution about as he found it and the nation at peace. The worst fear is that Reagan, seeking affection, will have disaster thrust upon him.

Part Seven

THE FUTURE OF AMERICAN FOREIGN POLICY

The future of American foreign policy is fraught with challenges and uncertainties but also with possibilities. A multitude of trends in world politics are unfolding and at often accelerating rates. The global agenda has become crowded with new issues and problems that have taken their place alongside others that have retained their customary prominence. Collectively, these emergent realities exert pressure for adaptations in American foreign policy even as the continuation of old problems inhibits new departures from America's traditional approaches to developments beyond the water's edge.

The essays in Part I of this book described the historical patterns of American foreign policy—both the policy goals and instruments used to realize them—that have shown remarkable consistency and continuity since the immediate aftermath of World War II. But trend is not destiny, and, unless one is willing to make the dubious assumption that the future is somehow determined by the past, we must consider the possibility that the

United States will evince some modification of its previous behavior in some policy arenas, even while manifesting consistency with the past in others.

Or will it? Will elected and appointed officials in Washington cope with the pressing new problems on the global horizon with imaginative new approaches? Or, instead, will tomorrow's policies resemble today's, with the assumptions on which past policies have been based continuing to color visions of the future?

Predicting the future of American foreign policy, as policy planners necessarily must, is a difficult task. Precise prediction is not a reasonable expectation when the subject is as complex and multifaceted as a global power's response to unforeseen external and internal developments. What we *can* contemplate, however, are those factors that are most likely to influence the response of the United States to the global challenges it faces.

What are those factors? *Perspectives on American Foreign Policy* is organized around five central determinants of America's past and present behavior, and hence those that will also determine its future orientation. How the United States has acted and will continue to act abroad is rooted in the ways change, or its absence, occurs within the various dimensions of the external world (Part II), American society at large (Part III), the confines of its governmental structures (Part IV), the kinds of decision-making processes encouraged by the roles embedded within these structures (Part V), and the personal characteristics of American policy makers (Part VI). Captured within each of these five source categories or "master variables" is a large number of forces that influence what goals the United States will pursue abroad, and how and with what tools they will be pursued. Some of these forces promote policy innovation. Others promote policy continuity. But they all operate simultaneously and collectively either to constrain the nation's capacity for foreign policy change or to facilitate it.

In contemplating the future of American foreign policy, therefore, it is useful to weigh the evidence, opinion, and theory discussed in the five parts of the book and to ask, "How are these influencing factors likely to interrelate to shape the policies the United States will forge to cope with problems beyond its borders?" Will the forces encompassed within the source categories converge in such a way as to reinforce policy outcomes similar to those of the past? Or will they come together in such a way as to stimulate new policy patterns and not just marginal adjustments to old ones? If the latter is the case, to which forces should we turn to best anticipate whether change will occur? In other words, which source category exerts the greatest influence, relative to the others, on American foreign policy; which is most potent in stimulating change in American foreign policy—or in inhibiting it?

Thinking in such terms forces us not only to contemplate the future but also to reflect on how the central variables within the source categories that provide the framework of this book perform. For instance, it is instructive to ask "Will changes in America's external environment—in the form of a technological breakthrough in Soviet military capabilities or another war in the Middle East, for example—promote reorientations in American policy? Or will departures more likely emanate from domestic political conditions, such as a radical shift in American public opinion or in the strength and operation of the national economy? Or is change more likely to result from a reorganization of the foreign affairs government and of the policy-making roles that it helps to define and sustain? Or, again, is a fundamental transformation most likely to occur through the election of a political maverick whose character, personality, and predispositions are quite unlike those of the leaders normally responsible for making foreign policy?" Posing these questions also raises two related questions: "How probable is it that the sorts of changes in the source categories posited here, or that might be conceived, actually will occur? And what will be the likely consequences for American foreign policy?"

PERSPECTIVES ON THE FUTURE OF AMERICAN FOREIGN POLICY: AN OVERVIEW

Perspectives on American Foreign Policy will have succeeded in its purpose if it stimulates questions such as those asked above, and if it informs judgments about how those questions are best answered. For ultimately both the questions and answers are critical to an understanding of the past and to an informed anticipation of the future.

The future of American foreign policy remains problematic, nevertheless. No analyst—regardless how experienced, astute, or informed—can characterize fully and confidently the shape and content of American foreign policy for the rest of this decade and beyond. More realistic are efforts to project the general thrust of American foreign policy in the relatively near future, and to anticipate the issues that seem destined to stimulate future policy debate about appropriate objectives and instruments.

To stimulate thinking along these more modest lines, Part VII contains three essays that seek, each in its own way, to describe the environment in which future U.S. policy will evolve and with which American leaders will have to grapple.

The first is an official U.S. government publication entitled *The Global 2000 Report to the President,* a document that received wide attention and provoked heated controversy following its publication during the 1980 presidential campaign. Long in preparation by an army of experts, the study is the first government effort to research systematically interdependent trends in population growth, resource consumption, and environmental stress from an international, not just national, perspective. The findings paint a picture of a challenging, even alarming, future global environment if present trends are not arrested. The issues discussed in the report thus define an agenda for the discussion of foreign policy priorities by identifying problems that must be confronted. Inasmuch as a prophet's most important tool is a good memory, those seeking a picture of the global future should be mindful of the trends discussed in this report, for they address some salient if disturbing developments that have surfaced in the recent past. Reproduced here is a summary of the findings that emerged from the full, 2000-plus page report to the president.

The approach to understanding the future underlying *The Global 2000 Report* is known as *persistence forecasting*. Another technique is to argue that future policy choices will be determined most by the operating assumptions decision makers maintain, and to predict or assume that leaders' beliefs today will define the confines of external behavior tomorrow. From this perspective, the goals that will guide America's policy patterns in the future will arise from policy makers' current beliefs and images about the world and America's place in it.

Henry Steele Commager's article, "Misconceptions Governing American Foreign Policy," builds on this approach. Commager contends that America's future policy, whether wise or foolish, will depend on how the assumptions on which it rests fit emergent realities. In a far-reaching and historically informed review, he contends that the assumptions about world affairs and America's world role made in the aftermath of World War II remain neither appropriate nor warranted (if ever they were). The thesis is all the more provocative, since it addresses many of the themes introduced in earlier discussions and clearly challenges the foundations on which the persistent patterns of postwar American foreign policy have been built. However troublesome, the questions raised in this timely critique deserve thought, because, for better or worse, the future will be influenced by the assumptions about contemporary reality that policy makers embrace.

Finally, Stanley Hoffmann's essay, "Foreign Policy: What's to Be Done?", looks at both the domestic and international context in which future priorities will be set. Hoffmann advances a number of timely prescriptions for what American foreign policy should seek to accomplish in the years ahead. Although policy makers and others may differ with Hoffmann's personal, albeit compelling, list of policy recommendations, many of the debates over future issues seem likely to be couched in terms of the choices he poses, for he displays sensitivity to constraints as well as opportunities. Furthermore, the issues raised promise to remain salient, and the postures assumed toward them will therefore shape the direction of American foreign policy in the decade ahead and beyond.

30

THE GLOBAL 2000 REPORT TO THE PRESIDENT

Entering the Twenty-First Century

PREPARED BY THE COUNCIL ON ENVIRONMENTAL QUALITY AND THE DEPARTMENT OF STATE

I f present trends continue, the world in 2000 will be more crowded, more polluted, less stable ecologically, and more vulnerable to disruption than the world we live in now. Serious stresses involving population, resources, and environment are clearly visible ahead. Despite greater material output, the world's people will be poorer in many ways than they are today.

For hundreds of millions of the desperately poor, the outlook for food and other necessities of life will be no better. For many it will be worse. Barring revolutionary advances in technology, life for most people on earth will be more precarious in 2000 than it is now—unless the nations of the world act decisively to alter current trends.

This, in essence, is the picture emerging from the U.S. Government's projections of probable changes in world population, resources, and environment by the end of the century. . . . They do not predict what will occur. Rather, they depict conditions that are likely to develop if there are no changes in public policies, institutions, or rates of technological advance, and if there are no wars or other major disruptions. A keener awareness of the nature of the current trends, however, may induce changes that will alter these trends and the projected outcome.

Rapid growth in world population will hardly have altered by 2000. The world's population will grow from 4 billion in 1975 to 6.35 billion in 2000, an increase of more than 50 percent. The rate of growth will slow only marginally, from 1.8 percent a year to 1.7 percent. In terms of sheer numbers, population will be growing faster in 2000 than it is today, with 100 million people added each year compared with 75 million in 1975. Ninety percent of this growth will occur in the poorest countries.

The Global Report to the President: Entering the Twenty-First Century, Vol. 1, *Summary Report* (Washington, D.C.: U.S. Government Printing Office, 1980), pp. 1-5.

While the economies of the less developed countries (LDCs) are expected to grow at faster rates than those of the industrialized nations, the gross national product per capita in most LDCs remains low. The average gross national product per capita is projected to rise substantially in some LDCs (especially in Latin America), but in the great populous nations of South Asia it remains below $200 a year (in 1975 dollars). The large existing gap between the rich and poor nations widens.

World food production is projected to increase 90 percent over the 30 years from 1970 to 2000. This translates into a global per capita increase of less than 15 percent over the same period. The bulk of that increase goes to countries that already have relatively high per capita food consumption. Meanwhile per capita consumption in South Asia, the Middle East, and the LDCs of Africa will scarcely improve or will actually decline below present inadequate levels. At the same time, real prices for food are expected to double.

Arable land will increase only 4 percent by 2000, so that most of the increased output of food will have to come from higher yields. Most of the elements that now contribute to higher yields—fertilizer, pesticides, power for irrigation, and fuel for machinery—depend heavily on oil and gas.

During the 1990s world oil production will approach geological estimates of maximum production capacity, even with rapidly increasing petroleum prices. . . . The richer industrialized nations will be able to command enough oil and other commercial energy supplies to meet rising demands through 1990. With the expected price increases, many less developed countries will have increasing difficulties meeting energy needs. For the one-quarter of humankind that depends primarily on wood for fuel, the outlook is bleak. Needs for fuelwood will exceed available supplies by about 25 percent before the turn of the century.

While the world's finite fuel resources—coal, oil, gas, oil shale, tar sands, and uranium—are theoretically sufficient for centuries, they are not evenly distributed; they pose difficult economic and environmental problems; and they vary greatly in their amenability to exploitation and use.

Nonfuel mineral resources generally appear sufficient to meet projected demands through 2000, but further discoveries and investments will be needed to maintain reserves. In addition, production costs will increase with energy prices and may make some nonfuel mineral resources uneconomic. The quarter of the world's population that inhabits industrial countries will continue to absorb three-fourths of the world's mineral production.

Regional water shortages will become more severe. In the 1970–2000 period population growth alone will cause requirements for water to double in nearly half the world. Still greater increases would be needed to improve standards of living. In many LDCs, water supplies will become increasingly erratic by 2000 as a result of extensive deforestation. Development of new water supplies will become more costly virtually everywhere.

Significant losses of world forests will continue over the next 20 years as demand for forest products and fuelwood increases. Growing stocks of commercial-size timber are projected to decline 50 percent per capita. The world's forests are now disappearing at the rate of 18–20 million hectares a year (an area half the size of California), with most of the loss occurring in the humid tropical forests of Africa, Asia, and South America. The projections indicate that by 2000 some 40 percent of the remaining forest cover in LDCs will be gone.

Serious deterioration of agricultural soils will occur worldwide, due to erosion, loss of organic matter, desertification, salinization, alkalinization, and waterlogging. Already, an area of cropland and grassland approximately the size of Maine is becoming barren wasteland each year, and the spread of desert-like conditions is likely to accelerate.

Atmospheric concentrations of carbon dioxide and ozone-depleting chemicals are expected to increase at rates that could alter the world's climate and upper atmosphere significantly by 2050. Acid rain from increased combustion of fossil fuels (especially coal) threatens damage to lakes, soils, and crops. Radioactive and other hazardous materials present health and safety problems in increasing numbers of countries.

Extinctions of plant and animal species will increase dramatically. Hundreds of thousands of species—perhaps as many as 20 percent of all species on earth—will be irretrievably lost as their habitats vanish, especially in tropical forests.

The future depicted by the U.S. Government projections, briefly outlined above, may actually understate the impending problems. The methods available for carrying out the Study led to certain gaps and inconsistencies that tend to impart an optimistic bias. For example, most of the individual projections for the various sectors studied—food, minerals, energy, and so on—assume that sufficient capital, energy, water, and land will be available in each of these sectors to meet their needs, regardless of the competing needs of the other sectors. More consistent, better-integrated projections would produce a still more emphatic picture of intensifying stresses, as the world enters the twenty-first century.

At present and projected growth rates, the world's population would reach 10 billion by 2030 and would approach 30 billion by the end of the twenty-first century. These levels correspond closely to estimates by the U.S. National Academy of Sciences of the maximum carrying capacity of the entire earth. Already the populations in sub-Saharan Africa and in the Himalayan hills of Asia have exceeded the carrying capacity of the immediate area, triggering an erosion of the land's capacity to support life. The resulting poverty and ill health have further complicated efforts to reduce fertility. Unless this circle of interlinked problems is broken soon, population growth in such areas will unfortunately be slowed for reasons other than declining birth rates. Hunger and disease will claim more babies and young children, and more of those surviving will be mentally and physically handicapped by childhood malnutrition.

Indeed, the problems of preserving the carrying capacity of the earth and sustaining the possibility of a decent life for the human beings that inhabit it are enormous and close upon us. Yet there is reason for hope. It must be emphasized that the Global 2000 Study's projections are based on the assumption that national policies regarding population stabilization, resource conservation, and environmental protection will remain essentially unchanged through the end of the century. But in fact, policies are beginning to change. In some areas, forests are being replanted after cutting. Some nations are taking steps to reduce soil losses and desertification. Interest in energy conservation is growing, and large sums are being invested in exploring alternatives to petroleum dependence. The need for family planning is slowly becoming better understood. Water supplies are being improved and waste treatment systems built. High-yield seeds are widely available and seed banks are being expanded. Some wildlands with their genetic resources are being protected. Natural predators and selective pesticides are being substituted for persistent and destructive pesticides.

Encouraging as these developments are, they are far from adequate to meet the global challenges projected in this study. Vigorous, determined new initiatives are needed if worsening poverty and human suffering, environmental degradation, and international tension and conflicts are to be prevented. There are no quick fixes. The only solutions to the problems of population, resources, and environment are complex and long-term. These problems are inextricably linked to some of the most perplexing and persistent problems in the world—poverty, injustice, and social conflict. New and imaginative ideas—and a willingness to act on them—are essential.

The needed changes go far beyond the capability and responsibility of this or any other single nation. An era of unprecedented cooperation and commitment is essential. Yet there are opportunities—and a strong rationale—for the United States to provide leadership among nations. A high priority for this nation must be a thorough assessment of its foreign and domestic policies relating to population, resources, and environment. The United States, possessing the world's largest economy, can expect its policies to have a significant influence on global trends. An equally important priority for the United States is to cooperate generously and justly with other nations—particularly in the areas of trade, investment, and assistance—in seeking solutions to the many problems that extend beyond our national boundaries. There are many unfulfilled opportunities to cooperate with other nations in efforts to relieve poverty and hunger, stabilize population, and enhance economic and environmental productivity. Further cooperation among nations is also needed to strengthen international mechanisms for protecting and utilizing the "global commons"—the oceans and atmosphere. . . .

. . . The Global 2000 Study may be seen as . . . a reconnaissance of the future; its conclusions are reinforced by similar findings of other recent global studies. . . . All these studies are in general agreement on the nature of the problems and on the threats they pose to the future welfare of humankind. The available evidence leaves no doubt that the world—including this Nation—faces enormous, urgent, and complex problems in the decades immediately ahead. Prompt and vigorous changes in public policy around the world are needed to avoid or minimize these problems before they become unmanageable. Long lead times are required for effective action. If decisions are delayed until the problems become worse, options for effective action will be severely reduced.

31

MISCONCEPTIONS GOVERNING AMERICAN FOREIGN POLICY

HENRY STEELE COMMAGER

W*hen society requires to be rebuilt, there is no use in attempting to rebuild it on the old plan.*

No great improvements in the lot of mankind are possible, until a great change takes place in the fundamental constitution of their modes of thought.

John Stuart Mill's admonitions are still valid. Since the Truman Doctrine of 1947—perhaps since Hiroshima and Nagasaki—the United States has been locked into a Cold War whose temperature has fluctuated over the years, and now threatens to become incandescent. The origins of that war have fascinated a generation of historians whose disagreements are by now irremediable, perhaps because the explanations are not to be found so much in unraveling the tangled skein of history as in probing the philosophical and psychological assumptions that were uncritically adopted at the beginning of hostilities, and that have not yet been subjected to serious re-examination by those in power.

How are we to explain our obsession with communism, our paranoid hostility to the Soviet Union, our preoccupation with the Cold War, our reliance on military rather than political or diplomatic solutions, and our new readiness to entertain as a possibility what was long regarded as un-thinkable—atomic warfare?

Can we avoid the "unthinkable" and rebuild a world of peace and order without a change in the "fundamental constitution of [our] modes of thought"—modes of thought themselves largely responsible for the crisis that glares upon us with relentless insistence from every quarter of the horizon?

Some of those assumptions have long enjoyed the dignity of official endorsement; some have been eroded in principle but linger on in official ideology—and are held together by passionate emotional harmony; some

This chapter appeared originally as "Foreign Policy: Outmoded Assumptions," in *The Atlantic Monthly*, 249 (March, 1982): pp. 12, 14–17, 22. Copyright © 1982, by The Atlantic Monthly Company, Boston, Mass. 02116. Reprinted with permission.

are sustained by interests so deeply entrenched that they seem invulnerable to criticism. As a body, the catechism of assumptions resembles in many respects that of the Moral Majority: it is rooted in emotion rather than in reason; it is negative rather than positive in its objectives; it is inspired by fear rather than by confidence; it is inconsistent and even contradictory in logic.

Consider some of those assumptions that have proved most tenacious.

First is the assumption that the world is divided between two great ideological and power groups, one dedicated to freedom, the other to slavery. History appointed the United States to represent and defend the first. The Soviet Union, whether by appointment or not is unclear, represents the second. These two worlds have been, for [over] thirty years, locked in fateful combat.

This simplistic picture has, over the years, been badly distorted by developments that do not fit its logic: the conflict between China and Russia; our own almost nonchalant rapprochement with China; the emergence of a new power bloc in the Middle East; and the growing reluctance of many members of the "free-world" coalition to respect either the freedom or the morality to whose defense we are committed. None of these developments has as yet persuaded many Americans to modify their original conviction that communism is the inveterate enemy.

A second assumption is implicit in the first: that communism, especially the Soviet variety, is not only dedicated to the enslavement of men but is godless and deeply immoral. Therefore the Soviet Union can never be relied upon to keep its word; it is engaged in ceaseless aggrandizement; it makes a mockery of international law and human dignity, and trusts only force. From all this it follows that for us to substitute diplomatic negotiations for military power would be to fall into a trap from which we could not extricate ourselves.

This assumption, to be sure, has deep roots in our history and our psychology. Though perhaps no other nation of modern times has had such spectacular success at the diplomatic table as the United States, Americans have long deluded themselves with the notion that their diplomats—invariably virtuous and innocent—have been consistently seduced and betrayed by wily Old World diplomats. This is, needless to say, fantasy. The Treaty of Paris of 1783 represented a spectacular triumph of American diplomats over both the British and the French, and the new nation found itself not thirteen independent states hugging the Atlantic but a vast empire. Twenty years later Jefferson intended to secure no more than New Orleans, but found that, thanks to Napoleon's impatience, the Treaty of 1803 doubled the territory of the United States without war and almost without cost. No one really won the War of 1812, but American diplomats won the negotiations at Ghent, and after that treaty, and the Battle of New Orleans, Europe left America alone. In 1871, the United States collected substantial awards from Great Britain for her violations of neutrality during the Civil

War—violations of international law that were tame compared with those we now commit as a matter of course. In 1898, we dictated our own terms to Spain; and if in 1919 Wilson was not able to get all the Fourteen Points into the Treaty of Versailles, he did get his associates to set up a League of Nations, which we subsequently scuttled. Certainly we were in command in 1945, dictating terms not only to Germany and Japan but to our allies as well—terms characterized on the whole by magnanimity. Yalta, which most Americans have been led to believe a diplomatic defeat, was no such thing: in the military circumstances of February, 1945 (when American forces had not yet crossed the Rhine), it constituted an American success.

As for violation of international law, treaties, and agreements, and of the territorial integrity of weaker nations, the record of the Soviet Union is indeed deplorable. Whether it differs greatly from the American record depends, no doubt, upon the point of view. Little need to rehearse that record: suffice it to say that the CIA has at least tried to be as subversive as the KGB in many parts of the globe, that intervention in Cuba, the Dominican Republic, and Guatemala was no less in violation of law than the Soviet invasions of Hungary and Czechoslovakia, and that a ten-year undeclared war in Vietnam, with casualties of some two million, both military and civilian, and bombardment with three times the tonnage dropped on Germany and Japan in World War II contrasts unfavorably with the much-condemned Soviet invasion of Afghanistan.

Nothing surprising about all this except that a people brought up, for the most part, on the New Testament should so readily ignore the question raised by Matthew: "Why beholdest thou the mote that is in thy brother's eye, but considerest not the beam that is in thine own eye?"

A third assumption is rooted in the second: that the Soviet Union is the mortal enemy of the United States and that her animosity is implacable. This assumption, implicit in innumerable statements by President Reagan and Secretary of Defense Caspar Weinberger, dictates most of our current political and military programs. The term "dictates" is appropriate, for we no longer appear to be masters of our own destiny or even in control of our policies, but react with almost Pavlovian response to the real or imagined policies of the Soviet Union. Clearly, our reaction to the Polish crisis is animated more by hostility to the Soviet Union than by compassion for Poland.

In all this we rarely ask ourselves what the Soviet Union has to gain by destroying the United States. In the past neither czarist nor Communist Russia has been an "enemy" of the United States, and in the twentieth century Russia was allied with or associated with the United States in two major wars. Nor do many Americans pause to acknowledge that the Communists have more ground for fearing the United States than we have for fearing them: after all, American military forces invaded the Soviet Union at Archangel and Vladivostok to prevent the Bolshevik takeover and remained on Russian soil for well over two years: had Communist forces invaded the United States in, let us say, Alaska or Florida, we would not be quite so forgetful.

That the ideological conflict between the Soviet Union and the United States is deep and perhaps irremediable cannot be denied. It is sobering to recall that during the early years of the nineteenth century—and, indeed, again during our Civil War—much of Europe looked upon the United States as we now look upon the Soviet Union, and with more justification. The new American republic did indeed threaten the peace and security of Old World nations. Republicanism, democracy, constitutionalism, and social equality challenged all Old World monarchies and class societies. That challenge was practical—millions of Europeans found refuge in America—and it was philosophical, as well. Listen to Prince Metternich, the greatest and most powerful European statesman of his generation, excoriate the United States for proclaiming the Monroe Doctrine:

These United States . . . have suddenly left a sphere too narrow for their ambition, and have astonished Europe by a new act of revolt, more unprovoked, fully as audacious, and no less dangerous than the former [against Britain]. They have distinctly and exactly announced their intention to set not only power against power, but, to express it more exactly, altar against altar. In their indecent declarations they have cast blame and scorn on the institutions of Europe most worthy of respect. . . . In permitting themselves these unprovoked attacks, in fostering revolutions wherever they show themselves, in regretting those which have failed, in extending a helping hand to those which seem to prosper, they lend new strength to the apostles of sedition, and re-animate the courage of every conspirator. If this flood of evil doctrines and pernicious examples should extend over the whole of America, what would become of our religious and political institutions, of the moral forces of our governments, and of the conservative system which has saved Europe from complete dissolution?

Nor was this paranoia confined to spokesmen of autocratic countries. Here is what the leading British journal of its day—*Blackwood's Edinburgh Magazine*—had to say of Lincoln's Emancipation Proclamation:

Monstrous, reckless, devilish. . . . It proves . . . [that] rather than lose their trade and custom, the North would league itself with Beelzebub and seek to make a hell of half a continent. In return this atrocious act justifies the South in hoisting the black flag . . . And thus . . . we are called upon to contemplate a war more full of horrors and wickedness than any which stands recorded in the world's history.

The exacerbation of anti-Russian paranoia by this administration is not in fact in the mainstream of American experience. We have had less excuse for it than any other major nation, for since 1815 we have never been threatened by external aggression by any nation except Japan nor, except for the Civil War, by serious ideological conflicts.

One current crisis dramatizes the wisdom of President Washington's warning, in his Farewell Address:

... nothing is more essential than that permanent, inveterate anti-pathies against particular nations . . . be excluded; and that in place of them just and amicable feelings towards all should be cultivated. The nation which indulges towards another an habitual hatred or an habit-ual fondness is in some degree a slave. It is a slave to its animosity or to its affection . . . Antipathy in one nation against another disposes each more readily to offer insult and injury . . .

It is perhaps this enslavement to our own animosity that explains a fourth major assumption—one we might call the Dr. Strangelove syndrome: that we could fight and "win" an atomic war, that the loss of 50 million to 100 million lives would be "acceptable," that the Republic could survive and flourish after such a victory. An atomic war is no longer "unthinkable"; perhaps it never was: after all, we are the only nation ever to use the atomic weapon against an enemy. Now spokesmen of both our parties have declared that in an "emergency" we would not hesitate to use it again. In all this we are reminded of the moral of slavery: when a "necessary evil" becomes necessary enough, it ceases to be an evil.

This philosophy is a product, or a by-product, of a fifth assumption: that the most effective way, and perhaps the only way, to counter the threat of communism is neither political, economic, nor moral but quite simply military, and that the mere threat of overwhelming military might will per-suade all rivals to abandon the field.

This is, to be sure, a familiar maxim: it was Voltaire who observed that God is always for the big battalions. But there is an older wisdom. More than three centuries ago Francis Bacon wrote, "Walled towers, stored arsenals, and armories, goodly races of horse, chariots of war, elephants, ordnance, artillery and the like—all this is but a sheep in lion's skin, except the breed and disposition of the people be stout . . ."

That is still true, though we must rephrase it to comport with modern weaponry. The futility of reliance on superiority in nuclear arms should have been clear as early as 1949, when the Russians astonished most of the "experts" by detonating their own atomic bomb a decade earlier than had been expected. Certainly it should be clear by now that the Russians can produce anything that we can produce, and that the notion of "winning" an arms race is fantasy. The hope—perhaps the only hope—of avoiding a nuclear war lies not in adding another $1,500 billion to the $2,000 billion we have already spent on the military since the close of World War II but in mutual abandonment of that race, and a cooperative program of systematic reduction of existing nuclear arms.

As for security, that is indeed to be found in the "stoutness" and the disposition of the people—in their courage, intelligence, and resourceful-ness, and in the preservation and nurture of that common wealth with which Nature has endowed them. The most serious threat to national secu-rity is in the wastage of human and the exhaustion of natural resources. It is in permitting our industrial and technological enterprises, our transportation system, our financial health, to deteriorate, our cities to decay into slums, our schools to fail of their primary functions of education, our society to be ravaged by poverty, lawlessness, racial strife, class hostilities, and injustice. It is in a leadership that lacks prudence, wisdom, and vision. It is in a society whose leaders no longer invoke, and whose people no longer take seriously, those concepts of public virtue, of the pursuit of happiness, and of the fiduciary obligation to posterity that were the all-but-universal precepts of the generation that founded the Republic.

A sixth assumption is a by-product of the fifth: that the security of the United States is bound up with and dependent on whatever regimes throughout the globe are ostentatiously anti-Communist. Our record here is a dismal one, yet instead of repudiating that record, the present administration seems determined to outstrip it. We persist in regarding South Korea and Taiwan as not only friends but allies; we practically forced Pakistan to accept billions of dollars for arms; we have abandoned all pretense of holding aloof from the tyrannical regimes of Chile and Argentina; we even conjure up a distinction between "authoritarian" and "totalitarian" regimes, whose only real distinction is whether they are authoritarian on our side or not. The vocabulary of this administration, as of Nixon's, inevitably conjures up what Thucydides said of the corruption of language in the Athens of his day: "What used to be described as a thoughtless act of aggression, was now regarded as the courage one would expect to find in a party member . . . fanatical enthusiasm was the mark of a real man . . . anyone who held violent opinions could always be trusted . . . and to plot successfully was a sign of intelligence."

To many of the peoples of the Third World, and even of the European world, the United States appears to be what the Holy Alliance was in the early nineteenth century. The analogy does not favor the United States, for while the Holy Alliance, for all its interventions in Spain and Italy and Greece, had the good sense to keep out of distant continents, the United States does not. What our interventions throughout the globe—Vietnam, Cambodia, Angola, Nicaragua, El Salvador, and Iran—have in common with those of the Holy Alliance is their failure.

Much of our new "imperialism" is rooted in a seventh assumption: that the United States is not only a Western but an African and an Asian power.

That the United States is a world power is incontestable. Clearly, too, it is by virtue of geography an Atlantic power and a Pacific power, and it is by virtue of history something of a European power—a fact convincingly vindicated by participation in two world wars. But the United States is no more an Asian power than China or Japan is an American power. We have never permitted an Asian power to establish a military presence in the American continents. We bought Alaska from Russia, and the 1912 Lodge Corollary to the Monroe Doctrine extended that doctrine to "any Government, not

American." It was the illusion that we could control the internal politics of China that distracted us from a recognition of reality for a quarter-century: certainly the greatest blunder in the history of American diplomacy. Even now, notwithstanding the commonsense reversal of that misguided policy by Nixon and Kissinger, we have not yet wholly rid ourselves of the purblind notion that we can, and should, "play the China card"—a notion that in its arrogance and in its vulgarity must represent the low-water mark of American foreign policy.

Another corollary of our reliance on the military for security is dramatized by an eighth assumption: that to achieve security it is proper for government to conscript science and scholarship for the purposes of war, cold or not; that, in short, the scientific, philosophical, and cultural community should be an instrument of the State for secular purposes.

This principle was not embraced by those who founded the Republic nor, for that matter, by the philosophers of the Enlightenment in the Old World. During the American Revolution, Benjamin Franklin joined with the French minister of finance, Jacques Necker, to decree immunity for Captain Cook because he was "engaged in pursuits beneficial to mankind." In the midst of the Napoleonic Wars, the French Institute conferred its gold medal on the great British scientist Humphrey Davy, and while the war was still raging, Sir Humphrey crossed the Channel to accept that honor. "If two countries are at war," he said, "the men of science are not." Napoleon himself shared this view: during his victorious campaign in Germany, he spared the university city of Göttingen from bombardment because it was the home of the greatest of classical scholars, Christian Heyne. And it was Napoleon, too, who, at the request of Joseph Banks of the Royal Society, freed the great geologist Dolomieu from the dungeons of Naples. Edward Jenner, the discoverer of the smallpox vaccine, put it for his whole generation: "The sciences are never at war. Peace must always preside in the bosoms of those whose object is the augmentation of human happiness." . . .

A ninth assumption, perhaps the most intractable of all, is that any of the fundamental problems that confront us—and other nations of the globe—can be resolved within the framework of the nation-state system. The inescapable fact, dramatized by the energy crisis, the population crisis, the armaments race, and so forth, is that nationalism as we have known it in the nineteenth and much of the twentieth century is as much of an anachronism today as was States Rights when Calhoun preached it and Jefferson Davis fought for it. Just as we know, or should know, that none of our domestic problems can be solved within the artificial boundaries of the states, so none of our global problems can be solved within the largely artificial boundaries of nations—artificial not so much in the eyes of history as in the eyes of Nature. Nature, as the dispenser of all resources, knows no boundaries between North and South Dakota or Kansas and Nebraska, no boundaries, for that matter, between Canada, the United States, and Mexico, and very few between the two Americas, Europe, Asia, and Africa. Every major problem that confronts us is global—energy, pollution, the destruction of the oceans and the seas, the erosion of agricultural and forest lands, the control of epidemics and of plant and animal diseases, famine in large parts of Asia and Africa and a population increase that promises to aggravate famine, inflation, international terrorism, nuclear pollution, and nuclear-arms control. Not one of these can be solved within the limits of a single nation.

Even to mitigate these problems requires the cooperation of statesmen, scientists, and moral philosophers in every country. Americans should find it easier to achieve such cooperation than did the peoples of Old World nations, for they are the heirs and the beneficiaries of a philosophy that proclaimed that *all* men were created equal and endowed with unalienable rights to life, liberty, and the pursuit of happiness.

Of all the assumptions I have discussed, that which takes nationalism for granted is perhaps the most deeply rooted and the most tenacious. Yet when we reflect that assumptions, even certainties, no less tenacious in the past—about the very nature of the cosmic system, about the superiority of one race to all others, about the naturalness of women's subordination to men, about the providential order of a class society, about the absolute necessity of a state church or religion—have all given way to the implacable pressure of science and of reality, we may conclude that what Tocqueville wrote well over a century ago is still valid:

> The world that is rising into existence is still half encumbered by the remains of the world that is waning into decay; and amid the vast perplexity of human affairs none can say how much of ancient institutions and former customs will remain or how much will completely disappear.

If some of our ancient institutions do not disappear, there is little likelihood that we shall remain.

32

FOREIGN POLICY: WHAT'S TO BE DONE?

STANLEY HOFFMANN

I

What kind of strategy would respond to the international situation many Americans find so ominous today? A few guidelines, at least, can be useful, first about preconditions for effective policy, then about priorities.

One precondition is the need to minimize discontinuity. The American system of government, with its concentration on the president, and the absence of a permanent bureaucracy at the top, is always prone to sudden changes of course. When presidents do not make it to a second term, the risk of hairpin turns increases. When a new president also is of a different party from his predecessor's, and there is a big shift in Congress, the temptation to repudiate the past and to put Creation in the present is overwhelming. But nothing is more destructive of confidence abroad, more dangerous and ultimately more confusing at home. It is a way both of raising excessive hopes in the electorate, and of telling many voters to burn what they once adored.

In the not so long term, this aggravates the voters' distrust of politics and politicians, and injects cynicism where trust should be, apathy where what John Stuart Mill called "the invigorating effect of freedom" ought to be felt. Many of the new initiatives, announced not because they are part of a well thought through policy, but because they demonstrate the desire for novelty and symbolize the new priorities, are likely either to backfire . . . or to go out of control. . . .

Allies and adversaries alike are unhelpfully upset; insofar as one of our goals is to induce more predictable behavior from our foes, our own unpredictability entails a change of signals, the throwing of new wrenches into the negotiations (as in the case of the Law of the Sea Conference), the raising of new conditions, the failure to pick up dangling threads (as the sad story of

An abridged version of Stanley Hoffmann's "Foreign Policy: What's to Be Done?" *The New York Review of Books* 28 (April 30, 1981): pp. 33–39. Some footnotes have been deleted or renumbered as appropriate. Reprinted with permission from *The New York Review of Books.* Copyright © 1981 NYREV, Inc.

SALT II since 1972 shows). Allies keep worrying about the wondrous new initiatives we will invent, the new slogans we will float, and above all the new demands we will make. . . .

A second proposition is that an effective foreign policy presupposes solid domestic underpinnings. It requires, on the one hand, an economic basis. This means a gradual reduction of inflation, allowing for a return to steady growth. A mere injection of money into the economy, by worsening inflation, would once more lead the government and the Federal Reserve authorities to put on the brakes and to provoke a recession. But a strictly monetarist attempt to break inflation by shock therapy followed by several years of recession and high unemployment would be unpalatable politically, at home and abroad. It also means an energy policy that reduces American dependence on imports from the Middle East, and thus decreases the imbalance of bargaining power between producers and consumers, reduces the weight of oil prices for developing, oil-importing countries, and thus helps to save them from increasingly more staggering indebtedness and falling rates of growth. It means, in the third place, a policy of industrial reconversion, to avoid, instance after instance, the bleak choice between bankruptcy and bailouts, between collapse and protectionism. . . .

A sound domestic political basis is also necessary. It entails, first, a reorganization of the executive which makes of the State Department the clear center of decision, negotiation, and execution. . . .

We need, in the second place, more of an effort to include important members of Congress, from both houses and parties, into the policy process, from the start. And we need, above all, a president keen on educating the public. . . . President [Reagan] is, in the words of Mr. Meese, excellent as a "management communicator." To be a good educator, he would have to be a bit more: he would have not only to inspire confidence, to be lucid in spelling out goals and priorities, but above all to be able to make Americans recognize and accept the reality and effects of complexity. He would have to see to it that their legitimate thirst for respect, their concern for honor and pride do not degenerate into the kind of machismo that, at best, is no more than posturing but, at worst (especially when rationalized by slogans, wrapped in spite or paternalism, and acted out by a mix of ignorance and arrogance), could make some Americans far more ashamed than proud. In this respect, the president's fondness for American exceptionalism, displayed in his inaugural address, does not bode well.

II

The goal of American foreign policy ought to be not merely the containment of Soviet expansionism but the management and steering of inevitable change. Not all changes are welcome, nor are all changes irresistible or unavoidable. But what is utterly unrealistic is a Metternichian attitude that equates stability with the status quo: what is almost as unrealistic is one that tolerates only the kind of peaceful, orderly change which not even Americans have always experienced in their history.

A few things appear certain, even to one whose skepticism about waves of the future, necessary trends, and philosophies of history is total. Complete and permanent repression is not a safe method of government. Even in countries with very old traditions of iron rule, expert in insulating their peoples from contamination and contact, the spirit and the contagion of criticism and ethnic assertiveness may be felt. Indeed the Soviet Union is probably, along with South Africa, the society whose present "formula" is, in the long run, the most unworkable. Nations such as Chile and Brazil, in which formidable inequities, extreme contrasts of poverty and wealth, rapid growth without benefit for the poor are maintained only by police methods and the control of all organizations by the state, face a stormy future. Countries such as Taiwan and South Korea, with increasing prosperity and rapidly expanding middle classes but no political safety valve, risk having the lid blown off—as happened in Iran. New countries such as Zaire, Ethiopia, or Uganda, whose precarious unity can no longer be assured by the battle against foreign masters, which are wracked by every kind of internal heterogeneity and ruled by small and greedy cliques, are breeding grounds for rebels and tempting preys for meddlers.

Many of the potentially most unstable countries happen to be clients or allies of the US—they range from Guatemala to Pakistan and the Philippines, from Haiti to Morocco and Egypt, from El Salvador to Saudi Arabia and Indonesia. Our twin worries, in years to come, will have to be to prevent explosions in such places from becoming manifestations of anti-Americanism, opportunities for Soviet influence; and to prevent explosions and disruptions in the Soviet universe from leading to general war. The one thing we will not be able to do, however hard we try, is to prevent explosions. Rather than direct aggression, it is the exploitation of revolutionary conditions, either through subversion or through encouragement of local revolutionary groups, which is the most likely form of Soviet expansion. In Afghanistan, indeed, it was such exploitation which, having been a failure, led to aggression.

In other words, the key issue—for the rest of the century—is the issue of revolution. And it so happens that, of all major powers in history, we may well be among the least well prepared to cope with it—since our only revolutionary experience was national not social, and since it is against the excesses and local incrustations of capitalism that many revolutions are likely to occur. To try to "coopt" change by rhetoric . . . will not get us very far. To excommunicate it will get us nowhere. In some countries, such as the Dominican Republic, democratic governments have survived with US encouragement. But to try crassly to manipulate other societies in a quest for progressive moderates, for benevolent centrists, has become a depressing ritual, since in many places such centrists are either ineffectual or the first victims of the contending extremes, and since nothing weakens their legitimacy more than an ardent embrace by us.

If we see in every revolution in which there is a trace of Soviet involvement a test between us and Moscow, we will stagger from one self-fulfilling prophecy to another in the worst possible conditions—we will either face endless military quagmires (or "pacification" campaigns), or risk dangerous escalations in order to "win" on more favorable ground, or fail. To see in every place where there is an opportunity for our opponents a deliberate target already chosen by them would also be self-defeating because it would allow them to divert attention, through propaganda, from their own exactions; and because it would radicalize large numbers of people, even in countries friendly to us. It is the US, not the Soviet Union, which would appear as the greatest threat to the independence of third world countries, should our interventions on behalf of the status quo turn us into heavy-handed protectors of shaky regimes, and should we behave as self-appointed geopolitical policemen.

Obviously, in a world of 170 states, sweeping generalizations are of little use. But a valid guideline would be, wherever we are closely associated with a regime, to encourage timely reform (by this I mean not only economic and social measures, such as land reform, by which we tend to get hypnotized, but above all the sharing of political power, which is what most discontented groups want, since political power conditions their future); for what is destabilizing is not such reform, but immobility. And we should distance or dissociate ourselves from a regime when it resists reform and dooms itself to upheaval, thus becoming a burden to its people and a liability to us.

In all cases where we are not particularly close, we should give no encouragement to regimes that trample the human rights for whose defense we stand (such as the current regimes in Argentina and Chile). And we should—as Carter did in Nicaragua and Zimbabwe—accept ungrudgingly radical new regimes, even if some of the groups that fought for power received support from "unfriendly" sources, as in Angola or Mozambique. We should then use our resources, our influence, and our skills to protect our main interests, to encourage these regimes to have normal relations with us, and to make it clear that it is to their advantage to avoid vicious treatment of internal opponents. When we treat such regimes, from the outset, as delinquents, and try to quarantine or to "destabilize" or to starve them, we foster both unnecessary hostility and the kind of internal reaction that strengthens extremism, paranoia, and repression.

What about Saudi Arabia, some will say? I see no reason to make an exception in that case. The US has to take account of the current regime's legitimate needs for arms and to have cooperative relations with it; but it must also quietly anticipate the possibility that through revolution, or mere succession, a new regime may appear, which will decide to cut down oil production for purely Saudi reasons. (Note that this case has to be distinguished from that of a deliberate effort, by the USSR or by a coalition of Middle Eastern states, to "strangulate" Western economies.) The US would be in a tragic position if it had to choose between economic disaster and a military intervention that could be economically futile and would be politically catastrophic. The Saudi sword over our heads is an added, powerful incentive for a combined energy policy of the US, its European allies, and Japan. It is not a reason for abandoning these guidelines.

III

In the world as it is, American foreign policy will have to be complex and to take advantage of complexity. This has several implications. The first is the end of unilateralism. The diffusion of power, in the third world as well as among the industrial countries, the appearance of new regional actors, the ability of the lesser ones either to combine their interests in a variety of groups and bodies, or to appeal to their bigger neighbors or to distant powers for protection against outside threats—all of this makes it impossible for the US to impose its own concerns (or obsessions), so to speak, from above and outside, and to assume that it is in the higher interest of others to share and to heed them. In this sense, the battle over the Panama Canal treaties was highly symbolic; it was a battle about accepting the end of the colonial era.

If we face major threats in parts of the world we deem essential—the Persian Gulf, Central America—we have no other recourse than to enlist the support of the main states in the area. If we want them to give priority to the threat of invasion or subversion by the Soviets or their proxies, and to make sure that our own military assistance does not end up supporting the local ambitions and grievances of the states we assist, we must also cooperate with the countries of each area in order to help them resolve intra-regional disputes. We can have a unilateral Central American policy only at the cost of antagonizing not only Mexico (a nation of growing importance for our future) but Venezuela, the other democratic republics of the area and of Latin America—and even some of the authoritarian ones, whose distaste for radicals is matched by their dislike for the big stick of Washington. To be sure, in a case such as that of El Salvador, the countries in the region may disagree on the best solution. But most of them agree on what would be the worst one—American military intervention—and we could do far worse than enlist their cooperation in the search for a political compromise.

In the Middle East, we have found that even Arab countries divided over Camp David agreed in their reluctance to provide us with bases—not because of the decline of our power, but because of our failure to use it in the one case, the Arab-Israeli dispute, that concerns them all. . . . It would be in our interest to enlist the support of our European allies . . . as well as that of all the non-rejectionist Arab states in the search for a solution of the Palestinian issue.

In the case of Southern Africa—Namibia, the future of South Africa itself—the cooperation of European states, especially Britain, and of key Black African countries will be indispensable; any rapprochement with South Africa will be shortsighted.

What this requires is a willingness on our part not merely to share the burdens and divide labor in a task defined by us but to devise a policy together. This does not mean encouraging selected allies whose own designs could prove deeply divisive in a given part of the world (as Iran did under the Shah, as the King of Morocco tends to be because of his Western Sahara adventure). It does require regional efforts aimed at coping with local threats . . . and providing such groupings with assistance, rather than shortcircuiting them with our own forces. Insofar as these would be needed, as against a Soviet threat of invasion in the Middle East, to have available a quickly deployable force stationed outside the area would be preferable to the permanent stationing of ground forces in it. The theoretical advantage in deterrent and war-fighting power permanent ground forces might enjoy would be smaller than the political costs of stationing them in so unstable an area where the winds of nationalism are so strong. . . .

Another implication of complexity is the need for selectivity, because of the limits on American power. The US must have both "power politics" goals—to preserve from aggression the territory of its allies and to preserve access to vital natural resources—and "world order" goals—to preserve chances for a humane and reasonably prosperous world. But, especially if America's economy does not recover speedily, the means at our disposal will have to be used intelligently. A world-wide crusade, stretching the meaning of security to extend to the internal order of states, or making of "friendly" states an essential ingredient of a tolerable international milieu, is clearly beyond our means, as well as likely to be counterproductive. But a policy of accommodating change and accepting revolutions, while more modest in its goals, still ought to make use of varied incentives to promote such important objectives as nonproliferation, the protection of human rights, and the improvement of economic conditions in developing countries.

IV

With respect to security, selectivity means concentrating our resources on improving the state of readiness and the equipment of our conventional forces, at the cost of returning to a peacetime draft if this appears necessary to build up adequate reserves. We need, also, more abundant means of air and naval transportation for the rapid deployment, reinforcement, and supply of our conventional forces. The navy needs anti-submarine protection and air defense against Soviet attack submarines and planes, and more ships for the Persian Gulf; but vulnerable supercarriers and revamped old battleships with cruise missiles are a dubious investment. All this is far more important than strengthening our nuclear forces. Our main problem there, the vulnerability of Minuteman missiles by the mid-1980s, is significant far less for its military effects—as an incentive for a Soviet strike, or a military disaster should Moscow strike—than for its psychological ones, the effects on our own perceptions and on those of our allies. And it can be dealt with by several possible policies.

First, we could try to negotiate a new agreement with Moscow to allow missile site defense, at a time when Soviet missiles are likely to become vulnerable to American strikes also. This would make sense only when ballistic missile defense is technically safe, and if there is an arms control agreement limiting the number of warheads each side can use to overwhelm the other side's defenses. In any case, it may not be to our overall advantage, since it would protect a far greater portion of the Soviet nuclear arsenal than of ours (land-based missiles constitute only one-fourth of ours, but four-fifths of theirs).

We could, alternatively, make Minuteman missiles mobile, underground or, should this prove to be financially and politically too costly, on submarines near the coast. Neither the MX nor a new strategic bomber is necessary. It is more important to deprive the Soviets of the one advantage their alleged war-fighting strategy can theoretically count on than to increase or improve our own nuclear war-fighting capacities beyond our regular program, which includes already air-launched cruise missiles and more accurate missiles on Minuteman and on our nuclear submarines. The latter, as well as most of our planes, would in any case survive a Soviet attack on Minuteman.

It may be argued that deterring a Soviet conventional attack on our European allies, or in the Persian Gulf area, requires an American ability to strike first with nuclear weapons, which would be aimed at Soviet military targets. But, on the one hand, there are many other targets besides Soviet missiles; and on the other hand, technological progress is going to make Soviet missiles vulnerable anyhow, without the MX or a new strategic bomber. To use the experts' jargon, we already have, and will increasingly have, "counterforce capabilities," and while the Soviets may have a temporary advantage, it is neither decisive (given the formidable risks the Soviets would incur if they attacked our land-based missiles) nor irremediable.

What we surely need is "crisis stability," which means forces neither so vulnerable as to tempt the other side to strike first, nor "so provocative to the other side as to induce the attack it seeks to deter."[1] An American policy of piling up the MX, a new strategic bomber, cruise missiles, middle-range missiles in Europe, and perhaps ballistic missile defenses, would be provocative. Moreover, to concentrate on strategic rather than on conventional forces would put the main burden of conventional rearmament on Bonn and Tokyo, with disastrous results, including bitter and divisive reactions both within Germany and Japan and from neighboring powers. To go for both a conventional and a strategic arms build-up would put an enormous burden on the economy and divert resources from other forms of power and other policies.

A selective policy means, above all, a new attempt at establishing a mixed relationship with Moscow. The preconditions are clear: First, we need to improve the military balance in Europe, with respect to NATO's conventional and middle-range nuclear forces. There is no justification for a doomsday view of the current conventional balance in Europe, but the trends of the 1970s are disturbing. The Warsaw Pact forces have a considerable lead in artillery, armored vehicles, attack helicopters, and offensive chemical warfare; their equipment is standardized; they have shorter lines of communication, and the number of long-range aircraft available to them has increased. NATO forces have an advantage in precision-guided munitions, anti-tank weapons, and tactical aircraft. But they can no longer expect to compensate for their quantitative inferiority with qualitative superiority, in view of Soviet progress in quality; and above all, they must try to overcome their opponents' current advantage in being able to build up their forces much faster. NATO needs more "prepositioned" stocks in Europe, quicker reinforcement capacity, and increased reserves.

As for middle-range nuclear weapons capable of hitting the Soviet Union, their need arises from the rapid deployment of the mobile and precise Soviet SS20 missiles, and from the Soviet construction of the Backfire bomber—weapon systems unmatched so far by NATO. The purpose of these Soviet weapons seems to be to make it possible for the Warsaw Pact countries to wage a purely conventional war in Europe, in the hope that the US would be deterred from the first use of its strategic, long-range nuclear weapons against Soviet territory by the fear of Soviet retaliation on the US, and that NATO would be deterred from resorting to its own short-range nuclear weapons (most of which could not reach the Soviet Union) by the ability of new Soviet missiles and bombers to destroy NATO's military objectives, including troop concentrations and nuclear installations. The NATO decision, in December, 1979, to deploy 108 mobile middle-range Pershing missiles and 464 ground-launched cruise missiles capable of reaching the Soviet Union means that the Soviet Union would, in invading Western Europe with conventional forces, expose itself to nuclear attack launched from Europe on its own territory; and the burden of initiating a strategic, intercontinental nuclear war would then rest on the USSR, not on Washington.

A second precondition is a Soviet willingness to move toward a generally acceptable solution in Afghanistan, one that would include withdrawal of Soviet troops. Large-scale, overt American arming of the Afghan resistance, untied to any diplomatic offer of a political solution, is likely to be counterproductive: it would incite the Soviets to dig in (and help justify their fake rationale for invading), and it would require a commitment to the Pakistan regime that could harm both our relations with India and our nonproliferation policy. . . .

A third precondition would be Soviet restraint in the aggressive use of force in other parts of the world—no more Afghanistans, and no invasion of Poland.

V

The objectives of a new relationship with Moscow cannot be the same as those of détente in the 1970s. Then, we hoped for a swift reduction of the burden of armaments, and we hoped to convert Moscow to our notion of international stability. Moscow hoped to bring about a reduction of America's presence and influence in the world, and to obtain a kind of political condominium. But we can no more prevent the Soviets from trying to affect the "correlation of forces," by exploiting opportunities in the third world, or by trying to drive wedges between the Western Europeans and ourselves, than they can prevent the reassertion of American influence and the resistance of Americans and others to the Soviet dream of a world run by the two superpowers together. In other words, each side had excessive expectations; and each one should learn from the experience: the Soviets, that the tilt in "correlation" can go either way, and that political condominium is beyond their reach; we, that agreements with Moscow mean neither ideological demobilization on their part nor a Soviet endorsement of the status quo. However, neither the mutual disillusionment of recent years, nor the new American mood of confrontation, nor the change in the military balance makes a revised policy of détente (under that or any other name) unadvisable or absurd.

As I have suggested before, the aim of foreign policy ought to be to make it possible for each of the two powers to play its own game, in such a way as not to violate the vital interests of the other. What is involved is not a fading away but a taming of the competition; not an explicit code of conduct demanded of the other side, but a change in the means and intensity of the contest, and a clear understanding both of what each side deems intolerable and of what measures it would take against the other if the intolerable should occur. . . .

A second objective is the pursuit of arms control. . . .

The present reaction against arms control in this country is a typical example of the tendency to throw away a tool because it has failed to do a job we were probably quite wrong to expect it to do—whether it is restraining competition in the third world or stopping the Soviet build-up—rather than appreciating what it can do. The fact is that without a limit on the number of warheads each type of missile can carry, the threat to our land-based missiles would become far worse, and it would be futile to invent schemes to make land-based mobile missiles: the more holes we would dig, the more warheads Moscow could aim at.

Bringing about strategic arms limitations and a comprehensive test ban soon would make the future arms race both more predictable and more restricted. It would allow us to concentrate, in our military efforts, on the more serious problem of conventional forces. It could provide the basis for the negotiation of serious discrete issues arising in the near future. These issues include: ballistic missile defense; antisatellite weapons; land-based missile vulnerability; verifying the number of mobile land-based missiles (should their increasing vulnerability, on both sides, lead each power to seek solace in such mobility); and curtailing ground and sea launched cruise missiles.

In building cruise missiles, we may repeat the mistake we made when we failed to push hard for a curb on MIRV at a time when we were ahead. In the long run, unlimited cruise missiles may become a curse for us, if the Soviets should multiply conventional as well as nuclear cruise missiles. Arms control could save both sides from a costly and dangerous drive for superiority.

Moreover, negotiating limitations on or reductions of both strategic and middle-range European-based nuclear weapons is a political prerequisite for the acceptance by the West Germans of the new NATO missiles I have described above. The NATO program of December 1979 needs both a military rationale and a political base. The willingness to negotiate is the only way of containing the wave of nuclear pacifism that has spread over part of the British and West German Left and over the smaller Western European countries, where the new American emphasis on counterforce war . . . and the ominous rise in mobile and precise nuclear weapons in the two alliances that face each other in the middle of Europe have reawakened the latent fear of a nuclear war fought over Europe.

VI

A last objective in our policy toward Moscow would be a renewed search for agreement on matters of mutual benefit. Economic cooperation can be one of them, especially with respect to the development of Soviet energy resources. The pursuit of a joint nonproliferation policy is another. There may be a joint interest in political cooperation in the Middle East, an area from which it is impossible to exclude either great power, which neither one can dominate, where each one finds its clients either troublesome or unreliable, and where the risks of confrontation far exceed the advantages of stirring the pot of troubles.

We face two Soviet threats. One is military—capacities for aggression (neither unlimited nor universal) and the ability to provide arms to groups and governments supported by Moscow. The other is political—the ability to exploit or exacerbate revolutionary tendencies or conflicts in the third world. But the Soviet Union has little to offer to countries in quest of economic development and political self-reliance. Its control over its Eastern European satellites is shaky and costly, its influence over distant clients is often temporary, and it suffers from political and economic rigidities which could cripple its effectiveness as a superpower or oblige it to sink its energies into drastic, painful, and unsettling internal reform. Against the Soviet military and political threat, against a Soviet temptation to find in external adventures a diversion from the domestic problems, we must follow a multiple strategy. We should combine defense measures, preventive diplomacy, and policies aimed at increasing the capacity for national and collective independence of other countries. We should also preserve possibilities of mutual arrangements with Moscow, given the waste of resources the arms race entails, the perils of confrontation, the fact that a large number of issues require some cooperation, and the Western ability to affect Soviet choices.

We should not let ourselves either be obsessed by Soviet strengths or lulled by Soviet weaknesses. The former are manageable. The latter are real, but not less serious than the present economic weaknesses of the noncommunist world in general and of the United States in particular (such as the decline of American productivity). And we could make our own economic weaknesses worse if, emulating Lyndon Johnson's mistakes in the mid-Sixties, we combined vast military expenditures with tax cuts and if our nonmilitary industries were obliged either to hide behind disastrous protective barriers or to succumb to the competition of countries that invest fewer financial and human resources in defense.

The directions suggested here are not those which our . . . leaders are inclined to follow. But they may find that their own analysis—which makes of the Soviet-American conflict the omnivorous issue of our time, and attributes past difficulties with allies and clients to our earlier failure of will and power—is far too simple-minded. They may come to see that the projection of a bipolar grid on regional disputes and internal turbulence all over the world is unsuccessful; that their neo-nationalism and their emphasis on military power antagonize more nations than are impressed; that their dislike of North-South bargains is putting the US at a disadvantage; that their view of Soviet expansionism is too militant to be widely shared by those who also deem Moscow dangerous. Then, perhaps, a chance would come for a more constructive approach.

The twin perils of the 1980s are a mismanagement of our contest with the Soviet Union, which may occur if its leaders feel altogether confident in its might, trapped by an unreformable and creaky system at home, and entirely cornered and surrounded abroad; and a mismanagement of the world economy, which the risks of a prolonged recession in the West and the shaky condition of the international financial and monetary systems might well provide. Against these dangers, the fundamentalist reaction that now prevails in the US has little to offer; it may indeed contribute to them. . . .

NOTE

1. *Challenges for US National Security*, Carnegie Panel on US Security and the Future of Arms Control, January 1981, p. 56.

INDEX

COMPILED BY
LUCIA WREN RAWLS
JOSEPH SAUSNOCK, III

Aaron, David, 189, 482
ABM. See Anti-ballistic missile
Acheson, Dean, 32, 197, 472, 490
Action-channels, 415
Action-reaction cycle, 205
Advanced Developing Countries
  (ADCs), 156
Advanced Industrial Countries
  (AICs), 121
Afghanistan, 26, 28, 29, 40, 151, 190,
  194, 213, 216, 443, 525
  Soviet invasion of, 43, 91, 153, 172,
  173, 175, 190, 191, 193, 210–
  211, 314, 512
Africa, 11, 124, 191, 507, 522
Agee, Philip, 312
Agricultural exports, U.S., 138, 140,
  158
Agricultural trade, 140–141
Agriculture, U.S. Department of, 122
AID. See International Development,
  Agency for
Allen, Richard, 275–276, 277, 484,
  486, 487
Alliances, 75, 100, 105, 107–110, 121,
  128, 129, 130, 197, 216, 217,
  220
Allison, Graham T., 290, 351, 363n,
  364, 365, 410–423 et passim,
  490
Ambrose, Stephen E., 4–5
American exceptionalism, 519

American foreign policy. See Foreign
  policy, post-WW II American
Angola, 25, 29, 40, 187, 198, 328–329
Anti-Americanism, 163, 190
Anti-ballistic missile, 57, 59
Anticommunism, 4–6, 13, 14, 36, 97,
  179, 193, 303, 515
Antihegemonal alignment, 26
ANZUS pact, commercial sales to,
  94n
Appeasement, 177
Arab-Israeli conflict, 87, 99, 232, 278
Argentina, 515
Armed forces, political use of, 62–78
  et passim
Arms control, 202, 368, 394, 514, 525–
  526
Arms Control and Disarmament
  Agency (ACDA), U.S., 95n, 230
Arms Export Control Act (AECA), 89,
  90
Arms race, 12–13, 17, 35, 43, 181, 182,
  205, 207, 309, 514, 516
Arms sales, 18, 515
Arms transfer policies, 90, 91, 92, 153,
  232, 290
Armstrong, Hamilton Fish, 176–177
Asia, American policies toward, 36,
  91, 507
Asymmetrical response. See Contain-
  ment
Atlantic Charter, 19, 151

Atomic bomb, 12, 21
Austrian State Treaty, 433
Authoritarian regimes, 124, 183, 185
  as distinct from totalitarian, 515
AWACS (Airborne Warning and Control System), 59, 174, 228, 232–234, 236, 237, 276

B–1 bomber, 200
B–52 bomber, 59
Backfire bomber, 459, 525
Baker, James, 485, 486
Balance of payments, 82–83, 135, 144, 146, 154
Balance of power, 21, 27, 33, 105, 106, 107, 116, 186, 191, 204, 456, 459
  challenges to, 28
  classical, 106, 201
  continental, 33
  correlation of forces and, 29, 204
  European, 33, 116
  and foreign affairs agenda, 127, 131
  global, 20, 38, 199
  psychological, 113–114
  Soviet challenges to, 22–199
  and Stalin, 19
  and system stability, 120
  U.S.-Soviet strategic nuclear balance, 73, 254
Balance of terror, 181
Balance of trade, 135, 141
Ball, George, 350
Ballistic missile defenses, 56, 58–59
  layered system for hard site defense, 58
Bank lending, U.S. private to Third World, 160
Barber, James David, 428, 437
Barnet, Richard J., 178, 181, 183, 230
Bay of Pigs, 77, 306, 307, 380, 435, 476
Behrman, Jere R., 157
Belgium, 87, 136
Benign neglect, 184
Bennis, Warren, 433
Berlin crisis, 26, 71, 74, 399
Bipolarity, 100–101, 104, 105, 107, 108, 110–115, 148, 200–201, 309

Bipolycentrism, 100
Blechman, Barry M., 8, 78n, 91, 95n, 165
Blumenthal, Michael W., 359
Bolshevik Revolution, 17, 512
Bolton, John, 331
Boundaries, significance of, 516–517
Brandt Commission, 150
Brandt, Willy, 150
Brazil, 138, 148
Bretton Woods system, 133, 142, 144, 145, 162, 197
Brezhnev, Leonid, 25, 31n, 175
Brezhnev Doctrine, 191
Brown, Harold, 49, 61n, 390
Bruck, H. W., 396
Brzezinski, Zbigniew, 177, 178, 181, 182, 182n, 184, 185, 186, 188, 246, 268–269, 270, 280n, 285, 290, 390, 442, 443, 479–481, 482, 484, 485
Bundy, McGeorge, 125, 177, 252, 257, 264, 265, 270, 278n, 279n, 452
Bundy, William, 177
Bunker, Ellsworth, 72
Bureaucracy, 295, 349, 350, 351, 384, 398, 399, 433, 439, 440
  competition within, 253–255, 292, 354, 356, 360, 365, 397, 414
  and international negotiations framework, 110, 117, 129, 357
  parochialism in, 254, 283, 288–289, 293, 301, 349, 350, 353, 354, 357, 414, 440
  politics of, 352–363 et passim, 467, 470, 471, 475
  pursuit of independent goals, 125
  role of, 245, 283–284, 289, 331, 356, 358, 359
Bureaucratic insubordination, 295–297, 410–411, 422
Bureaucratic Politics Model, 349, 350, 351, 356, 364–378 et passim, 410–423 et passim
Bureau of Politico-Military Affairs, U.S. Department of State, 189
Bush, George, 312, 329, 485, 489

Caddell, Pat, 495

Cabinet diplomacy, 104
Cabinet politics, 470, 475
Cambodia, Vietnamese invasion of, 153
Camp David Accords, 79, 441
Canada, 123, 143
Cancún Summit, 150
Carnegie Endowment for International Peace, 188
Carrying capacity of the earth, 507–508
Carter, Jimmy, 6, 33, 37, 49, 90–91, 128, 171, 172, 175, 188, 189, 191, 192, 194, 210–211, 228, 230, 238, 247, 268, 269, 277, 285–286, 290, 292, 293, 311–312, 331, 335–337, 390, 397, 398, 432, 435, 439, 441, 442, 443, 492n, 496, 497, 500
   management style of, 478–482
Carter Doctrine, 213
Casey, William J., 300, 316
Castro, Fidel, 66
Center for Defense Information, 92, 95n
Central America, 152, 165
Central Intelligence Agency (CIA), 13, 248, 299–318 et passim, 329, 419, 512
   charter reforms of, 310–318
   and covert actions, 299, 302–306, 310
   and domestic surveillance, 302, 303, 310
Centrally planned economies. See Second World
Chalmers, Robert, 253–254
Chamoun, Camille, 68–69
Chile, 458, 515
China, People's Republic of (PRC), 17, 29, 36, 107, 181, 182, 309, 380, 461
Church, Frank, 25, 323, 328, 437
Churchill, Winston, 257
C³I (Command, Control, Communications and Intelligence), 48, 54
Civilian defense, 48, 57, 60
Clark, William P., 246, 267, 277, 487–489, 493n

Clifford, Clark, 177
Cline, William, 155
Coalition for a Democratic Majority, 230
Coalitions. See Alliances
Cohen, Bernard C., 174, 225, 227
Cohen, Stephen D., 349, 350
Colby, William, 312
Cold War, 6, 8, 13, 16–18, 26, 27, 62, 79, 100, 176, 177, 199, 301, 315, 351, 401, 405
   causes of, 17, 18, 19, 20
   and Soviet Union, 6, 100, 198
   See also Containment; Soviet Union; Détente
Collective security, 93
Colonialism, 37–38, 134, 150, 203, 522–523
Commager, Henry Steele, 504
Commerce, U.S. Department of, 122
Committee on the Present Danger, 202, 230, 238
Common Fund, 157
Communism, 13, 17, 38, 112–113, 152, 181, 189, 229, 301, 307, 380, 432, 437, 459–460, 510, 511, 513, 514
   See also Anticommunism
Comparative advantage, 155
Compartmentalization, Soviet strategy of, 24, 28
"Competitive depreciation" (of currencies), 139–140
Congress, U.S., 29, 89, 128, 187, 194, 197, 223, 229, 245–246, 248, 254, 309, 315, 340
   assertiveness of, 320–343 et passim
Connally, John, 495
Consensus building, 442
Consistency in foreign policy. See Foreign policy, post-WW II American
Containment, 14, 20, 21–23, 26, 29, 33, 38, 47, 79, 97, 114, 123, 148, 151, 153, 171, 178, 179, 180, 181, 182, 183, 187, 189, 191, 197, 203, 304, 307, 380, 388, 519–520
   critique of, 175–195 et passim

history of, 16–31 *et passim*
See also Détente; Soviet Union; Truman Doctrine; Kennan, George F.
Continuity in foreign policy. See Foreign policy, post-WW II American
Conventional Force, 43–44, 124
Correlation of Forces. See Balance of power; Linkage
Council on Foreign Relations, 176, 179, 192
Counterforce strategy, 35, 524
Counterinsurgency, 36, 384
Countervalue strategy, 55
Crisis, 445, 449, 462–463
Crisis Communication Center, 399
Crisis management, 275, 435, 489, 524
Cronin, Thomas E., 249, 430
Cruise missiles, 54, 523, 526–527
Cuba, 10, 70
and Soviet Union, 25, 153, 191
Cuban Missile Crisis, 17, 26, 151, 186, 351, 416–422 *et passim*, 435
Cyprus, 76
Czechoslovakia, 71

Deaver, Michael, 485, 486, 494
Decision, defined, 251
Decision-making, 250–251, 253, 258, 294, 296, 347, 348, 349, 353, 364, 366, 367, 371, 372, 373, 382
contexts of, 351, 435, 444–445
problem, defined, 393–394
problem definition, 393, 396–397, 398
problem recognition, 393, 395–396, 398, 404
Decision overload, 400
Defense, U.S. Department of, 10, 80–81, 122, 247–248, 286, 360, 367
Defense expenditures, U.S., 180, 188, 200, 213, 220, 292
Defense Programs Review Committee, 475

"Definition of the situation," 396
Deforestation, 506, 507. See also Global problems
DeGaulle, Charles, 123
Democracy, 12, 112, 185, 392, 410–411
Departments, U.S. See Individual entries on U.S. government agencies
Dependence, 134, 136
Desertification, 507. See also Global problems
Destler, I. M., 247, 282–283, 289
Détente, 23, 24, 25, 26, 28, 114, 128, 153, 182, 189, 194, 198, 200, 309–310, 459, 461
defined, 37
as U.S. policy, 248
See also Containment; Soviet Union
Deterrence, 7, 56, 57, 82, 107, 108, 123, 186, 392
nuclear, 35, 45–46, 49, 124
Developing countries. See Third World
Diem, Ngo Dinh, 381, 385
Dienbienphu, 151
Diplomacy, 105, 287
Directed energy weapons, 58–59
Direct investment, 136, 154, 160, 161
Disarmament, unilateral, 46
Disarmament organizations, 231
Dollar, U.S.
depreciation of, 135, 138, 146
as reserve currency, 134, 135, 142–143
Domestic actors, 126
Domestic conflict, 112, 151
Domestic politics, 129, 400–401
Dominance, of strong states, 125–126
Dominican Republic, 8, 10, 13, 66–67, 124
Domino theory, 198, 380, 452
See also Communism
Doppelgänger effect, 433
Draper, Theodore, 385
Drew, Elizabeth, 229, 495
Dulles, Allen, 303–306, 307, 435

Dulles, John Foster, 22, 32, 197, 286, 379, 432, 433, 434, 443, 450, 462, 473, 474, 490

Eastern Europe. *See under* Europe
East Germany, 71
East-West confrontation, 37, 40, 123, 148, 151, 164, 188, 191, 198, 200, 203, 204
Ecology, 182. *See also* Environment, problems of
Economic markets, 138, 157
Economic Policy Group, 355
Economic Support Funds (ESF), 81, 88, 93n
Egypt, 29, 42, 79, 87, 94n, 161, 213, 442
Eisenhower, Dwight D., 21, 170, 223, 250, 252, 253, 254, 264, 434, 435, 438, 443, 470, 495
management style of, 472–474, 476, 490, 491n
Eisenhower Doctrine, 89
Elections, and U.S. foreign policy, 173, 439, 495, 498
Ellsberg, Daniel, 226, 423
El Salvador, 151, 153, 228, 234–236, 237
Embargoes, grain, 141
Emerging countries. *See* New Nations; Third World
Emigration, Soviet policies on, 128
Energy, 122, 159, 506
nuclear, 35
Energy dependence, U.S., 159–160
England. *See* Great Britain
Environment, problems of, 122, 505, 508
See also Global problems
Environmental degradation, 163
See also Global problems
Equanimity, doctrine of, 184, 186, 190
Equilibrium, among states, 105, 116
Equivalence, concept of, 45
Escalation, 29, 36, 49, 50, 53, 55, 56, 124
Ethiopia, 29, 40, 153, 161, 191
Eurocurrency markets, 147

Europe, 87, 109, 123, 181, 190
Eastern, 17, 26, 34, 42, 123–124, 149, 177
rearmament of, 79
Western, 139
European Common Market, 122, 139
Exchange rates, 138, 139, 140, 142–143, 144, 145–146, 147
Ex Com, 414, 415, 417, 420
Executive agreements, 324, 327
Executive Committee of the Cabinet (EXCAB), 291
Executive-Congressional relations, 439
Executive fatigue, 383–384
Executive Order
No. 11905, 312
No. 12036, 313
No. 12333, 317
Executive privilege, 325
Executive secrecy, 333
Expansion, U.S. *See* Globalism and U.S. foreign policy
External source category, 97–102 *et passim*, 125, 198

"Fair" trade, 139
Falk, Richard A., 178, 202
Falkland Islands, 489
Farer, Tom J., 184–185
Finland, 17
First World, defined, 149, 150
Food
and interstate agenda, 127, 505, 506
issue of, 158–159, 163, 361
Food stocks, U.S. holdings of, 158
Force, use of, 119, 123, 126, 127, 217, 285
See also Foreign policy, post-WW II American; Political realism
Ford, Gerald R., 89, 230, 268, 311, 312, 333, 335, 338, 434, 496, 500
Foreign affairs agenda, 122, 127, 130, 131, 227, 351, 354, 370, 392, 394, 445
Foreign aid, U.S., 89, 141, 153, 161–162, 197

Foreign Assistance Act (FAA) (1961),
89
Foreign direct investment, U.S. *See*
Direct investment
Foreign Military Sales (FMS), 80, 83,
86, 92, 94*n*
Foreign Military Sales Credit Program
(FMSCR), 80–81, 83, 84, 88,
94*n*
Foreign policy, post-WW II American
alternatives, 37
assumptions underlying, 510–517 *et
passim*
beliefs about, 11, 172, 198, 207–211
consensus on, 175, 214, 238, 244,
288, 303, 308, 309
conservative influence on, 33, 175
continuity of, 1–2, 4, 27, 32–33, 38,
70, 122, 190, 198, 221, 244, 267,
269, 271, 272, 283, 286, 292,
348, 349, 501, 502
credibility of, 233
defined, 243
détente as, 37
diplomatic language in, 386
discontinuity in, 518–519
domestic context of, 104, 120–121,
122, 127, 169, 179, 284–300,
383, 389, 519
economic policy in, 286, 290
electoral influence on, 225
elitist model of, 171, 173, 174
executive dominance in, 244, 246
future of, 501–528 *et passim*
goals of, 4–5, 7–9, 115, 116, 162–
163, 184–185, 248. *See also* Ambrose, Stephen E.; Globalism;
Anticommunism; Contain-
ment; Interventionism
ideological conflicts and, 104, 513
institutional influences on, 243–244
momentum of, 384
and the national interest, 115–118,
284
post-Vietnam era and, 208
pragmatism in, 111
and public opinion, 170, 172, 173,
177, 188, 197, 213–214, 238
racism in, 386

revisionist view of, 170
security assistance and, 79
sense of mission in, 117
sources of, 1-5, 97, 169–174 *et passim*, 349–351. *See also* External
source category; Governmental source category; Individual
source category; Societal
source category
and Soviet foreign policy, 36. *See
also* Soviet Union
structural problems of, 103–106.
See also Policy-making process
use of force as instrument of, 123
Foreign policy establishment, 175–
176, 178, 179, 187, 188, 189,
195
Foreign Service, U.S., 361, 381
Foreign trade, liberalization of, 197
Forrestal, James V., 288
Forrestal, Michael V., 252
Forty Committee, 457, 458, 475
Fourteen Points, 19
Fourth World, defined, 149
Fowler, Henry, 125
Fragmentation policy, 360
France, 11, 12, 123, 136, 139
Free, Lloyd, 172
Freedom of Information Act, 329
Free enterprise, 12
Free trade, 135, 137, 139, 151
"Free world," 179
Freeze movement, nuclear, 439, 527
Fulbright, J. William, Jr., 434, 439,
453, 454

Gaddis, John Lewis, 6, 30*n*
Gaither Committee Report, 253–254
Gallup poll, 213
Game theory, 100, 386
Gelb, Leslie, 151, 178, 180, 181, 184,
187, 189, 194, 247, 268
General Agreement on Trade and
Tariffs (GATT), 122, 130, 141–
142, 163, 197
General System of Preferences (GSP),
156
Geneva Summit, 433
George, Alexander L., 427–428, 432

Germany, 11, 12, 42, 62, 123, 136, 143, 197
Gershman, Carl, 171
Glassboro Summit, 308, 457
Globalism and U.S. foreign policy, 4–5, 13, 14, 20, 97, 109, 116, 152, 170, 200, 204, 214, 218, 221, 351, 515–516, 521
Global problems, 122, 163, 166–167, 189, 506, 507, 508, 517, 527
    See also Murphy Commission
Global trends, 403, 505–509 et passim
Global 2000 Report to the President, 166, 503–504
Goldwater, Barry, 451
Government agencies and domestic constituencies, 361, 400–401
Governmental Politics Model, 418
Governmental source category, 243–249 et passim
Great Britain, 11, 12, 87, 123, 136, 143
Great Depression, 140, 154, 197, 257
"Great man" theories of history, 425
Great Society, 33, 454
Green Revolution, 158, 508
Greenstein, Fred, 491
Group of 77, 150
Group-think, 382–383, 433
Gruening, Ernest, 453, 454
Guatemala, 124
Guerilla warfare, 257
Gulf of Tonkin Resolution, 309, 323, 452, 453, 454

Haig, Alexander M., Jr., 232, 246, 261, 274, 275, 277, 359, 442, 484, 485, 486, 487, 489, 490, 493n
Halberstam, David, 176
Halperin, Morton, 363n, 365, 368
Harriman, W. Averell, 72, 380
Helms, Jesse, 496
Helsinki agreement, 25
Hermann, Charles F., 351, 373
Hermann, Margaret G., 426–427, 432
Herter, Christian, 32
Hickenlooper Amendment, 161
"High politics," 101–102, 119, 127, 200–201, 203
    See also Political realism

Hilsman, Roger, 246, 363n
Ho Chi Minh, 452
Hodgson, Godfrey, 179, 187
Hoffmann, Stanley, 31n, 132n, 165, 178, 181, 185, 186, 187, 192, 193, 203, 504
Holbrooke, Richard, 178, 187, 189
Holsti, Ole R., 172, 173
Hong Kong, 138
Hoopes, Townsend, 176, 178
Hoover Commission, 470
Hoover, Herbert, 196
Hoover, J. Edgar, 254
Howard, Michael E., 61
Hughes, Barry B., 224
Hughes-Ryan Amendment, 310, 315, 328
Hughes, Thomas L., 178, 188, 192
Human rights, 16, 24, 25, 90, 185, 189, 193, 521
Hunter, Robert E., 181–182, 189
Huntington, Samuel P., 178, 338–339

ICBM. See Inter-Continental Ballistic Missile
Ideologies, impact of, 105, 182, 208, 222
IMF. See International Monetary Fund
"Imperial presidency," 244, 248–249, 309, 320–343 et passim
Impoundment, 325
Independent Commission on International Development Issues, 150
India, 138
Individual factors, 425–428 et passim, 462–467
Individual source category, 425–428 et passim
Indochina. See Vietnam
Indonesia, 29, 161, 388
Industrialized countries, 123, 134
Inflation, U.S., 137, 140, 145, 146, 147.   See also Dollar
Institute for International Social Research, 217–218
Integrated Program for Commodities (IPC), 157

Integration, political, 120, 271
Intelligence system, U.S., 299, 300,
    301–304, 307–308, 312, 315,
    316, 317, 318
Interagency coordination process,
    355, 406, 457, 466, 475
Inter-Continental Ballistic Missile
    (ICBM), 53, 57, 58, 523
Interdependence, 35, 101–102, 127,
    129, 182, 337, 403, 404
  complex, 119–132 *et passim*, 201,
    205
  economic, 121, 127, 134, 154
Interior, U.S. Department of, 122
Intermestic politics, defined, 248,
    299–318 *et passim*
International Development, Agency
    for (AID), 161
International economic policy, 133,
    349, 350, 352, 356, 359, 360,
    361, 362
  bureaucratic politics of, 355–363
Internationalism, U.S. *See* Globalism;
    Public opinion
International Labor Organization
    (ILO), 162
International Military Education and
    Training Program (IMET), 81,
    84, 88, 94n
International Monetary Fund (IMF),
    122, 130, 139, 143, 144, 145,
    150, 163
International organizations. *See*
    Transnational organizations
International Rubber Agreement, 157
International Sugar and Coffee
    Agreements, 157
International system, concept of. *See*
    External source category
International Trade Commission
    (ITC), 361
International Wheat Agreement, 157
Intervention, military, 164, 179
Interventionism, U.S., 5, 8, 10, 97,
    124, 152, 203, 205, 234, 459,
    512, 522
Iran, 26, 42, 62, 87, 151, 153, 213, 216
  hostage rescue mission, 269, 274,
    390, 393, 397, 481

seizure of U.S. hostages, 152, 173,
    210–211, 213, 284–288, 313–
    314
Iraq, 29, 69
Isolationism, U.S., 5, 10, 152, 180, 188,
    196, 203, 204–207, 214
  post-Vietnam, 153–154, 179, 215,
    218, 220, 309
Israel, 79, 88, 89, 94n, 161, 438, 442
Issues, hierarchy of, 119–120, 121,
    122, 125, 126, 127
Italy, 11, 136, 460

Jackson, Henry, 230, 233–234, 263,
    332
Jackson-Vanik Amendment, 24
Janis, Irving, 373
Japan, 11, 12, 28, 94n, 135–136, 137,
    139, 143, 148, 181, 190, 217,
    437, 513
Jervis, Robert, 396
Jewish lobby, in U.S., 438
Johnson, Lyndon B., 32, 176, 307, 309,
    412, 433, 434, 444, 449–455 *et
    passim*, 457, 470, 494
Johnson, Richard T., 474, 482–483,
    491n
Joint Chiefs of Staff, 367, 368, 388
Jordan, 1970 civil war in, 70
Justice, U.S. Department of, 122

Kahn, Herman, 459
Kaplan, Stephen S., 8, 78n, 95n, 165
Keeny, Spurgeon M., Jr., 8
Kennan, George F., 6, 18, 21, 22, 30n,
    46, 178, 180, 182, 183n, 194,
    197, 204, 205
Kennedy, Edward M., 495
Kennedy, John F., 22, 27, 31n, 117,
    252, 253, 258, 263, 307, 380,
    412, 415, 417, 418, 420, 434,
    435, 437, 441, 443, 454, 457,
    470, 495
  management style of, 475–478, 481,
    483
Kennedy, Robert F., 414, 421
Kenya, 213
Keohane, Robert O., 101, 132n, 403,
    405

Kessler, Allen, 399, 408*n*
Key currency, 142
Khrushchev, Nikita, 18, 70, 72
Kissinger, Henry A., 28, 31*n*, 37, 101,
　　103*n*, 122, 124, 132*n*, 175, 186,
　　187, 188, 230, 246, 266, 267,
　　270, 278*n*, 279*n*, 283–284, 285,
　　293, 370, 371, 434, 441, 443,
　　455–462 *et passim*, 475, 478,
　　481, 485, 490
Koenig, Louis, 432
Komer, Robert, 264–265
Korea, 8, 10, 21, 22, 26, 66, 88, 138,
　　141, 149, 151, 435, 515
Krasner, Stephen D., 351

Labor, U.S. Department of, 122
Lake, Anthony, 178, 180, 187, 189
Laos, 66, 68, 70, 381
　　See also Armed forces
Latin America, 36, 89, 506, 507
　　U.S. exports to, 154
Law of the Sea Conference, 132
Leadership, 425–428
　　constituencies of, 438–441
　　and delegation of authority, 443
　　images of, 429–431
　　influence of birth order on, 436
　　influence of characteristics of, 431–
　　　438
　　influence of historical period on,
　　　437–438
　　interest and training in foreign af-
　　　fairs, 434–436
　　nature of, 429–431
　　personalities of, 351, 431
　　political socialization of, 436–438
　　political style, 433
　　staff selection of, 433
　　types of
　　　"crusaders," 427, 433, 448–449,
　　　　462–464
　　　"pragmatists," 427, 432, 448–449,
　　　　462–464
　　view of the world, 431–433
League of Nations, 177, 442, 512
Lebanon, 8, 10, 34, 68, 69, 489
Legalism, as U.S. approach, 116

Legitimacy, political, 104, 105, 111,
　　112, 113
Less developed nations. *See* Third
　　World
Levgold, Robert, 192
Liberalism, 192
Liberal-populist governing coalition,
　　188
Lichtheim, George, 177
Linkage, 22, 24, 28–29, 126, 131, 184,
　　202, 461
　　and complex interdependence,
　　　125–127, 128, 129, 131
　　and correlation of forces, 29, 526
　　See also Balance of power
"Look-down" radar planes, 59
Low Altitude Defense System
　　(LOAD), 57–58
　　See also MX missile
"Low politics," 101–102, 119, 127, 201
Luce, Henry, 13

MacArthur, Douglas, 62, 437, 472
McCarthy, Eugene, 307–308, 379, 402
McCone, John, 417
McGovern, George, 204, 230, 238
McNamara, Robert S., 252, 384, 388,
　　414, 420, 452, 453
McNaughton, John, 452
McNeill, William, 392
Management and Budget, U.S. Office
　　of (OMB), 286–287
Manning, Bayless, 179, 183–184, 300
Mansfield, Mike, 305–307
Manshel, Warren Demian, 178, 184,
　　187
Marshall Plan, 244, 392
Marxism, in new nations, 113, 170
Mass media, 222–241 *et passim*
　　news defined, 238
Mathieson, John A., 102
Mayagüez Affair, 188, 340
Meany, George, 204
Meese, Edwin, 275–276, 485–486
Mexico, 138, 152, 160
Middle East, 11, 25, 70, 91, 94*n*, 99,
　　159–160, 161, 506, 521
Milbrath, Lester, 222, 227–228, 239

Military Assistance Program (MAP),
81, 83, 84, 85, 94n
Military Assistance Service Funded
(MASF), 81, 84, 85, 94n
Military-industrial complex, 13, 82,
170, 173, 182, 223, 250
Misperception, 394, 396, 408n
in Soviet-American relations, 205
Missile gap, 202, 252
Missiles, Soviet long-range theater nu-
clear (SS-4, SS-5, SS-20), 54,
525
Mondale, Walter F., 324
Monetary system, international, 127,
140, 143, 144, 519
Monroe Doctrine, 33, 152, 515
Morgenthau, Hans J., 6, 98, 119, 130,
132n, 460
Morse, Wayne, 453, 454
Most-favored-nation (MFN) principle,
141
Moynihan, Daniel P., 185, 187, 188
"Muddling through" model, 258n
Multilateralism, 214
Multinational corporations, 121, 127,
128, 134, 135, 161, 203, 216
Multiple advocacy, 475
Multiple Independently Targetable
Re-entry Vehicle (MIRV), 52,
394
Multipolarity, 22, 105, 106, 107–115
Multi-reserve currency system, 143
Munich syndrome, 177, 198
Murphy Commission, 290, 311, 353,
402–403
Muskie, Edmund, 191–192, 269
Mutual Assured Destruction (MAD),
6, 7, 48, 49, 52, 56, 58, 59, 60n
See also Keeny, Spurgeon;
Panofsky, Wolfgang
Mutual hostages, 47, 52, 59
MX missile, 57, 58, 200

National attributes, 170–171
National interest, 6, 32–39 et passim,
98, 101, 115–118, 129–130,
166–167, 169, 197, 198, 224–
225, 285, 341, 349, 355–356,
360, 397

Nationalism, and world order, 105,
111, 181, 185, 214, 221, 516,
517, 523, 528
National liberation movements, 18
National security. See Security, national
National Security Act (1947), 288, 302
National Security Assistant, 260–281
et passim, 288–289, 293, 443,
467
changed character of, 264, 266, 277
inaccessibility to Congress, 263
responsibilities of, 262–263, 265,
267, 268, 270, 275, 277
role of, 246, 247, 262
National Security Council (NSC), 255,
260, 265, 266, 269, 273, 285,
288, 289, 301–302, 355, 359
National Security Policy, 271
NATO (North Atlantic Treaty Organ-
ization), 26, 28, 44, 45, 83, 94n,
100, 108, 116, 162, 183, 197,
231, 524, 527
Nelson Amendment, 89–90
Netherlands, 136
Neustadt, Richard E., 254, 259n, 264,
364, 410, 412
Neutron bomb, 55
New Economic Policy (1971), 244
New International Economic Order
(NIEO), 130, 131, 150, 163, 203
Newly Industrialized Countries
(NICs), 138, 139, 149
New nations, 104, 106, 111–113. See
also Third World
New Zealand, 140
Nicaragua, ouster of Somoza in, 153
NIEO. See New International Eco-
nomic Order
Nigeria, 160
Nitze, Paul, 230
Nixon Doctrine, 22, 30n, 89, 153, 309
Nixon, Richard M., 10, 14, 22, 24, 32,
89, 176, 177, 238, 266, 309, 320,
340, 354, 371, 380, 438, 441,
443, 462, 470, 473, 496, 515
management style of, 474–476, 478,
481, 484
Nonaligned Conference (Havana), 190
Nonaligned world. See Third World

Non-military issues, 125, 127
Non-proliferation Treaty (NPT), 109, 368
Nonstate actors, 124
Nonzero-sum game, international politics as, 201
North, 150
  See also Industrialized countries
North Atlantic Treaty Organization. *See* NATO.
North-South confrontation, 37, 39, 123, 134, 150, 164, 188, 200, 203, 204, 527
North-South trade issues, 128
NSC-68, 21–22, 392. *See also* containment
Nuclear Test Ban Treaty (1963), 109, 441
Nuclear Utilization Target Selection, (NUTS), 8, 49, 52, 60n
Nuclear Utilization Theorists (NUTs), 6, 7, 60n
Nuclear war, 47–61 *et passim*, 151, 458, 510, 514
  estimates of fatalities of, 53
  fear of, 202
  limited, 50, 231
  MAD character of, 50
  risks of general, 114
  as winnable, 35
Nuclear weapons
  compared to atomic bomb, 50, 52, 54, 55
  consequences of use of, 45, 46, 49, 50–51, 52, 53, 54, 56, 76, 124
  interest groups and, 231–232, 237
  parity and, 229
  policy on use of, 174, 228, 231–232
  protests against, 231
  tactical, 35, 54
Nye, Joseph S., Jr., 101, 132n, 403, 405

OECD (Organization for Economic Cooperation and Development), 122, 148, 159
Ogburn, Charlton, 395
Oil, 35, 127, 206, 506
  crisis (1973–1974), 14, 128, 133, 138, 145

and United States, 12, 148, 159
Olympic boycott, U.S., 26
Oman, 87, 213
OMB. *See* Management and Budget, U.S. Office of
OPEC (Organization of Petroleum Exporting Countries), 124, 127, 145, 147, 149, 153, 157, 159, 206, 360
Open-door policy, 152
Operational code, 432
Orderly Marketing Agreements, 137
Organizations, and foreign policy making, 287, 297, 348–349, 395, 397–401, 403–407
  See also Policy-making process
Ottawa Economic Summit (1981), 151
Overkill, 45
Overseas Private Investment Corporation (OPIC), 161

Paige, Glenn D., 396
Pakistan, 42, 66, 76, 87, 267
Palestinian question, 26
Panama Canal treaties, 165, 441, 482, 522
Panofsky, Wolfgang K. H., 8
Parties, political, and foreign policy, 208–209, 218
Peace Corps, 161
Peacekeeping Operations (PKO), 81
Pentagon. *See* Defense, U.S. Department of
Pentagon Papers, 309
People's Republic of China. *See* China
Perceptions, role in foreign policy, 99–100, 119, 171, 175, 182, 408n, 468
Percy, Charles, 235
Pershing II missiles, 54–55
Persian Gulf, 79, 87, 159–160
Personality, role in foreign policy, 351, 431, 448, 468–489 *et passim*
Petroleum. *See* Oil
Philippines, 161
Phoenix Program, in Vietnam, 36
Physicians for Social Responsibility, 50, 231
Pipeline (Soviet-European), 489

Pipes, Richard, 230
Platt, John, 404, 406, 408n
"Plausible Denial," defined, 312
Poland, 42, 62, 512
Policy-making process, 223, 246, 250–258, 273–274, 278, 287, 294–295, 296–297, 300, 350, 352, 353, 354, 366, 414–416, 443, 463–490 et passim
 information "leaks" in, 253–254, 256, 267
 multiple channels in, 120, 121–122, 129
 multiplicity of actors in, 255, 272, 284, 289, 291, 293–294, 466
 pluralist model of, 173–174
 reorganization of, 467
 and roles in, 349–351
 use of "back channels" in, 266
 See also Rational Actor Model
Political culture, 171
Political economy, 101
Political realism, 98–99, 101, 119–132 et passim, 188, 199, 206, 523
 focus on politico-military issues, 127
 political processes of, 131
Politicization, defined, 128
Polycentrism, 100
Pool, Ithiel de Sola, 132n, 399, 408n
Population, problems of, 122, 136
 growth of, 163, 505, 507, 508
 See also Global problems
Populism, 33
Portugal, 87
Poseidon submarine, 52
Power
 distinction between influence and, 222, 223, 358–359
 nature and use of, 98, 105, 106–107, 116, 117, 165, 180–181, 523
Prediction, nature of, 403, 502–503, 504
President
 and abuse of power, 320, 321, 343
 dependency of, on bureaucracy, 444
 experience in foreign affairs, 435–436
 "honeymoon" period with Con-gress, 445
 models and types (of management styles), 427–428, 469–490 et passim
  collegial, 469–470, 477–478
  competitive, 469–471, 474–476
  formalistic, 467–470, 472
 power of, 252–253, 273, 286, 310, 373
 role conception of, 271, 273, 274, 278, 320, 322, 323, 327, 340, 343, 364, 369, 415–416, 467
 and style of policy making, 271, 354, 466–490 et passim
Presidential Directive 13 (PD-13), 90–91
Pressure groups. See Special-interest groups
Pre-theory (of James N. Rosenau), 2, 9n
Preventive diplomacy, 384, 527
Protectionism, 137, 139, 142, 159
 See also Trade
Public Law 480 (Food for Peace), 161
Public opinion,
 characteristics of, 198–203, 337, 341, 358, 400, 439, 449
 cleavages in, 114, 198–201, 208, 225, 226, 236
 surveys of, 213–221 et passim
 variations in, 191, 198, 218–220

Ransom, Harry Howe, 248
Rapid deployment force, 523
Rational Actor Model, 251, 296, 349, 351, 365, 411–413, 417, 419–420
Ravenal, Earl C., 206
Reagan, Ronald, 148, 164, 171, 198, 210–211, 231, 234, 238, 247, 260–261, 274–278, 311, 315–316, 396, 398, 428, 431, 433, 437, 441, 485–488, 494–504 et passim, 519
 management style of, 484–490 et passim, 498–499
Realism. See Political realism
Regionalism, 388
Repression, U.S. opposition to, 185, 520

Resources, 91, 122, 156–157, 163, 505, 506, 508, 514–515
Reston, James, 441
Revisionism, 18
Revolution, in new nations, 111, 520
Rockefeller, Nelson, 458
Rogers, William P., 266, 286
role, as concept, 284, 347–351 *et passim*, 384, 398, 399, 479
    See also President; State, Secretary of
Roosevelt, Franklin D., 434, 436, 441, 470, 495, 497
    management style of, 470–471, 483, 484
Roosevelt, Theodore, 442
Rosati, Jerel A., 350
Rosenau, James N., 9*n*, 97–98, 102*n*, 170, 172, 173
Rostow, Eugene, 230
Rostow, Walt Whitman, 265–266, 270, 403, 451, 452
"Rule of non-collision," 186, 190
Rumania, 71
Rusk, Dean, 32, 115, 250, 271, 286, 443, 452

Safire, William, 433
SALT I (Strategic Arms Limitation Talks), 24, 25, 350, 367–369, 458, 459
    and the Johnson Administration, 367–369
SALT II, 25, 29, 174, 194, 200, 202, 228–231, 236, 272, 369–371
Sapin, Burton, 396
Satellite reconnaissance capabilities, 17
Saudi Arabia, 87, 174, 232–234, 521–522
Schell, Jonathan, 392
Schlesinger, Arthur M., Jr., 322–323, 339, 412
Scowcroft, Brent, 267, 270, 278*n*
Seamless web model, 125–126
SEATO. *See* Southeast Asia Treaty Organization
Second World, defined, 149
    domestic opinion in communist states, 124

Security, military, 119–125, 130, 131, 165, 181
Security, national, 81–82, 101, 102, 176, 180, 194, 226, 514–515
Security assistance, 74, 79, 80, 81, 82–83, 84–85, 86–89, 94*n*
Security assistance policy, U.S., 8–9, 79–95 *et passim*
Security policy, U.S., 222–241 *et passim*
Select Committee on Intelligence, role of, 328
Semmel, Andrew K., 8–9, 79*n*, 95*n*
Senior Review Group, 475
Separation of powers, 254, 300, 321, 322, 331, 341
Sewell, John W., 102
Shulman, Marshall, 180, 182, 183, 188
Shultz, George P., 261, 277–278, 489
Singapore, 138
Sino-American rapprochement, 99
Sino-Soviet dispute, 202, 481, 511
Sixth Fleet carriers, 76
Skybolt, 414
Smith, Adam, 173
Smith, Bromley, 263, 265
Smith, Gerard, 266–267
Snyder, Richard C., 396
Societal source category, 169–174 *et passim*
Somalia, 213
Sorensen, Theodore C., 259*n*, 313, 339, 414
South. *See* Third World
Southeast Asia, 34
Southeast Asia Treaty Organization (SEATO), 162, 381, 453
South Vietnam. *See* Vietnam; Vietnam War
South Yemen, 153
Soviet Union, 42, 47, 53, 58, 62, 69, 71, 83, 149, 182, 183, 193, 332, 402, 432, 443, 459, 460, 485, 510, 512, 517, 519, 522, 523–524, 525
    defense expenditures of, 199, 202
    expansionist tendencies of, 5–6, 20, 24, 113–115, 123, 153, 190, 198, 316
    foreign policy, 36, 307

government, nature of, 40–46 *et passim*, 193, 204, 206
military superiority of, 27, 45, 52, 313, 402
problems for, 204
Statement of Basic Principles of, 24
U.S. relations with, 11, 128, 173, 186, 190, 192, 193, 202, 207, 300, 301, 305, 306–309, 314, 317–318, 458, 459, 462, 521–522, 524–526
Space-based ballistic missile system, 59
Special Assistant for National Security Affairs. *See* National Security Assistant
Special Drawing Rights (SDRS), 143
Special-interest groups, 170, 173, 180, 222–241 *et passim*, 438
Spengler, Oswald, 455
Sphere of influence, 17
Sri Lanka, 162
Stalin, Joseph, 12, 18
Standard operating procedures (SOPs), 350, 351, 366, 399, 412, 413, 416, 420
START (Strategic Arms Reduction Talks), 232
State-centric approach, 119
State, U.S. Department of, 13, 80, 116, 122, 230, 247–248, 282–298, *et passim*, 359, 361, 379, 380, 384, 519
Secretary of, 247, 282, 283, 284, 443, 467
Stealth bombers, 59
Steel, Ronald, 179
Stewart, Louis, 436
Stimson, Henry L., 386–387, 389
Stockholm Environment Conference (1972), 130
Stockpiles
nuclear, 47, 49, 52
resource, 156
of U.S. weapons, 49, 83
Stoessinger, John G., 427, 432
Strategic Air Command aircraft, 76
Strategic doctrine, 47, 107, 223
Strategic Triad, 57, 200

Strategic weapons, 25, 50–51, 110
Strategy, military, 35, 48, 107
Strauss, Robert, 273
Submarine-Launched-Ballistic Missile (SLBM), 52, 200
Sub-Saharan Africa, 89
Suez, 87, 151
Surgical strike, 53, 385
Switzerland, 143
Symmetrical response. *See* Containment
Szanton, Peter, 290

Taft, Robert, 14
Taiwan, 66, 72, 88, 138, 141, 149, 515
Tanzania, 185
Tariffs. *See* Trade
Taylor, Maxwell D., 252, 452
Technology, 50, 104
Technology Assessment, Congressional Office of, 53
Terms of trade, commodity, 127, 156–158
Terrorism, international, 34, 124, 152, 198
Textiles, import restraints on, 141
Thailand, 66, 68
Theater Nuclear Warfare (TNW), 55
Third World, 6, 8, 17, 22, 25, 39, 123, 130–131, 149, 205–206, 520–521
issues of concern to, 37–39, 140–141, 145, 154, 161, 185
Soviet influence in, 26, 91, 182, 198
U.S. relations with, 34, 93, 148–167 *et passim*, 178, 190, 192, 207
See also New Nations
Thompson, James C., Jr., 350
Thurow, Lester C., 401
Tito, 71
Tokyo Round, 142
Totalitarianism, 180, 184
Trade, 121, 129, 136, 137–139, 140, 142, 149, 154–156, 204, 332
Traditionalism. *See* Political realism
Transgovernmental relations, 120, 128–130
Transnational actors, 120, 121, 125, 126, 127, 131

Transnational organizations, 120, 126, 127, 128, 130–131, 196
Transnational relations, 120, 128–130, 178
Treasury, U.S. Department of, 122, 362, 363
Trident II submarine-launched ballistic missile, 200
Trigger price mechanism, 355
Trilateral Commission, 121, 238
Trilateralism, 186, 190
Tripolarity, 100, 461
Trujillo, Rafael, 66
Truman, Harry S., 5–6, 12, 197, 252, 301, 430, 470
  management style of, 471–472, 490, 491n
Truman Doctrine, 5–6, 79, 89, 184, 188, 307, 392
Turkey, 62, 89, 332
Turner, Stansfield, 313

U-2 aircraft, 415, 418, 421–422
Ullman, Richard H., 178, 180, 184, 186
UNCTAD (UN Conference on Trade and Development), 157
Unilateralism, public opinion on, 215
United Nations, 19, 130, 131, 132, 150, 162, 185, 196, 216
United States
  economic dependency of, 133, 136, 141, 147, 149, 160
  post-WW II preeminence of, 133, 136, 148, 214
  strategic goals of, 151
  world role of, 52, 115–116, 191, 196, 214, 244, 271, 285, 389
  See also Foreign policy, post-WW II American; Globalism
United World Federalists, 196–197
Urban defense, 57
U.S.S.R. See Soviet Union

Vance, Cyrus R., 165, 175, 177, 188, 268, 269, 272, 285, 286, 442, 443, 479–481, 484
Verification Panel, 475

Veto, legislative, 330–332
Vietnam, 10, 13, 14, 27, 29, 32, 70, 71, 124, 151, 192, 308–309, 334, 373, 379–389 et passim, 450–455 et passim, 475
Vietnam War, 22, 36, 64, 66, 81, 125, 165, 171–172, 177, 179, 187, 208, 405
  domestic context of, 8, 117, 197–198, 208, 308, 350
Voluntary export restraints, 137

Wallace, Henry, 14
War, 119, 130, 197, 516
  ecological effects of, 123
  economic, 12, 123
  obsolescence of, 182
  threat of, 214
War-fighting targeting doctrines, 48
Warnke, Paul C., 178, 181, 183, 184, 188, 194
War Powers Act (1973), 236, 309, 326, 327, 332, 338, 340
Warsaw Pact, 100, 524–525
Washington Special Actions Group, 457, 475
"WASP elite," 179
Watergate, 180, 333–334, 341, 439, 462
Watts, William, 172
Weinberger, Caspar, 275–276, 486, 487, 512
Welsh, Richard, 312
Western Europe. See under Europe
West Germany, 137, 148, 183
Whitman, Marina V. N., 186
Wilson, Woodrow, 176, 442, 512
"Window of vulnerability," 53
World Bank (International Bank for Reconstruction and Development), 163
World federalists, 196–197
World Food Conference (1974), 130
World gross national product, U.S. share of, 138
World order, 105, 113, 181, 196, 204, 389
World view, new consensus on, 177

Yarmolinsky, Adam, 180
Yemen, 29
Yom Kippur War (1973), 87
Young, Andrew, 189
Yugoslavia, 17, 42, 71, 185

Zero-sum game, international politics
 as, 20, 105, 199
Zimbabwe, 165
Zionism, as "racism," 216
Zygmunt, Nagorski, Jr., 186